Legal Secretary's

Complete Handbook

Also by Mary A. De Vries

Prentice Hall Style Manual

The Complete Word Book

The New American Dictionary of Abbreviations

The Office Sourcebook

The New Robert's Rules of Order

The New American Handbook of Letter Writing

Complete Secretary's Handbook, 6th ed. (revisor)

Professional Secretary's Encyclopedic Dictionary, 4th ed. (revisor)

The Complete Office Handbook

The Practical Writer's Guide

Legal Secretary's Encyclopedic Dictionary, 3rd ed. (revisor)

Guide to Better Business Writing

New Century Vest-Pocket Secretary's Handbook

The Prentice Hall Complete Secretarial Letter Book

Secretary's Standard Reference Manual and Guide

Legal Secretary's Complete Handbook

Fourth Edition

Mary A. DeVries

Legal Consultant

Carolyn W. Baldwin, Partner
Baldwin & de Séve
Attorneys at Law

PRENTICE HALL
Englewood Cliffs, New Jersey 07632

Prentice-Hall International, Inc., *London*
Prentice-Hall of Australia, Pty. Ltd., *Sydney*
Prentice-Hall of Canada, Inc., *Toronto*
Prentice-Hall of India Private Ltd., *New Dehli*
Prentice-Hall of Japan, Inc. *Tokyo*
Prentice-Hall of Southeast Asia Pte., Ltd., *Singapore*
Editora Prentice-Hall do Brasil Ltda., *Rio de Janeiro*
Prentice-Hall Hispanoamericana, S.A., *Mexico*

© 1992 by

PRENTICE-HALL, INC.

Englewood Cliffs, NJ

10   9   8   7   6   5

Library of Congress Cataloging-in-Publication Data

De Vries, Mary Ann.
  Legal secretary's complete handbook / by Mary A. De Vries. — 4th ed.
    p.   cm.
  Rev. ed. of: Legal secretary's complete handbook / by Besse May Miller.
3rd. ed. c1980.
  Includes index.
  ISBN 0-13-529876-8
        1. Legal secretaries—United States—Handbooks, manuals, etc. I. Miller, Besse May
Legal secretary's complete handbook. II. Title
KF319.M54   1992
651'.934—dc20
                                                                    92-8332
                                                                    CIP

ISBN 0-13-529876-8

PRENTICE HALL
Professional Publishing
Englewood Cliffs, NJ 07632

Simon & Schuster. A Paramount Communications Company

Printed in the United States of America

Contents

Foreword by Carolyn W. Baldwin   xxix

Preface to the Fourth Edition   xxxi

Part 1. General Duties in the Law Office   1

1. Working in a Law Office   *3*

You and the Lawyer—3

    1.1. The Law-Office Team—3
    1.2. Ethics in the Law Office—3
    1.3. Legal Training—4
    1.4. Requirements for Admission to the Bar—4
    1.5. Law Degrees—5
    1.6. Specialization—6
    1.7. Building a Practice—7
    1.8. The Lawyer's Outside Activities—10
    1.9. The Lawyer's Relationship with Clients—10
    1.10. Fees—10

Organization and Personnel of a Law Firm—11

    1.11. Kind of Business Organization—11

1.12. Personnel in a Law Office—12
1.13. The Secretary's Duties—13
1.14. Deportment—14

The Law-Office Layout—14

1.15. Physical Layout—14
1.16. The Furniture—15

Law-Office Automation—16

1.17. Telephone Equipment—16
1.18. Filing and Retrieval Equipment—17
1.19. Mailing Equipment—17
1.20. Photocopy Machines—18
1.21. Facsimile Machines—18
1.22. Bookkeeping and Accounting Equipment—19
1.23. Dictation Equipment—19
1.24. Word Processing Equipment—20

Stationery Supplies—21

1.25. Inventory Management—21
1.26. Types of Paper—21

The Computer in the Law Office—21

1.27. Computer Hardware—22
1.28. Computer Software—24
1.29. Computer Security—25
1.30. The Computer as a Word Processor—25
1.31. The Computer in Document Assembly—26
1.32. The Computer in Desktop Publishing—27
1.33. The Computer in File Management—27
1.34. The Computer in Database Management—28
1.35. The Computer in Addressing and Mailing—29
1.36. The Computer in Billing and Bookkeeping—30

2. Opening Client Files and Creating Documents   32

A New Matter—32

2.1. New Case, or Client, File—32
2.2. The Secretary's Role—33
2.3. Routing of New Case Report—33

Word Processing in the Law Office—35

    2.4. The Looseleaf Formbook—35
    2.5. Understanding Dictated Material—35
    2.6. Errors in Dictation—36
    2.7. Pairs of Words That Cause Confusion—37
    2.8. Recurring Phrases, Clauses, and Paragraphs—39
    2.9. Take-ins, or Inserts—39

Production of Documents—40

    2.10. Rules for Formatting the Document—40
    2.11. Checking the Document—43
    2.12. Copying the Document—43

3. Contacts with Clients and Other Callers   *44*

Basic Guidelines—44

    3.1. Introduction to the Client—44
    3.2. Basic Precepts That Must Be Observed—45

Contacts in Person—46

    3.3. Contacts in Person with Clients—46
    3.4. Client Arrives Without an Appointment—46
    3.5. Stranger Wants Legal Advice—48
    3.6. Client Is Early for an Appointment—50
    3.7. Client Is Hysterical—50
    3.8. Client Offers Invitation—50
    3.9. Client Offers Presents and Payment for Work—51
    3.10. Client Wants to See File—51
    3.11. Sales People and Job Hunters Want to See Lawyer—52
    3.12. Impatient Client Waits for Lawyer Who Is Late—53
    3.13. Important Client Is Unreasonable—54

Contacts over the Telephone—54

    3.14. Importance of Telephone Contacts—54
    3.15. Rules of Telephone Courtesy—55
    3.16. Placing Calls for the Lawyer—55
    3.17. Long Distance, or Toll, Calls—56
    3.18. When Clients Place Toll Calls—56
    3.19. Answering Calls for the Lawyer—58
    3.20. Making Notes of Incoming Calls—58

3.21. Screening Calls for the Lawyer—58

3.22. Finding Out the Purpose of a Call—60

3.23. The Caller Who Wants Legal Advice over
      the Telephone—61

3.24. An Irate Client Calls—62

3.25. Client or Prospective Client Asks What a Fee Will Be—62

3.26. An Unscrupulous Vendor Calls—62

3.27. Your Telephone Conversation—63

3.28. Desk Telephone Lists—63

4. Reminder Systems and Practices   *66*

The Diary—66

4.1. What Is a Diary?—66

4.2. Diaries You Should Keep—67

4.3. How to Make Up Diaries—69

4.4. How to Make Entries About Legal Work—69

4.5. How to Obtain Information for Entries—70

4.6. Checklist of Entries to Make in Diary—71

4.7. Checklist of Entries of Work Accomplished—73

Tickler Card Files—74

4.8. Use of Tickler Card File—74

4.9. Use of Tickler Card File with Diary—74

Follow-Up Files—75

4.10. Use of Follow-Up Files—75

4.11. Checklist of Material to Be Placed in Follow-Up Files—75

4.12. Operation of Follow-Up System—76

Reminding the Lawyer of Things to Do—77

4.13. Necessity for Reminder—77

4.14. How to Remind the Lawyer of Appointments—77

4.15. How to Remind the Lawyer of Things to Do—77

4.16. How to Remind the Lawyer of Court Work—79

5. Filing in the Law Office   *80*

Organization of Material—80

5.1. Classification of Files—80

Electronic Filing—82

    5.2. Modern Filing Systems—82

Numerical System of Filing: Clients' Files—82

    5.3. What Is the Numerical System of Filing?—82
    5.4. How to Use the Numerical System in a Law Office—82
    5.5. Assigning Numbers According to Type of Case—84
    5.6. How to Transfer Numerical Files—85

Alphabetical System of Filing: Client Files—86

    5.7. What Is the Alphabetical System of Filing?—86
    5.8. How to Use the Alphabetical System—86
    5.9. How to Transfer Alphabetical Files—87

Other Files—87

    5.10. Personal Files—87
    5.11. General Correspondence Files—88
    5.12. Periodicals, Bulletins, and Other Printed Matter—88

Physical Setup of Files—88

    5.13. Preparation of Material for Filing—88
    5.14. How to Type Index Tabs and Labels—89
    5.15. How to Arrange Papers in File Folders—92
    5.16. Preparation for Closing a File—93
    5.17. Control of Material Taken from the Files—93

6. Handling Legal and Business Correspondence   *100*

Letter Formats—100

    6.1. Letter Formats—101
    6.2. Opinion Letters—101
    6.3. Punctuation—106

Principal Parts of the Letter—106

    6.4. Dateline—106
    6.5. Reference Line—106
    6.6. Personal Notation—107
    6.7. Inside Address: Forms of Address—107
    6.8. Inside Address: Business Titles or Position—109
    6.9. Inside Address: Forms for Addressing Women—109
    6.10. Inside Address: Letter and Envelope Street Address—111

6.11. Attention Line—112

6.12. Salutation—112

6.13. Subject Line—114

6.14. Complimentary Close—114

6.15. Signature—114

6.16. Identification Line—115

6.17. Enclosure Notation—116

6.18. Mailing Notation—116

6.19. Copy-Distribution Notation—118

6.20. Postscript—118

6.21. Continuation-Page Heading—119

6.22. Enclosures—119

Effective Letter Writing—120

6.23. Six Ways to Improve Your Letters—120

6.24. Trite Terms to Avoid—120

6.25. Unnecessary Words and Phrases—125

6.26. Two Words with the Same Meaning—126

6.27. Favorite Words and Expressions—126

6.28. Big Words Versus One-Syllable Words—127

6.29. Sentence Length—127

Letters the Secretary Writes—128

Letters Written Over the Secretary's Signature—128

6.30. Acknowledgment of Correspondence Received
       During Employer's Absence—128

6.31. Letters Calling Attention to an Error in an Account—133

6.32. Reply to Notice of Meeting—135

6.33. Letters Calling Attention to Omission of Enclosures—136

6.34. Follow-Up Letters—136

Letters the Secretary May Write for Employer's Signature—137

6.35. Letters of Appreciation—137

6.36. Letters of Sympathy—140

6.37. Letters of Congratulations—141

6.38. Letters of Introduction—143

6.39. Letters of Invitation—144

6.40. Letters of Acceptance—146

6.41. Letters of Declination—147

Contents

7. How to Keep Books and Records   *149*

How to Keep Books in the Law Office—149

    7.1. System of Bookkeeping in the Law Office—149
    7.2. Basic Principles of Double-Entry Bookkeeping—150
    7.3. Simple Rules to Remember—151
    7.4. Cash Journal—151
    7.5. General Ledger—153
    7.6. Subsidiary Ledger—154
    7.7. Posting to the General Ledger—155
    7.8. Trial Balance—157
    7.9. Taking a Trial Balance of Accounts Receivable—157
    7.10. Profit and Loss Statement—158
    7.11. Drawing Account—158
    7.12. Payroll Record—158
    7.13. Capital Account—161

Time and Cost of Professional Services—161

    7.14. Records Required to Find Time and Cost of Services—161
    7.15. Finding Out the Cost of a Lawyer's Time—161
    7.16. Daily Time Sheet—162
    7.17. Posting the Time Charges—162

Billing the Client—162

    7.18. Preparation of the Bill—162
    7.19. Charges Made to Clients—167

Petty Cash Fund—167

    7.20. How to Handle a Petty Cash Fund—167

8. Using References in Legal Research   *169*

Legal Research—169

    8.1. Electronic Research—170

Statutes and Codes—170

    8.2. Compilations of Laws—170
    8.3. How to Find a Law—171

Reports of Decided Cases—171

    8.4. Scope and Organization of Reports—171

8.5. How to Use the Reports and Reporters—173
8.6. How to Find Alternative Citations—174
8.7. Other Publications of Decisions—174
8.8. Looseleaf Services—175

Books That Classify the Law—176

American Digest—176

8.9. Scope and Organization of the Digest System—176
8.10. How to Use the Digest System—177

Shepard's Citations—177

8.11. Purpose of Shepard's Citations—177
8.12. How to Use Shepard's Citations—178

Corpus Juris Secundum System—180

8.13. Scope and Organization of System—180
8.14. How to Use Corpus Juris Secundum System—181
8.15. How to Cite—182

American Jurisprudence and American Law Reports—182

8.16. Scope and Organization of American Jurisprudence and
        American Law Reports—182

Federal and State Codes—182

8.17. Federal Codes of Regulations and State Codes—182

Form Books—183

8.18. Practice Manuals—183
8.19. Books of Legal Forms—183

Treatises—183

8.20. Purpose of Treatises—183

Other Reference Sources—184

8.21. Basic Reference Books—184
8.22. Useful Reference Books for Names and Addresses—184

Part 2. Preparing Legal Instruments and Documents   187

9. Handling Legal Instruments   *189*

The Legal Instrument—189

9.1. What Is a Legal Instrument?—189
9.2. Parties to an Instrument—190
9.3. How to Prepare Legal Instruments—190

Execution of an Instrument—191

9.4. What Is "Execution" of an Instrument?—191
9.5. Testimonium Clause—191
9.6. Signatures—194
9.7. How to Fit the Signatures on the Page—194
9.8. Sealing an Instrument—195
9.9. Attestation Clause—196

Acknowledgments—198

9.10. Importance of Acknowledgments in the Law Office—198
9.11. Laws Governing Acknowledgments—198
9.12. Essentials of an Acknowledgment—199
9.13. How and Where to Place the Acknowledgment—203
9.14. Who May Make an Acknowledgment—204
9.15. Who May Take an Acknowledgment—204
9.16. Authentication—205

Affidavits—205

9.17. What Is an Affidavit?—205
9.18. Distinction Between Affidavit and Acknowledgment--206
9.19. Essentials of an Affidavit—206
9.20. Authentication—207
9.21. Preparation of Affidavit—207

Notaries Public—209

9.22. What Is a Notary Public?—209
9.23. Following the Letter of the Law When You Notarize a Paper—210
9.24. What to Look for When You Notarize a Paper—211

Recording Legal Instruments—212

9.25. Purpose in Recording Instruments—212
9.26. Distinction Between Recording and Filing—212
9.27. What the Secretary or Paralegal Does—212

10. How to Prepare Legal Papers   *215*

Preparation Guidelines—215

10.1. Number of Copies—215
10.2. Paper—215
10.3. Margins—216
10.4. Paragraphs—216
10.5. Numbering Pages—216
10.6. Marginal and Tabular Stops—217
10.7. Tabulated Material—217
10.8. Responsibility and Distribution Line—217
10.9. Line Spacing—218
10.10. Standard Rules for Spacing—218
10.11. Space for Fill-ins—219
10.12. Underscoring—219
10.13. Quotations and Other Indented Material—220
10.14. Drafts—223
10.15. Correction of Errors—223
10.16. Copying—223
10.17. Collating—225
10.18. Conforming—225
10.19. Ditto Marks—225
10.20. Legal Backs—225
10.21. Printed Law Blanks—226

11. How to Handle Powers of Attorney and Wills   *227*

Powers of Attorney—227

11.1. What Is a Power of Attorney?—227
11.2. Parties to a Power of Attorney—227
11.3. Forms of Powers of Attorney—228
11.4. Statements and Clauses—228
11.5. Directions for the Preparation of a Power of Attorney—228

Wills—229

11.6. What Is a Will?—229
11.7. Who Are the Parties to a Will?—230
11.8. Forms and Kinds of Wills—231
11.9. Pattern of the Contents of Wills—232
11.10. Title—233
11.11. Introductory Paragraph—233
11.12. Revocation Clause—233

11.13. Text, or Body—233
11.14. Payment of Debts and Funeral Expenses—235
11.15. Dispositive Clauses—235
11.16. Trust Provisions—235
11.17. Residuary Clause—235
11.18. Appointment of Executor—236
11.19. Appointment of Guardian—236
11.20. Precatory Provisions—236
11.21. Testimonium, or Signature, Clause—237
11.22. Attestation Clause and Witnesses' Signatures—237
11.23. Preparing a Will—237
11.24. Signature Page and Preceding Page of a Will—238
11.25. How to Gauge and Test the Page Length—240
11.26. Witnessing a Will—240
11.27. Copies of Wills—240
11.28. Capitalization and Punctuation—241
11.29. "Dos and Don'ts" in Preparing a Will—241
11.30. Codicil—242
11.31. Red-Inking a Will—243

Part 3. Preparing Court Papers   **245**

12. Understanding Courts and Their Functions   *247*

Court System and Procedure—247

12.1. The Word "Court"—247
12.2. Court Procedure—248
12.3. What Happens in Court—249
12.4. Court Personnel—250
12.5. American Court System—252
12.6. Jurisdiction—255
12.7. Inferior Courts—257
12.8. Superior Courts—257
12.9. Courts of Special Jurisdiction—258
12.10. Courts of Intermediate Review—259
12.11. Supreme Appellate Courts—259
12.12. Distinction Between Equity and Law—260
12.13. Judges and Justices—261

12.14. The Trial Lawyer—262
12.15. Clerk of the Court—263
12.16. Clerk's Index System—263
12.17. Clerk's Permanent Record—264
12.18. Clerk's Minute Books—265
12.19. Court Calendar and Calendar Number—265
12.20. Calendar Call—265
12.21. Term of Court—266

Progress Records—267

12.22. How to Keep a Progress Record of Court Matters—267
12.23. Physical Features of a Suit Register—267
12.24. When and How to Open a Case in the Suit Register—268
12.25. What to Enter—269
12.26. Form and Sufficiency of Record—269
12.27. Closing the Record of a Case—273

13. Handling Court Papers   274

Parties to an Action—274

13.1. Party Bringing or Defending a Lawsuit—274
13.2. Parties to a Cross Action—275
13.3. Party Intervening—275
13.4. Parties on Appeal—275
13.5. Amicus Curiae—276
13.6. Who May Be Parties to a Lawsuit—276

Verifications—279

13.7. What Is a Verification?—279
13.8. Who May Verify a Pleading?—279
13.9. Forms of Verification—279
13.10. How to Format a Verification—280
13.11. How to Administer the Oath to Person Verifying a Pleading—284

How to Prepare Court Papers—284

13.12. Paper—284
13.13. Heading or Caption—284
13.14. How to Prepare the Caption—285
13.15. Captions on Papers Filed in Federal District Court—287
13.16. Indentions—289

Contents

13.17. Number of Copies—290
13.18. Numbering Pages—290
13.19. Conforming Copies—290
13.20. Use of Legal Backs—290
13.21. Folding—290
13.22. Printed Litigation Blanks—291

Practice and Procedure—291

13.23. The Secretary's Responsibility—291
13.24. Variations in Practice and Procedure—291

14. How to Prepare Court Papers   *292*

Summons and Complaint—293

14.1. Plaintiff's First Pleading—293
14.2. Analysis of a Complaint—294
14.3. How to Prepare the Complaint—295
14.4. Analysis of a Summons—297
14.5. How to Prepare the Summons—297
14.6. Return Day of Summons—299
14.7. Alias Summons; Pluries Summons—300
14.8. What to Do with the Summons and Complaint—300

Notice of Appearance—301

14.9. Analysis of a Notice of Appearance—301
14.10. How to Prepare a Notice of Appearance—302
14.11. What to Do with the Notice of Appearance—302

The Answer—302

14.12. Defendant's First Pleading—302
14.13. Analysis of an Answer—305
14.14. How to Prepare the Answer—305
14.15. Methods of Service of Answer on Plaintiff's Attorney—309
14.16. What to Do with the Answer—311

Motion to Dismiss—312

14.17. Analysis of a Motion to Dismiss—312
14.18. How to Prepare the Motion to Dismiss—313
14.19. What to Do with the Motion to Dismiss—313

Motion for More Definite Statement—317

14.20. Analysis of a Motion for More Definite Statement—317

14.21. How to Use Motion for More Definite Statement—317

14.22. Parts of Motion for More Definite Statement—317

14.23. How to Prepare the Motion for More Definite Statement—318

14.24. What to Do with the Motion for More Definite Statement—318

Other Motions—321

14.25. Examples of Other Motions—321

14.26. Return Day of Motion—322

14.27. Information You Need to Prepare the Motion—322

14.28. What to Do with the Motion and Affidavit—324

Affidavit for Use in Court—325

14.29. Analysis of an Affidavit—325

14.30. How to Prepare an Affidavit for Court Use—325

Motions or Assented to Motions (Stipulations)—326

14.31. Analysis of a Stipulation—326

14.32. How to Prepare a Stipulation—329

14.33. What to Do with Stipulations—330

Discovery (Interrogatories, Request for Production of Documents, Request for Admissions, Notice of Deposition)—330

14.34. Forms of Discovery—330

14.35. Interrogatories—331

14.36. How to Prepare Interrogatories—331

14.37. Request for Production of Documents—331

14.38. Request for Admissions—331

14.39. Depositions—332

Notice of Trial—332

14.40. Noticing a Case for Trial—332

14.41. Note of Issue—332

14.42. What to Do with a Note of Issue—332

Requests for Findings and Rulings—336

14.43. Analysis of Findings of Fact and Conclusions
       (or Rulings) of Law—336

14.44. How to Prepare Findings of Fact and Conclusions
       (or Rulings) of Law—336

14.45. What to Do with Findings of Fact and Conclusions
     (or Rulings) of Law—337

Instructions to the Jury—337

14.46. Nature of Instructions to the Jury—337
14.47. How to Prepare Instructions to the Jury—338

Orders—338

14.48. Proposed Orders—338
14.49. How to Prepare an Order—339
14.50. What to Do with an Order—339

Judgments and Decrees—342

14.51. Analysis of Judgments and Decrees—342

15. How to Handle Records on Appeal, Briefs, and Citations   345

Procedure for Review—345

15.1. Rules of the Reviewing Court—345
15.2. Methods for Review by a Higher Court—346
15.3. Diary Entries—347
15.4. Change in Caption of Case—347
15.5. Designation of Parties to an Appeal—348
15.6. Notice of Appeal—348
15.7. Service on Opposing Counsel—350

Contents and Preparation of the Record on Appeal—350

15.8. What Is a Record on Appeal?—350
15.9. Assignment of Errors and Instructions to the Clerk—352
15.10. Who Prepares the Record?—352

The Brief—353

15.11. Nature of a Brief—353
15.12. Preliminaries to Preparing a Brief—353
15.13. Time Element—354
15.14. Preparation of a Brief—354
15.15. Application for Oral Argument—356

Citations—360

15.16. What Is a Citation?—360
15.17. Accuracy of Citations—360

15.18. Research—361
15.19. Official Reports and the National Reporter System—361
15.20. How to Cite a Constitution—362
15.21. How to Cite Statutes and Codes—362
15.22. How to Cite Cases in Official Reports and Reporters—363
15.23. Named Reporters—365
15.24. String Citations—365
15.25. How to Cite an Unpublished Case—365
15.26. How to Cite Slip Decisions—365
15.27. How to Cite Treatises—366
15.28. How to Cite Law Reviews—366
15.29. How to Cite Legal Newspapers—366
15.30. Underscoring and Italicizing—366
15.31. Spacing of Abbreviations—367
15.32. Placement of Citations—367
15.33. Illustrations of Citations—368

Part 4.   Assisting in Specialized Practice   **371**

16. Assisting in Partnership Formation and Incorporation   *373*

Corporations—374

16.1. What Is a Corporation?—374
16.2. Steps in the Organization of a Corporation—375
16.3. Who May Form a Corporation?—376
16.4. State of Incorporation—376
16.5. Memorandum, or Checklist, Preliminary to Preparation
       of Incorporating Papers—377
16.6. Reservation of Name—378
16.7. Incorporation Papers—380
16.8. Preparation of the Articles of Incorporation—380
16.9. Execution of the Incorporation Papers—383
16.10. Filing the Incorporation Papers and Payment of Fees—384
16.11. Necessity and Purpose of Organization Meeting—386
16.12. Preparation for the Organization Meeting—387
16.13. Corporate Outfit—387
16.14. Waiver of Notice of Organization Meeting—389
16.15. Preparation of Bylaws—390

16.16. Minutes of First Meeting of Incorporators—392
16.17. Minutes of First Meeting of Directors—392
16.18. Resolution Opening a Bank Account—392
16.19. Preparation of Stock Certificates—393

Partnerships—393

16.20. What Is a Partnership?—393
16.21. How a Partnership Is Formed—393
16.22. Preparation of Partnership Agreement—394

17. Acting as Corporate Secretary   *395*

Duties and Responsibilities—395

17.1. What the Secretary and Paralegal Will Do—395

Corporate Meetings—396

17.2. Kinds of Meetings—396
17.3. Preparation for Meeting—397
17.4. Meeting Folder—397
17.5. Notice of Stockholders' Meeting—398
17.6. Waiver of Notice of Stockholders' Meeting—398
17.7. Quorum at Stockholders' Meeting—398
17.8. Proxies and Proxy Statement—399
17.9. Notice of Directors' Meeting—400
17.10. Quorum at Directors' Meeting—400
17.11. Preservation of Notice—401
17.12. The Agenda—401
17.13. Reservation and Preparation of the Meeting Room—401
17.14. Directors' Fees—402
17.15. Material to Take to Meetings—402
17.16. Drafting Resolutions Before Meetings—403
17.17. Preparation for Taking Notes at Meetings—403
17.18. Taking Notes at Meetings—405

Minutes—406

17.19. The Minutes—406
17.20. Arrangement of Contents of Minute Book—406
17.21. Content of Minutes—407
17.22. Preparation of Draft of Minutes—407
17.23. How to Prepare Minutes in Final Form—408

17.24. Correction of Errors in Minutes—409
17.25. Certified Extract of Minutes—409
17.26. Indexing of Minutes—410

Issuance and Transfer of Stock of a Small Corporation—412

17.27. Authority to Issue Certificate—412
17.28. Stock Certificate Book—412
17.29. Original Issue and Transfer of Stock—412
17.30. Issuance of Certificate of Stock—414
17.31. Transfer of Certificate—415
17.32. Separate Form of Assignment—416

The Corporation Calendar—416

17.33. Need for a Corporation Calendar—416
17.34. How to Keep the Corporation Calendar—418
17.35. Where to Get Dates for the Corporation Calendar—418

Change of Corporate Name—419

17.36. When the Corporate Name Is Changed—419

Corporation Forms—420

17.37. Model Corporation Forms—420

18. Assisting in Real Estate Practice and Foreclosures   *430*

Real Estate Instruments—430

18.1. Pattern Followed for Each Instrument—430

Real Property Descriptions—431

18.2. How Land Is Described—431
18.3. Section and Township Description—431
18.4. Metes and Bounds Description—433
18.5. The Plat System—433
18.6. How to Prepare Real Property Descriptions—435
18.7. How to Check Land Descriptions—436

Deeds—436

18.8. What Is a Deed?—436
18.9. Parties to Deed—436
18.10. Forms of Deeds—437
18.11. Kinds of Deeds—437

18.12. Printed Form of Deed—438
18.13. Information Needed for Form—438
18.14. Deeds Prepared by Computer—440
18.15. Statements and Clauses in Deeds—440
18.16. State Taxes—443
18.17. Cancellation of Stamps—443
18.18. Recording of Deed—443
18.19. How to Prepare a Deed—444

Mortgages—447

18.20. What Is a Mortgage?—447
18.21. Parties to a Mortgage—447
18.22. Designation of the Parties—447
18.23. Forms of Mortgages—448
18.24. Purchase Money Mortgage—449
18.25. Printed Mortgages—449
18.26. Information Needed for Mortgage or Deed of Trust—450
18.27. Computer-Prepared Mortgages and Deeds of Trust—451
18.28. Statements and Clauses in Mortgages—451
18.29. State Tax—454
18.30. How to Prepare a Mortgage—454

Leases—454

18.31. What Is a Lease?—454
18.32. Parties to Lease—455
18.33. Classification of Lease—455
18.34. Printed Form of Lease—456
18.35. Standard Lease Clauses—456
18.36. Standard Clauses in Commercial Leases—457
18.37. Style of Computer-Prepared Lease—458
18.38. Execution, Acknowledgment, and Recording of Lease—458
18.39. How to Prepare a Lease—459

Purchase and Sale Agreements—459

18.40. What Is a Purchase and Sale Agreement?—459
18.41. Need for a Purchase and Sale Agreement—460
18.42. Types of Contracts of Sale of Land—460
18.43. Parties to a Purchase and Sale Agreement—461
18.44. How to Prepare a Purchase and Sale Agreement—461

18.45. Information Needed for Form—461
18.46. Earnest Money—462
18.47. Escrow for the Sale of Real Property—463

Title Closings and Evidence of Title—463

18.48. What Is a Title Closing?—463
18.49. Evidence of Title—464
18.50. Abstract of Title—464
18.51. Opinion of Title—465
18.52. Mechanics and Materialman's Liens—467
18.53. Hazardous Substances—467
18.54. Certificate of Title—467
18.55. Title Insurance Policies—467
18.56. Torrens Certificate—468
18.57. Preparations for Closing—468

Preparation of Closing Statement—470

18.58. What Is a Closing Statement?—470
18.59. How to Calculate Adjustments—471
18.60. Example of Calculation of Tax Adjustment—474
18.61. Example of Calculation of Interest Adjustment—474
18.62. Example of Calculation of Insurance Adjustment—475
18.63. Example of Calculation of Rent Adjustment—475
18.64. Miscellaneous Payments—475

Foreclosure Actions—476

18.65. What Is a Foreclosure Action?—476
18.66. Papers Necessary for Institution of Foreclosure Action—477
18.67. Information Needed to Prepare Papers in Foreclosure Action—477
18.68. Venue—477
18.69. Parties to a Foreclosure Action—478
18.70. Fictitious Names—478
18.71. Description of Note or Bond—479
18.72. Description of Mortgage—479
18.73. Description of Property—479
18.74. When Is a Mortgage Considered in Default?—480

Procedure in Foreclosure Action—480

18.75. Title Search for Foreclosures—480
18.76. Preparation of Complaint—480

Contents

18.77. Number of Copies—481
18.78. Preparation of Summons—482
18.79. Filing and Service of Complaint and Summons—482
18.80. Follow-up of Process Service—482
18.81. Party Sheet—482
18.82. Other Steps in Foreclosure Proceedings—483
18.83. What to Do in Foreclosure Action—484

19. *Assisting with Probate and Estate Administration*   *486*

Administration of Estate—486

19.1. Distinction Between Executor and Administrator—486
19.2. The Lawyer's Part in the Administration of an Estate—487
19.3. Estate Taxes—488

Probate of Will—488

19.4. The Personal Representative's Right to Act—488
19.5. Probate of Will—488
19.6. Parties to a Probate Proceeding—489
19.7. Copy of Will and Affidavit—489
19.8. Petition for Probate of Will—491
19.9. Transfer Tax Affidavit—491
19.10. Citation and Waiver in Probate Proceeding—493
19.11. How to Handle a Waiver of Citation—493
19.12. How to Handle a Citation—494
19.13. Preparations for Hearing—494
19.14. Notice of Probate—495
19.15. Deposition of Witnesses to the Will—495
19.16. Oath of Personal Representative—496
19.17. Decree Admitting Will to Probate—496
19.18. Letters Testatmentary—497
19.19. Notice to Creditors—497

Appointment of Administrator—498

19.20. Application for Letters of Administration—498
19.21. Parties—498
19.22. Who Has Prior Right to Letters of Administration?—499
19.23. Necessary Papers in Application for Letters of Administration—499
19.24. How to Handle a Petition; Oath; Designation of Clerk—499
19.25. Renunciation—500

19.26. Citations—500
19.27. Notice of Application for Letters of Administration—501
19.28. Letters of Administration—501

20. Handling Commercial Collections   *502*

Collection Procedures—502

20.1. Commercial Law Lists—502
20.2. Office Procedures Affecting Collections—503
20.3. How to File Collection Matters—503
20.4. Acknowledgment of Claim—504
20.5. Collection Letters—504
20.6. Reports to the Forwarder—506
20.7. Installment Payments—506
20.8. Record of Collections—506
20.9. Remitting—506
20.10. Fees—510
20.11. Forwarding an Item for Collection—510

Uncontested Suit—511

20.12. When the Lawyer Recommends Suit—511
20.13. Complaint and Summons—512
20.14. Preparation and Service of a Summons
       and Short-Form Complaint—512
20.15. Information Needed to Draw a Complaint and Summons—513
20.16. Judgment by Default—514
20.17. How to Prepare a Judgment by Default—514

Part 5.   Legal Facts and Secretarial Aids   **517**

Forms of Address: Honorary and Official Positions   *519*

Chief Justice, U.S. Supreme Court—519
Associate Justice, U.S. Supreme Court—519
Retired Justice, U.S. Supreme Court—520
Chief Justice, Chief Judge, State Supreme Court—520
Associate Justice, Highest Court of a State—520
Presiding Justice—520
Judge of a Court—521
Clerk of a Court—521

Latin Words and Phrases   *523*

Glossary of Legal Terms   *533*

Courts of Record and Judicial Circuits   *575*

    I. Federal Courts of Record in the United States and Their Members—575
    II. State Courts of Record in the United States and Their Members—576
    III. Judicial Circuits and the States and Territories in Each Circuit—583
    IV. States and Territories and Judicial Circuit in Which Each Is Located—584

Index   *585*

Foreword

Today's law firms vary greatly in size and specialty, ranging from the sole practitioner personally handling all of the matters that come into the law office, usually with the assistance of a secretary and perhaps a paralegal, to very large firms employing hundreds of lawyers with clerical and paraprofessional staff and having branch offices nationally and internationally.

Law firms are increasingly specialized. Large firms have departments for various specialties, such as tax law, real estate, estate planning, trusts, bankruptcy, patent law, domestic relations, personal injury, commercial law, and criminal law. Smaller firms tend to focus their practice on one or more areas of law, or each lawyer may have his or her own interest and expertise.

Your employer may be a lawyer but may not work in a conventional law firm. You may be employed in the office of a corporate counsel, a municipal "solicitor," or a state or federal department of justice. Or you may work with a lawyer whose major activity is more akin to managing a business than to the practice of the usual client-oriented law firm. In these situations there is only one client—the corporation, city, state, or business.

The employer's requirements for secretarial and clerical assistance will vary with the size, complexity, and age of the firm. A sole practitioner, especially one who has been in practice for a relatively short time, will look to his or her secretary to set up filing, billing, and other office systems or to maintain and improve existing ones. Large firms, on the other hand, will have an extensive division of labor and well-established ways of doing things, which you will be expected to learn and follow. Some will have handbooks detailing their procedures. Training of new employees will be institutionalized, and you may be responsible to a supervisor who is not a lawyer.

Whatever the size or type of firm, there are basic concepts common to the practice of law. As you prepare correspondence and documents you will begin to learn something about the kind of practice in which your employer is engaged. This does not make you a lawyer, and you should *never* give legal advice, but it will help you to take accurate telephone messages; to respond intelligently to clients' calls, especially when the lawyer is not available; and to ensure that materials are properly organized and handled.

In most firms lawyers have some individual latitude and may want certain matters handled in a particular way. But individual peculiarities must give way to the need for common codes for filing, record access, billing, and backup of client services.

Before using any of the procedures described in this book, find out if your office already has established a method for accomplishing the particular task. If so, you should become thoroughly familiar with the existing system.

Electronic technology has affected the law office as it has every other aspect of modern business and professional practice. You may find that you will know or learn more than your employer about new developments in computer and communications technology that could improve the efficiency of the office. If you think there may be a better way of doing something, you may be right. But don't implement something new until you check with others who may be affected by your new system, especially your employer. Lawyers usually do not have much time to spend learning elaborate new systems and may choose to continue with a "horse and buggy" system simply because they know how to use it.

This book takes into account the variations that exist among lawyers and the firms they represent. It provides a detailed look at practices and procedures that are common in the legal profession and thereby aims to increase the knowledge and skill you need to function intelligently in a modern law firm.

Carolyn W. Baldwin

Preface to the Fourth Edition

This revised fourth edition of the *Legal Secretary's Complete Handbook* takes a step into the computerized legal profession of the 1990s. The number of changes that have been made is evident in the table of contents and the index. There you will find completely new topics that move the book into the computer age, such as "The Computer in Database Management" and "Facsimile Machines," as well as revisions that modernize outmoded discussions and terminology, such as the "Motion for More Definite Statement" replacing the former "Demand for bill of Particulars" and the "Motion to Dismiss" replacing the former "Demurrer."

To help those who have been using the third edition in following the sequence of major topics in this edition, we have retained the same general chapter structure.

In Part 1, the former first chapter ("Working in a Law Office") has been reorganized into two introductory chapters, the first of which considers key aspects of the modern law office, including law-office automation and the use of computers. The second chapter looks at procedures in opening client files and in creating documents. Chapter 3 discusses contacts with clients and other callers. Chapters 4 and 5 explain reminder systems and filing systems. Chapter 6 covers legal and business correspondence, Chapter 7 reviews bookkeeping and other record-keeping practices, and Chapter 8 looks at legal research.

Part 2 moves into a discussion of handling legal instruments and documents, including affidavits and acknowledgments (Chapter 9), and preparing legal papers (Chapter 10). Chapter 11 reviews powers of attorney and wills.

Part 3 concerns court papers, with Chapter 12 explaining court systems and procedures and Chapters 13 and 14 discussing the preparation and processing of court papers. Chapter 15 looks at records on appeal, briefs, and citations.

Part 4 examines some important areas of specialized practice, such as partnership formation and incorporation (Chapter 16), corporation activities (Chapter 17), real estate (Chapter 18), probate and estate administration (Chapter 19), and commercial collections (Chapter 20).

Part 5 provides useful legal facts and secretarial aids: forms of address for honorary and official positions, Latin words and phrases, a glossary of legal terms, and tables of state and federal courts and judicial circuits in the United States.

A wealth of new information has been introduced covering everything from computerized filing to interrogatories. Examples of new topics include automation in the law office, the computer in document assembly, the use of databases, handling unscrupulous vendors, computer-generated billing, electronic research, computer-generated legal forms, current styles for court papers, explanation of discovery, requests for admissions, depositions, Subchapter S corporations, steps in dissolving a corporation, explanation of mechanics and materialman's liens, estate taxes, and the distinction between consumer and commercial collections.

In addition to adding new topics, we have thoroughly checked and updated the previous edition. Procedures and practices have changed in many cases, and sometimes a new format or a completely new form is required for certain things. Among the modernized forms you will find a new matter (case) report, a fax transmission form, a complaint, a summons, a notice of appearance, a certificate of service, an assented to motion, a notice of deposition, an affidavit of service by mail, a page from a brief, a page from incorporation papers, a deed, and a real estate closing statement. Readers are cautioned, however, that all illustrations and examples throughout the book are samples only. Often facts have been changed to fictionalize or modernize an example. Moreover, requirements may vary from one jurisdiction to another, and you should always consult local rules and practices for precise wording and format of any document or element within a document.

The wide range of legal information in this fourth edition is intended to be useful to both beginning and veteran legal secretaries, paralegals, and other coworkers in the legal profession. Recent important changes in the law and the practice of law have been incorporated in the book wherever possible. To achieve this, a team of experts (see Acknowledgments) pooled their knowledge and efforts to correct and update the entire book line by line and page by page. The result is a collection of essential information that should vastly enhance the skills and professional capabilities of all of those associated with law-office activities in the 1990s.

Mary A. De Vries

Acknowledgments

The work of a revisor is often measured by the team assembled to undertake the revision process. In preparing the fourth edition of the *Legal Secretary's Complete Handbook,* I was especially fortunate to have the help of some extraordinary professionals with impressive credentials. Many professional people and organizations, in fact, made important contributions to this edition, providing a rich supply of practical advice, guidance, literature, and encouragement.

In particular, I want to thank Ashley S. Lipson, managing partner, Coleman, Lipson, and Bradford, P.C., in Farmington Hills, Michigan. Lipson, author of *Law Office Automation for Paralegals, Administrators, and Legal Secretaries* as well as numerous articles, reviewed the third edition and prepared an extensive critique, including not only corrections in the third edition and suggestions for detailed revision but also many pages of important new material to be incorporated into the fourth edition. His keen insight and practical commentaries were invaluable.

Several other individuals participated in the revision process by providing reviews of or correcting chapters in the previous edition. I greatly appreciated the many helpful revision suggestions of Deborah E. Larbalestrier, twice past president of the American Paralegal Association and a member of the Advisory Board of the University of West Los Angeles School of Paralegal Studies. I'm also grateful to Max Moses, executive vice president, Commercial Law League in Chicago, who reviewed and corrected Chapter 20 on commercial collections. Special thanks are due to Margaret Watkins, paralegal, Baldwin & de Séve in Concord, New Hampshire, who played an especially important role in the revision work by conducting ongoing research and providing line-by-line corrections and additions throughout the entire project. The book has benefited enormously from the contributions of these talented professionals and would have suffered considerably in their absence.

Above all, it is impossible to imagine how the book could have been prepared without the counsel of Carolyn W. Baldwin, partner,

Baldwin & de Séve in Concord, New Hampshire. Ms. Baldwin, who also had participated in the revision of the third edition, accepted the difficult task of serving as legal consultant throughout the project, a demanding position that required her to review thousands of facts and figures in depth and supply substantial new information in all of the chapters. I deeply appreciate her dedication and tireless efforts to make the fourth edition the most accurate and up-to-date handbook available, and I sincerely thank her for this generous and impressive contribution.

None of these individuals, however, is responsible for any errors that may have resulted from my own efforts during the complex process of putting all the pieces together or during the final stages of production.

Mary A. De Vries

Part 1

GENERAL DUTIES IN THE LAW OFFICE

1. Working in a Law Office

2. Opening Client Files and Creating Documents

3. Contacts with Clients and Other Callers

4. Reminder Systems and Practices

5. Filing in the Law Office

6. Handling Legal and Business Correspondence

7. How to Keep Books and Records

8. Using References in Legal Research

1 Working in a Law Office

An understanding of what a law office is like and how it functions is necessary to perform your duties intelligently. You need to know what is expected of you in a law office, the training and effort necessary for a lawyer to build a successful practice, the organization and personnel of a law firm, and the type of equipment and services you will use.

YOU AND THE LAWYER

1.1. The Law-Office Team

Successful offices function through effective teamwork. If you are employed in a law office, you are a member of the team whether you work for one or several attorneys. Like all of the other people on the team, you will be expected to pull your share of the load and, to do that, will need to understand the lawyer's work and take an active interest in it. Moreover, you will need to be loyal and discreet and be governed by high standards in all of your actions. Those who work in a law office, in addition to being able to think and write accurately, must have initiative, administrative ability, judgment, and a deep sense of responsibility.

1.2. Ethics in the Law Office

People who work in a law office are bound by the same code of ethics as their employers. You and other members of the law-office team cannot solicit business for the lawyer, and must regard everything you know about a client or a case as confidential. You and your coworkers must therefore never divulge the contents of a written document in the office without

3

permission from the lawyer. Also, you must never talk outside the office about a case even if the remarks are merely an anecdote.

Although it may be tempting to entertain friends with interesting tidbits about socially prominent clients, it is necessary to resist such temptations since irreparable harm could result from mentioning anything about what is transpiring in a case. Suppose that a lawyer should dictate an application for injunction against removal of certain property from the county so that he or she can levy upon it. If anyone would mention this, the owner of the property, especially in a small town, might hear about it and remove the property before the order is served. Information received from clients in the course of work is "privileged communication" (see section 1.9).

To help you understand the matter of ethics more fully, read the American Bar Association's (ABA's) Code of Professional Ethics or the rules of professional conduct developed for the state(s) in which your employer practices. Every law office should have copies of both. For the ABA code, write to the American Bar Association, 750 North Lake Shore Drive, Chicago, IL 60611.

1.3. Legal Training

A lawyer spends many years in training for admittance to the bar. This usually includes four years in college, three years in law school, and a state examination. A practicing lawyer finds that competition is keen; practice is arduous for almost all lawyers and not always lucrative.

1.4. Requirements for Admission to the Bar

Each state has its own requirements for admission to the bar. In every state the requirements include four factors: academic training, legal training, moral character, and belief in and loyalty to the U.S. form of government.

In almost all states the applicant for admission to the bar must take an examination, even though he or she is a law school graduate. Graduates of a few schools have been admitted without examination in some states. Admission to practice in one state does not license the attorney to practice in another state. He or she must comply with the rules that each state has for admission of an attorney applicant. Many states, however, have reciprocal agreements and will admit an attorney from another state without examination, or with a limited examination, after he or she has practiced a specified time, provided the applicant meets other requirements. Some states require that every attorney applicant take an examination.

License to practice in one or more states does not admit the lawyer to practice in the federal courts. To be admitted to practice in the U.S. Supreme Court, an attorney must have practiced three years immediately preceding application in the highest court in his or her state or territory.

An attorney may obtain special permission, sometimes called *pro hac vice*, to argue a particular case before a court in which he or she is not licensed to practice. This often happens in criminal cases when the accused wants a nationally famous criminal lawyer to represent him or her in the state in which the accused is to be tried.

1.5. Law Degrees

The law degrees obtainable and the abbreviations of them follow. Notice that in some cases the abbreviation of the Latin word *juris*, meaning "law," is used. (The LL.D. is sometimes conferred as an honorary degree.)

Bachelor of Laws	LL.B.; B.L.
Bachelor of Civil Law	J.C.B.; B.C.L.
Master of Laws	LL.M.; M.L.
Doctor of Laws	LL.D.; J.D.
Doctor of Law	Jur.D.
Doctor of Civil Law	J.C.D.; D.C.L.
Juris Civilis Doctor	J.C.D.
Doctor of Jurisprudence	J.D.
Juris Doctor	Jur. D.; J.D.
Jurum Doctor	J.D.
Doctor of Juristic Science	J.S.D.
Doctor of Both Laws	J.U.D.

Traditionally, after three years of study, law schools conferred a bachelor's degree, generally the LL.B. But in recent years, in recognition of the length of study required, most schools now confer a doctor of jurisprudence degree or its equivalent.

1.6. Specialization

General practitioners in law, as in medicine, are gradually disappearing. Specialization in law is more prevalent in large cities than in small towns. If you work for a specialist or are assigned to a particular department in a large firm, your work will probably be in only one field: corporate law (Chapters 16 and 17), real estate matters and foreclosures (Chapter 18), probate matters (Chapter 19), or some other specialized field such as taxation, administrative law and practice, or domestic relations.

The trend toward specialization results from the lawyer's inclination and liking for a special field and from the human impossibility of becoming expert in every field. Specialization is a great timesaver for both the lawyer and the staff. The lawyer who handles a tax matter as incidental to his or her other practice must spend hours doing research on a problem that a tax specialist could dispose of in a few minutes, because the specialist deals with the same problem every day.

Administrative Law

Increasingly, the practice of law involves dealing with government entities—federal, state, county, and municipal. Government agencies administer the statutes within their jurisdiction. They have authority to make decisions, issue orders, and hold hearings on appeals of administrative decisions.

Administrative agencies at the federal level, for example, might be the Social Security Administration, National Labor Relations Board, Environmental Protection Agency, and Internal Revenue Service. At the state level there are agencies with similar authority. At the county and municipal levels you will find planning and zoning commissions, tax abatement boards, and county commissioners and city councils.

Practice before regulatory agencies may be an important part of the lawyer's work. Each agency has its own rules and procedures, set up under the authority of its particular statute. Hearings are less formal than court trials, and there is no jury. Administrative tribunals may consist of three or more members, or the matter may be heard by a single hearing officer or administrative law judge. Whatever the structure, appeal is statutory and is usually directly to an appellate-level court, not to a trial court.

Codes of regulations are published by administrative agencies. At the federal level it is called the Code of Federal Regulations (CFR). State agencies' regulations may be called Code of Administrative Rules or a similar title. County and municipal boards will administer zoning ordinances, building codes, health regulations, and ordinances pertaining to any number of matters.

Matters before administrative agencies may be either *quasi judicial;* that is, they are making a decision on a particular matter based on the law and implementing regulations, or *quasi legislative;* that is, they are revising the rules and regulations. In either case, it is important to prepare thoroughly for administrative hearings, because their decisions have the force of law, and the record before the agency will serve as a basis in the event the decision is appealed.

1.7. Building a Practice

Graduating from law school and being admitted to the bar does not mean that the lawyer will succeed in building a worthwhile practice. He or she must have not only the necessary training and knowledge of law but also a personality that will attract clients, gain their confidence, and hold it.

Traditionally, lawyers were not permitted to advertise under the Canons of Ethics or the more recent Code of Professional Responsibility of the American Bar Association, but the U.S. Supreme Court has struck down this prohibition as unconstitutional. State courts and bar associations have established standards and guidelines for advertising. However, lawyers have always been able to engage in practices such as sending out announcement cards stating that they are engaged in the practice of law at a certain address. Lawyers also send these announcements when they join a new firm or move the offices. Figure 1.1 illustrates an announcement when the lawyer first enters practice; Figure 1.2, when he or she resumes practice; and Figure 1.3, when he or she moves the offices. (See pp. 8-9.)

It is helpful for the secretary to compile and maintain a permanent list of people that may be sent announcements. The list may be maintained by computer for ease in regularly entering additions or changes (some secretaries also maintain a three-by-five-inch index card file or Rolodex).

Announcements may be mailed to the groups listed below.

Friends and acquaintances. You will have to depend primarily on the lawyer to compile this list initially, but you can maintain it by adding the names of contacts that he or she makes that you know about and by keeping the addresses on the list up to date.

ROLAND ADAMS

ANNOUNCES THE OPENING OF HIS OFFICE

FOR THE PRACTICE OF LAW

AT

210 EAST 45TH STREET

NEW YORK, N.Y. 10017
—
212-432-1000

Figure 1.1.   Announcement When Entering Practice.

One West Avenue
Chicago, Illinois 60616

Donald T. Lewis, having completed his term as a
Justice of the Supreme Court of the State of Illinois, announces
his return to the practice of law with the firm of

Wilson & Lewis

January 15, 19__   *312-665-4000*

Figure 1.2.   Announcement When Resuming Practice.

Members of the local bar. Most state bar associations publish lists of
their members with addresses and telephone numbers. The telephone directory, classified section, will contain information on local law firms.

DOUGLAS, HART & MORRIS

ANNOUNCE THE REMOVAL OF THEIR OFFICES TO

400 MARKET STREET

SAN FRANCISCO, CALIFORNIA 94105

WHERE THEY WILL CONTINUE THE GENERAL PRACTICE

OF LAW UNDER THE FIRM NAME OF

DOUGLAS, HART, MORRIS & WEBER

AUGUST 1, 19_ _   415-010-1000

Figure 1.3. Announcement of Removal of Offices.

Martindale-Hubbell Law Directory contains a list of lawyers and their addresses in the United States and Canada, but not all lawyers are included. Every law library and many law offices have this directory, which contains a wealth of useful information about law and lawyers in various jurisdictions. Time spent becoming familiar with its organization and contents is well worthwhile.

County officials. Each state publishes a "bluebook," directory, register, or roster that contains the names of county officers, state officers, judges, members of the Senate and House, and names of departments and administrative offices. Probably, a more accessible source for the names of county officials is the clerks' office in the county courthouse.

Classmates. You can get the names and addresses of the lawyer's college and law-school classmates from the permanent secretary of his or her class. If there is no permanent class secretary, write to the alumni secretary who will refer you to the proper source for the information or send it to you.

Clients. The name of each client should be added to the announcement list.

1.8. The Lawyer's Outside Activities

The legal profession is a public service; its purpose is the administration of justice. Therefore, the lawyer's first interest in outside activities is usually the work of the bar association—that is the lawyer's duty as a member of the profession. But the lawyer also takes a wholehearted interest in civic affairs—the school, church, charities, and any movement that will improve the community. The lawyer's position in the community demands that he or she participate in its affairs. Participation is the lawyer's duty; paralegals, legal secretaries, and other personnel should make it theirs. This should include reading the reports of the bar association and keeping informed about what is going on locally and nationally. In addition, you can be alert for news items of interest to the lawyer that you can call to his or her attention. The lawyer will appreciate your interest and your willingness to help by doing things beyond the scope of your actual duties.

1.9. The Lawyer's Relationship with Clients

A lawyer is a fiduciary whose relationship with a client is one of trust and confidence. Lawyers represent clients' interests to the best of their ability. They do not use their position of trust and confidence to further personal or private interests. They never discuss the client's business with outsiders but consider it strictly confidential. So sacred is the relationship between lawyer and client that information given to a lawyer by a client is a *privileged communication;* that is, the lawyer can rarely be compelled to testify concerning it.

1.10. Fees

A fairly standard charge is made in many communities for certain items of work, including drawing deeds and mortgages, examining abstracts, evicting tenants, obtaining default divorces, foreclosing mortgages, organizing corporations, and probating estates, providing these matters have no unusual complications. Time is a major consideration in billing, although each office has its own method of determining fees. In any case, an accurate record of the time spent on each item is always important.

The type of fee charged is important to you for record and bookkeeping purposes (Chapter 6). Fees are classified as follows:

Single retainer. The client retains the lawyer for a specific case and agrees to pay a specified fee. Usually, the retainer is paid in advance.

Yearly retainer. Many organizations are constantly in need of legal advice and have numerous legal matters to be looked after. They retain lawyers on an annual basis. When a client is on a yearly retainer basis, you should know whether a specific matter is covered by the retainer or is to be charged for separately.

Contingent fee. In certain types of cases the lawyer may agree to take a case for a client for a percentage of the amount recovered. The fee is contingent on the successful outcome of the case. Contingent fees are customary in personal injury cases, especially if the client is unable to pay for the lawyer's time except out of the damages he or she might recover.

Referral, or forwarding, fee. Frequently, a case is referred to a lawyer by an out-of-town firm. The American Bar Association, however, disapproves of referral fees unless the lawyer receiving the fee has performed work or incurred responsibility and the client is made aware of the fee.

Collection charges. The collection of commercial items is a special branch of law practice (Chapter 20). Often there is a standard charge for collection cases, based on a percentage of the amount collected, with an additional fee if suit is necessary.

ORGANIZATION AND PERSONNEL OF A LAW FIRM

1.11. Kind of Business Organization

Formerly, state statutes did not permit lawyers to incorporate—a lawyer either practiced alone or entered into a partnership with one or more lawyers. Most states now permit lawyers to form professional corporations or professional associations. When firms are incorporated, the letters *P.C.* or *P.A.* will appear on the letterhead after the name of the firm. The lawyer's highly personal obligation to his or her clients is not affected by incorporation.

A law firm frequently consists of a senior partner or partners, a junior partner or partners, and associate lawyers. Even if a lawyer does not have a partner, he or she frequently has associates. They are paid a salary and do not share in the firm's profits, nor are they responsible for its obligations. When lawyers' names are listed on the letterhead of a law firm or on the door of a law office, a line sometimes separates one group of names from another group. The names below the line are the names of associate lawyers who are not members of the firm.

In any law firm, whether large or small, a designated partner or director is responsible for the smooth functioning of the organization. Generally, this partner is called the "managing partner." All of the service departments—accounting, filing, word processing, maintenance of the court docket—are under his or her supervision.

1.12. Personnel in a Law Office

One of the many compensations of working in a law office is the type of people with whom you are associated. The prestige and dignity of a law office demand that every position in the firm be filled by a person of intelligence and refinement.

The particular division of labor will depend on the size of the firm— from a sole practitioner to hundreds of lawyers in numerous branch offices. Usually, the fewer the lawyers, the more varied will be the tasks of the legal secretary and other office personnel. The number of persons in a particular position will depend on the size of the firm and volume of work. One person alone may fill several positions in a small firm or if the volume of work is small. Although actual job titles may vary from one firm to another, the following list illustrates the variety of positions that exist in many firms:

Partners or directors (in a professional corporation)

Associate lawyers

Managing clerk

Law clerks

Docket clerks

Firm business manager

Office manager

Paralegals

Supervisor of secretaries

Supervisor of equipment and machines

Secretaries

Proofreaders

Receptionist

Bookkeepers

Clerks

File clerk

Mail clerk

Telephone operators

Computer operators

Messengers

Paralegals, or legal assistants, have become important additions to the personnel of a law firm. They usually have a college background including paralegal studies or they may have completed a paralegal training program. Some firms prefer to train their most experienced legal secretaries to become paralegals. The paralegals' education and training enable them to help lawyers perform many tasks, such as handling legal research and analyses, drafting and preparing legal documents, interviewing clients and witnesses, organizing and maintaining dockets and files, and conducting real estate closings. Paralegal duties vary widely from office to office; members of the profession are found in all sectors of society, including law firms, courts, business and financial institutions, and government.

1.13. The Secretary's Duties

In a small law office the work and responsibilities of all service departments fall on the secretary. In a large office, such responsibilities may be divided among secretaries and other personnel. In any case, secretaries must be familiar with the various responsibilities so that they can cooperate with other departments. In addition to handling word processing duties and operation of facsimiles and other equipment, the secretary in a law office may perform some or all of the following tasks:

1. Writing letters (Chapter 6)
2. Making appointments (Chapters 3 and 4)
3. Taking and placing telephone calls (Chapter 3)
4. Filing (Chapter 5)
5. Maintaining the diary and tickler file (Chapter 4)

6. Keeping account of charges, disbursements, and collections (Chapter 7)
7. Following office cases on court calendars (Chapter 13)
8. Maintaining the court docket or suit register (Chapter 12)
9. Greeting clients (Chapter 3)

1.14. Deportment

The dignity of a law firm should be maintained at all times by its personnel. An impression of refinement is reflected in knowledge of professional customs and practices, good manners, and personal appearance. For anyone who aspires to work in a law office, politeness, friendliness, graciousness, and consideration for others should be well-established habits. The customs and practices in the legal profession that secretaries, paralegals, and other members of the law-office team should know are covered throughout this book.

THE LAW-OFFICE LAYOUT

1.15. Physical Layout

The ideal suite of law offices consists of a reception room, a workroom, a library, a file room, a conference room, and a series of private offices. Additionally, a suite would include restrooms, lounges, and kitchen areas and might provide exercise grounds and fitness quarters. In a small law office the reception room, workroom, and file room may be combined as a general office; the law books may be in various offices, and there may be no conference room, but each lawyer *always* has a private office. The confidential nature of legal matters and the desire of clients for privacy demand this. Paralegals also may have individual offices, especially when they are expected to deal directly with clients. (See section 1.1 for a description of the law-office team.)

Glass partitions so common to business offices are not used in law offices because they do not ensure privacy. Large law offices usually have a series of private suites, consisting of an office for the lawyer and an office for his or her secretary. Lawyers sometimes share facilities, with each lawyer conducting his or her practice as a sole practitioner. Some law firms also have satellite offices in suburbs and smaller communities, with personnel using computer modems (section 1.27) and facsimiles (section 1.21) to communicate from various locations away from the main office (telecommuting). Some very large firms have offices in major centers throughout the country and even in foreign countries; some have offices in several cities in their home states.

Here are some suggestions you can make about the layout of a suite of law offices when you are asked for ideas:

1. If the workroom is also the waiting room, arrange the furniture so that it is not necessary for people passing in and out of the general office to enter the part used as a workroom.

2. The secretary should be located as near as possible to the lawyer to whom he or she is assigned.

3. Paralegals often need private quarters since their duties may involve confidential matters such as interviewing clients and prospective clients.

4. A private exit from the lawyer's office is desirable so that a client does not have to leave through the reception room where other people are waiting. It also enables the lawyer to come and go without being observed.

1.16. The Furniture

Furniture is selected not only for a dignified and pleasing appearance but for its functional value. Appropriate furniture must be used for each task. Computer furniture, for instance, would be appropriate and necessary for a secretary or word processing operator but would be inappropriate for personnel who do not use such equipment.

With greater emphasis on ergonomics in the workplace—adapting working conditions for the benefit of workers—modern offices frequently select chairs that are designed to reduce fatigue and stress. The type of filing equipment and other storage containers that are used depends on the nature of the filing system. Even when there is a large central file department, each individual or office usually has traditional file cabinets for localized use. The arrangement of furniture and cabinets is often determined by the general office layout (section 1.15) as well as the location of computers and other equipment, cables, and various peripherals and accessories.

LAW-OFFICE AUTOMATION

A well-equipped law office will have modern equipment to handle all tasks from telecommunications to filing to word processing. This will include telephone equipment (section 1.17), filing and retrieval equipment (section 1.18), mailing equipment (section 1.19), photocopy machines (section 1.20), facsimile machines (section 1.21), bookkeeping and accounting equipment (section 1.22), dictation equipment (section 1.23), and word processing-computer equipment (sections 1.24 and 1.27).

1.17. Telephone Equipment

The type of telephone system used in a law office is primarily determined by the size of the firm—the number and location of offices. Two common systems are the pushbutton, or "key," desk telephone system and the telephone-exchange system. The newer equipment is digital, and signals are transmitted in varying discrete steps based on bits (binary digits). Switching systems, whereby outside telephone lines are all connected to a central facility rather than to the individual telephones, are generally called PBX systems or CBX if computerized. PBX systems are more common in large organizations and key systems in small or medium-sized firms. As features become similar on both types, however, the distinction between systems is becoming blurred. Two switching systems—Centrex and Direct Inward Dialing (DID)—provide separate telephone numbers for individual telephones. Callers then dial a person directly rather than call a central operator at the firm. Integrated Services Digital Network (ISDN) standards aim to standardize the digital PBX systems.

Modern technology has merged traditional telephone service with other services such as voice mail (answering service), paging, least-cost routing (of dialed calls), call forwarding (of incoming calls to another number), and telephone-cost accounting (automatic recording of time and costs per customer). Services and equipment accessories are numerous and change frequently, with ongoing advances in many areas such as cellular telephone technology for cars and other vehicles. The telephone lines themselves may be used for various subscriber services such as telex, facsimile, and electronic-mail transmission. (See Chapter 3 for procedures in telephone contacts with clients.)

1.18. Filing and Retrieval Equipment

Although some equipment and containers, such as metal and wood filing cabinets, have changed very little over the years, other large storage and retrieval systems are now electronically controlled. Law firms with large central file departments may have one or more automated features to their storage and retrieval functions. Indexes are commonly maintained by computer, but the actual transport of a container in some systems is accomplished by entering the file number on a numerical keyboard. A device then locates and physically moves a shelf or container in and out.

Computers are widely used in document storage and retrieval through floppy-disk or hard-disk storage (section 1.33). Some desk units, for example, can store data on disks, scan and read documents, and print out a hard (paper) copy with a laser (or other) printer. One desktop optical filing system has a screen for viewing while indexing, storing, cross-referencing, and retrieving documents. It has a built-in scanner and uses an erasable or nonerasable optical disk and a high-quality laser printer. (See Chapter 5 for filing procedures and systems.)

In the field of micrographics, document-miniaturization equipment may be used to reduce storage-space requirements when extensive material must be stored for long periods. With the proliferation of personal computers, however, this method is less popular than floppy-disk storage. *Microfilm* reduces images onto rolls of film; *microfiche* reduces images onto film sheets. A *reader* is a machine that enlarges the images to normal size on a televisionlike screen. A *reader-printer* can additionally print one or more copies of the document. The miniaturization technique frequently relies on computer-assisted retrieval.

1.19. Mailing Equipment

Law firms may or may not have a separate mail room but usually have at least some basic mailing equipment such as a postal scale, postage meter, opener, and date-time stamp. A large law firm may have addressing equipment, sorting bins, collating machines, folding and inserting machines, and other equipment designed for extensive mailing. Usually, such equipment is designed for record-keeping purposes as well. Postal machines, for example, may automatically post mailing costs to individual client accounts.

Messages and documents may be sent through the U.S. Postal Service or by way of private-delivery services, many of which, like the postal service, have overnight express capability. Voice-mail systems and voice-data systems provide message storage and transmission via the telephone lines. Computer mail service relays messages over the telephone lines or through direct wiring of one terminal to another (local area network [LAN]). Law firms with one or more branch offices, nationally or internationally, may lease lines from common carriers for a direct link between offices in the different locations. These lines can be used for regular telephone communications as well as for other fast messaging such as facsimile transmission. (See Chapter 6 for models and procedures in preparing business correspondence.)

1.20. Photocopy Machines

Photocopiers are widely used in all law offices to make accurate and legible copies in lieu of carbon copies and to provide at least one copy of any document for the client's file. Small-volume copying is handled most efficiently in-house, whereas volume, multiple copying may best be sent to an outside copy shop or printer (large law firms may have their own in-house print shop).

The size and capability of copy machines varies from small, relatively slow, desktop personal copiers to large, high-speed, office machines that rival small printing presses in both speed and capability. Two-sided copying, reduction or enlargement, color copying, editing, and other advanced features are available on the more expensive machines. Nearly all copiers use plain paper, such as bond typing paper. Service contracts are commonly purchased for regular maintenance and servicing of photocopy equipment.

1.21. Facsimile Machines

Law firms, particularly those with branch offices, use facsimile machines to send letters and to transmit exact duplicates of documents. With a significant reduction in price of equipment during the early 1990s, smaller firms have also made greater use of facsimile machines (mail services and other businesses now routinely offer facsimile transmission for those who do not want to purchase a machine).

Facsimile operation is relatively simple. With many machines the sender places the document in a tray or cylinder, calls the appropriate telephone number, and pushes a "transmit" button. A *transceiver* refers to a machine that can both send and receive messages. The most recent machines can transmit a page of copy or graphics in mere seconds.

Small, portable machines may weigh as little as a few pounds and are less than a foot wide. With an adapter they can be plugged into a car's cigarette lighter. New models use plain paper as opposed to special thermal paper. Other models double as a copier, and some have a built-in electronic telephone book and a security password feature to keep out junk mail. A sequential broadcast feature enables the same message to be sent sequentially to many receivers, using preprogrammed telephone numbers. The *PC fax* is a computer with an external fax card or a fax modem. Incoming transmissions are stored in the computer and printed out on a computer printer. This system is more complicated than a regular fax, and the computer is unavailable for other use while it is being used for messaging.

1.22. Bookkeeping and Accounting Equipment

Most bookkeeping, billing, payroll, and other accounting work is handled by computer in the modern law office (section 1.36). Computer software is available for virtually all bookkeeping and accounting functions from recording receipts and disbursements to preparing financial statements. In the integrated office, the accounting function is usually linked directly to other activities. With certain telephone systems, for example, time and charges for calls are computed automatically and appear on the law firm's telephone bill along with a code designating the client to whom a call was placed.

Other machines used in accounting are also commonplace in a law office, for example, calculators and checkwriters. *Printing calculators* have a roll of paper on which entries are printed. (See Chapter 7 for procedures in keeping books and records.)

1.23. Dictation Equipment

With machine dictation, the lawyer can dictate whenever it is convenient, and the secretary can transcribe the information later. Transcription may be eliminated with future machines, however, as automatic voice-to-typed document becomes available. (See sections 2.5-2.9 in Chapter 2 for details on handling dictated material.) Dictation equipment varies in size and capability from very small pocket-portable machines to desktop or central units. Material is often stored on standard, mini, micro, or even nano cassettes. The latest technology is digital.

Whereas with individual models each person has a complete unit on his or her desk, with a central system the recorder is in one area and the dictating and transcribing units are in various offices. More than one person can be using a central system at the same time from within or outside the firm (via the telephone lines). Only the secretary handles the media with a central unit. With portable or desktop models, both dictator and transcriber handle the media.

Modern equipment has many useful features such as automatic cassette changing (when one cassette is full), dual-track cassettes (for making changes on the second track without rerecording the message), verbal insertion (space on disk can be opened up to insert other data verbally), voice activation (machine stop and start at the sound of the dictator's voice), security (other dictators cannot access your message), telephone dictation (use of the system from another location), routing (sending dictation to people within a word processing center), central voice file (ability to organize, store, and retrieve messages by voice), and priority designation (ability to assign priorities to work).

1.24. Word Processing Equipment

Many machines such as dictation equipment, typewriters, and computers (sections 1.30-1.36) are part of the overall word processing function in a law firm. Although computers are used for correspondence (Chapter 6) and document preparation (sections 1.30-1.32) in most law firms, electronic typewriters are still used for such text preparation in some offices and are often used for preparing envelopes, multiple-part and fill-in forms, and other specialty tasks in firms of all sizes and stages of technological advancement.

In many law firms electric typewriters are being replaced by electronic models that function in much the same way as a computer. Although text-storage capacity (memory) is usually much less than that of a computer, other features are similar such as automatic centering and automatic text wrap (automatic movement to the next line without carriage return). High-end models can interface with a full-size screen the same as a computer monitor and may have hard-disk drives and graphics capability. Low-end models may have only a tiny window to view one or two lines of text before the material is printed on paper. Like a computer, electronic typewriters require proper daily upkeep and periodic maintenance. Law firms often purchase service contracts from the dealer or manufacturer to cover routine servicing and repairs. (For a description of word processing by computer, see section 1.30.)

STATIONERY SUPPLIES

1.25. Inventory Management

Often it is the secretary's responsibility to order stationery and other office supplies. To be certain such items are reordered in adequate time before the supply is depleted, it is important to maintain accurate records of the quantity on hand at all times, with projected reorder dates clearly marked on a calendar or inventory chart as a reminder.

1.26. Types of Paper

Law offices use a variety of paper including letterheads and matching envelopes, continuation sheets, photocopy and facsimile paper, and legal pads, as well as miscellaneous items such as envelopes, various notes and memos, invoices, tractor and other computer paper, and so on. A *continuation sheet* is a sheet of paper of the same size and substance as the letterhead that is used for additional pages of a letter. The page may have no heading or may have the firm name engraved or printed at the top or bottom.

Standard 8 1/2-by-11-inch paper is generally accepted throughout the legal system for correspondence and documents. Some jurisdictions have adopted the 8-by-10 1/2-inch size as standard. Consult the clerk of the court or the court rules to determine proper sizes for court papers in your jurisdiction. Invoices, memos, note paper, and other miscellaneous items are used in various sizes. Legal backs or covers may be used for certain documents such as wills or deeds but are generally omitted.

THE COMPUTER IN THE LAW OFFICE

Computers range from individual laptop units to free-standing, desktop personal computers (PCs) to large mainframe systems with various workstations connected to a central processing unit. The chief components of a computer system (section 1.27) include the keyboard, floppy disk drives or hard disks, central processing unit, monitor, and printer. Systems that use the telephone lines for activities such as database research (section 1.34) require a modem (section 1.27). An *optical scanner* is a device that "reads" data and feeds it directly into the computer where it can be processed the same as any other text that would be entered by keyboard. A *mouse* is a small, handheld device that you can move around a desk or other surface that will simultaneously move text and illustrations in your document. *Surge protectors* protect the sensitive equipment from erratic power. *Software* (section 1.28) refers to programs that instruct the hardware to perform certain tasks such as accounting. The operating system software tells the hardware what to do.

Virtually all law offices have computers, although sizes and capabilities vary with the needs of the particular office. Although typewriters (section 1.24) are often used for filling out multiset and other forms, typing envelopes and labels, and performing other miscellaneous small tasks, correspondence (Chapter 6) and document drafting (sections 1.30-1.32; sections 2.10-2.12 in Chapter 2) are usually done by computer or word processor (a computer dedicated to text preparation).

Many of the tasks that were previously considered as separate, relatively unrelated operations are now accomplished using a computer. Legal secretarial training includes developing computer skills, especially word processing (section 1.30) and file management (section 1.33). Any additional computer skills you may need to acquire will depend on your aptitudes and the needs of your employer.

By the 1990s local area networks had become the most popular design for office computing. In the integrated law firm today, it is often difficult to separate computer activities from other work such as dictation. The future all-purpose workstation, in fact, will likely integrate into a single unit the computer, facsimile, copier, image scanner, telephone, high-speed laser printer, and dictation equipment.

1.27. Computer Hardware

Disks

Computer systems display, edit, store, retrieve, and print data. Disk drives read information from and write information onto disks. Personal computers have at least one floppy-disk drive, and many also have one or more hard disks, which can store large amounts of data, or an additional floppy-disk drive. The first disk drive is referred to as *A*, the second as *B*, the third as *C*, and so on. Information can be stored on the hard disks or on the removable floppy disks, which are available in sizes of either 5 1/4 or 3 1/2 inches. A high-density floppy disk can store up to 1.44 megabytes (M) of data (1 byte = 8 bits = [about] 1 character; 1 megabyte = 1 million bytes). Typically, information on a hard disk is backed up (copied) onto a floppy disk that is removed and stored in a secure place. This represents a safeguard should something happen to the hard disk that would cause the information there to be lost.

Monitor

The monitor, where information is viewed, is sometimes called a screen, display screen, or CRT (cathode ray tube). Monitors may display data in color or in monochrome (e.g., black and white or a single color such as green or amber on black, or the reverse).

The *cursor* is a bright dot or line that you see moving on the monitor as you type. Operators can move it around the screen while editing by striking certain keys on the keyboard or by moving a handheld device called the mouse over a hard surface. Which process is easier—using keys or a mouse—is a matter of ongoing debate.

Keyboard

The keyboard resembles a typewriter keyboard, typically in the familiar Query layout of keys, with the addition of some keys for special functions, such as entering commands quickly with one keystroke. Other keys are used to move the cursor up, down, left, or right or to accomplish other tasks. Commonly, ESC (escape) is used to escape from the present screen. ALT (alternate) is used in conjunction with other keys to change data to underlining, italic type, bold face, subscript or superscript, and the like. CTL (control) is used with other keys to enter different commands. Another special key is the scroll key, which causes a document to move from page to page on the screen.

Central Processing Unit

The central processing unit (CPU) controls operations and processes information. It has two types of memory: (1) random-access memory (RAM) and read-only memory (ROM). Information from a program that is loaded into the computer is temporarily copied into RAM, where you can call it onto the screen for viewing, add to it, or change it in some other way. However, the proper keystrokes to save the material (store it on a floppy disk or hard disk) must be used before turning off the computer, or the editing will be lost. ROM is permanent memory used to instruct the CPU in communicating with the monitor, keyboard, and printer.

Computer speed is measured in megahertz (MHz). An 80286 microprocessor, for example, may run at 12 MHz whereas an 80386 microprocessor may run at a faster speed of 20 MHz (1 hertz = 1 cycle per second; 1 megahertz = 1 million hertz).

Printer

Printer technology has tried to wed speed with quality. The principal types of computer printers are the dot matrix printers (fast but lower quality depending on the dots per inch that it can print—the more dots, the better the quality); daisywheel printers (usually slow but typewriter-quality print for text only—no graphics); inkjet printers, or plotters (good quality, used mainly for graphics); and the laser printer (the most expensive but, through laser technology, able to combine speed and high quality).

Modem

Modems are devices that are connected to the telephone for transferring information from one computer to another via the telephone lines. A modem operates at a speed measured in bauds or bits per second (bps). New modems have speeds of 4,800 to 9,600 bits per second of data transferred (the baud rate). Since costs increase the longer it takes to transmit data over the telephone lines, the faster the modem is, the more economical the function will be.

1.28. Computer Software

The precise steps to take in starting a computer, running programs, creating files, and printing out documents depends on the equipment (hardware) you use and the particular programs (software) that are run on the computer to do some task such as accounting or document preparation. Each computer operating system provides detailed instructions (documentation) for tasks such as entering commands, formatting disks, creating and organizing files on disks, making backup copies, and so on.

A software program that coordinates the work of the components of a system and enables it to perform certain tasks is called *operating-system software;* a program that enables you to do certain work such as editing or accounting is called *applications software*. Only software that matches the requirements of your hardware (operating system, computer type, memory capacity, type monitor, type disk, and so on) can be run on your computer. Applications programs for work such as text editing have detailed instructions—some better than others—to tell you what keys to use for specific tasks.

Software programs are available for word processing (sections 1.30-1.32), such as preparing documents and writing letters, articles, or books; spreadsheet activities (section 1.36), such as handling finance, accounting, and scheduling; database usage (section 1.34), such as handling storage, research, and report preparation; graphics (section 1.22), such as preparing charts, diagrams, and other illustrations; telecommunications (sections 1.27 and 1.35), such as sending and receiving data from other electronic equipment; desktop publishing (section 1.32), such as producing magazines, newsletters, bulletins, and other documents; and programming (section 1.34), such as creating your own database or other program.

1.29. Computer Security

Protecting your data from loss or theft remains a problem in many firms, although passwords, keylocks, and other protective measures provide fair to good security. Special security programs are also available to prevent the computer from being used by unauthorized people.

To prevent loss from theft, fire, and other problems, backup disks should always be made and stored in secure places. A *computer virus* is a program that "infects" an existing program file and is designed to erase or damage your hard-disk files. The best safeguard against a computer virus is not to copy material from bulletin boards or allow anyone else to run or copy programs on your computer. Careful operators assume that an outside program could contain a virus. As another safeguard, you also can purchase an antivirus program such as FluShot (IBM) or Virex (Macintosh).

1.30. The Computer as a Word Processor

Whether your computer is used only for text preparation or also for various administrative functions such as computerized docketing or electronic mail, processing text with a computer or a word processor is a major activity in a law office. Preparing correspondence (Chapter 6) and documents (section 1.31) by computer or high-end electronic typewriter (section 1.24) is relatively fast and easy. The chief advantages over a conventional typewriter are that repetitive material—both text and formats—can be saved in the computer memory and copied into successive documents; proofreading can be accomplished with the assistance of a spell-checker—dictionaries and grammar-checkers are also available; editing and error correction can be achieved on the screen—before the information is transferred to paper—eliminating the need to retype entire pages if an error is found; and stored documents can be retrieved faster by means of simple keystrokes (see section 1.33). In addition, special features enhance the ease of production. A merge feature, for example, will insert data from one document into another so that it can be printed out as a single document. (For more on word processing in the law office, see sections 2.4-2.12 in Chapter 2.)

To create a document, most operators first prepare a draft and view it on the monitor, where it can be edited using the cursor or a mouse to highlight copy that is to be moved, deleted, or revised or corrected in some way. (See also sections 2.10-2.12 in Chapter 2.) Since computers have a wordwrap feature that automatically moves copy to a new line, the return key is used only to designate a new paragraph or a new line at a particular place.

Characters, paragraphs, and entire pages can be formatted by selecting options that instruct the computer on appearance. You can specify type style (bold, italic, underlining, and so on); left and right paragraph indent; space between lines; style for lists and outlines; style and placement of running heads and page numbers; page margins and length; number of columns; centering; and numerous other aspects of document appearance. With many word processing software programs you can save the format specifications used for letters and each type of legal document in stylesheets, which can be stored in the computer's memory for recall later when you want to prepare another document using the same specifications.

Many programs automatically save a document in its original state before editing. The initials BAK at the end of a filename refer to a backup copy of the original data. If the edited version is accidentally lost, you can return to the backup of the initial version and reedit it.

1.31. The Computer in Document Assembly

Although document-assembly capability may exist in your word processing program (section 1.30), separate more powerful document-assembly software is available for law firms and other organizations. Document assemblers combine word processing with the logic capabilities of a language compiler. They are used to create documents ranging from simple to complex.

As a high-level language, a document assembler asks familiar English-language questions that appear on the monitor, and you type your reply. The questions are used by the computer to organize, format, write, and print out the desired document. With this type of program the computer does more of the thinking and planning and creating than would be the case with a typical word processing program.

1.32. The Computer in Desktop Publishing

Desktop publishing is an extension of word processing (section 1.30) in that it enables you to process text (and graphics) in a more elaborate format. With desktop publishing software it is possible to create typeset-quality documents (section 1.31) such as a brief, a newsletter, or even a book.

With a graphics card and monitor, a PC may be able to run a desktop publishing program, essentially duplicating a dedicated desktop publishing terminal. Because desktop publishing programs are able to create documents of professional appearance, they likely will be used more and more in law firms in the future.

1.33. The Computer in File Management

The computer occupies a prominent position in the file-management function of a law office. (See Chapter 5 for guidelines and filing procedures in a law office.) Many of the various documents that are produced must be stored and accessible for rapid retrieval. Although conventional paper storage cannot be eliminated entirely, electronic filing reduces storage-space requirements substantially and also provides for easier and faster location of documents. Depending on the size of the law firm, information may simply be stored on disk, or the computer may be used to index and control a large paper filing system.

Law firms have a vast amount of documents, correspondence, and associated material to retain in an indexed or nonindexed system. Computerized docketing is now common in law firms of all sizes. An effective computer system can contribute greatly to better file management. Computerized filing uses floppy disks or hard disks as the medium on which to store electronic files. A hard disk in particular provides for massive amounts of storage as well as immediate access to files. Floppy disks, although having less capacity than a hard disk, are a convenient and inexpensive means of storage. Since floppy disks must be brought to the computer and inserted in a disk drive, however, access to files on floppy disks involves more time than with a hard disk, which is already in the computer.

Depending on your software, information to be filed electronically must be given an alphanumeric or numeric filename. A more descriptive name, or identifier, should be written on a floppy-disk label to correspond to any paper file-folder label containing hard copies of the document in question. (Most computerized systems are used in conjunction with a manual paper file system.) Follow the rules of your software for naming files and, within those parameters, follow your firm's system. To load a file into the computer, you type the name of the file you wish to see, and it will appear on the monitor. You can then review it, edit it, print it out, or once again store it in the computer's memory.

To organize files on a hard disk you need to instruct the computer to set up directories and subdirectories. Individual document files are then stored within the appropriate directory/subdirectory. To call up a file, you must specify the drive letter (A, B, and so on) and directory name, as well as the filename, where the document is stored (DISK DRIVE\DIREC-TORY\SUBDIRECTORY\FILE).

1.34. The Computer in Database Management

Database management systems (DBMSs) are software programs that enable you to monitor a *database,* which is a store of files. The DBMS will do many organizational tasks such as sort and categorize information. It can be used for case management, accounting (Chapter 7), and numerous other activities in a law firm. Database packages can be purchased or created (a programming language, such as Lotus or dBase IV, designed to create databases is required for you to develop your own). You might, for example, create a database, or storage file, of master forms used in your office.

Original, or master, files are documents saved for future use as well as storage. Such a document may be loaded from storage into the computer and then copied on screen. The copy, not the master, would then be edited in preparation for printout or other transmission. (By modem, documents can be transmitted over the telephone lines to other locations.)

Forms files are vital to legal practice, and most law firms have their own file of master forms, both on disk and in hard copy. Commercial systems with forms files are also available for different areas of practice, such as estate planning. Although adjustments may be needed to tailor commercial forms to your requirements, the forms provide the basis for an excellent in-house database. (See also section 2.4 in Chapter 2.)

Numerous commercial databases are available to supplement databases created in-house, for example, Lexis, which has several million cases and other documents on file, and Westlaw, which has a variety of legal data, including U.S. Supreme Court (and other court) opinions and the Federal Register. The American Bar Association (ABA) has a database called ABA/net, which provides a variety of services for lawyers, such as electronic communication with other lawyers nationwide, in addition to access to the ABA databank. A *relational database,* typical in accounting work, combines two or more files such as payroll, billing, and purchase orders, into a single database file. In conducting legal research, access to the appropriate database can save considerable time that would be spent in manually searching books and documents for required facts. (See section 8.1 in Chapter 8 for more about electronic research.)

Rather than purchase a commercial package, for a charge users can access many timesaving databases, such as Dialog, Westlaw, or Lexis, by using a modem for contacting the database and requesting the data over the telephone lines. Special software is needed to make the necessary contact and file transfer, as well as a password provided by the vendor. An on-line search is triggered by supplying key words on your subject that the computer can search for to provide the information you want. The better your queries, the more successful and economical the results will be.

1.35. The Computer in Addressing and Mailing

Both short and long address lists can be maintained on disk in any desirable type of arrangement—by name, by region, by type of application, or by any other useful categorization. Search routines enable users to locate specific names in a file. Mailing-list programs are a type of data-management system designed to make entering, editing, and organizing of data easy and efficient. Files and lists can be created, sorted, and printed in hundreds of customized formats. Some firms create their own list-management program, whereas others prefer to purchase a reliable commercial program.

Some commercial software, for example, such as address and telephone-book software, enables users to organize and produce listings for various needs including address books, mailing lists, telephone lists, envelopes, file cards, and Rolodex files.

The merge feature of many programs including word processing software, whereby information from two or more files may be produced in a single document, is important in mailing-list printouts. Whereas a letter or document may be generally standard, the names of people, places, and certain other facts or clauses may change from one document to another. Names from an address list, for instance, might be merged with a form letter or document. To merge addresses with other information, it is necessary to tell the program where the information is filed (drive, directory, and so on), which names or other data to print, and where they are to be inserted.

The computer is also used in mailing activities through electronic messaging. *Electronic mail (E-mail)* refers to communication between computers that either are connected in-house (LANs) or are connected by a telecommunications link such as the telephone lines, usually via a subscriber service or a service establishment offering E-mail messaging.

Messages for E-mail transmission are created on the computer the same as any other message. (See Chapter 6 for models of business and legal correspondence.) Unlike facsimile transmission, though, E-mail cannot handle graphics, signatures, and the like. To transmit the message over the telephone lines to a receiving computer, the sender must have a modem. Since messages are stored at the receiving end in an "electronic mailbox" (computer memory), they may be sent at any time, earlier or later rather than at hours of peak usage. If privacy is a concern, users should determine whether others have access to stored messages at the receiving end.

E-mail senders and receivers must both use the same computer service. Law firms, for example, could use the ABA/net service, where they would likely find many other lawyers using the same service. Since services usually charge for time used, the shorter the message and the faster the modem, the less the transmission will cost.

1.36. The Computer in Billing and Bookkeeping

Law firms have been a major beneficiary of electronic bookkeeping and invoicing. The spreadsheet—a grid with rows and columns that intersect to form cells—in particular has reduced errors while also reducing time requirements in various applications in the law firm. Spreadsheets are used for anything from balancing the books to preparing budgets to generating reports. Law firms often benefit as well from other features of spreadsheets such as the ability to evaluate "what-if" questions. (See Chapter 7 for procedures in keeping books and records in a law office.)

Spreadsheets, as they appear on screen, provide an outline with rows of columns. The two basic steps in creating a spreadsheet are (1) to label the columns and rows and (2) to enter the formulas (calculations) to be performed by the spreadsheet. The spreadsheet software being used will have detailed instructions on steps to follow, data to be entered, and results to be expected. For extensive spreadsheet work, you may need greater RAM, a math coprocessor, and a mouse (to point to the cells on the spreadsheet that you want to change, format, or modify).

Most of the records-management function in a law firm can be handled by computer, including accounts receivable and payable, the general ledger, payroll, cost accounting, tax reporting, and billing. Commercial accounting programs are available for specific areas of financial and accounting activity, such as law-firm budgeting or payroll processing, or for virtually all key aspects of accounting in one program, for example, purchase orders, invoicing, graphics, report generation, budgeting, cash management, general ledger, accounts receivable and payable, and auditing. Billing programs often enable users to bill in any of thousands of formats, compiling the records you entered as you worked. Other programs track weekly business expenses and cash advances and reimbursements and then calculate and print out expense reports.

The Internal Revenue Service requires that all records based on computerized systems be maintained along with a complete description of the computerized portion of the accounting system. The records must be maintained as long as they may be material in the administration of any internal revenue law (see Revenue Procedure 86-19, 1986-1 C.B.558, for further information).

2 Opening Client Files and Creating Documents

To work effectively in a law office it is necessary to understand the proper procedures to follow in processing new matters and creating various legal documents. These two basic functions—opening new case files and creating documents—are described in this chapter. Other important practices and procedures in a law office are described in Chapters 3 through 8.

A NEW MATTER

2.1. New Case, or Client, File

When a new matter is received in a law office, it must be processed in a routine manner before the lawyer actually begins to work on it. In the well-organized law office, a new client file is made immediately on every matter received. The lawyer who interviews the client obtains the following information:

1. Name, address, and telephone number of the client

2. Name of opposing party and his or her address and telephone number, if known

3. Attorney for opposing party, if any

4. Referral source for client (another attorney, another client, television, advertisement, and so on)

Occasionally, these data are given to the secretary by the client when leaving the office, but it is usually more diplomatic for the lawyer to make a note of the information.

2.2. The Secretary's Role

The secretary's first job is to get the information from the lawyer as soon as the client leaves the office so that a new client file can be created. A case, or client, file also calls for one or more of the following items of information, which the lawyer should indicate to the secretary:

1. The general nature of the case, such as general litigation, probate, or foreclosure
2. Whether the case is on an annual retainer basis or is a single case. This affects the bookkeeping (Chapter 7)
3. Whether the client is new or old
4. Whether stenographic services are to be billed separately or included in the overall fee
5. Name of the junior partner or associate and the paralegal to be assigned to the case

Standard forms are available for new client files, or attorneys can devise their own (see Figure 2.1 on next page). Frequently, the lawyer completes the information. When the report is filled out, it is ready to be routed.

2.3. Routing of New Case Report

The routing procedure varies with the office, but the following sequence is practical and can be adapted to the requirements of any office. If you are a secretary in a small office, instead of routing the new case report you will take the steps indicated by this procedure.

1. File department. A file number is assigned, and a file is opened with data entered in the computer. File clerk initials. (Chapter 5)
2. Accounting department. A ledger sheet for the client and case is opened, after which disbursements may be made for and charged to the case. Bookkeeper initials. (Chapter 7)

CAROLYN W. BALDWIN
ATTORNEY-AT-LAW

NEW MATTER REPORT

```
                                        **********************
                                        *                    *
                                        *  Case #_____   *
CLIENT NAME & ADDRESS:                  *  Date _____     *
                                        *  Referred by:      *
_____        *                    *
                                        *  _____   *
_____        *  _____   *
                                        *  _____   *
_____        *                    *
                                        **********************
_____
                                        WORK:  _____
_____
                                        HOME:  _____
```

BRIEF DESCRIPTION OF CASE: _____

_____

OPPOSITE SIDE; NAME & ADDRESS:

_____

_____   TELEPHONE:

_____

_____   _____

```
FEE ARRANGEMENT: _____         *********************
                                         *                   *
_____          *   SPECIAL NOTES   *
                                         *                   *
RETAINER/DEPOSIT: _____         *   _____   *
                                         *                   *
ADDITIONAL INFORMATION: _____        *********************

_____          *********************
                                         *                   *
_____          *   DISK STORAGE    *
                                         *                   *
_____          *   _____   *
                                         *                   *
_____          *   _____   *
                                         *                   *
_____          *   _____   *
                                         *********************
```

Figure 2.1.   New Case Report

In a large firm there might be other departments, such as the litigation department, or committees, such as the budget committee, to which the report should be routed.

The new case is then returned to the filing department and filed. The mechanics of processing the case have been completed, and the attorney, the paralegal, and the secretary are ready to work on it. The matter might consist of drawing an instrument (Part 2), in which event the file will soon be closed (Chapter 5); or it might involve litigation (Part 3) that extends over a period of years; or it might be a matter in a specialized field of law (Part 4), such as organizing a corporation (Chapter 16). Regardless of the nature of the case, the secretary will handle the word processing and paperwork and, very probably, will have contact with the client either in person or by telephone (Chapter 3).

The subsequent chapters of this book will show you how, in a professional manner, to do any task that might arise in connection with the case.

WORD PROCESSING IN THE LAW OFFICE

2.4. The Looseleaf Formbook

Although forms are generally stored by computer, every law office should also have a looseleaf binder to hold copies of each kind of instrument used frequently in the office. The copy should show not only the style in which the instrument is prepared but also the wording used by the lawyer. Referring to a looseleaf book is sometimes more convenient than retrieving a form from the computer memory and may be faster than reference to a practice manual or to the file of a case that contains a similar instrument. Arrange the papers logically in the binder in the same order as they are stored in the computer file.

2.5. Understanding Dictated Material

Although many lawyers do a lot of their work on their own computers or word processors, others rely on dictation for correspondence and document preparation. Dictation may be taken in shorthand at least part of the time in some law offices, but dictating equipment has taken over much of this work (see section 1.23 in Chapter 1). These machines free the secretary for other work while the lawyer is dictating and enable the lawyer to dictate at times and places when the secretary is not available.

A well-trained legal stenographer could take dictation and transcribe it accurately without a notion of the meaning of the sentences, but she would consider her job boring and arduous. The dictated material is rarely monotonous and is intensely interesting to the secretary who understands what is being dictated. One of the objects of this book is to clarify what would otherwise be jargon to you.

Another difficult feature of dictation in a law office is the length of the material dictated. Frequently, dictation on one matter lasts three to four hours. Again, an understanding of what is being dictated changes the arduous task into a pleasant one. Being able to follow the lawyer's thought also enables you to transcribe dictation more accurately, thus saving time and eliminating rewrites.

2.6. Errors in Dictation

As a rule, lawyers are excellent dictators. They think clearly and express themselves fluently, thus enabling the secretary to follow their trend of thought. Sentences in legal work, however, may be long and involved, and the best of dictators sometimes makes errors in grammar and sentence structure.

Some of the responsibility for the English in the document is yours, and it is up to you to catch obvious errors. One of the most common errors is the omission of a main verb or a conjunction when a parenthetic clause intervenes. To detect an inaccuracy in sentence structure, read the independent clause in the sentence without the intervening subordinate clauses or parenthetic material. If you are following the dictator's thought you will immediately realize something is wrong with the sentence, and you should call the sentence to the dictator's attention, because you cannot supply the omission. As an example, analyze the following sentence.

> The courts below have decided, [although this plaintiff failed to bring her action within the time limit because an alternative remedy, which as against the employer was exclusive, was apparently granted to her by a statute] yet the courts are powerless to afford her any relief if under the express terms of the statute the action is now barred.

The words in brackets are parenthetic. Without the intervening parenthetic clause, the sentence reads: "The courts below have decided, yet the courts are powerless. . . ." In this instance, the dictator may have intended to follow the material in brackets with the conjunction *that* but, intent on the point he or she was making, lost sight of the sentence structure. In any case, the secretary realizes the sentence is incomplete but cannot supply the missing words. Perhaps the dictator intended to say ". . . decided . . . against the plaintiff; yet the court . . . ."

Another common error, and one you can easily detect and correct, is the repetition of the conjunction *that* in introducing a single clause when a phrase or clause intervenes between *that* and the clause it introduces. For example, in the sentence cited above, the dictator might easily have preceded and followed the bracketed material with *that,* instead of omitting it.

Another common slip on the part of the dictator that you must guard against is calling the plaintiff "defendant" and vice versa. You are more likely to detect this slip when listening to machine dictation than when taking dictation. If you have any doubt about which is accurate, check with the dictator.

2.7. Pairs of Words That Cause Confusion

Many words used frequently in legal dictation and written material sound alike or look alike. Some of them have similar but not exact meanings, and it is difficult to judge from the sense which is the correct word. A list of pairs of words that are confusing follows. It is limited to words used frequently in legal work and does not include words the secretary should have become thoroughly familiar with in school or in other fields of work, for example, *affect, effect.* (Basic computer spell-checkers catch only misspellings but would not distinguish, for instance, between simple errors such as *the* when *them* is intended. Definitions of the words in this list that have a special legal significance are included in the glossary of legal terms in Part 5. The secretary should constantly be alert to possible misuse or misspelling of the following terms and question the dictator when there is any doubt.

abjure, adjure

act, action

adverse, averse

appellate, appellant

apperception, perception

arraign, arrange

atonement, attornment

avoid, void

avoidable, voidable

case, cause

casual, causal

casualty, causality

cite, site, sight

collision, collusion

comity, committee

cost, costs

corporal, corporeal

curtesy, courtesy

descent, dissent

defer, differ

depositary, depository

devisable, divisible

devisor, devisee

disburse, disperse

dower, dowry

drawer, drawee

estop, stop

in re, in rem

interpellate, interpolate

judicial, judicious

jura, jurat

malfeasance, misfeasance, nonfeasance

mandatary, mandatory

payor, payee

persecute, prosecute

plaintiff, plaintive

precedence, precedents

prescribe, proscribe

presence, presents

return, writ

situate, situated

state, estate

status quo, in statu quo

thereon, therein

therefor, therefore

tortious, tortuous

transferor, transferee

vendor, vendee

2.8. Recurring Phrases, Clauses, and Paragraphs

Many phrases, clauses, and short paragraphs are used over and over again in legal work. The lawyer's familiarity with them causes him or her to dictate them at a high rate of speed. Often, the lawyer will not dictate the entire clause or paragraph but will dictate only the first few words and the secretary completes it when transcribing. These phrases, clauses, and paragraphs vary with the field of practice and the wording varies with the state and, to a lesser extent, with the office. As soon as you recognize one that is used in your office, put it in the computer memory to be recalled and inserted when needed.

2.9. Take-ins, or Inserts

Every office has a system of marking books, documents, drafts, or photocopies to indicate what is to be copied or inserted in another document, and you will be expected to learn and follow that system. If photocopies are not used, the marks are usually made lightly in pencil in a book or other original document and should be erased after the material has been proof-read. The following is one system of marking material to be copied:

1. The signs < > indicate that the matter within them is to be omitted.
2. A number in a circle indicates that the matter to be copied begins or ends at that point. Odd numbers indicate the beginning; even numbers, the end. Thus ① . . . ② would mean copy from the point marked ① to the point marked ②.

3. Crosses (XX) indicate that the matter between them is to be underscored.

4. To signify that something once erased, or marked for omission, is to remain, the word *stet* is written in the margin and dots are placed under the word or words to be retained. (Printers also use this method of marking.)

Figure 2.2 illustrates a page marked for copying.

PRODUCTION OF DOCUMENTS

The lawyer's secretary assists in the preparation of a wide variety of materials, including briefs, forms of deeds, mortgages, and other instruments. The following pages explain what you should know about composition in order to prepare legal documents. (See also sections 1.30-1.32 in Chapter 1.)

2.10. Rules for Formatting the Document

Make photocopies for reference purposes, but always send the original to the court. In layout of documents, observe the following rules (see also sections 1.30, 1.31, and 1.32 in Chapter 1):

1. Set the line width at approximately six inches (some lawyers like a justified right margin; others do not).

2. Set paragraph indents about five to ten spaces or the equivalent on your computer.

3. Place headings and subheadings in the position they are to occupy on the final printed page, and capitalize headings consistently.

4. Leave a margin of at least one inch on all four sides.

5. Set off quoted material from the rest of the text by indenting it from the left margin or from both the left and the right margins. Indent lists of items in a similar manner. Space above and below extracts and lists to separate them from the rest of the text copy. (Permission to quote must be requested for copyrighted material. Use the credit line provided by the copyright owner as a footnote.)

6. Follow your word processing program instructions to create footnotes. This will guarantee that all notes have textual references

84   **Ill.**   **93 NORTH EASTERN REPORTER, 2d SERIES**

the sink and suddenly became dizzy and after reaching his room he vomited for about two hours. He reported that Dr. Smith was called who only talked with his daughter-in-law and did not examine him but pronounced with a grin "indigestion." Mr. Jorn called another doctor, a Dr. Palmer, who made a thorough examination and said it was not indigestion. Mr. Jorn also related that when he became dizzy at the sink that his daughter-in-law in a sassy fashion told him to get away as though his sickness was not altogether unexpected. He also reported that she had tampered with a bottle of his medicine. Was Mr. Jorn's process of thinking on the subject of his being poisoned by his son's wife so fantastic that it could reasonably be denominated as insane delusion? A complete answer to this inquiry can be found in the case of Owen v. Crumbaugh, 228 Ill. 380, at page 401, 81 N.E. 1044, at page 1051, 119 Am. St.Rep. 442, 10 Ann.Cas. 606, where the court used this language: "Whatever form of words is chosen to express the legal meaning of an insane delusion, it is clear, under all of the authorities, that it must be such an aberration as indicates an unsound or deranged condition of the mental faculties, as distinguished from a mere belief in the existence or nonexistence of certain supposed facts or phenomena based upon some sort of evidence. A belief which results from a process of reasoning from evidence, however imperfect the process may be or illogical the conclusion, is not an insane delusion. An insane delusion is not established when the court is able to understand how a person situated as the testator was might have believed all that the evidence shows that he did believe and still have been in full possession of his senses. Thus, where the testator has actual grounds for the suspicion of the existence of something in which he believes, though in fact not well founded and disbelieved by others, the misapprehension of the fact is not a matter of delusion which will invalidate his will. Stackhouse v. Horton, 15 N.J.Eq. 202; Potter v. Jones, supra [20 Or. 239, 25 P. 769, 12 L.R.A. 161]; Martin v. Thayer, 37 W.Va. 38, 16 S.E. 489; Mullins v. Cottrell, supra [41 Miss. 291]."

[2, 3] The trial judge wrote a short memorandum opinion giving his reasons for sustaining the validity of testator's will. It was his observation that the lay witnesses who testified for the defendant had a better opportunity to observe the testator than the doctors who appeared for the plaintiff, and accordingly their opinions were entitled to greater weight. The chancellor's findings should not be disturbed unless they are palpably wrong. A careful reading of the record convinces us we cannot so hold. The trial judge who sees and hears witnesses is in a much superior position to find the truth than the reviewing court who has before it only the printed page. Well worth repeating in this connection is the language of the Judge of the Supreme Court of Missouri in the case of Creamer v. Bivert, 214 Mo. 473, 113 S.W. 1118, 1120. "He (Trial Court) sees and hears much we cannot see and hear. We well know there are things of pith that cannot be preserved in or shown by the written page of a bill of exceptions. Truth does not always stalk boldly forth naked, but modest withal, in a printed abstract in a court of last resort. She oft hides in nooks and crannies visible only to the mind's eye of the judge who tries the case. To him appears the furtive glance, the blush of conscious shame, the hesitation, the sincere or the flippant or sneering tone, the heat, the calmness, the yawn, the sigh, the candor or lack of it, the scant or full realization of the solemnity of an oath, the carriage and mien. The brazen face of the liar, the glibness of the schooled witness in reciting a lesson, or the itching overeagerness of the swift witness, as well as honest face of the truthful one, are alone seen by him. In short, one witness may give testimony that reads in print, here, as if falling from the lips of an angel of light, and yet not a soul who heard it, nisi, believed a word of it; and another witness may testify so that it reads brokenly and obscurely in print, and yet there was that about the witness that carried conviction of truth to every soul who heard him testify."

We are of the opinion that the decree entered herein should be affirmed.

· Decree affirmed.

Figure 2.2.   Page from Law Book Marked for Copying

and are numbered consecutively. Court-case citations, however, commonly are referenced in the text itself, in brackets.

7. Avoid references to specific pages in the text if possible. When pages must be referenced, be sure to fill in the numbers before the final printout of the document.

8. Always date drafts and final documents.

Front Matter

Front matter of a book, report, or some other larger document includes a title page and table of contents. There might also be a list of tables and illustrations and a preface or an introduction. The *title page* should show the document's title, who is submitting it, and the date, as well as the name of the court, case heading, and docket number if it is a court document. Center items on the space left after any edge taken up by a binder. Keep at least four line spaces between each item and two spaces between additional lines in a single item. The *table of contents* should list chapter and topic numbers and titles to the left and page numbers to the right. Center it on the page area left after the binder edge. Set up a list of tables or illustrations in the same manner. A *preface* or an *introduction* should be set up the same as a text page.

Bibliographies

Bibliographies are always typed at the end of a document in alphabetical order. Indent the second and other additional lines instead of the first one, for example:

Doe, John. *Modern Law Offices*. Chicago:
ABC Press, 1990.

Smith, Jane. "Secretarial Techniques."
Law Journal, June 1990, p. 7.

Tables

Follow your word processing program instructions for the creation of tables. Single-space long tables on separate sheets. Use symbols or superior letters to mark footnotes in the body of the table and place the actual notes directly beneath the table. Refer to each table in the text (for example: "see table 3"). Give each table a number and title. Most writers use only horizontal (not vertical) rules to set off column heads from the body of the table. Type items in the left column flush left with an initial capital only. Important words in table titles and crossheads should be capitalized.

2.11. Checking the Document

Every document should be checked carefully for errors and consistency. If a word can be spelled or abbreviated in more than one correct form, choose the one you prefer and use it consistently. On the first reading, make a list of your selections of optional spellings to guide you toward consistency. Here is a checklist of things to examine for errors and consistency:

1. Spelling
2. Punctuation
3. Inconsistencies in spelling, punctuation, use of italics, bold face, capitals, and in paragraph indentions and spacing
4. Transposition of lines
5. Page numbers
6. Continuity from page to page

If the material to be proofread is technical or lengthy, like a deed, have someone read the original (including punctuation marks, capitalization, italics, and so on) to you slowly enough so that you can follow.

2.12. Copying the Document

At least one copy of any document should be made for the client's file. Additional copies may be prepared as needed for other purposes. (See also section 1.30 in Chapter 1). For small jobs, photocopies are generally made in-house. Larger jobs, such as very long documents or those requiring numerous copies, may best be sent out to a copy/print shop or a printer (or to an in-house print shop, if available).

3 Contacts with Clients and Other Callers

Every caller is a potential client, and every client with a small matter is a potentially valuable client. Because of the importance of contacts with clients and other callers, all members of the law-office team must constantly strive to maintain the proper attitude and conduct in handling contacts both in person and by telephone.

Certain situations requiring tact and diplomacy arise repeatedly during a secretary's contacts with clients and other callers. Basic guidelines govern the handling of these situations, but the application of these guidelines varies with your personality, the office in which you work, and the individual client or caller. In this chapter we give fundamental instructions and make suggestions about how to handle difficult phases of contacts in person and over the telephone.

BASIC GUIDELINES

3.1. Introduction to the Client

In law offices where a team spirit prevails, the lawyer always introduces a client to the paralegal assigned to the case and to the lawyer's secretary. The format is the same as for any social introduction, except in introducing dignitaries and older persons, a basic rule is that lower ranking persons are introduced *to* higher ranking persons, which means the name of the person of higher occupational status in mentioned first.

A secretary is always introduced *to* an executive (Mr. Ross, this is my secretary, Jeanne Franklin). The lawyer explains to the client that the secretary always knows where to reach him or her and that if the client telephones when the lawyer is out, the secretary will answer any questions or try to get an answer from another member of the firm. In an emergency, the secretary will get in touch with the lawyer. In addition, the lawyer explains to the client that he or she has the utmost confidence in the secretary, who necessarily knows about the client's problem. The client gradually comes to know the secretary personally and to have a high regard and respect for the secretary's efficiency. The secretary's contacts thus promote the goodwill of the client and are of inestimable value to the lawyer.

3.2. Nine Basic Precepts That Must Be Observed

Good manners, judgment, and discretion should control your attitude in contacts with clients and other callers. Your tone of voice should always be warm, cordial, and respectful, without subservience. Your tone of voice is especially important over the telephone, because you cannot show your interest by your facial expressions. Guard against the tendency to let your voice become mechanical and without expression.

On a new job the lawyer will probably give you explicit instructions about certain clients, but he or she will expect you to observe the following precepts without instructions:

1. Find out the name of a caller, and if it is the policy in your office to do so, inquire about the purpose of the call. If you recognize the caller, greet the person by name.

2. Never discuss with one client the affairs of another.

3. Guard against letting your knowledge of a client's legal difficulties color your attitude toward the client.

4. Never give legal advice.

5. Maintain the goodwill of the caller and make his or her contact with the firm pleasant and satisfactory.

6. Judge which clients your employer will welcome, which he or she wants to avoid, which should be seen by another lawyer in the firm, and which you should take care of yourself.

7. Make explanations to those callers whom the lawyer will not see, without antagonizing the person.

8. Be prepared to handle emotional or difficult callers.

9. Although all calls are important, learn which ones take priority and which ones warrant interruption of a meeting or other caller.

CONTACTS IN PERSON

3.3. Contacts in Person with Clients

You must be prepared to handle certain situations that occur frequently in law offices. You might make a mistake, but you may be sure the lawyer will back you up in the presence of a visitor. If the lawyer thinks you have made a mistake, he or she will tell you so privately and will point out to you how you should have handled the matter. The following are typical situations:

1. A client arrives without an appointment, and the lawyer cannot see the person (section 3.4).
2. A client arrives without an appointment, but the lawyer will see the person (section 3.4).
3. A stranger wants legal advice (section 3.5).
4. A client is early for an appointment (section 3.6).
5. A client is hysterical (section 3.7).
6. A client invites you to dinner (section 3.8).
7. A client gives you a present or offers payment for work done for him or her (section 3.9).
8. A client wants to see a file (section 3.10).
9. A salesperson wants to see the lawyer (section 3.11).
10. An important client waits for a lawyer who is late for the meeting because of court delays, forgetfulness, or something else (section 3.12).
11. An important client is repeatedly obnoxious, demeaning, and demanding (section 3.13).

Here are some suggestions on how to handle these difficult situations.

3.4. Client Arrives Without an Appointment

A client, Ms. Franklin, asks to see Mr. Perry, the attorney.

Secretary: Good afternoon. May I help you?

Franklin: Yes, I'm Marsha Franklin. I'd like to see Mr. Perry. Is he in?

Lawyer Cannot See the Client

Secretary: Yes, he's here, but he'll be with a client until after closing time. Could anyone else help you?

Franklin: No, I have to see him. I'm from out of town, so I didn't make an appointment because I didn't know when I'd get here. It would only take a little while.

Secretary: I'm very sorry, but he asked me not to interrupt him or make any more appointments for this afternoon. Could you come some other day? I'd be glad to make a future appointment.

Franklin: Well, I don't know when I'll be back this way again, and it's very important.

From this point, a secretary must depend on his or her own judgment about whether the client is someone the lawyer would want to make an exception for or whether the secretary should dismiss the client as inoffensively as possible. Someone who has been a secretary for a long time might be able to induce the client to see another lawyer in the office. In any case, it is important to follow instructions without offending the client.

A new secretary probably should ask to be excused and find another lawyer in the firm to come out and speak with the client. Another lawyer could also indicate whether Mr. Perry should be notified that Ms. Franklin is there. A new secretary should hesitate to take the responsibility of turning away an out-of-town client. Under the circumstances, no reasonable attorney could censure a secretary for letting him or her know a client is in the office. If the client were not from out of town, however, the secretary should insist politely but firmly that it is not possible to disobey instructions. In that case, if the person does not want to make an appointment or to see anyone else, the secretary could suggest taking a message so that the lawyer can call the client as soon as possible.

Lawyer Will See the Client

Secretary: I'm sorry, Mr. Watson, I didn't note your name on Mrs. Hall's appointment book for today. What time did you have an appointment?

The secretary knows the client did not have an appointment, but this is a diplomatic way of bringing to his attention that he should always make an appointment in advance. It also prompts him to tell the secretary the amount of time the interview will require. The secretary's voice should be especially friendly and courteous.

Watson: I didn't have an appointment today, but I'll take only a few minutes of her time.

Secretary: I'm sure Mrs. Hall will be glad to see you for a few minutes, Mr. Watson. Won't you have a seat? Would you care to look at the paper while you're waiting?

The phrase "for a few minutes," said without emphasis, lets the client know the lawyer is busy and that he should be brief.

If Mrs. Hall is alone when Mr. Watson arrives without an appointment, the secretary, after asking him to be seated, would take the file to Mrs. Hall and tell her that Mr. Watson is waiting and would like to see her for a few minutes.

If Mrs. Hall is in conference and will be finished within a short time, the secretary would inform the client of this and ask him to wait. If Mrs. Hall will be busy for some time and it is all right to interrupt her, the secretary would call her on the interoffice telephone and ask if she would come outside to see Mr. Watson for a few minutes. If Mrs. Hall cannot be interrupted for some time, the secretary could make this suggestion to the client:

Secretary: I'm sorry, Mrs. Hall isn't free right now. Do you have some other business in town you could attend to and come back in about one hour?

3.5. Stranger Wants Legal Advice

Someone the secretary has never seen before comes into the office. The following conversation might take place:

Secretary: How do you do. May I help you?

Jones: I'd like to see Mr. Smith.

Secretary: May I have your name please?

Jones: Jones—Robert A. Jones

Secretary: I don't believe you have an appointment, do you, Mr. Jones?

Jones: No.

Secretary: Have you consulted Mr. Smith before?

Jones: No, I haven't.

Secretary: May I ask who referred you to him?

Up to this point the secretary did not know whether or not Mr. Jones was calling about a legal matter, but the answer to the last question should enable the secretary to classify the caller.

Jones: A friend of mine, George King—Mr. Smith handled a case for him once.

Secretary: Oh, yes, Mr. King.

Depending on the practice in your office, you may be expected to find out the general nature of the person's problem.

Secretary: And may I ask the nature of your problem, Mr. Jones?

Jones: I need help drawing up a deed.

Secretary: I'm sure Mr. Smith can help you, but he isn't free right now. Could I make an appointment for you to see him later today, say, 4:45 this afternoon?

Jones: Couldn't I wait now?

Secretary: I'm afraid he'll be busy for some time, and then he has another appointment. It would be better if you could come back. Would tomorrow be more convenient?

Jones: No, I guess this afternoon would be better.

Secretary: I'm sorry Mr. Smith can't see you now, but I'll put you down for 4:45 this afternoon.

Jones: I'll be here then.

The secretary should also get the telephone number and mailing address of Mr. Jones so that if the lawyer cannot keep the scheduled appointment she can notify him at once. If the appointment had been made for several days in advance, the secretary would give Mr. Jones the lawyer's card as a reminder. A telephone conversation with a stranger who calls for an appointment would be handled in a similar way.

3.6. Client Is Early for an Appointment

A nuisance in a law office is the client who always arrives considerably ahead of appointment time and expects to carry on a conversation with the secretary until time for the appointment. In such cases you should offer the client a newspaper or magazine and continue with your work. Discussion with the client not only would be a waste of your employer's time, it is not good form. This does not mean that you should be unfriendly or refuse to acknowledge remarks made by the client; it does mean you should discourage the client from conversing with you. A law firm should take this potential problem into consideration when arranging the seating in the reception room. If visitors are seated directly in front of or very near the secretary's desk, they will be more inclined to carry on a conversation.

3.7. Client Is Hysterical

Sometimes a distraught client becomes emotional or even hysterical in the office. Female secretaries should ask for male assistance in calming a hysterical male caller, and male secretaries should seek female assistance in helping a female caller. Both male and female secretaries should not hesitate to ask for additional help or advice from someone else such as an older, more experienced member of the legal staff.

3.8. Client Offers Invitation

A basic rule of office conduct is that office life and social life must be kept apart. This rule is particularly applicable to the contact between a lawyer's secretary and his or her clients. If the social contact proves disagreeable in any way, the unpleasantness may be reflected in the professional contact and may even result in loss of the client. A secretary, therefore, should not accept social invitations from clients whom he or she has met in the lawyer's office. You may make an exception to this rule and accept an invitation from a client whom you have known a long time provided you first ask the lawyer if it is all right for you to do so.

3.9. Client Offers Presents and Payment for Work

Often the secretary is required to do some special work for out-of-town clients or associate counsels and is offered a present or payment for the work. Gifts of flowers, candy, or the like may be accepted without permission from the lawyer. It is also appropriate to accept Christmas presents, with your employer's consent, provided they are not very expensive, but a secretary should never accept expensive personal gifts from a client. Also, it is never appropriate to accept a gift from an opposing client, such as an opposing litigant or opposing party in negotiations, even though the differences have been resolved.

You would not accept payment for work done for a client or associate counsel when the work is done on the lawyer's time. When client or counsel requests you to work overtime or at night on a special job not connected with your work, however, you are entitled to payment. But you should consult your employer before agreeing to do the work.

The acceptance of payment for work done after hours on a matter connected with your job requires careful consideration. It is permissible, although not always desirable, to accept payment, provided you are offered a lump sum and are not asked the price of your services and provided your employer is willing. Many secretaries feel that extra payment by the client or associate counsel is in the nature of a gratuity and do not wish to accept it for this reason. On the other hand, clients and associate counsel are genuinely appreciative of the extra effort on their behalf and are merely trying to show their gratitude. Refusal of their offer might offend them. You should be guided by the extent of the service and your employer's views.

3.10. Client Wants to See File

Frequently, clients stop in the office to look over papers in a file. Different firms may have different policies regarding access to client files, and it is important to know your firm's policy. Although some firms require the lawyer handling a case to approve all requests to see information in files, it usually is not necessary to disturb the lawyer for this reason. Ask the clients exactly what papers they would like to examine, and if they are entitled to see them, remove them from the file and hand them over. Clients are entitled to examine papers that are theirs, such as mortgages and deeds. They also are entitled to examine other papers of which they have personal knowledge or that are of public record, such as court papers and transcripts of testimony taken in their presence. They are not entitled to examine the lawyer's working papers or any other papers of which they do not have personal knowledge.

A secretary should never hand an entire file to a client without express permission. Clients are not supposed to take any papers out of the office, unless the lawyer gives permission. Even then, with documents generated by the lawyer, it is better to make a photocopy of the document for the client, if appropriate, and keep the original in the office. Original material brought in by a client, however, should be returned to the client and a photocopy made for the office files.

3.11. Sales People and Job Hunters Want to See Lawyer

Salespersons are frequent visitors to law offices. You will soon learn to distinguish between those the lawyer is interested in seeing and those who are not welcome.

Law Book Sales People

Law books, services, and periodicals are some of the tools with which a lawyer works, and he or she may be interested in buying them from time to time. Some lawyers, therefore, may want to see those who sell this material, if time permits. You will soon become familiar with the names of the various publishing houses and with their sales representatives. Unless instructed otherwise, you may let a law-book salesperson see the lawyer at the time of the call, if convenient, or you can make a future appointment. It is to the advantage of the salesperson to talk to the lawyer when he or she is not distracted or pressed for time. If you make an appointment the lawyer cannot keep, it is important to be prompt in notifying the salesperson before he or she comes to the office.

Other Sales People

Although practically all office buildings have large signs prohibiting sales people, they occasionally get into your office. They read the name of the firm on the door, walk in, and ask to see one or more members of the firm. Often there is no visible means of detecting who the caller is. When you ask salespeople who referred them to the attorney, they will probably be evasive and will tell you that they will require only a few minutes of the attorney's time. A rule that must be strictly observed is: never bring strangers into the lawyer's private office unless you are positive they are not salespeople or unless the lawyer has told you to do so.

Job Hunters

Law students seeking part-time or temporary work and other job hunters may stop at the office and ask to see one of the lawyers. If no positions are available, inform the job hunter of this, briefly describe the situation in your law office, and invite the job hunter to leave a resumé for future reference. If the person insists on speaking with an attorney, and one of the lawyers is free, you can call that lawyer on the interoffice telephone and ask if he or she is able to speak with the applicant for a few minutes. If no one is free to see the job hunter, advise the appropriate attorney later that someone stopped by and show the attorney a copy of the resume before filing it.

3.12. Impatient Client Waits for Lawyer Who Is Late

If an impatient client is waiting in the office for a lawyer who has been detained, perhaps in court or in another meeting, or who has simply forgotten the appointment, make a special effort to accommodate the client. Usually, a secretary should not allow a delay to exceed fifteen or twenty minutes before taking action.

If you know where the attorney is or why the attorney is late, explain the delay. If possible, make a telephone call to the appropriate location to find out how much longer the lawyer will be delayed. If the lawyer has simply forgotten the appointment, however, and is in a location or situation where he or she can be interrupted, call the lawyer and discreetly explain that the client is waiting. After you have determined approximately how long the delay will be—or if it is impossible to determine this—apologize to the client for the inconvenience, state that the lawyer was unavoidably delayed and whether you were able to determine how much longer the delay will be, and then offer to reschedule the appointment for an appropriate later time if the client does not want to wait.

If the client has indicated that the matter is urgent, ask if he or she would like to have you inquire whether another lawyer in the firm is available. After you have done all you can to satisfy the client with a new appointment or an opportunity to see someone else, emphasize that you know the lawyer will deeply regret the unfortunate delay and inconvenience to the client.

3.13. Important Client Is Unreasonable

Occasionally, a client takes advantage of his or her importance to the firm and may be obnoxious, demanding, or even demeaning to the secretary. Most firms do not want to lose important clients and expect their secretaries to handle a certain amount of thoughtlessness or rudeness as calmly and pleasantly as possible, although no one is ever expected to endure excessive rudeness, sexual harassment, or any other form of abuse.

Sometimes a quiet, courteous comment followed by involvement in your other work will put a stop to unreasonable demands or obnoxious remarks. But if the demands or unpleasant behavior continues, you should seek assistance from another member of the firm. You might state, "Let me see if I can find someone who is free to answer that question [or to help you with that]." Rather than speak openly over the telephone, excuse yourself and briefly step into another office where you can speak freely and privately. If it is not possible to interrupt the lawyer in charge of the important client's affairs at that time, consult the lawyer's assistant or another attorney in the firm who is authorized to deal more firmly or forcefully with a client who is clearly taking advantage of his or her financial importance to the firm.

CONTACTS OVER THE TELEPHONE

3.14. Importance of Telephone Contacts

Telephone contacts are of paramount importance in a law office. The secretary must know how to answer and make calls smoothly and how to take messages for the lawyer as well as what to say. Here, the fundamentals of telephone techniques are provided with examples on handling telephone calls in the following situations:

1. A stranger telephones for an appointment but is reluctant to divulge the nature of his or her business (section 3.22).

2. A caller wants legal advice (section 3.23).

3. An irate client telephones while the lawyer is out (section 3.24).

4. A client or prospective client asks the fee for certain services (section 3.25).

5. An unscrupulous vendor calls (section 3.26)

3.15. Rules of Telephone Courtesy

The following simple rules constitute the basis of courteous and efficient telephone usage:

1. Answer calls promptly.

2. When you leave your desk, arrange for someone to take your calls. Leave word where you can be reached and when you will return.

3. Keep pad and pencil handy.

4. In asking a caller to wait, say, "Will you please hold while I get the information," and wait for the reply. Then press the hold button. When you return to the telephone, thank the caller for waiting. If it will take you some time to get the information, offer to call back.

5. If you have to put down the receiver for any reason, do it gently.

6. Do not interrupt or be impatient. Listen attentively. Do not make the other party repeat because of your inattention.

7. Do not try to talk with a pencil or cigarette in your mouth. (Most offices now do not allow employees to smoke in the office except perhaps in a rest lounge or other such designated area.)

8. When you have finished talking, say, "Thank you, Mr. Smith," or "Good-bye," pleasantly and replace the receiver gently. Let the caller hang up first.

3.16. Placing Calls for the Lawyer

Although many attorneys prefer to place their own calls, you should know the proper procedure to place the call for your employer. The correct practice to follow when you place calls for the lawyer has developed from expediency. When *you* place the call, it is your privilege to get the person called on the line before connecting your employer.

Assume that you are calling Ms. Hardy for the lawyer, Mr. MacDonald. When you get Ms. Hardy's secretary on the line, you would say, "Is Ms. Hardy there, for Mr. MacDonald?" Then Ms. Hardy's secretary would put her employer on and trust to your good judgment and care to see that Mr. MacDonald comes on the line promptly. (When she calls your employer, you should reciprocate the courtesy.) When Ms. Hardy comes on the line, say, "Just a moment for Mr. MacDonald," press the hold button, and inform Mr. MacDonald which line to pick up for Ms. Hardy's call.

A secretary must be extremely careful not to keep the person called waiting for the lawyer to take the call. On the other hand, a secretary must be sure that the lawyer does not hold the phone needlessly. When you are calling a person whose secretary is cooperative and dependable, there is no difficulty because you and she can connect your employers simultaneously.

There is an exception to this procedure. If you call a close friend or a person to whom deference is due by the lawyer, connect the lawyer as soon as you talk to the secretary at the other end of the line. Tell the lawyer that the person he or she is calling will be on the line immediately and let the lawyer receive the call directly. Some secretaries follow this procedure at all times.

3.17. Long Distance, or Toll, Calls

A record must be kept of every long distance, or toll call that is placed from your office (see Figure 3.1). After you fill in the details of a call on the form used for recording telephone calls, give the form to the lawyer who made the call so that he or she can initial it. Some secretaries have the authority to initial it for the lawyer. Depending on the practice in your office, the form may then be sent to the bookkeeper. Modern telephone systems may have cost-accounting features for automatic recording of time and costs per client. (See Chapter 1 for a description of the modern law office.)

3.18. When Clients Place Toll Calls

Clients may ask permission to place a telephone call, and most people will use their telephone charge card if the call is not a local one. If they do not do this, keep a record of these calls and bill the client for them, unless special circumstances make it more diplomatic for the law firm to charge the call to overhead.

525			JULIUS BLUMBERG, INC., LAW BLANK PUBLISHERS 80 EXCHANGE PLACE AT BROADWAY, NEW YORK	

RECORD OF TELEPHONE CALLS

Month of .... 19____

Date	Telephone No.	Name and Address	Time	Remarks

Courtesy Julius Blumberg, Inc.

Figure 3.1.   Record of Telephone Calls.

3.19. Answering Calls for the Lawyer

If a secretary calls and tells you that her employer wants to speak with a certain lawyer in your office, ask her to wait a moment and announce the call to the lawyer in your office. You might say to the secretary, "One moment, please," and tell the lawyer that "Mr. Harris of ABC is calling." The lawyer will then pick up the telephone and wait until Mr. Harris is connected with him or her. Or perhaps the other secretary has learned that you are cooperative and puts Mr. Harris on the line at the same time that you connect the call with your employer.

3.20. Making Notes of Incoming Calls

It is important that the lawyer be informed of every call that comes in for him or her whether or not the caller leaves a message. It is important not to depend on memory for this but to make a note immediately, recording the caller's name, company, time and date of the call, telephone number of the caller, and any message. If your office does not have printed forms for this purpose, you might suggest that some be ordered. Most are inexpensive and are convenient, easy to read, and neat. Many are carbonless duplicates so that you can keep a record of incoming calls at the same time that you prepare a message slip for the lawyer (see Figure 3.2). Keep a pad of the forms on your desk and on the desk of everyone in the office who takes telephone messages.

Firms handle billing for long distance calls in different ways. Some charge only the most costly calls directly to clients (on the theory that it is more expensive to bill most such calls than include them in general overhead). Others track all calls and either pass through charges to the client or charge a standard amount. In a small office that tracks calls, the secretary generally is responsible for maintaining records, matching the number called with the client, and so forth. Many telephone systems have computerized features that record the number called, the time and duration of the call, and the station from which the call is made (see sections 1.3 and 1.8 in Chapter 1). Some of this information will appear on monthly telephone bills. In larger firms an accounting department handles the actual billing, and calls are simply noted in the client's file.

3.21. Screening Calls for the Lawyer

A lawyer usually expects the secretary to screen calls; otherwise, the calls do not go through the secretary but are put through directly to the

To_____

Date_____Time_____A.M.
                                        P.M.

WHILE YOU WERE OUT

Mr._____

of_____

Phone_____

TELEPHONED		PLEASE CALL HIM	
CALLED TO SEE YOU		WILL CALL AGAIN	
WANTS TO SEE YOU		RETURNED CALL	

Message_____

_____

_____

_____

_____

Operator

No. 585—Julius Blumberg, Inc., 80 Exchange Place, New York

Figure 3.2.   Telephone Message Memo.

lawyer. A polite way of asking who is calling is "May I tell Ms. Adams who is calling?" Or, "May I ask who is calling?" A legitimate caller seldom objects to giving his or her name.

If callers do not want to give their names you have the right to insist, politely but firmly, that they do so. In fact, a secretary is usually expected to screen calls and find out if the lawyer is willing to talk before putting the call through. If a caller insists on withholding his or her name, you might say, very politely, "I'm very sorry, but Ms. Adams has someone with her at the moment. If you'd rather not give your name, I'd suggest you write to her and mark you letter 'personal.' I'll be glad to see that she gets it promptly."

3.22. Finding Out the Purpose of a Call

A secretary may be expected to find out why a person wants an appointment with the lawyer. When this is the policy, it can pose a delicate problem in the law office, because callers are often reluctant to disclose the nature of their legal business. Knowledge of what a client wants, however, frequently enables the secretary to save considerable time not only for the lawyer but also for the prospective client. This situation is illustrated by the following conversation between a secretary and Mr. Goldman, the caller:

Secretary: Samuels and Rolff.

Goldman: This is Henry Goldman. I'd like an appointment to see Mr. Samuels, please.

Secretary: I'm Carol Brownstein, Mr. Samuels's secretary, and I'll be happy to arrange an appointment for you. What date and time would you like to see Mr. Samuels?

Informing the caller that you are the lawyer's secretary gives the client an opening to tell you the nature of his or her business. But this caller did not respond in the manner the secretary desired.

Goldman: I'd like to see him on Tuesday afternoon, say around two o'clock.

Secretary: Mr. Samuels will be busy part of the afternoon on Tuesday, Mr. Goldman. About how long will you need for your appointment?

This gives the caller another opportunity to state the nature of his business, but Mr. Goldman is still elusive.

Goldman: I won't need more than an hour of his time. How about two to three?

Now comes the difficult part. When the office policy is to find out what the caller wants, you must do it diplomatically. The "voice with a smile" is especially important here.

Secretary: In connection with a client's visit, Mr. Goldman, it's often necessary for Mr. Samuels to have certain forms or information available. So that I'll have everything ready for your appointment on Tuesday, could you give me a general idea about the nature of your business? I don't need to know any of the details, of course, just a brief statement.

By giving him a good reason for your inquiry and assuring him that you are not interested in details, you have asked him, in a gracious and courteous manner, for a brief statement concerning his appointment. Perhaps he states that he wants a divorce. You know that Mr. Samuels will not handle the case but that it will be turned over to a junior member of the firm.

Secretary: Mr. Davidson of this office usually handles those matters and confers with Mr. Samuels when necessary. It would really be better for you to see Mr. Davidson on Tuesday. If that's satisfactory, I'll arrange the appointment with Mr. Davidson instead of Mr. Samuels.

Or perhaps Mr. Goldman states that he has a small collection matter he wants Mr. Samuels to handle. Your office does not handle collections except for retainer clients.

Secretary: I'm sorry, Mr. Goldman. As much as Mr. Samuels would like to help you, he doesn't handle collections. However, Robert Ames, a member of the bar located in this building, would no doubt be happy to handle the matter for you. Would you like his telephone number?

There are innumerable situations, but by exercising discretion and diplomacy, you will soon be able to handle them all.

3.23. The Caller Who Wants Legal Advice over the Telephone

Sometimes a caller wants to ask the lawyer for his or her legal opinion over the telephone. Lawyers can rarely answer a legal question without thoroughly understanding the problem that gives rise to it. Try to find out the general nature of the problem presented, and if it is an area handled by the lawyer, suggest that the caller make an appointment to see the lawyer.

Explain that the lawyer will need to discuss the problem in more detail before he or she can be of help. The caller should take the hint that free legal advice cannot be obtained over the telephone. If the caller asks for *your* legal opinion, state that you are sorry but you are not able to answer the questions and that it will be necessary for the caller to discuss the matter with an attorney. It is, in fact, illegal for someone who is not a lawyer to give legal advice.

3.24. An Irate Client Calls

Occasionally, a client who is annoyed about something telephones while the lawyer is out. It is usually advisable to avoid making explanations to the caller. Simply tell the person that you will ask the lawyer to call as soon as he or she returns—and then be certain to tell the lawyer promptly about the call. No matter how expert a secretary is or how tactful and diplomatic, some things must be handled by a lawyer, and angry clients belong at the top of the list.

3.25. Client or Prospective Client Asks What a Fee Will Be

Many clients and prospective clients try to find out over the telephone what the lawyer will charge for certain services. A lawyer's secretary should *never* quote fees; that is for the lawyer to do. In fact, the lawyer does not even like to quote fees until he or she is thoroughly familiar with the amount of work involved. The fee for drawing a simple will, for example, is not as much as the fee for drawing a will that involves a trust or complex estate planning provisions. When a client asks you what a fee will be, offer to make an appointment with the lawyer. If the client does not want an appointment, offer to have the lawyer call the person. Mention that the initial consultation is free, provided that this is the firm's policy.

3.26. An Unscrupulous Vendor Calls

Unless secretaries personally know a caller or a caller's company, they should not give out any information about the law firm or its equipment, particularly serial numbers or specifications. Such information is often used as a basis for shipping unsolicited and unwanted supplies such as photocopier paper or toner or typewriter ribbons. As a precaution, do not readily believe callers who claim that something has already been ordered (always check the records to verify the order) and that your name is needed for confirmation. Later the caller may claim that *you* placed the order.

Beware of comments such as "We're sending your toner right away; we just want to verify your address. . . . Thank you. And your name is . . . ?" Or, "Hi, this is the company that just sold you your new fax machine. We need to verify the serial number for our records." Often you can expose such practices by asking for the person's name, company name, telephone number, and the purchase order number, stating that you will return their call after checking your own records. They may give a false name but usually will not reveal their telephone number or other information that might lead authorities to them.

3.27. Your Telephone Conversation

When you have to make a telephone call for the lawyer, plan your conversation before placing the call. Know your facts and the points you want to cover. If necessary, have an outline of them before you while you talk. Have all records and other material before you.

Identify yourself immediately to the person to whom you are speaking: "This is Carol Smith, Mrs. Newton's secretary," or, "This is Carol Smith at Boyle and Matthews."

Keep your telephone conversation brief but not to the point of curtness. Take time to address people by their names and title and to use expressions of consideration such as "Thank you," "I'm sorry," and "I beg your pardon."

3.28. Desk Telephone Lists

You should keep a Rolodex or similar directory on your desk or a listing in your computer with up-to-date information on the name, address, and telephone number of any of the following that apply to your firm or office needs:

Law Business Numbers

Attorneys associated in current cases (temporary listing)

Attorneys available for various kinds of matters your office does not handle

Attorneys on opposite side of current cases (temporary listing)

Auctioneers

Bonding companies

Collection agencies

Consuls

Court reporters

Courts

Custodians

Deputy sheriffs or process servers

Detectives

Engineers

Fast printing and copying services

Handwriting experts

Investigators

Law journals

Law stationers

Libraries

Marshals

Newspapers

Photographers

Printers

Translators

Office Administration Numbers

Airlines

Building manager or superintendent

Car rental agencies

Computer hotline

Emergency calls (fire, police, ambulance, and so on)

Express mail service

Fast-messaging services (telex, electronic mail, etc.)

Messenger service

Office supply stores

Post office

Railroads

Residences of office employees

Taxis

Time of day

Travel agency

Equipment repairs

Weather

Lawyer's Personal Telephone Numbers

Bank

Dentist

Doctors

Family (residence, business, schools)

Florist

Friends the lawyer calls frequently

Garage

Insurance agent

Organizations to which lawyer belongs

Restaurants lawyer frequently visits

Resorts or clubs lawyer frequently visits

Services (dry cleaner, tailor, etc.)

Stockbroker

Stores in which lawyer frequently trades

Theater ticket agency

4 Reminder Systems and Practices

In a law office certain things must be done at certain times. The need for an infallible system of reminders is imperative, because failure to take legal action within the time required may have irreparable consequences. For any reminder system—computer or manual—to function properly, the secretary must keep it accurately and must refer to it each day. The simplest system that works is invariably the best.

Three reminder systems are described in this chapter: (1) the diary, (2) the card tickler file, and (3) follow-up files, none of which is a complete substitute for the other. Some lawyers keep their personal diaries on their computers (see section 4.1). Suggestions are made at the end of the chapter on methods of reminding the lawyer of his or her appointments and things to do.

THE DIARY

4.1. What Is a Diary?

A diary is not only a record of what is actually accomplished; it is kept from year to year and furnishes a permanent record of appointments, dates that cases were tried, and time spent with clients in or out of office or in court. The diary has a separate page printed for each day in the year. Many standard yearbooks are designed for lawyers, and calendar reminder systems are available for computerized operations. The important thing is that they should have space for work actually done and the time consumed doing it as well as space for appointments and matters to be attended to. In many law offices, especially those in which several attorneys practice, time records and charges are kept on charge sheets (see Chapter 7). In such instances it is not necessary to use a diary that provides space for work done and time consumed.

Figure 4.1 on the next page illustrates a page from a lawyer's manual diary. See also the Daily Time Page illustrated in Chapter 7 (Figure 7.4), which serves as an appointment book and as a convenient place to record all services and charges connected with a client's business. An electronic calendar system is described below, and Chapter 12 describes suit registers, or court dockets. The latter are progress records of litigation; advance entries in the diary are essential as reminders to take the necessary action.

Computerized Diaries

Software for diary/calendar programs provides a number of benefits that a manual system lacks. Not only can appointments, deadlines, holidays, paydays, and the like be recorded electronically, but schedules of your choice, such as weekly or monthly listings, can be selected and printed out. Specific types of dates, such as meeting dates or staff vacation dates can also be selected and printed out. Calendar-creator programs enable you to print out individual calendar sheets either upright or sideways in a variety of styles from daily to quarterly to annually. Since program features and requirements vary among software vendors, follow the instructions provided with the calendar or docket software used in your firm.

Although a computerized calendar or docket system may provide essential organizational capability for a large firm with complex scheduling needs, a traditional manual system may be adequate or even easier to maintain in a small office with relatively simple scheduling needs. Also, since the input of dates in an electronic system is subject to keyboarding errors, a firm must consider whether the recording and scheduling process could be provided more accurately with a manual diary system. Even when an electronic system is desired, secretaries commonly maintain some form of backup desk calendar as well.

4.2. Diaries You Should Keep

Two or more diaries are required, one for each lawyer for whom you work and one for you, but the entries are not completely duplicated. In each lawyer's diary, enter all of his or her appointments and important deadlines.

Saturday, APRIL 20   112th Day

9:45 - Dept. 2 - Hill v. Pruitt   Trial

(ax. - 7230 - chg. Dennis v. City)

4:30 - Construction Committee Meeting

Last day to file Op. Br. - Yale V. City
Pay jury fee Deposit - Clifford v. Morris

Clients Name and Address	Work Done	Time
Hill (John V.)	Briefing	2 hrs.
115 Hilltop Lane	Trial	4 hrs.

Figure 4.1.   Page from Lawyer's Diary.

If the lawyer so requests, note personal days to remember, such as a spouse's birthday. (If the important days are not noted, the lawyer may inadvertently make conflicting engagements.) Do not enter in the lawyer's diary items that are merely reminders to you, such as days on which checks should be written. Watch the lawyer's diary closely for appointments he or she makes without telling you.

In your diary, enter notations of your own business activities and appointments, as well as the lawyer's appointments and the things you will have to remind him or her about.

4.3. How to Make Up Diaries

Keep a list of items that go in the diary year after year (see section 4.6). As soon as diaries for the forthcoming year are available, enter all of the recurring items, events, and appointments under the appropriate date. In preparing the diaries, work from the list, not from the previous year's diary, because dates for events change. For example, if the board meetings of a corporate client are held on the first Monday of every month, the actual dates vary from year to year. In making an entry, be certain the date is not Sunday or a holiday. Enter notations of additional appointments and things to do as soon as you learn about them.

In your diary, enter time-consuming tasks that must be done by a certain date sufficiently *in advance* to permit the work to be finished on time. Also make an entry under the date on which the action must be taken. The practice of making advance entries is very important and will save you and the lawyer the strain of having to prepare material on short notice. It is not usually necessary to make advance entries in the lawyer's diary—you can remind him or her of work to be done. (See section 4.15.) Underline or highlight important due dates and deadlines.

Advance notice of payments of large sums should also be entered in the diary. The lawyer's funds might be low, or he or she might want to negotiate renewal of a loan.

4.4. How to Make Entries About Legal Work

Under the date on which a step must be taken, make an entry setting forth (1) the title of the matter, (2) the time and place for the step, and (3) the nature of the act to be performed, fully described. If you keep the diary for more than one lawyer, also include the initials of the lawyer or lawyers interested. The third example of entries, below, indicates that a brief must be prepared. This entry should also be made under an advance date (see above), with a notation of the date the briefs must be ready. Form the habit of making entries in the diary immediately upon learning that they should be made. Allow no telephone calls or other interruptions to interfere.

Examples of Entries

Jonathan Maxwell Estate—pay on account New York Estate Tax to obtain benefit of 5% discount. RSF

R. V. Robertson Co.—Clerk's Office, U.S. Courthouse, Foley Square—Order to show cause returnable why certain claims should not be compromised. NEL

Dixon v. Rogers (both actions)—Last day to serve and file reply briefs. RSF:NEL

4.5. How to Obtain Information for Entries

Information necessary to make these entries is obtained in various ways:

1. Observe the dates and the places mentioned in papers that your firm prepares and in those served on it by opposing counsel. For example, an order in the R. V. Robertson Co. case would read in part:

   "ORDERED that the plaintiff or his attorney show cause, . . . at the office of the Clerk of the United States District Court for the Southern District of New York in the United States Court House, Foley Square, Borough of Manhattan, City of New York, on the 18th day of July, 19.., at 10:30 o'clock in the forenoon. . . ."

   Obviously, you know that a diary entry should be made under the date of July 18 and that the place is the Clerk's Office, U.S. Court House, Foley Square.

2. Observe the date a notice is served on your office or that your office serves a notice.

3. Calculate the time prescribed by law or rules of court for answering, replying to, or moving to dismiss or correct a pleading when a pleading is served on your office. You can get this information from the practice rules of the court.

4. Calculate the time for taking any step when the time limit for that step runs from some other act of which you have notice. A typical court rule will read like this:

> Any < specific pleading > must be filed within < x > days of or filing of < service or filing of another pleading >.

> *Example:* A response to a complaint is due thirty days after it is served on April 20. Mark the response for May 10 to be safe.

It would be impossible to set forth here all of the instances and time limits that affect litigation; not only are they numerous, but they vary with the state. Knowledge of them is gained by experience and study. The lawyer is responsible for knowing them and instructing you accordingly; *you* are responsible for making notations in the diary in accordance with his or her instructions and for asking the lawyer to give you those instructions. A few diaries have an appendix of timetables of procedure and court rules for specific states, which are very helpful to the legal secretary. Ask the lawyer or the firm's managing attorney for diary dates whenever you do not have them or do not know how to calculate them.

5. Watch for appeal periods—notice is rarely given. After your employer has lost a case, he or she will have a limited time within which to appeal.

4.6. Checklist of Entries to Make in Diary

Here is a checklist of the items that the secretary might enter in the appropriate diary. Although this list includes personal and social entries, some lawyers may prefer not to enter social or personal items on their business calendars.

Appointments

Clients, in and out of office

Doctor and dentist

Court Work

Deadlines for filing pleadings and serving copies on opposing
   counsel

Deadlines for serving notices in probate court

Hearings

Pretrial conferences with court and opposing counsel

Return dates on summons, orders to show cause, and the like

Trial dates

Family Dates (if requested by lawyer)

Anniversaries

Birthdays

Father's Day

Mother's Day

Holidays (usually already printed on calendars)

Christmas

Easter

Election Day

Independence Day

Labor Day

Memorial Day

New Year's Day

President's Day

Religious holidays

Thanksgiving

Valentine's Day

Meetings

Bar association meetings

Board of directors' meetings

Club meetings

Committee meetings

Stockholders' (also called shareholders') meetings

Payment Dates (if requested by lawyer)

Bar association dues

Contributions

Insurance premiums

Interest on notes payable and maturity dates

Periodic payments such as salaries, rent, allowances to children, tuition

Renewal Dates (if requested by lawyer)

Automobile registration

Driver's license

Hunting and fishing licenses

Subscriptions to periodicals

Tax Dates

Federal estate tax returns for clients

Federal income tax returns and payment dates for clients' and lawyer's personal tax

Social security tax returns and payments

State and local taxes

Unemployment tax and disability contribution returns and payments

Withholding tax returns and payments

4.7. Checklist of Entries of Work Accomplished

Although most offices keep a separate time sheet, diary entries of work accomplished and associated time might include:

Appointments

Arguments

Closings

Conferences

Dictation

Hearings

Interviewing witnesses

Research

Some stenographic work

Some telephone calls

Trials

TICKLER CARD FILES

4.8. Use of Tickler Card File

Some lawyers use a computer calendar or reminder system whereas others use a tickler card file in addition to a calendar. A tickler card file has a tabbed guide for each month of the year and 31 tabbed guides, one for each day of the month. The daily guides are placed behind the current month guide. Memoranda are made on cards or slips, which are filed behind the daily guide according to the date on which the matter is to be brought up.

4.9. Use of Tickler Card File with Diary

Generally, secretaries in law offices do not like to depend on tickler cards as reminders for deadlines, hearings, trial dates, and other legal work. It is too easy to lose or misplace a small 3" x 5" card or slip, and the resulting damage might be irreparable. Furthermore, tickler cards do not constitute a permanent record of the day's activities as a diary does.

However, tickler files can be used satisfactorily in conjunction with a diary when desired. They reduce the work necessary in making diary entries. Recurring items can be put on one card, and the card can be moved from week to week, month to month, or year to year. Thus if a certain check is made out each Friday, you can make one card and move it each week, instead of making 52 entries in your diary. Also, you can put all necessary information on the card so you or anyone else can attend to the task without referring to any other material. Tickler cards are also particularly useful for indefinite date follow-ups. If the lawyer has told you he or she wants to do a certain job some time within the next few months, you can make a card and move it from time to time if the lawyer does not do the task when you first bring it to his or her attention. The tickler system is also used to provide periodic review of files that are relatively inactive.

A tickler card file *does not* take the place of a diary for noting appointments. All appointments, even regularly recurring ones, should be entered in the diary and the computerized docketing system; otherwise, whenever you want to make an appointment, you will have to look not only in the diary but also at the tickler.

Refer to the diary every afternoon for the following day and to the tickler each morning.

FOLLOW-UP FILES

4.10. Use of Follow-Up Files

If all matters in a law office that had to be followed were entered in the diary, it could become so cluttered that it would lose its usefulness. Therefore, letter- or legal-size follow-up files, like tickler card files, may be a useful supplement to a manual or computerized diary or reminder system (see section 4.1). A brief notation or reminder is placed in a tickler card file while the material itself remains in its proper place in the regular files. In a full-size manual follow-up file, a photocopy of correspondence or other material is often placed in the follow-up folder while the original material remains in the regular files. Both the card and file-folder systems, then, accomplish a similar purpose for those who choose to supplement their manual or computer diary/calendar reminders and their docket software. Although either system is useful for an office that is not fully computerized, a firm that is geared toward electronic filing might prefer to avoid the duplicate effort of a parallel hard-copy follow-up system.

4.11. Checklist of Material to Be Placed in Follow-Up Files

Court cases are preferably followed through the diary, but the following matters may be followed through hard-copy follow-up files:

1. Matters that are referred to other lawyers, law clerks, or paralegals in the office for information, comment, or action

2. Correspondence or memoranda awaiting answer

3. Collection letters (see chapter 20)

4. Covering letter enclosing documents sent by registered mail, until receipt is received

5. Requests for acknowledgments of documents and so on

6. Receipts for documents left with court clerks or other officials for recording

7. Letters to Register of Deeds, or other officials, enclosing papers for recording, to be kept until papers are returned and delivered to client

8. Letters to abstract company

4.12. Operation of Follow-Up System

Numerous types of equipment for follow-up purposes are available, including filing cabinets, desk file drawers, and portable boxes. Many secretaries use the hard-copy follow-up file system described here in a container apart from the regular hard-copy files. The only equipment necessary is a file drawer or box and file folders.

1. Make a set of file folders consisting of (a) 12 folders labeled from January through December, (b) 31 folders labeled from 1 through 31, and (c) 1 folder marked "Future Years."

2. Arrange the folders labeled by days in numerical order in the front of the file, and place in them copies of the follow-up material for the current month. The folder labeled for the current month is at the back of the other monthly folders ready to receive any material to be followed up in the same month next year. Immediately following the numerical daily folders is the folder for the coming month, followed by the folder for the succeeding month, and so on.

3. Make an extra copy of correspondence or memoranda that require a follow-up. Mark on the extra copy the date on which it is to be followed up.

4. Place copies of material that is to be followed up in the current month in the proper date folders. Each day transfer the empty daily folder back of the folder for the coming month. Thus you always have 31 daily folders for follow-ups, part of them for the remain-

ing days in the current month and part of them for the first part of
the coming month. Place copies of material that is to be followed
up more than 30 or 31 in the future in the proper month folder,
regardless of the day of follow-up.

5. On the first of each month, transfer the material from the folder
   for that month into the folders labeled by days. To avoid filing
   material for follow-up on Saturdays, Sundays, or holidays, reverse
   the folders for those days so that the blank side of the label faces
   the front of the file. (See Figure 4.2 on next page.)

REMINDING THE LAWYER OF THINGS TO BE DONE

4.13. Necessity for Reminder

It is advisable for a secretary in a new job to ask the lawyer if he or
she likes to be reminded of things to be done and if he or she has a preference
as to the method. The lawyer's diary shows appointments and things to do.
For many lawyers, placing the manual diary open at the current date or
leaving a printout in a conspicuous place on his or her desk is sufficient.

4.14. How to Remind the Lawyer of Appointments

In the late afternoon, or the first thing in the morning, place on the
lawyer's desk a typed schedule or printout of his or her appointments, giving
all pertinent information. Before the time of the appointment, give the
lawyer the file and other material he or she will need for it.

4.15. How to Remind the Lawyer of Things to Do

To remind the lawyer of a task, place the file on his or her desk with
a memo if necessary. For example, if a real estate closing is scheduled for
the 29th and papers must be drawn for it, put the file on the lawyer's desk
about the 27th with a memo that the closing is scheduled for the 29th.

If the lawyer has told you that he or she wants to do a certain thing in
connection with a matter, attach a reminder to the file. Suppose that the
lawyer said, "If we don't receive that information from Robinson by Friday,
I want to obtain a stipulation postponing his case another week." On Friday,
if the information has not been received, you would prepare a memo ("You

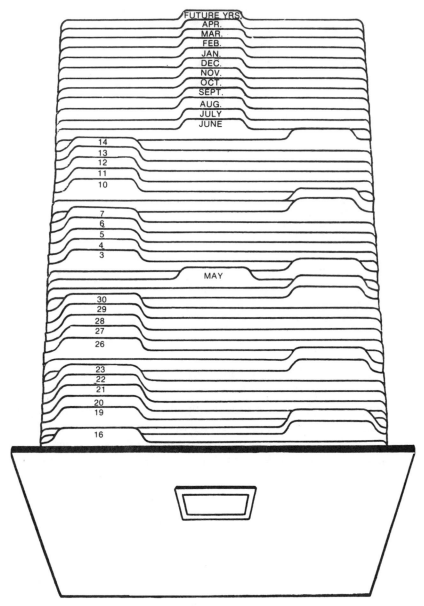

Figure 4.2. Diagram of Follow-Up Files.

wanted to obtain a stipulation to postpone this case") and attach it to the Robinson file before placing it on the lawyer's desk. If you have the necessary information, you may prepare the stipulation and give it to the lawyer with the file. This procedure, however, would depend on your experience and the lawyer's wishes in connection with delegating such duties to you.

Some lawyers make a practice of calling their secretaries into their office the first thing every morning to dispose of correspondence and to discuss pending matters and things to be done. This is the ideal arrangement. For the discussion, take with you a list of things to be done and any material pertaining to them, as well as your notebook.

4.16. How to Remind the Lawyer of Court Work

In a large office a diary of court cases is maintained by the managing clerk under the supervision of the managing attorney. Although each lawyer in charge of a matter is presumed to know its status, it is the duty of the managing clerk to follow the status of the matter, to furnish information regarding the status, and to aid in securing prompt and orderly disposition of court matters. In a comparatively small office, you, as secretary to the senior partner or to the managing partner, may have this responsibility.

From your manual or computer diary records, send a written notice to the lawyer in charge sufficiently in advance to permit him or her to make preparations necessary to take the indicated step. The lawyer in charge of the matter should return the written notice to you with a notation of the action taken.

Another method of reminding the lawyers in your office about pending court work is to print out or type the entries from your diary each week for two weeks in advance, making as many copies as necessary to circulate among the lawyers. Each lawyer then checks the cases in which he or she is interested. You will recall that the diary entries include the initials of the interested lawyers.

Some offices also use a large wall calendar showing a full year. Significant dates are recorded on it, especially relative to matters in litigation.

If you are secretary to a lawyer who receives a notice from the managing clerk, or from the secretary to the managing partner, check your diary and see that preparations necessary to take the required action are made.

5 Filing in the Law Office

Lawyers usually want specific file folders, papers, or letters in a hurry, and one of the secretary's most important duties is to produce them promptly. No matter what system of filing is used, the accuracy with which you file determines whether you will be able to find the desired material without extended searching and fumbling. A paper misplaced even temporarily can cause embarrassment and can even mean a lost client.

Your filing system should be so well organized that someone other than you can find papers when needed. You might know where a paper is because you put it there, but no one else will be able to locate it. "Memory" filing is not a filing system.

In this chapter we classify the material to be filed and describe the methods appropriate to the material. We also tell how to prepare the material for filing and how to arrange the papers so that disorderly files and unnecessary searching will be avoided.

ORGANIZATION OF MATERIAL

5.1. Classification of Files

It is expedient to segregate files pertaining to clients' business from files pertaining to personal and office-administration matters. The following classification of files is appropriate for the typical law office:

1. *Clients' business.* Files in this category include all matters relating to clients, with the exception of commercial collections when handled in volume. Some offices separate the material into litigation and nonlitigation matters. Other offices segregate files relating to a particular field of law if a large part of the practice is in a

specific field. Still other offices segregate matters relating to a retainer client with a large volume of business. In a small law office, the files for each client can be kept together with separate folders for each matter. Most offices, however, segregate inactive client files from the active ones (see section 5.6). Since clients' files constitute by far the major part of the files in a law office, the detailed explanations in this chapter of the numerical and alphabetical systems of filing relate to clients' files.

2. *Commercial collections.* When a fair volume of commercial collections is handled, the files are segregated from other clients' business because of the close follow-up on these cases. Chapter 20 describes fully the system of filing used for these cases.

3. *Personal files.* The lawyer's personal files contain material relating to the lawyer's personal business matters, correspondence, and outside activities, such as bar association committees.

4. *General correspondence files.* This is the miscellaneous or catch-all category. These files contain correspondence not relating to clients' business or to the lawyer's personal matters. Correspondence about a case the lawyer does not accept would be filed here.

5. *Office-administration files.* This category might include personnel applications and records, correspondence about office equipment, correspondence with law-book publishers, and the like.

6. *Periodicals, bulletins, and so on.* Every office accumulates pamphlets, booklets, periodicals, and the like that contain information likely to be needed in the future. These items are library materials that may be filed by subject in file cabinets, in pamphlet boxes, or in looseleaf binders, as the material requires or as the lawyer prefers.

7. *Other files.* You may need files (other than the general correspondence or office-administration files) for material such as sample legal forms. Although forms are generally kept on the computer, secretaries often keep a set of sample forms in a looseleaf notebook or in file folders. Some material must not be destroyed (e.g., stock certificates) and is kept in a fireproof company safe or fireproof locked file.

ELECTRONIC FILING

5.2. Modern Filing Systems

The modern law office uses the computer extensively for electronic storage of files on hard disks and diskettes. The computer is also used for indexing hard-copy and other types of files, such as a cross-index for a numerical file or an index for files in large information storage and retrieval systems of central file departments. Section 1.4 in Chapter 1 describes the different filing systems, including electronic, optical disk, and micrographic storage, and section 1.9 describes the use of the computer for file management in a law office.

NUMERICAL SYSTEM OF FILING: CLIENTS' FILES

5.3. What Is the Numerical System of Filing?

Under the numerical system of filing, each file is given a number and positioned in numerical sequence. Although this system lends itself well to electronic filing and large file systems, it is an indirect system since it must be used in connection with a cross-index that has the subject and number of each file listed alphabetically. Such indexes are usually maintained by computer since the search-and-find procedure is handled rapidly and it is easy to insert new files and delete old ones electronically.

The advantages of the numerical system are the rapidity and accuracy of refiling and the opportunity for unlimited expansion. The disadvantages are the need to maintain an auxiliary index and the need to make two searches (at least some of the time) when material is withdrawn, first a search of the alphabetical index and then a search of the numerical file. Even when the numerical digits represent categories or subjects that sometimes make it possible to identify a file without consulting an index, it is still necessary to maintain the index for those occasions when this is not possible.

5.4. How to Use the Numerical System in a Law Office

Although different-size firms may use different systems, one method of numerical filing is to give a key number to a client instead of to a case. Each case for that client is given the client's key number plus an identifying number or letter. An explanation of one way to set up and maintain such a filing system follows.

1. Assign a key number to the client in numerical sequence. His or her general file has this number. Then assign an identifying letter to each matter that is not litigation. For example, client Sloan & McKinley, Inc., has a file of general correspondence, a profit-sharing plan for employees, and a suit against The Baker Co. You give the general file the number 85, the profit-sharing file the number 85-A, and the suit the number 85-1. The next suit will be 85-2. (If you prefer, you might identify all files by number or all by letter instead of using numbers for the suits and letters for the nonsuit files.)

2. Make entries on the computer under each name that appears in connection with the matter. In some instances, for example estate matters, your client's name does not appear in the subject of the file; nevertheless, an entry should be made in the client's name. Note the title of the case, the number assigned to it, and the client's name if it does not appear in the title. In a matter of litigation, the entry under the defendant's name will read *defendant ads. plaintiff,* instead of plaintiff vs. defendant. If the matter is not a suit or claim, note in addition to the client's name, an identifying description of the subject matter. For example:

   Sloan & McKinley, Inc.
   Profit-Sharing Plan

3. When there is more than one item under a client's name, place them in this order: general; nonlitigation, arranged alphabetically according to subject; and litigation, arranged alphabetically according to opposing party. Suppose a client has a general file and five other files. The index entries will be arranged as follows.

Sloan & McKinley, Inc.	52
Sloan & McKinley, Inc—Arbitration	52-B
Sloan & McKinley, Inc.—Legislation	52-C
Sloan & McKinley, Inc.—Profit-Sharing Plan	52-A
Sloan & McKinley, Inc. vs. Harvey	52-2
Sloan & McKinley, Inc. ads. Watson	52-1

4. Put any hard-copy file folders in numerical sequence according to key number. If there is more than one file for a client, arrange those bearing identifying letters in alphabetical sequence; follow with those bearing identifying numbers in numerical sequence. Thus all folders pertaining to one client are together; all of his or her nonlitigation matters are together, and all suits and claims are together.

5. When a client brings a case to the office, give the client a key number and assign the case an identifying letter or number. Reserve the key number, without identifying letters or numbers, for the client's general correspondence.

6. Reserve a key number for miscellaneous clients, who might want a letter written for them or have some small matter involving only one or two papers. These matters can be filed under the same key number, but they should be indexed like other files.

5.5. Assigning Numbers According to Type of Case

When files are separate according to type of case, a group of numbers is set aside for each category. Cases involving litigation, for example, will be numbers 1 through 199; probate cases, 200 through 299; and so on. The client does not have a key number.

Another method of numbering when files are separated according to type of case is for each category to have a separate sequence of numbers. There might be, for example, a Claim 485 and a Probate 485. In the hard-copy files, different colored labels or folders should be used for each category.

Six digits might be used in assigning numbers. The first digit would correspond to one of the nine categories of law, for example:

1. Litigation
2. Probate (and Estate Planning)
3. Corporate (and Business)
4. Real Estate
5. Tax
6. Labor
7. Motor Vehicle

8. Administrative Agency

9. Other

The second and third digits represent the year the file was opened. The fourth digit represents the quarter of the year the file was opened. The final two digits are sequential. For example, 189,302 refers to the second litigation file opened in the third quarter of 1989. To avoid setting up a separate file system for retired files, simply place a small c (closed) in front of the file number, both on the label and on the index entry, for example, c189,302.

5.6. How to Transfer Numerical Files

Lawyers rarely destroy a file. The procedure followed by many firms is to retain in the office as many closed hard-copy files as space permits and to save computer files on floppy disks. Hard-copy files are sometimes saved on microfilm.

Law files are not retired periodically but are closed when a matter is presumably completed. A file that was opened in 1992 might be completed and ready for retirement in 1993, whereas a case opened in 1995 might remain active until the year 2000 or longer. Old files should be stripped periodically. Some items that can be removed with minimal lawyer supervision are unused portions of yellow pads, multiple photocopies, and interim (not complaint) pleadings that are filed and kept by the court. Hard-copy retired files should contain no original documents. They should be copied and returned to the client.

Ideally, you should process a file for retirement as soon as you are informed that the matter has been completed, without permitting an accumulation. But this is a job that secretaries are inclined to postpone until there is a lull in the work. As soon as you are informed that a matter has been completed, stamp any hard-copy file jacket "closed." Then when time permits, you can withdraw all closed cases and process them for retirement.

Here are the steps in processing a hard-copy file for retirement or storage.

1. Delete from the active index all entries relating to the closed case and insert them alphabetically in the closed-file index. Some offices, however, prefer to keep entries for inactive files in the master list so that the secretary need look only in one place to see if something is active or inactive.

2. Withdraw from the hard-copy files all jackets or folders holding papers that relate to the completed case. Your index will indicate whether there are extra copies or printed papers that have been removed from the regular files. Documents in the office safe will not be sent to storage. They will be returned to the client, or other appropriate disposition will be made of them.

3. Arrange the closed files numerically, just as they were filed in the active files. (Closed files may also be filed numerically even when an alphabetical system is used for current, open files.)

4. Over time, certain materials initially retained in the closed files can be withdrawn and disposed of. However, a secretary should never destroy any material without authorization from the lawyer.

ALPHABETICAL SYSTEM OF FILING: CLIENT FILES

5.7. What Is the Alphabetical System of Filing?

Although medium-size and large law firms may be entirely computerized, small firms sometimes maintain files alphabetically, by client name. Under the alphabetical system of filing, the folders are filed alphabetically according to name or subject. A cross-index is not necessary with this system of filing but can be used if desired. The principal advantage of the alphabetical system is that it is not necessary to look up a file number in a cross-index when papers or folders are filed or withdrawn. The disadvantages are that the system does not lend itself to hard-copy expansion as readily as the numerical system and requires more shifting of file folders.

5.8. How to Use the Alphabetical System

Each client has a general file and each of his or her matters has a separate file. All matters of a specific client are filed under the client's name. The order of arrangement of the hard-copy folders is similar to that of the index entries in a numerical system. The general folder comes first and is followed by the nonsuit files arranged alphabetically according to subject. These files are followed by the litigation files arranged alphabetically according to opposing party. The various matters of client Rossiter & Grossberg, Inc., might be labeled and filed as follows:

Rossiter & Grossberg, Inc.—General

Rossiter & Grossberg, Inc.—Arbitration—T. F. Lewis

Rossiter & Grossberg, Inc.—Arbitration—J. B. Maxwell

Rossiter & Grossberg, Inc.—Profit-Sharing Plan

Rossiter & Grossberg, Inc. ads. Goldman, Inc.

Rossiter & Grossberg, Inc. vs. Donaldson Sound Systems, Inc.

If the active files of a client are very numerous, they might be numbered and an index entry made of that client's files.

5.9. How to Transfer Alphabetical Files

When alphabetical files are closed or transferred to storage, a cross-index entry *must* be made. The simplest method of transferring them is to assign the file a transfer number and make cross-index entries for each party connected with the matter. The files are then stored in numerical order.

Some offices transfer alphabetically, however. Hard-copy file drawers are numbered, and the drawer number in which the file is placed is indicated on the cross-index entry. Each year's transferred files may be filed together alphabetically. However, this entails shifting of files from drawer to drawer unless ample space under each letter is kept open for files to be stored under that letter in the future.

OTHER FILES

5.10. Personal Files

The personal file in a law office is a combination name and subject file, and the alphabetical system of filing is used for it. No cross-index is needed.

File all correspondence together under the first letter of the correspondent's last name, according to date. Thus correspondence with Mrs. Pomeroy and with Mr. Hill will be in the same file. If the lawyer has prolific correspondence with a certain person, set up a separate file for that correspondent. Also, make a separate file for each separate business matter and outside activity. Thus if the lawyer is on the Grievance Committee of the American Bar Association, there will be a file named "American Bar Association—Grievance Committee" under the letter *A*.

Close these files periodically but save from the subject files such as the "American Bar Association—Grievance Committee" any material that is pertinent to the forthcoming year. Transfer the closed files to storage. (See section 5.9.)

5.11. General Correspondence Files

The alphabetical system should be used for correspondence files, and they are operated in the same manner as the personal files. File according to name of the correspondent. No cross-index is necessary. Also, close and transfer these files periodically by the same method used to close and transfer the lawyer's personal files.

5.12. Periodicals, Bulletins, and Other Printed Matter

File these items by subject in the firm's library in a filing cabinet (need not be fireproof), in looseleaf binders, or in pamphlet boxes, according to the firm's preference and the nature of the material. This material will consist of government bulletins, specialized newsletters and other publications, articles, advertisements, catalogs, and any other material of this nature that the lawyer wants to keep. Miscellaneous items such as announcements of changes in law firms, announcements from law schools, and the like can be kept in the general correspondence files. Periodically, you should review the files and discard material that is out of date. Check with the lawyer to establish how long this material should be kept.

PHYSICAL SETUP OF FILES

5.13. Preparation of Material for Filing

To prepare material for filing, do the following:

1. Segregate papers belonging in different files: client's matters; personal; general correspondence.
2. Check to see if the lawyer has initialed the paper for filing or otherwise indicated that he or she has seen the material. In some offices the lawyer clips papers into the folder to indicate that they

have been reviewed. (In offices with more than one attorney, there should be a firm rule that no paper is to be filed until the responsible attorney has reviewed it.)

3. Check through all papers that are clipped or stapled together to see whether they should be filed together.

4. Remove all paper clips.

5. Mend torn papers with cellophane tape.

6. See that all legal documents have been conformed.

7. Mark on all court papers the date they were filed with the clerk of the court or served on opposing counsel. (This information may have been stamped by the clerk of the court on the back of the paper and so may not be evident when the paper is fastened to the folder unless noted on the face of the paper.)

8. Note on the paper where it is to be filed. Write the key and identification number in the upper right corner; for a name or subject file, write the name or subject in color in the upper right corner.

9. Punch a hole or holes in the *exact* place where the paper should be fastened to the folder.

10. When fastening the paper in the folder, check the number and name on the paper being filed with the number and name on the folder.

11. Sort unfiled material into categories and keep it nearby in one or more folders to save time spent in searching for unfiled items.

12. Fold oversized papers so the written material is on the outside.

13. Use follow-up files (see chapter 4) to avoid needless searching for items needing follow-up.

14. In looseleaf books, file the latest material at the front to avoid paging through everything when searching for current items.

5.14. How to Type Index Tabs and Labels

For best results in typing tabs, guides, and folder labels, observe the following rules:

1. Use the briefest possible designations. Abbreviate, omitting punctuation whenever possible. Index tabs need to be legible only at normal reading distance. Guide labels should be legible at two to three feet. File-drawer labels should be legible at six feet.

2. Use initial caps whenever needed. Full caps, especially in elite and pica type, do not increase the legibility of label designations; they decrease the amount of light background around the letters and make reading more difficult. Do not underline.

Folder Labels

The most important part of a folder label is the eighth of an inch immediately below the top or, for folded labels, the scoring (the place at which the label is folded for positioning on the folder tab). Frequently, this space is the only part visible in the file. Therefore, start at the first typing space below the top. Typing should also begin in the first or second typing space from the left edge of the label, except for one or two chapter designations. If this is done, all folder labels in the file drawer will present an even left margin. (See Figure 5.1.)

Use initial caps and indent the second and third lines so that the first word of the first line will stand out.

In typing labels for a numbered subject or name file, leave space between the number and the first word; type the subject in block form. Avoid exceptionally long file numbers if possible.

Guide Labels

For file guide labels, use the largest type available. Begin the typing as high on the label as the guide tabs will permit. Center one- and two-chapter designations. Start all other designations in the second typing space from the left edge. Use abbreviations or shortened forms and omit punctuation, except for large numbers such as 10,000.

File-Drawer Labels

In preparing labels for file drawers, use the largest type available. Center the typing on the label and leave a double space above and below detailed reference information. It is better to print file-drawer labels in large letters because type is not legible at a distance.

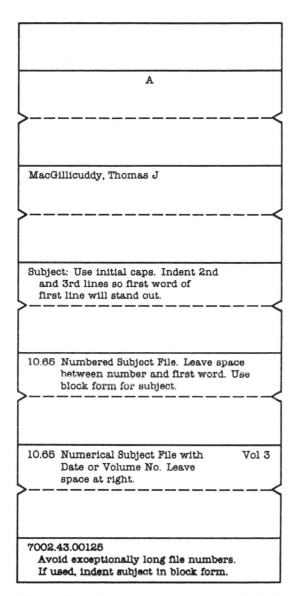

Figure 5.1. Proper Arrangement for Label Designations.

Source: *Complete Secretary's Handbook*, 6th Edition, by Lillian Doris and Bess May Miller, revised by Mary A. De Vries, © 1988, 1983, 1977, 1970, 1960, 1951. Reprinted by permission of the publisher, Prentice-Hall, Inc., a Division of Simon & Schuster, Englewood Cliffs, N.J.

5.15. How to Arrange Papers in File Folders

A file in a law matter consists of at least two parts: correspondence and formal documents, whether they be court papers or legal instruments such as agreements, leases, and the like. Each hard-copy file must have a correspondence folder and a document folder, both of which are kept together in a file jacket. It does not matter what kind of folder is used. When the lawyer prefers to have papers fastened into the folder, it has to be firm enough to serve as a backing sheet to which the papers may be fastened with a clip that permits removal when desired. Correspondence and papers are filed in their respective folders according to date, usually with the latest on top, although some lawyers prefer the reverse order. If correspondence pertains to a particular document, it may be filed with the document, with or without a photocopy in the correspondence folder. Always keep the correspondence folder on top of the document folder in the jacket.

A file might consist of more than two parts. Separate folders, for example, might be used for briefs and law memoranda; drafts; extra copies; miscellaneous memoranda such as interoffice memos, notes made by the lawyer, and so on. If a file contains both legal instruments (agreements, contracts, and the like) and court papers, a separate folder may be made for each one. If a case has papers filed in more than one court, a separate folder would be made for each court. A law file might also contain a folder for "hold papers," that is, papers belonging to the client other than those kept in the safe. The "hold papers" should not be fastened in the folder. Always indicate in the index entry the folders that are made up in each case. For example, an index entry might indicate that a blue book, a file for duplicates, and a paper file all have been made in the case. (*Blue book* denotes the folder in which important papers, such as wills and agreements, are filed; *paper file* denotes the folder for miscellaneous memoranda.)

As a file grows, it is broken down into volumes, with all letters together in one or two folders, all court papers together, and so on. Hard-copy law files frequently become so voluminous that two or more jackets are required. All of the jackets in a particular case should have the same number. On each jacket, write the classification of the contents of that jacket—that is, the folders that are in the jacket—so that you will not have to open more than one jacket to find the desired papers. Some offices make a separate index entry for each jacket.

Figure 5.2 (pages 94 and 95) illustrates another kind of folder used for matters that will not become too voluminous. The outside cover gives a full history of the case from opening to closing. Every step in the litigation is shown on the cover so that information required in a hurry will be available at a glance.

A similar folder, generally used for contract or real estate matters, is illustrated in Figure 5.3 on pages 96 and 97,. The folder in Figure 5.4 (page 98) can be adapted for special documents like cases on appeal, briefs, and memoranda of law.

5.16. Preparation for Closing a File

When closing a file, go through it carefully and remove duplicate copies, blank paper, paper clips, and all nonessential material. If a file has several jackets, you might be able to combine the contents into one jacket. Papers and folders in a closed file may be packed more tightly than those in an active file. Remove any original documents so that they can be copied and the original returned to the client while you still have a current address for the client. At this time you should also remove any interim drafts still in the file.

5.17. Control of Material Taken from the Files

To control folders taken from your hard-copy files, use guides the same height as the file folders but of different-colored stock, with the word *out* printed on the tab (see Figure 5.5 on page 99). The *out* guide provides space on which to make an entry of the date, the material taken, who has it, and date it should be returned. Place the guide in the files where the removed material was located.

In a private office you would not put an *out* guide in the file every time you withdraw material for the lawyer. You would use the guide under these circumstances: (1) Someone outside the immediate office wants the material, (2) the lawyer expects to take the material out of the office, for example, when he or she goes on a trip, and (3) you expect your employer to keep the material a week or so, perhaps to prepare a brief.

When a paper is removed from a folder, make a note of the removal and insert it in the folder. Many law offices have a rule (and it is a good one) that no one may remove a paper from a folder except the person responsible for the filing. Some offices have a check-out system whereby a 3"x5" slip must be filled out by anyone removing a file other than the secretary or the

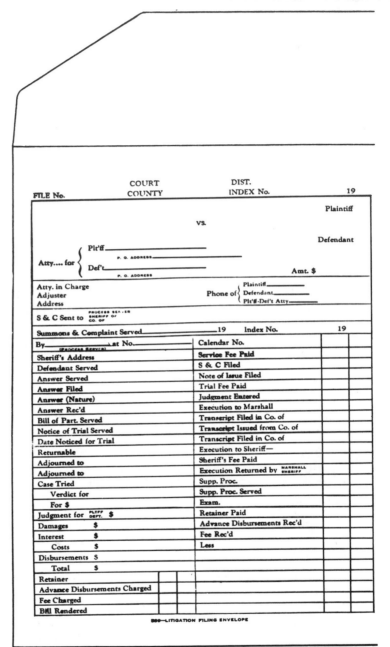

Figure 5.2. Litigation Filing Envelope.

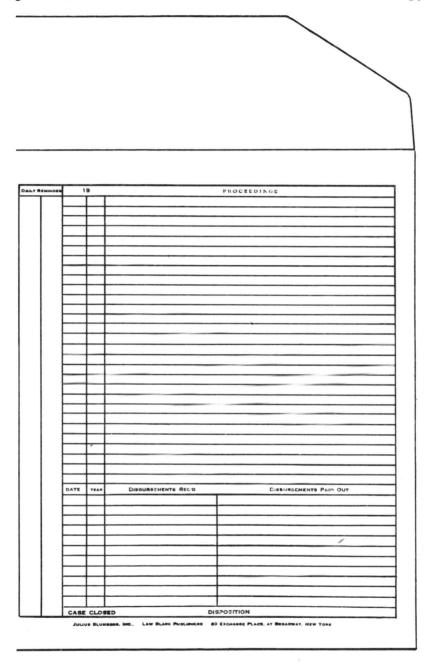

Figure 5.2. Litigation Filing Envelope. *(cont.)*

File #_____ Closing Date_____ Place_____
Client_____ Phone_____
Client's Address_____
Property_____ Municipality_____
Map_____ Block_____ Lot_____
(Seller) (Buyer) Atty._____ Phone_____
Purchase Price or Mortgage $

	Prep.	Ord.	Recvd.	Rec.	Bk.	Pg.	Delvd.
Contract							
County Search							
Tax & Assessment Search							
Planning Board Search							
Improvement Search							
Corp. Status Report							
Trenton Search							
Estate or Inher. Tax							
Prelim. Title Binder							
Survey (or Affidavit)							
Chancery Abstract							
Tenement House Bd.							
Mtg. Estoppel Letter							
Tax Bills							
Fuel Verification							
Water Adjustment							
Rent							
Fire Policy Adj.							
Liability Policy Adj.							
Fire Policies or End.							
Liability Policy or End.							
State Tax Stamps							
Deed							
Affidavit of Title							
Corp. Resolution							
Bond							
Mortgage							
Cancellation-Dischge. of Mtg.							
Satisfaction or Release—Mtg.							
Escrow							
Final Title Cert.							
Title Ins.							
Miscl.							

JULIUS BLUMBERG INC. LAW BLANK PUBLISHERS   80 EXCHANGE PLACE AT BROADWAY, NEW YORK

S 598 Docket Envelope

Courtesy Julius Blumberg, Inc.

Figure 5.3.   Docket Envelope—Litigation or Real
                          Estate.

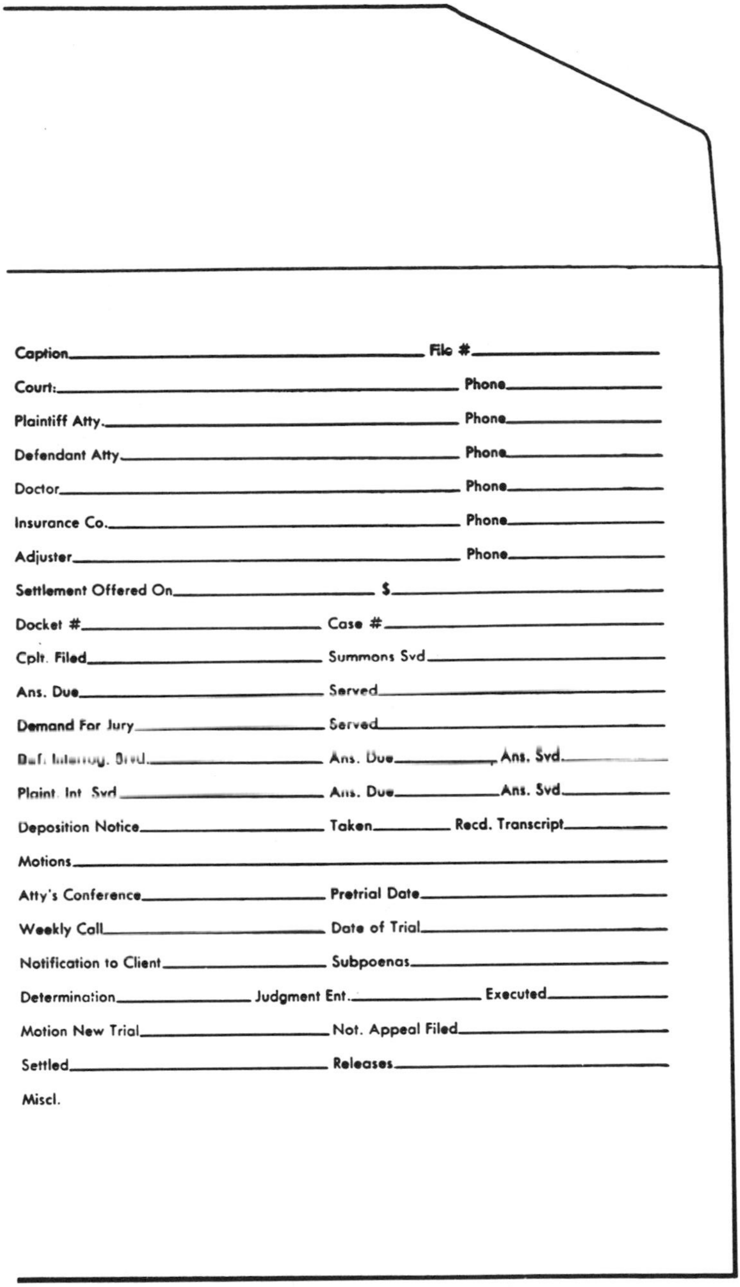

Caption_____ File #_____

Court:_____ Phone_____

Plaintiff Atty._____ Phone_____

Defendant Atty_____ Phone_____

Doctor_____ Phone_____

Insurance Co._____ Phone_____

Adjuster_____ Phone_____

Settlement Offered On_____ $_____

Docket #_____ Case #_____

Cplt. Filed_____ Summons Svd_____

Ans. Due_____ Served_____

Demand For Jury_____ Served_____

Def. Interrog. Svd._____ Ans. Due_____Ans. Svd._____

Plaint. Int. Svd._____ Ans. Due_____Ans. Svd._____

Deposition Notice_____ Taken_____ Recd. Transcript_____

Motions_____

Atty's Conference_____ Pretrial Date_____

Weekly Call_____ Date of Trial_____

Notification to Client_____ Subpoenas_____

Determination_____ Judgment Ent._____ Executed_____

Motion New Trial_____ Not. Appeal Filed_____

Settled_____ Releases_____

Miscl.

Figure 5.3. Docket Envelope—Litigation or Real
Estate. *(cont.)*

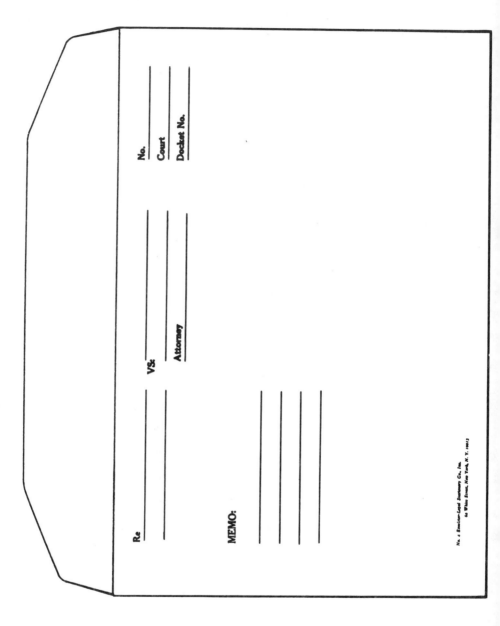

Figure 5.4. Multipurpose Docket Envelope.

Source: Courtesy of Exclesior-Legal Stationery Co., Inc.

Figure 5.5.   Out Guide.

Source: *Complete Secretary's Handbook*, 6th Edition, by Lillian Doris and Bess May Miller, revised by Mary A. De Vries, © 1988, 1983, 1977, 1970, 1960, 1951. Reprinted by permission of the publisher, Prentice-Hall, Inc., a Division of Simon & Schuster, Englewood Cliffs, N.J.

lawyer. The slip should state the file name and number, a description of the material removed, who removed it, the date it was removed, the expected return date, and any pertinent remarks.

6 Handling Legal and Business Correspondence

The written communication that goes out of a law office represents the lawyer and his or her firm. If the composition is awkward or confusing and if the mechanical presentation is careless, inaccurate, or unpleasing to the eye, the lawyer's good work is apt to suffer and might be lost. The secretary can greatly enhance the effectiveness of all written communication by setting it up attractively and typing it accurately and neatly.

LETTER FORMATS

The style of letter used in a law firm will depend on the image the firm wants to convey. Section 6.1 illustrates three business styles (and one personal style) that range from modern to traditional. Once a style is selected, format instructions can be entered on computer stylesheets for automatic setup of all letters thereafter. Repeated closings, headings, paragraphs, or addresses can be handled with only a few keystrokes by saving such material in the form of macros. Different addresses can also be merged with a form letter through the use of the merge function provided by some software. Standard letters or paragraphs should be saved in a forms file from which they can be retrieved and copied into future letters without retyping from scratch each time. Many offices now add a computer code to all letters and documents so that they can be easily recalled when needed for reference or revision.

6.1. Letter Formats

The illustrations of different styles in which letters are formatted in the law office include the full-block, block, modified-block, and official-personal formats.

Full-Block Format

The distinguishing feature of the full-block style of letter is that there are no indentions; all structural parts begin flush left. The complimentary close and dateline, for example, are aligned with the paragraphs at the extreme left rather than shifted to the right. (see Figure 6.1, p. 102)

Block Format

In the block style everything is flush with the left margin except the dateline and reference line, which are either flush right or slightly right of the page center, and the complimentary close and signature lines, which are slightly right of the page center. (see Figure 6.2, p. 103)

Modified-Block Format

The modified-block style is the same as the block style except that the first line of each paragraph is also indented (about five to ten character spaces or a half inch). Carryover lines in an address should always be indented about three character spaces. (see Figure 6.3, p. 104)

Official-Personal Format

The official-personal style is sometimes used for personal letters written to acquaintances. The distinguishing feature of this style of letter is that the inside address is placed below the signature, flush left with the left margin, instead of before the salutation. The identification line and enclosure notations, if any, are typed two line spaces below the last line of the address. (see Figure 6.4, p. 105)

6.2. Opinion Letters

Opinion letters are formal letters giving a professional opinion to a client on some legal question. Each law firm has its own method of setting them up, usually in the style that is used for ordinary letters. These letters

[L E T T E R H E A D]

April 5, 19XX

Mr. Carl B. Ryan
Ryan Communications Center
2216 East Street
Chicago, IL 60616

Dear Mr. Ryan:

Re: FULL-BLOCK LETTER FORMAT

This is an example of the full-block letter used in
many law offices because of its modern appearance.

As you can see, there are no indentions. Everything,
including the date and the complimentary close,
begins at the left margin. Since the dictator's name
is given in the signature, it is not necessary to
include his or her initials in the identification
line.

If you have any questions, Mr. Ryan, please don't
hesitate to let us know. We appreciate your interest.

Sincerely yours,

James P. Trout

dj

Figure 6.1.   Full-Block Letter Format.

[L E T T E R H E A D]

April 5, 19XX

Your reference 24,131P

Ms. Annette Carson
Carson & Hunt
114 Oceanside Avenue
Miami, FL 33100

Dear Ms. Carson:

Re: BLOCK LETTER FORMAT

Some law firms prefer the block letter over the
full-block letter because of its somewhat more
traditional appearance.

Paragraphs are aligned with the left margin, as in
the full-block style. But the dateline, reference
line, complimentary close, and signature lines begin
slightly to the right of the page center. Since the
dictator's name is given in the signature, it is not
necessary to include his or her initials in the
identification line.

If you have any questions, Ms. Carson, please don't
hesitate to let us know. We appreciate your interest.

Sincerely yours,

John D. Evans
Manager

km

Figure 6.2.   Block Letter Format.

[L E T T E R H E A D]

                                        April 5, 19XX

Messrs. Adams and Smith
35 Fifth Avenue
New York, NY 10003

Dear Sirs:

              Re: MODIFIED-BLOCK LETTER FORMAT

     This is an example of the modified-block letter.
Conservative firms choose it because of its traditional
appearance.

     As you can see, it resembles the block style,
except that the first line of each paragraph also is
indented, and the subject line is centered (or it may
be indented the same as the paragraphs). The dictator's
initials do not appear in the identification line
since his or her name is typed in the signature. The
transcriber's initials often appear only on the
copies.

     If you have any questions, please don't hesitate
to let us know. We appreciate your interest.

                              Sincerely yours,

                              Jennifer Clark
                              Correspondence Manager

Figure 6.3.   Modified-Block Letter Format.

[L E T T E R H E A D]

April 5, 19XX

Dear Jane:

    This letter is an example of the official-personal
letter. It is used in many personal letters written
by lawyers and looks unusually attractive on
executive-size letterhead.

    The body of the letter is the same as that of a
modified-block letter. There is no subject line,
however, and the identification line is omitted from
personal letters.

    If you have any questions, Jane, please don't
hesitate to let me know. I appreciate your interest.

                    Sincerely yours,

                    George E. Thomas

Mrs. Jane W. Baker
18 Hillside Avenue
Minneapolis, MN 55405

Figure 6.4. Official-Personal Letter Format.

are generally signed by a partner with the firm name (see the example in section 6.14), because they represent advice from the firm and not merely from the lawyer who dictated the letter.

6.3. Punctuation

Either mixed or open punctuation may be used in the structural parts of a letter. *Mixed punctuation,* the most common, means no end-of-line punctuation in the inside address; however, there is a colon after the salutation and a comma after the complimentary close. *Open punctuation* means the omission of punctuation marks after the inside address, salutation, and complimentary close, unless a line ends in an abbreviation. Open punctuation is used most often with the full-block format.

PRINCIPAL PARTS OF THE LETTER

6.4. Dateline

Offices commonly date letters the day they are dictated, not the day they are transcribed. Follow the practice in your office. If you are asked to date letters the day they are transcribed, adjust references to time made in the dictation, such as "today" or "yesterday."

Write the date conventionally, all on one line (November 15, 19XX). Do not use *d, nd, rd, st,* or *th* following the day of the month (*not* November 15th, 19XX), and do not abbreviate or use figures for the month (*not* 11/15/XX). Also, do not spell out the day of the month or the year, except in very formal letters or invitations (*not* November fifteenth, Nineteen hundred and . . .).

6.5. Reference Line

If a file reference is given in an incoming letter, include a reference line in your reply. Place your own reference beneath the incoming reference. When letterheads have a printed notation such as *In reply please refer to,* type the reference line after it. Otherwise, type it about two line spaces beneath the date, aligned with the date on the left.

Your file 2211-51

Our File 7-085-92

June 19, 19XX

Our Order 77C-41

6.6. Personal Notation

A letter or envelope should not be marked "Personal" or "Confidential" as a device to ensure its delivery to a busy person. These words should be used only when no one but the addressee is supposed to see the letter. Put the word *Personal* or *Confidential* about four line spaces above the address. (In the official-personal style of letter, place the notation at the top of the letter.) The notation should be written in solid capitals and underlined on the envelope, positioned about two line spaces below the return address. On the letter the word usually has an initial capital and may be underlined.

6.7. Inside Address: Forms of Address

A person's name is important. If it begins with *Mac,* it should be written that way, not *Mc.* The same is true of firms and companies. Some law firms omit the comma between names of the members of the firm (*Bell Wilson Nelson Adams*); others insert the ampersand between each name (*Bell & Wilson & Nelson & Adams*). Some companies include *Company, Co., The, Inc.,* or & as part of the official name. One should always write a name the way the owner writes it and should not guess as to the spelling but should verify the name from incoming correspondence, the files, or some other source.

Titles

Generally, the following forms apply (for the correct forms of addressing persons in official judicial positions, see "Forms of Address," Part 5).

Always precede a name by a title unless initials indicating degrees or the abbreviation *Esq.* follows the name. The use of a business title or position such as *vice president* or of the abbreviation *Sr.* or *Jr.* after a name does not take the place of a title such as *Ms.* or *Dr.* (see section 6.8).

Mr. David Henderson, President (*not* David Henderson, President)

Esquire never precedes a name and is never used with any other title, not even with *Mr.* In business correspondence *Esquire* is used only to address high-ranking professional people who have no other title, but many law offices always address a lawyer as *Esquire.* However, you must be guided by the instructions of the person dictating the correspondence. Clerks of courts and justices of the peace are properly addressed as *Esquire.* But it is not proper to use *Esquires* after a firm name composed of two or more last names.

Dr. John W. Parsons (*not* Dr. John W. Parsons, Esq.)

Nora S. Manley, Esq. (*not* Ms. Nora S. Manley, Esq.)

Harold M. Davis, Jr., Esq. (*not* Mr. Harold M. Davis, Jr., Esq.)

Messrs. or *Mesdames* is used for addressing a firm of attorneys, as *Messrs. Jackson, Bell & Hunt.* It may be used in addressing a business firm when the names denote individuals only but not in addressing corporations or other business organizations that bear impersonal names or designations.

Messrs. Fenwick & Fenwick (*not* Messrs. Martin Fenwick & Sons)

Mesdames Kelly and Bartless (*not* Mesdames Kelly and Bartlett, Inc.)

Initials or abbreviations indicating degrees and other honors are sometimes placed after the name of the person addressed. Use only the initials of the highest degree; more than one degree may be used, however, if the degrees are in different fields. In that case, place the degree pertaining to the person's profession first. A scholastic title is not used in combination with the abbreviation indicating that degree, but another title may be used in combination with abbreviations indicating degrees, such as *The Reverend Maxwell B. Hart, D.D., LL.D.*

Janis E. Lewis, Ph.D. (*not* Janis E. Lewis, A.B., A.M., Ph.D.)

Dr. Morris Glass (*preferred*) or Morris Glass, M.D. (*not*
  Dr. Morris Glass, M.D.)

Professor Robert E. Kline (*not* Professor Robert E. Kline, Sc.D.)

6.8. Inside Address: Business Titles or Position

The designation of a business position follows the name. It does not take the place of a title.

Mr. John King, President (*not* John King, President *or* President John King)

Do not abbreviate business titles or positions such as *president, secretary,* or *sales manager. Mr., Ms., Mrs.,* or *Miss* precedes the individual's name, even when the business title is used. If a person's business title is short, place it on the first line of an address; if it is long, place it on the second line.

Ms. Donna Ullman, President
Ullman & Prince Company
1000 West Avenue
Cleveland, OH 44100

Ms. Donna Ullman
Vice President, New Product Development
Ullman & Prince Company
1000 West Avenue
Cleveland, OH 44100

The modern trend, however, is to omit the business title, particularly if it makes the address run over four lines.

Hyphenate a title when it represents two or more offices.

Secretary-Treasurer (*not* Secretary Treasurer)

If a letter is addressed to a particular department in a company, place the name of the company on the first line and the name of the department on the second line.

In addressing an individual in a firm, corporation, or group, place the individual's name on the first line and the company's name on the second line.

6.9. Inside Address: Forms for Addressing Women

Follow these forms in addressing unmarried, married, widowed, and divorced women.

Unmarried Woman

Use *Ms.* when you are addressing an unmarried woman, unless you know that she prefers *Miss*.

Married Woman

In formal social situations, a married woman is addressed by her husband's full name preceded by *Mrs*. In business or informal social-business situations, she is addressed by her first name and her married last name, preceded by *Ms.*, unless she has requested another form of address.

Widowed Woman

A widow is addressed the same as a married woman socially and in business.

Divorced Woman

In formal social situations, if a divorced woman has retained her married last name, she is addressed by *Mrs.* and her maiden name combined with her married last name (no first name). If she has resumed her maiden name, however, she should be addressed by her first name and her maiden name preceded by *Miss*. In business or informal social-business situations, she may be addressed by her first name with either her married last name or both her maiden name and married last name combined or her maiden name only, as she prefers, preceded by *Ms.* in any case.

When One Spouse Is Titled

It is not proper to address a married woman by her husband's title. In formal social situations, address her as *Mrs. James A. Altman* or *Mrs. J. A. Altman*. If she is addressed jointly with her husband, the correct form is *Dr. and Mrs. James Altman* or *Judge and Mrs. James A. Altman*. When the woman is titled but her husband is not, keep her title: *Dr. Helen and Mr. James A. Altman*. If both are titled, use both titles: *Drs. James A. and Helen Altman* or *Dr. James A. and Dr. Helen Altman*.

Gender Unknown

When you do not know whether an addressee is a man or woman, use the person's first name without a title: *Leslie J. Weingarten, Dear Leslie*

Weingarten. Women in official or honorary positions are addressed just as men in similar positions except that *Madam, Ms., Mrs.,* or *Miss* replace *Sir* or *Mr.* See "Forms of Address," Part 5.

6.10. Inside Address: Letter and Envelope Street Address

The inside address and the address on the envelope are the same, although in addressing for postal optical character reading (OCR), the Postal Service requires the following format, in all capitals, for the envelope. The address on the letter would be written in the conventional style, as illustrated in Figures 6.1-6.4.

```
AJK: 2011-R-92
WILSON & LEVINSON
ATTN TC JOHNSON
35 E 96 ST  RM 1000
MILWAUKEE WI 12345
```

The following instructions for writing the address are common, although various authorities give different rules for writing it. Do not precede the street number with a word or sign.

60 Fourth Avenue (*not* No. 60 Fourth Avenue *or* #60 Fourth Avenue)

Spell out the numerical names of streets and avenues if they are numbers of 12 or under. When figures are used, do not follow with *d, st,* or *th.* Use figures for all house numbers except *One.* Separate the house number from a numerical name of a thoroughfare with a space, a hyphen, and a space.

16 West Tenth Street

16 West 13 Street

One Ninth Avenue

2 Sixth Avenue

143 - 91 Street

If a room, suite, or apartment number is part of the address, it should follow the street address. This position facilitates mail delivery. If the address is an office building instead of a street, the suite number may precede the name of the building.

600 Tulip Drive, Room 214 (*not* Room 214, 600 Tulip Drive)

2020 O'Shea Building

Never abbreviate the name of a city. States, territories, and possessions should be abbreviated by their official two-letter designations (*IL, OH, CA,* and so on).

The zip code should appear on the last line of the address following the city and state. One or two spaces should be left between the last letter of the state and the first digit of the code.

Even if there is no street address, keep the city and state on the same line.

Use a post-office box number, if you have it, instead of the street address.

6.11. Attention Line

Strictly business letters addressed to a firm are often directed to the attention of an individual by the use of an attention line, in preference to addressing the letter to the individual. This practice marks the letter as a business rather than a personal letter and ensures that it will be opened in the absence of the individual to whose attention it is directed.

Place the attention line two line spaces below the address. The word *of* is not necessary. The attention line has no punctuation and is not underscored. When a letter addressed to a firm has an attention line, the salutation is *Ladies and Gentlemen* because the salutation is to the firm, not the individual. It is permissible to direct the letter to the attention of an individual without including his first name or initials, if they are unknown.

Attention Henry R. Walters (*preferable*)

Attention Mr. Walters (*permissible*)

6.12. Salutation

Capitalize the first word and the person's name and title in the salutation. Capitalize *Dear* when it is used as the first word of the salutation: *Dear Margaret, My dear Margaret.*

Use a colon following the salutation. A comma is used in social letters, particularly in those written in longhand.

Mr., Ms., Mrs., and *Dr.* are the only titles that are abbreviated.

Forms of Salutation

The form of salutation varies with the tone of the letter and the degree of acquaintanceship between the lawyer and the client. The trend today is toward the less formal salutation: *Dear Ms. Saunders, Dear Mary.* If a letter is addressed to a company or group, make it plural and address both men and women: *Ladies and Gentlemen* (see also section 6.7 for the use of *Messrs.* and *Mesdames*).

It is not proper to use a designation of any kind after a salutation.

Dear Mr. Wilson (*not* Dear Mr. Wilson, C.P.A.)

The salutation in a letter addressed to an unmarried man and woman is *Dear Sir and Madam* (formal) or *Dear Mr. King and Ms. Rawlings* (informal). Name the highest ranking person first.

To a married couple, the salutation in a social situation is *Dear Mr. and Mrs. Nash, Dear Dr. and Mrs. Nash*, or *Dear Dr. and Mr. Nash.*

In business, when writing to a married couple as business partners at work, use *Dear Mr. Nash and Ms.* [or *Mrs.* if she prefers] *Nash, Dear Dr. Nash and Ms. [or Mrs.] Nash*, or *Dear Dr. Nash and Mr. Nash.*

In business, when writing to a married couple at home, use *Dear Mr. and Mrs. Nash, Dear Dr. and Mrs. Nash*, or *Dear Dr. and Mr. Nash.*

It is not proper to use a business title or designation of position, such as director, in a salutation. (Honorary and official titles, such as *chief justice*, are frequently used in a salutation, however.)

Dear Mr. Franklin (*not* Dear Secretary *or* Dear Secretary Franklin)

If a letter is addressed to a firm of lawyers with an attention line to an individual lawyer, the salutation is nevertheless to the firm and not to the individual.

Follow a title with the last name.

Dear Professor Johnston (*not* Dear Professor)

Salutation in Letters Addressed to Women

Do not use *Ms., Miss,* or *Mrs.* as a salutation unless it is followed by a name. But Madam is used without a name (*Dear Madam*).

Dear Ms. MacDonald (*not* Dear Ms.)

If a letter is addressed to a firm of women and the salutation is *Ladies* or *Mesdames*, do not use *Dear* or *My dear* (not *Dear Ladies*).

The salutation to two women with the same name is *Dear Mesdames Smith* (both married), *Dear Mss. Smith* (married or unmarried), or *Dear Ms. Smith and Mrs. Smith* (if those are their preferred titles).

6.13. Subject Line

In any letter, a subject line makes it unnecessary for the writer to devote the first paragraph of the letter to a routine explanation of its subject. In correspondence about law matters the subject line is a necessity as well as a convenience. Correspondence may be filed according to subject, and not according to the name of the correspondent, and frequently, it is difficult to deduce from the letter the matter to which it refers.

Traditionally, lawyers have placed the subject line above the salutation. But since the subject is actually part of the body of the letter, it should follow the salutation, two line spaces below, and in the legal profession is preceded by *Re* or *In re* (see "Latin Words and Phrases," Part 5), which may be followed by a colon or not, as desired.

6.14. Complimentary Close

The form of complimentary close varies with the tone of the letter and the degree of acquaintanceship between the lawyer and the client. In the interchange of letters between lawyer and client, observe how the client closes the letter and be guided by his or her taste.

Familiar informal closes are *Sincerely, Sincerely yours, Cordially, Cordially yours, Regards, Best regards,* and *Best wishes*. Familiar formal closes are *Yours very truly, Yours truly, Very sincerely yours, Respectfully* (to officials and dignitaries), and *Respectfully yours* (to officials and dignitaries).

6.15. Signature

Firms of attorneys frequently sign letters with the firm name, particularly if the letter expresses a professional opinion or gives professional advice. In some offices the firm name is typed on the letter and the lawyer who dictated it signs his or her name. Write the firm name in all capitals and exactly as it appears on the letterhead.

BLACK, HALL & POINTER

By *Edgar R. Black*

A letter signed in the firm name is written in the first person plural, not the singular.

Many letters are signed by the dictating attorney or by a partner without having the firm name appear in the signature. The purpose of typing a signature is to enable the recipient of the letter to decipher a difficult signature. There is no need, therefore, for the lawyer's name to be typed in the signature if it is printed on the letterhead. If a firm has alternate forms of signatures, the dictator will include his or her preference. When the signature of the dictator is typed, spell it exactly as the person signs his or her name.

Right:

Richard P. Miller

Richard P. Miller

Wrong:

Richard P. Miller

R. P. Miller

In a block, modified-block, or official-personal format, the typed signature should never extend beyond the right margin of the letter.

No title except *Miss or Mrs.* should precede either the written or typed signature, and those titles are used only when the woman prefers to be addressed as such. However, *Ms.* or *Mr.* (as well as *Miss* or *Mrs.*) may be included if the signer's gender would otherwise be unknown: *(Ms.) R. V. Bentley.*

6.16. Identification Line

The identification line shows who dictated a letter and who typed it. The dictator's initials are in all capitals and the transcriber's in small letters

(*KVT:jc*). The only purpose of this identification is for reference by the firm that is writing the letter. It does not belong on the original of a letter, but many firms put it there to save the time of adding it later to the file copies.

The usual position of identification marks is two line spaces below the last line of the signature, flush with the left margin. If the dictator's name is typed on the letter, there is no need for his or her initials to appear in the identification marks.

6.17. Enclosure Notation

When a letter contains enclosures, put the abbreviation *Enc., Encl.*, or *Encs.* flush with the left margin one or two line spaces beneath the identification line. If there is more than one enclosure, indicate the number. If the enclosures are of special importance, identify them. Some offices require that any enclosure be identified somewhere in the letter. If an enclosure is to be returned, make a notation to that effect also.

RPE:es
Enc. 2

RPE:es
Enc. Cert. ck. $2,350
Mtge.—Fenton to Struthers

RPE:es
Enc. Policy 35 4698-M (to be returned)

6.18. Mailing Notation

When a postal letter is sent by any method other than regular postal delivery, type a notation of the exact method on the envelope in the space below the stamps and above the address. Make a similar notation on the copy of the letter.

Private-delivery services each have their own requirements and forms to be completed for mailing. Facsimile, electronic-mail transmission, and other fast messaging using the telephone lines have still other requirements. Subscriber services provide codes that senders must use to effect transmission. Telephone numbers are specified in transmission forms such as facsimile. (See Figure 6.5 for a sample facsimile transmission form.) The type of mail or other transmission is stated on the letter immediately below

Telephone
603.225.2585

Telecopier
603.226.4692

Baldwin & de Séve, Attorneys at Law

46 South Main Street
Concord, NH 03301

Carolyn W. Baldwin*

Richard J. de Séve
Admitted in
New Hampshire
& Maryland

FAX TRANSMISSION FORM

NOTE: The information contained in this facsimile
message is intended only for the use of the individual
or entity named below. If you are not the intended
recipient or an employee or agent of the intended
recipient who is responsible for delivering it to the
addressee, you are notified that any dissemination,
distribution or copying of this communication is
strictly prohibited. If you have received this
communication in error, please immediately notify the
sender by telephone (collect) and return the FAX to
the above address by U.S. mail. Receipt by anyone
other than the intended recipient is not a waiver of
any attorney-client or work-product privilege.

To:_____

_____

FAX number_____ Date_____

Number of pages (including cover sheet): _____
If a complete transmission is not received, please
telephone immediately (603) 225-2585.

Special instructions/notes:

* Of Counsel to:
McGregor, Shea &
Doliner
18 Tremont Street
Boston, MA 02108

Figure 6.5. Facsimile Transmission Form.

the enclosure notation (see the example in section 6.19) unless other requirements are specified by a particular service.

    rcf
    Enc. Bylaws
    By United Parcel 2nd Day Air

A fax, modem, or other time-based transmission notation commonly specifies the time as well.

    Fax: 4:05 p to 602-785-4291

    Mod: 2:00 p to [access number]

6.19. Copy-Distribution Notation

When a copy is to be sent to another person, type the distribution notation flush with the left margin, below all other notations. The word *Copy* or the abbreviation *c* (any type of copy) may be used; some writers use *cc* (*carbon copy*) for all types of copies. Other notations are *pc* (photocopy), *fc* (fax copy), *and rc* (reprographic copy). The abbreviation *bc* (blind copy) refers to a copy sent to someone without the addressee's knowledge. Therefore, those initials should appear only on the copy going to the blind-copy recipient and on the file copy.

The various notations (identification marks, enclosure notation, mail notation, copy-distribution notation) may all be stacked single-spaced or double-spaced, depending on available space in the letter.

    SRE:ng
    Enc. Articles of Incorporation
    By Dix Express Overnight Service
    Copies: J. V. Buford
             M. M. Solomon

6.20. Postscript

When it is necessary to add a postscript to a letter, place it two line spaces below the last notation on the letter. The left margin of the postscript should be indented when paragraphs in the letter are also indented. Put the dictator's initials after the postscript in all capitals.

6.21. Continuation-Page Heading

Law firms generally have continuation sheets, loosely called second sheets, with the firm name (but usually no address) printed on them for use when a letter runs more than one page. If your office does not have printed continuation sheets, use a plain sheet of paper the same size and quality as the letterhead. Write enough descriptive matter at the top of the succeeding pages to make them recognizable if they should become separated from the opening page. Include at least the name of the addressee (omit the person's title), the number of the page, and the date. Access codes or subscriber codes may be included, depending on the type of transmission. Data may be stacked or spread across the page.

Joseph Shawnley
May 1, 19XX
page 2

Joseph Shawnley, May 1, 19XX, page 2

Joseph Shawnley   May 1, 19XX   page 2

6.22. Enclosures

In mail processed by machine (e.g., postal or private-delivery material), fasten enclosures together with staples. Pins or metal clips might injure the hands of employees, and the clips might damage processing equipment.

1. *Enclosures the size of the letter.* These enclosures are easily folded and inserted, with their accompanying letters, into ordinary commercial envelopes or envelopes provided by the delivery service. If an enclosure consists of two or more sheets, staple them together, but do not fasten the enclosed material to the letter itself. In a small envelope, fold the enclosure and then fold the letter and slip the enclosure inside the last fold of the letter. Thus when the letter is removed from the envelope, the enclosure comes out with it. For an example of a form to accompany facsimile transmissions that states the number of pages, or enclosures, see Figure 6.5.

2. *Enclosures larger than the letter.* These enclosures include briefs, abstracts, and other documents too large to fit into a commercial envelope of ordinary size. They are mailed in large envelopes that will accommodate both the letter and the enclosure.

3. *Enclosures smaller than the letter*. When enclosures are considerably smaller than the letter, staple them to the letter in the upper left corner, on top of the letter. If two or more such enclosures are sent, put the smaller one on top.

EFFECTIVE LETTER WRITING

We do not all have the talent that makes an outstanding letter writer, but we can improve the style and effectiveness of our own letters by studying those written by experts. Careful planning and highly developed techniques make those letters outstanding. This section will help you develop techniques that will improve the quality and persuasiveness of your letters.

6.23. Six Ways to Improve Your Letters

The language of a letter should be natural, just as though the writer were talking to the reader. Unfortunately, lawyers are frequent offenders against this basic requirement of letter writing, and their staffs are inclined to follow their style.

Here are six suggestions that will help you write letters in simple, straightforward language. When you draft a letter for your own or the lawyer's signature, if you follow these suggestions, he or she should be favorably impressed by the clarity and effectiveness of your letter.

1. Never use stilted or trite phrases (section 6.24).
2. Avoid unnecessary words or phrases (section 6.25).
3. Do not use two words with the same meaning for emphasis (section 6.26).
4. Avoid favorite words or expressions (section 6.27).
5. Do not use big words or "legalese" when a short, familiar word will do (section 6.28).
6. Use short sentences whenever possible (section 6.29).

6.24. Trite Terms to Avoid

Here is a list of expressions that are stilted or trite and hence not good usage.

Acknowledge receipt of. Use *we received.*

Advise. Used with too little discrimination and best reserved to indicate actual advice. Often *say, tell,* or *let you know is better.*

BAD: We *wish to advise* that your case has been set for trial on November 15.

BETTER: Your case has been set for trial on November 15.

As per; per. Correctly used with Latin words *per annum* and *per diem.*

ALLOWABLE: $5 *per* page.

BETTER: $5 *a* page.

BAD: As *per* our telephone conversation.

BETTER: *In accordance with* our telephone conversation.

BAD: *Per* our agreement.

BETTER: *According to* our agreement.

At all times. Often used with little meaning. Better to use *always.*

POOR: We shall be pleased to talk with you *at all times.*

BETTER: We will *always* be happy to welcome you in our office.

At this time. Also unnecessary in most cases. Try *at present* or *now.*

POOR: We wish to advise that we have no further information *at this time.*

BETTER: We are sorry that we have no further information *at present.*

At your convenience; at an early date. Trite, vague, and unnecessary in most cases. Be specific.

INDEFINITE: Please notify us *at an early date.*

BETTER: Please let us know *within ten days* (or *by the first of next month*).

VAGUE: We should appreciate hearing from you *at your convenience.*

BETTER: We would appreciate hearing from you *by the tenth of June, 19XX.*

Beg. Avoid expressions such as *beg to state, beg to advise, beg to acknowledge.*

POOR: In answer to yours of the 10th inst., *beg to state* . . .

BETTER: In answer (or *response* or *reply*) to your letter of May 10 . . .

Contents carefully noted. Contributes little to a letter.

POOR: Yours of the 5th received and *contents carefully noted.*

BETTER: The instructions outlined in your letter of June 5 have been followed in every detail.

Duly. Unnecessary.

POOR: Your request has been *duly* forwarded to our offices in Washington.

BETTER: Your request has been forwarded to our offices in Washington.

Enclosed please find. Needless and faulty phraseology. The word *please* has little meaning in this instance, and the word *find* is improperly used.

POOR: *Enclosed please find* draft of the contract.

BETTER: *Enclosed is* (or *We are enclosing* or *We enclose*) a draft of the contract.

Esteemed. Too flowery and effusive.

POOR: We welcomed your *esteemed* favor of the 9th.

BETTER: Thank you for your letter of April 9.

Favor. Do not use the word *favor* in the sense of letter, order, or check.

POOR: Thank you for your *favor* of October 5.

BETTER: Thank you for your *letter* of October 5.

Handing you. Out of place in correspondence today.

POOR: We are *handing you* herewith an affidavit signed by R. M. Davis.

BETTER: *Enclosed is* (or *We are enclosing*) an affidavit signed by R. M. Davis.

Have before me. A worn-out expression.

POOR: I *have before me* your complaint of the 10th.

BETTER: *In answer* (or *response* or *reply*) to your letter of November 10th . . .

Hereto. Trite.

POOR: We are attaching *hereto* a copy of the agreement.

BETTER: Attached is a copy of the agreement.

Herewith. Often redundant.

POOR: We enclose *herewith* a copy of the charter.

BETTER: Enclosed is (or *We are enclosing*) a copy of the charter.

In re. Avoid except in subject line. Use *regarding* or *concerning*.

POOR: *In re* our telephone conversation of this morning . . .

BETTER: *Supplementing* (or *Confirming* or *Regarding*) our telephone conversation of this morning . . .

Inst. Avoid the abbreviation of the word *instant* and the word *instant* itself.

POOR: Your favor of the 6th *inst.* (or *instant*) . . .

BETTER: Your letter of *June 6* . . .

Our Mr. Becker. Say, *our associate Mr. Becker* or just *Mr. Becker*.

POOR: *Our Mr. Becker* will call on you next Tuesday, May 10.

BETTER: *Our associate Mr. Becker* will call on you next Tuesday, May 10.

Proximo. A Latin word meaning "on the next." Better to give the exact name of the month.

POOR: The meeting will be held on the 10th *prox.* (or *proximo*).

BETTER: The meeting will be held *December 10.*

Recent date. Vague and unbusinesslike. Give the exact date if known; otherwise, say *recent letter* rather than the stiff wording *letter of recent date.*

VAGUE: Your letter of *recent date.*

DEFINITE: Your letter of *June 2.*

Same. A poor substitute for one of the pronouns *it, they,* or *them.*

POOR: Your letter of the 5th received. We will give *same* our immediate attention.

BETTER: Thank you for your letter of March 5. We will make the requested arrangements immediately.

State. Often too formal. Omit or use *say, tell,* or *let you know.*

POOR: We wish to *state* that the meeting is . . .

BETTER: The meeting is . . .

Take pleasure. A trite expression. Omit or use *are* [or *will be*] *pleased, happy,* or *glad.*

POOR: We *take pleasure* in arranging reservations for you.

BETTER: We *will be happy* to make the arrangements for you (or *We will make the arrangements for you*).

Thanking you in advance. Discourteous and implies that your request will be granted.

POOR: Please mail me any information you may have concerning the ARS bill. *Thanking you in advance* for the favor, I remain . . .

BETTER: I will appreciate any information you can send concerning the ARS bill.

Ultimo. A Latin word meaning *the preceding month.* No longer used in modern correspondence.

POOR: Yours of the 9th *ultimo* (or *ult.*) received.

BETTER: We have received your letter of *June 9.*

Under separate cover. Be specific and give the method of shipping.

POOR: We are sending you *under separate cover* a copy of the record.

BETTER: We are sending you a copy of the record by Express Mail.

Valued. Too effusive and suggestive of flattery. Better to omit.

POOR: We appreciate your *valued* suggestion given to Mr. McCall.

BETTER: We appreciate your suggestion given to Mr. McCall.

Wish to say; wish to state; would say. All are examples of needless, wordy phrases and can be omitted.

POOR: Referring to your letter of the 10th, *wish to say* that we cannot make the necessary arrangements before the first of December.

BETTER: In response to your letter of March 10, we regret that we cannot make the necessary arrangements before December 1.

6.25. Unnecessary Words and Phrases

Many letter writers add unnecessary words to their comments because of an erroneous idea that the padding gives emphasis or rounds out a sentence. For example, letter writers frequently speak of "*final* completion," *month of* January," or "*close* proximity." The completion must be final or it is not complete; January is obviously a month; incidents in proximity must be close.

Here is a list of some padded phrases frequently used in business letters. The italicized words are unnecessary and should be omitted.

The material came *at a time* when we were busy.

Houses appreciate *in value* with time.

During *the year of* 1991.

The radio cost *the sum of* $150.

At a theater party *held* in New York.

In about three months' *time*.

The problem *first* arose when the machine malfunctioned.

A *certain* article entitled *"Day's End."*

The *close* proximity of your shop.

He arrived at *the hour of* noon.

There is merit to both *of them*.

In *the state of* Illinois.

The jar is made *out* of glass.

During *the course of* our conversation.

Perhaps it may be better to leave now.

His uniform *and invariable* policy is as follows.

Someone *or other* is at fault.

I am now *engaged* in writing a book.

He entered by *means of* the elevator.

The car sells for *a price of* $18,000.

6.26. Two Words with the Same Meaning

Some letter writers think that if one word does a job, two words add emphasis. Although speakers and writers sometimes intentionally repeat facts for emphasis, in the following examples the second word makes the thought less effective.

sincere and good wishes

the first and foremost

appraise and determine the worthwhile things

our experience together and contacts in a civic association

deeds and actions

feeling of optimism and encouragement

we refuse and decline

unjust and unfair manner

advise and inform

at once and by return mail

immediately and at once

we demand and insist

right and proper consideration

assume obligation or responsibility

6.27. Favorite Words and Expressions

Avoid acquiring favorite words or expressions. They become habitual. For example, a lawyer might easily overwork the word *records*. One letter might say, "According to our records, the grace period will expire next Monday," and "The enclosed is for your records." A skillful letter writer would simply say, "The grace period will expire next Monday," and "The enclosed copy is for you."

6.28. Big Words Versus One-Syllable Words

Some people think a large vocabulary of big words marks them as learned, but simple, short words usually do the best job. Others use unfamiliar terms known only to other members of their profession (e.g., "legalese"). This does not mean that a large vocabulary or specialized terminology is not an asset. The more words you have, the more clearly and forcibly you can express yourself. But avoid words unfamiliar to laypersons if other familiar words are available, and do not excessively use words of many syllables unless there is a reason for it. Why say *propertied interests* when you mean *rich* or *wealthy people* or *utilize* for *use* or *annihilate* for *wipe out* or *transcend* for *go beyond* or *prior to* for *before?*

6.29. Sentence Length

Since the aim of a letter is to transfer a thought to the reader in the simplest manner with the greatest clarity, avoid long, complicated sentences. Lawyers probably disregard this technique of good letter writing more than most people. Break up overlong, stuffy sentences by making short sentences out of dependent clauses. Here is an example of one sentence containing more than a hundred words.

> Believing the physical union of the two businesses to be desirable and in the best interests of the stockholders of each corporation, the boards of directors have given further consideration to the matter and have agreed in principle on a new plan that would contemplate the transfer of the business and substantially all of the assets of the A Company to B in exchange for shares of common stock of B on a basis that would permit the distribution to the A Company stockholders of one and one-half shares of B common stock for each share of A Company common stock.

The cumbersome sentence could be rewritten in four short sentences and reduced to 67 words.

> The boards of directors of companies A and B thought a merger desirable and in the best interests of the stockholders. They finally agreed on a new plan. The business and substantially all assets of A will be transferred to B in exchange for B common stock. A stockholders will get one and one-half shares of B common stock for each share of A common stock.

LETTERS THE SECRETARY WRITES

Of necessity, the lawyer's dictation time is limited. He or she must spend most of the time in conferences, in court, or in research. So the time reserved for dictating must be used for the more important work—contracts, briefs, examinations, and the like. The lawyer cannot afford to use that time for personal notes, letters of congratulations, complaints to stores he or she deals with, and so on.

Secretaries must be prepared to take over this function when possible. They should be able to answer an invitation, send a follow-up letter, set up an appointment, and compose various other routine messages—on their own. The model letters below cover a variety of miscellaneous communication the lawyer's secretary will be called on to compose from time to time—whether under the secretary's signature or the employer's. Once the secretary selects the type of letter that is needed, the rest is only a matter of typing or, if it is a repetitive type of letter, using a computerized form and making appropriate adjustments.

If you are asked to send copies of documents to clients, follow firm policy in either stamping the document "For Your Information" or adding a simple covering letter: "Here is the [document] you requested. Please let us know if we can provide any additional information." In either case, note on the file copy of the document that a copy was sent, to whom, and the date.

LETTERS WRITTEN OVER THE SECRETARY'S SIGNATURE

6.30. Acknowledgment of Correspondence Received During Employer's Absence

Acknowledgment of a letter received during your employer's absence is a business courtesy. These letters fall into two classes: (1) an acknowledgment without answering the letter, and (2) an acknowledgment that also answers the letter.

Acknowledgment without Answer

The pattern for these letters is simple.

1. State that your employer is out of the city or away from the office.

2. Give the expected date of his or her return.

3. Assure the writer that his or her message will receive attention when your employer returns.

4. If the delay may cause inconvenience to the writer, add a note of apology.

Do not refer to your employer's illness when explaining an absence from the office, unless the addressee already knows the lawyer is ill. Simply state: "Because of Mr. Bentley's absence from the office, he will not be able to attend . . ."

Dear Mr. Sloan:

Since Ms. Franklin is away from the office this week, I am acknowledging your letter of January 6 concerning the housing project. I'll bring it to her attention as soon as she returns, and I know that she will contact you promptly.

Please accept my apologies, Ms. Sloan, for this unavoidable delay.

Sincerely,

Acknowledgment that Also Answers

The important factor in answering, as well as acknowledging, a letter during your employer's absence is to know the facts. Here is a suggested pattern:

1. Identify the incoming letter.

2. State that your employer is away.

3. State the facts that answer the letter.

4. If appropriate, or desirable, state that your employer will write when he or she returns.

Dear Mrs. Smith:

Your letter reminding Mr. Williams of the Rotary Club luncheon on October 17 has arrived during his absence from the office.

Mr. Williams plans to return to Louisville on the 16th and expects to attend the luncheon. If there are any changes in his plans, Mrs. Smith, I'll let you know immediately.

Sincerely,

Letters Concerning Appointments

Here is a pattern that a letter arranging an appointment should follow:

1. Refer to the purpose of the appointment.
2. Suggest, or ask the person to whom you are writing to suggest, the time, place, and date.
3. Ask for a confirmation of the appointment

Employer Asks for Appointment: You Want to Fix the Time

Dear Mr. Jefferson:

Mr. Black will be in Los Angeles for a few hours on Tuesday, March 22. He would like to discuss with you the recent Supreme Court decision in the McNally case.

Will it be convenient for Mr. Black to call at your office at three o'clock on March 22?

Sincerely,

You Have to Let the Other Person Fix the Time

Dear Mrs. Kennedy:

Mr. Billings is returning from Canada the end of this week and would like to discuss with you the result of his conference with the president of the Kittering Corporation.

Would you please ask your secretary to telephone me at 624-9200 and let me know when it will be convenient for you to see Mr. Billings? Thank you.

Sincerely yours,

You Ask Someone to Come in to See Your Employer: You Want to Fix the Time

Dear Mr. Penman:

Ms. Adams would like to see you on Monday, February 27, at two o'clock in her office, Room 201, to complete arrangements for the rental of your summer cottage.

Please let me know whether this time is convenient. Thank you very much, Mr. Penman.

Sincerely,

You Have to Let the Other Person Fix the Time

Dear Mr. and Mrs. Farrington:

The papers in connection with the trust you are creating for your daughter are now complete, except for your signature. Mr. Lewis would like you to come to his office early next week to sign them. Would you please telephone me so that we can set up an appointment for you to do this?

Thank you.

Sincerely,

Reply to Letter Asking Your Employer for Appointment: You Fix a Definite Time

Dear Mr. Smith:

Mrs. Benjamin will be glad to see you on Monday, December 27, at two o'clock in her office, Room 1000, to discuss with you the program for the annual convention. She will be looking forward to seeing you then.

Sincerely,

You Want to Let the Other Person Fix the Time

Dear Ms. Glass:

Mr. Logan will be glad to see you some time during the week of March 3, to talk about the installation of the elevator in his residence at 20 West Street.

If you will telephone me at 221-1000, Mr. Glass, we can arrange a time that will be convenient for you and Mr. Logan. Thank you.

Sincerely,

Your Employer Signs the Letter

Dear Mr. Birdsell:

I'll be happy to talk with you when you are in Denver next week. Would it be convenient for you to come to my office at ten o'clock Thursday morning, November 5? I believe this hour would give us the best opportunity to discuss your project without interruption.

It will be a pleasure to see you again, Mr. Birdsell.

Cordially yours,

You Have to Postpone Fixing a Definite Time

Dear Mr. Edwards:

This is in answer to your letter asking for an appointment with Mr. Finley.

He is away from the office now and is not expected back until the end of the month. However, I'll write to you just as soon as I know when he will be able to see you, Mr. Edwards.

Sincerely yours,

You Have to Say No Politely

Dear Mr. Shotts:

Mrs. Smith has considered very carefully all that you said in your letter of December 21. If there were any possibility that a meeting with you would be helpful, she would be glad to see you; however, she does not believe that would be the case and has asked me to let you know and to thank you for writing.

Sincerely yours,

6.31. Letters Calling Attention to an Error in an Account

In calling attention to an error in an account, avoid giving the impression that you are complaining. These letters fall into four classes: (1) when the amount of an item is incorrect, (2) when the total is incorrect, (3) when returned merchandise has not been credited, and (4) when an item not purchased is charged to the account.

When the Amount of an Item Is Incorrect

Here is a workable outline that covers the necessary points.

1. Give the name and number of the account.
2. Describe the item and tell how it is incorrect.
3. State your version of what the item should be, giving any documentary information you have.
4. Ask for a corrected statement, or enclose a check for the correct amount and ask that the error be rectified on the account.

Ladies and Gentlemen:

The June statement of Elton M. Randall's account no. 15836 shows a charge of $99.80 on May 5 for stationery. Evidently, the figures were transposed. The amount should be $88.90, as shown by sales slip no. O-511C-002.

Please send us a corrected statement, and we will be happy to send our check for the proper amount promptly upon receipt.

Thank you.

Sincerely yours,

When the Total Is Incorrect

Follow the same pattern as when the amount of an item is incorrect.

Ladies and Gentlemen:

The June statement of Laura R. Hudson's account no. 733-4221-7776 shows a balance of $56.90. I believe this amount should be $46.90.

The debits and credits shown on the statement agree with Ms. Hudson's records. I would appreciate it, therefore, if you would check your total again. If you find that the statement should be for $46.90, please send Ms. Hudson a corrected statement. Thank you.

Sincerely yours,

When Returned Merchandise Has Not Been Credited

Follow the same pattern as when the amount of an item is incorrect.

Ladies and Gentlemen:

On May 4 Harold K. Whitsall, whose account number is R2HF1107, returned for credit a pair of bookends purchased from you on May 2. The price was $67.50, including tax.

Mr. Whitsall's June statement does not show this credit. A credit slip was given to him, but unfortunately, it has been misplaced. Mr. Whitsall would appreciate it if you would verify the credit and send him a corrected statement.

In the meantime, I am enclosing Mr. Whitsall's check for $146.25, the amount of the statement less the price of the returned merchandise.

Sincerely yours,

When an Item Not Purchased Is Charged to the Account

These letters should include the following points.

1. Name and number of the account
2. Description of the item charged in error, including the price and the date charged.
3. Any additional pertinent information that you have

4. A request that the charge be investigated

5. A request for a corrected statement

Ladies and Gentlemen:

The June statement of Anita Bergman's account 413-9276-3302 shows a charge of $48.35 on May 15 for two books. Ms. Bergman charged two books for $48.35 on May 10 and one other book for the same amount on May 20, but she did not charge anything on May 15. The three books that she bought on May 10 and 20 were properly charged to her account.

Ms. Bergman does not know why the charge was made against her account. Please investigate and let her know what happened. Naturally, she is concerned that someone might have used her account without her permission.

If the charge was made through clerical error, please send her a corrected statement. Thank you.

Sincerely yours,

6.32. Reply to Notice of Meeting

Sometimes the secretary knows whether his or her employer plans to attend a meeting; at other times it is necessary to find out what the lawyer's plans are. A letter replying to a meeting notice covers the following points:

1. Repeat the time, date, and place of the meeting

2. State whether the lawyer plans to attend the meeting.

3. Give a reason if he or she does not plan to attend.

Dear Mr. Brown:

Mr. Morris plans to be present at the meeting of the Finance Committee on Tuesday, October 26, at 9:30 a.m., in your office.

Sincerely yours,

Dear Mr. Brown:

Mr. Morris has the notice of the meeting of the Finance Committee on Tuesday, October 26, at 9:30 A.M. Unfortunately, previous business appointments will prevent him from attending this meeting.

Sincerely yours,

6.33. Letters Calling Attention to Omission of Enclosures

When an enclosure mentioned in an incoming letter is omitted, you should notify the sender. Here is the pattern your letter should follow:

1. Identify the incoming letter and enclosure.

2. State that the enclosure was omitted.

3. Ask that the enclosure, or a copy of it, be sent to you.

Dear Ms. Boyd:

In your letter of March 3 to Ronald Pearson you said that you were enclosing a copy of the tentative program for the meeting of the Sales Executives Club in May. The program, however, was not enclosed.

Since Mr. Pearson's reply to your letter will be governed by the tentative program, I would appreciate it if you would send a copy of the program right away.

Thank you very much, Ms. Boyd.

Sincerely,

6.34. Follow-Up Letters

If correspondence in your follow-up files (see chapter 4) is not answered by the follow-up date, trace the letter for a reply. Your letter should cover the following points:

1. Identify the letter. Identification by date is not sufficient because your correspondent does not know what you are writing about.

2. Offer a reason for the recipient's failure to reply, without casting reflection on him or her.

3. Enclose a copy of your original letter, unless it was very short. If so, simply repeat the contents in your follow-up letter.

Copy of Original Letter Not Enclosed

Ladies and Gentlemen:

On February 2 we ordered from you six copies of your latest bulletin "Practicing Attorneys' Letter," but we have not yet received an acknowledgment of the order.

Since our first order evidently went astray, please consider this a duplicate.

Sincerely yours,

Copy of Original Letter Enclosed

Since this is a follow-up of a letter requesting a favor, it is written for the lawyer's signature.

Dear Mr. Fonda:

In the rush of work you probably have not had time to answer my letter of October 25 about using some of your practice ideas in our Bar Association Journal, with credit to you. On the chance this letter did not reach you, however, I'm enclosing a copy of it.

I would like very much to include your ideas in the next issue. This will be possible if I have your reply by December 15.

Thanks very much, Mr. Fonda.

Sincerely,

LETTERS THE SECRETARY MAY WRITE
FOR EMPLOYER'S SIGNATURE

6.35. Letters of Appreciation

A letter of appreciation should reflect genuine sincerity and honest gratitude; it should not reflect merely the writer's desire to conform with the rules of etiquette. The tone should be one of friendly informality.

Dear Ms. Wyckoff:

I want to thank you for taking time yesterday to talk with Fred Duxbury, the person I recommended to you for a sales position with your firm.

I spoke with him again this morning, and he is enthusiastic about the prospect of joining your organization. He was particularly impressed by what you told him, and he appears eager to tackle the job.

Although I have grown wary of recommending people, I cannot help feeling that in this case I was justified in suggesting that you meet Mr. Duxbury.

Sincerely yours,

For Assistance to Firm, Club, or Association

Dear Mr. Hardy:

The Society for Advancement of Management is deeply indebted to you for your inspiring remarks made at its annual conference. The members of the society will long remember your message as having contributed immeasurably to the success of the meeting.

As chairman of the conference, I am particularly indebted to you for your kindness in agreeing to speak. I sincerely hope the society will be honored again at some future conference by your presence on the speaker's platform.

I also look forward to having lunch with you in the near future, Mr. Hardy, and hearing more about your ideas.

Sincerely,

For Hospitality

Dear Ms. Cartwright:

This is my first day in the office after my long northern trip. Everything considered, it was an extremely pleasant trip, and the luncheon visit with you in Buffalo helped to make it so. Thank you again for rearranging your plans on such short notice to include me in your day.

I hope that something will bring you through the South before the year is over, Ms. Cartwright, and that you will include a day in Birmingham.

Best regards,

For Message of Congratulations

Dear Tom:

I appreciate your kind words about my efforts to guide the recent Credit Management program. It was a lot of fun, and I only hope that all the participants in our discussion enjoyed this exchange of ideas as much as I did.

Your making a special effort to attend, despite adverse circumstances, made me feel very good. I was glad you were able to be there, since it is likely we will be working together on similar programs for a long time to come. I hope so.

Thanks for your thoughtful note, Tom.

Cordially,

For Message of Sympathy

Dear Mr. Poindexter:

On behalf of the personnel of Stone & Westerly, I want to thank you for your kind letter of sympathy upon the death of our president, Jonas MacIntyre.

It is true that this organization has sustained a shock and a great loss in the sudden passing of Mr. MacIntyre. But by holding to the high standards he represented, we believe we will be paying him the most appropriate tribute.

Your friendship, as manifested in your letter, gives us encouragement as we undertake this task.

Very sincerely yours,

6.36. Letters of Sympathy

In any letter written to express sympathy, sincerity and tact are the most important qualities. Avoid words or sentiments that could distress the reader. Do not philosophize about the meaning of death or quote scripture or poetry. A letter of sympathy should not be long and involved. The length is based on (1) the degree of friendship between writer and reader, (2) the situation that prompts the letter, and (3) the tastes and temperament of the reader.

Upon Death

Dear Mrs. Cullen:

Every member of our firm was shocked and saddened at the sudden death of your husband.

Although sympathy is small consolation, even when it comes from the hearts of those who share your sorrow, I want you to know how keenly John's loss is felt by everyone here. I don't need to tell you of the respect and admiration in which he was held by all who worked with him.

Other members of the firm join me in this expression of our deep sympathy, Mrs. Cullen. We only wish it were within our power to alleviate the sadness that has come to you and your family.

Very sincerely yours,

Upon Personal Injury or Illness

Dear Larry:

I just learned of your painful injury and want to send you my best wishes for a speedy recovery.

Since you will be confined to your home for a few days, I believe you will enjoy reading a new book that has given me a number of pleasant hours. I'm sending it along with this note.

Cordially,

6.37. Letters of Congratulation

The outstanding qualities of an expression of congratulations are (1) brevity, (2) naturalness of expression, and (3) enthusiasm. Trite, stilted phrases indicate a lack of sincerity and destroy the individuality of the letter.

The following illustrations of congratulatory messages are suitable for numerous occasions that occur frequently in business.

Upon Professional or Civic Honor

Dear Mr. Guyote:

I was very pleased to learn that you are the new secretary of the Omaha Chamber of Commerce. I can think of no one better qualified for this important work, and I know you will make an outstanding success of it.

Whenever I can be of assistance in any way, Mr. Guyote, you will find me glad to cooperate.

Cordially yours,

Upon Promotion

Dear Mr. Moore:

I just learned of your appointment as division superintendent of the Santa Fe Railroad.

At this time when you have such good reason to be proud and happy, may I add my sincere congratulations. I was very glad to hear of your promotion, Mr. Moore, and wish you every success in your new position.

Cordially yours,

Upon Retirement from Business

Dear Ms. Forest:

Thirty-eight years of helpful counsel to your associates and wise leadership in your community is a record of service that few people achieve. It is also a record that deserves a sincere word of gratitude from those you have helped so generously during all these years.

We will miss your steady hand, but we know how fully you have earned the first leisure time of your 38 years in Mansfield.

Congratulations on your outstanding record of service, Ms. Forest, and best wishes for many happy years ahead.

Sincerely yours,

Upon Speech, Article, or Book

Dear Mr. Conwell:

Last night I read your excellent article in the June issue of *The American Banker*. You have presented the soundest treatment of bank credit problems that I have ever seen.

I congratulate you on this fine article, Mr. Conwell. Many others, I'm sure, have learned as much from your constructive analysis as I have.

Cordially yours,

Upon Outstanding Community Service

Dear Mayor Fry:

As a citizen of Oakland, I want to express my sincere appreciation for the many things you have done to make it a better city in which to live.

Probably, yours has seemed like a thankless task at times, but the satisfaction of a big job well done is no small reward in itself.

Certainly, that satisfaction is yours in abundant measure as well as the pleasure of knowing that you have the gratitude of every citizen who stands for honest and efficient city government.

Sincerely yours,

Upon Business Anniversary

Dear Mr. Shell:

On the eve of your 40th business anniversary, I want to extend to you my congratulations on your record of achievement and my sincere best wishes for the future.

Your 40 years in business represent not only a career of the highest ethical standards but also one of genuine service to this community. You have won the respect, confidence, and admiration of the people of Clinton, Mr. Shell, and you have every right to be proud of the reputation you've earned.

Yours sincerely,

Letters of Seasonal Good Wishes

Dear Mrs. Larson:

My association with you during the past year has been so enjoyable that I want to send you this word of good wishes for a happy and successful 19XX.

I hope that the coming year will afford more opportunities for pleasant contacts between your firm and mine and that I'll have the pleasure of further visits with you.

Sincerely yours,

6.38. Letters of Introduction

The letter of introduction may be prepared for direct mailing to the addressee or for delivery in person by the one introduced. In the latter case the envelope should be left unsealed as a courtesy to the bearer. When there is sufficient time for the letter to reach its recipient before the arrival of the person introduced, the preferable practice is to send the note directly to the addressee.

The letter is ordinarily written in a spirit of asking a favor. It should include the following points:

1. The name of the person being introduced
2. The purpose or reason for the introduction
3. All relevant and appropriate details, personal or business
4. A statement that any courtesy shown will be appreciated by the writer

Introducing a Personal Friend

Dear Jim:

My good friend and former neighbor Don Parker will present this note to you when he stops in Omaha on his way to the Pacific Coast.

Don is head of the advertising staff of Fall River Air Service, and I am sure that you and he will have much to discuss. In fact, it's because I think you both will enjoy a visit that I'm writing.

I'll appreciate any courtesy you may extend to Don during his brief stop in Omaha. Thanks, Jim.

Regards,

Introducing a Business or Professional Associate

Dear Mr. Samson:

This letter will be handed to you by my friend and associate Harvey Lister, a well-known writer of articles on business.

Mr. Lister is preparing a book in which he hopes to outline the development of the textile industry during the last half century. He believes that through a talk with you he could obtain both information and inspiration that would be valuable to him in his work.

Since you are the authority on your particular phase of the industry, he has asked for an introduction to you. I'll appreciate any courtesies you may show him, Mr. Samson, and I know he will too.

Thanks very much.

Sincerely,

6.39. Letters of Invitation

The letter of invitation should be cordial and gracious in tone, entirely free of stilted formality. It should be complete in detail, telling when, where, and, if the occasion is essentially business, why.

To Attend Banquet, Luncheon, or Entertainment

Dear Suzanne:

Can you join me for lunch at the Fifth Avenue Hotel next Monday about 12:30 p.m.?

Anne Steel will be with me for the day, and I'd like to have you meet her. Aside from the fact that she is someone you would enjoy knowing, the contact might prove helpful from a business standpoint. Anne plans to add several new departments to the Boston and Worcester stores.

I'd have written you this note earlier, but I didn't learn until today that she would be in town next week. I hope you can make it, Suzanne.

Best wishes,

To Give Address or Informal Talk

Dear Mr. Connelly:

The subject of "How to Write Good Business Letters" is an interesting one to every business and professional person. For a long time I've intended, when it came my turn to arrange a program for the Professional Club, to invite a real authority in the field to talk to the club on that subject.

My turn came today, when I was asked to arrange the program for Tuesday noon, November 17. I know of no other person as well qualified as you to speak on the technique of writing business letters, and I'm hoping very much that you will find it possible to accept my invitation.

Our luncheon meetings are held in the Banquet Room of the Hotel Cleveland. They begin at 12:15 p.m. and are usually over about 1:30 p.m. The talks range from 30 to 40 minutes.

If you can be our guest on the 17th, Mr. Connelly, you'll receive a most enthusiastic welcome.

Sincerely,

6.40. Letters of Acceptance

A personal letter accepting an invitation should convey appreciation and enthusiasm. If the invitation has left certain details—such as time and place—to the convenience of the recipient, the acceptance must deal specifically with these points. Otherwise, a brief note is sufficient.

Accepting Invitation to Banquet, Luncheon, or Entertainment

Dear Jack:

I'll be delighted to be your guest at the Business Association on Thursday, October 12. For several months I've hoped I might hear John Parson's widely discussed talk on "Personality in Client Contact," and the opportunity to hear it in your company will make it doubly enjoyable.

As you suggest, I'll be in the Claremont lobby a few minutes after twelve. Thanks for thinking of me, Jack.

Best regards,

Accepting Hospitality for an Overnight Visit

Dear Roger:

Nothing could have been more welcome than your letter inviting me to stay with you during my weekend in Portland. I'm happy to accept.

It's very thoughtful of you and Mrs. McGuire to extend the hospitality of your home, and I look forward to seeing you next Saturday.

Cordially,

Accepting Speaking Invitation

Dear Mr. Walton:

I'll be happy to speak to the Rotary Club on Monday, June 26. Thank you for asking me.

The subject you suggest is satisfactory, and I'll do my best to give your members an interesting half-hour. I know that prompt adjournment is an important requirement of most luncheon clubs, and I assure you that my remarks will be confined to the allotted time.

I'll be glad to meet you in the Biltmore lobby at 12 o'clock, Mr. Walton, and I look forward with pleasure to the visit with members of your club.

Cordially yours,

Accepting Membership in Professional or Civic Organization

Dear Ms. Lane:

Your cordial invitation for me to join the Hyattville Community Association pleases me very much, and I accept with pleasure.

I realize your membership includes many dedicated members of the community, both in academic ranks and in business circles. I'm highly complimented at the opportunity to become associated with such a group.

Sincerely yours,

Accepting Invitation to Serve on Civic or Professional Committee or Board

Dear Mr. Faber:

I was both pleased and complimented to receive your letter yesterday.

It will be a pleasure to serve on the Planning Committee for the "Better Burlington" campaign, and I'm looking forward to a pleasant association with you and Ms. Harper in this work.

Sincerely,

6.41. Letters of Declination

Letters of declination should include an expression of regret and an expression of appreciation for the invitation. An explanation of the circumstances that prevent acceptance helps to show that the regret is sincere. The message must combine cordiality with tact.

Declining Invitation to Banquet, Luncheon, or Entertainment

Dear Evelyn:

Only this morning I accepted another invitation to be a guest at the Acceptance Banquet. This makes it impossible for me to enjoy your hospitality.

It's a pleasure, however, to know I'm going to see you during that week. Thank you, Evelyn, for your kindness in remembering me in arranging your table.

Cordially,

7 How to Keep Books and Records

Although the practice of law is a profession and not a business, the successful lawyer today practices his or her profession in a businesslike way. The lawyer maintains an orderly system of accounts that shows whether a fee is adequate for the time spent on a case, what percentage of overhead bears to his or her income, and the like.

This chapter describes the fundamentals of bookkeeping in the lawyer's office. It also identifies records that will show the lawyer immediately the cost of his or her services.

HOW TO KEEP BOOKS IN THE LAW OFFICE

7.1. System of Bookkeeping in the Law Office

In addition to checkbooks, the records usually maintained are a cash journal, a general ledger, and a subsidiary accounts receivable, or clients', ledger, all of which are usually kept by computer. Most offices have a bookkeeper or accounting department to maintain the firm's accounting records. Usually, the lawyer is responsible for daily, weekly, or monthly time-sheet reports, and the secretary is responsible for seeing that these reports reach the designated person in time. Nevertheless, it is helpful to a secretary to have a general understanding of the principles and rules of bookkeeping.

7.2. Basic Principles of Double-Entry Bookkeeping

In every double-entry system records are kept by accounts. An account is a formal record of related transactions maintained in a general ledger. Entries are made in a file (computerized system) or book (manual system) of original entry and are posted to the appropriate accounts in the ledger. Posting merely means transferring items from a file or book of original entry to a ledger account. This posting process is handled by assigning each account a number and arranging the accounts in numerical order in the general ledger. Each account has a debit column and a credit column. The debit is the left column and the credit is the right column.

In double-entry bookkeeping every transaction must be recorded in two accounts—as a debit in one account and a credit in another.

Debits and Credits

A few principles for debit and credit are all you need to be able to understand the bookkeeping records that are ordinarily kept in a law office. Application of these rules will be explained later.

1. A debit *increases* asset accounts. Cash (bank account), accounts receivable, furniture and fixtures, and other property owned by the firm are assets.

2. A debit *increases* expense accounts such as salaries, office supplies, and taxes.

3. A debit *decreases* the capital account. The money the lawyer puts into the bank when he or she opens a law office is shown in the capital account. It is decreased when the lawyer withdraws any of that money or when he or she incurs a loss in carrying on the practice.

4. A debit *decreases* an income account.

5. A debit *decreases* liability accounts. Accounts payable is a liability account. So is any other item the firm owes.

6. A credit does exactly the reverse of a debit.

These principles may be expressed as a formula as follows:

Debit—*Increases* assets and expense accounts.
    Decreases capital, income, and liability accounts.

Credit—*Decreases* assets and expense accounts.
Increases capital, income, and liability accounts.

7.3. Simple Rules to Remember

Since almost all transactions in a law office involve either bank deposits or bank withdrawals, or charging clients for services and receiving payment from them, you will have no difficulty in understanding entries if you remember the four rules that follow.

1. Cash received (bank deposits) is always debited to the bank account in which it is deposited and therefore must be credited to another account.

2. Cash payments (bank withdrawals) are always credited to the bank account on which the check is drawn and therefore must be debited to another account.

3. Accounts Receivable is always debited when bills for services are sent to a client, and the amount charged must be credited to the Services Charged account.

4. Accounts Receivable is always credited when a client pays for services, and the payment must be debited to the Services Charged account.

7.4. Cash Journal

In a law office the file (computerized system) or book (manual system) of original entry commonly used is the cash journal. It is a chronological record of every cash or other transaction that passes through the office. It is supplemented by a record of the lawyer's time (described in the section "Time and Cost of Professional Services"), from which billings are made. The usual journal sheet in a software package consists of 16 to 18 columns. Appropriate headings, which will vary with the office, are written in the columns. An acceptable form of journal sheet has the lines numbered at each side to facilitate following the line across the sheet. In addition to spaces for date, description of item, and check number, the cash journal sheet in a law office will usually include the columns described in the following sections, for the purposes indicated:

Cash (Firm Bank Account), Debit

All deposits of money belonging to the firm are entered here.

Cash (Firm Bank Account), Credit

All checks drawn on the firm bank account are entered here.

Trust Fund Account, Debit

All receipts of money belonging to clients are entered here. Large advances by clients for expenses are also usually deposited in the trust account and, therefore, are entered in this column. Collections of commercial items for clients (Chapter 20) are deposited to the trust account. Separate funds should be used when the firm is either executor or trustee of a client's estate or trust. (See also section 7.18 for more about trust accounts.)

Trust Fund Account, Credit

All checks drawn on the trust fund account are entered here.

Accounts Receivable, Debit

All charges made to clients are entered here.

Accounts Receivable, Credit

All payments made by clients are entered here.

Accounts Payable, Debit

All payments made on accounts owed are entered here. Law firms have few outstanding accounts payable. Therefore, this column is frequently omitted, and the payments on accounts owed are entered in the General Ledger (debit) column, from which the detail entry is posted to the debit column of the control account in the general ledger.

Accounts Payable, Credit

All accounts owed are entered here. As indicated before, this column may be omitted and entries made instead in the General Ledger (credit) column, from which the detail entry is posted to the credit column of the control account in the general ledger.

Services Charged, Debit

All payments made by clients for services are entered here.

Services Charged, Credit

All charges made to clients for services are entered here.

General Ledger, Debit, and General Ledger, Credit

These columns are for accounts that do not have separate columns of their own, such as Furniture and Fixtures, Library, and Accounts Payable. Expenses that occur only occasionally, such as rent, insurance, and entertainment, are entered in the General Ledger column. The entries are posted in detail to the respective accounts in the general ledger.

Fees Earned

All income from fees is entered here. Only one journal column is necessary because all entries are credits.

Tax Expense

Taxes the firm pays are entered here. They include the firm's share of the social security tax, unemployment tax, use and occupancy tax, and others. All entries are credits.

Overhead Expense

There may be any number of columns for overhead expenses, such as Office Supplies, Utilities, and Telephone. The breakdown depends on the need and number of columns. All entries are debits.

Miscellaneous Expense

Expenses that cannot be readily classified and have no account of their own in the ledger are entered here. All entries are debits.

7.5. General Ledger

The general ledger contains all of the accounts, including the control account for the individual client accounts. The entries in the journal are posted to the accounts affected. The cash journal shows what transactions took place on a certain date, whereas the ledger shows the recorded status of each specific account at any time.

The accounts in the ledger are arranged numerically and grouped in the following order in the general ledger to facilitate the preparation of financial statements.

Assets (Bank Accounts, Furniture and Fixtures, Accounts Receivable, etc.)

Liabilities (Accounts Payable, Loans Payable, etc.)

Capital (Proprietorship)

Income

Expense

The general ledger will have accounts for the following columns shown in the cash journal (section 7.8): Cash (Firm Bank Account), Trust Fund Account, Accounts Receivable, Services Charged, Accrued Withholding Tax, Accrued Federal Insurance Contributions, Fees Earned, Tax Expense, Telephone, Office Supplies, Salaries, and Miscellaneous Expense in which any miscellaneous expense may be entered in detail. The general ledger will also have accounts for items that are entered in the General Ledger column, such as Rent, Insurance, Petty Cash, and Accounts Payable.

In addition, it will have some accounts that are not immediately affected by the journal. They will have been opened when the files (computerized system) or books (manual system) were set up. Entries are usually made in them only once a year, when the accounting files or books are closed. They generally include a Capital (proprietorship) account, Profit and Loss, Accumulated Depreciation, Depreciation, Bad Debts, and others. The closing entries, which are posted to these accounts, are usually made by the accountant.

7.6. Subsidiary Ledger

The subsidiary accounts receivable ledger is the most important record in the law office—accounts receivable is the lawyer's largest asset. The Accounts Receivable account in the general ledger is a "control" account; it summarizes the individual accounts in the subsidiary ledger. Its balance equals the sum of the balances of the individual accounts in the subsidiary accounts receivable ledger. The control account simplifies getting a trial balance and, especially, detecting any error that might be made in posting to the wrong side of the individual accounts that it controls. The accounts are kept in alphabetical order according to the client's name.

Unless a separate record is kept of the hours worked on a case (see the sections under "Time and Cost of Professional Services"), it is desirable that the client's ledger sheet should have columns for this information. It should also have separate columns for disbursements and charges for services and a column for payments. Figure 7.1 on page 156 shows a form of client's ledger sheet suitable for a law office. The specific layout of items on the form will depend on the accounting software package used by the law firm.

An attorney's daily time record is illustrated in section 7.17. Information can be picked up from that record and brought into the client's ledger sheet (Figure 7.1). Thus the ledger sheet will reflect the actual time spent by the attorney handling any particular phase of the matter.

As soon as a new case is received, a ledger sheet should be opened for it. Because of the manner in which lawyers bill their clients, a separate sheet is opened for each case. Thus a client with three cases pending would have three sheets in the ledger. Information necessary to open the account can be taken from the New Matter Report (see "A New Matter" in Chapter 2).

The column for disbursements and the column for services charged are debit items. Postings are made to these columns from the cash journal.

7.7. Posting to the General Ledger

Recording items from the cash journal in the affected accounts in the ledger is called *posting*. The items in the Accounts Receivable column should be posted daily to the client's subsidiary ledger account, so that charges for disbursements are apparent when the lawyer decides to bill the client. (See the sections under "Billing the Client.") The other items may be posted monthly. The items in the General Ledger column must be posted individually to the accounts affected. Only the totals of the other columns are posted to the corresponding accounts.

The following procedure is used in posting from the cash journal to the accounts in the general ledger. With electronic spreadsheets, calculations previously made manually are performed automatically.

1. Each column in the journal is totaled and then the debit and credit columns. The totals of the debit and credit columns must equal

Nature of Case: (3)
Escrow Agreement, Real Estate

Name of Client   Kenneth Harrison
Address   1800 Seventh Avenue
Berkeley, California 94710

| Date | Lawyer | Hours | | Description | Debits | | Credits | Balance |
		Partner	Staff		Disburse-ments	Service		(credit)
Mar.8	R.S.E.	1.25		Conference with client				
9				Abstract of title	20.			
12	L.E.T.		2.50	Examination of Abstracts				
13	R.S.E.	1.00		Conference with Smith Attorney				
14				Deposit for Trust			1,350.	(1,350.)
18	L.E.T.		2.50	Draft Agreement				
19	R.S.E.	1.25		Conference with Smith Attorney				
21	L.E.T.	1.00		Drawing deed				
23	R.S.E.	.50		Conference with client				
24	R.S.E.	1.25						
	L.E.T.		1.25	Closing				
24				Ch. R.D. Smith settlement	780.			
25				Services		550.		(550.)

Figure 7.1. Client's Ledger Sheet.

156

each other. If they do not, there is an error in the entries or in addition.

2. The totals from all columns except the General Ledger are posted to the corresponding accounts in the general ledger as a debit or credit, as indicated in the column. Previously, the individual items in the Accounts Receivable column were posted to the respective clients' accounts. The total of the Accounts Receivable column is posted to the control account in the general ledger.

3. The individual items from the General Ledger column are posted to the respective accounts in the general ledger as a debit or credit, as indicated in the column. In a manual system, a checkmark is placed by each item to show that it has been posted.

4. In a manual system, a double red line is drawn under the total of each column that has been posted. The next entries will be below these lines, and new totals will not include the figures above the red lines.

7.8. Trial Balance

The process of listing the titles of the accounts in the ledger and showing the balance of each, whether debit or credit, is known as taking a trial balance. The purpose is to determine whether the total debits equal the total credits and to establish a basic summary for financial statements. With a computerized spreadsheet system, a trial balance can be produced almost instantly on demand.

7.9. Taking a Trial Balance of Accounts Receivable

When a trial balance is taken, the accuracy of the accounts in the clients' subsidiary ledger should also be proved. The computer will add the debit balances and the credit balances, if any, and subtract the credits from the debits. The result should be the same as the balance shown in the Accounts Receivable control account in the general ledger. If it is not, an error was made in posting.

In taking the balance of accounts receivable, both the disbursement entries and the charges for services are debits, whereas the payments received are credits.

The Services Charged account is in reality a reserve set aside for the collection of accounts receivable for services and should be in balance with the amounts that are receivable for services.

In taking a trial balance of the accounts receivable, a separate listing should be made of the accounts receivable for advances made by the attorney for clients' expenses, indicated on the client's ledger sheet as Disbursements. After deducting from the total listing of all receivables the amount of receivables for expense, the balance should equal the credit balance in the Services Charged account, unless there are certain prepayments in the accounts receivable balances in the form of advance retainers or trust deposits. Every debit to Accounts Receivable *for services rendered* is reflected in the credits to Services Charged.

7.10. Profit and Loss Statement

A profit and loss statement shows the lawyer whether he or she made a profit or lost money over a given period. It also shows the amount of each type of expense. The accountant usually prepares this statement by computer after closing the files or books for the period. However, a profit and loss statement can be generated almost immediately by computer at any time.

7.11. Drawing Account

Each partner of the firm has a drawing account from which he or she withdraws funds for personal remuneration. All of the entries are on the debit side. These accounts are closed out at the end of the accounting period, usually by the accountant.

7.12. Payroll Record

An individual account for each employee should also be kept, to facilitate reports to the state and federal governments and the preparation of the withholding receipt that must be given to each employee. Figure 7.2 is a form used for this purpose when employees are paid weekly. The precise layout of data will depend on the particular computerized or hard-copy form used by the law firm. A payroll form provides space for recording and accumulating taxes withheld for remittance to the Internal Revenue Service and for the annual withholding statement. It also includes any other withheld

PAYROLL

NAME								PHONE		SOCIAL SEC. NO.			NO. OF EXEMPTIONS		
ADDRESS															
DATE 19	PERIOD PAID FOR	RATE	EARNINGS			DEDUCTIONS						NET PAID	CHECK NUMBER
			REGULAR	OTHER	TOTAL	W.H. TAX	FICA W.H.	OTHER W.H.	TOTAL				
JAN.													
TOTAL JANUARY													
FEB.													
TOTAL FEBRUARY													
MAR.													
TOTAL MARCH													
TOTAL 1ST QUARTER													

Figure 7.2. Payroll Record.

159

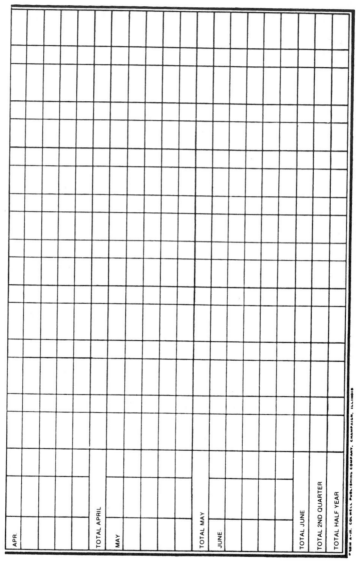

From Daily Log for Lawyers, Courtesy Colwell Publishing Company.

Figure 7.2. Payroll Record. *(cont.)*

accounts such as insurance and retirement. These entries are posted from the cash journal.

7.13. Capital Account

It takes money to open a law office and operate it before the fees are received. The money the lawyer puts up for this purpose is known as *capital*. It is entered in the debit column of the Firm Bank Account and in the credit column of the Capital account. Any change in the Capital account—addition or subtraction—must be reflected in the closing entries made at the end of the year.

TIME AND COST OF PROFESSIONAL SERVICES

7.14. Records Required to Find Time and Cost of Services

The records required to ascertain the cost of the lawyer's service on a specific case are the daily time sheet and the client's ledger (kept in connection with bookkeeping).

7.15. Finding Out the Cost of a Lawyer's Time

In figuring the profit and loss in a law office for accounting purposes, the lawyer's time is not counted, but the lawyer who practices his or her profession in a businesslike manner wants to know the cost of the time spent on a case. The fee charged may be more than the cost, giving the lawyer a profit, or it may be less, resulting in a loss. But at least the cost of the lawyer's time is a basis for a fair fee. Even when a client is on a yearly retainer or when the lawyer accepts a case on a contingent basis, he or she wants to know the cost.

The cost per hour of a lawyer's time is arrived at by adding the lawyer's drawing account to the overhead and dividing by the number of hours he or she expects to be working during the year. If there is more than one attorney practicing for the firm, the overhead is proportioned among them, including the associates, on the basis of their drawing accounts. The senior member of the firm, who has the largest drawing account, is thus charged with a larger proportion of the overhead than a junior member. This is as it should be since he or she has a better office, a higher paid secretary, and the like. Salaries paid associate attorneys are not included in overhead for the purpose of calculating the cost of services; the associate's cost to the firm is figured in the same manner as the cost of a partner's service.

7.16. Daily Time Sheet

The daily time sheet is the starting point for the billing process. To arrive at the cost of a job, each lawyer in the office should keep a daily time sheet. The diary illustrated in Figure 4.1 (see Chapter 4) can be used as a time record. Figure 7.3 illustrates another form. These forms do not provide for an estimated fee, but this is covered by the new matter report illustrated in Figure 2.4 (see Chapter 2). In some offices the secretaries and the paraprofessionals also keep time sheets. The time spent on each matter is posted to the client's ledger account and is considered in calculating the fee.

7.17. Posting the Time Charges

The time charges are posted to the client's ledger account (Figure 7.1) from the daily time sheet, showing which lawyer did the work. The posting process is usually handled by computer (see the sections under "How to Keep Books in the Law Office"). When the lawyer is ready to fix the fee, he or she will ask for the time spent on the case by each attorney. The lawyer knows the cost per hour and can thus calculate the cost to the firm of the services rendered. The fee may be more or less than the cost.

Some law firms do not post the time to the client's ledger account but keep it on a computer service ledger sheet (see Figure 7.4, p. 164). Only the disbursements, service charges, and payments appear on the client's ledger account.

BILLING THE CLIENT

7.18. Preparation of the Bill

Clients are usually billed regularly, often monthly, throughout the process of their case. Especially with new clients, the lawyer requests and receives a retainer that is drawn upon as work progresses. The retainer is placed in a trust account, and checks are drawn against it as charges are incurred. The secretary or billing clerk will prepare a draft bill, and the

878—Attorney's Daily Record

Printed by Julius Blumberg, Inc., 80 Exchange Place, at Broadway, New York

DAILY RECORD OF_____DAY_____DATE_____19___

TIME	Kind of Work	MATTER	TIME	Kind of Work	MATTER
9 a.m.			2 p.m.		
.10			.10		
.20			.20		
.30			.30		
.40			.40		
.50			.50		
10 a.m.			3 p.m.		
.10			.10		
.20			.20		
.30			.30		
.40			.40		
.50			.50		
11 a.m.			4 p.m.		
.10			.10		
.20			.20		
.30			.30		
.40			.40		
.50			.50		
12 m.			5 p.m.		
.10			.10		
.20			.20		
.30			.30		
.40			.40		
.50			.50		
1 p.m.			6 p.m.		
.10			Remarks:		
.20					
.30					
.40			Evening		
.50					
2 p.m.					

C—Consultation with client; I—Interview with others; T—Telephone conversation; D—Dictation; W—Work; L—Looking up Law; M—Miscellaneous

Courtesy Julius Blumberg, Inc.

Figure 7.3. Attorney's Daily Time Sheet.

				CHARGE RECORDS NO. 325
City Bank #56 Lester Trust				
DATE	LAWYER	PARTNER HOURS	STAFF HOURS	
19__ 3-6 3-8	S.E.T. R.L.A.	2:30	7:15	Preparation of Draft Examination of Draft

Figure 7.4.   Service Ledger Sheet.

lawyer will generally review it before it is finalized and submitted to the client.

Trust accounts are used for funds that do not belong to the firm. Money held for the client pending settlement of a case or closing of a real estate transaction, for example, and most retainers are deposited in the Trust account. These funds must *never* be mingled with firm accounts. The lawyer is required to account for them separately and in considerable detail. Any use of money in the Trust account for other than the purpose for which it is being held is a serious violation of law as well as of ethical standards.

Law firms may have printed bill heads or use letterhead stationery. Small firms sometimes print out the firm's name and address by computer at the same time the invoice is generated. The general practice is to make an original and two copies—the original and a return copy for the client and a copy for the invoice file. The bills are frequently numbered and filed in the invoice file according to file number or alphabetically by client. If they are not numbered, they are filed according to date. See Figure 7.5 for a sample computer-generated invoice.

Carolyn W. Baldwin
Attorney at Law
Ralph Pill Marketplace
22 Bridge Street
Concord, NH 03301

Invoice submitted to:

Mr. and Mrs. John Smith
123 Market Street
Concord, NH 03301

May 31, 1990
In reference to: Timber Trespass

		Amount
	CBaldwin @ 100	
5/7/90	- Initial phone conference with Fred Jones	NO CHARGE
	Phone call to Mr. Smith	
	Phone call to Mrs. Smith	
5/8/90	- Phone call to Mr. Jones	100.00
	Confirming letter to Mr. and Mrs. Smith	
	Letter to Young	
	- Office conference with Mr. Black	50.00
5/10/90	- Phone conference with Mr. Edwards	20.00
	- Phone conference with Mr. Black	20.00
5/11/90	- Phone conference with Mr. Edwards	50.00
	re: damage appraisal	
5/14/90	- Phone conference with Mr. Black	10.00
	- Office conference re: photos	100.00
	View video	
5/16/90	- Phone conference with Atty. Lawrence	50.00
	Phone call to Mr. Edwards	
	Phone call to Mr. Black	
5/17/90	- Phone conference with Mr. Edwards	20.00
5/18/90	- Letter to Atty. Lawrence	50.00
	SUBTOTAL: [4.70	470.00]

Figure 7.5. Invoice.

Mr. and Mrs. Smith
Page 2

			Amount
	Paralegal @ $35		
5/15/90	- Research, Strafford County Registry		94.50
	SUBTOTAL:	[2.70	94.50]
	RdeSeve @ $85		
5/15/90	- Review of Landclearing Ucc Filings, corporate documents		85.00
	SUBTOTAL:	[1.00	85.00]

		Hours	
	For professional services rendered	8.40	$649.50
	Additional charges:		
	Paralegal		
5/15/90	- Mileage: 89.0 Miles		22.25
	SUBTOTAL:	[	22.25]
	Total costs		$ 22.25
Total time and expense charges			$671.75
5/16/90	- Retainer		($500.00)
	Balance due		$171.75

Figure 7.5.   Invoice. *(cont.)*

7.19. Charges Made to Clients

Fees for services and disbursements made on behalf of a client are charged to his or her account. (See Figure 7.1.) The disbursements, which are itemized in the bill, include:

Recording fees

Court costs

Fee paid process servers

Revenue or documentary stamps

Postage, when for heavy certified mail; also when a special job requires sending a large number of letters

Overnight or fast mail charges

Stenographic services, when an out-of-the-ordinary amount of clerical work is required

Long distance telephone calls and facsimile

All fees paid for investigations, accountings, abstracts, etc.

Photocopies in quantity

PETTY CASH FUND

7.20. How to Handle a Petty Cash Fund

Keep a petty cash fund in the office to pay for any small incidental expenses that may arise, such as postage due on incoming mail or any other item too small to warrant writing a check. The size of the fund will vary according to the demands made upon it, but it should be large enough to last about a month. Keep the money in a safe place because you are responsible for it. Never mix this money with your own funds; never make change from it unless you can make the exact change; and *never* borrow from it.

Keep a running record of expenditures made from the fund. As each expenditure is made, no matter how small, enter the date, the amount, the purpose for which spent, and the client and case to which it is chargeable. When the fund gets low, add up the expenditures and write a check, payable to yourself, for the total—that is, the amount necessary to bring the petty cash fund up to its original figure. Attach the record to the check when you give it to your employer for his or her signature. Mark the record "Paid— (*date*)—, Ck. No.____"; initial it; and file it. Then start a new running account for future expenditures from the fund.

8 Using References in Legal Research

Without legal reference material the lawyer could not function. Before drawing an agreement, bringing a court action, undertaking to defend a lawsuit, advising a client—before making a move of any kind—the lawyer "looks up the law." The material, both printed and electronic, that enables a lawyer to do his or her job efficiently includes the following:

Statutes, codes, and regulations

Reports of decided cases and administrative rulings

Books that classify the law

Form books

Treatises and looseleaf services

Computerized databases, which contain all of the above
   —and more

LEGAL RESEARCH

Lawyers use both printed reference material and computerized databases in their research. Law firms that have access to one or more databases may rely heavily on electronic research, although printed books and other material are still necessary for everyday reference to statutes and case law in the firm's jurisdiction, administrative regulations, forms, and commonly used references. This chapter describes the principal reference material available to lawyers.

8.1. Electronic Research

A database is a collection of documents such as statutes, court decisions, administrative materials, or commentaries. The procedures followed in electronic research vary according to the requirements of the particular database. Each database has its own identifier that is used to designate the database to be searched.

Familiar databases in the legal profession include WESTLAW, LEXIS, PHINET, and VERALEX. Users must follow the instructions provided by the database to retrieve the desired information. WESTLAW, for instance, specifies that a case citation must be entered in the following form to retrieve information from the Shepard's database:

SH 313 So.2d 712

The Shepard's information for the case reported at 313 So.2d 712 will then be displayed. (For more about Shepard's citations, see sections 8.11 and 8.12.)

STATUTES AND CODES

8.2. Compilation of Laws

The laws enacted by the Congress of the United States and the various state legislatures are systematically sorted and arranged in chapters and subheads to facilitate their use. The compilations, known as *statutes* and *codes,* usually contain, also, the Constitution of the United States and of the particular state. See "Approved Method of Citing Compilations of Statutes and Codes" in Part 5.

Every lawyer has the compilation of his or her own state or has access to it through a computerized database. Law firms that practice in several states have access to the compilations for those states. Nearly all lawyers have access to the United States Code or, more commonly, one of the commercially produced annotated versions such as United States Code Annotated (West) or U.S. Code Service (Lawyer's Cooperative); law association libraries and law college libraries usually have the compilations of every state. The compilations are kept up to date by pocket parts and supplements.

8.3. How to Find a Law

If you examine the arrangement of the compilation for your state, you will find that the preface contains useful explanatory material. Every compilation contains a general index, and some of them also have an index in each volume. The indexes vary in their completeness and usefulness, but with a little perseverance, it is possible to find the desired section of the law. After searching the compilation, a researcher would search the supplements and pocket parts (inserts in a slot at the back of a volume), if any, and all session laws since the date of the latest supplement. A particular section of the law might have been amended or repealed since the compilation, or a new law on the subject might have been enacted.

When a lawsuit involves a statute, the court's judicial interpretation and construction of that statute also become a part of the law. You will notice that the notes in annotated compilations (see figure 8.1, p. 172) include references to the published opinions that relate to the statutes. If the compilation is not annotated, it is necessary to look elsewhere (see "Books That Classify the Law") to locate judicial interpretations of the statutes.

REPORTS OF DECIDED CASES

8.4. Scope and Organization of Reports

When a point of law has once been settled by a judicial decision, it forms a precedent for the guidance of the courts in similar cases. The decisions are published in order that they may be readily accessible to the lawyers and the courts. Every practicing attorney must have access to the published reports of decisions in his or her own state, either in the official state reports or the appropriate reporter of the National Reporter System. See section 15.22 in Chapter 15.

Preceding the opinion in a case is a brief statement of each point of law determined by the case. These statements are known as the *syllabus,* or the *headnotes.* In the reporters, the headnotes are numbered, and the part of the opinion that covers a particular headnote is numbered to correspond with the headnote number. Thus if you are interested only in a statement made in headnote 3, you turn to the "[3]" in the opinion.

Each series of reports or reporters is numbered consecutively. Additional volumes of the reporters in the National Reporter System are pub-

198.23 Personal liability of executor, etc.

If any executor shall make distribution either in whole or in part of any of the property of an estate to the heirs, next of kin, distributees, legatees or devisees without having paid or secured the tax due the state under this chapter, or obtained the release of such property from the lien of such tax he shall become personally liable for the tax so due the state, or so much thereof as may remain due and unpaid, to the full extent of the full value of any property belonging to such person or estate which may come into his hands, custody or control.

Historical Note

Derivation:

Comp.Gen.Laws Supp.1936, § 1342 (96).

Laws 1933, c. 16015, § 16.

Prior Laws:

For complete text of the Inheritance and Estate Tax Laws of 1931, see Appendix to this chapter.

Cross References

Apportionment of estate taxes, see § 734.041.
Determination of amount by commissioner and payment thereof as discharging executor, see § 198.19.

Law Review Commentaries

Vexing probate problems. Judge William C. Brooker, 31 Fla.Bar J. 75 (February 1957).

Library References

Taxation ⟨=890.

C.J.S. Taxation § 1169.

Notes of Decisions

I. Protection of tax liens

The commissioner of taxation, under his rule-making power contained in §§ 198.08 and 199.03, and granted to aid in the proper enforcement of said §§ 198.01 et seq., 199.01 et seq., should adopt rules and regulations designed to protect the state's interest through tax liens in bank account subject to payment to foreign personal representatives under circumstances which might well have the effect of a loss of the state's lien in this connection. 1959 Op.Atty.Gen. 059–7, Jan. 15, 1959.

From West's Florida Statutes Annotated, Vol. 10A (St. Paul: West, 1971), p. 25.

Figure 8.1. Excerpt from Annotated Compilation.

lished several times a year; volumes of the official state reports, less often. In arranging the books on a library shelf, leave an empty shelf, or part of a shelf, after the last volume of a series so that you will not have to shift the books when additional volumes are received. Keep the advance sheets (see section 15.22 in Chapter 15) in consecutive order after the last volume of the series. When a new bound volume is received, destroy the advance sheets that are covered by it.

8.5. How to Use the Reports and Reporters

Finding a case in a report or reporter when you have the volume and page number needs no explanation. But the second series of a reporter must not be confused with the first series. If the lawyer tells you that a case is in "76 Northeastern," this does not mean "76 Northeastern Second" (76 N.E. 255; 76 N.E.2d 255). Each report and reporter has a list of the cases cited in it with the cases arranged alphabetically under the name of plaintiff and defendant. For example, *Abbott v. Bralov* is also listed as *Bralov; Abbott v.* Since a reporter covers more than one state, it contains a general table of all cases reported, followed by a separate table for each state. Thus if you know the volume and the name of either party to a case, you can easily find the page number where the opinion begins.

In the back of each reporter is a digest of the cases reported in that volume, arranged according to subject. The lawyer might know the substance of a decision and the approximate time it was decided but be unable to recall the name of the case. You can refer to the volume or volumes covering the approximate time of the decision and, under the appropriate subject in the digest, you will be able to locate the desired case. This might involve searching several volumes and is not a desirable method of research, but sometimes it is necessary.

You can find the names of the justices of the appellate courts in the front of the reports and reporters. The name and location of the attorneys in a case are given immediately following the syllabus, preceding the opinion.

Reporters for Federal Cases

Federal cases can be located in the following reports or reporters:

U.S. Reports (*U.S.*): official reporter of the U.S. Supreme Court; also Supreme Court Reporter (*S. Ct.*) and Lawyer's Edition (*Law. Ed.*)

Federal Reporter (*F.*, *F.2d*): for federal circuit courts of appeal

Federal Supplement (*F. Supp.*): for federal district courts

8.6. How to Find Alternative Citations

When the lawyer has a citation to a case in an unofficial reporter, he or she may require the official citation. Occasionally, the reverse is true. There are several ways to find alternative citations to state court cases. (1) The table of cases in the state or regional digest generally gives alternative citations. It is necessary to have the correct case when looking up an alternative citation; there are sometimes two or more cases under the same name. (2) The *National Reporter Blue Book* and the blue books for state and regional reporters are compilations of tables of alternative citations. The blue books generally are found only in relatively large libraries. (3) *Shepard's Citations* lists the alternative citations preceded by a lowercase "s" indicating "same case." Look up the citation you have in the appropriate volume of *Shepard's* to find the alternative citation by this method.

8.7. Other Publications of Decisions

In addition to state reports and the National Reporter System, there are several other types of publications of decisions.

Selected Cases Series, Annotated

Selected cases series limit the cases reported to (1) decisions that deal with questions upon which there is a conflict of law, (2) decisions that deal with novel questions, and (3) decisions that are outstanding by reason of their treatment of the question involved and their review of the authorities. The decisions are reported in full, with headnotes, and are fully annotated. They thus may be used not only as a report of the decision but also as a guide to other cases in point and as a source of original research.

American Law Reports is the only current selected series of American cases. The series is the merger of, or successor to, all previous selective cases series. The following diagram shows the development that resulted in the current series. The diagram gives the abbreviations by which the publications are cited. The full titles, in the sequence in which they appear in the diagram, are as follows:

Lawyers' Reports Annotated

Lawyers' Reports Annotated, New Series

Lawyers' Reports Annotated, Third Unit

American Decisions

American Reports

American State Reports

American and English Annotated Cases

American Annotated Cases

American Law Reports

L.R.A.→L.R.A. (N.S.)→L.R.A. (3d Unit)
Am Dec→Am. Rep.→Am. State Rep.   } Ann. Cas. } A.L.R.

Am. & Eng. Ann. Cas.

The volumes are identified by year of publication and by letter: 1916A, 1916B, and so on.

Subject Reports

Some reports publish only those decisions that relate to a particular subject or topic of law. Among the series of subject reports are the American Federal Tax Report (AFTR) and American Labor Cases (ALC).

8.8. Looseleaf Services

Most law firms that practice extensively in a particular area of the law, such as federal taxation, corporation law, labor law, environmental law, and the like, subscribe to one or more looseleaf services in their areas of specialization. For example, Commerce Clearing House publishes *Standard Federal Tax Reporter, Trade Regulation Reporter, Federal Energy Guidelines, Labor Law Reports*; the Bureau of National Affairs publishes *Family Law Reporter, Labor Relations Reports,* and *Environmental Law Reporter* and Prentice Hall publishes the *Federal Tax Course.*

The looseleaf services provide frequent updating of information in areas of the law that are constantly changing. They include reports of court decisions, both state and federal; reports of pertinent decisions of agencies; reprints and explanations of agency regulations; and text and summaries of proposed or enacted legislation in a particular field.

Another important looseleaf service found in many law offices is *U.S. Law Week,* published by the Bureau of National Affairs. This service reports all U.S. Supreme Court decisions as soon as they are handed down and lists case names and docket numbers of all cases currently before the Court. It also summarizes important state and lower federal court decisions as they are handed down, along with federal agency rulings and federal statutes. Consult the "how to use" card in the general law section binder for detailed instructions on research in *Law Week.*

Your office will receive releases to be filed in each service to which the firm subscribes. They are usually issued weekly and should be filed promptly to keep the service up to date. Each release contains detailed filing instructions that must be followed meticulously to avoid mistakes.

BOOKS THAT CLASSIFY THE LAW

The books that classify the law enable the lawyer to pick from among the millions of cases those that are on point with the legal problem that confronts him or her. These books, because of their nature, are sometimes called *books of index.* They include digests, encyclopedias, texts, citators, and tables of cases. The lawyer uses them initially as a lead and also to direct him or her to other cases in point. Among the books most commonly used are the *American Digest,* state and regional digests, *Corpus Juris* and *Corpus Juris Secundum, American Jurisprudence, American Law Reports* (section 8.7), and *Shepard's Citations.*

AMERICAN DIGEST

8.9. Scope and Organization of the Digest System

Digests are published for every state and for all regional reporters except Northeast and Southwest. In addition, there is the *Federal Practice Digest* and the *Supreme Court Digest.* All state and federal cases are brought together in the American Digest System. Because of its broad scope, this system is awkward to use to find case law of a particular jurisdiction. The American Digest is cumulated into a Decennial Digest every ten years and supercedes the General Digest for that period. At the beginning of each 10-year period, a new General Digest Series begins. Each volume of the General Digest Series contains a reference to all cases on every topic published during the period covered by that particular volume. Thus each volume of the General Digest Series contains the topic *Judgment*. By the end of the ten-year period the General Digest may contain forty to fifty volumes, most of which must be searched to find all of the cases on a given topic decided during the period since the last decennial cumulation.

A detailed fact index constitutes part of each digest. The index is contained in volumes entitled "Descriptive Word Index." The descriptive words are listed in bold type in alphabetical order. Different situations involving the fact element are listed in lighter type and refer to the place in the digest where cases in point may be found. The reference is by means of topic and key number.

An analysis precedes each main topic. The digest of cases are grouped according to the point of law involved, and each point is given a key number. Each digest also contains a table of cases, by plaintiff and defendant, with complete citations to the National Reporter Systems and to official state reporters where they have been published. This is an alternative and often quicker way to find alternative citations than to use the blue books mentioned in section 8.6.

8.10. How to Use the Digest System

Suppose that you are interested in the priority over other claims of an allowance by the executor to a widow. The first step in finding the authorities through the digest system is to get the key number. There are three methods of getting the key number:

1. If you already have at least one case in point, from the key numbers in the headnotes in the reporters, which correspond to the key numbers in the digests

2. From the Descriptive Word Index

3. From the analysis that precedes each topic

SHEPARD'S CITATIONS

8.11. Purpose of Shepard's Citations

To prove a point, the lawyer cites a decision contained in a published opinion. Before citing the case he or she wants to know something of its history and subsequent treatment. The lawyer is interested in knowing whether the case has been appealed to a higher court and whether it was affirmed or reversed; whether it has been followed in many other cases; and whether it has been overruled in a subsequent case. *Shepard's Citations* is designed to give the lawyer this information. It is easy to "shepardize" a case, and a lawyer never cites a case as authority without first shepardizing it. *Shepard's* also shepardizes statutes, showing where they have been interpreted by state and federal courts.

8.12. How to Use Shepard's Citations

An explanation of how to use *Shepard's* appears in the front of each volume, along with a list of abbreviations used. Figure 8.2 illustrates a page from the Federal Reporter Citations.

Illustrative Case[1]

Let us assume that by reference to a digest, encyclopedia, textbook, or other unit of legal research you have located the case of *Hanover Star Milling Co. v. Allen & Wheeler Co.*, reported in volume 208 of the Federal Reporter on page 513, dealing among other things with the property right that a complainant has in a trademark.

Figure 8.2 is a reproduction from Shepard's Federal Reporter Citations. Note the volume of reports to which the citations apply (vol. 208) in the upper right corner of the page.

An examination of the bold-face type numbers within the page locates the page number (513) in the seventh column of citations. This is the initial page of the case under consideration. Following this page number you will find the citation "sLRA1916D 136" indicating that the same case "s" is also reported in 1916D Lawyers Reports Annotated 136.

In obtaining the history of this case you will observe that upon appeal to the United States Supreme Court, it was affirmed "a" in 240 United States Reports "US" 403, 60 Lawyers Edition of United States "LE" 713, 36 Supreme Court Reporter "SC" 357, 1916 Decisions of the Commissioner of Patents "'16 CD" 265. Wherever there are parallel sets of reports covering the same citing case, these citations immediately follow each other.

---

[1] Acknowledgment is made to Shepard's Citations, Inc., for this explanation.

SPECIMEN PAGE—Shepard's Federal Reporter Citations, 1938 Bound Volume

FEDERAL REPORTER Vol. 208

The callout boxes indicate:

- Same case reported in Lawyers Reports Annotated
- Affirmed by United States Supreme Court
- Followed to paragraph one of the syllabus
- Citations in parallel sets of reports grouped
- Cited in Illinois Appellate Court Reports prior to their inclusion in National Reporter System
- Cited in units of the National Reporter System and cases to correspond in the State Reports
- Cited in case in National Reporter System not reported in State Reports
- Cited in notes of Annotated Reports System

For later Citations see (1938-1953) Bound Supplement, current issue of Cumulative Supplement and intervening Advance Sheet — 1175

Figure 8.2. Page from Shepard's Federal Reporter Citation.

Source: Reprinted from *Shepard's Federal Reporter Citations*, volume 208, page 1175, copyright 1938 by Shepard's/McGraw-Hill, Inc. Further reproduction is strictly prohibited.

Also, by examining the abbreviations preceding the citations, it can be seen that this case has been followed "f", explained "e", and harmonized "h" in subsequent cases in the Federal Reporter.

The next citation covers the reference "215F^{1}495." The small superior figure "^{1}" in advance of the citing page number 495 indicates that the principle of law brought out in the first paragraph of the syllabus of the cited case is also dealt with in 215 Federal Reporter 495.

Assuming you are primarily interested in the principle covered in paragraph one of the syllabus, we find the additional citations that contain the superior figure "^{1}" in advance of the citing page number include numerous other cases that deal with this particular point of law and are reported in the Federal Reporter; Federal Reporter, Second Series "F2d"; Federal Supplement "FS"; Appeal Cases District of Columbia "ADC"; Decisions of the Commission of Patents and United States Patents Quarterly "PQ."

In addition to the citations in point with paragraph one of the syllabus, there are several citations to other paragraphs of the syllabus of this case in cases reported in the Federal Reporter; Federal Reporter, Second Series; and the notes "n" of the American Law Reports "ALR." Thus the citations dealing with a point of law in any particular paragraph of the syllabus may be referred to instantly without examining every citation to the case.

This case has been cited by the courts of Illinois, New York, Texas, and Wisconsin. These citations are arranged alphabetically by the state reports with the corresponding reference in the National Reporter System. The citation 266 Southwestern Reporter (SW) 533 is a case decided in the Court of Civil Appeals of Texas and not reported elsewhere. This case has also been cited in the notes of 1914C Annotated Cases 932 (AC'14C932n).

By examining this same volume and page number in the 1938-53 Bound Supplement, latest issue of the Cumulative Supplement, and intervening Advance Sheet, all subsequent citations to this case will be found.

CORPUS JURIS SECUNDUM SYSTEM

8.13. Scope and Organization of System

The Corpus Juris Secundum System consists of Corpus Juris Secundum and Corpus Juris. The system is a complete statement of the body of American law in encyclopedic form, broken down into approximately 430 titles. The authorities cited in the notes in the Secundum are the cases decided since that title in the Corpus Juris was written. If there are earlier cases on the point, footnote references in Corpus Juris Secundum direct the searcher to the precise page and note in Corpus Juris where they will be found. The absence of a footnote reference to Corpus Juris indicates there are no earlier cases. Thus, although the text of Corpus Juris is being superseded by Corpus Juris Secundum, Corpus Juris remains a vital part of the lawyer's library because of the footnotes.

The titles embraced by the system are alphabetically arranged. Judicially defined words, phrases, and maxims are alphabetically interspersed through the titles. The backbone of each volume shows the first and last words in that volume and also the volume number. Volume 72 of Corpus Juris is a complete descriptive word index to all volumes of Corpus Juris. Each volume of the Secundum has an index to the titles contained in that volume. There is also a five-volume general index arranged alphabetically.

8.14. How to Use Corpus Juris Secundum System

There are three methods of finding the discussion and supporting authorities in the Corpus Juris Secundum System.

1. *The fact, or descriptive, word index.* Find the descriptive word in the index to the title in the back of the volume. If you are interested in the extent of an implied agency, for example, your title would be *Agency.* In the index you will find "Implied agency," with the section and page number where implied agency is discussed. At the head of the section is an analysis of points covered in the section, which enables you to narrow your search. Each volume of Corpus Juris does not contain an index. If the title in which you are interested has not been published in the Secundum, look for the descriptive word in volume 72, "Descriptive-Word Index and Concordance," of Corpus Juris.

2. *The general analysis preceding each title.* At the beginning of each title is an analysis, or breakdown, of the contents of the title. The topics are in bold-face capitals and are numbered with roman numerals. Each of the topics has a subanalysis. Judge which topic should cover the point in which you are interested, and then look at the subanalysis for the specific point. "III Creation and Extent of Relation" should cover implied agency. In the subanalysis of

that topic, you will find " 24, Implied Agency—p. 1045." If you cannot judge which topic should cover your problem, you can look at each of the subtopics, but this is a slower method of research.

3. *Words and phrases alphabetically arranged throughout the set.* If an important word or words in your problem can be picked out, you can refer to those words in Corpus Juris Secundum and find cross-references to many related topics in which the words have meaning or importance.

8.15. How to Cite

Cite by volume number, title, and page and section number.

57 C.J., Set-Off and Counterclaim, p. 376, 22

24 C.J.S., Criminal Law, p. 147, 1606

AMERICAN JURISPRUDENCE AND AMERICAN LAW REPORTS

8.16. Scope and Organization of American Jurisprudence and American Law Reports

The Lawyers Co-operative Publishing Company has completely revised its encyclopedia *American Jurisprudence* and has published it as a second edition, referred to as "AmJur2^d." It is cross-referenced to American Law Reports (ALR) and to the Lawyers Edition (Law. Ed.) of the U.S. Supreme Court Reports. The format differs slightly from Corpus Juris and Corpus Juris Secundum, but it serves much the same purpose. Few law offices have both encyclopedias, but most have one of them.

FEDERAL AND STATE CODES

8.17. Federal Codes of Regulations and State Codes

Rules such as the Code of Federal Regulations (CFR) and state codes have the force of law and are very important when a matter includes a regulatory agency. Often they are annotated, just like statutory compilations. Note that a statutory compilation is sometimes called a code (e.g.,

California code). But a code of rules should be distinguished from a statutory code.

FORM BOOKS

8.18. Practice Manuals

Practice manuals contain forms of pleadings, which the lawyer usually follows when dictating. Since the wording of pleadings differs with the state, a practice manual is used only in the state for which it is prepared. With the aid of a practice manual you can draft many pleadings without dictation. The forms always indicate by italics, by parentheses, or in some other manner the wording that must be changed with each case, such as names, dates, and various clauses applicable to a particular situation. In addition to the complete forms, the manuals contain many clauses applicable to various circumstances that may be substituted for the clauses contained in the complete form.

8.19. Books of Legal Forms

Books of legal forms contain forms of instruments and documents as distinguished from litigation papers. Although the statutes prescribe the wording of many instruments, books of legal forms are generally useful for all states. They call attention to statutory requirements and often give forms for each state. *Current Legal Forms,* published by Matthew Bender, New York, for example, is one of the best known sets of legal forms. It gives forms of acknowledgments, deeds, mortgages, and wills that meet the requirements of each state. It is a multivolume set, published in looseleaf format and updated periodically. Some form books, however, cover only forms in one particular field. In giving instructions for the preparation of a legal instrument, the lawyer will frequently tell you to copy certain forms or clauses from a form book. You should also maintain standard forms in your computer library.

TREATISES

8.20. Purpose of Treatises

Treatises expound the theory of the law in particular areas and cite key cases that illustrate the state of the law on a given point in various jurisdictions. Some are supplemented, usually annually, by pocket parts or paper supplements. Others are published in a looseleaf binder format and are supplemented by replacement and added pages and sections at intervals as the publisher deems necessary. These supplements must be carefully filed as soon as they are received, just as the looseleaf services are filed.

OTHER REFERENCE SOURCES

8.21. Basic Reference Books

There are a few books that provide basic information to all personnel in the law office. The following list may be supplemented in your office by essential books for the jurisdiction and specialty in which the firm practices. Always order the latest edition of any reference book.

Legal Research in a Nutshell, West, or *How to Find the Law,* West

Ballentine's Law Dictionary, with Pronunciations, Lawyer's Co-operative, or *Black's Law Dictionary,* West

Law Dictionary for Non-Lawyers, West

Webster's New Collegiate Dictionary, Merriam-Webster

A Uniform System of Citations, Harvard Law Review

Court rules of the jurisdiction

8.22. Useful Reference Books for Names and Addresses

The following reference books are useful for confirming the spelling of names and the accuracy of addresses. Specialized and local references also exist and should be acquired when needed for a particular practice or locality.

Official City Directory

Telephone directories

Zip code directories

The Bar Register

Congressional Directory

Directory of Directors in [City]

The Law List (British)

The Lawyer's List

Martindale-Hubbell Law Directory

Moody's Manuals

State legislative manuals

Official Register of the United States

Poor's manuals

Rand McNally Bankers Directory

World almanacs

Part 2

Preparing Legal
Instruments and Documents

---

9. Handling Legal Instruments

10. How to Prepare Legal Papers

11. How to Handle Affidavits, Powers of
    Attorney, and Wills

9 Handling Legal Instruments

More than three-fourths of most law practice relates to matters that are not litigated. This practice involves, among other things, the preparation of numerous legal instruments. In this chapter we give basic information about legal documents generally. Because you will probably have to notarize many of these legal instruments, we also describe the duties of a notary.

THE LEGAL INSTRUMENT

9.1. What Is a Legal Instrument?

A *legal instrument* is a formal written document, such as a deed, bill of sale, lease, contract, agreement, or will. It gives formal expression to a legal act or agreement. Although both legal instruments and court papers are referred to as legal documents, a legal instrument is not to be confused with a court paper. A *court paper,* or *pleading* as it is called professionally (see Chapter 13), constitutes a step in bringing or defending a lawsuit and is prepared and filed for the information of the court, whereas a *legal instrument* is designed for the use of the parties who sign it and constitutes evidence of the intent of a person or of an agreement between parties.

A legal instrument is not a step in a court action, but it is frequently the basis of one. If one of the parties to a legal instrument does not abide by its provisions, the other party may sue to enforce the provisions of the instrument. Copies of a legal instrument are used frequently as exhibits in court actions.

9.2. Parties to an Instrument

Those who acquire a right, undertake an obligation, or give up a right, as evidenced by a written instrument, are the *parties* to the instrument. A party may be an individual, a partnership, a corporation, or a governmental entity. Almost all instruments have two or more parties, but there are some, such as assignments and powers of attorney, that have only one signatory.

All parties who have a common interest in the subject matter of the document are grouped together and are usually referred to throughout the instrument by a descriptive identification instead of by name. An expression occasionally used is "party (parties) of the first part" and "party (parties) of the second part." More commonly, the term may be a description such as *buyer-seller, grantor-grantee, lessor-lessee,* or any term appropriate to the party's interest in the subject matter of the instrument. There may be more than one party in a group designated by a descriptive term. You will notice that the instrument illustrated in figure 9.1 has two parties of the first part but only one of the second part.

9.3. How to Prepare Legal Instruments

Although certain instruments, such as deeds and wills, may be set up in a special style, agreements or contracts generally vary only slightly in

Witness the hands and seals of the said parties this _____ day of

_____, 19_____.

In the Presence of:

_____ L.S.

_____

_____ L.S.
                                                Buyers

_____

_____ L.S.
                                                Sellers

Figure 9.1.   Testimonium Clause, Signature and Seal
for Individuals, Witnessed.

form, no matter what the subject matter is. Hence general formats may be stored in the computer for ready access. Many specific instruments are illustrated throughout this book (see the index). Figure 9.2 on pages 192-193 illustrates a skeleton of a form of agreement used by many law offices. It is easily adaptable to any general agreement or contract. Always make duplicate originals for the parties to the contract and a copy for your file. If the lawyer wants an extra copy, he or she will tell you. Agreements may be printed out on paper with or without a ruled margin. If the lawyer has a preference, he or she will specify it.

EXECUTION OF AN INSTRUMENT

9.4. What Is "Execution" of an Instrument?

Technically, *execution of an instrument* is doing that which is required to give effect or validity to the instrument and, therefore, includes signing and delivery. In law-office parlance, execution more frequently refers merely to the signing of an instrument by the party or parties described in it. Legal instruments must be executed with a certain formality. Some or all of the following formalities attach to the execution of various instruments: sealing, witness or attestation, acknowledgment, and notarization, each of which is discussed below.

9.5. Testimonium Clause

The *testimonium clause* is the clause with which an instrument closes. It immediately precedes the signature. It is a declaration by the parties to the instrument that their signatures are attached in testimony of the preceding part of the instrument. The testimonium clause is not to be confused with the *witness* or *attestation* clause (section 9.9). The testimonium clause relates to the parties themselves, whereas the witness or attestation clause relates to those who sign the paper as witnesses, not as parties to the instrument.

Often, the testimonium clause will guide you in setting up the signature lines. It will indicate (1) what parties are to sign the instrument, (2) what officer of a corporation is to sign, (3) whether the instrument is to be sealed, and (4) whether a corporate seal is to be attested. From the following clause, which is a form commonly used, you know that the president of the

THIS AGREEMENT, entered into on the ___ day of
_____, 19—, by and between _____ CORPORATION,
a corporation organized and existing under and by virtue of
the laws of the State of _____, and having its office
at _____, _____, hereinafter referred to as
"_____," and THE _____ COMPANY, a corporation organized and existing under and by virtue of the laws of the
State of _____, and having its office at _____,
_____, hereinafter referred to as "_____,"

W I T N E S S E T H :

WHEREAS _____
_____; and
WHEREAS _____
_____
_____.
THEREFORE, in consideration of the premises
_____
_____,

IT IS AGREED:

1. _____
_____
_____ .

2. _____
_____.

IN WITNESS WHEREOF the parties hereto have on the
day and year first above written caused these presents to be

(Continued on following page)

Figure 9.2.   Agreement between Two Corporations
with Seals Attested.

(Continued from preceding page)

executed in their behalf and in their corporate names respectively by their proper officers hereunto duly authorized
and their respective corporate seals to be hereto attached
by like authority.

(Corporate Seal)   _____CORPORATION

                                             By _____
ATTEST: President

_____
             Secretary
                                             THE _____COMPANY

(Corporate Seal)
                                             By _____
ATTEST: Vice President

_____
             Secretary

(Number page in center, one-half inch from bottom.)

Figure 9.2.   Agreement between Two Corporations
with Seals Attested. *(cont.)*

corporation is to sign, that the seal is to be affixed, and that the secretary of
the corporation is to attest the seal.

IN WITNESS WHEREOF, The Bentley Corporation has caused its corporate
seal to be hereto affixed, and attested by its secretary, and these presents to be signed
by its president, this 26th day of October, 19XX.

On the other hand, from the following clause, also commonly used,
you know that the instrument is not to be sealed.

IN TESTIMONY WHEREOF, the parties hereto have duly executed this
agreement this 14th day of May, 19XX.

The introductory words to the testimonium clause, *in witness whereof, in testimony whereof,* and the like are sometimes typed in solid caps. The word following is lowercase unless it is a proper name. A comma usually follows the introductory words. Since the wording is fairly standard, clauses can be stored in the computer for recall and modification as required.

9.6. Signatures

An instrument recites who will sign it. As a general practice, lines are inserted for signatures. The first line of signature appears four line spaces below the body of the instrument, slightly to the right of the center of the page. There should be a line for the signature of each person who must sign the instrument. There are no special requirements for the spacing of signature lines, except that sufficient space should be allowed for average-size handwriting, and the lines should be evenly spaced. Three or four line spaces between lines are practical.

Frequently, the descriptive identification of the parties signing is placed under the signature lines, along with the name of the party signing, for example, "Buyer," "Seller," or whatever identification was used in the instrument. The lawyer will probably instruct you about how many signature lines to use for each party, but you will also know from the content of the instrument what signature lines are necessary. Figure 9.1 illustrates signature lines and identification of the parties.

When a corporation is a party to an instrument, the instrument is signed in the name of the corporation by the officer or officers authorized to execute it. The name of the corporation should be in solid caps, with sufficient space beneath it for a signature and "By" with a line for the signature. Under the signature line, insert the title of the corporate officer who is going to sign the instrument. The testimonium clause usually recites the title of the officer who is supposed to sign the instrument. The corporate seal is placed at the left margin, parallel to the signature (see Figure 9.2).

When a partnership is a party, the name of the partnership should be in solid caps, with sufficient space beneath it for the signature and "By" with a line for the signature. Since partnerships do not have officers, there will be no title under the signature line.

9.7. How to Fit the Signatures on the Page

Arrange the body, or text, of the instrument so that at least two lines appear on the page with the signatures. The signatures must all be on the same page unless there are so many that they require more than a full page. To comply with these requirements you must gauge carefully the length of the document. Use the formatting options of your word processing program to adjust pages as needed. If necessary, do the following:

1. Adjust the top and bottom margins.

2. If you are using paper without ruled margins, leave wider or narrower left and right margins.

3. If the last line of a paragraph is full length, adjust the right margin of that paragraph so that at least one word carries over to another line, thereby taking up an extra line. Or, if a paragraph ends with one word on a line, adjust the margin so that it is not necessary to carry over the one word, thereby saving a line of space.

4. Triple-space between paragraphs.

5. Leave less space between the text of the instrument and the signatures.

6. Leave less space between the signatures

9.8. Sealing an Instrument

The practice of affixing a seal to an instrument originated in the days when only a few people could write their names. Written instruments were marked with sealing wax, which was impressed with a ring or other device. This seal was the mark of the person making the instrument and took the place of his signature. The process of affixing the seal is referred to as *sealing the instrument,* and the instrument becomes a *sealed instrument.* Figure 9.2 illustrates signatures to a sealed corporate instrument.

Historically, the sealed instrument had a twofold significance: (1) Under the statutes of limitations, the time during which suit could be brought on a sealed instrument was longer than on an unsealed instrument. (2) Suit on a contract could not be defended on the basis that it was without consideration, because the consideration of a sealed instrument could not be questioned. (If an instrument is to be sealed, the testimonium clause will so indicate.) Most jurisdictions have now abolished this distinction between sealed and unsealed instruments relating to the statute of limitations. In most instances, a mere recital that an instrument is sealed will not serve as substitute for the showing of consideration. In many jurisdictions, it is no longer necessary to seal deeds and wills or other documents signed by individuals. But the corporate seal retains its importance to attest to a corporate act.

The Corporation Seal

Almost all corporations adopt a formal seal. It is engraved on a metal plate and impressed by this means on the paper. The seal usually recites the name of the corporation and the year and state of incorporation. It is often kept in the custody of the clerk of the corporation who is, in many instances, the lawyer. The secretary may be responsible for seeing that the seal is properly filed and available when corporate documents requiring it are to be signed. As a practical matter, a corporation's bylaws usually provide that any instrument signed on behalf of the corporation will be impressed with the corporate seal. An officer of the corporation impresses the seal on the instrument when it is signed. In many cases the corporate secretary must bear witness, or "attest" to the fact that the imprint on the paper is the seal of the corporation. Whenever the testimonium clause recites that the seal is to be *attested,* insert the ATTEST line on the left side of the page, opposite the signature lines, as shown below:

ATTEST

_____

                                                  Secretary

The attest by the officer of a corporation to its seal is not be confused with the attestation or "witness" clause, which relates to the subscribing witnesses (see Figure 9.3).

An Individual's Seal

The wax seal formerly used by individuals has been replaced by the word *seal* or *L.S.* (abbreviation for *locus sigilli,* meaning "place of the seal"), or any other scroll or mark. At the end of the signature lines on an instrument that must be sealed, the words *SEAL* or *L.S.* should appear in solid caps.

9.9. Attestation Clause

Frequently, the signatures to an instrument must be witnessed to make the instrument legal. The act of witnessing the signature to a written instrument, at the request of the party signing the instrument, is *attestation.* The witness is called a subscribing witness, because the person signs his or her name as a witness. A legend or clause that recites the circumstances

```
              IN WITNESS WHEREOF, we, the lessors and the
         lessee, have hereunto set our hands and seals to the fore-
         going lease, consisting of twenty-two pages (22), on this
         day of April 19--.


Signed, sealed, and delivered )
                              )
by lessors in the presence of:)
                              )
                              )
                              )
_____ )
                              )    _____ L. S.
                              )
_____ )
                                   _____ L. S.
                                          Lessors

Signed, sealed, and delivered )
                              )
by lessee in the presence of: )
                              )    _____ L. S.
                              )          Lessee
_____ )
                              )
                              )
                              )
_____ )
```

Figure 9.3. Legend and Signature Lines for Two
Groups of Witnesses.

surrounding the signing of the instrument often precedes the signature of
the attesting witnesses and is called the *attestation clause*. The wording of
the attestation clause varies from a simple "In the presence of" to the lengthy
clause used in wills (see Figure 11.3 in Chapter 11).

The legend and the lines on which witnesses sign appear opposite the
lines for the signatures of persons who will execute the instrument. When
parties to an instrument do not sign at the same time, different people witness
the signature. The instrument then carries signature lines for each of the
witnesses, with an identification of the parties whose signatures each group
is witnessing (see Figure 9.3).

ACKNOWLEDGMENTS

9.10. Importance of Acknowledgments in the Law Office

An acknowledgment is a familiar tool in the law office, and the staff should acquire an intimate knowledge of it. An *acknowledgment* is the act by which a person who executes a legal instrument declares to an officer, designated by statute, that he or she is the person who executed the instrument and that he or she did so for the purposes stated in the document. In a law office the term signifies both the declaration of execution and the officer's written certificate of the declaration. It is common practice for a legal instrument to carry a certificate of acknowledgment, because almost all states require the acknowledgment of an instrument before it can be recorded or filed. Also, when an instrument is introduced in court as evidence, the certificate of acknowledgment is usually sufficient proof of the authenticity of the instrument.

9.11. Laws Governing Acknowledgments

Many states have adopted the Uniform Acknowledgment Act, and in these states the law governing the use of acknowledgments and the form of the certificate are similar. Otherwise, the law varies with the state. Some of the statutes are very precise in their requirements, and they must be adhered to strictly. The acknowledgments illustrated in Figures 9.4 through 9.8 on pages 198-201 show you how acknowledgments are set up and will give you a general idea of the wording of various forms of acknowledgment. They are not supposed to be copied word for word. The lawyer will either dictate or make available to you a form of the acknowledgment he or she wants you to use. Make an extra copy for your looseleaf book of forms for future reference and add it to the forms in your computer.

A principle of law governing acknowledgments is this: The law of the state where the instrument is to be recorded or used, not the law of the state where the instrument is executed, governs. Thus if your office is in New York and you prepare an instrument that is to be recorded in Florida, the form and wording follow the Florida statutes, although the certificate will show that the acknowledgment was made in New York. But if you send an instrument to Florida to be signed and returned for recording in New York, the certificate of acknowledgment will follow the New York law, although it will show that the acknowledgment was made in Florida.

9.12. Essentials of an Acknowledgment

In many states accepted forms of certain legal instruments have been established by statute. In particular, the forms of deeds, wills, and acknowledgments are often set forth in legislation and can be relied on as acceptable in courts within the state. Although acknowledgments vary with the state, they all have certain basic essentials. The following basic essentials are apparent in the acknowledgments illustrated in Figures 9.4 through 9.8.

Venue

An acknowledgment always begins with a recital of the venue, that is, the name of the state and county in which the acknowledgment is made. In Kentucky, Massachusetts, Pennsylvania, and Virginia the venue recites the name of the commonwealth instead of the state; in Louisiana, the parish instead of the county. The statement of the venue appears in solid caps and bracketed. If it is followed with *ss.*, the abbreviation for *scilicet* (*sc*, though correct, is not used in legal papers), the abbreviation may be capitals or small

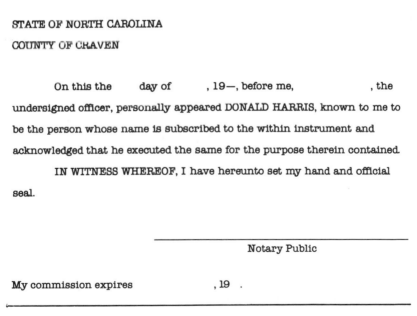

Figure 9.4.   Certificate of Acknowledgment of Individual.

STATE OF NEW MEXICO

COUNTY OF MORA

      I, MARY SMITH, a notary public in and for the said state and county, duly commissioned and sworn, hereby certify that JOHN COLE and PHYLLIS COLE, his wife, who are to me personally known, this day appeared before me personally, and severally acknowledged that they signed, sealed, and delivered the foregoing deed for the purposes therein stated. The said PHYLLIS COLE, wife of said JOHN COLE, being duly examined by me, separate and apart from her said husband, did declare that she signed, sealed, and delivered the said deed freely and voluntarily, and without compulsion by her said husband, with intention to renounce and convey all dower or other right, title, and interest in the property thereby conveyed, for the uses and purposes therein stated.

      IN WITNESS WHEREOF, I have hereunto set my hand and official seal this 30th day of April, 19—.

                               _____

                                          Notary Public

My commission expires   , 19 .

Figure 9.5.   Certificate of Acknowledgment by Husband and Wife—Separate Examinations

letters and is followed by a period. Technically, a colon should also follow because scilicet means "to wit," but few law offices observe this technicality, and many firms now omit the abbreviation entirely.

Date of Acknowledgment

     An acknowledgment always recites the date on which the acknowledgment is made. The certificate of acknowledgment has blank spaces for the day of the month. Leave a blank space for the name of the month, too,

STATE OF MICHIGAN
COUNTY OF BARRY

I hereby certify that on this day before me, an officer duly authorized
in the state aforesaid and in the county aforesaid to take acknowledgments,
personally appeared WALTER HUTCHINS and ALLEN AVERY, to me known
and known to be the persons described in and who executed the foregoing
instrument as president and secretary, respectively, of Hartshorne Company,
Inc., a corporation named therein, and severally acknowledged before me
that they executed the same as such officers, in the name of and for and on
behalf of the said corporation.

IN WITNESS WHEREOF, I have hereunto set my hand and affixed my
official seal this   day of September, 19—.

_____
                                              Notary Public

My commission expires   , 19 .

Figure 9.6.   Certificate of Acknowledgment by
Corporation—Two Officers.

if you are preparing the instrument near the end of the month. Although a
client is supposed to sign and acknowledge an instrument on the 30th of
April, he or she might not get into the office until the first day of May. The
date of the acknowledgment does not necessarily coincide with the date of
the instrument, but the date of an acknowledgment must *never* precede the
date the instrument was signed.

Designation of Person Making Acknowledgment

The name of the person making the acknowledgment always appears in the certificate in solid caps. If the person making the acknowl-

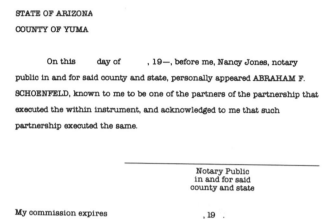

STATE OF ARIZONA
COUNTY OF YUMA

On this   day of   , 19—, before me, Nancy Jones, notary public in and for said county and state, personally appeared ABRAHAM F. SCHOENFELD, known to me to be one of the partners of the partnership that executed the within instrument, and acknowledged to me that such partnership executed the same.

_____
Notary Public
in and for said
county and state

My commission expires   , 19 .

Figure 9.7.   Certificate of Acknowledgment by Partnership.

STATE OF OHIO
COUNTY OF PIKE

On this the   day of   , 19—, before me,   , the undersigned officer, personally appeared HAROLD PETERSON, known to me to be the person whose name is subscribed as attorney-in-fact for MICHAEL M. HATFIELD, and acknowledged that he executed the same as the act of his principal for the purposes therein contained.

IN WITNESS WHEREOF I hereunto set my hand and official seal.

_____
Notary Public

My commission expires   , 19 .

Figure 9.8.   Certificate of Acknowledgment by Attorney-in-Fact.

edgment is making it in a capacity other than that of an individual, that capacity is also stated, but not in solid caps. When a person makes an acknowledgment as secretary of a corporation, for example, the designation is written ". . . WILLIAM FOLEY, secretary of Fenton Instruments, Inc., . . ." The person who makes the acknowledgment does not sign the certificate.

Signature and Designation of Officer Taking Acknowledgment

The officer who takes an acknowledgment signs the certificate. A blank line for his or her signature appears four line spaces beneath the body of the certificate. Insert his or her title underneath the line. In many states the certificate also recites the name and full title of the officer taking the acknowledgment. If you do not know who is to take the acknowledgment, leave a blank space long enough for the average name to be inserted in handwriting.

Date of Expiration of Commission

Many states require that an acknowledgment taken by a notary public show the date of the expiration of his or her commission. On acknowledgments to be used in those states, insert "My commission expires_____, 19__," two lines spaces below the signature. Notaries usually have a rubber stamp showing the expiration date of their commission, and the typed line is not necessary except as a reminder that the date of expiration must appear on the certificate.

Notary's Seal

In almost all cases, the certificate of acknowledgment must also bear the notary's seal, especially if the instrument is acknowledged outside the state where it is to be recorded. In some states, a justice of the peace may take an acknowledgment and swear witnesses. The requirements for becoming a justice of the peace differ slightly from those for becoming a notary public, as do the functions of the officer.

9.13. How and Where to Place the Acknowledgment

Acknowledgments are usually double-spaced. They follow the signatures. Although there is no rule of law governing the placement of an acknowledgment on the page, it is desirable that the entire acknowledgment be placed on the signature page of the instrument, even if single spacing is necessary to accomplish this. If the entire acknowledgment cannot be placed on the signature page it is preferable to begin it on that page. In the case of some instruments, such as a power of attorney that authorizes the conveyance of any interest in real estate, it is practically mandatory for the acknowledgment to appear on the same page as the signatures. The suggestions given in section 9.7 for fitting signatures on the page are applicable to fitting the acknowledgment on the page.

9.14. Who May Make an Acknowledgment

Any person who signs an instrument is qualified to acknowledge it, and this person acknowledges it in the same capacity that he or she signed. A person who signs an instrument in his own behalf acknowledges it as his act in his individual capacity (Figure 9.4). If husband and wife sign, each makes an acknowledgment, but in almost all states only one certificate of acknowledgment is necessary (Figure 9.4). See also section 9.18.

The officer of a corporation acknowledges that the corporation executed the instrument, and the acknowledgment associates the acknowledger with the corporation. In those states that require a corporate instrument to be signed by two officers, each officer acknowledges the instrument but both acknowledgments are included in the same certificate (Figure 9.6).

A partner acknowledges that an instrument was executed by the partnership (Figure 9.7).

An attorney-in-fact (see section 11.2) acknowledges that he signed the principal's name and his own as attorney-in-fact (Figure 9.8).

A subscribing witness may also acknowledge an instrument. The wording of an acknowledgment by a subscribing witness (someone who signs a document as a witness to the affiant) differs considerably from an acknowledgment made by a party to the instrument. The lawyer will dictate the acknowledgment or give you a form to follow.

9.15. Who May Take an Acknowledgment

The statutes in the various states designate the officers before whom an acknowledgment may be made or who may "take acknowledgments."

These officers include, among others, judges, clerks of courts, and notaries public. Usually, the secretary or paralegal in a law office is appointed notary public, so he or she may take acknowledgments of clients to instruments prepared in the office. (See "Notaries Public" for the qualifications and duties of a notary public.)

9.16. Authentication

Instruments are frequently acknowledged in one state and recorded in another. Some states require that instruments acknowledged outside the state must have the notary's certificate of acknowledgment authenticated by a designated official, usually the clerk of the county court in which the notary public is registered. The clerk's *authentication* is a certification to the effect that the notary is authorized to take acknowledgments and that the signature on the certificate of acknowledgment is his or hers. The statutes usually prescribe the wording of the certificate of authentication. If your office is in a state that requires authentication of the notary's certificate, prepare the certificate of authentication in accordance with the statute in your state. (The lawyer will dictate it or give you a form to follow. Make a copy for your looseleaf notebook and add it to your computer file.) Your letter forwarding the instrument for acknowledgment should point out that the authentication, as well as the certificate of acknowledgment, should be signed.

AFFIDAVITS

9.17. What Is an Affidavit?

An *affidavit* is a written statement of facts sworn to by the person making the statement in the presence of an officer authorized to administer the oath. A party making a statement in writing may *affirm* the statement in lieu of swearing to it in most jurisdictions. This right was originally reserved only for those whose religion forbade their taking an oath. In general, the affiant or deponent may swear or affirm, as he or she chooses. The person makes the affidavit to help establish or prove a fact. Affidavits are used to prove, among other things, identity, age, residence, marital status, and possession of property. They are also an essential part of court motions (see Chapter 14).

9.18. Distinction Between Affidavit and Acknowledgment

An affidavit is a complete instrument within itself, but an *acknowledgment* is always part of, or an appendage to, another instrument. The purpose of an affidavit is to prove a fact, whereas the purpose of an acknowledgement is the declaration by the person making it that he or she signed this instrument to which the certificate of acknowledgment is attached. An affidavit is sworn to, but an acknowledgment is not. The maker signs an instrument, whether it is a deed, an affidavit, a power of attorney, or other. The officer (usually a notary public) signs an acknowledgment or the jurat, whichever is appropriate.

9.19. Essentials of an Affidavit

Some affidavits are written in the first person and some in the third person, but they all have the following basic essentials.

Venue

When an affidavit is used in a court case, it is always preceded by the caption of the case (see Chapter 14). The affidavit itself begins with a recital of the venue.

Name of Affiant

The name of the person making the affidavit is written in solid caps.

Averment of Oath

The introduction to the affidavit avers that the affiant was sworn, or made under oath.

Statement of Facts

The body of the affidavit is a narrative of the facts that the affiant wants to state.

Signature of Affiant

The affiant always signs the affidavit, even those that are written in the third person.

Jurat

A *jurat* is a clause in an official certificate attesting that the affidavit or deposition was sworn to at a stated time before an authorized officer. It is often referred to as the "sworn to" clause. The form of jurat varies slightly in the different states. In a few states, the jurat recites the title of the officer and the state, or state and county, in which he or she is authorized to act. In a few other states, the name of the affiant is repeated in the jurat.

The form of the jurat is essentially the same as the form of the acknowledgment.

STATE OF NEW HAMPSHIRE
COUNTY OF MERRIMACK

Appeared before me the above-named John Jones, known to me or satisfactorily proven to be the same, and swore that the statements made in the foregoing affidavit are true to the best of his knowledge and belief, this   day of   19 .

_____

Notary Public/Justice of the Peace

My commission expires   , 19 .

Signature of Notary

The notary signs immediately beneath the jurat and affixes his or her seal and the expiration date of commission. In some states the expiration date precedes the signature.

9.20. Authentication

If the affidavit is to be used in a state other than that in which it is made, an *authentication* of the officer's signature and authority is sometimes necessary. The procedure is the same as when an acknowledgment is authenticated.

9.21. Preparation of Affidavit

Directions for the preparation of an affidavit for use in a court case are given in Chapter 14. The directions given here apply to affidavits that are not to be used in a court case. (See Figure 9.9) Inquire about the number of copies to make.

1. The venue is typed like the venue on an acknowledgment.
2. Double-space.
3. Give the affiant's name in solid capitals.
4. The signature line appears at the right for the affiant to sign.
5. Usually, the jurat is typed on the left half of the page (see Figure 9.9), but in a few jurisdictions the practice is to type it across the entire page.
6. The signature line for the notary public (or other officer who is to administer the oath) appears immediately beneath the jurat, at the

---

STATE OF KENTUCKY

COUNTY OF ELTON

    JOHN A. BARNES, being duly sworn, deposes and says:

    He is the Secretary of Timberlane Corporation, and that no stockholder of said Corporation has filed with the Secretary thereof a written request (other than such written request or requests as may have heretofore expired or been withdrawn) that notices intended for him shall be mailed to some address other than his address as it appears on the stock book of the said Corporation.

                                             Secretary

Sworn to before me this

    day of   , 19_ _

         Notary Public

My commission expires   , 19 .

Figure 9.9.   An Affidavit.

left margin of the page. If the jurat is typed across the page, place the signature line on the right half of the page.

7. Beneath the signature line insert the officer's title. In some states the officer's authority to act in the particular political subdivision is required. For example: Notary Public in and for the County of *Los Angeles,* State of California."

8. Insert "My commission expires   " (when required) two line spaces beneath the officer's title if the jurat appears on the left half of the page. If the jurat is typed aross the page, the expiration dateline is placed at the left margin, parallel to the officer's signature and title.

NOTARIES PUBLIC

9.22. What Is a Notary Public?

A *notary public* is a commissioned officer of the state whose powers and duties consist, among others, in administering oaths, certifying to the genuineness of documents, and taking acknowledgments. In some states a notary is authorized to act only in the county in which he or she is commissioned; in others, the notary is qualified to act throughout the state. Almost all law offices have a notary public, and, frequently, the secretary or paralegal is the notary. Lawyers in some states, for example, New Jersey and New York, have de facto notarial authority, but they must generally qualify, register, and have a notarial seal or stamp. The eligibility requirements are not stringent, relating primarily to age and residence. If your office wants you to be commissioned as a notary, write to the official in your state who appoints notaries for an application blank. In some states, the application must be endorsed by a member of the legislature, a judge, or some other designated official. If this is the case, it will be indicated on the application blank.

After the commission is received, order a notary's seal and stamp. Then register your commission with the clerk of the court (or other designated official) in your county, so that the officer can authenticate your certificate of acknowledgment on papers that are to be recorded in another state.

In some states a justice of the peace performs many of the functions of the notary. The justice of the peace may administer oaths, take acknowledgments, and so forth. The requirements for eligibility and the means of acquiring the commission are similar to those for a notary. The justice of the peace may or may not have an official seal. He or she no longer has any judicial functions, although the justice of the peace is still a judicial officer. In either case, the functions and methods of appointment are entirely statutory.

9.23. Following the Letter of the Law When You Notarize a Paper

A commission as a notary public is a trust; it confers certain powers upon you and requires that you perform certain duties. In exercising those powers and duties, you should fully observe the "letter of the law." In a law office your principal duty as a notary public will be taking acknowledgments.

Notice that all of the certificates of acknowledgment previously illustrated (Figures 9.4 through 9.8) recite that the person making the acknowledgment "personally appeared" before the notary. This is true of all forms of acknowledgment in every state. You, therefore, should never take an acknowledgment without the actual appearance of the individual making the acknowledgment. In fact, it is illegal to do so. If a client's spouse signs an instrument at home and wants to acknowledge it over the telephone, politely but firmly decline to take the acknowledgment and state the reason for your refusal.

Acknowledgments also recite that the individual "acknowledged" that he or she signed the instrument. You do not administer an oath to a person making an acknowledgment, but ask: "Do you acknowledge that you executed this instrument as attorney-in-fact for Henry J. Cromwell?" or a similar question, depending on whether the acknowledgment is being made by an individual in his or her own behalf, by an officer of a corporation, by a partnership, or by an attorney-in-fact.

Acknowledgments also recite that the notary knows, or has satisfactory evidence, that the person making it is the person "described in and who executed" the instrument. You must have satisfactory evidence of the identity of a person whose acknowledgment you take. In taking acknowledgments made by clients, though, you are not likely to have difficulty in this respect. A notary who willfully makes a false certificate that an instrument was acknowledged by a party to the instrument is guilty of forgery.

A certificate of acknowledgment also shows the date it is signed by the notary. One should never postdate or antedate a certificate since to do so would constitute fraud and deceit in the exercise of one's powers.

Some states require that a wife be examined by a notary "separate and apart" from her husband. This is especially true with reference to instruments relating to real estate. If the state in which an instrument is to be recorded has this requirement, follow the statutory procedure strictly. Do not take the wife's acknowledgment in the presence of her husband. Figure 9.5 illustrates a certificate in a state requiring a separate acknowledgment by the wife.

9.24. What to Look for When You Notarize a Paper

A notary must exercise special care to see that documents he or she notarizes are executed correctly. If the papers are not in conformity with the requirements of the office where they are to be recorded, they will be rejected. You would not read an instrument that you notarize, but you must read the acknowledgment and also glance over the instrument. Observe the following details when taking an acknowledgment.

1. If the instrument recites that it is "under seal," be certain that the signature to the instrument is followed by "L.S." or "Seal."

2. When a corporation is a party to an instrument, be certain that the corporate seal is impressed on the instrument if required; seals are usually required on corporate instruments.

3. Fill in all blanks in the instrument and in the certificate of acknowledgment.

4. Be certain to show the date of the expiration of your commission, when required.

5. Be certain to impress your notarial seal on the certificate, when required.

6. Be certain that rubber stamps you use make legible imprints. A black stamp pad is preferable because the black ink photocopies more distinctly than other inks.

7. Be certain to have the clerk of the court (or other designated official) authenticate your certificate of acknowledgment if authentication is required.

RECORDING LEGAL INSTRUMENTS

9.25. Purpose in Recording Instruments

Legal instruments are frequently recorded in a public office, and the record is available to anyone who is interested. The purpose of recording an instrument is to provide constructive notice to the world that the recorder has a certain legal interest, thereby protecting himself against those who might claim otherwise. For example, *A* wants to purchase some property from *B*. He learns from the public record that *C* holds a mortgage on the property. *A* purchases the property, but he makes legal arrangements that will protect not only his own interests but those of *C* as well.

9.26. Distinction Between Recording and Filing

The terms *record* and *file* are used loosely. They are not synonymous and should not be used interchangeably. If an instrument is to be *recorded,* it is given to an official designated by the state statute. The official copies the instrument in a book, thereby preserving it perpetually. This record furnishes authentic evidence of the existence of the instrument. After the official records the instrument, he or she stamps upon it the date and the number and page of the record book in which it is recorded and returns it to the person who gave it to him or her, usually the lawyer. When a paper is *filed,* it is placed in the custody of a designated official, who enters upon the paper the date of its receipt and keeps it in his or her office, where it is available for inspection.

Legal instruments are generally recorded whereas court papers are always filed. In some states, however, certain legal instruments are filed and recorded in the abstract; that is, only a summary of the essential parts is recorded. The official designated to record legal instruments varies with the locality. He or she might be the county clerk, the town clerk, a register or recorder of deeds, or some other official. Instruments that are recorded or filed are also appropriately indexed so the record or file can be easily located.

9.27. What the Secretary or Paralegal Does

Any instrument must be "in recordable form" for the particular state in order to be recorded. When the lawyer asks you to have an instrument recorded, be sure you know not only what official is to record it but also *where* it is to be recorded. For example, although your office is located in Adams County and the client signs the paper there, if the instrument relates to property located in Brown County, the instrument must be recorded in Brown County, not in Adams County.

If your firm uses legal backs (see section 10.20), the firm name and address will probably appear on it. If no legal back is used, the firm name may appear on the paper used for the instrument. If not, type or print it on the back of the document.

If the instrument is to be recorded in a place located near your office, take it in person to the office of the proper official. He or she will give you a receipt for it and return it to your office after recording it. You will have to pay a recording fee, which is fixed by the state statutes. In addition to a recording fee, a transfer tax must be paid in most jurisdictions before any real estate transaction will be recorded (see Chapter 18).

In some places, the recording office will bill your firm periodically for recording. Otherwise, pay the fee out of petty cash or take a blank check to the recording office and fill in the amount when you are told what the recording fee will be.

When it is necessary to mail the instrument to the recording office, send it by certified mail, return receipt requested, with a covering letter. The letter should be addressed to the designated official and should describe the instrument sufficiently to identify it. You will also have to enclose a check for the fee or request that a bill be mailed. Note that the official usually will not record the instrument until the fee is received. A model letter for this purpose appears on the following page.

Place the receipt from the recording official, or a copy of your covering letter to him, in your follow-up file so that you may follow up if the instrument is not returned within about two weeks. When it is returned, send it to the client with a covering letter (unless, for some reason, the instrument is to be kept by the lawyer). After an instrument has been recorded, there is no need to send it by certified mail.

November 14, 19XX

CERTIFIED
RETURN RECEIPT REQUESTED

James P. Frost, Esq.
Clerk of the County Court
DeKalb, IL 60115

Sir:

Enclosed for recording is a lease dated November 14, 19XX between
Hilary Ross and Edmond Butler. Also enclosed is our check for $ . . .
to cover the cost of recording this instrument.

Thank you.

Sincerely,

OAKLAND & RUBIN

By
B. B. Oakland

Enc.

10 How to Prepare Legal Papers

One of the most common and most important duties in a law office is the preparation of legal papers. Printed forms are often used in drawing up legal instruments and some court papers. However, whether a preprinted form is available either in hard copy or, more commonly, in the firms' computer database, or whether you must prepare the legal paper from scratch, accuracy is essential. The directions in this chapter are general and apply to all legal papers. Directions that are peculiar to a specific document are given when that document is discussed

PREPARATION GUIDELINES

10.1. Number of Copies

An original, your file copy, and a varying number of photocopies of all legal documents are necessary. Frequently, one or more of the copies are to be a *duplicate original,* or *triplicate original,* which means a copy is to be signed and treated in all respects as though it were an original copy. The lawyer will tell you how many copies to make. Instructions are usually given in this manner: "two and four," meaning an original, a duplicate original, and four copies; or, "one and five," meaning an original and five copies, no duplicate original being necessary.

10.2. Paper

Use the paper required by your computer printer or photocopier, usually in a twenty-pound weight. The kind of paper used also depends on the document being prepared and varies with the office. See the discussion of specific documents; see also the list of stationery supplies in chapter 1.

10.3. Margins

Begin five to six double spaces from the top of the paper and make a habit of allowing the same number of spaces on each document. By following this practice, you know that every page of a document starts at the same place on the paper and has the same number of lines. Appropriate margins can be set in your word processing program.

Bottom Margin

Leave a margin of one to two inches at the bottom. In a neatly prepared legal document, the copy on every page ends exactly the same number of lines from the bottom of the page.

Left Margin

Leave a margin on the left of about one and a quarter or one and a half inches.

Right Margin

Leave a right margin that is consistent with the left margin. Adjustments may be made as required by the particular document.

10.4. Paragraphs

Indent paragraphs one-half to one inch, or follow the indention requirements of your office.

10.5. Numbering Pages

Number pages of legal documents about one-half inch from the bottom or top of the page in the center of the text area or in the upper right corner flush right with the right margin of the text. A centered number may or may not be preceded and followed by a hyphen: -4-. If the first page is not numbered, the numbering begins with 2. Pagination of some documents such as wills and deeds shows the total number of pages in the document: page 2 of 4. The computer will insert each number in exactly the same position on the pages so that when the pages are collated, the numbers will overlie one another.

10.6. Marginal and Tabular Stops

Pica type is used most frequently in law offices. With a computer, the tab stops are set automatically and can be easily changed as required from paragraph to paragraph.

10.7. Tabulated Material

When portions of a paper or letter are tabulated or itemized, the items are usually preceded by a number or letter followed by a period. Begin each line of the tabulated text about two spaces to the right of the number. The first letter of each listed item is capitalized. When the sentences are incomplete, no punctuation is used after each item, as shown in Figure 10.1. Full sentences would be followed by a period. Follow your word processing program instructions for list formatting.

10.8. Responsibility and Distribution Line

In the upper left corner of the file copy or at the bottom, add a notation of the number of copies made, the date, the initials of the person dictating, and your initials. If the material is prepared by computer, add the computer filename. Follow the practice of your office, however, if a different procedure is required.

I have revised the affidavit you returned, I hope in accordance with your recommendations. If you find it satisfactory as now drawn, may I ask you:

1. To swear to it before a notary and have the notary affix his or her seal and notarial stamp

2. To fill in the last column of Schedule B as to the months for which payments are in default on each vehicle

3. To return the affidavit with five forms of the conditional sale contract

---

Figure 10.1.   Tabulated Items.

2-3
7/23/92
ERJ:sm
pc/60-5 benjm.nts

This indicates that one original and a duplicate original and three copies, one of which is for the files, were made on July 23, 1992, and that the document was dictated by ERJ to sm.

10.9. Line Spacing

Most legal work other than correspondence is double-spaced, although one and one-half line spaces or single spacing may be acceptable in some cases such as when a double-spaced acknowledgment will not fit on the page with signatures acknowledged (see Chapter 9). Quotations may also be single-spaced. Triple-space, however, before and after all double-spaced indented material, and triple-space drafts.

10.10. Standard Rules for Spacing

Usage has established the following rules for spacing (although exceptions are sometimes made in computer preparation).

After a comma	1 space
After a semicolon	1 space
After every sentence	2 spaces
After a colon	2 spaces
Before or after a dash (two hyphens)	No space
Before or after a hyphen	No space
Between quotation marks and the matter enclosed	No space
Between parentheses and the matter enclosed	No space
Between any word and the punctuation following it	No space
After an exclamation mark used in the body of a sentence	1 space
After a period following an abbreviation or an initial	1 space

After a period following a figure or letter at the beginning of a line in a list of items	2 spaces
Between periods used as ellipsis points	1 space
Before and after *x* meaning "by," for example, 3" x 5" card	1 space
Before or after an apostrophe in the body of a word	No space
Between the initials that make a single abbreviations, for example, *C.O.D.* (but see "Citations" in Chapter 15)	No space

10.11. Space for Fill-ins

When a date is to be filled in later, leave a space instead of typing a line for the fill-in.

June , 19XX	3 spaces
This day of June, 19XX	6 spaces

Do not leave the blank for a later fill-in at the end of a line, because it will not be noticeable.

10.12. Underscoring

If your equipment does not provide italic type, underscoring, or underlining, in typewriter or computer material is equivalent to italics in printed material. The underlining is continuous and not broken at the spacing between words. If your printer will not print in italics, the following use of underscoring in legal work is recommended.

1. Underscore for emphasis. The person dictating indicates when emphasis is desired.
2. Underscore material that is italic type in the original.
3. Underscore to indicate Latin words and phrases, or abbreviations of them. Unfamiliar words of other foreign languages are also underlined.
4. Underscore titles of books, brochures, plays, movies, and paint-ings.

Do not, however, underscore foreign words that have become a part of the English speech through continuous use. (The *United States Government Printing Office Style Manual* has a list of anglicized foreign words that should not have diacritics and should not be italicized.) In the list of Latin words and phrases in Part 5, those terms that should not be underlined or italicized are given in roman type. Some words are roman when standing alone but are italicized when used as part of certain phrases, for example, "caveat" and *caveat emptor*.

Some material, such as headings, is prepared in a bold type. If your printer will print in bold, follow the instructions of your word processing software.

10.13. Quotations and Other Indented Material

Some material should be set off as a block apart from the rest of the text. With a computer such formatting instructions are usually made through adjustments in the paragraph options of the word processing program.

Margins and Paragraphs

The left margin of blocked quotations of eight or more lines (extracts) and other displayed material should be indented one-half to one inch. The beginning of a paragraph within the material should be indented an additional one-half to one inch. If a quotation begins in the middle of a paragraph, however, the initial indention is omitted.

The right margin of indented material either may be the same as the principal right margin or indented about one-half to one inch the same as the left margin.

Short lines of indented material may be indented one to one and one-half inches.

> The American Bar
> The Bar Register
> The Lawyer's List

Line Spacing

Quotations are usually spaced the same as the rest of the text. Triple-space before and after double-spaced extracts; double-space before and after single-spaced extracts.

Quotation Marks

When quoted material is indented, do not enclose it in quotation marks. When the material is *not* indented, but is part of the regular text, place double quotation marks at the beginning and end of the quotation and at the beginning of each new paragraph within the quoted material. Change any double quotation marks within the material to single quotation marks, thus conforming to the rule that quotations *within* quotations are enclosed in single quotation marks. In extracts, however, change single quotation marks to double quotation marks since opening and closing marks are not used in blocked quotations.

Errors

Copy quotations exactly, even obvious errors. Indicate any errors in the same way that you do in making an exact copy of any material (see section 10.16).

Italics

If words in the original are in italics, use italic type if provided by your printer; otherwise underscore the words. If words that are not in italics in the original are italicized or underscored at the direction of the person dictating, add the words "Italics ours" or "Emphasis ours" in parentheses at the end of the quotation. Frequently, part of a quoted passage is italicized and the person dictating wants to emphasize another part of it. In that case, put "Italics theirs" in parentheses immediately following the original italicized passage and add the words "Emphasis ours" in parentheses at the end of the quotation. In Figure 10.2 on page 222 the word *records* was italicized in the original. The rest of the underscoring was added by the dictator for emphasis.

How to Show Omissions

Omissions of part of a quotation are indicated by the use of ellipsis points. They may be periods or, less frequently, asterisks and are usually in groups of three. There should be a space between each period or asterisk, except before the period that signifies the end of a sentence.

In using ellipsis points, remember that they take the place of words and place them accordingly. Thus if a quotation begins in the middle of a sentence, there is no space between the quotation mark and the first ellipsis

The pertinent part of the opinion rendered by the Copyright Office at our request reads as follows:

> The Copyright Office does not undertake to pass upon his [the author's] rights, leaving the question to the courts in case of dispute. It simply <u>records</u> (italics theirs) his claims, and by this recording gives him certain rights <u>provided his claims can be substantiated</u>....

> ... this [copyright] is taken out in the name of the publisher rather than of the author, as the contract itself is really a license to sell from the publisher to the auther [sic]. It is also the duty of the publisher to take all necessary steps to effect renewals ....

> An auther should be "guided" by his publisher in all questions of copyright. (Emphasis ours.)

We contend that this opinion strongly supports the contention of the petitioner.

Figure 10.2.   Exact Copy of Quoted Material

point, but there is a space between the final ellipsis and the following word. If an entire sentence is omitted, four ellipsis points are used, the first representing the period at the end of the sentence. Punctuation is placed in the same relation to the ellipsis points as if they were words.

You may indicate omission of one or more entire paragraphs by a separate line of three to five centered ellipsis points about five spaces apart or by four ellipsis points at the end of the last sentence preceding the omission. Some law offices use a single group of three to five asterisks centered on a separate line.

Figure 10.2 illustrates a quotation with periods showing omissions. (It also shows errors that were in the material being copied. See section 10.16.) Notice that the first paragraph begins in the middle and is thus not indented; there are one or more paragraphs omitted after the first one; the next paragraph begins and ends in the middle of a sentence; the last paragraph is quoted in full. Notice that there are four periods at the end of the second paragraph since one represents a period at the end of the sentence.

10.14. Drafts

Lawyers expect to make changes in drafts; therefore, it is important to triple-space all dictated material. Extracts copied from books or other documents may be double-spaced or single-spaced in the draft. Leave wide margins, and type the date, the initials of the dictator and your initials, and the word *DRAFT* in all capital letters in the upper left corner of the first page. If there is a second or a third draft, indicate this fact. Follow the usual practices for form and style except with reference to line spacing and margins.

Speed is more desirable than neatness in a draft, but accuracy must not be sacrificed. Although a lawyer expects to make changes in a draft, careless transcription of his or her dictation is annoying and is not tolerated any more than it would be in a final copy. Before correcting a draft, study the corrected page, noting the following:

1. Portions marked for omission
2. Additional material to be inserted
3. Transpositions
4. Corrections in spelling, punctuation, and the like

Note carefully the changes in each sentence before making corrections. Difficult handwriting between lines of typing and in the margins may often be deciphered quickly by referring to the scratched-out wording of which the handwritten matter is usually a revision.

10.15. Correction of Errors

If an insertion or deletion does not jibe with the other material, you are misinterpreting it, or the lawyer has overlooked something. When you detect an error of this kind, or any error other than typographical, in a draft you are correcting, check with the lawyer. If you cannot locate the lawyer and you cannot get a clarification, use your best judgment in making the change and call it to the lawyer's attention later when you return the work.

10.16. Copying

If you are inserting in a new document portions of an executed document, signed letter, extracts from books, or the like, the following instructions apply (see Figure 10.1 for a copy of quoted material).

1. Copy exactly, even obvious errors, because the copy purports to be a "true and exact" copy.

2. Indicate obvious errors copied from the original as follows: (a) Italicize or underline an incorrect letter or figure. (b) Put "sic" in brackets after apparently or obviously incorrect words or phrases. (c) Show an intentional omission by ellipsis points as explained in section 10.13; show an unintentional omission that appears in the original by enclosing a question mark in brackets in the position where something is missing.

> agreement entered into the 31*th* day of May . . .
> upon rec*i*ept . . .
> I give, devise and bequest [sic] unto . . .
> meeting of the United [?] Assembly in Paris . . .

3. Copy line for line as far as practicable.

4. When the document is completed, proofread it for punctuation, underlining, full capitals, hyphens, and so on.

5. If material to be copied is lengthy, an optical scanner enables one to copy text from a source such as a book directly into the computer.

See section 2.23 in Chapter 2 for the method by which the lawyer gives instructions for copying certain material.

Punctuation and Capitalization

Punctuation in legal documents should be handled the same way as it is with other material, such as correspondence (see chapter 6). There are, however, a few exceptions to general rules of capitalization. Names, for instance, are usually given in all capitals in legal papers. Often the first letter of words pertaining to specific papers are capitalized, such as *Warranty Deed.* The word *versus* (*v.* or *vs.*) is usually written in all lowercase letters. Court and venue names are usually given in all capitals, as are the titles of legal papers such as *AGREEMENT.* Your files will have many examples to follow if you are in doubt, and the lawyer will instruct you further when more than one procedure is permissible.

Letterheads

When part of a letterhead is copied, state in all capitals and in brackets [LETTERHEAD OF . . . .].

10.17. Collating

Every legal paper of two or more pages should be collated. *Collating* is the process of organizing a set of pages in the correct sequence. The task is facilitated by the use of a rubber finger or a pencil eraser. Photocopy machines often have collating trays for automatic collating of copied materials.

10.18. Conforming

Duplicates of originals are usually made by photocopy machine. Such duplicate copies should be stamped "COPY" or photocopied on paper that already is marked "COPY." There is no need to "sign" copies made by photocopier.

10.19. Ditto Marks

Ditto marks are not permissible in a legal document. They are used in exhibits and schedules but not in the document to which the exhibits and schedules are annexed. Ditto marks may sometimes be used in drafts to save time, although a computer can quickly copy and insert text that is frequently repeated. In any final copy, the language *must* be repeated.

10.20. Legal Backs

Legal instruments such as wills or deeds are occasionally backed with a manuscript cover called a *legal back* made of thick paper about nine by fifteen inches. Certain data, referred to as the *endorsement,* are typed on the back of the cover. The contents of the endorsement vary with the instrument but usually include a brief description of the instrument and the names of the parties to it. The attorney's name and address are usually printed or engraved in the space provided. The inside cover contains verifications, affirmations, and affidavits of service. The appropriate ones are used for any particular case.

10.21. Printed Law Blanks

Although many law blanks are kept in the computer, printed blanks are still used in drawing up legal instruments and some court papers. Law blank printers publish a catalog showing the numbers and titles of the blanks that they print. Each law blank has its title and, usually, the printer's catalog number, printed in small letters in the upper left corner. Frequently, the secretary or paralegal can fill in these blanks without any dictated instructions from the lawyer. When it is necessary to provide the material to be inserted in the blanks, the lawyer usually handwrites the material on a photocopy of the appropriate blank, thus eliminating any confusion about where each insertion should be made.

"Z" Ruling

Frequently, the material typed on a printed form does not fill the space provided. To protect the instrument from alteration, a "Z" ruling, as illustrated here, may be added with pen and ink in the unused space.

11 How to Handle Powers of Attorney and Wills

Chapters 9 and 10 gave basic information about legal instruments and how to prepare legal papers. This chapter reviews two representative instruments that are a part of the work in every law office.

POWERS OF ATTORNEY

11.1. What Is a Power of Attorney?

A *power of attorney* is a written instrument giving authority to the agent appointed to act in the name and on behalf of the person signing it. Authority may be given to another to borrow money; collect debts; manage, lease, sell, or mortgage real estate; prosecute a suit at law; and for almost any other purpose.

11.2. Parties to a Power of Attorney

The person who gives the authority to another to act for him or her is called the *principal*. The principal may be an individual, a corporation, or a partnership, but principals must be capable of performing the act they authorize another to perform for them.

The person to whom authority is given is the *agent,* or *attorney-in-fact*. The latter designation does not imply that the agent is a lawyer. An attorney-at-law may be an attorney-in-fact, but an attorney-in-fact is not necessarily an attorney-at-law.

11.3. Forms of Powers of Attorney

A power of attorney is either general or limited. A *general power of attorney* is broad in scope and enables the agent to transact almost any business for the principal, whereas under a *limited power of attorney*, the agent's power is limited to a specified act or acts.

The forms and extent of authority of powers of attorney are established by statute. A power of attorney can be terminated by the principal at any time.

A *durable power of attorney* survives the incompetence or death of the principal. A durable power of attorney includes words such as: "This power of attorney shall not be affected by the subsequent disability, incompetence, or death of the principal." The exact wording is often set forth in the statutes of the jurisdiction. A durable medical power of attorney gives the agent authority to make medical decisions for the principal if he or she is not able to do so.

11.4. Statements and Clauses

Except with respect to the powers granted by the instrument, all powers of attorney are similar. No state requires a specific form. At one time a power of attorney always began with the words *Know all men by these presents,* or simply *Know all men,* written in solid caps. In modern practice, attorneys drop this introductory phrase in an effort to simplify legal documents.

After a recital of the parties and their residences, the powers granted by the instrument are set forth. This portion of the instrument is most important and requires careful and expert phrasing so that powers granted may be clearly and precisely defined. The lawyer dictates the recital of powers or gives you a special form to follow.

A power of attorney ends with a testimonium clause, which is similar to the testimonium clause in any instrument (see section 9.5 in Chapter 9). Those relating to real estate are always acknowledged.

11.5. Directions for the Preparation of a Power of Attorney

Unless instructed otherwise, follow these directions when preparing a power of attorney.

1. Make an original for the attorney-in-fact and as many copies as are needed, including a copy for your files.
2. Use letter-size paper.

3. Place the responsibility marks on the office copy only.

4. Double-space if the power is one page; otherwise single-space.

5. Be certain to have at least two lines of typing on the signature page.

6. Prepare signature lines for only the principal or principals.

7. If the powers granted relate to the conveyance of real estate, the instrument must be prepared with the formalities required for a deed. Follow directions in Chapter 18.

8. If the powers granted do not relate to real estate, ask the lawyer if the power of attorney is to be witnessed and acknowledged. If so, follow instructions in Chapter 9. Durable powers of attorney are always witnessed and acknowledged.

9. Collate. (Some copy machines have this capability.)

10. If a legal back is used, endorse it as illustrated in Figure 11.1 (p. 230).

11. Check to see that the principal's signature agrees with the name typed in the instrument.

12. After the instrument is signed, and acknowledged if necessary, conform copies to original (see section 10.18 in Chapter 10).

13. If a power of attorney relates to real property, it is recorded like any conveyance. Sometimes, however, it is not recorded until the attorney-in-fact exercises the power granted. Ask the lawyer for instructions about recording.

14. The lawyer will tell you whether the original of the power of attorney is to be delivered directly to the attorney-in-fact or to the principal.

15. Make a notation on your office copy of the distribution of the original and copies.

WILLS

11.6. What Is a Will?

A *will* is the disposal of one's property to take effect after death. At one time only real estate was disposed of by will, personalty being disposed of by testament. The distinction between the terms *will* and *testament* is no

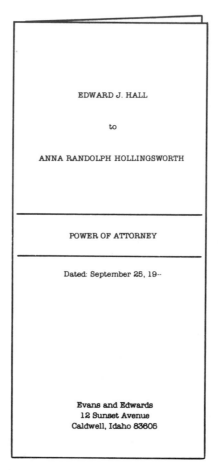

Figure 11.1. Endorsed Back of Power of Attorney.

longer of legal significance, and the terms are frequently used interchangeably.

11.7. Who Are the Parties to a Will?

Only testators are parties to a will.

Testator

The *testator* is the person who makes the will—who disposes of the property and issues the instructions to be carried out after his or her death.

A testator must be of sound mind and of the age required by the state statutes. In the majority of states, the age requirement is eighteen.

The law of the state where the testator resides (his or her domicile) controls with respect to personality, but with respect to real estate, the law of the state where the property is situated controls.

Beneficiaries

Beneficiaries are not parties to the will but are the ones who benefit from it. A *devisee* is one to whom real estate is willed, whereas a *legatee* is one to whom personalty is bequeathed. Like *will* and *testament,* the terms *devisee* and *legatee* are frequently used interchangeably, but a careful lawyer does not use the terms loosely in the wills he or she drafts.

11.8. Forms and Kinds of Wills

None of the states requires that a will and testament follow any specific wording, but the statutes do provide for certain formalities in its execution.

Oral Wills

Oral wills, known as *nuncupative wills,* are recognized only under very limited circumstances in almost all of the states. Written wills are far more common

Handwritten Wills

A will may be written entirely in the testator's handwriting and without the usual formalities of execution; such a will is called a *holographic will* and is acceptable in about half of the states. In other states, a handwritten will is admitted to probate only if it is executed with the same formalities required of "typewritten" wills. You will be concerned principally with the formal written will, typed or computer prepared and executed in the lawyer's office. (Although it is possible to buy printed forms of wills, they are not used in a law office.)

Reciprocal Wills

Wills made by two or more persons with reciprocal testamentary provisions in favor of one another are called *reciprocal wills.* Reciprocity in estate planning is not favored. Attorneys often add an article to a will providing that even though a husband and wife may each be executing a will at the same time, such an act is not to be construed as being mutual or reciprocal.

Living Will

A *living will* is a document that states whether life-sustaining treatment of a person shall be withdrawn or withheld in cases of an incurable or irreversible condition that will cause death in a relatively short time and when the individual is no longer capable of making decisions about his or her medical treatment. The living will is prepared for a person before the individual reaches this state and while the person is still able to articulate that he or she does not want life-prolonging measures to be applied or continued when there is no hope of recovery.

11.9. Pattern of the Contents of Wills

Although no two wills are alike in detail, they are all drafted from similar patterns. The outline given below is generally followed in properly drawn wills. The explanation in the succeeding paragraphs will enable you to recognize each part and clause.

1. Title
2. Introductory paragraph
   a. Revocation clause
3. Body or text
   a. Payment of debts and funeral expenses
   b. Dispositive clauses
      i. Devises
      ii. Bequests
      iii. Trust provisions
      iv. Residuary clause
   c. Appointment of executor/personal representative
   d. Appointment of guardian/conservator
   e. Precatory provisions
4. Testimonium clause

5. Signature and seal
6. Attestation clause
7. Witnesses' signatures
8. Self-proving acknowledgment (if provided for by statute)

11.10. Title

The *title* merely identifies the document as "Last Will and Testament of John Jones" or "First Codicil to the Last Will and Testament of John Jones." It is stated in solid caps, underscored, and arranged symmetrically, beginning about six double spaces from the top of the page. See Figure 11.2 (p. 234).

11.11. Introductory Paragraph

In the introductory paragraph, the testator sets forth his or her name and residence and recites that he or she does "hereby publish and declare this my Last Will and Testament." Introductory clauses also frequently recite the mental capacity of the testator to make a will, that is, "of sound mind and disposing memory."

11.12. Revocation Clause

The *revocation clause* specifically revokes all former wills. Wills do not always include this clause, even though the testator has made other wills, because the act of executing a new will normally has the effect of revoking prior wills. The revocation clause is either a part of the introductory paragraph or is a separate paragraph, usually near the end of the will.

11.13. Text, or Body

The *text,* or *body,* of the will disposes of the testator's property, appoints his or her executor, and expresses wishes of the testator that are not necessarily mandatory. The provisions in the body of the will are often referred to as *articles,* or *items,* and are numbered. There are no firm rules as to numbering schemes, but the following are among those commonly used.

In the center of the page: ARTICLE I, ARTICLE II, etc.; ITEM I, ITEM II, etc.

THE LAST WILL AND TESTAMENT OF

DAVID C. BRAUN

I, DAVID C. BRAUN, of Laconia, County of Belknap, State of New Hampshire, do hereby declare this my Last Will and Testament, and hereby revoke any and all wills and codicils heretofore made by me.

FIRST: I direct that all of my just debts and funeral expenses be paid as soon as practicable after my decease.

SECOND: I give and devise my farm located in the town of Meredith, County of Belknap, State of New Hampshire, to my son, RICHARD, and his heirs and assigns forever.

THIRD: I give and bequeath to my daughter, ANNE, fifty (50) shares of common stock of United States Steel, Inc.

FOURTH: I give and bequeath the following sums of money to the following persons, to-wit:

(a) The sum of Seven Hundred Fifty Dollars ($750) to ROBERT JONES of Allentown, Georgia.

(b) The sum of One Thousand Dollars ($1,000) to EDNA JONES of Ellisville, Florida.

FIFTH: I give and bequeath to the MERCHANTS' LOAN AND TRUST COMPANY, a corporation, organized under the laws of

-1-

Figure 11.2.   First Page of Will.

At the side of the page: FIRST:, SECOND:, etc.; First:, Second:, etc.; or, in a short will, 1., 2., etc.

The various articles might have subparagraphs that are also numbered (1), (2), etc. or (a), (b), etc., and they in turn might also be subdivided. If you use numbers for subparagraphs, use letters for sub-subparagraphs and so on. The left margin of sub-subparagraphs is usually indented about ten spaces or about one inch.

The will must maintain a consistent numbering system, and you should watch for inconsistencies. If a certain article contains more than twenty-six bequests, you should choose numbers rather than letters for the subparagraphs in all of the articles.

11.14. Payment of Debts and Funeral Expenses

The first paragraph in the body of a will usually directs an executor to pay debts, expenses of last illness, and funeral expenses. This provision is normally not necessary, because the law requires the executor to pay these debts, but it is customarily included.

11.15. Dispositive Clauses

The dispositive clauses are the provisions that express the testator's will as to what will be done with his or her property—the provisions that dispose of the property. Disposal of real property is a devise; disposal of personal property may also be a devise or, in some states with older probate codes, a bequest or legacy. In a carefully drawn will, the testator will "give and devise" real property; "give and bequeath" personal property; and "give, devise and bequeath" both real and personal property.

11.16. Trust Provisions

The testator may will property to an institution, or an individual, "in trust for the following purpose. . . ." A testamentary trust, which comes into being upon the death of the testator, is usually created when the testator wants the beneficiary to receive the income from it during his or her life, or until he or she reaches a certain age, or until the happening of some other contingency. Wealthy testators frequently set up endowment funds in trust for charitable and educational purposes. The trust provisions of many wills are very explicit and, therefore, lengthy. They constitute part of the dispositive provisions of the will.

11.17. Residuary Clause

The residuary clause is that part of the will that disposes of all of the testator's property not otherwise devised or bequeathed, ". . . all the rest, residue, and remainder. . . ." A residuary clause is an essential part of the will. Specific or general devises and bequests have priority over the residuary clause, and it is therefore the last dispositive provision of a properly constructed will. No set form of wording is necessary.

11.18. Appointment of Executor

Someone must see that the provisions of the testator's will are carried out after his or her death. The testator appoints an *executor*, or *personal representative*, in his or her will for this purpose. The executor may be an individual or an institution, such as a bank. Frequently, the testator appoints more than one executor, or he or she may appoint an alternate, in the event of the incapacity or refusal of his or her first choice to act. The paragraph naming the executor may follow the dispositive provisions (bequests) of the will or may appear in the first or second article.

11.19. Appointment of Guardian

If a testator is the surviving parent, he or she will probably appoint a *guardian* of the "person and property" of his or her minor children. Or the testator might choose to appoint one guardian for the person of the children and another, increasingly referred to as a *conservator,* for their property. The paragraph appointing a guardian normally follows the paragraph appointing an executor.

11.20. Precatory Provisions

Precatory provisions in a will are those in which the testator expresses words of desire, expectations, hope, or recommendation that certain action will be taken by the executor—generally in connection with establishing a trust for a named beneficiary. A testator may state, for example, that he "wishes and requests" or "has the fullest confidence in" his or her executor doing this or that.

Unfortunately, expressions like these often result in litigation to determine testator's intention. Were these words meant to impose an obligation that testator must carry out, or were the words a mere recommendation that testator use his or her discretion in creating or not creating a particular trust?

The carefully drawn will should clearly spell out the testator's intentions rather than just use precatory provisions capable of more than one interpretation.

11.21. Testimonium, or Signature, Clause

The testimonium, or signature, clause to a will is similar to the testimonium clause in any written instrument (please refer to section 9.5 in Chapter 9).

11.22. Attestation Clause and Witnesses' Signatures

All states require that a will be witnessed, but the required number of witnesses varies. The attestation clause (see section 9.9 in Chapter 9) to a will recites that the will was witnessed at the request of the testator and that it was signed by him or her in the presence of the witnesses, who subscribed their names in the presence of the testator and in the presence of each other. Holographic wills are seldom witnessed. In states that provide for it, a self-proving acknowledgement is added.

11.23. Preparing a Will

Many wills are short, but some are very long and involved, ranging from ten to fifty or more pages. With a word processor, the preparation should cause no difficulty. Copy should begin and end at the same point on every page, except the last one, and yet there must be continuity from page to page, which means that no page should end with a paragraph or sentence. The purpose of the continuity is to avoid the omission, or the possible insertion, of a page. Some lawyers even require that the last word on each page be hyphenated. The placement of the signature with reference to the testimonium and attestation clauses is of prime importance in a will. Page numbers are placed at the bottom of pages and often indicate the total number of pages in the document: Page 2 of 4. (See item 8 in section 11.29.) See Figures 11.2 (p. 234) and 11.3 (p. 238) for examples of the first and last pages of a will.

If you are asked to copy lines from another source, watch for differences between the will you are preparing and the form you are following, such as a change from singular to plural or from his to her.

made in this will and including any property over which I have a power of

appointment, hereby defined as my residuary estate, I give, devise and

bequeath to my daughter, JANE, her heirs and assigns forever.

IN WITNESS WHEREOF, I have signed my name at the end of this

my Last Will and Testament and affixed my seal this   day of May, 19—.

_____ [L.S.]

The foregoing instrument, consisting of ten typewritten
pages, including this page, was signed, published and
declared by DAVID C. BRAUN to be his Last Will and
Testament in the presence of us, who, at his request, in his
presence and in the presence of each other, have subscribed
our names as witnesses.

_____ of _____

_____ of _____

_____ of _____

(Number page in center, one-half inch from bottom.)

Figure 11.3.   Last Page of Will.

11.24. Signature Page and Preceding Page of a Will

The placement of the signature often presents a problem. Good
practice makes the solution obligatory in some respects, permissible in
others.

It is obligatory that at least one line of the testimonium clause be on
the same page as part of the will (see Figure 11.4). In other words, a new
page cannot begin with the testimonium clause, because this arrangement
would increase the possibility of the loss of a page, or permit the insertion
of a page without detection.

IN WITNESS WHEREOF, I have signed my name at the

—8—

Figure 11.4. One Line of Testimonium Clause on
Page with Part of Text of Will.

It is obligatory that at least one line of the attestation clause be on the
page with the signature (see Figure 11.5). The purpose of this requirement
is to tie in the witnesses' signatures with that of the testator.

IN WITNESS WHEREOF, I have signed my name at the
foot and end of this My Last Will and Testament and affixed
my seal this   day of May, 19—.

_____ [L.S.]

Signed, sealed, published and declared by the said

—9—

Figure 11.5. One Line of Attestation Clause on Page
with Signature.

The most desirable setup of the signature page is to have at least three lines of text on the page with the testimonium clause, the signature, and the attestation clause and witnesses' signatures (see Figure 11.3). It is permissible, though not desirable, to have the signature and attestation clause on a page containing only one line of the testimonium clause.

11.25. How to Gauge and Test the Page Length

Unless a will is very short and simple, a draft, triple-spaced, is always printed out so that the final copy can be manually paged. With a word processor, adjustments can be made quickly and easily.

11.26. Witnessing a Will

When a will is drawn up and executed in your office, you will probably be asked to witness it. The procedure of witnessing a will is somewhat formal. The general practice is for the testator to "publish" the will in the presence of the witnesses by declaring that the document is his or her will. The testator also asks the witnesses to witness the signing of it. The testator not only signs the will but signs or initials the left margin of the other pages. Each witness signs in the presence of the testator and of each other, and no one leaves the room while the will is being signed, witnessed, and acknowledged. You will notice from Figure 11.3 that space for the address of the witness is provided. The address is important because the witness will be called upon to prove the will after the testator's death, unless it is a self-proving will. For a will to be self-proving, and thereby admitted to probate without testimony of any witnesses, the final page should be in affidavit form. Statutes usually specify the form required.

11.27. Copies of Wills

It was previously customary in many law offices for the secretary to certify the copies of a will. This certification was not for the purpose of the formal affidavit required when the will is probated (see Chapter 19) but for authentication of the copies. Today, a secretary would make photocopies of the executed will and mark the copies as such or would copy the will on paper with the word COPY already printed on it.

11.28. Capitalization and Punctuation

You will notice from Figure 11.2 that all names are written in solid caps. The words *Last Will and Testament* are capitalized in the will and in the attestation clause. In the phrases *make, publish and declare* and *give, devise and bequeath,* no comma precedes the conjunction *and.* Many lawyers prefer that *executor* and *trustee* be capitalized. You will notice from Figure 11.3 that the words *IN WITNESS WHEREOF* are written in solid caps and are followed by a comma. These arrangements are arbitrary but are followed extensively in law offices that give considerable attention to these details.

11.29. "Do's and Don'ts" in Preparing a Will

Unless instructed otherwise, follow these directions when preparing a will.

1. Print out a draft unless the will is only a few pages.
2. Make an original and two copies of the final version, the original and one copy for the testator and the other copy for your files. (If a bank or other institution is named executor, ask if an extra copy is to be made for it.)
3. Use a very good quality, letter-sized bond paper.
4. Place the responsibility line at the top of the office copy only. (See section 10.8 in Chapter 10.)
5. Double-space, except the attestation clause.
6. Print out the same number of lines on each page.
7. Number each page about one-half inch from the bottom of the page.
8. In pagination, indicate the total number of pages (Page 2 of 4) or precede and follow the page number with a hyphen (-2-).
9. Triple-space between the text of the will and the testimonium clause.
10. Single-space the attestation clause. Indent it about three spaces from the regular left margin, indenting the first line about five spaces or one-half inch. Run the attestation clause all the way over to the right ruled margin of the paper.

11. Start the first witness line three line spaces below the attestation clause, at the left margin, and underscore for 25 spaces; then type "residing at" and underscore for another 25 spaces.

12. Triple-space between the witness lines.

13. Collate.

14. Check and double-check spelling of names.

15. Endorse the back, if used, as shown in Figure 11.6.

16. If real estate devised by the will is described, have someone compare the description with you.

17. Bind firmly and securely.

18. Have the will signed and witnessed.

19. Conform copies to original. (See section 10.18 in Chapter 10.)

20. Copy the will as described in section 11.27.

21. If your office is to retain the original of the will for safekeeping, give the testator a receipt, signed in the firm's name by one of the lawyers or yourself, reading as follows: "The will of   , dated   , is in our possession for safekeeping."

22. Enclose the original in an envelope marked "Last Will and Testament of   , dated   ."

23. If an institution is named executor, forward a conformed copy with covering letter.

24. If a copy of a former will by the testator is in your file, note on it that a later will, of a certain date, has been executed.

11.30. Codicil

After making a will, a testator might decide to delete, add, or change certain provisions. He or she does this by means of a codicil, which is a supplement to the will. A codicil is written and executed with the same formality as the will. It is not attached to the will but rather should be placed in a separate envelope marked "Codicil to Last Will and Testament of   , dated   ." A testator may make more than one codicil.

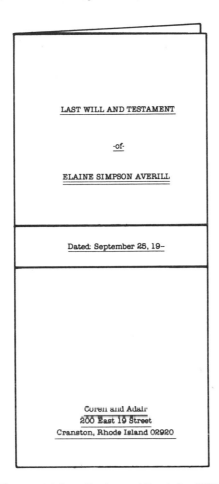

Figure 11.6.   Endorsed Back for Will.

11.31. Red-Inking a Will

Although the procedure is not common, some attorneys like to *red-ink* a will. The usual method of red-inking is as follows:

1. Draw *double* red lines (a) under the name of the testator in the introductory paragraph and on the cover, (b) under each article number, and (c) under "IN WITNESS WHEREOF."

2. Draw *single* red lines (a) under each name appearing in the will, (b) under "Executor" and "Trustee," and (c) under everything

appearing on the cover, including the engraved name of the law firm but excepting the name of the testator, which has double lines under it.

Part 3

PREPARING COURT PAPERS

12. Understanding Courts and Their Functions

13. Handling Court Papers

14. How to Prepare Court Papers

15. How to Handle Records on Appeal, Briefs, and Citations

12 Understanding Courts and Their Functions

A large part of the work in a law office concerns the functions of the court. Therefore, an understanding of the organization of courts and their functions is not only desirable but necessary.

COURT SYSTEM AND PROCEDURE

12.1. The Word "Court"

The word *court*, as it relates to the practice of law, is commonly used in these senses:

Court refers to the person or persons assembled under authority of law, at a designated place, for the administration of justice. These persons are the judge or judges, clerk, marshal, bailiff, reporter, jurors, and attorneys, and they constitute a body of the government. Thus when the lawyer's secretary states that his or her employer "is in court this morning," it means that the lawyer is appearing before this duly assembled body in the interest of a client. It is not necessary that all of these persons be present to constitute a court—court is frequently held without a jury.

Court refers to the authorized *assembly* of the persons who make up the court. Thus "Court will be held . . ." means that the judge, clerk, attorneys, and so on will gather together to administer justice. Or "Judge Smith's court . . ." means the clerk, attorneys, jurors, and so on over which Judge Smith presides.

Court refers to the judge or judges themselves, as distinguished from the counsel or jury. Thus we have the expressions "In the opinion of the Court . . . ," "May it please the Court . . . ," "The Court stated. . . ." In this sense, the word is written with a capital because it is personified when it stands for the judge.

Court is used occasionally to refer to the chamber, hall, or place where court is being held. Thus a spectator is present "at court," in the courtroom, but the defendant is "in court" because he or she is part of the assembly. Not all proceedings occur in a courthouse, however, and advances in telecommunications will further change how and where hearings take place.

Court is always included in the name of a specific court and is capitalized in an official court name: Probate Court, Essex County. Neither probate nor court is capitalized if reference is made to probate courts *generally:* "Petitions for letters of administration are filed in probate court."

12.2. Court Procedure

Court proceedings are generally conducted for and in behalf of the litigants by attorneys-at-law. It is permissible for an individual party to a lawsuit to represent himself or herself in court (a corporation usually must appear by attorney), but a layperson seldom has the required technical knowledge. Court actions consist of a series of written statements of the claims and defenses of the parties to a court action. These written statements are known professionally as *pleadings*.

In almost all states, a civil legal proceeding is commenced when the first pleading is filed with the clerk of the court by the person bringing the suit. The plaintiff—the person bringing the suit—makes a written statement in clear and concise language of the facts that caused him or her to bring the suit. The designation of this first pleading varies with the court; it might be called a *complaint,* a *declaration,* a *libel,* or a *petition.* In some states the first pleading in an equity action is designated as a *bill in equity* or a *bill of complaint.* A summons, or its equivalent, is then issued and served on the person against whom the action is brought—usually called the *defendant.* The defendant answers the summons and complaint, defending himself or herself by raising legal arguments or by denying the facts stated by the plaintiff in the complaint. When the case is finally submitted to the court for a decision, the judge decides controversies about legal points; a jury, or a judge acting in place of a jury, decides questions of fact. See Chapter 14 for pleadings that might be filed in a civil action.

12.3. What Happens in Court

Court proceedings vary in elaborateness and formality from a simple hearing in the judge's office, called *chambers,* to a full-dress jury trial. A hearing may also occur via teleconference. A common feature of all court proceedings is the dignified demeanor of all participants and the respect accorded the presiding judicial officer.

In an informal hearing in chambers, only the judge (or on occasion the special master assigned), the litigants, and their attorneys are present. In a more formal courtroom hearing, the litigants, their attorneys, and the presiding judge will be joined by the clerk of court, the court reporter, and one or more bailiffs.

If you attend a jury trial, you are likely to see the following procedure at every session of the trial. Before the judge arrives, the plaintiffs and their attorneys and the defendants and their attorneys will be present in the courtroom along with the court reporter, a bailiff, and any members of the public who want to attend. All present stand while the jury is brought into the courtroom and seated in the jury box. Everyone then rises at the order of the bailiff and remains standing until the judge has entered the courtroom and is seated behind the bench.

The clerk declares the court in session and announces the first case to come before the court at this particular session. The plaintiff, if it is a civil case, or the prosecution, if it is a criminal case, begins by making an *opening statement.* This is a brief outline of the case to be presented and the evidence expected to be brought before the court. Sometimes the defense attorney will make an opening statement immediately after that of the prosecution or plaintiff. The prosecution or the plaintiff, again depending on whether it is a criminal or civil case, then presents the evidence he or she has to support his or her side of the case. Witnesses are called and questioned in turn by the plaintiff's attorney or the prosecution as the case may be.

When the prosecution has completed the questioning of a witness, the defendant's attorney has a turn to cross-examine the same witness. When the defendant has completed cross-examination, the prosecution or plaintiff may ask further questions of the witness on what is called *redirect examination.* Redirect is limited to questioning on matters brought up on cross-examination. Occasionally, redirect examination is followed by a *recross-examination* by the defendant's attorney. Upon completion of the evidence for his or her side, the plaintiff or prosecution rests.

The same routine is followed for the defendant's *case in brief*. The attorney may make a brief opening statement and proceed to present the evidence. At the end of the defendant's evidence, the prosecution or plaintiff may present rebuttal witnesses. Evidence will be limited to matters raised by the defendant's witnesses. When both sides have completed presenting all their evidence, the attorneys present their *closing arguments* to the jury. The plaintiff or prosecution argues first. He or she reviews the evidence presented and describes to the jury in detail his or her theory of the case and reasons for believing that they should find in the plaintiff's favor. When the plaintiff has completed his or her argument, the defendant or defense attorney then presents a closing argument.

Finally, before the jury retires to deliberate on the evidence, the judge *charges* the jury. He or she describes to the jury the issues they must decide and outlines for them the law of the jurisdiction on which they must base their decision. After this, the jury retires to deliberate. They may upon occasion ask the judge for further instructions. Otherwise, the case is complete when they return with their verdict. In a criminal case, if the jury returns a guilty verdict, the judge may sentence the defendant immediately upon the return of the verdict, or he or she may defer sentencing.

12.4. Court Personnel

Various personnel are involved in court proceedings.

Judge

The *judge* is responsible for the conduct of the proceedings. Although the judge's rulings are subject to exception and appeal to a higher tribunal, they may not be actively questioned while the trial proceeds. As the evidence is presented, the judge rules on objections and makes certain limited instructions to the jury. After the evidence is completed, the judge instructs the jury about the law. If a trial is without a jury, the judge is also the finder of fact as well as the determiner of law.

Jury

The *jury* may consist of as few as 6 or as many as 12 individuals, and sometimes alternates in addition. Their function is to listen to the evidence, to make determinations of fact when testimony conflicts, and to apply the law to those determinations as instructed by the judge.

Court Reporter

The *court reporter* records verbatim every word spoken in the court-room. Even conferences at the bench between the judge and attorneys are often recorded by the court reporter at the judge's request or at the request of the attorneys. A number of methods are currently in use for reporting court proceedings. Some reporters use computer-aided transcriptions that can provide an immediate transcript as the trial proceeds. Traditional methods include the stenotype machine, conventional shorthand, a regular taperecorder, and a special type of tape recorder in which the reporter repeats each word spoken into a special kind of microphone, identifying the speaker at the same time.

Clerk of Court

The *clerk of court* is responsible for scheduling the trials and seeing that all matters in the court run smoothly. He or she is the administrative officer of the court. The clerk reads the indictment at the beginning of the trial but may have no other spoken function during the trial. He or she is responsible for seeing that the jury is cared for and that their questions are relayed to the judge while they are deliberating.

Bailiffs

The *bailiffs* are responsible for preserving order in the court, under the direction of the clerk.

Attorneys

All *attorneys* are officers of the court. An attorney is responsible for presenting the evidence in the most favorable light for his or her client. The attorney must abide by the rules of the court and defer to the ruling of the judge whether or not he or she agrees with it at the time.

Plaintiff or Prosecution

The *plaintiff* or *prosecution* initiates the lawsuit. He or she bears the burden of preparing the case and presenting the evidence to the jury to support the case.

Defendant

The *defendants* are not obligated to present any evidence. If the defendants believe the plaintiff's or prosecution's evidence is so weak that the jury cannot find in his or her favor, they may decline to present evidence on their own behalf. Ordinarily, however, defendants present evidence to show that the plaintiff's or prosecution's evidence is insufficient to support the case he or she is trying to make.

Witnesses

One or more *witnesses* may be called by either side in a lawsuit. Often witnesses are *sequestered,* that is, they are not permitted to come into the courtroom to hear testimony preceding theirs. They may testify voluntarily or they may be subpoenaed by either side. Each witness undergoes direct examination by the side that calls the witness and also cross-examination by the opposition. Some witnesses may be *expert witnesses,* hired by one side to bring testimony to the jury on matters beyond the experience of the ordinary person. Examples of people called as expert witnesses are doctors, engineers, and psychiatrists, depending on the type of case.

Plaintiffs and Defendants

Both *plaintiffs* and *defendants* are usually present during the trial of their case. They may or may not testify in their own behalf. There is no requirement that they do so. Each can assist his or her attorneys in many ways, both during preparation of the case and during the trial itself, by supplying information about people and events involved.

12.5. American Court System

The *American court system* consists of federal courts plus the various court systems of all of the states. The courts of the District of Columbia and Puerto Rico are part of the federal court system, although both are now organized along lines similar to state court systems. The Supreme Court of the United States is the highest tribunal—the apex in the hierarchy of courts, both federal and state. There is no appeal from its decisions.

State Courts

The system of *state courts* follows a fairly consistent pattern, indicated in Part 5, "Courts of Record and Judicial Courts." Each system consists of the state's highest appellate court and of courts of original jurisdiction, that is, courts where suits are initiated. States with a large volume of cases also have intermediary appellate courts to relieve the congestion of cases in the highest court. A case is brought and tried in a lower court and may be appealed to a higher court having appellate jurisdiction until it reaches the state's highest appellate court or, in some cases, the United States Supreme Court.

Under some of the state systems, the state is divided into circuits or districts with a court for each. Usually, court is held in each county seat, and the judges travel the "circuit" to the county seats to hold court. Other states have only one superior, or trial, court, which is composed of geographical divisions. The distinction is reflected in the wording of the captions on court papers. Mississippi, for example, is divided into seventeen judicial circuits, with a separate court for each. The captions on the court papers read:

IN THE CIRCUIT COURT OF THE FIRST JUDICIAL DISTRICT
OF HINDS COUNTY, MISSISSIPPI

On the other hand, there is only one superior court of Massachusetts, which is composed of divisions according to counties. The captions on the court papers read:

COMMONWEALTH OF MASSACHUSETTS
ESSEX, ss   SUPERIOR COURT

In many jurisdictions the courts are also divided into parts, for the purpose of facilitating the court's work. There is no standard principle upon which the division is based. For example, the Chancery Court of Davidson County, Tennessee, is divided into Part One and Part Two, and members of the Nashville bar can bring their suits in either part. The caption designates the part. In Kings County, New York, Part One of the Supreme Court (which is the trial court in New York State) is the part in which all cases are called when they appear on the ready day calendar (see section 12.19). The judge presiding in Part One sends cases to the different trial parts. After a case is assigned to a certain part, that part is designated in the caption.

The courts in one state have no control over, or relation to, the courts in another state—the hierarchy in each state is complete. Where they can assume jurisdiction (see below), federal district courts will apply the law of the state in which they sit in cases where federal law is not at issue. The United States Supreme Court is the final arbiter in all cases involving federal constitutional or statutory law.

Federal Courts

When the United States first adopted its Constitution, a rivalry and jealousy existed among the states that made up the Union and between the federal government and the respective state governments. The citizens of one state were fearful that they would not receive a fair verdict from a judge or jury in another state. The federal government feared that the state courts would not interpret and enforce the national laws to the best of their ability. To avoid any miscarriage of justice that might result from interstate antagonism, the Congress provided for a *federal system of courts* for the trial of cases involving federal laws and interstate commerce and, also, cases involving *diversity of citizenship*—cases brought by a citizen of one state against a citizen of another state.

The federal system of courts consists of the Supreme Court of the United States, 11 circuit courts of appeal, 90 district courts, a court of claims, a customs court, and a tax court. (See Part 5, "Courts of Record and Judicial Circuits.") The United States is divided into 11 judicial circuits—10 are comprised of several states each, and there is in addition the District of Columbia circuit.

United States District Court

The *district courts* are the trial courts of general federal jurisdiction. Each state has at least 1 district court, and some of the larger states have as many as 4. There is also a United States Small District Court in the District of Columbia. In all, there are 89 district courts in the 50 states plus one in the District of Columbia. In addition, the Commonwealth of Puerto Rico has a United States district court with jurisdiction corresponding to that of district courts in the various states.

At present each district court has from 1 to 32 federal district judgeships, depending on the amount of judicial work within its territory. Only one judge is usually required to hear and decide a case in a district court, but in some kinds of cases, three judges must be called together to comprise the court. In districts with more than one judge, the judge senior in commission who has not reached his seventieth birthday acts as the chief judge. There are in all 385 permanent district judgeships in the 50 states and 15 in the District of Columbia. There are 3 judgeships in Puerto Rico. Except in certain territories, district judges hold their offices during good behavior as provided by Article 3, Section 1, of the Constitution. Congress, however, may create temporary judgeships with the provision that when a vacancy occurs in that office, such vacancy will not be filled. Each district court has a clerk, United States attorney, a United States marshal, one or more United States magistrates, referees in bankruptcy, probation officers, and court reporters and their assistants.

Cases from the district court are reviewed by the United States Court of Appeals except that injunction orders and special three-judge courts, certain decisions holding acts of Congress unconstitutional, and certain criminal decisions may be appealed directly to the Supreme Court.

12.6. Jurisdiction

The laws of the United States provide that certain causes of action (lawsuits, cases) must be brought in one court, and others in another. The authority of a court to hear a particular cause of action and to render a binding decision is called *jurisdiction*. Without jurisdiction, a court's orders and rulings may be meaningless. To hear a case, a court must have jurisdiction *in personam* (of the person) or *in rem* (of the thing and subject matter jurisdiction).

In Personam Jurisdiction

This means that a court must have jurisdiction over the *litigants* (the person or persons bringing the suit and those defending it). For example, if the litigants live in different cities in the same county, the county court rather than a city or municipal court has jurisdiction. A New York court generally would not have jurisdiction over a citizen of Mississippi in a suit brought by a New York citizen. Foreclosure actions could be brought only in the county in which the property is located unless the Mississippi citizen is physically present and duly served with process in New York State. There are a number of exceptions to this rule, however. So-called long-arm statutes give a court jurisdiction over a citizen of another state who has done certain kinds of acts in the state where the court sits.

In Rem Jurisdiction

In rem jurisdiction means that the court must have jurisdiction over the physical property, usually real estate, in controversy.

Subject Matter Jurisdiction

Subject matter jurisdiction is an absolute prerequisite to a court's involvement in the case and is statutorily or constitutionally defined. Jurisdiction depends on several factors: nature of the case, amount involved, location of the property. A magistrate's court has jurisdiction over a traffic violation, for example, but cannot try a person for murder. A suit for damages caused by an automobile collision cannot be brought in a probate court.

Original Jurisdiction

Some courts have *original jurisdiction,* whereas others have appellate jurisdiction. Suits are commenced and tried only in courts of original jurisdiction, which are usually the lower courts. After a case has been decided in a court of original jurisdiction, it may be brought into a higher court having appellate jurisdiction for another decision. Appellate courts have original jurisdiction over some matters.

Sphere of Authority

The term *jurisdiction* is also used to refer to the *sphere* of a court's authority, as distinguished from the authority itself. Thus we might say that the jurisdiction of a district court is limited to that particular district; of a state supreme court, to that particular state. The decisions of a particular court prevail within that court's jurisdiction, although they might be in conflict with the decisions of a court in another jurisdiction—another sphere of authority.

Limitations on Jurisdiction

Limitations on the jurisdiction of each court vary too much to attempt to give more than a general summary here. Furthermore, it is the lawyer's job to know in which court a particular action should be brought. But the secretary, paralegal, and other staff should have a general understanding of jurisdictional limitations so that they will understand why a case is brought in a certain court. Any classification of courts is necessarily incomplete and, also, overlapping, but for our purpose we arbitrarily classify courts as (1) inferior, (2) superior, (3) courts of special jurisdiction, (4) courts of intermediate review, and (5) supreme appellate courts. The general jurisdiction of each class is given below.

12.7. Inferior Courts

The most common *inferior courts* are justice courts, small claims courts, and a class of courts whose jurisdiction is confined to misdemeanors and violations of city ordinances. Courts of this class are variously called police, magistrate's, municipal, district, or recorder's courts. All inferior courts have a very narrow jurisdiction. In criminal matters, they are restricted to decisions on misdemeanors or minor infractions and preliminary hearings or inquiries in felony cases. In civil actions, they have jurisdiction over actions involving small amounts only, the amount varying with the sate. In Texas, for example, small claims courts have jurisdiction over claims of $500 or less; in Indiana small claims courts have jurisdiction of claims for $2,000 or less. Inferior courts are usually courts not of record; that is, their proceedings are not recorded. Sometimes the judge of an inferior court is not a lawyer. The decisions of these courts are subject to review or correction by higher courts. Actually, circuit and district courts are "inferior" to appellate or supreme courts, but the term is usually applied to the courts of limited jurisdiction described here.

12.8. Superior Courts

The highest state courts of original jurisdiction are *superior courts*. They are usually designated as circuit, district, or superior courts. (In New York, for example, the highest court of original jurisdiction is called the supreme court.) They have original jurisdiction in the first instance and are the courts where cases outside the jurisdiction of inferior courts are tried originally. They also have appellate jurisdiction over some matters arising in inferior courts, in certain state and local administrative agencies, and, in many states, probate matters. They control or supervise the lower courts by writs of error, appeal, or certiorari.

In some states, superior courts have one or more departments or divisions that have jurisdiction over special matters. The Superior Court of New Jersey, for example, has a law division for the trial of actions at law and a chancery division for hearing equity matters; in California, a department of each superior court acts as a probate court. Other states have courts of special jurisdiction for probate matters.

12.9. Courts of Special Jurisdiction

Courts of special jurisdiction are courts of original jurisdiction over certain restricted matters. Some states have courts of special jurisdiction in some fields; other states, in other fields. The most common courts of special jurisdiction are probate courts, criminal courts, chancery courts, juvenile courts, county courts, and municipal courts in large cities.

Probate courts have jurisdiction over the probate of wills, administration of a decedent's estate, and guardianship of minors and insane people.

Criminal courts have original jurisdiction over criminal cases. Criminal trial courts may be called *oyer & terminer* (hear and determine).

Chancery courts have jurisdiction over equity or chancery matters and apply rules of chancery law. See section 12.12 for the distinction between equity and law.

Juvenile courts usually have exclusive original jurisdiction over all neglected, dependent, or delinquent children under age 18.

County courts have widely diverse jurisdiction in the different states. In Oregon, for example, they are courts of criminal jurisdiction; in Florida, they have jurisdiction over misdemeanors, over violations of city and county ordinances, and in civil actions where the amount in controversy does not exceed $2,500; in Mississippi, they have concurrent jurisdiction with circuit and chancery courts if the amount involved does not exceed $10,000.

Municipal courts in large cities are frequently courts of record and have concurrent jurisdiction with superior courts, if the amount involved does not exceed a stated sum, usually not more than $3,000.

Family courts exist in several states. Their jurisdiction varies, but typically, proceedings deal with child abuse and neglect, child support, paternity establishment, permanent termination of custody by reason of permanent neglect, juvenile delinquency, and family offenses. The family court may be a division or a department of a court of general jurisdiction.

Land courts in some states have exclusive original jurisdiction over matters pertaining to applications for registration of title to land in the state or commonwealth and foreclosure and redemption of tax titles. They have original jurisdiction over writs of entry and various petitions for clearing title to real estate and petitions regarding zoning, bylaws, and regulations.

They have original concurrent general equity jurisdiction in land questions except for questions of specific performance of contracts relative to same, and they have original jurisdiction, concurrent with the supreme, superior, and probate courts of declaratory judgment proceedings.

12.10. Courts of Intermediate Review

Courts of intermediate review are established to relieve congestion in a state's highest appellate court. They are indicated in Part 5, "Courts of Record and Judicial Circuits," by an asterisk. Some states have more than one court of intermediate review. These courts exercise appellate jurisdiction only, except that in some states they have original jurisdiction to issue writs of mandamus, certiorari, habeas corpus, and the like. They have jurisdiction of matters of appeal from the final judgments, orders, or decrees of superior courts, usually in both law and chancery matters. The appellate jurisdiction of intermediate courts is frequently restricted. The Georgia Court of Appeals, for example, which is a court of intermediate review, does not have jurisdiction over appeals involving the Georgia Constitution or the United Sates Constitution. The appellate courts of Illinois do not have jurisdiction over criminal appeals other than misdemeanors. In New Jersey and New York, divisions of the superior court exercise intermediate jurisdiction.

12.11. Supreme Appellate Courts

There is only one *supreme appellate court* in each state. These courts are courts of last resort in their respective states. (In Oklahoma, the Criminal Court of Appeals, and in Texas, the Court of Criminal Appeals, are courts of last resort in criminal cases.) The jurisdiction of these courts is appellate, their original jurisdiction, if any, being limited to the issuance of writs of mandamus, certiorari, habeas corpus, and the like.

The highest court in 46 states is designated as the *supreme court*. The designations in the four other states are as follows:

Maine and Massachusetts	Supreme Judicial Court
Maryland	Court of Appeals
New York	Court of Appeals
West Virginia	Supreme Court of Appeals

12.12. Distinction Between Equity and Law

The word *equity* means "fair dealing," and that is the purpose of the system of legal rules and procedures known as equity. Remedies at the common law in England were frequently inadequate to give the wronged party a fair deal. He would then take his case to the King's Chancellor, who tempered the strict letter of the law with fairness. As a result of this practice, chancery courts, in which equity is practiced, were established, presided over by a chancellor instead of a judge. Cases heard in equity are not tried before a jury, whether or not there is a formal separation of cases at law or in equity. A few states still have courts of chancery, as indicated in Part 5, "Courts of Record and Judicial Circuits." Other states do not separate cases in equity from cases at law but apply equity principles when appropriate. In the majority of states, equity and law are organized under a single court, which has two dockets—one in equity and one in law. The Federal Rules of Civil Procedure, which govern all federal courts, have combined the two.

Ordinarily, law actions have for their object the assessment of damages, but a court of equity goes further and attempts to right the wrong itself or to give the complainant what he or she bargained for. Among the more common equity actions are injunction suits, specific performance, partition suit, rescission of a contract, reformation of a contract, and all matters relating to trusts and trustees.

During its development, equity has established certain fundamental principles or maxims, which the lawyer frequently uses in dictating briefs. Among them are the following.

1. *He who seeks equity must do equity.* If I seek the return of property I was induced to sell through fraud, I must offer to return the purchase price.

2. *He who comes into equity must come with clean hands.* If I induce you to breach a contract and to make one with me instead and then you breach the contract with me, a court of equity will not compel specific performance of your contract with me.

3. *Equity will presume that to be done which should have been done.* If I unlawfully take possession of your cow, a calf from that cow will belong to you, because a court of equity will presume that I was holding the cow for you.

4. *Equity aids the vigilant, not those who slumber on their rights.* Where the statute of limitations (see Part 5, "Statutes of Limitations in Number of Years") has not run out, but a claimant has delayed unreasonably in bringing suit, a court of equity may bar the claim by reason of such delay.

5. *Equity follows the law.* Except where the common law is clearly inadequate, equity follows the precedents of the common law and the provisions of the statutes. Thus if a deed is void by common law or statute, the mere fact that a holder has given valuable consideration for it will not make the deed valid in equity.

6. *Equity regards substance rather than form.* Common law is normally governed by legal form. Corporations, for example, are regarded in law as artificial beings, separate from their stockholders, directors, and officers. To accomplish justice, equity may disregard the corporate fiction and examine the substance of the dispute. For example, several men sold out a fish business and agreed not to go into the fish business in the same locality. They immediately formed a corporation to carry on a fish business in competition with the purchaser. The court ignored the corporate entity and granted an injunction against the violation of the agreement not to compete.

Equity is a superior and more powerful remedy than *law* since it provides extraordinary relief in the form of injunctions, mandamus, and so on. But it is not a remedy that is available to everyone. Two showings are commonly required: (1) that the seeker has no available remedy at law and (2) that immediate or irreparable harm will result unless equitable relief is granted.

12.13. Judges and Justices

Insofar as power, authority, and duty are concerned, there is no distinction between a *judge* and a *justice*. The statutes in each state specify whether the members of each court in that state will be designated as judges or justices. In the majority of states, the members of the highest appellate courts are called justices, whereas the members of the trial courts are judges. Part 5, "Courts of Record and Judicial Circuits," shows the technical designation of the members of each court listed there.

The lawyer often prepares orders and decrees for the court's approval. It is important, therefore, for you to know whether the technically correct designation of the court is judge or justice, because these papers always contain the court's title, either in the heading or in the signature. Almost all of them commence with a heading similar to the following:

Present:
> HONORABLE DAVID M. WILSON,
>> Justice.

Present:
> HONORABLE MARGARET R. MADISON,
>> United States District Judge.

See Chapter 14 for an explanation of orders and decrees and Figures 14.21, 14.22, and 14.23 for approved styles of setting them up.

It is also important for you to know whether a member of a court is a judge or a justice when writing and speaking to or about him or her. Part 5, "Forms of Address," gives the correct forms of address, salutation, and complimentary close in letters to judges, justices, and clerks of courts.

12.14. The Trial Lawyer

As with many professions, the legal profession is becoming increasingly specialized. In some countries, notably England, the legal profession is divided into two distinct categories: *barristers*, who actually try cases in court, and *solicitors*, who attend to other legal matters for their clients. In this country, we have no such formal separation. Many lawyers, however, do no trial work whereas others engage in litigation almost exclusively. Trial lawyers may further specialize in criminal or civil cases.

The secretary and paralegal who work with a trial lawyer will have closer contacts with the court than those who work with attorneys who do not engage in active litigation. Whether a trial lawyer is involved chiefly in civil or criminal cases, the paralegal in particular may be involved in factual investigation, interviewing of witnesses, and preparation of certain documents for trial. The secretary to a trial lawyer will be required to keep track of the status of the case, at every stage, and to help the lawyer prepare for trial in whatever way the attorney directs.

12.15. Clerk of the Court

The secretary's and paralegal's contacts with the court are chiefly through the *clerk*. Almost all correspondence is addressed to the clerk (see the chart in Part 5 for the correct form of addressing clerks of courts); the clerk answers inquiries, written or telephoned, about pending court cases, court rules, the calendar, and any other matters pertaining to his or her office. The clerk of a court and the personnel in the clerk's office can be of considerable help to a secretary or paralegal. It is frequently necessary to look up something in the records of the clerk's office or to telephone for information regarding a case. It behooves both secretary and paralegal to maintain cordial relations with the personnel in the clerk's office at all times.

Although the systems of keeping records in clerks' offices vary in detail because of statutory requirements and custom, they are similar in format. A brief example of one way that these records are kept in the state(s) in which a firm regularly practices will contribute to the ability of all law-office personnel to deal effectively with the clerk's office.

12.16. Clerk's Index System

The clerk receives all court papers—complaints, answers, amendments, motions, appearances, and the like. As soon as the summons and complaint, or other first pleading, is filed, the clerk assigns an *index number,* also called a *docket number* and an *action number,* to the case. The numbers are consecutive. In some courts, an initial is used to indicate the court in which the case is filed, for example, *S* for Superior, *C* for Circuit, *P* for Probate. In courts that have separate law and equity divisions, the letter *L* or the letter *E* will be a part of the index number. In some courts, the successive numbering of cases starts over at the beginning of each year, and the number includes the year. Thus the index number might read 80S-1328, or 1328/80, or 1328-1980, indicating that the case was filed in 1980. When a clerk uses this system of numbering, the year is as important as any part of the number. The clerk keeps a cross-index of the cases, arranged alphabetically according to the name of the plaintiff and, also, in some courts, a cross-index arranged according to the name of the defendant.

How to Use the Index or Docket Number

If you file the first pleading, get the index number from the clerk of the court or from the clerk's records so that you can enter it in your office file. If an attorney in your office files the paper, he or she should get the number and give it to you; otherwise, ask for it. To find an index number in the clerk's records, look in the plaintiff's index under his or her name. You should procure the index number as soon as possible after it is assigned to a case.

After an index or docket number is assigned to a case, you *must* include that number on all papers thereafter prepared in the case in that court. Before filing a paper or giving it to an attorney to file, check to see that the proper index number is endorsed on it.

Finally you must have the index number in order to get information about the status of a case.

12.17. Clerk's Permanent Record

Some courts keep a record with the contents of all case files; others list the contents in the front of a file folder, sequentially by the date filed. A permanent record kept by the clerk of the court is usually called the *docket* or the *register*. It contains a record of all legal papers filed in the suit. The cases are entered consecutively according to index number, a case to a page. The clerk enters on the docket sheet the index number, the title of the case, the names and addresses of the attorneys, and the date the summons was served. He or she also enters on the docket sheet all subsequent proceedings.

How to Use the Register

Although the lawyer keeps his or her own record of the information in the clerk's register, it is sometimes necessary to consult the register to check on dates that papers were filed by opposing counsel. Besides, an attorney is frequently interested in the developments in a case in which he or she is not representing any of the litigants. The lawyer is usually interested in knowing the status of cases immediately preceding his or hers on the court calendar, to judge when his or her case will be reached.

If you want information on any case in court, look in the alphabetical index under the plaintiff's name and get the index number, unless you already have the number. Then turn to that page number in the docket and read the entries made there. If you want to read the original papers on file, give the clerk the index number and ask him or her to get them for you.

12.18. Clerk's Minute Books

The clerk maintains abstracts of all court orders, sometimes in a *minute book,* numerically according to index number. He or she might have separate books for law, chancery, divorce, and the like.

How to Use the Minute Book

If you want any information about the court's orders in a case, you can get it by consulting the court's records. You must have the index number to do this. Usually, the clerk's office will give you the information over the telephone.

12.19. Court Calendar and Calendar Number

The *court calendar* is a list of cases that are ready to be brought to the attention of the court. When Notice of Trial, or Note of Issue, is filed (see sections 14.17-14.21 in Chapter 14), the clerk of the court assigns the case a *calendar number* and places it on the general court calendar. Successive numbers are given to successive cases. The purpose of the calendar number is to have the case come up for trial in its turn. Do not confuse it with the index number, which will continue to appear on papers prepared for the case. After the clerk gives a case a calendar number, it must await its turn to be called for trial in numerical order. From the cases on the general calendar, the clerk prepares a list of cases for the court to hear each day. The cases on the list are "called" before the court on a certain date.

12.20. Calendar Call

Courts may or may not use a traditional "call" of cases. If it is used, such a list of cases to be called before the court is referred to as the *daily call* in courts in which cases are called daily and as the *weekly call* in courts in which cases are called weekly. The lists may be published in the local law journal, so the lawyers will know when their cases are to be called before the court. Lists also may be distributed to law offices by the clerk's office. Both sides are supposed to be in court when the case is called. If the plaintiff responds and the defendant does not appear, there will be a judgment or decree by default. If the defendant is ready and the plaintiff does not appear, the case will be dismissed for want of prosecution (DWP).

Answering the Calendar Call

In some offices the secretary or paralegal answers the calendar call to save the lawyer's time. The cases will be called by calendar number and by title. When your case is called, answer "Ready"; or when the lawyer is trying a case in another court, "Ready subject to engagement." Then explain to the court that the lawyer is trying a case in another court but will be available at a later hour. The lawyer will not send you to answer the calendar call if he or she is not ready and must ask for an adjournment. If the case has been settled out of court, you will answer "Settled."

After all of the cases on the list are called, they are called for trial in turn. There is no need, however, for the lawyer to sit through the trial of other cases. You, or whoever is answering the call for the lawyer, may wait in the courtroom until a reasonable time before the lawyer's case is about to be reached for trial and then telephone him or her to come to court to try the case. But despite the best efforts of lawyers and judges, it is impossible to forecast accurately the length of any given trial. Cases may settle at any time even after the trial has begun, or the trial may be prolonged beyond anyone's expectations. Cases that are not reached (that are not heard because the cases ahead of them run longer than expected) may be "bumped" or rescheduled to another list several weeks or even months later.

Pretrial Conference or Stipulation

Some courts have dispensed with the traditional call of the list in favor of the *pretrial conference* or *pretrial stipulation*. In a pretrial conference, counsel for the parties meet with a judge or in some cases the court clerk to determine the exact issues to be decided, the probable length of trial, whether the judge or jury will take a view of the locus (of an accident, for example), and so forth. Before or sometimes in place of a pretrial conference, lawyers may exchange a pretrial stipulation that informs the court about the number of witnesses, length of trial, issues to be determined, requirements for a view, and so on. When the traditional call of the list is not used, court clerks notify attorneys of trial assignment dates by mail.

12.21. Term of Court

The designated period prescribed by law during which a court may sit to transact business is known as a *term of court* or *term time*. The periods during the term when the court actually sits are known as *sessions*. The terms are usually designated by the time they commence, for example, *November term*. A term of court is also referred to in various jurisdictions as *general term* or *trial term,* meaning the term during which cases are tried.

PROGRESS RECORDS

12.22. How to Keep a Progress Record of Court Matters

In every law office a record is kept of the progress of all matters with which it is concerned that are pending in court, whether the matter is a litigated case, a foreclosure, an estate administration proceeding, or a special proceeding. This record saves time that would be required to examine all of the papers in the file. A quick examination of the record shows the status of the matter. Also, just before term time the lawyer can quickly examine the records of all pending cases as a double-check on things to be done. The record is variously called a *suit register,* a *register of actions,* or a *docket,* but the objectives and procedure are the same. The following sections explain the procedure for keeping this record and refer to it, for convenience, as the suit register.

12.23. Physical Features of a Suit Register

The progress record of an action may be prepared on printed forms designed for the purpose or on plain paper. The form used depends on where the records are kept. The records are commonly computerized but may be kept in a looseleaf binder, the client's file folder, or a portable tray or cabinet.

Malpractice insurance carriers require detailed systems and backup systems for keeping track of matters in court. Firms with extensive litigation practice keep suit registers or docket control information by computer. They may also use a large wall calendar and individual lawyers' diaries as well as the file itself.

A progress record kept in the client's file may be maintained either by writing the entries on the folder itself or by typing them on a sheet placed in the front of the folder. If the record is kept on a loose sheet, colored paper is desirable because it is more easily distinguished from the other papers in the file folder. Figure 12.1 on page 268 illustrates a sheet appropriate for maintaining a record in the client's file folder.

COURT_____	HALL and DOBB	OFFICE NAME_____
DOCKET NO._____	10 SLATE STREET BOSTON, MASS. 02178	OUR FILE NO._____
SERVICES		ATTACHMENTS
	VS.	

DATE OF WRIT_____
RESPONSIBLE ATTY._____   RETURN DAY_____
ATTY. TO BE NOTIFIED_____   FORM OF ACTION_____
PLAINTIFFS ATTY._____   AD DAMNUM_____
DEFENDENT ATTY._____   NATURE OF CASE_____
TRUSTEE ATTY._____

COPY WITHIN	DATE FILED	DESCRIPTION	TRIAL LIST

Figure 12.1. Progress Record Sheet.

12.24. When and How to Open a Case in the Suit Register

A suit register sheet is not opened on every matter in the office—only on court matters. Therefore, the record is opened when the first paper is filed in court or when a paper is served on your office, indicating that the case is pending in court. In opening the record, enter (1) the court in which the action is pending; (2) the full title of the case, as it appears on the summons and complaint or other first paper filed; (3) nature of the proceeding, that is, "Suit on note," "Divorce," "Petition for letters of administration," and the like, as indicated by the new matter slip (see Chapter 2); (4) amount demanded, if any; (5) names, addresses, and telephone numbers of all opposing counsel; (6) name of the attorney in your office who is handling the matter; (7) court index number as soon as available; and (8) calendar number, as soon as available.

All of the above information is put at the top, and the entries follow. Each entry is dated at the left side of the sheet. Figure 12.2 on pages 270 and 271 illustrates a suit register record.

12.25. What to Enter

Some offices record only court papers and orders in a suit register. The office record is then actually a duplicate of the court docket kept by the clerk of the court; hence, the name "office docket." Many offices enter all written, formal steps in connection with an action. It is often a matter of practice and judgment as to what to enter. Obviously, you would not enter "Received phone call from plaintiff's attorney asking when we thought case would be reached; told him we had no definite estimate." That does not affect the progress of the case. But, also obviously, you would enter "Filed motion for particulars on _____" when the motion was filed with the court and served on the opposing counsel. The best rule is to use your own judgment as to what actually affects the progress of the action and to enter too much rather than too little. If you are in doubt about the advisability of making an entry, ask the lawyer in charge.

12.26. Form and Sufficiency of Record

In making entries in the suit register give complete information. Describe the matter entered with particularity, but not in great detail. Observance of the following directions will help you make complete and accurate entries:

1. Date all entries.
2. Avoid abbreviations.

SUPREME COURT—NEW YORK COUNTY

INDEX NO. 19000-19—

ATLANTIC CORPORATION,

Plaintiff,

-against-

JACKSON MILLS CORPORATION,

Defendant.

ACTION FOR $250,000 FOR BREACH OF CONTRACT FOR FAILURE
TO COMPLETE DELIVERY OF JEEPS AND TRUCKS PURSUANT TO
TERMS OF WRITTEN AGREEMENT DATED MAY 26, 19—.

John Barnes, Esq.,
Attorney for Plaintiff,
211 E/W 76th Street
New York, N.Y. 10019

Baker & Bookman,
Attorneys for Defendant
Partner in Charge: Mr. Hill
Principal Assistant: Ms. Jones

19—		
July	13	Summons and verified complaint served on defendant.
August	1	Obtained stipulation extending defendant's time to answer or move with respect to complaint to and including August 21, 19—.
	21	Served verified answer to complaint on attorney for plaintiff and obtained "copy received."
	21	Served demand for a verified bill of particulars.
	31	Signed stipulation extending plaintiff's time to serve on a verified bill of particulars to and including September 20, 19—.
Sept.	19	Gave "copy received" on plaintiff's verified bill of particulars.
	20	Served note of issue noticing this case for trial for the October 19— Term to be tried by Court with a jury on attorney for plaintiff and obtained "copy received"; filed original with County Clerk of New York County and obtained Index No. 19000-19—; filed copy with Trial Term Calendar Clerk, and obtained Jury Contract Calendar No. 17000.
Oct.	6	Ms. Jones attended on call of Contract Jury Reserve Calendar and this case was adjourned by consent to the Reserve Calendar of the Contract Jury Calendar for the November 19— Term.
Nov.	10	Ms. Jones attended on call of Contract Jury Reserve Calendar and this case was adjourned by consent to the Reserve Calendar of the Contract Jury Calendar for the February 19— Term.

(continued)

Figure 12.2. Suit Register Record.

(continued)

19–		
Feb.	9	Mr. Barnes attended on call of Contract Jury Reserve Calendar and requested the Court to set this case down for a day certain because two important witnesses must come from Japan; the Court marked this case for the head of the Reedy Day Calendar for trial on March 5, 19–.
March	5	Mr. Barnes attended on call of Day Calendar and this case was assigned to Mr. Justice Carter, at Trial Term, Part X.
	5	Mr. Barnes reports that a jury was picked and the trial commenced at 2:00 P.M. and is to continue on March 6, 19– at 10:00 A.M.
	6	Mr. Barnes reports that the trial went on all day and is to continue on March 7, 19–.
	7	Mr. Barnes reports that plaintiff rested, Court reserved decision on motions to dismiss and defendant's case was commenced to be continued on March 8, 19–.
	8	Mr. Barnes reports that defendant rested, the usual motions for a directed verdict were made and decision reserved, both sides summed up to the jury and the Court is to charge the jury on March 9, 19– at 10:00 A.M.
	9	Mr. Barnes reports that after the Court's charge, the jury retired, and after four hours deliberation returned a verdict in favor of defendant, the Court denied plaintiff's motions to set the verdict aside and for a new trial, etc.
	12	Entered judgment dismissing plaintiff's complaint with costs as taxed in the sum of $435.00.
	12	Served judgment with notice of entry and copy of bill of costs as taxed on attorney for plaintiff and obtained "copy received"
April	17	Plaintiff paid judgment for costs as taxed amounting to $435.00 and we filed a satisfaction of said judgment.

Figure 12.2. Suit Register Record. *(cont.)*

271

3. When an action is commenced by the service of a summons only, open the record immediately, but you cannot enter the nature and substance of the action until the complaint is received. Enter this information opposite the title as soon as the complaint is received.

4. When an answer or notice of appearance is served on your office, enter the name of the attorney, his or her address and telephone number, and the party the attorney represents.

5. As soon as you know the court index number, enter it opposite the title. Also enter it on the index tab if you keep a record that has a visible index. As a condition precedent to proper filing, the court index or docket number must be placed on every paper that is filed. The individual who files the paper on behalf of your office must get the index number from the clerk of the court or from the court's docket and give it to you so that you can enter it on the record. Make a practice of checking the suit register weekly for any missing index numbers.

6. Keep the entries opposite the title up to date, including index number, substitutions of attorneys, changes of addresses, office file number, and the like.

7. In describing petitions, orders, and stipulations, enter a notation as to when they are verified, signed, entered, or dated, respectively, and by whom.

8. When entering stipulations, enter "Obtained stipulation . . ." if your office is granted something by it; enter "Signed stipulation . . ." if your office gives a right. If your office represented the plaintiff, for example, the entry of the stipulation illustrated in Figure 14.10 would be:

> Signed stipulation with Fenton & Jacobs, dated September 25, 19XX, extending time of Creative Classics, Inc., to answer to October 13, 19XX.

If your office represented Creative Classics, Inc., the entry would read:

> Obtained stipulation from Richards & Russell, dated September 23, 19XX, extending time to answer to October 13, 19XX.

Some stipulations, for example, a stipulation for continuance, are both "obtained" and "signed."

9. Enter the name of the attorney from your office who attends motions, calls of calendar at trials, hearings, arguments of appeals, and the like, and the disposition of the respective matters.

10. Enclose in quotation marks any entry from a law journal or similar publication with a reference to the date and page of the publication, because the date of the event is often different from the date upon which the event is announced in the publication.

11. When cases are settled out of court, enter the amounts paid, dates of payment, data concerning exchange of general releases, if any, and the like.

12. When judgment is entered, enter the amount of the judgment, the amount of costs, and payment received, if any.

13. Examine the diary (Chapter 4) each day for the day just past, to be certain that a report and entry have been made for everything listed there.

12.27. Closing the Record of a Case

When a case is closed, copy the entry from the active records to a closed file disk, if the register is computerized and your firm maintains such information on disk. Alternatively, a firm may retain paper copies only, filed alphabetically by the first-named plaintiff, the decedent in the case of an estate, or the principal corporation or individual named in a special proceedings. The court also retains its public record of the case.

13 Handling Court Papers

Pleadings and supporting papers, such as affidavits and bills of particulars, are commonly called *court papers* or *litigation papers,* as distinguished from the legal documents or instruments described in Chapter 9. Court rules require that they be set up in a particular style, and those who prepare court papers must always consult local rules and practice.

An understanding of the various parties that may become involved in a legal action and their designations is essential to the preparation of a court paper. An explanation concerning the parties, therefore, is given first in this chapter. General instructions applicable to the preparation of all court papers follow. Detailed instructions for the preparation of specific papers are given in subsequent chapters.

PARTIES TO AN ACTION

13.1. Party Bringing or Defending a Lawsuit

The party who brings a lawsuit—the one who has a cause of action—is the *plaintiff.* He or she is the one who complains. In some states the party bringing the action is called the *petitioner* or *complainant* when the suit is an action in equity. When the action is an appeal from an administrative agency or local board, the party bringing the suit may be called the *appellant* or *petitioner.* In most states, however, especially those whose rules of procedure follow the model of the federal rules, the party who brings an action in equity is known as the *plaintiff,* just as in actions at law. The party against whom suit is brought is the *defendant.*

13.2. Parties to a Cross Action

In some cases, the defendant's interest cannot be defended properly by answering the plaintiff's complaint or by a counterclaim. An airline, for example, was the defendant in a wrongful death action. The complaint alleged that the plane was improperly designed and was not safe for its intended use. The airline claimed that if defective and hazardous conditions existed in the plane, they were caused by the failure of the airplane manufacturer to keep its guarantee that the plane would be free from defect in design.[1]

In these circumstances, under the federal rules of civil procedure, the defendant becomes a third-party plaintiff. The airline manufacturer, the party who is impled, is a third-party defendant. State rules tend to follow federal practice.

13.3. Party Intervening

The issues raised by a lawsuit may sometimes adversely affect a third party who is not initially named as a party to the litigation. The third party may request the court's permission to *intervene* by filing a "motion to intervene" or "complaint in intervention." The third party is called an *intervenor* or, in some states, a *third-party plaintiff* or *defendant,* as the case may be. While negotiations for a contract were in progress, for example, the employee who was negotiating the contract as agent for his employer suddenly quit the employer and closed the contract in his own behalf. The former employee later sued to enforce the contract. His former employer claimed that the former employee was his agent and was permitted to intervene to assert his interest in the contract. He became a party to the action as an *intervenor.*[2]

13.4. Parties on Appeal

The party who loses a lawsuit or is dissatisfied with a judgment or court order may appeal to a higher court. See Chapter 15 for designation of parties on appeal.

---

[1]Blue et al. v. United Air Lines, Inc. et al., 98 N.Y.S. (2d) 272.

[2]Patterson v. Pollock, et al., 84 N.E. (2d) 606.

13.5. Amicus Curiae

An *amicus curiae* (Latin for "friend of the court") is not, strictly, a party to the lawsuit. He or she is a person who has no inherent right to appear in the suit but is allowed to participate to protect his or her own interests. Leave to file a brief as *amicus curiae* is frequently granted to a lawyer who has another case that will be affected by the decision of the court in the pending case. An *amicus curiae* might also volunteer information for the benefit of the judge. In adoption proceedings, for example, the guardian of a child might seek permission to appear as *amicus* for the purpose of presenting evidence about which the court should be informed and that might lead the court to refuse the order of adoption. The most common *amicus* is an organization representing interests that might be affected by the appellate decision in a given case. Public interest groups, trade or business associations, and the like frequently request (and are granted) leave from the court to file *amicus* briefs.

13.6. Who May Be Parties to a Lawsuit

A party to a lawsuit may be an individual, a partnership, a corporation, or an association. A *guardian ad litem* is a person, often but not exclusively a lawyer, who represents a minor or incompetent in court proceedings. In several states a *guardian ad litem* is appointed by the court to represent the interests of children in domestic relations cases where custody is at issue.

Minors and Incompetents

An individual ordinarily sues on his or her own behalf, but minors (frequently referred to as infants) and incompetents (persons of unsound mind or habitual drunkards) are legally incapable of bringing a legal action. If the minor or incompetent has a legally appointed guardian, the suit is often brought by the guardian. Otherwise, depending on the state, a suit is brought on behalf of a minor or incompetent by his or her "next friend" or by a guardian *ad litem* appointed by the court for the special purpose of the litigation. The fact that the plaintiff sues by his or her guardian or next friend is indicated in the caption of the case and is alleged in the pleadings. If a minor or an incompetent is the defendant in a suit, he or she answers by a guardian *ad litem* or next friend. In

Louisiana a minor is represented by a *tutor* and a mentally incompetent person by a *curator*.[3]

The expressions commonly used are as follows:

WILLIAM HENDRICKS, a minor, suing by his father and next friend, ARNOLD HENDRICKS

JAMES LEWIS, guardian ad litem of WILLIAM HENDRICKS, an incompetent

JILL NEWTON, by her next friend LLOYD T. CRAFT

JEFFREY CROSS, by FRANCIS ADLER, guardian by appointment of Orphans' Court of Baltimore City

Executors, Administrators, Trustees, Personal Representatives

Often a plaintiff has a cause of action, not for a wrong against the plaintiff in his or her individual capacity but for a wrong against the plaintiff in his or her representative capacity as executor, administrator, trustee, or personal representative. The action is then brought by the plaintiff in that capacity. The capacity in which the action is brought is indicated in the caption and is stated in the introductory sentence of the pleadings. An executor sues "as executor of the last will and testament of Lynda Smith, deceased." An administrator sues "as trustee under will of Lynda Smith." Actions are also brought against, and defended by, executors, administrators, personal representatives, and trustees of estates and trusts.

Husband and Wife

In some actions if a married person sues, the spouse joins in the complaint. The caption indicates, and the first paragraph of the pleading declares, the relationship. If the husband has the cause of action, the suit is brought by John Rogers and Mary Rogers, his wife; if the wife has the cause of action, the suit is brought by Mary Rogers and John Rogers, her husband. The same practice is followed when a married person is sued. In the caption of all pleadings, except the complaint and in the endorsements on the back

---

[3]Louisiana law is based on the French Civil Code, unlike the law in all other states, which is based on English common law. The law of the Province of Quebec is also derived from the civil law, but the rest of Canada follows the common law tradition.

of a court paper (see section 13.15), the Latin phrase *ex uxor,* or *et ux.,* may be substituted for "and John Rogers, her husband."

Partnerships

When a party to an action is a partnership, that fact is indicated in the caption and declared in the first paragraph of the pleading.

Expressions similar to the following are used in the caption.

ADAM JACKSON and DAVID HAMMOND, doing business as a partnership under the name of JACKSON and HAMMOND,

KENNETH AVERY and DONALD PLANTE, d/b/a AVERY & PLANTE, a partnership

MERVIN CARSON and ANDREW BOWKER, individually and as copartners doing business under the firm name and style of BOWKERS

The stock statement in the pleading is ". . . Henry Daniels and Joseph Farnsworth are now, and at all times mentioned were, copartners, doing business under the fictitious firm name and style of Daniels-Farnsworth Company, a copartnership, and have filed the certificate and published the notice as required by *(insert code or statute section).* . . ."

Corporations

When a litigant is a corporation, its corporate existence is alleged in the first paragraph of the complaint. The wording of the allegation depends on whether the corporation is a domestic corporation, incorporated in the state where suit is brought, or a foreign corporation, incorporated in a state other than that in which suit is brought.

In some states, a party's corporate existence is also indicated in the caption, as follows:

Domestic corporation
    WESTERN LOAN COMPANY, INC., a domestic corporation.

Foreign Corporation
    WESTERN LOAN COMPANY, a corporation organized and existing under and by virtue of the laws of the State of
    _____.

VERIFICATIONS

13.7. What Is a Verification?

A *verification*, which is really an affidavit, is a sworn statement by a qualified person that the allegations contained in a pleading are true. The statutes require that many pleadings and supporting papers be verified or supported by an affidavit, and some law firms follow the practice of verifying all pleadings whether or not the statute requires it. The litigation papers commonly verified are answers, petitions, and bills of particular. If a complaint if verified, the answer *must* be verified.

A verification always recites the venue and always has a jurat, or "sworn to" clause. One of the duties of a notary public is to administer the oath to a person verifying a pleading. (See section 13.11 for directions about administering the oath.) The verification is usually written on a separate page but may occur on the last page of the pleading or at least begin on the last page of it, if desired. No rule of law or court governs. Some legal backs have verifications printed on the inside, but the verifications are generally typed.

13.8. Who May Verify a Pleading?

Generally, the verification is by a party to the action, but under some conditions an agent or the attorney for a party to an action may verify a pleading. The attorney will tell you who is going to verify the pleading.

13.9. Forms of Verification

There is a special form of verification appropriate for each capacity in which the person verifying the pleading (called the *deponent* or the *affiant*) might make a verification. Figures 13.1, 13.2, 13.3, and 13.4 (pp. 280-283) illustrate verifications by an individual, an officer of a domestic corporation, an officer of a foreign corporation, and an attorney for a party to the action. They are included here to give you an understanding of the general content of a verification and to show you how one should be set up. If you use them as a pattern, get a lawyer in your office to approve the wording or provide the wording and format he or she wants you to use. You will notice that if an agent or attorney verifies, he or she states, in addition to the allegation ordinarily used:

STATE OF INDIANA

COUNTY OF KNOX

ALBERT F. MAXWELL, being duly sworn, deposes and says: That he is one of the defendants herein; that he has read the foregoing answer and knows the contents thereof, and that the same is true of his own knowledge, except as to the matters therein stated to be alleged upon information and belief, and as to those matters he believes it to be true.

_____

Sworn to before me this
21st day of June, 19--.

_____
Notary Public

My commission expires   , 19   .

Figure 13.1.   Verification of Answer by Individual.

1. The grounds of the agent's or attorney's belief as to all matters not stated upon his or her knowledge
2. Why the verification is not made by the party to the action

The last two paragraphs of a verification by an attorney or an agent change with the facts, but otherwise the wording of the verifications as indicated in these illustrations remains practically the same in every action.

The venue of the verification depends on where the verification is made.

13.10. How to Format a Verification

Observe the following points with reference to the preparation of verifications:

STATE OF MAINE   )
                   : SS.
COUNTY OF OXFORD   )

     LEONA J. CROWLEY, being duly sworn, deposes and says: That she is the treasurer of Taylor & Benson, Inc., the plaintiff in the above entitled action; that she has read the foregoing complaint and knows the contents thereof; that the same is true of her own knowledge, except as to matters therein stated to be alleged upon information and belief, and as to those matters she believes it to be true.

Given under my hand and seal this
     day of September, 19-.

                Notary Public
My commission expires   , 19   .

Figure 13.2.   Verification of Complaint by Officer of Domestic Corporation.

1. Although many secretaries leave no space between the longest line of typing and the bracketing of the venue, its appearance can be improved by leaving one or two spaces.
2. The abbreviation for scilicet (ss), if used, may be lowercase or in caps, followed by a period or by a period and a colon.
3. There are three line spaces between the venue and the body of the verification.
4. The name of the deponent is in solid caps.

STATE OF MARYLAND

COUNTY OF CHARLES

    EDGAR O. BRECKENRIDGE, being duly sworn, deposes and says:
That he is a vice president of Ferris Manufacturing Company, Inc., the
defendant in the above entitled action; that he has read the foregoing answer
and knows the contents thereof; that the same is true to his own knowledge,
except as to the matters therein stated to be alleged on information and
belief, and that as to those matters he believes it to be true.

    That this verification is made by deponent and not by defendant
because defendant is a foreign corporation organized under the laws of the
State of Delaware and deponent is an officer thereof, to wit: a vice president;
that the sources of deponent's knowledge and the grounds of his belief as to
all matters therein alleged upon information and belief consist of _____

_____

_____

                                          _____

Sworn to before me this

    day of   , 19--.

_____

My commission expires   , 19   .

Figure 13.3.   Verification of Answer by Officer of
Foreign Corporation.

    5. There are three line spaces between lines of signature and the jurat,
       which is at the left of the page.

    In Figure 13.3, the month in the jurat, as well as the day of the month,
is filled in by the notary. Whenever you prepare a paper for signature near

STATE OF KANSAS   )
                  :   ss.
COUNTY OF BARTON)

WAYNE B. BOVEY, being duly sworn, deposes and says: I am an attorney at law and a member of the firm of Castle & Yale, attorneys for the plaintiff in the above entitled action. I have read the foregoing complaint and know the contents thereof and the same is true of my own knowledge except as to the matters therein alleged to be upon information and belief, and as to those matters I believe it to be true.

This verification is made by deponent and not by plaintiff because plaintiff is a foreign corporation and none of its officers are within the City of Great Bend and County of Barton where I reside and have my offices for the transaction of business.

The sources of my information and the grounds of my belief as to all matters in said complaint stated to be alleged upon information and belief are correspondence with persons representing plaintiff and an examination of a file with reference to this account.

_____

Subscribed and sworn to before me this   day of

, 19-.

_____
                                    Notary Public

My commission expires   , 19   .

Figure 13.4.   Verification of Complaint by Attorney for Plaintiff.

the end of the month and are not certain that it will be signed before that month expires, leave the month blank, so that it will not have to be changed if the verification is not sworn to until the following month.

13.11. How to Administer the Oath to Person Verifying a Pleading

Unlike an acknowledgment of the execution of a legal instrument (Chapter 9), the verification of a pleading must be sworn to. If you are a notary in a law office, it will be your duty to administer the oath to the person verifying the pleading. The proper procedure is to stand and raise your right hand and ask the verifier to do the same. Then administer the oath in the following, or similar, words: "Do you solemnly swear that the contents of the foregoing instrument subscribed by you are the truth, the whole truth, and nothing but the truth, so help you God?" The verifier should answer "Yes" or "I do."

If the verifier's religion forbids him or her to swear, use the word *affirm* instead of *swear*. The word *affirmed* should also be substituted for *sworn to* in the jurat.

You will notice from the preceding illustrations of verifications that, unlike the case with acknowledgments (Chapter 9), the verifier signs the verification as well as the instrument that precedes it. The jurat follows the verifier's signature. As notary public, you will sign the jurat and affix your notary seal and show the date your commission expires, if required in your state.

HOW TO PREPARE COURT PAPERS

13.12. Paper

Pleadings and supporting papers are usually prepared on 8 1/2-by-11-inch paper.

13.13. Heading or Caption

All court papers have a heading, or caption, which is written on every separate document, although several documents might be bound together. The caption consists of four main parts.

Jurisdiction and Venue

Usually, the *jurisdiction,* that is, the name of the court in which the case is brought, and the *venue* are recited together in phraseology similar to this:

IN THE DISTRICT COURT WITHIN AND FOR
CLARK COUNTY, STATE OF WASHINGTON

IN THE DISTRICT COURT OF ALBANY COUNTY
WYOMING

In a few states the venue is recited separately from the jurisdiction, thus:

STATE OF ILLINOIS

                                    IN THE CIRCUIT COURT
COUNTY OF COOK   THEREOF

The Title of the Case

This gives the names and designations of the various parties to the action (see sections 13.1-13.6). The heading that appears on the summons and complaint is used throughout the action until it is appealed, unless (1) there should be a change of parties by amendment or (2) there is more than one plaintiff or defendant. In the latter case, it is necessary to show only the first-named plaintiff and the first-named defendant, followed by appropriate words indicating that there are others, such as *et al., et ux.,* or *et vir.*

The Index Number

The index, docket, or action number is assigned by the clerk of the court (see section 12.16 in Chapter 12). Although it is not known at the time the first paper is filed in court, it must be included on all later papers.

Title of the Pleading

Each litigation paper has a designation or title, such as Petition, Complaint, or Motion for_____. The common practice is to include the title in the heading or just beneath it. But all offices do not follow this practice.

13.14. How to Prepare the Caption

Court rules specify the information that goes into the caption, but only a few courts regulate the style in which the caption must be typed. A few examples of caption styles are illustrated in Figure 13.5 on pages 286-289. But it is important to examine the rules of court and forms set forth in

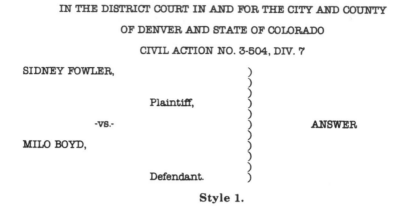

IN THE DISTRICT COURT IN AND FOR THE CITY AND COUNTY

OF DENVER AND STATE OF COLORADO

CIVIL ACTION NO. 3-504, DIV. 7

SIDNEY FOWLER,

　　　　　Plaintiff,

　　　　　　-vs.-　　　　　　　　　　　　　　ANSWER

MILO BOYD,

　　　　　Defendant.

Style 1.

Figure 13.5.　　Examples of Caption Styles.

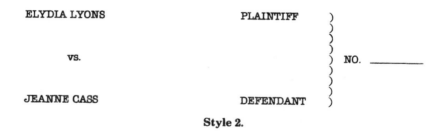

IN THE CIRCUIT COURT OF THE FIRST JUDICIAL DISTRICT

OF HINDS COUNTY, MISSISSIPPI

ELYDIA LYONS　　　　　　　　　　　PLAINTIFF

　　　　vs.　　　　　　　　　　　　　　　　　　NO. _____

JEANNE CASS　　　　　　　　　　　DEFENDANT

Style 2.

Figure 13.5.　　Examples of Caption Styles. *(cont.)*

practice manuals for your particular jurisdiction to determine how a pleading should be styled. Ask the lawyer to designate the style he or she wants
you to follow.

　　1. Note carefully the capitalization, punctuation, alignment, and
　　　　spacing.

Figure 13.5.   Examples of Caption Styles. *(cont.)*

2. Notice the placement of each part of the caption with reference to the other parts. For example, in style 3 the title of the document follows the caption whereas in other styles the title of the document may be typed at the right of the title of the case.

13.15. Captions on Papers Filed in Federal District Court

It is mandatory that the caption on all papers filed in federal district courts set forth the name of the court, the title of the case, the file number,

STATE OF WISCONSIN   :   CIRCUIT COURT   :   MILWAUKEE COUNTY

OTTO F. NORTHUP,

                              Plaintiff

                    vs.   COMPLAINT

JULIA ROCKWOOD,

                              Defendant.

Style 4.

Figure 13.5.   Examples of Caption Styles. *(cont.)*

IN THE DISTRICT COURT OF THE THIRD JUDICIAL DISTRICT OF THE
STATE OF IDAHO, IN AND FOR THE COUNTY OF ADA

```
----------------------------------------------------x
MARGOT SHIPLEY,                                     :
                                                   :
                              Plaintiff:            :        No. _____
                                                   :
                    -vs.-                           :        COMPLAINT
SUZANNE ELKRIDGE,                                  :
                                                   :
                              Defendant.            :
                                                   :
----------------------------------------------------x
```

Style 5.

Figure 13.5.   Examples of Caption Styles. *(cont.)*

SUPREME COURT OF THE STATE OF NEW YORK

COUNTY OF NEW YORK

```
-----------------------------------------------------x
                                                     :
ROSE KAPLAN,                                         :        No. .................
                                                     :
                                                     :
                Plaintiff,                           :        COMPLAINT
                                                     :
        vs.                                          :
                                                     :
ANITA ADDIS,                                         :
                                                     :
                                                     :
                Defendant.                           :
-----------------------------------------------------x
```

Style 6.

Figure 13.5.   Examples of Caption Styles. *(cont.)*

and the designation of the paper being filed. The title of the case is frequently boxed, but it is not mandatory that the caption be typed in any particular style.

13.16. Indentions

Indent paragraphs about one inch. Never block-paragraph a court paper.

The left margin of quotations and other indented material should be one-half to one inch to the right of the principal left margin; the beginning of a paragraph of indented material should be indented an additional one-half inch.

The right margin of indented material should be about one-half to one inch to the left of the principal right margin.

Spacing

The body of all court papers should be printed out double-spaced. Quotations and descriptions may be single-spaced, but many courts prefer that this material also be double-spaced.

Single-space names of parties in the caption.

Single-space the line of signature and address and, also, the name and address of opposing counsel, when it appears on the court paper.

13.17. Number of Copies

When preparing court papers, always make an original for the court, a copy for each opposing party or his or her attorney, and a copy for your file. All courts require the original; some also require an extra copy. It may be necessary to make additional copies and also duplicate originals. When this is the case, the person dictating will tell you how many copies to make. If you are in doubt as to the number of copies needed, inquire.

13.18. Numbering Pages

Number pages of court papers about one-half inch from the bottom in the center of the page or in the upper right corner.

13.19. Conforming Copies

After the original and duplicate originals are signed, conform the copies (see section 10.18 in Chapter 10).

13.20. Use of Legal Backs

Legal backs are rarely, if ever, used for court papers. (In many jurisdictions legal backs are used only for documents such as wills and deeds that will be retained for long periods. The copy, or copies, that are served on opposing counsel may also be bound, but the office copy that you keep in your file is not.) When endorsement on the back of pleadings is required, the secretary should follow local practice as set forth in court rules or state practice manuals.

13.21. Folding

Court papers may be folded into document form before they are filed in court or served on opposing counsel. Your office copy is not usually folded. In many courts, however, there is a trend away from document folding and over to flat filing, because the uselessness of folding legal papers into document form and then having to unfold them for reference is now widely realized. Therefore, the secretary should not fold court papers unless instructed to do so.

13.22. Printed Litigation Blanks

Although forms are generally stored in the computer and can easily be modified to suit a particular case, printed forms for some court papers are still available. When they are used, the same care should be taken in filling them in that is taken with all printed forms.

PRACTICE AND PROCEDURE

13.23. The Secretary's Responsibility

Masters of pleadings are usually stored in the computer, and complete documents can be retrieved by the secretary as needed. Some attorneys also have their own PCs or terminals and will draft pleadings, documents, and correspondence. When there is a centralized source of information, the lawyer may pull together the necessary pieces and customize them as required. The secretary then may be asked to correct and prepare the final draft. Generally, the secretary's responsibilities might consist of (1) keeping an accurate calendar and record of the proceedings, (2) preparing the pleadings in a professional manner, and (3) relieving the lawyer of details. The better you understand the pleadings and motions involved in a typical case, the better you will be able to assist the lawyer.

13.24. Variations in Practice and Procedure

The rules of civil practice and procedure vary in detail not only in the various states but, to a lesser extent, in various jurisdictions within a state. A fundamental variation is the requirement with respect to the service and filing of pleadings. In the majority of jurisdictions, a copy of every pleading and supporting paper must be served on opposing counsel, and the original filed in court. When a copy of the initial pleading is served with the summons, as is often the case, it is served on the defendant because there is no counsel of record at that time. Check court rules in your jurisdiction as well as state practice manuals. *Opposing counsel* refers to the counsel for each adverse party. Thus if the rules require service on opposing counsel and there is more than one adverse party, sufficient copies of the paper are prepared to permit service of a copy on counsel for each party.

14 How to Prepare Court Papers

This chapter focuses on preparing court papers under the federal rules. The secretary and paralegal can adapt the illustrations given here to other pleadings and supporting papers. Keep in mind, however, the variations in practice and procedure discussed in Chapter 13. Each jurisdiction has its own rules, which may be similar although not identical to the federal rules, and you should be familiar with the basic elements of local rules and practice. Remember also that local courts in some jurisdictions have requirements that are not statewide.

The Federal Rules of Civil Procedure, adopted by the federal courts in 1938, were designed to reduce the complexities of common law pleading. Under the federal rules, and now in most state jurisdictions, the distinction between law and equity is abolished in the pleadings, and all initial pleadings are called *complaint.* The federal rules also abolished the *demurrer,* replacing it with a less formal *motion to dismiss.* The purpose of the federal rules is to demystify the process and make it more uniform so that people moving from one jurisdiction to another can understand what is happening without being experts in the procedure of the particular court.

With a few notable exceptions, most states have adopted the Federal Rules of Civil Procedure, with some changes, for use in their own courts. Among the states that have not adopted a version of the federal rules are New York and California. The federal rules are used in all federal courts, but each federal court has some rules applicable only to its own jurisdiction. These rules differ from one district to another.

Most courts will accept filings only on 8 1/2-by-11-inch paper, and all court documents are filed flat. Legal backs are no longer used, and courts generally prefer not to have notations on the backs of papers where it is necessary to search for them. Basic formats are typically stored in the computer, along with headings, certificates of service, and stock segments of various pleadings.

The normal sequence of documents to be expected in a lawsuit is as follows:

Summons and complaint

Appearance

Answer

Motion to dismiss

Motion for more definite statement

Other motions

Objections to motions

Affidavits

Memoranda of law

Stipulations

Discovery (interrogatories, request for production of documents, notice of deposition)

Requests for findings of fact and rulings of law (for bench trials)

Jury instructions

Proposed order

SUMMONS AND COMPLAINT

14.1. Plaintiff's First Pleading

The *first pleading* by the plaintiff is a formal and methodical specification of the facts and circumstances surrounding the cause of action. It sets forth in detail the grounds upon which the plaintiff is suing the defendant and asks the court for damages or other relief. The lawyer will usually instruct you on the preparation of a complaint, except very simple ones. The phraseology for various pleadings is standard, although the lawyer must provide information on the facts and circumstances.

The plaintiff's first pleading is called the *complaint* in the majority of states; the *petition,* the *writ,* or the *declaration* in a few states. In those states where a distinction still exists between actions at law and in equity, the first pleading in equity actions is called the *bill of complaint* or *petition*. (We use the term *complaint* to refer to the first pleading regardless of the terminology in the various states.)

14.2. Analysis of a Complaint

Although complaints necessarily differ in detail, they follow a standard pattern. A complaint consists of the following parts:

1. *Caption.* The caption (see Chapter 13) to the complaint designates the court in which the action is brought and lists the full names of all plaintiffs and defendants. It does not show the clerk's index or docket number because that is not available at the time the complaint is prepared.

2. *Introduction.* The opening paragraph of the complaint simply states: "The plaintiff, by his attorney, John Jones, complaining of the defendant, alleges as follows:" or words to that effect.

3. *Identification of the parties.* This includes their addresses and legal status (for corporations or other nonhuman entities).

4. *Jurisdiction and venue.* See section 13.13 in Chapter 13.

5. *Statement of the facts.*

6. *Statement of the claim setting forth the cause of action or legal basis of the plaintiff's claim.* This may take the form of one or more *counts*. Each count usually incorporates the facts set forth in the statement of facts. A cause of action, or count, is composed of one or more *allegations*. They are statements that the plaintiff expects to prove. Complaints in certain actions must contain standard allegations, which will be incorporated in computerized forms or taken from a practice manual. For example, when a domestic corporation is the plaintiff, the allegation will allege the corporate status in a form similar to the following:

   That at all times hereinafter mentioned, the plaintiff was and still is a domestic corporation, organized and existing under and by virtue of the laws of the State of . . .

   When a corporation is the defendant, the allegation is introduced by the words "Upon information and belief . . ."

7. *Prayer for relief, or statement of the relief requested.* The prayer, or "wherefore" clause, is the final paragraph of the complaint and "demands" judgment against the defendant for a specified sum or, in equity actions, "prays" for other relief to which the plaintiff believes he or she is entitled. The language used in equity gives the prayer its name. The complaint will also demand interest if the action is for a definite amount of money owed by the defendant, as when the action is on a stated account or a promissory note.

8. *Signature.* Either the plaintiff or his or her attorney must sign the complaint. In some instances, both must sign the initial pleading. Usually, the original must be signed manually. In federal courts, pleadings must be signed by an attorney in his or her individual name, not in the firm name.

9. *Verification.* The law in the various states specifies which complaints must be verified, but some lawyers follow the practice of having all complaints verified. The verification is signed before a notary public. (See "Verifications" in Chapter 13.) In place of verification, federal and most state court rules now impose an automatic responsibility upon the signer of any pleading to ascertain first the truth and validity of any facts or claims by conducting a reasonable inquiry. The best known example is Rule 11 of the Federal Rules of Civil Procedure.

14.3. How to Prepare the Complaint

Simple forms of complaint, such as complaints in actions for goods sold or in actions on promissory notes, are often left to the secretary or paralegal to draw. Computers have eased the job considerably, since standard complaints can be easily retrieved and modified, as necessary. In addition to storing standard complaints in the computer, make an extra copy of the complaint in each kind of action for your looseleaf book of forms.

Figure 14.1 on page 296 illustrates the first page of a complaint. Follow the general directions for the preparation of litigation papers (Chapter 13). The following directions relate specifically to the preparation of a complaint:

1. Number the counts or causes of action.

2. Number the paragraphs consecutively.

3. Add a line for the signature and "Attorneys for Plaintiff" underneath it.

UNITED STATES DISTRICT COURT
FOR THE
DISTRICT OF [STATE]

. . . .   Civil Action
                                        .   No. _____
A,   .
                                        .
            Plaintiff,   .
                                        .
        v.   .
                                        .
B, C, and D   .
                                        .
            Defendants.   .
                                        .
. . . .

COMPLAINT

For their Complaint (a) seeking costs and damages pursuant to the
Comprehensive Environmental Response, Compensation and Liability Act of
1980 ("CERCLA"), as amended, 42 U.S.C. s.9601 et seq.; the [state] Oil
Spillage in Public Waters Statute RSA 146-A; the [state] Hazardous Waste
Management Program RSA 147:48 et seq. and 147-A; and the common law of
nuisance, strict liability, and negligence, (b) seeking injunctive
relief pursuant to Section 7002 (a)(1)(B) of the Resource Conservation
and Recovery Act ("RCRA"), 42 U.S.C. s.6972 (a)(1)(B), and (c) seeking a
declaration of their rights to future damages pursuant to 28 U.S.C.
s2201 and RSA 141:22, plaintiffs allege as follows:

PARTIES

1.   Plaintiff A is a corporation duly organized and existing

Figure 14.1.   Complaint.

4. Place the verification, when required, preferably on the last page of the document, or at least start it on the last page, but you may prepare it entirely on a separate sheet. There is no rule of law about this. The lawyer will tell you who is to verify the complaint.

5. Place the name, address, and telephone number of the firm representing the plaintiff after the verification (or the signature if there is no verification), if court rules so require.

6. Collate, and make an original for the court, a copy for each defendant, and a copy for your files.

14.4. Analysis of a Summons

A *summons* is not, strictly, a pleading, but it is an essential part of every lawsuit. It is the first paper that is served on the defendant, sometimes being served before the preparation of the complaint. It notifies the person named in the summons that suit has been brought against him or her and commands that person to appear in court or answer the complaint by a certain date. Although the secretary to the plaintiff's attorney prepares the summons, it is generally issued and signed by the clerk of the court.

A summons consists of the following parts:

1. *Caption.* See Chapter 13.

2. *Body.* This commands the defendant to answer the complaint within the time specified.

3. *Signature and seal of the clerk of the court.* (In New York the plaintiff's attorney issues the summons.)

14.5. How to Prepare the Summons

A printed form of summons (see Figure 14.2, p. 298) may be used unless there are numerous parties plaintiff or parties defendant.

1. If the name of a court is printed on the form, make certain that it is the court in which the action is being filed.

2. Style the caption exactly like that of the complaint. List the names of all parties in full.

3. If there are numerous parties, follow the required form instead of using a printed form. The form will be in the practice manual or

United States District Court

_____ DISTRICT OF _____

A   SUMMONS IN A CIVIL ACTION

       v.   CASE NUMBER:

B, C, and D

      TO: (Name and Address of Defendant)

     YOU ARE HEREBY SUMMONED and required to file with the Clerk of this Court and serve upon

PLAINTIFF'S ATTORNEY (name and address)

an answer to the complaint which is herewith served upon you, within _____ days after service of this summons upon you, exclusive of the day of service. If you fail to do so, judgment by default will be taken against you for the relief demanded in the complaint

                          ATTACHED:
                          Notice/Consent to Proceed
                          Before U.S. Magistrate

_____   _____
Clerk   Date

_____
Deputy Clerk

Figure 14.2.   Printed Form of Summons.

court rules and after first use should be added to your computer file.

4. Endorse the back of the original summons and of each copy, unless the summons is stapled to the complaint. The endorsements need not list all of the parties. It is sufficient to show the name of the first plaintiff and the name of the first defendant, with appropriate words indicating that there are others.

5. Make an original for the court, a copy for each defendant, and a copy for your file. An extra copy of the summons must be filed in court in those jurisdictions that require an extra copy of pleadings to be filed. In some jurisdictions, and under specified circumstances, service may be made by certified mail. The return receipt is evidence of service.

14.6. Return Day of Summons

The civil practice and procedure codes and statutes provide the date by which, or the time within which, a defendant must respond to a summons by filing a notice of appearance or an answer. The final day for the defendant's appearance is designated as the *return day* of the summons. Thus if the defendant is required to answer "within 20 days" from the service of the summons, the twentieth day is the return day. In some jurisdictions certain days, designated as *return days* or *rule days,* are set aside for filing papers in court. In these jurisdictions, the rules provide that the defendant must appear "by the next rule day"; otherwise, the defendant must appear on the following rule day. Thus the return date is always a rule day.

These return dates are very important and should always be entered in your diary and on the attorney's calendar, if that is his or her preference, whether your office is serving the summons or has received a summons for a client.

How to Compute the Time

The statutes and codes provide how the time should be computed. The usual method is to exclude the date from which the period begins to run but to include the last day of the period. If it falls on Sunday or a legal holiday, the next business day is the return date. Intermediate Sundays or holidays are included in the computation, unless the period allowed is less than seven days. The period begins to run the day the summons is served, not the day it is dated. This method of computation of time applies to the time for filing all pleadings as well as to the return day of the summons.

14.7. Alias Summons; Pluries Summons

If the original summons is not served on all of the defendants for any reason, the clerk will issue another summons, designated as an *alias summons*. It is prepared like the original summons, except that *alias* precedes *summons*. If the alias summons is not served, and it is necessary to issue a following summons, the third one is designated as a *pluries summons*.

14.8. What to Do with the Summons and Complaint

Follow this procedure with a summons and complaint:

1. Prepare the complaint and, when required, the verification.
2. Have the original complaint signed and verified, after approval by the lawyers.
3. Make the required copies.
4. Prepare the summons.
5. Attach a copy of the summons to each copy of the complaint. Place the complaint against the inside of the cover, if one is used, so that the verification printed on the inside cover will read as a continuation of the complaint. Put the summons on top of the complaint. Do not attach the original summons to the original complaint.
6. Open a case in the suit register (Chapter 12) and computerized schedule and make the appropriate entry.
7. File the original complaint in court, have the clerk of court issue (sign, seal, and date) the original summons, and pay the required fee.
8. Make a note of the index or docket number assigned by the clerk of the court and put it on all subsequent papers prepared by you in that particular case.
9. Make copies of the signed summons before delivery for service.
10. Give the original of the summons, together with a copy of the summons and a copy of the complaint for each defendant, to the

process server for service on the defendants. In some jurisdictions the copies are given to the clerk of the court at the time the original summons is issued, and he or she, in turn, delivers them to the sheriff for service. Where allowed, service may also be made by certified mail.

11. Notice that the summons has a space for the return that the process server fills in after serving the summons. In many jurisdictions the process server will complete an affidavit of service and return the summons to the plaintiff's attorney for filing with the court. In other jurisdictions the process server should get in touch with you as soon as he or she serves the summons and complaint, for the purpose of making the affidavit of service. The affidavit should be made on the same day that service is made. If the affidavit of service is on a separate sheet, it should have a regular caption, like that on the complaint, but if the affidavit is made on the back of the summons, no caption is necessary.

12. File the original summons and proof of service in court. If the summons is not filed within the time permitted by the practice rules, a new summons must be served.

13. Mark on the office copy the date service is made and by whom or photocopy the return of service for your file before filing it with the court.

14. Enter in your diary and on the lawyer's calendar, if appropriate, the return date of the summons. The period begins to run the date the summons is served, not the date it is prepared.

15. If you are employed by the lawyer for the defendant, enter in your diary and on the lawyer's calendar the return day of summons. This is very important. Failure to file an appearance by the date might mean a default judgment.

NOTICE OF APPEARANCE

14.9. Analysis of a Notice of Appearance

The defendant appears by filing a *notice of appearance* with the clerk of the court and serving a copy of it on the plaintiff's attorney. It is a statement that the defendant appears by his or her attorney. Thereafter, copies of all pleadings are served on the attorney appearing for the defendant, if service is required. In some jurisdictions the notice of appearance is addressed to the attorney for the plaintiff; in others, to the clerk of the court. Figures 14.3 and 14.4 illustrate state and federal notices of appearance.

Under the federal rules, an attorney's signature on a pleading serves as an appearance, and no separate appearance is necessary. In some jurisdictions the defendant or his or her attorney responds to a summons and complaint by filing a notice of appearance. In some jurisdictions, and in the federal rules, an answer signed by the defendant or his or her attorney and timely filing obviates the need for filing an appearance form.

14.10. How to Prepare a Notice of Appearance

Many courts have a printed appearance form that they supply to attorneys who practice in their jurisdictions. These forms should be used when they are available. Otherwise, a stock printed form may be used or the notice may be produced from a computer forms library.

1. Style the caption the same as that of the summons.
2. Add a signature line for the attorney, with his or her address underneath. When a printed form is used, place the attorney's name underneath the line for the signature so that the opposing counsel will have no difficulty in deciphering the signature.
3. Prepare an original for the court, a copy to be served on the opposing counsel, and a copy for your office file.

14.11. What to Do with the Notice of Appearance

A notice of appearance is never verified because it contains no statements of fact. Otherwise, your responsibilities with respect to the notice are the same as with respect to the answer.

THE ANSWER

14.12. Defendant's First Pleading

The modern summons contains a notice to the defendant to appear in court or to file and serve an answer to the plaintiff's complaint within a

_____ ss   THE STATE OF [NAME]   _____ Court

APPEARANCE/WITHDRAWAL

[] COURT

[] JURY   Docket No.

_____ v. _____

Of: _____   OF: _____

_____   _____

Returnable on the first Tuesday of

APPEARANCE	WITHDRAWAL
Please enter my appearance as: [] counsel for: _____ _____	Please enter my appearance as: [] counsel for: _____ _____
[] Pro se	Notice of withdrawal sent to my clients on _____ at the following address: _____ _____

I hereby certify that duplicates of this notice were:
                    [] delivered
                                    to:
                    [] mailed

_____

on _____
                    Date

    Signed _____
                    Print or type name
    Address _____
            _____
    Telephone _____

Figure 14.3.   Notice of Appearance: State.

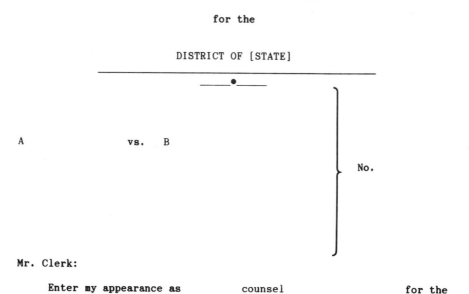

UNITED STATES DISTRICT COURT

for the

DISTRICT OF [STATE]

A   vs.   B

                                                              No.

Mr. Clerk:

        Enter my appearance as   counsel   for the
Defendant, B,

                                        in the above-entitled case.

        Dated at [city, state]
on the   day of   , 19   _____

                                        Address _____

Figure 14.4.   Notice of Appearance: Federal.

specified time. If the summons directs the defendant only to appear, he or she may do so by filing an appearance with the clerk of the court (see section 14.16). If a copy of the complaint is served with the summons, the defendant is directed to file and serve his or her answer. The filing and service of an answer by the defendant constitute his or her appearance in court. Failure to meet the established deadlines subjects the defendant to a judgment by default in favor of the plaintiff.

As soon as a client brings a summons to your office, enter in your diary and on the attorney's calendar, as appropriate, the time by which he or she must appear and answer. It is your responsibility to see that no default judgment is taken against a client of your office because of your negligence.

14.13. Analysis of an Answer

The *answer* is the defendant's formal written statement of his or her defense, signed by the defendant's attorney. It admits, denies, answers, or responds to some or all of the allegations of the complaint and sets forth the grounds of the defendant's defense. It may also set up claims the defendant has against the plaintiff as *counterclaims*.

The answer consists of the following parts:

1. Caption
2. Introduction
3. Responses to allegations of the complaint
4. Affirmative defenses
5. Counterclaims, if any
6. "Wherefore" clause; prayer, if answer contains a counterclaim
7. Signature of attorney for defendant
8. Verification if the complaint is verified

14.14. How to Prepare the Answer

The lawyer will provide the answer for the secretary, but it is the secretary's responsibility to set it up in a professional manner. Follow the style adopted by the firm or the style illustrated in Figure 14.5 on pages 306 and 307. See also Figure 14.6 (page 308).

BMM:r   4/22/--   1-2-1

IN THE CIRCUIT COURT OF THE ELEVENTH
JUDICIAL CIRCUIT OF FLORIDA, IN AND FOR
DADE COUNTY.

--x
                                                            :
GEORGE N. CARR and
HELEN R. CARR,   :   Index No. 11660-19--

              Plaintiffs,   :

       vs.   :

PRINCE DISTRIBUTING CORPORA-   :
.TION, a corporation, and CONTEM-
PORARY CLASSICS, INC., a
corporation,

                                                    :
              Defendants.
                                                    :
--x

ANSWER

The defendant Prince Distributing Corporation, answering the
amended complaint herein by his attorneys, Parker & Madison.

       1. Admits _____
_____
_____ .

       2. Denies that he has knowledge or information sufficient to form a
belief as to the allegations contained in the paragraph of the complaint
designated "SECOND."

(Continued on following page)

Figure 14.5.   Answer.

FOR A FIRST SEPARATE AND COMPLETE
DEFENSE, DEFENDANT ALLEGES:

3. On information and belief _____

_____ .

FOR A SECOND SEPARATE AND PARTIAL
DEFENSE, DEFENDANT ALLEGES:

4. _____

_____ .

FOR A DISTINCT SEPARATE AND AFFIRM-
ATIVE DEFENSE AND BY WAY OF A
COUNTERCLAIM, DEFENSE ALLEGES:

5. _____

_____ .

WHEREFORE, defendant demands that the complaint be dismissed

with costs and asks judgment in the amount _____

                                    _____
                                            John Jones, Esq.
                                            Jones & Smith
                                            100 Elm Street
                                            Greentown, Florida
                                            904-222-3333

I hereby certify that a copy of the foregoing

Answer of the Defendant has been served on _____

_____, Esq., Attorney for the Plaintiff, by

first-class mail this _____ day of _____,

19___.

                                    _____ _____

(If verification required, type on this page or on separate sheet.)

Figure 14.5.   Answer. *(cont.)*

UNITED STATES DISTRICT COURT
DISTRICT OF [STATE]

CIVIL ACTION NO. C9926304D

```
                                    )
   A                                )
                                    )
                    Plaintiff,      )
                                    )
   v.                               )
                                    )
   B, C, and D,                     )
                    Defendants.     )
                                    )
```

ANSWER, CROSSCLAIMS AND COUNTERCLAIMS OF

_____ C _____

NOW COMES THE DEFENDANT, C, and submits the following answer and crossclaims and counterclaims.

ANSWER

1. C is without knowledge or information sufficient to form a belief as to the truth of the allegations contained in paragraph 1 of the Complaint.

2. C admits the allegations contained in paragraph 2 of the Complaint.

3. C is without knowledge or information sufficient to form a belief as to the truth of the allegations that defendant B is a

Figure 14.6.   Answer, Crossclaims, and Counterclaims.

1. Use 8 1/2-by-11-inch paper or that required by the practice of the court.

2. Style the caption the same as that on the complaint, but if there are numerous parties, the title of the case may be shortened on most subsequent documents by adding *et al., et ux,* or *et vir.* However, some documents, like a judgment, will require the parties' names in full.

3. Place the index or docket number on the answer, at the right of the box.

4. Make the title of the document "Answer."

5. Number the paragraphs consecutively throughout, each response bearing the same number as the allegation. The last paragraph, which is the "wherefore" clause, is not numbered. Do not start a new series of numbers for the paragraphs in each separate defense.

6. Add a line for the signature of the attorney.

7. Verify the answer if the complaint is verified.

8. In most jurisdictions, place the attorney's name, address, and telephone number after the signature.

9. Notice that the caption differs from the caption on the complaint in that it shows the court's index or docket number.

10. Notice that the certificate of service on the plaintiff's attorney appears after the signature or on a separate sheet and must also be signed by the defendant's attorney. (See Figure 14.7, p. 310.)

11. After signatures, make an original for the court, a copy to serve on each plaintiff's attorney, and a copy for your file.

14.15. Methods of Service of Answer on Plaintiff's Attorney

Although practice may vary with the jurisdiction, the answer is generally served on the plaintiff's attorney by (1) handing the attorney a copy or leaving it at the attorney's office with his or her clerk or other person in charge of the office; (2) by mailing it to the attorney; or (3) by faxing it to the attorney, when he or she so stipulates. No regular process server is necessary in the majority of jurisdictions.

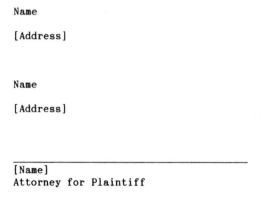

UNITED STATES DISTRICT COURT
DISTRICT OF [STATE]

A   )
)   Civil Action No.
              Plaintiff,   )   C-32-594-D
)
       v.   )
)
B   )
)
              Defendant.   )

CERTIFICATE OF SERVICE

       I hereby certify that on this   day of   1989, I have

caused a true copy of plaintiff's foregoing Motion for Summary Judgment,

together with a supporting memorandum, attachments, and Proposed Order,

to be delivered by first class mail to:

              Name

              [Address]

              Name

              [Address]

              _____
              [Name]
              Attorney for Plaintiff

Figure 14.7.   Certificate of Service

Proof of Service

The attorney on whom the answer is served, or you if you are authorized, writes on the back of the original a receipt similar to the following example.

Copy received . . . . (date). . . . .
. . . . (Firm name). . . . .
Attorneys for . . . . (name of client). . . . .

Many offices have rubber stamps for this purpose. When service is mailed, receipt is assumed.

In most jurisdictions the attorney whose office is serving the answer includes the following certificate at the end of the pleading, after the signature.

I do hereby certify that copy hereof has
been furnished to . . . .
by mail (or delivery), this . . . . day
of . . . . , 19 . . . . . .

14.16. What to Do with the Answer

Follow this procedure with an answer:

1. Prepare the answer, and verification, if required.
2. Have the answer signed, and verified, after approval by the attorney.
3. Notarize the verification.
4. See that a copy is served on the plaintiff's attorney.
5. Be sure that affidavit or certification of service is included.
6. File the original in court, with the fee, if required. (Fees for an answer are not common, unless the defendant demands a jury.)
7. Make an entry of the service and filing in the suit register and computerized schedule.
8. If you are employed by the attorney on whom the answer is served, make a notation on your copy of the date it was served; also make an entry in the suit register and computerized schedule.

9. Enter in your diary and the lawyer's calendar, if appropriate, the date by which the next action must be taken.

MOTION TO DISMISS

14.17. Analysis of a Motion to Dismiss

The function served by what used to be a *demurrer* is now served by a motion to dismiss for failure to state a case on which relief may be granted. A *motion to dismiss* is a pleading that raises an issue of law, not of fact. It objects to defects that are apparent from the pleading itself. Instead of denying facts alleged in the complaint, as an answer does, a motion to dismiss takes exception to the complaint because it is insufficient on some legal ground. For example, a defendant may move to dismiss a complaint on the ground that the plaintiff does not have legal capacity to sue. But a motion to dismiss is not a pleading to be used by the defendant only. A plaintiff may move to dismiss the defendant's answer or a cross-complaint. Each cause of action (count) or each defense is addressed separately.

A motion to dismiss consists of the following parts:

1. Caption
2. Introduction
3. Grounds of motion, each stated separately
4. Points and authorities
5. Signature of attorney with address and telephone number
6. Attorney's certificate of good faith when required
7. Certificate of service on other attorneys or parties

The statutes name the grounds for a motion to dismiss. These grounds usually include, among others, the following: (1) that the court has no jurisdiction; (2) that the plaintiff has no legal capacity to sue; (3) that the complaint (or answer) is ambiguous, unintelligible, uncertain. A motion to dismiss is supported by legal points and authorities sustaining the grounds of the motion.

14.18. How to Prepare the Motion to Dismiss

The motion to dismiss for failure to state a claim upon which relief may be granted is prepared like any other motion except that it does not require verification or an affidavit because it does not allege any facts.

Figures 14.8 and 14.9 on pages 314 and 315 are standard styles for a motion to dismiss. Figure 14.10 (page 316) illustrates the points and authorities supporting a motion.

1. Print out on the size paper specified by the court.

2. Style the caption the same as that on the complaint, but you may shorten the title of the case.

3. Place the index or docket number on the motion at the right of the box.

4. Make the title of the document "Motion to Dismiss."

5. Number the grounds for dismissal of each cause of action or count (or each defense) consecutively, beginning with 1.

6. Add a line for the attorney's signature.

7. Omit the verification because a motion to dismiss does not allege or aver facts.

8. Include the attorney's certificate of good faith in jurisdictions where it is required by the court rules. The certificate reads:

> I hereby certify that this motion is filed in good faith and not for the purpose of delay. In my opinion the grounds are well taken.
>
> _____
> Attorney for . . . .

9. Make an original for the court, a copy for the opposing party's counsel, and a copy for your file.

14.19. What to Do with the Motion to Dismiss

Follow this procedure with a motion to dismiss:

1. Prepare the motion and the points and authorities.

2. Get the attorney to sign the original and also the certificate of good faith, if required.

3. Serve a copy on the attorney for the opposing party.

IN THE SUPERIOR COURT OF THE STATE OF CALIFORNIA

IN AND FOR THE COUNTY OF LOS ANGELES

AUDREY SLOANE,	)	No. 14788
Plaintiff,	)	
vs.	)	MOTION TO DISMISS
DOUGLAS SLOANE,	)	
Defendant.	)	

Comes now the above named defendant, DOUGLAS

SLOANE, and moves to dismiss Count One of the complaint of AUDREY

SLOANE on file herein upon the following grounds and each of them:

I

That Count One of said complaint fails to state

facts sufficient to constitute a cause of action against

this defendant.

II

That Count One of said complaint fails to state

facts sufficient to constitute a cause of action against

this defendant in this, that it affirmatively appears there-

from that the purported cause or causes of action therein

set forth are barred by the provisions of §§ 339(1), 343

Figure 14.8.   Motion to Dismiss (First Page).

IV

That Count One of said complaint is ambiguous

for each of the reasons heretofore set forth for its uncer-

tainty.

V

That Count One of said complaint is unintelli-

gible for each of the reasons heretofore set forth for its

uncertainty.

COUNT TWO

Defendant demurs to Count Two of said complaint

upon the following grounds and each of them:

I

(Continue as in Count One.)

WHEREFORE, this demurring defendant prays that

this motion to dismiss be sustained without leave to amend and that

he be dismissed with his costs.

JOSEPH SCHAEFFER
Attorney for Defendant

I hereby certify that this motion to dismiss is filed

in good faith; that it is not filed for the purpose of delay,

and in my opinion the grounds are well taken.

JOSEPH SCHAEFFER
Attorney for Defendant

Figure 14.9.   Motion to dismiss (Last Page).

POINTS AND AUTHORITIES

POINT ONE

A PARENT IS NOT BOUND TO COMPENSATE THE OTHER

PARENT FOR THE VOLUNTARY SUPPORT OF HIS CHILD WITHOUT AN

AGREEMENT FOR COMPENSATION.

Civil Code § 208

POINT TWO

AS BETWEEN THE PARENTS OF MINOR CHILDREN, THEIR

RESPECTIVE OBLIGATIONS OF SUPPORT OF EACH OTHER AND TO THE

MINOR CHILDREN MUST BE DETERMINED IN THE PROCEEDING FOR

DIVORCE, AND IN THE ABSENCE OF SOME SPECIFIC PROVISION TO

THAT EFFECT, THE FATHER WHO HAS BEEN DEPRIVED OF THE

CUSTODY OF THE MINOR CHILDREN IS NOT OBLIGATED FOR THEIR

SUPPORT.

Calegaris v. Calegaris, 4 Cal. App. 264, 87 Pac. 561;

Ex Parte Miller, 109 Cal. 643, 42 Pac. 428;

Lewis v. Lewis, 174 Cal. 336, 163 Pac. 42.

Respectfully submitted,

_____

JOSEPH SCHAEFFER
Attorney for Defendant

Figure 14.10.   Points and Authorities Supporting
Motion to Dismiss.

4. See that admission of service is endorsed on the back of the original, if required.

5. File the original in court with the fee, if required.

6. Make an entry of the service and filing in the suit register and computerized docket.

7. If you are employed by the counsel on whom the motion is served, make a notation on the back of your copy of the date and hour the motion was served and an entry in the suit register and computerized schedule.

MOTION FOR MORE DEFINITE STATEMENT

14.20. Analysis of a Motion for More Definite Statement

In some jurisdictions a party to an action obtains more specific information by filing a motion for more definite statement. The procedure is like that in any other motion. The adverse party, if the court so orders, amends his or her pleading in accordance with the order. In most jurisdictions discovery (section 14.34) proceeds without court order unless a party refuses to cooperate voluntarily.

14.21. How to Use Motion for More Definite Statement

Under the federal rules the *demand for bill of particulars* was abolished, leaving the liberal *discovery* rules (section 14.34) to accomplish this purpose. In jurisdictions that retain the motion, it is used to obtain the specific details of a claim made by one party against another, especially when the claim is based on an account. (See section 14.20.) A party demands that the adverse party furnish him or her with a statement of the details, called a *bill of particulars,* within a specified time (or within the time provided by statute). He or she may ask the court for an order for the bill of particulars, in which case the procedure is like that in any other motion. The demand is addressed to the opposing counsel.

14.22. Parts of Motion for More Definite Statement

The motion consists of the following parts:

1. Caption
2. Salutation
3. Introduction
4. Details demanded
5. Dateline
6. Signature of attorney demanding the bill
7. Name and address of attorney on whom the demand is made

14.23. How to Prepare the Motion for More Definite Statement

Usually, the lawyer provides the details for the motion. Unless instructed otherwise, follow Figure 14.11 for style.

1. Use the same caption as that on the complaint; the title of the case may be shortened.
2. Number consecutively and indent the details demanded.
3. Place the dateline at the left margin, three line spaces beneath the last numbered paragraph.
4. Add a line for the signature of the attorney demanding the bill. Beneath the signature line, indicate the party he or she represents.
5. Include the name and address of the counsel to whom the demand is addressed at the left margin, several spaces beneath the signature. If the attorney's name is given in the salutation, this is not necessary.
6. Omit the verification.
7. Collate, and make an original for the court (some courts require an extra copy), a copy to serve on each opposing counsel, and a copy for your file.

14.24. What to Do with the Motion for More Definite Statement

Proceed with the motion as follows:

1. Prepare the motion.
2. Ask the attorney to sign it.

JMH:p 8/23/-- 1-2

SUPREME COURT OF THE STATE OF NEW YORK

COUNTY OF RICHMOND

```
------------------------------------------------------------------x
                                                                  :
WARREN D. CANNON and                                              :
REGINA M. CANNON,                                                 :  No. _____
                                                                  :
                                       Plaintiffs,                :
                                                                  :
                                                                  :
                    -against-                                     :
                                                                  :
MODERN DIE COMPANY, and                                           :
C & M PRESS, INC.,                                                :
                                                                  :
                                                                  :
                                       Defendants                 :
                                                                  :
------------------------------------------------------------------x
```

DEMAND FOR BILL OF PARTICULARS

SIRS:

PLEASE TAKE NOTICE that the above named defendants hereby demand that the plaintiffs serve upon the attorneys for the defendants within ten days a Bill of Particulars showing in detail the following:

(1) The date and the time of day of the occurrence as closely as the plaintiffs can fix it.

(2) Its location, identifying as closely as possible the display counters and the place on the floor between them as described in paragraph FIFTH of the complaint.

(Continued on following page)

Figure 14.11.   Demand for Bill of Particulars.

(Continued from preceding page)

      (3) A statement of the injuries and a description of those claimed to be permanent.

Dated, New York, August 23, 19--,

                                       Yours truly,

                                       JARRELL & GROSSET,
                                       Attorneys for Defendants,
                                       Box 2000,
                                       New York, N. Y. 10006

TO:

TARA & TARA,
  Attorneys for Plaintiffs,
    4700 East Drive,
      New York, N. Y. 10016

Figure 14.11. Demand for Bill of Particulars. *(cont.)*

3. See that a copy is served on the opposing counsel.

4. Be sure that a receipt or certificate of service is endorsed on the back of the original.

5. Make a diary and calendar entry of the date the motion must be served.

6. File the original in court, if required by court rules.

7. Make an entry of the service and filing in the suit register and computerized schedule.

8. If you are employed by the attorney on whom the motion is served, make a notation on the back of your copy of the date and hour of service. Enter in your diary and the attorney's calendar, if appropriate, the date by which the motion must be served. Also make an entry in the suit register and computerized schedule.

OTHER MOTIONS

14.25. Examples of Other Motions

A *motion* is an application for an order addressed to the court or to a judge by a party to a lawsuit. Whenever an attorney wants the court to take any action in a pending case, he or she "moves" the court to take that action. Motions are numerous and varied. They include:

Motion for summary judgment

Motion for change of venue

Motion to strike

Motion for new trial

Motion for leave to amend

Motion to set cause for trial

Unless a motion is made during a hearing or trial, it is in writing. The motion is always served on the opposing counsel so that he or she will have a chance to contest it.

A *motion* states the papers and proceedings upon which the motion is brought and also the grounds of the motion. The supporting papers usually include an affidavit that is attached to the notice of motion.

Some jurisdictions have special terms of court at which all motions are heard. In crowded jurisdictions the contested motions are heard in one part, and *ex parte* motions (see "Glossary of Legal Terms"), of which the opposing counsel has no notice, are heard in another part. Although *ex parte* motions are rare, and rarely granted, you should acquaint yourself with the part in which they are heard, if there is a distinction in any of the courts in your locality.

Motions based on facts require an affidavit signed by the person asserting the facts. Motions asking for a decision on a legal point require supporting memoranda of law.

Unless the motion is assented to, the party opposing the motion must file an *objection* (see Figure 14.13) within a specified time of the date when the motion is filed. Ten days is a common deadline, except for motions for summary judgment, which generally allow a longer response time. The secretary should be aware of these deadlines and see that they are properly entered in the diary and calendar. Failure to respond to a motion in a timely fashion could lead to a default or a granting of the motion without hearing.

For an example of an objection to a motion, see Figure 14.12.

14.26. Return Day of Motion

Court rules require that the opposing party respond to the motion within a given time, usually ten days. If the opposing party does not respond, the motion may be granted or decided by the court without a hearing. Motions in some jurisdictions give the date the attorney will move the court for entry of the desired order. This date is the *return day* of the motion; the motion is *returnable* on that day. The practice rules provide that the notice must be served on the opposing counsel a specified number of days, or a reasonable time, before the return day of the motion. Some jurisdictions that do not have special terms of courts for motions set aside certain days in the month as "motion day," on which day all motions are returnable. You should become familiar with (1) the motion days in the various courts and (2) how many days of notice are required.

14.27. Information You Need to Prepare the Motion

The lawyer will draft some motions, but you should be able to prepare many of them upon instructions from him or her. You will need the following information:

1. *Style of case.* The style will be stored in the computer; you can also get it from the complaint or other papers in the file.

2. *Papers and proceedings upon which the motion will be based.* The lawyer usually provides this.

3. *Grounds upon which the motion will be made.* The lawyer will provide this, except when the grounds are standard. For example, a motion to strike is always on the ground that portions of the pleadings are "sham, irrelevant and redundant." (The standard wording of the clause varies with the court.)

4. *Return day of motion.* If you do not know how to calculate the return day, in jurisdictions where this is necessary, ask the lawyer. (See section 14.26.)

JMH:p 12/15/– 2-1

IN THE CIRCUIT COURT OF THE FIRST JUDICIAL DISTRICT

OF HINDS COUNTY, MISSISSIPPI

ADAM SHALLOHE,	PLAINTIFF	)
		)
VS.		) NO. _____
		)
		)
RICHARD RAMSEY,	DEFENDANT	)

AFFIDAVIT OPPOSING MOTION

STATE OF MISSISSIPPI
COUNTY OF HINDS

GRANT F. RIGGS, being duly sworn, deposes and says: He is an
attorney and counsellor at law, associated with the firm of Messrs. Hettinger
& Pomona, attorneys for the defendant herein, and that he has knowledge of
all of the facts hereinafter set forth.

[Set forth facts here.]

WHEREFORE, your deponent prays that plaintiff's motion be denied,
with the costs of this motion.

_____

SWORN TO AND SUBSCRIBED before me, this the 15th day of
December, 19--.

_____

Figure 14.12.   Objection to Motion: supporting Affidavit.

5. *Time motion will be heard.* Usually, court practice rules set aside a certain hour at which motions will be called. If you are not familiar with this time in the various courts, ask the lawyer or consult the rules. The notice will read "at . . . o'clock in the . . . . . noon, or as soon thereafter as counsel can be heard." Motions, however, are not always heard.

6. *Where the motion will be heard.* Motions are usually heard in the court where the case is pending. In some jurisdictions specific terms, parts, departments, or divisions are set aside for motions.

7. *Name of affiant and date of supporting affidavit,* if the motion is based on an affidavit, as it usually is. The lawyer will give you this information. Probably, he or she will draft the affidavit before instructing you about the notice.

8. *A statement that the moving party has sought the concurrence of opposing counsel for the requested relief,* which concurrence has been refused.

14.28. What to Do with the Motion and Affidavit

A motion is frequently supported by an affidavit (see "Affidavit for Use in Court"), as appears from the wording of the motion. When this is the case, your responsibilities, after preparation of the motion and affidavit, are the following:

1. After approval by the lawyer, see that a copy is served on the opposing counsel.

2. See that the receipt of service is on the back of the original. If the papers are served by mail, prepare a certificate of service by mail.

3. Enter the return day of motion in your diary and on the lawyer's calendar, if appropriate.

4. File the original, with proof of service, in court.

5. Make entries of service and filing in the suit register and computerized schedule.

6. If you are employed by the attorney on whom the papers are served, make a notation on the back of your copy of the date and hour of service. Enter in your diary and on the lawyer's calendar

the return day of motion. Also make an entry in the suit register and computerized schedule.

AFFIDAVIT FOR USE IN COURT

14.29. Analysis of an Affidavit

The discussion in Chapter 9 of affidavits for use other than in court cases is applicable to all affidavits. The content of an affidavit for use in court cases always relates to the case. It differs from *verification* in that the affiant swears that facts stated in the affidavit are true, whereas the verifier swears to the truth of statements made in a pleading to which the verification is attached.

An affidavit for use in court cases consists of the following parts:

1. Caption
2. Title
3. Venue
4. Body
5. Signature of affiant
6. Jurat
7. Signature and seal, or stamp, of notary public

14.30. How to Prepare an Affidavit for Court Use

An affidavit for court use is prepared like any other affidavit (Chapter 9) with this important exception: It is preceded by a caption like the one on the complaint. It differs from a verification in form in that it is complete, with caption, whereas the verification is actually a part of the pleading that it verifies.

1. Use the size paper required by the court or what is customary in your office.
2. Use the same caption as that on the complaint and include the index or docket number. The title of the case may be shortened.
3. After the box, give the recital of the venue.
4. Add a line for the signature.

5. Place the jurat at the left of the page.

6. Add a line for the notary's signature.

7. Word the endorsement according to what the affidavit is about. It might be "Affidavit in Opposition" or "Affidavit of Service by Mail" or some other subject. If another paper is bound in the back with the affidavit, the endorsement will also include the title of that paper.

8. After approval by the lawyer, have the affiant sign the original affidavit.

9. Notarize the original, and make an original for the court, a copy for the opposing counsel, and a copy for your file.

See Figure 14.12 for an affidavit in opposition prepared for court use.

MOTIONS OR ASSENTED TO MOTIONS (STIPULATIONS)

14.31. Analysis of a Stipulation

Attorneys for opposing parties frequently make agreements respecting certain phases of a lawsuit. The agreement might be an accommodation to the opposing counsel, such as an extension of the time in which to file a pleading, if that is permitted in the jurisdiction without court order; it might be an agreement that will save time in court, such as an agreement admitting certain facts.

These agreements between counsel are called *stipulations*. A stipulation is usually an agreement among the attorneys for all of the parties to an action. It could settle a case or one or more issues in a case, or it might be simply an agreement between the attorney for the plaintiff and the attorney for a defendant, the other parties defendant not being interested in the particular stipulation.

Simple motions that do not dispose of the case may be assented to and will normally be granted by the court without hearing. Federal and many state court rules require that the movant (the party making the motion) certify that he or she has sought agreement from the opposing side on any motion except one that would dispose of the case. (See Figure 14.13.)

```
                    UNITED STATES DISTRICT COURT
                       DISTRICT OF [STATE]


*****************************************
                                        *
A,                                      *
        Plaintiff                       *
                                        *
             v.                         *          Civil Action No.
                                        *          C-44-692-33-D
B,                                      *
                                        *
        Defendant                       *
                                        *
*****************************************
```

ASSENTED TO MOTION TO ENELARGE TIME

NOW COMES the defendant and respectfully requests that the deadlines for the parties responding to any motions or discovery on either side be enlarged by two weeks due to the fact that settlement negotiations have been undertaken that make it probable that the case will be resolved in the near future.

Although this enlargement of time is requested by the defendant, counsel for the plaintiff concurs in the filing of the Motion and joins in the request that the enlargement be granted.

Figure 14.13. Assented to Motion.

Because of the nature of this Motion, no memorandum of law is required.

Respectfully submitted,

B,

By its attorneys,

[Firm Name]

Date:_____   _____
                                            [Attorney Name]
                                            [Address]
                                            [Telephone]

I hereby certify that on the above date a copy of the foregoing motion was mailed, first class, postage prepaid, to [Name], Esquire, and [Name], Esquire.

_____
[Name]

Figure 14.13.   Assented to Motion. *(cont.)*

Although stipulations are filed in court (except in those few jurisdictions where no papers are filed until note of issue), the court is usually not required to approve the motion except in domestic relations cases.

A stipulation consists of the following parts:

1. Caption
2. Body
3. Dateline
4. Signatures of attorneys for all interested parties (by the parties themselves in domestic relations cases)

14.32. How to Prepare a Stipulation

The wording of all stipulations about a particular step in the litigation is substantially the same. The lawyer does not usually draft the simple stipulations; he or she will say, "Draw up a stipulation in the Jones case extending our time to answer until March 10"; or "Draw up a stipulation in the Smith case to set for trial on March 18." You can get the wording from a practice manual and maintain it among other forms in the computer. Whenever you prepare a stipulation of a different kind, file a copy in the computer. The lawyer will draft some stipulations, such as those admitting certain facts. It is customary for the attorney seeking the stipulation to prepare it.

1. Use the same caption as that on the complaint; the style of the case may be shortened.
2. State in solid caps: "IT IS HEREBY STIPULATED AND AGREED."
3. When there is more than one stipulation in the same document, state each one in a separate numbered paragraph.
4. Provide a signature line for each attorney or firm of attorneys that is stipulating. Indicate the party represented by the stipulating attorney, thus: "Attorney for Defendant Bernard Lowe" or "Bernard Lowe, by his attorney."
5. Make an original for the court and a copy for all interested attorneys as well as a file copy.

14.33. What to Do with Stipulations

Follow this procedure with stipulations:

1. Prepare the stipulation.
2. Ask the attorney to sign the original and make copies.
3. Deliver copies to the opposing counsel who is stipulating and ask for his or her signature on the original and your office copy, giving the opposing counsel a copy that was signed at your office.
4. If the stipulation sets a date for future action, make an entry in your diary; on the lawyer's calendar, when appropriate; and in the computer scheduling system.
5. Make an entry in the suit register (see Chapter 12).
6. If you are employed by the attorney who did not prepare the stipulation, make an entry in your diary and in the suit register and computerized schedule when you receive a copy of the stipulation.

DISCOVERY
(INTERROGATORIES, REQUEST FOR PRODUCTION OF
DOCUMENTS, REQUEST FOR ADMISSIONS, NOTICE OF
DEPOSITION)

A complaint does not contain all of the minute details or particulars of the plaintiff's claim against the defendant. The defendant is entitled to those details so that he or she may prepare the proper answer and defend himself or herself in the trial of the case. Likewise, the plaintiff may need more definite information from the defendant before he or she can adequately prosecute the case. The methods by which this information is obtained vary with the state and also with the kind of action. This process is called *discovery*. The Federal Rules of Civil Procedure permit liberal discovery in federal courts, and many states have adopted similar discovery rules. Some states, however, permit more limited discovery than is allowed under the federal rules.

14.34. Forms of Discovery

Discovery may take the form of a motion for more definite statement, sometimes called "demand for a bill of particulars" (sections 14.20-14.23), which is essentially a motion; interrogatories (sections 14.35-14.36), requests for production of documents (section 14.37); requests for admissions (section 14.38); and depositions (section 14.39).

14.35. Interrogatories

Interrogatories are questions propounded in writing by one side in a lawsuit to the other. They are served, usually by mail, and the court rules give the respondent a certain amount of time in which to answer (30 days under federal rules). Neither the interrogatories nor the answers are filed with the court unless they are used at trial.

14.36. How to Prepare Interrogatories

Follow this procedure with interrogatories:

1. Make the caption the same as that on the complaint.
2. Number the interrogatories and begin each one on a new line. Many jurisdictions require that space be left after each question so that the answer may be inserted directly on the original.
3. Note that as the name implies, interrogatories are usually in the form of questions, and each interrogatory is followed by a question mark. (Store the interrogatories in the computer for recall and use in similar lawsuits.)
4. Preferably, place the affidavit on the last page of the interrogatories, but it may be on a separate page.
5. Make an original, one or more copies for the person to whom they are addressed (follow court rules), and a copy for your files.

14.37. Request for Production of Documents

Requests for production of documents are similar to interrogatories and are often appended to them. They are simply a request to submit specified documents that may support (or damage) a party's case in court. They are served and responded to like interrogatories.

14.38. Request for Admissions

When one side believes that certain facts are not in dispute or cannot be adequately refuted by the other party, a request for admissions is submitted. The opposing party has a specified time to respond (30 days under the federal rules).

14.39. Depositions

Depositions are oral question-and-answer sessions in which the deponent responds, under oath and on the record, to questions propounded by the other side's attorney. A professional stenographer is usually hired to record and transcribe the session. The secretary will prepare a *notice of deposition* (see Figure 14.14), will make arrangements with the stenographer, and will see that the conference room is prepared for the deposition.

NOTICE OF TRIAL

14.40. Noticing a Case for Trial

The clerk of court is responsible for scheduling judges and courtrooms and for trying to get all parties together at the same time. Many courts now call a pretrial conference, often before discovery is complete, to bring the parties together and set a schedule for the preliminaries, to get an estimate of trial time, and to set a tentative date for the trial. Most courts prepare their own trial notices.

14.41. Note of Issue

The *note of issue* is a printed or computerized form that you can easily complete without directions from the lawyer. (Figure 14.15 illustrates a completed form.) It is important to remember that if an "at issue" notice is not received within the specified time, the court may dismiss the action for lack of progress. Many courts control the trial docket from start to finish, however, thus abolishing the entire procedure. When "at issue" documents do exist, though, a good computer docketing system is invaluable.

14.42. What to Do with a Note of Issue

Follow this procedure with a note of issue:

1. Note that telephone numbers of attorneys should be included in the note of issue and *must* be included in some jurisdictions.

UNITED STATES DISTRICT COURT
FOR THE
DISTRICT OF [STATE]

```
. . . . . . . . . . . . . . . . . .
                                  .
A,                                .
                                  .
          Plaintiff,              .
                                  .
     v.                           .          Civil Action
                                  .          No. 10-255-D
B, C, and D,                      .
                                  .
          Defendants.             .
                                  .
. . . . . . . . . . . . . . . . . .
```

NOTICE OF DEPOSITION

TO:

[Names and Addresses]

PLEASE TAKE NOTICE that, on Monday, April 15, 19.., at 11:00 a.m., at the offices of [Name], [Address], Plaintiff A will take the deposition upon oral examination of Defendant B by a person or persons

Figure 14.14.   Notice of Appearance.

to be designated by B pursuant to Federal Rule of Civil Procedure

30(b)(6) as having the most knowledge of the following:

> Activities conducted by B with respect to [Name] located at
> [Address], during the period March 1, 19.., to the present,
> including but not limited to the following: (a) activities to
> insure compliance with B's agreements with [Name], (b) activities
> related to the contamination of the property located at [Address]
> (the "Property"), and (c) activities related to preventing
> contamination at the Property.

The examination will be taken before a person qualified to

administer oaths and will continue from day to day until completed. You

are invited to attend and cross-examine.

By its attorneys,

_____

[Attorneys' Names]
[Firm Name]
[Address]
[Telephone]

Dated:

Figure 14.14.   Notice of Appearance. *(cont.)*

B 537—Note of issue and certificate of readiness: Uniform Rules, 22 NYCRR 202.21(b), 1-86.   JULIUS BLUMBERG, INC., PUBLISHER 62 WHITE STREET, NEW YORK, N. Y. 10013

Calendar No. (if any) ....
Index No. ....
.... Court, ...County, N. Y.

NOTE OF ISSUE

For use of Clerk

....
Name of Judge assigned
NOTICE FOR TRIAL
☐ Trial by jury demanded
  ☐ Of all issues
  ☐ Of issues specified below
    or attached hereto
☐ Trial without jury

Filed by attorney for ....
Date summons served ....
Date service completed ,...
Date issue joined   ....

Plaintiff(s)

against

NATURE OF ACTION OR SPECIAL PROCEEDING

☐ Tort: ☐ Motor vehicle negligence
           ☐ Medical malpractice
           ☐ Other tort
☐ Contract
☐ Contested matrimonial
☐ Uncontested matrimonial
☐ Tax certiorari
☐ Condemnation
☐ Other (not itemized above) specify...

☐ This action is brought as a class action
☐ This is a medical malpractice action: panel procedures prescribed by court rules pursuant to Jud. § 148-a.
  ☐ have been completed   ☐ have not been completed
Amount demanded $...
      Other relief ....

Defendant(s)

Special preference claimed under...

on the ground that...

Insurance carrier(s), if known:...

Attorney(s) for Plaintiff(s)
Office & P.O. Address:

Phone No.:

Attorney(s) for Defendant(s)
Office & P.O. Address:

Phone No.:
NOTE: Clerk will not accept this note of issue unless accompanied by a certificate of readiness, or, in a medical malpractice action, unless, where applicable, the certificate of readiness previously has been filed and the panel procedures prescribed by court rules pursuant to section 148-a of the Judiciary Law have been completed.

Figure 14.15. Note of Issue.

Courtesy Julius Blumberg, Inc. Forms may be purchased from Julius Blumberg, Inc., New York, NY 10013, or any of its dealers. Reproduction prohibited.

2. Make each sentence a separate paragraph.

3. Do not staple in a legal back, but provide an endorsement on the printed form.

4. Include an affidavit of service and file it with the court.

5. Make an original for the court, a copy to serve on each opposing counsel, and a copy for your file.

REQUESTS FOR FINDINGS AND RULINGS

14.43. Analysis of Findings of Fact and Conclusions (or Rulings) of Law

At the trial of a case before a judge (nonjury trial), certain facts are determined from the pleadings and evidence. Certain rules of law are applicable to those facts. After the trial of a case by the court without the jury, the attorneys submit a statement of the facts and applicable rules of law. This statement is designated *findings of fact and conclusions (or rulings) of law*. In other jurisdictions, the court directs counsel for both sides to prepare findings of fact and conclusions (or rulings) of law. In some jurisdictions the court directs counsel for only one party to prepare the statement; the opposing counsel then has a specified time within which to file objections and submit his or her proposed findings. The secretary's and paralegal's duties are the same in either situation.

14.44. How to Prepare Findings of Fact and Conclusions (or Rulings) of Law

The lawyer drafts the findings of fact and conclusions (or rulings) or law.

1. Make the caption the same as that on the complaint.

2. Title the document "Plaintiff's (or 'Defendant's') Requests for Findings of Fact and Conclusions (or Rulings) of Law."

3. Enumerate the findings of fact, beginning with FIRST, or 1.

4. Enumerate the conclusions (or rulings) of law, beginning with FIRST, or 1.

5. Place the dateline below the last conclusion (or ruling) of law, at the left margin.

6. Make an original for the court, a copy for each counsel, and a copy for your file.

14.45. What to Do with Findings of Fact and Conclusions (or Rulings) of Law

Follow this procedure with the findings and conclusions:

1. Note that before the trial, the attorney will draft the findings of fact and conclusions (or rulings) of law.

2. See that a copy is served on the opposing counsel. (A judgment is sometimes prepared and served at the same time. See "Judgments and Decrees.")

3. See that a receipt of copy is acknowledged, or make an affidavit of service by mail.

4. Enter in your diary and on the lawyer's calendar, if appropriate, the date by which the opposing counsel must file objections and submit proposed findings (usually done simultaneously by both parties).

5. Submit the original, with proof of service on opposing counsel, to the judge who tried the case.

6. Make an entry of the service on submission to the judge, of the signing, and of the filing in the suit register and computerized schedule.

INSTRUCTIONS TO THE JURY

14.46. Nature of Instructions to the Jury

When a case is tried by a jury, the court instructs or *charges* it regarding the law applicable to the action. Counsel for both sides submit to the court instructions that they want the court to give the jury. The court may give an instruction as proposed by counsel, may modify it, or may refuse to give it. Counsel may take exception to instructions given to the

jury at the request of the opposing counsel or to a modification of, or refusal
to give, an instruction that he or she proposed.

14.47. How to Prepare Instructions to the Jury

Many offices keep computerized or printed forms of stock instructions, but the lawyer will draft others.

1. Prepare each instruction on a separate sheet of paper.
2. Number each instruction for identification purposes.
3. Identify the party submitting the instructions, thus, "Plaintiff's Instruction No. . . . " (This may be placed at the top or bottom of the charge; numbers are inserted later in the order in which the charge is given.)
4. Omit the caption.
5. Do not staple the instructions in a legal back and do not endorse.
6. Make an original for the judge, a copy for the opposing counsel, and an office copy.

ORDERS

14.48. Proposed Orders

Every direction of a court, judge, or justice, made or entered in writing and not included in a judgment or decree, is called an *order*. The only basic difference between an order and a judgment or decree is that the latter are final decisions in a lawsuit. An order may be interim, addressing some procedural point, or it may be final. Orders are made upon motion of counsel or by the court. In many cases the lawyer prepares an order for the judge to consider as the order of the court. It may be presented at trial, after the evidence is in. Sometimes a proposed order is attached to a motion that disposes of a particular issue.

A proposed order may be submitted at the end of a trial. It is always served on the opposing counsel by hand or by mail.

If an order is entered while the court is sitting, it is called a *court order*. If it is signed by a judge, or justice, in his or her chambers or elsewhere while the court is not in session, it is called a *judge's order*. Both have the same legal effect, but in many jurisdictions there is a distinction in the form and wording.

14.49. How to Prepare an Order

The caption of an order entered *while the court is sitting* usually differs from the caption of the pleadings in two respects.

1. It shows the term and name of the court, where the court is sitting, and the date, in a single-spaced legend at the right of the page.

2. The name of the presiding judge precedes the box. The order also has a space for the judge's signature and the initials of his title: U.S.D.J. (United States District Judge); J.S.C. (Justice of Supreme Court); J.C.C. (Justice of City Court); J.M.C. (Justice of Municipal Court), and so on. In some courts the word *enter* precedes the signature.

    Enter, _____
                    J.S.C.

When an order is signed by a judge *while the court is not sitting,* the caption is similar to that on the complaint. "Enter" does not precede the signature as is the case with court orders in many courts. Give the judge's title in full instead of the initials. (Figure 14.16 on page 340 illustrates a judge's order.) Although an order to show cause is a court order, it is prepared like a judge's order. In all other respects an order is prepared like the pleadings.

If a notice is attached to the order, as is frequently the case, endorse the back "Order and Notice of Entry" (or "Notice of Settlement" or whatever the notice is called). Place the copy of the order that the judge is to sign on top of the set of papers, but in the other sets place the notice on top.

14.50. What to Do with an Order

Generally, when the judge instructs counsel to "settle order on notice," proceed as follows (but follow local rules and procedures where different):

1. Prepare the following papers: (a) *Proposed order*. Make an original for the court; one for each opposing counsel, one to be served with the notice of settlement, and one to be served after the order is entered. When the order is signed, everyone gets a copy. (b) *Notice of settlement*. Make a copy for each opposing counsel and

IN THE CIRCUIT COURT FOR JEFFERSON COUNTY, ALABAMA

JASPER FREIGHT LINES,   )
)
           Plaintiff,   )
)
        v.   )   IN EQUITY
)   NO. 5487-X
LILLIAN STACY,   )
)
           Defendant.   )

PROPOSED ORDER

The plaintiff above named having duly moved for an order

_____

_____

_____ ;

NOW, after reading and filing the _____

_____ ,

on motion of Page & Newton, Esqs., attorneys for the plaintiff, and no one

appearing in opposition thereto, it is hereby

ORDERED by the Court that _____

_____ .

Dated this 6th day of July, 19____.

_____
                              Circuit Judge

Figure 14.16.   Proposed Order.

an office copy. The notice is not filed in court. (c) *Notice of entry*. Make a copy for each opposing counsel and an office copy.

2. Staple the notice of settlement on top of the proposed order, a copy for each opposing counsel.

3. See that service is made on the opposing counsel and that receipt of service is acknowledged on the original of the order.

4. Enter in your diary and on the lawyer's calendar, if appropriate, the date the proposed order will be submitted to the court.

5. Make an entry of the service of notice of settlement in the suit register and computerized schedule.

6. Staple the notice of entry on top of the order, a copy for each opposing counsel.

7. Note that the lawyer will take to court the original of the proposed order and the copies that are stapled with the notice of entry.

8. If the judge does not sign the order immediately, make a follow-up entry in your diary and follow the law journal closely to see when the order is entered.

9. As soon as the order is signed, see that conformed copies with the notice of entry are served on the opposing counsel *immediately*. Prompt service of the settlement of order is very important, because the opposing counsel's time to take an appeal begins to run when service is made, not when the order is entered.

10. Make an entry of the order and of the service in the suit register and computerized schedule.

11. Make an entry in your diary and on the lawyer's calendar of the last day to appeal from the order.

12. If you are employed by the attorney on whom the notice of entry is served, make entries in the suit register, on the computerized schedule, in your diary, and on the lawyer's calendar.

When the judge instructs counsel to submit an order, it is not necessary to serve a copy of the order on the opposing counsel before submitting it the court or judge. No notice of settlement is necessary.

1. Make an original of the order for the court, a copy for the opposing counsel, and an office copy.

2. Make a copy of the notice of entry for each opposing counsel and an office copy.

3. Proceed as in steps 6 through 12 above, following local rules and procedures where different.

JUDGMENTS AND DECREES

14.51. Analysis of Judgments and Decrees

A decision by a court, after a trial or hearing, of the rights of the parties is a *judgment*. Broadly, any adjudication by a court of law or of equity is considered a judgment, but, technically, an adjudication by a court sitting in equity is a *decree*. The words *judgment* and *decree* are often used synonymously by the statutes, especially in states where the civil procedure codes have abolished the formal distinction between law and equity. A decree usually directs the defendant to do or not to do some specific thing, as opposed to a judgment for money damages in a court of law. The sentence in a criminal case is the judgment.

A decree or judgment is *interlocutory* when it leaves unsettled some question to be determined in the future; for example, a temporary injunction is an interlocutory decree, or it may be called an order. A decree or judgment is final when it disposes of the case, leaving no question to be decided in the future. The parties, however, may appeal to a higher court from a final judgment or decree and sometimes for an interlocutory order. The execution of the judgment is stayed pending the higher court's decision.

A judgment is sometimes entered "on the pleadings" upon motion of counsel, before a trial of the cause is reached. For example, the plaintiff moves the court to strike the answer of the defendant and direct judgment for the plaintiff. More frequently, judgment is not entered until the case has been tried and findings of fact and rules of law have been made. (See "Requests for Findings and Rulings.") In most jurisdictions the clerk of the court prepares the judgments, but in some cases the prevailing lawyer does. A judgment is similar in style to a court order. See Figure 14.17 for the style of a decree.

IN THE DISTRICT COURT IN AND FOR THE CITY AND COUNTY
OF DENVER AND STATE OF COLORADO
CIVIL ACTION NO. 3-504, Div. 7

CAROLINE BILLINGS FRY,

                       Plaintiff,

          -vs-   INTERLOCUTORY DECREE IN
                                           DIVORCE.

DOUGLAS MONROE FRY,

                    Defendant.

THIS CAUSE, coming on to be heard on this 9th day of January, 19–,
upon its merits, the plaintiff being represented by Jones & Fairmount,
attorneys of record, and the defendant appearing by Crystal & Gwinner,
attorneys of record, and the Court having examined the full record herein,
finds that it has jurisdiction herein; and having heard the evidence and the
statements of counsel, the Court now being fully advised

DOTH FIND that a divorce should be granted to the
plaintiff herein upon the statutory grounds of _____
_____ .

IT IS ORDERED, ADJUDGED and DECREED by the Court, that an
absolute divorce should be granted to the plaintiff, and an Interlocutory
Decree of Divorce is hereby entered, dissolving the marriage of plaintiff and
defendant six months after the date of this Interlocutory Decree.

IT IS EXPRESSLY DECREED by the Court that during such six months
period after the signing of this Interlocutory Decree the

(Continued on following page)

Figure 14.17.   Interlocutory Decree of Divorce.

(Continued from preceding page)

parties hereto shall not be divorced, shall still be husband and wife, and neither party shall be competent to contract another marriage anywhere during such period, and the Court during all of said period does hereby retain jurisdiction of the parties and the subject matter of this cause and upon motion of either party, or upon its motion, for good cause shown, after a hearing, may set aside this Interlocutory Decree.

It is further ORDERED, ADJUDGED and DECREED by the Court that defendant shall pay into the Registry of the District Court on the _____

_____ .

It is further ORDERED, ADJUDGED and DECREED by the Court that the sole care, custody and control of the minor children, Lester Douglas Fry and Julia Caroline Fry, is hereby awarded to the plaintiff as a suitable person to have such care and custody until the further order of the Court, with the defendant to have reasonable visitation rights.

The Court FURTHER DECREES that after six months from the date hereof this Interlocutory Decree shall be and become a Final Decree of Divorce and the parties shall then be divorced, unless this Interlocutory Decree shall have been set aside, or an appeal has been taken, or a writ of error has been issued.

Done in open Court this 9th day of January, 19--.

BY THE COURT,

Judge.

APPROVED AS TO FORM:

Crystal & Gwinner
Attorneys for Defendant.

Figure 14.17. Interlocutory Decree of Divorce. *(cont.)*

15 How to Handle Records on Appeal, Briefs, and Citations

The party who loses a lawsuit, or who is dissatisfied with a judgment or court order or decree, may ask a higher court to review the decision of the lower court with the hope that the higher court will reverse or modify the lower court's decision. When a case is appealed, the lawyers for each party file a *brief* with the appellate court in support of their contentions. This chapter describes the procedure for review by a higher court. It also gives the fundamentals that affect your part in the preparation of a brief. Illustrations show the layout and appearance of briefs.

PROCEDURE FOR REVIEW

15.1. Rules of the Reviewing Court

The procedure for taking a case to a higher state court is governed by the rules of the highest state tribunal. These rules are based on the civil practice acts or codes of civil procedure and may be found in an appendix to the act or code or in compilations of the rules of court. They may also be obtained in pamphlet form from the clerk of the appellate court or from the state judicial council. The United States Supreme Court makes the rules for appeals to it and, also, for appeals from federal district courts to federal courts of appeal. Criminal convictions may also be appealed. There are special rules for criminal appeals, but the procedure is essentially similar to appeals in civil cases.

You can find in these rules the information you need to do your part of the appellate work in accordance with the court's requirements. The rules provide, among other things, for the following:

1. Methods for review
2. Forms of notice of appeal
3. Content of the record on appeal
4. Form of testimony (question and answer, narrative, or abstract)
5. Preparation and format of record
6. Preparation and format of brief
7. Time allowed for filing and service of papers
8. Method of service on opposing counsel
9. Number of copies required by the court
10. Costs

15.2. Methods for Review by a Higher Court

In the majority of states the method for requesting review by the higher tribunal is by filing a notice of appeal from the lower court to the higher court. In a few states the method is by a petition to the higher court for a writ of error. At one time, chancery cases were reviewed by means of an appeal and law cases by means of a writ of error. This distinction in appellate procedure now exists in very few states. Regardless of the method for review, the procedure is loosely referred to as *taking an appeal* or *appealing a case*. The use of the term *appeal* here embraces both appeals and writs of error.

A case may also be referred to a higher court, under special circumstances, by means of extraordinary writs, such as *certiorari, mandamus, habeas corpus, prohibition, quo warranto,* and *stay writs*. These writs eliminate the necessity of hearings and trials in the lower court.

Not all cases in which a notice of appeal is filed are accepted for review by the appellate court. Some matters, especially criminal cases, may be appealed as of right. In some states civil cases may be heard on appeal at the discretion of the appellate court.

In some states the appeal is to an intermediate appellate court (see section 12.10 in Chapter 12) and then to the highest state court. In states that do not have intermediary appellate courts (and in certain cases even if they do), the appeal is direct from the trial court to the highest court. The procedure for taking an appeal to an intermediate appellate court is similar to, but not exactly the same as, taking an appeal to the highest state tribunal. The main variations are in the details, such as the time allowed for the various steps taken, disbursements to be paid, the form of the appeal documents, and the number of copies that must be filed with the court. Check the rules of the intermediate appellate court.

15.3. Diary Entries

The reviewing court's rules require that an appeal must be perfected according to a strict timetable. It is your duty to make diary entries of the schedule so that there will be no slipup on the part of your office. You should also note the progress of the appeal in the suit register and computerized schedule (see Chapter 12). The rules of some courts provide for return days of appeals, just as they do for pleadings (see section 14.26 in Chapter 14). Other courts consider the date on which the record on appeal is filed as the date from which the time for filing motions and briefs will run. You can get the appropriate timetable from the reviewing court's rules, or the lawyer will give it to you. Dates by which the following steps must be taken should be entered in the diary.

1. Filing notice of appeal by appellant
2. Ordering of the transcript of the pertinent proceedings
3. Filing of additional instructions by appellee
4. Filing of record on appeal in reviewing court
5. Appellee's motion to quash or dismiss an appeal, or for summary affirmance
6. Hearing of motions
7. Filing of appellant's brief
8. Filing of appellee's brief
9. Filing of appellant's reply brief
10. Oral argument

15.4. Change in Caption of Case

From the time the record is filed with the appellate court, the caption of the case will change. The caption on all motions and briefs filed thereafter will show the name of the appellate court and its docket number; the designation of the parties may change to show their appellate status, depending on the practice in the particular state. The lower court's index or docket number of the case is no longer indicated.

15.5. Designation of Parties to an Appeal

In almost all states the party appealing is referred to as the *appellant,* and the party opposing the appeal is referred to as the *appellee* or the *respondent.* When the defendant in the lower case is the appellant, the title of the case may be reversed. Thus *John Smith v. Alfred Jones* becomes *Alfred Jones v. John Smith.* Eight methods of designating parties on appeal in the caption are shown in Figure 15.1. In cases in which review is by petition for a writ, the party appealing is designated as the *petitioner* and the other party as the *respondent.*

Although the designation of the parties may change in the title of the case, the briefs sometimes refer to the parties by their designation in the lower court. (Some rules require this designation.) Or the brief might refer to a party by the lower court designation on one page and by the appellate court designation on the other page. The change in designation is very confusing, and the lawyer might inadvertently refer to the defendant-appellant instead of plaintiff-in-error. Before you prepare a brief, fix firmly in your mind the designation of the parties in both the trial and appellate courts so that you will be able to recognize any error in the designation of parties.

15.6. Notice of Appeal

Under the rules of a typical state, the filing of a *notice of appeal* with the clerk of the court whose order is appealed from gives the appellate court jurisdiction, and an appeal is deemed to have commenced. The time usually allowed for filing a notice of appeal is 20 to 30 days (check the court rules) after mailing a copy of the judgment with notice of entry.

You can get the format of the notice of appeal from the court rules or from a form book, or the lawyer will provide a form to follow. Set it up in the same manner, and use the same kind of paper as for other court papers. Some courts may require that the notice of appeal be filed on a form supplied by the clerk of court. Bind the notice of appeal in the format required by the rules in your particular jurisdiction.

STYLES OF DESIGNATION OF PARTIES ON APPEAL BY DEFENDANT TO
HIGHEST STATE COURT WHEN TITLE OF CASE IN LOWER COURT WAS

Joseph Smith, Plaintiff, vs. William White, Defendant

Style 1 (Names reversed)

William White,
    Appellant,
vs.
Joseph Smith,
    Appellee.

Style 5 (Names not reversed)

Joseph Smith,
    Appellee,
vs.
William White,
    Appellant.

Style 2 (Names not reversed)

Joseph Smith,
    Plaintiff and Respondent,
vs.
William White,
    Defendant and Appellant.

Style 6 (Names not reversed)

Joseph Smith,
    Respondent,
vs.
William White,
    Appellant.

Style 3 (Names not reversed)

Joseph Smith,
    Plaintiff and Appellee,
vs.
William White,
    Defendant and Appellant.

Style 7 (Names reversed)

William White,
    Appellant and Defendant,
vs.
Joseph Smith,
    Respondent and Plaintiff.

Style 4 (Names reversed)

William White,
    Plaintiff-in-Error
vs.
Joseph Smith,
    Defendant-in-Error.

Style 8 (Names reversed)

William White,
    Defendant Below, Appellant,
vs.
Joseph Smith,
    Plaintiff Below, Appellee.

Figure 15.1. Methods of Designating Parities on
Appeal in the Caption.

1. Make the caption the same as that on the pleadings.
2. Have the attorney for the party who appeals sign the notice of appeal.
3. Make an original, a copy for each appellee, and a copy for your files (but see number 4).

4. Serve a copy on the counsel for the appellee and file the original, with proof of service, with the clerk of the court. In some states the rules do not require service of notice of appeal on the opposing counsel, but a copy is usually given to the opposing counsel for his or her file. In other states the rules require that the notice be filed in duplicate, with one containing the proof of service.

15.7. Service on Opposing Counsel

Service of all papers and notices required by the rules of the appellate court may be made by leaving them in the office of the opposing counsel, during regular office hours with a person in charge of the office or by depositing them, securely sealed and postpaid, in the post office directed to such attorney at his or her usual post office address. Proof of service is made by affidavit. The lawyer's secretary will probably mail the document and, therefore, make the affidavit, when service is made by mail. Placing the properly sealed and addressed document in an "outgoing basket" to be dispatched by the mail clerk in your office is not in compliance with the statute. You must actually do what the affidavit of service says. Figure 15.2 illustrates one form of affidavit of service by mail. If the wording of the affidavit used in your office differs, make an extra copy for your form book. In all cases, however, consult the rules of the court regarding the preparation of any material.

Notice that the affidavit is preceded by the caption of the case. When this affidavit is copied into the record on appeal, the caption will be omitted, but the recital of venue will be included.

CONTENTS AND PREPARATION
OF THE RECORD ON APPEAL

15.8. What Is a Record on Appeal?

A *record on appeal* is a copy of the pleadings, exhibits, orders, or decrees filed in a case in the lower court, and a transcript of the testimony taken in the case. The purpose of the record is to inform the appellate court of what transpired in the lower court. The court rules specify that the record

THE STATE OF [NAME]

SUPREME COURT

_____

No..............................

_____ v. _____

 I hereby certify that on the   day of   19
I sent one copy of the   brief in the above-entitled action
to each counsel of record and sixteen copies to the Clerk-Reporter of
the Supreme Court, [Address].

    _____

    Attorney for_____

Figure 15.2. Affidavit of Service Mail.

must be abbreviated as much as possible so that the judges will not have to wade through a mass of extraneous material. The appellate court does not need to be informed about matters that are not pertinent to the decision of the questions before it. Furthermore, the larger the record, the more expensive it is.

15.9. Assignment of Errors and Instructions to the Clerk

Consult the rules of the court for specific procedures. Generally, within a certain number of days after the notice of an appeal is filed (the number being specified by the rules) the appellant files *assignments of error and directions to the clerk* for making up the transcript and record on appeal. In cases where the court has some discretion about whether to accept an appeal, the schedule runs from the date the court accepts it (agrees to hear it). The assignments of error and directions to the clerk may be combined in one document. Elsewhere, in New Hampshire, for example, what is described here as "assignment of errors" is included in the notice of appeal as "questions presented."

The purposes of an *assignment of errors* are to apprise the appellate court of the specific questions presented by the appellant for consideration and to inform the opposite party of the matters of error relied on so that discussion may be limited and concentrated on those points.

The *directions to the clerk* designate the portions of the proceeding and evidence to be included in the transcript of record—those portions pertinent to the questions before the appellate court. The appellee might consider that other portions of the record will throw light on the questions to be reviewed by the court. If so, the appellee files additional directions and cross assignments.

In lieu of directions to the clerk, the parties may file written stipulations with the clerk designating the contents of the record.

Preparation

The directions for preparing the notice of appeal apply also to assignments of error and instructions to the clerk (see section 15.6). The originals are filed with the clerk of the court, and copies are served on the counsel for the appellee. Proof of service of these documents on the opposing counsel is filed with the clerk and included in the transcript of record.

15.10. Who Prepares the Record?

The clerk of the court or the appellant prepares the record from the directions to the clerk filed by the parties. The common practice is to employ a court reporter to make up the transcript. Consult the rules of the court for the proper procedure.

THE BRIEF

15.11. Nature of a Brief

Black's Law Dictionary gives the following complete, yet concise, definition of a *brief:* "A written or printed document, prepared by counsel to serve as the basis of an argument upon a cause in an appellant court, and usually filed for the information of the court. It embodies the law which the counsel desires to establish, together with the arguments and authorities upon which he rests his contention." *Brief* is short for *brief of argument.*

The brief must contain a history of the appealed case, a statement of the questions or points involved, and the argument. The history is a concise statement of the essential facts, without argument. It states the purpose of the litigation and contains a chronological enumeration of the pleadings, the issues, and the judgment of the trial court, giving references to applicable pages of the transcript. The questions or points should be stated as concisely as possible. Each one is numbered and set forth in a separate paragraph and is usually followed by a statement of whether it was answered in the negative or the affirmative by the trial court. The section of the brief entitled "Argument" contains a division for each of the questions involved, with discussion and citation of authorities.

15.12. Preliminaries to Preparing the Brief

Before the lawyer dictates the brief, he or she briefs cases to be used in support of his or her position. This means that the lawyer makes a summary, digest, or abstract of a case, quoting pertinent parts from the court's opinion. Prepare each summary on a separate sheet of paper. Put the name of the case and the citation at the top of the sheet, double-space the lawyer's language, and indent and single-space the quotations. Firms that do a lot of litigation in a particular area of law will have standard sections of briefs and memoranda in the computer library for insertion as appropriate.

Check carefully the spelling of names and the volume and page number of each citation. After preparing the notes, have someone read back the quotations, if possible. If the book quoted from is a borrowed book that must be returned before the final brief is written, make a photocopy of the pages with material being quoted for retention.

15.13. Time Element

The court rules provide that the appellant must file his or her brief within a specified number of days after the record is filed and that the appellee has a specified number of days thereafter to file his or her brief. The appellant then has an additional time in which to file a reply brief. The timing is close. If the brief is to be printed, there is a deadline by which the manuscript must reach the printer. Unfortunately, many lawyers are inclined to put off the preparation of a brief until the last minute, and there is nothing you can do about it except remind the lawyer of the date the brief must be filed. Generally, observe the following procedures.

15.14. Preparation of a Brief

Draft

Prepare a rough draft of the material provided by the lawyer or assemble citations from the database. Occasionally, the lawyer will provide part of a brief and then, because of other matters, be unable to complete the work for a day or two. In the meantime, you should prepare the partial draft and place a copy on the lawyer's desk or in the files for reference when he or she is able to work again on the brief.

Number of Copies

After the lawyer revises the draft, make the corrections and print out a second draft or a final original, as the lawyer requests. The number of copies required for filing will be specified by the court rules. In addition, make a copy for each party to the appeal, including your office and, if it is the office policy, one for the client.

Format

Figure 15.3 illustrates a page from a brief. Notice also the following points about the makeup of a brief:

1. The questions or points are typed in solid caps or printed in bold face.
2. When several cases are cited in support of the same proposition, they are placed one under another unless they are in a quotation.

Smith v. Jones   Brief for Appellants   page 11

ARGUMENT

I

THE TRIAL COURT ERRED IN EXCLUDING PAROL EVIDENCE OFFERED BY THE
APPELLANTS ON THE NATURE OF RIGHTS GRANTED TO THE PLAINTIFFS TO "USE"
THE COMMUNITY DOCK.

At trial the lower court did not permit the defendants to introduce
parol evidence on the issues raised in the pleadings pertaining to the
nature and extent of the rights granted the back lot owners by the
developers. Since the developers did not clearly express their intent
in an unambiguous fashion, extrinsic evidence should have been admitted
by the court below. Failure to admit extrinsic evidence was reversible
error.

Extrinsic evidence may not vary clear and unambiguous terms of a
written instrument. Nashua Trust Co. v. Weisman, 122 NH 397, 445 A2d
1101 (1982). Where a written instrument is susceptible to more than one
interpretation or its intent cannot be ascertained from its language,
extrinsic evidence is admissible to interpret its terms. Ouellette v.
Butler, 125 NH 184, 480 A2d 76 (1984); 30 Am Jur 2d Section 1069, p.
210-211. Parol evidence should be admitted to explain the terms of a
writing where its meaning is subject to debate or in doubt.

An ambiguity may arise in either the employment of an unusual word
or from the uncertain application of an otherwise plain term.

> In short, an ambiguity, so far as the parol evidence
> rule is concerned, may arise from the use of words if
> their meaning is either doubtful or uncertain, and parol

Figure 15.3. Page from a Brief.

Table of Contents and List of Authorities Cited

A brief of more than 12 pages (consult the rules of the court) must have a table of contents and be prefaced by an alphabetical list of the authorities cited. The more powerful word processing programs will automatically alphabetize the cases. The pages are numbered with small roman numerals. Figure 15.4 illustrates a table of contents; Figure 15.5, the list of authorities. In this list the titles of the cases cited are not necessarily underscored or in italics.

Notice in the illustration (Figure 15.5) that there is no volume and page number cited for the case of *City of Miami Beach v. Perrell*. Sometimes a case is cited before the court's opinion is published in the reporter or even in the advance sheets. The page and volume numbers are then left blank. Should the opinion be published before the brief is filed, the reference may be inserted.

Cover and Binding

The cover of the brief contains the name of the court, the style of the case, identification of the brief (the party filing it), and the name and address of the attorneys representing the party filing the brief. When double covers are used, the brief is stapled at the side. Some rules specify different colors for the covers of the appellant's brief, the appellee's brief, and the appellant's reply brief. Figure 15.6 illustrates a brief cover.

Filing and Service

The rules specify the number of copies of the brief that must be filed with the clerk of the appellate court and the number of copies that must be served on the opposing counsel. Service on the opposing counsel may be by mail or in person. Proof of service must be made to the appellate court.

15.15. Application for Oral Argument

Although witnesses do not appear before appellate courts, the lawyers are permitted to argue the case before the court. In some cases the lawyer believes the brief is sufficient and does not choose to argue the case. In some states, if the lawyer wants to appear before the appellate court, he or she must make application for oral argument at the time the brief is filed. A copy

CONTENTS

Table of Authorities

Questions Presented   1

Statement of the Case   2

Statement of Facts   4

Arguments

    I.   THE TRIAL COURT DID NOT ERR IN THE EXCLUSION
        OF PAROL EVIDENCE   7

    II.   THE TRIAL COURT WAS CORRECT IN ISSUING A
        DIRECTED VERDICT IN FAVOR OF THE PLAINTIFFS   9

    III. THE TRIAL COURT WAS CORRECT IN HOLDING THAT
        THE CONDOMINIUM UNIT OWNERS MAY NOT ASSERT
        RIGHTS DERIVED FROM RSA 356-B AGAINST THE
        PLAINTIFFS   15

    IV. THE TRIAL COURT DID NOT COMMIT ERROR IN
        DENYING THE APPELLANT'S MOTION TO SET ASIDE
        VERDICT   17

    V.   THE TRIAL COURT IS NOT REQUIRED UNDER STATE
        LAW, THE RULES OF COURT, OR COMMON LAW TO MAKE
        SPECIFIC REQUESTS AND FINDINGS IN RESPONSE TO
        A PARTY'S REQUEST   19

Conclusion   19

Figure 15.4.   Table of Contents in a Brief.

AUTHORITIES CITED

<u>Allen</u> v. <u>Avondale Co.</u> (1988), 135 Fla. 6, 185 So. 137....... 28

<u>Barton</u> v. <u>Moline Properties</u> (1975), 121 Fla. 683, 164 So. 551, 103 A.L.R. 725... 30

<u>City of Coral Gables</u> v. <u>State ex rel. Worley</u> (1985), 44 So.2d 298... 18

<u>City of Fort Lauderdale</u> v. <u>Smith</u> (1970), 44 So.2d 302....... 107

<u>City of Miami Beach</u> v. <u>Daoud</u> (1962), 149 Fla. 514, 6 So.2d 847... 50, 110

<u>City of Miami Beach</u> v. <u>First Trust Co.</u> (1970), 45 So.2d 681... 31, 42, 50, 108

<u>City of Miami Beach</u> v. <u>Gulf Oil Corp.</u> (1980), 141 Fla. 642, 194 So. 236... 100

<u>City of Miami Beach</u> v. <u>Sun Oil Company</u> (1960), 141 Fla. 645, 194 So. 237.. 100

<u>City of Miami Beach</u> v. <u>Texas Company</u> (1950), 141 Fla. 616, 194 So. 368... 98

<u>Dade County</u> v. <u>Thompson</u> (1971), 146 Fla. 66, 200 So. 212..... 29

<u>De Carlo</u> v. <u>Town of West Miami</u> (1950), 49 So.2d 596...... 12, 110

<u>Downs</u> v. <u>Kroeger</u> (1967), 200 Cal. 743, 254 P. 1101........... 29

<u>Ehinger</u> v. <u>State</u> (1971), 147 Fla. 129, 2 So., 2d 35.......... 103

<u>Forde</u> v. <u>City of Miami Beach</u> (1981), 146 Fla. 676, 1 So.2d 642... 32, 36, 37, 101

<u>Glogger</u> v. <u>Bell</u> (1941), 146 Fla. 1, 200 So. 100.............. 100

<u>Green Point Savings Bank</u> v. <u>Board of Zoning Appeals</u> (1989), 281 N.Y. 534, 24 N.E.2d 319................................. 11

<u>Harrington</u> v. <u>Board of Adjustment, City of Alamo Heights</u> (Tex. 1989), 124 S.W.2d 401............................... 11, 16

Figure 15.5. List of Authorities Cited in Brief.

THE STATE OF [NAME]
SUPREME COURT

1990 TERM
MAY SESSION

No. 90-139

John J. Jones

v.

William Baker, Jane Collins, and Henry Davis,
d/b/a/ The Professional Association
Jane Collins, Secretary

BRIEF FOR THE DEFENDANTS
(APPELLANTS HEREIN)

Adam C. Hill (orally)
[Address]
[Telephone]

Nancy Hartshorne, Esq.
[Address]
[Telephone]

Figure 15.6. Cover for Brief.

of the application is served on the opposing counsel in the same manner that the brief is served.

CITATIONS

15.16. What Is a Citation?

A *citation*[1] is a reference to an authority that supports a statement of law or from which a quotation is taken. Citations occur most frequently in briefs, law memoranda, and opinion letters. The lawyer speaks of "citing a case," "a cited case," "citing a report," and the like. The references are principally to the following sources:

1. Constitutions, statutes, codes
2. Law reports
3. Texts and periodicals

A useful publication to have when preparing materials that include citations is a booklet called *A Uniform System of Citations,* published by the Harvard Law Review Association in Cambridge, Massachusetts. Use the most recent edition. Some state supreme courts, however, require a form of citation that differs from the Harvard system. Always check your own court rules to see how the official state reporters should be cited in appellate briefs.

15.17. Accuracy of Citations

The importance of accuracy of citations cannot be overemphasized. Citations may be checked by a computerized database such as AutoCite. If done manually, check and double-check the volume and page references and the spelling of names. Check against the original reports, not against notes. Check printed briefs against the original reports, not against manuscripts. A judge will be annoyed if he or she cannot find a case cited because you made a typographical error in the citation. Misspellings of the name of a well-known case marks the lawyer as either careless or ignorant. Errors

---

[1] Certain writs and summonses issued by courts are also known as citations.

in citations are always avoidable, and it is your responsibility to see that no negative reflection is cast upon the lawyer through your carelessness.

15.18. Research

Lawyers use both printed reference material and computerized databases to locate their references (see Chapter 8). Procedures in using electronic research vary according to the requirement of the particular database. Users of WESTLAW, LEXIS, PHINET, VERALEX, and other databases must follow the instructions of the particular database to retrieve the desired information. See section 8.1 (Chapter 8) for an example of the procedure required by WESTLAW to retrieve information from the Shepard's database.

15.19. Official Reports and the National Reporter System

All of the opinions of the highest state tribunals and of the United States Supreme Court and many of the opinions of intermediary appellate courts are published. Each appellate court has a reporter whose duty it is to see that the opinions are published in bound form at intervals. The publication under the direction of the state reporter is considered the official report of the court's opinion.

West Publishing Company publishes the opinions of the federal courts and the courts of every state, with those of several states published in the same bound volume. This system of reports, covering the entire country, is called the National Reporter System. (See "Reports of Decided Cases" in Chapter 8.) Some of the reporters are designated "Second Series." The designation is for numbering purposes and indicates that the numbers of the volume have started over with 1.

These reporters, which are unofficial reports of the courts' opinions, are published much sooner than the official reports. Some states have discontinued the publication of state reports and use the appropriate reporter of the National Reporter System as the official report. The Lawyer's Cooperative Publishing Company also publishes the decisions of the United States Supreme Court. Its publication is called *Supreme Court Reports, Lawyer's Edition*, and is cited as *Law. Ed.*

Before the opinions are published in bound volumes of the National Reporter System, they are published in weekly pamphlets known as advance sheets. (Some official reports also have advance sheets.) Thus the lawyer is informed immediately of the courts in which he or she is interested. The page numbers in the advance sheets correspond with the page numbers that will appear in the bound volumes.

15.20. How to Cite a Constitution

To cite a constitution, show the number of the article or amendment in roman numerals and the section number in arabic numerals. Give the date if the constitution cited is not in force.

U.S. Const. art IV, § 2

U.S. Const. amend. VI, § 2

Ga. Const. art XI, § 3

Ga. Const. art. II, § 1 (1875)

15.21. How to Cite Statutes and Codes

Whenever full reference to a federal statute is necessary, cite the date, chapter number, statute citation, and United States Code citation: Section 1 of the Act of June 13, 1934, c. 482, 48 Stat. 948, 40 U.S.C. 276b. Compilations of state statutes and codes are cited by chapter, title, or section number. *A Uniform System of Citation* (latest edition) gives the approved form of citing the latest compilation in each state; note that some states have more than one approved compilation.

When citing statutes and codes, observe these directions:

1. If a compilation in its preface gives the method of citing it, use that citation.

2. When the date is incorporated in the title of the compilation, show it.

3. When statutes or codes of one state are cited outside of that state, the name of the state is always indicated for identification purposes. For example, lawyers in New Hampshire cite the New Hampshire Revised Statutes Annotated as *R.S.A.*, but outside of the state the citation is *N.H. Rev. Stat. Ann.*

4. When citing an act or law that has been repealed and no longer appears in the latest compilation, give the date of the compilation cited.: *Ill. Rev. Stat. ch. 114, 88 (1889)*.

15.22. How to Cite Cases in Official Reports and Reporters

Cases in official reports and reporters are cited alike. Directions for citing cases must be considered in the light of applicable court rules. Some courts place considerable emphasis on how cases should be cited and whether citation to the National Reporter System should be included. The following directions are the rules of thumb used in many law offices. Examples of citations are given at the conclusion of the chapter.

Names of Parties

Follow this procedure for the names of parties:

1. Cite the name of the case as it appears in the running head of the report, not as it appears at the beginning of the opinion. Do not abbreviate the first word.

2. When the United States is a party, do not abbreviate to *U.S.* unless it is part of the name of a government vessel. (See Example 1.)

3. Do not substitute the initials of a government agency or a labor union for its full name in briefs. You may do so in other legal writing, however. (See Example 2.)

4. Use the first name of railways, but abbreviate the rest. (See Example 3.)

5. When *Co.* and *Inc.* are both part of a name, omit the *Inc.*

6. When the names of parties change completely on appeal, indicate the fact by the use of *sub. nom.* (See Example 4.) This direction does not apply when the names of the parties are merely reversed.

Volume and Page

Cite the volume and page number of the report or reporter in which the opinion is published. The reference is to the entire opinion and gives the page at which the opinion begins. A *spot page reference* follows when it is desired to call attention to a particular page, such as one from which a quotation is taken. (See Example 5.)

The designation *2d* must be included in the citation of a volume in a second series. A reference to *58 N.E.* is not the same as a reference to *58 N.E.2d.*

Date

Show in parentheses the year the decision is handed down by the court. It appears at the beginning of the court's opinion. Both *A Uniform System of Citation* and *Practice Manual of Standard Legal Citations* place the date at the end of the citation (see Example 1), but lawyers, when writing briefs, frequently place it between the title of the case and the volume reference (see Example 5). Many lawyers do not show the date of the decision unless it is relevant to the argument.

Jurisdiction and Court

When the name of the reporter does not indicate the jurisdiction, show the jurisdiction in parentheses preceding the date. (See Example 6.) Also show the name of the court deciding the case if it is not the highest court in the state. (See Example 7.) This is always necessary when only the unofficial reporter is cited.

Parallel Citations

Both the official and unofficial reports should be cited if available. Cite the official report first. (See Example 8.) When the case has not been published in the official reports, but will be in the future, cite the name of the official report, preceded and followed by blanks: ___ Miss. ___, 55 So.2d 447. (See Example 9.)

Federal Courts

When citing cases decided by the federal courts of appeals, show the circuit in parentheses. (See Example 10.) The District of Columbia circuit is indicated by *D.C.* (See Example 11.) When citing cases decided in the federal district court, show the district, but not the division, in parentheses. (See Example 12.)

Selective Case Series

In some law report series, such as *American Law Reports* and *Law Reports Annotated,* only certain cases are published. These series are cited by the year of publication, the *letter* of the volume (A, B, C, or D), and the page. (See Example 13.) In parallel citations, they follow the National Reporter citation. It is customary to cite selective case series in briefs for state courts but not in those for federal courts.

15.23. Named Reporters

Old court reports carry the name of the reporter. When citing cases in the U.S. reports before volume 91, always cite by the volume number and name of the reporter, not by the subsequently assigned consecutive U.S. number. To cite these volumes by the U.S. number is considered bad form. The following are the names of the old court reports and the number of volumes they reported.

4 of Dallas (cited as 1 Dall. 10)

9 of Cranch (cited as 1 Cranch 10)

12 of Wheaton (cited as 1 Wheat. 10)

16 of Peters (cited as 1 Pet. 10)

24 of Howard (cited as 1 How. 10)

2 of Black (cited as 1 Black 10)

23 of Wallace (cited as 1 Wall. 10)

When citing state cases, follow the local practice. In Massachusetts, for example, the early reports are often cited by the name of the reporter, whereas in North Carolina a rule of court requires that they be cited by the consecutive number. When the name reporter is used, indicate the jurisdiction and date in parentheses. (See Example 14.)

15.24. String Citations

When several cases are cited one after the other instead of on separate lines, the citation is referred to as a *string citation*. Separate the cases with a semicolon. (See Example 15.)

15.25. How to Cite an Unpublished Case

When citing a case that has not been reported, cite by name, court, the full date, and the docket number, if known. (See Example 16.)

15.26. How to Cite Slip Decisions

Each opinion of the United States Supreme Court is published separately as soon as it is handed down. This form of publication is called a *slip decision.* Slip decisions are printed by the U.S. Government Printing Office and also by two unofficial publishers, Commerce Clearing House and U.S. Law Week. (State appellate courts also publish slip decisions.) They are widely circulated and are frequently cited in briefs. Cite by number, court, date of decision, and source, if unofficial. (See Example 17.)

15.27. How to Cite Treatises

Cite treatises by volume number (if more than one volume), author, title of the publication, page or section number, and the edition in parentheses. If the editor is well known, his or her name follows the edition. Underscore or italicize the title of the publication. (See Example 18.)

Star Page

In a few well-known works, the paging of the original edition is indicated by stars in differently paginated editions. Cite by the star page. (See Example 19.)

15.28. How to Cite Law Reviews

Cite the volume and page number and the year. Underscore or italicize the title of the review. If an article is referred to, place it in quotation marks. Abbreviate *Law (L.)*, *Review (Rev.)*, and *Journal (J.)*. (See Example 20.)

15.29. How to Cite Legal Newspapers

When citing a case that has not been published in either the official or unofficial reports but has been published in a legal newspaper, give the name of the newspaper, the volume and page number, the column, the court, and the exact date of the decision. (See Example 21.)

15.30. Underscoring and Italicizing

Practices in underscoring and italicizing vary with the law office, but the following directions, some of which are arbitrary, are based on the practices followed by many lawyers (some computer printers do not have italics capability, and underscoring is used in those cases to designate italic type):

1. Italicize or underscore the names of the parties.

2. Note that the use of italics or underscoring for *v.* or *vs.* is optional; continuous italic type or continuous underscoring, however, requires less care in breaking at the desired points.

3. When a previously cited case is referred to in the text of the brief by part of the title used as an adjective, italicize or underscore it: "Under the authority of the *Daoud* case the Court held . . ." But when the reference is repeated under the same point of the brief, do not italicize or underscore it.

4. Italicize or underscore *case* or *cases* only when it is part of the usual name of the case.

5. Preferably, do not underscore words and expressions between citations of the same case that relate to its history, such as *affirmed* and *certiorari denied.* (See Example 22.)

15.31. Spacing of Abbreviations

In briefs and other legal writings the general practice is to close up the citation: *N.E.2d.*

15.32. Placement of Citations

Unless a citation is part of a quotation, it is indented and placed on the line following the quotation. If it runs over one line, the carryover line is indented additional spaces.

> ". . . should be denied, as proposed allegations would add nothing to the equity of the bill."
> *Volunteer Security Co.* v. *Dowl* (1947), 159 Fla. 767, 33 So.2d 150, 152.

When several citations are given in support of a point, list them one under the other (see Figure 15.5).

15.33. Illustrations of Citations

The following examples of citations illustrate the foregoing directions. Parts appearing in italics would be underscored if your computer printer lacks italics capability. Apparent inconsistencies in the style of things such as italics and placement of dates in these examples demonstrate the variations in accepted practice; however, in your office you should use the same style consistently throughout a brief. Also, consult the latest edition of *A Uniform System of Citation* for current citation style and follow local court practices and requirements.

1. *United States* v. *Texas & Pacific Motor Transport Co.*, 340 U.S. 450, 71 S. Ct. 422 (1981).

2. *United States* v. *Congress of Industrial Organization*, 334 U.S. 106, 68 S. Ct. 1349, 48 A.L.C. 1164, aff'd 77 F. Supp. 355, 48 A.L.C. 559 (D.C. Cir. 1948).

3. *Nashville, C. & St. L. Ry.* vs. *Walters* (1970) 294 U.S. 405, 55 S. Ct. 486.

4. *Blaustein* v. *United States*, 44 F.2d 163 (C.C.A. 3), certiorari denied *sub nom. Sokol* v. *United States*, 283 U.S. 838, 51 S. Ct. 486.

5. *Dyett* v. *turner* (U.S.D.C., D. Utah, Cent. Div., 1968) 287 F. Supp. 113; 114.

6. *Harrington* v. *Board of Adjustment, City of Alamo Heights* (Tex. 1989) 124 S.W.2d 401, 404.

7. *Rayl* v. *General Motors Corp.* (Ind. App. 1971) 101 N.E.2d 433 *Janice* v. *State*, 107 N.Y.S.2d 674 (Ct. Cl. 1951)

8. *People* v. *Davis*, 303 N.Y. 235, 101 N.E.2d 479.

9. *In re Fortune* (1991)____ Ohio St. ____, 101 N.E.2d 174.

10. *American Fruit Machinery Co.* v. *Robinson Match Co.*, 191 Fed. 723 (3rd Cir. 1911).

11. *Barbee* v. *Capital Airlines, Inc.* (D.C. Cir. 1971) 191 F.2d 507.

12. *Standard Oil Co.* v. *Atlantic Coast Line R. Co.* (W.D. Ky. 1990) 13 F.2d 633.

13. *Hanover Star Milling Co.* v. *Allen & Wheeler Co.*, 208 Fed. 513, 1916D L.R.A. 136 (7th Cir. 1913).

14. *Forward* v. *Adams*, 7 Wend. 204 (N.Y. 1831).

15. *Rubin* v. *Board of Directors of City of Pasadena* (1969) 16 Cal.2d 119, 104 P.2d 1041; *Harrington* v. *Board of Adjustment, City of Alamo Heights* (Tex. 1939) 124 S.W.2d 401; *Green Point Savings*

Bank v. *Board of Zoning Appeals* (1989) 281 N.Y. 534, 24 N.E.2d 319.

16. *Roe* v. *Doe,* No. 152 U.S. Sup. Ct., Jan. 10, 1952.

17. *Jones* v. *Smith,* No. 40, U.S. Sup. Ct., No. 21, 1988 (15 U.S. Law Week).

18. 2 Pomeroy, *Equity Jurisprudence* 428 (5th ed., Symonds, 1990).

19. 2 Bl. Comm. *358.

20. 42 *Yale L.J.* 419 (1989).

21. *Garden Park Apts., Inc.* vs. *Fletcher,* 127 N.Y.L.J. 703, col. 7 (Sup. Ct. Spec. Term Feb. 20, 1972).

22. *In re Morse* (1979) 220 App. Div. 830, 220 N.Y. Supp. 858, rev'd on other grounds, 147 N.Y. 290, 160 N.E. 374.

Part 4

ASSISTING
IN SPECIALIZED PRACTICE

16. Assisting in Partnership Formation and Incorporation

17. Acting as Corporate Secretary

18. Assisting In Real Estate Practice and Foreclosures

19. Assisting with Probate and Estate Administration

20. Handling Commercial Collections

16 Assisting in Partnership Formation and Incorporation

The work of forming a corporation and qualifying it to do business in more than one state is highly technical, requiring strict observance of specific laws and of federal laws if public issues of stock are involved.

The organization of a simple corporation with no public issues of stock is not particularly complicated and may be an assignment in any law office. The task offers secretaries and paralegals a chance to assume considerable responsibility, thereby relieving the busy lawyer. In the case of a complicated corporation, the lawyer may engage the services of a firm that specializes in incorporating, qualifying, and maintaining corporations. In that case, the secretary and paralegal have no part in the incorporating work.

A partnership is a much less formal entity than a corporation and may come into being without any legal consultation whatsoever. Most states have adopted the Uniform Partnership Act, which in general outlines the duties and obligations of partners to each other and particularly addresses partnership assets and debts when the partnership is dissolved. There are a number of instances in which a lawyer may be consulted before or after the formation of a partnership. The partnership will probably want to register its name with the secretary of state. The name is reserved in the same manner as that for a corporation or an unincorporated business.

The partners may want to draw up a formal agreement among themselves outlining the various duties and responsibilities of the partners. In partnerships in which one or more of the partners is a so-called limited partner, it is most common to draw up a formal agreement indicating the nature of the limited partner's participation. In a *limited partnership* the limited partners invest capital, have limited liability, and do not share in the management of the business. In a *general partnership* all partners have unlimited personal liability for the business obligations and are actively involved in the management.

The following sections examine the nature of partnerships and corporations and outline the duties of the law-office team in each case.

CORPORATIONS

16.1. What Is a Corporation?

A *corporation* is a device for carrying on an enterprise. It is an entity, a "legal person," separate and apart from the persons who are interested in and control it. The state authorizes its existence and gives it certain powers. It also has certain powers that it gives itself, within the limits prescribed by the state, when it goes through the formalities of organization. A corporation has fundamental characteristics that make it the most popular form of business organization. Probably, the most favorable aspect of the corporate form is the assurance of limited liability to the persons who put capital into the business. This means that an individual's personal assets cannot be reached to satisfy creditors of the corporation.

Corporations may be classified as public corporations, corporations not for profit, and corporations for profit, each class being organized under different statutes.

Public corporations include all of the subdivisions of the state, such as cities and towns, tax districts, and irrigation districts. They also include government-owned corporations, such as the Federal Deposit Insurance Corporation and Federal Savings and Loan Insurance Company.

Corporations not for profit are those organized for purposes other than the pecuniary gain of their members. Those who are interested in and control the corporation are referred to as its members, rather than its stockholders or shareholders as in a corporation for profit. These corporations include religious, civil, social, educational, fraternal, charitable, and cemetery associations. When a not-for-profit corporation receives tax-exempt status under the Internal Revenue Code, it is commonly referred to as a *nonprofit corporation.*

Corporations for profit, or *business corporations,* are corporations with capital stock that carry on an enterprise for profit. The organization procedure described in this chapter relates to a private business corporation but is adaptable to other corporations.

Most corporations fall into three categories: publicly owned corporations, close corporations, and professional corporations or associations. The *publicly owned corporation* sells its shares to members of the general public, either through the major stock exchanges or "over the counter." The *close,* or *closely held, corporation* is generally one that has a small group of stockholders (some states even permit only a single stockholder), often members of the same family, and all of whom are active in the business and constitute the board of directors and officers of the corporation. Many states now have special corporation laws that apply to this kind of corporation to make it easier for the corporation to operate. The *professional corporation,* in some states called the *professional association,* is one composed of a group of, say, doctors, lawyers, or dentists who practice their profession in corporate form as distinguished from individual or partnership form. Most states now have laws that permit various professions to incorporate their practices. The closely held and professional corporations represent most of the average attorney or corporate practice.

A corporation, once formed, may choose to be treated as a "C" corporation or as a "Subchapter S" corporation for federal income tax purposes. A corporation is automatically taxed as a "C" corporation unless its shareholders specifically elect to be treated as an "S" corporation. A "C" corporation is considered a separate entity from its shareholders for tax purposes, filing its own tax returns and paying tax on its own net income. An "S" corporation, however, treats its shareholders as if they were a partnership. The shareholders can elect to have the corporation treated as an "S" corporation by filing an election with the Internal Revenue Service on Form 2553, Election by a Small Business Corporation.

16.2. Steps in the Organization of a Corporation

To organize a corporation means to bring it into existence. Each state designates a specific department and official through which the lawyer must work. Certain steps are necessary. They involve routine procedure that you can follow at the lawyer's direction without detailed instruction.

The usual steps in the organization of a corporation are as follows:

1. Reservation of name
2. Preparation of incorporating papers, including articles of incorporation, certification of authority to issue stock from the state
   securities department, and corporate bylaws
3. Execution of papers
4. Filing of papers
5. First meeting of incorporators
6. First meeting of directors
7. Preparation of stock certificates

16.3. Who May Form a Corporation?

Those who unite for the purpose of forming a corporation are *incorporators*. They tell the lawyer the kind of business that the corporation will
engage in and other details the lawyer needs to know before he or she begins
the legal organization procedure. They also put up the capital for the
corporation.

States that have adopted the Model Business Corporation Act of 1969
prepared by the Committee on Corporate Laws, Section of Corporation,
Banking and Business Law, of the American Bar Association, or the
Revised Model Business Corporation Act of 1984, allow only natural
persons to incorporate. However, several states (including Illinois, Massachusetts, New Jersey, Pennsylvania, and West Virginia) allow corporations
to form corporations. Others (including Alabama, California, Delaware,
Florida, Iowa, Kansas, Louisiana, Oklahoma, Oregon, and Texas) allow
partnerships and associations to form corporations. Some states even allow
trusts and estates to form corporations.

Most states require only one incorporator, who need not be a citizen
or resident. But many states require that the incorporators be adults. No state
requires that the organizational meeting be held in that state. Most allow the
organizational meeting, if needed, to take place anywhere, although a few
states limit the location to the United States.

16.4. State of Incorporation

A state in which a corporation is organized is the *state of incorporation*. Usually, the lawyer will organize the corporation in the state in which

its principal office is located. But a corporation is not necessarily incorporated under the laws of the state in which its executive office is located, especially if it is to carry on business in more than one state. Each state has a corporation law under which private business corporations for profit are organized. The laws of some states are more favorable to corporations generally than those of other states. The lawyer may recommend to a client a state whose laws are most favorable to the proposed corporation. The cost of incorporating and the tax laws in each state are also taken into consideration. Therefore, the lawyer for whom you work might organize a corporation under the laws of a state far removed from your office. Delaware is the leading incorporating state.

In the state of incorporation, a corporation is known as a *domestic corporation;* in all other states, as a *foreign corporation.* (Corporations organized outside the United States are referred to as *alien corporations.*) Thus a corporation incorporated in Delaware is a domestic corporation there, but in New York and California, it is a foreign corporation.

16.5. Memorandum, or Checklist, Preliminary to Preparation of Incorporating Papers

Each lawyer has his or her own method of giving instructions about the preparation of incorporating papers. Often the attorney uses a "checklist for incorporation" to ensure that nothing will be overlooked. It also allocates responsibility between the attorney and the accountant. The checklist is then given to the secretary, who prepares the articles and other initial papers. In some cases a paralegal will do much of the routine work of preparing papers of a new corporation.

One method commonly followed involves the preparation of a preliminary memorandum. After the lawyer has a conference with the principals interested in forming a corporation, he or she drafts a memorandum of the conference. This memorandum covers all information necessary to the preparation of the articles of incorporation. It will include:

1. State of incorporation.
2. The corporate name selected by the principals, usually first and second choice.
3. Nature of business in which the corporation proposes to engage. This clause is known as the *purpose clause.* The lawyer may direct you to a form in the forms file or in a forms book for this clause.

4. Names and addresses of incorporators.

5. Names and addresses of directors.

6. Number of shares of stock each incorporator and director will hold, if any.

7. Designation of resident agent.

8. Location of principal office within the state of incorporation.

9. Fiscal year of the corporation.

10. Date for annual stockholders' meeting.[1]

11. Amount of capital with which the corporation will commence business (the corporation law in each state fixes a minimum amount).

12. Authorized capital stock and its breakdown (number of shares of common stock and of preferred stock; number of shares with par value and the par value of each; number of shares of no par stock).

13. Designations, rights, preferences, and all other details relating to preferred stock. This clause in the charter is known as the *stock clause*. It is frequently complicated, and sometimes several drafts of it are written before its provisions satisfy the principals.

This memorandum will serve as the basis for the organization of the corporation. With the help of the memorandum and appropriate forms, you will be able to complete the organization of a simple corporation without detailed instructions from the lawyer.

16.6. Reservation of Name

Deciding on a business name is a serious matter to which the incorporators and the lawyer give careful consideration. All of the states require that a corporation's name contain the words *company, corporation, incorporated,* or *limited* or abbreviations of them. Also, the majority of the states will not permit the use of the word *bank* or *trust* in the name of a corporation unless it is a banking institution. The chief importance of a name to the incorporators is that, as a business develops, its name acquires a value in itself, representing to a great extent the goodwill of the company. The state

---

[1]The words *stockholders* and *shareholders* often are used interchangeably.

laws and the courts generally protect the corporation's exclusive right to the use of its name. The state official will not accept for filing a charter or articles of incorporation if the name of the proposed corporation so closely resembles that of a corporation existing in the state that deception or confusion might result. Therefore, as soon as the lawyer drafts the memorandum described in the preceding paragraph, he or she will tell you to find out if the choice of name is available and, if so, to reserve it.

What to Do to Clear the Name

Call or write to the designated state official and ask if the chosen name is available. You have to ascertain if the proposed name is available not only in the state of incorporation but also in any states in which the corporation expects to do business.

In some states the state official will reserve a name for a specified period for the payment of a fee or as a courtesy. In the states that require a fee, enclose a check when you ask to have the name reserved. Send the check to the designated official as soon as you have a reply to your request.

Your letter might read as follows:

The Honorable James R. Clark
Secretary of State of Vermont
Montpelier, VT 05053

Sir:

Re: Franklin J. King, Inc.

Please let us know whether the above-styled name is available for a domestic corporation, which we are about to organize under the laws of your state. If so, please reserve it for us for a statutory period. Enclosed is a check for $____ in payment of the reservation fee.

Thank you.

Sincerely yours,

Warner & Croft

If the incorporators expect to qualify as a foreign corporation in another state, the first paragraph will be changed to read: ". . . foreign corporation, which we are about to qualify to transact business in your state." You may be able to get a response by telephone or facsimile.

16.7. Incorporation Papers

The next step in the organization of a corporation is the preparation of the proposed *articles of incorporation,* to be submitted to the designated public official for approval. The articles determine what the corporation is authorized to do, and the corporation cannot function until it has been approved by the proper official. The articles of incorporation are sometimes called *charters, certificates of incorporation,* or *articles of association,* depending on the terminology used in the state of incorporation. Most states provide printed forms that may be used; otherwise, the charter is drawn from models that have been approved by the public official with whom the papers must be filed. Standard forms should be stored in your computer to be retrieved to compile the sections for any particular corporate documentation.

The states have different requirements for the provisions of the charter, but all of the states require that they must contain special information with reference to the items set forth in the statutes.

16.8. Preparation of the Articles of Incorporation

The preparation of the average incorporation papers is largely routine, and you should be able to prepare it from the memorandum previously drafted, by using a form from your files as a model or by incorporating the information into your computerized form.

1. Use a good quality bond paper. Most states use letter-size paper.
2. If printed blank forms are used, follow the same procedure as in filling in any blank form. (See also section 10.21 in Chapter 10.)
3. When printing out the charter, always use pica (10 point) type and double-space it. These requirements are mandatory in nearly every state. Otherwise, there is no specific form in which the charter must be typed. Although you should have a form stored in the computer, Figures 16.1 and 16.2 illustrate the first and last pages of the articles and may serve as a model for style.
4. Each signer has a signature line.

ARTICLES OF INCORPORATION

of

FRANKLIN J. KING, INC.

ARTICLE I

Name

The name of the Corporation is FRANKLIN J. KING, INC.

ARTICLE II

Duration

The Corporation shall have perpetual existence.

ARTICLE III

Purpose

The Corporation is organized for the following purposes:

1. _____

_____

_____

2. _____

_____

_____

3. _____

_____

_____

Figure 16.1. First Page of Incorporation Papers.

ARTICLE X

Amendment

The Corporation may amend or repeal any provisions contained in these Articles of Incorporation, or any amendment hereto, by a majority vote of the shareholders of the Coprporation.

In WITNESS WHEREOF, the undersigned subscriber has executed these Articles of Incorporation this   day of   , 19   .

_____

[Name]

STATE OF FLORIDA

COUNTY OF

BEFORE ME, a notary public in and for said county and state, personally appeared [name], known to me and known by me to be the person who executed the foregoing Articles of Incorporation, and he acknowledged before me that he executed these Articles of Incorporation for the purposes set forth therein.

IN WITNESS WHEREOF, I have hereunto set my hand and affixed my official seal, in the state and county aforesaid, this   day of   , 19   .

_____

Notary Public

My commission expires   , 19

Figure 16.2. Last Page of Incorporation Papers.

5. If an acknowledgment is required, prepare the certificate of acknowledgment in the form required by the state of incorporation. The venue will recite the state and county where the incorporators sign, not the state of incorporation. The rules that govern the acknowledgment of any instrument govern the acknowledgment of incorporation papers. Remember that some states require acknowledgments taken outside the state to be authenticated. Therefore, if the acknowledgment is to be taken in a state other than the state of incorporation, determine if authentication is necessary. If all incorporators sign at the same time, one certificate of acknowledgment is sufficient, but if they sign at different times, there must be a separate acknowledgment for each. Some states do not require that all incorporators who sign must acknowledge the instrument.

6. Find out the number of copies required by law in your state. Make three extra copies—one to be kept at the principal office of the corporation, one for your file, and one for the minute book. (In some states an extra copy is required as an exhibit to the application for a permit to sell securities to the public. A copy of the charter must also be filed with the application to the Securities Exchange Commission if the stock is to be sold publicly.) Some states also require that a certified copy be filed in each county where the corporation owns real estate. You will also have to make an extra copy for some states in which the proposed corporation expects to qualify. Many states now accept a certificate of good standing from the appropriate official (usually the secretary of state) of the state of incorporation.

16.9. Execution of the Incorporation Papers

In a few states all copies of the papers required to be filed with the designated public official must be original copies, photocopies not being acceptable. In others, an original and duplicate originals or triplicate originals are acceptable. Some states will accept an original and photocopies.

If the papers are to be executed in your office, notify the incorporators that the papers are ready for signature and arrange a time for them to come in to sign. (It is advisable to do this as soon as you know when the papers will be ready, to avoid delay.) If some or all of the incorporators are to sign outside your office, send the document with a covering letter.

Each original, duplicate original, and triplicate original must be signed, but the photocopies need not be signed. The signature must be the same on each copy and must be written exactly as in the document. Thus if an incorporator signs his name *A. B. Johnson*, his name should not be written *Adam B. Johnson* in the document.

When acknowledgments are required, take the acknowledgment of the incorporators who sign in your office and notarize all signed copies. Conform the unsigned copies. (See section 10.18 in Chapter 10.)

16.10. Filing the Incorporation Papers and Payment of Fees

After the document has been executed, send the required number of copies to the proper state official with a letter of transmittal and a check in payment of the organization tax and fees. Your letter might read as follows:

Secretary of State
State of Vermont
Montpelier, VT 05053

Sir:

Re: Franklin J. King, Inc.

We are enclosing an original and two conformed copies of the Articles of Incorporation of Franklin J. King, Inc. Please record the original of the articles in your offices and certify and return to us the conformed copies.

We are also enclosing our check for $_____ covering (1) the organization tax, $_____; (2) the filing fee, $_____; (3) the recording fee, $_____; (4) certification of copy for recording, $_____; and (5) certification of one extra copy, $_____.

Thank you.

Sincerely yours,

Warner & Croft

Enclosures (4)

If the articles are acceptable, the public official will retain the original. He or she will mark the copy, or copies, to show that the articles have been filed, will endorse his or her approval upon it or attach a certificate of approval to it, and will return it, together with receipt for tax and fees, to your office. You will then do the following:

1. Conform your office copy, noting particularly the date of the official's filing marks. This date, rather than the date on which the articles were executed, is the date of incorporation.

2. Draw a check for the local filing fee and file the certified copy of the articles in the appropriate local office if required.

3. Note on your office copy the date the papers were filed locally.

4. Attach the tax receipt in the minute book.

Filing Form SS-4, Application for a federal Employer Identification Number

Form SS-4 should be filed with the Internal Revenue Service at the same time the articles of incorporation are submitted to the state. The federal Employer Identification Number will be needed when the corporation sets up a bank account. The letter of transmittal to the IRS (with a copy to the client) might read as follows:

Internal Revenue Service
P.O. Box 25866
Montpelier, VT 05053

Re: Franklin J. King, Inc.

Ladies and Gentlemen:

Enclosed is Form SS-4, an Application for Employer Identification Number, filed on behalf of the above corporation. Upon issuance of the number, please send the acknowledgement to this office at the letterhead address.

Thank you.

Sincerely,

Warner & Croft

Enc.

Copy: J. M. King

Filing Form 2553, Election by a Small Business Corporation

If the shareholders of a corporation decide to file an election with the Internal Revenue Service to be taxed as an "S" corporation, Form 2553 must be filed within 75 days after the start of the corporate fiscal year. The taxable year for a newly formed corporation starts on the first date it has shareholders, acquires assets, or begins doing business. If a valid election is timely, it is retroactive to the first day of the corporate year.

The following is a sample cover letter to the IRS:

CERTIFIED MAIL

Internal Revenue Service Center
Montpelier, VT 05053

Re: Franklin J. King, Inc.

Ladies and Gentlemen:

Enclosed for filing are an original and one copy of Form 2553, Election by a Small Business Corporation, with the consent of the shareholders of the above corporation to be treated as a small business corporation under Section 1372(a) of the Internal Revenue Code of 1954.

Please acknowledge on the copy that the original form was timely filed and return the copy to us in the preaddressed, stamped envelope.

Sincerely,

Warner & Croft

Enc.

Copy: J. M. King

16.11. Necessity and Purpose of Organization Meeting

From a practical, as well as legal, standpoint, a corporation cannot transact its business until details of its organization are completed. Therefore, as soon as the articles are approved and filed with the proper authorities, and other mandatory requirements of the law are complied with, an organization meeting is held.

The states do not all use the same terminology as to the participants in the organization meeting. There are at least four variations: (1) *incorporators,* (2) *incorporators and subscribers* (to the stock), (3) *shareholders* or *stockholders,* (4) *subscribers* (signers of the articles). In some states the organization meeting is a meeting of the directors named in the articles.

The actions taken at organization meetings are routine and are usually agreed upon in advance by the principals organizing the corporation. Frequently, therefore, no formal meeting is held, but a written consent is prepared to be signed by all of the incorporators.

16.12. Preparation for the Organization Meeting

The secretary and paralegal will have to make certain preparations for the organization meeting.

1. Obtaining a corporate outfit (see section 16.13)
2. Preparing a waiver of notice of meeting and obtaining signatures to it
3. Preparing the bylaws
4. Preparing the minutes of the first meeting of incorporators
5. Preparing the minutes of the first meeting of directors
6. Preparing the bank account resolution
7. Preparing the stock certificates
8. Preparing the resolution to elect Subchapter S status (if applicable)

16.13. Corporate Outfit

Simultaneously with the preparation of the papers, order a *corporate outfit.* This consists of a seal, minute book, stock certificate book, and a stock ledger. Today many domestic corporations no longer have seals unless they plan to do business in other states. Such materials may be obtained from any store that handles legal supplies. Some minute books contain printed forms for minutes and bylaws, but many lawyers object to the use of them. When you order the outfit, your letter should give all data necessary to the preparation of the seal and stock certificates. The following model letter indicates the necessary data, and Figure 16.3 on page 389 illustrates the compact kind of corporation outfit that is available from most legal suppliers.

City Stationery Company
803 33rd Street
Montpelier, VT 05053

Re: Franklin J. King, Inc.

Ladies and Gentlemen:

Please send us immediately the following corporation supplies:

1. Hand Seal (FRANKLIN J. KING, INC., A Vermont corporation, Incorporated 19..)

2. Minute Book with Filler

3. Stock Certificate Book (minimum number of certificates)

4. Stock Ledger

The following information is for your use in preparing the stock certificates: There are authorized to be issued 150 shares of capital stock (only one class authorized) having no par value, fully paid and nonassessable. FRANKLIN J. KING, INC., is a corporation of the state of Vermont and was incorporated in 19...

Please include your invoice when the supplies are mailed to us, and we will promptly send our check in payment.

Thank you.

Sincerely yours,

Warner & Croft

If there are two classes of stock, it is advisable to send a copy of the articles with the order. The supplier can then get the preferred stock clause, which is printed on the back of the stock certificate, directly from the articles. The certificate of common stock will be one color; preferred stock, another color.

Figure 16.3.   Corporation Outfit.

16.14. Waiver of Notice of Organization Meeting

The statutes require that the incorporators, directors, shareholders, or subscribers, as the case may be, must be given notice of the organization meeting, just as of any other meeting (see section 17.9 in Chapter 17), unless they waive notice. It is customary for them to waive notice of the organization meeting. It is your responsibility to prepare the waiver and obtain the signatures of the interested parties. (Forms 2 and 3 in section 17.36 of Chapter 17 illustrate waivers of notice of first meeting of incorporators and of first meeting of directors.)

16.15. Preparation of Bylaws

The bylaws of a corporation are the rules adopted to govern the corporation, its officers, directors, and stockholders. Like the charter, the bylaws usually follow a more or less routine pattern. Forms will be available in the computer, and the lawyer will draft special clauses or paragraphs peculiar to the corporation being organized and will prepare a memorandum that includes the following information:

1. Place of stockholders' meeting
2. Day and hour of annual meeting of stockholders
3. Time when notice of annual meeting of stockholders must be given (usually ten days before meeting)
4. Who may call special meetings of stockholders (usually president, vice president, or, upon request, two directors or holders of 25 percent of the outstanding stock)
5. Time when notice of special meeting of stockholders must be given (usually ten days before meeting)
6. Percentage of stock that constitutes a quorum (usually a majority)
7. Place of directors' meetings
8. When regular directors' meetings are to be held
9. Time when notice of regular meetings of directors must be given (usually three to five days before the meeting)
10. Who may call special meetings of directors (usually president, vice president, or, on request, two directors)
11. Time when notice of special meetings of directors must be given (usually three to five days before the meeting)
12. Number of directors to constitute a quorum
13. Officers who are to sign and countersign checks
14. Officers who are to sign and countersign stock certificates
15. When the fiscal year of the company ends

With the help of this memorandum and the organization papers, you will be able to follow a form and prepare the bylaws. Bylaws are too lengthy to be included here, but you may refer to the forms in your computer file or to any book of incorporating forms, or you may obtain a printed copy of the bylaws of corporations that are listed on a stock exchange. Figure 16.4 shows how the bylaws should be set up.

FRANKLIN J. KING, INC.

BYLAWS

ARTICLE I.

Office.

The principal office of the Corporation shall be located in the Borough of Manhattan, City of New York,

_____

_____

ARTICLE II.

Meetings of Stockholders.

Section 1. Annual Meeting. The annual meeting of the stockholders of the Corporation after the year 19

_____

Section 2. Inspectors of Election. The annual election of Directors shall be conducted by two inspectors

_____

_____

ARTICLE III.

Directors.

Section 1. Management. The property, business and affairs of the Corporation shall be managed by a

_____

_____

Figure 16.4. First Page of Bylaws.

16.16. Minutes of First Meeting of Incorporators

You can prepare minutes of the first meeting of incorporators without instructions from the attorney, by following a form. The purpose of the minutes is to place on record the filing date of the original of the articles; the filing date of a certified copy in the appropriate county office, where required; the election of directors; the presentation and adoption of the bylaws; and the authorization of the board of directors to issue capital stock of the corporation. Form 1 in section 17.36 of Chapter 17 is a form of minutes of the first meeting of a corporation. See also section 17.23 in Chapter 17. In some states corporations do not hold an incorporators' meeting but transact this business at the first meeting of directors, who are named in the articles.

16.17. Minutes of First Meeting of Directors

The purposes of the first, or organization, meeting of the board of directors are to elect officers, approve and ratify the acts of the incorporators, adopt a seal (if any), approve the form of stock certificate, open a bank account, designate a resident agent, and transact any other business that may properly come before the meeting. The preparation of such minutes is usually performed via a checklist of corporate resolutions stored in the computer.

16.18. Resolution Opening a Bank Account

The resolution of the board of directors authorizing the opening of a bank account must conform to the requirements of the bank in which the account is to be carried. (Note that a federal Employer Identification Number is needed before an account can be opened.) Banks usually have printed forms of these resolutions. Generally, the client takes care of the resolution and signature cards. If you are asked to perform this task, obtain the forms and signature cards and fill them in before the meeting. The necessary information is available from the memoranda prepared by the lawyer immediately after his or her original conference with the principals (see sections 16.5 and 16.15). The signature cards and resolutions must be signed by the appropriate individuals.

16.19. Preparation of Stock Certificates

The lawyer will tell you to whom stock certificates must be issued and the number of shares each stockholder must receive, or you will find this information in the checklist for incorporation. See Chapter 17 for directions about issuance of stock.

PARTNERSHIPS

16.20. What Is a Partnership?

When two or more individuals undertake an enterprise together, without the formalities of incorporation, they form a partnership. A corporation, as a legal entity, may also be a member of a partnership. But whereas a corporation is an independent legal entity, taxed separately from its shareholders (except in the case of Subchapter S corporations) and organizationally complex, a partnership is not.

There are two kinds of partners. A *full partner* shares in the profits and is fully liable for the debts of the partnership, both his or her personal assets and the partnership assets being reachable by creditors. The *limited partner* simply invests in the business but takes no part in the activities of the partnership. His or her share of the profits is specified by agreement and generally relates to the amount he or she has invested; the limited partner is liable for the losses of the business only to the extent of his or her investment. The corresponding businesses are *general partnerships* and *limited partnerships,* respectively. Most states have adopted a version of the Uniform Partnership Act, which establishes procedures and rules governing the organization and operation of both general and limited partnerships.

16.21. How a Partnership Is Formed

A partnership may be formed by a simple agreement between two or more parties to enter into a business together. Most partnerships, however, draw up an agreement among the partners, outlining their duties and liabilities throughout the existence of the partnership and at its termination. Standard clauses are generally stored in the computer. The partnership agreement will usually state:

1. The nature and place of business and the firm name

2. The time of beginning and the duration of the partnership

3. The contribution of each partner to the capital of the firm

4. The share of each in profits and losses

5. The powers of each partner in the conduct of the business

6. Provisions for its dissolution and the conclusion of its affairs

The agreement may be drawn up at any time, before or after the commencement of the business. Some states require partnerships to register with the state or county before transacting business.

16.22. Preparation of Partnership Agreement

A partnership agreement is a much less formal document than the charter of a corporation. There are rarely state law requirements about how it must be presented. In essence, it is a written contract among the partners, its form being dictated by the number of persons involved, the type of business they are about to enter, and various other factors. (See sections 16.20 and 16.21.)

The first item might be the name of the partnership and a brief description of the type of business it plans to carry on. The second item might outline the duration of the partnership and make provisions for carrying on the business after the death or withdrawal of one of the partners. Additional sections might describe the place of business and the overall purpose of the business in as much detail as the partners wish. Another section might deal with capital investment in the business by various partners, followed by a formula for sharing profits and losses. The duties of the partners might be outlined in detail. The final sections might outline the way the partnership business will wind up after its dissolution.

The partnership name may be reserved with the secretary of state in most states and registered to prevent another business from using the same name.

17 Acting as Corporate Secretary

The lawyer works closely with the corporate secretary. He or she is frequently a director and officer of the corporation, and many responsibilities that are ordinarily those of the corporate secretary are delegated to the lawyer. He or she drafts resolutions and makes the preparations for directors' and stockholders' meetings. The lawyer prepares the minutes of meetings and submits them to the corporate secretary for his or her signature. The lawyer is also responsible for seeing that certain matters, such as lease renewal, are attended to at certain times.

DUTIES AND RESPONSIBILITIES

17.1. What the Secretary and Paralegal Will Do

The lawyer's secretary and paralegal will likely have the following duties and responsibilities pertaining to the affairs of a corporate client.

1. Making all preparations for corporate meetings
2. Recording the minutes of the meetings
3. Issuing certificates of stock and handling ordinary stock transfers, if the corporation is small
4. Making a record of important documents and safekeeping them
5. Keeping the corporation calendar
6. Looking after details if the corporation changes its name

You will perform some of these duties on your own initiative without instructions from the lawyer; others you will undertake only with instructions from the lawyer and, at first, under his or her close supervision. If you are to be successful in the performance of these duties, you must be thoroughly familiar with the bylaws of the corporation.

Information Folder

When the lawyer has the responsibilities listed in the preceding paragraph, it is advisable to keep an information folder (or looseleaf notebook) pertaining to the corporation. In some law offices some or all of this information may be kept on the computer. The material makes available information needed at a moment's notice, without the necessity of removing a document from the safe or looking at the minutes or other records. The material will vary with the need but ordinarily includes the following:

1. Schedule of stockholders' meetings (showing when annual meetings are to be held, how special meetings are called, notice required, what constitutes a quorum)

2. Schedule of directors' meetings (showing how called, notice required, what constitutes a quorum)

3. Dividends (chronological record of dividends paid)

4. Number of stockholders

5. Record of incorporation

6. Bylaws

7. States in which the corporation is doing business

8. List of bank accounts (showing where located, who may sign checks)

9. Abstracts of indentures (including abstracts of special agreements such as option to purchase property)

CORPORATE MEETINGS

17.2. Kinds of Meetings

In addition to the organization meetings described in the preceding chapter, the kinds of corporate meetings are (1) annual stockholders' meetings, (2) special stockholders' meetings, (3) regular meetings of directors, (4) special meetings of directors, and (5) committee meetings. Especially in small, closely held corporations, the business of all of these meetings may be accomplished by consent without an actual meetings. In that case you will prepare a consent agreement for signature.

17.3. Preparation for Meeting

Preparations for meetings include the following activities:

1. Keeping a current meeting file
2. Sending notices of the meeting
3. Preparing the agenda
4. Reserving the meeting room and getting it ready
5. Arranging for payment of directors' fees
6. Preparing to record minutes

17.4. Meeting Folder

Keep a current folder for each forthcoming meeting, with the name and date of the meeting noted on the cover or tab. Keep in the folder all papers and documents pertaining to matters to be discussed at the meeting. As matters to be taken up at the meeting come before the lawyer, he or she examines them, makes whatever notes are necessary, arranges the material for presentation at the meeting, and gives you the material. Shortly before the meeting, the corporate secretary might submit a list of items for the agenda. File this material, together with the material given you by the lawyer, in the current meeting folder and make up the agenda for the meeting from it (see section 17.12).

Also place in the meeting folder all copies of calls, notices of meetings, a list of those to whom the notice was sent, drafts of resolutions to be taken up at the meeting, and possibly a skeleton of the minutes (see section 17.17). On the list of stockholders, show the number of shares owned by each one.

In addition to including the current material, keep in the folders on stockholders' and directors' meetings (1) a pamphlet copy of the corporation laws of the state in which the corporation is organized; (2) a copy of the articles of incorporation and bylaws, with amendments; and (3) other papers of a similar nature that may be needed at any stockholders' or directors' meetings. After the meeting has taken place, remove the current papers and file them in their respective location, leaving in the current file only the documents necessary for all meetings. The folder is then ready to receive material for the next meeting.

17.5. Notice of Stockholders' Meeting

The bylaws tell how and when notices of stockholders' meetings, both annual and special, must be sent. The secretary must follow those provisions closely. The notices are usually in writing, and the secretary mails them to the stockholders a certain number of days before the meeting, as specified in the bylaws.

Form and Content of Notice

The notice of a stockholders' meeting may be in the form of a postcard or of an announcement sent in a sealed envelope. The notice should specify the date, the place, the hour at which the meeting is to be held, and the purpose of the meeting.

An example of a notice of the stockholders' annual meeting and an example of a special meeting notice are given in section 17.37.

17.6. Waiver of Notice of Stockholders' Meeting

Notices of meetings are sent to all stockholders who have the right to vote. In small corporations, however, the stockholders frequently waive notice. In that case, prepare a waiver for the stockholders to sign either before or at the meeting. You can easily adapt form no. 2 in section 17.37 as a waiver of notice of stockholders' meeting.

When a stockholder waives notice, indicate that fact on the list of stockholders that is kept in the current meeting folder.

17.7. Quorum at Stockholders' Meeting

In a small corporation, the secretary has the responsibility of making sure that a quorum will attend the meeting; without a quorum the meeting cannot be held. If you have this responsibility, consult the bylaws to see what percentage of the stock ownership is needed to constitute a quorum. In business corporations the "majority" representation that is normally required is based on shares of stock and not on number of individual stockholders. For example, if a company has a total of 20 stockholders, 5 of whom own more than half the stock, those 5 stockholders would constitute a majority. Thus you can see the necessity for indicating on the stockholders' list the number of shares owned by each.

17.8. Proxies and Proxy Statement

Since it is impossible for all stockholders of a large corporation to attend meetings, it is customary for a stockholder who cannot attend to give some other person, or a committee, authority to vote his or her stock. This authority is known as a *proxy*. The word is also used to denote the person to whom the authority is given and the form on which the authority is given. The proxy form is sent to each stockholder with the notice of meeting.

In large corporations it may be necessary to furnish a written proxy statement to each person whose proxy is being solicited. The proxy statement must set forth the nature of the matters to be voted on under the proxy, whether the person giving the proxy has power to revoke it, and other information relating to the proxy. Proxy statements are technical legal documents, and the lawyer will draft the statement, which may be printed if there are to be a large number of proxies.

What the Secretary Does

Usually, the secretary of a small corporation does not send proxies with the notice of a meeting. If for any reason you anticipate that there will not be a quorum present, however, get proxies from stockholders who cannot attend, representing a sufficient number of shares to make up a quorum. Since small corporations do not list their stock, a proxy statement is not required.

Although large corporations commonly use printed proxy forms, proxies may be reproduced by any means. If only a few are required, photocopy them on letter-size paper, either plain or with the corporation's letterhead.

The proxy need not be witnessed or notarized. The signature should agree with the name in the stock certificate. The signature lines of proxy to be executed by a corporation should be prepared in the same manner as the signature to any instrument signed on behalf of a corporation (see Chapter 9).

As each proxy is received, check the stockholders' list in the current meeting file to show that the proxy has been received.

17.9. Notice of Directors' Meeting

Follow the provisions of the bylaws in sending notices of meetings to directors. Even if notice of a regular meeting is not required by the bylaws, it is advisable to notify the directors of the meeting. If a special meeting is to be called, telephone or fax the directors to determine whether the time is convenient for all of them. Send a written notice when the time of the meeting is definitely fixed.

The list of the directors that is kept in the current meeting folder should be tabulated, with columns showing the date each was notified; the date a follow-up notice, if any, was sent; and the replies.

Form and Content of Notice

Notices of directors' meetings are usually sent on the corporation's letterhead. A model should be stored in the computer.

The notice is sent in the name of the corporate secretary. It should specify the date, place, and hour at which the meeting is to be held. Whether or not it is required by statute or bylaws, the notice of a special meeting should state the purpose for which it is held.

An example of a notice of a directors' special meeting specifying the purpose of the meeting is given in section 17.37 (see model no. 9).

17.10. Quorum at Directors' Meeting

A directors' meeting cannot be held unless a quorum is present. Consult the bylaws for the number of directors necessary to constitute a quorum. A quorum at a directors' meeting differs from a quorum at a stockholders' meeting in that the representation is based on the number of directors and not on the amount of stock owned by them.

If you learn that a quorum will not be present, telephone those directors who expect to attend and arrange, with approval of the person calling the meeting, to have the meeting postponed. This is particularly important if the directors are coming from a distance.

A director cannot give a proxy for a directors' meeting. But corporate action may be taken without a formal directors' meeting when written consent is obtained from all or a majority of the directors.

17.11. Preservation of Notice

Keep a copy of every notice of meeting, with the date of mailing noted on it, in the current meeting folder. If the notice has been published in the newspapers, keep a clipping of the published notice and the name of the publication and dates of publication.

17.12. The Agenda

The *agenda* consists of an itemized list of matters to be brought up at a meeting. The secretary lists them from the accumulated material in the current meeting folder. The agenda should follow the order of business as set forth in the bylaws. A typical agenda prepared for a directors' meeting would include the following steps:

1. *Read minutes of last meeting.* (Attach a copy of the minutes of the previous meeting to the corporate secretary's copy of the agenda.)

2. *Submit the following statements.* (Here enumerate the reports of officers and committees to be presented to the meeting. Copies of the reports may be attached to the agenda.)

3. *Adopt resolution approving minutes of executive committee meetings.* (If minutes are long, copies may be made and attached to the agenda.)

4. *Business of the meeting.* (Here enumerate business to be acted upon, indicating each item by a summary of the resolution that is required.)

Begin preparation of the agenda several days before the meeting. Have it completely in order the evening before the meeting. Prepare a copy for each director. Attach to the agenda the exhibits, supporting papers, reports, and the like that contain the information necessary to supply the groundwork for discussion.

17.13. Reservation and Preparation of the Meeting Room

If a meeting is to be held in a room that is used for other purposes, notify the person who is responsible for the room to have it available at the time of the meeting. When you enter the date of the meeting in the corporation's calendar (see sections 17.33-17.35), also enter at an earlier date a reminder to reserve the room. This should be done in ample time to avoid conflict, the time of the advance notice depending on the demand for the room.

In preparing the room for the meeting, have it dusted, properly heated, and ventilated. See that sufficient coat hangers are available. Provide a pitcher of ice water and glasses as well as stationery, memo pads, and pens and pencils for each person who is expected to attend the meeting. Have a supply of paper clips and rubber bands on the table. Put an ash tray and matches at each place only if smoking is permitted. If any special equipment, such as slide projectors, recorders, or display materials, is to be used at the meeting, be sure it is assembled and operational by the time the meeting begins.

17.14. Directors' Fees

The fee payable to directors for attendance at a meeting is usually fixed by resolution adopted by the board of directors. When preparation for the meeting is the lawyer's responsibility, payment of the fees might be his or her responsibility also. In this case, arrange with the treasurer of the corporation to have the checks or cash at the meeting. If any payments are left over because of nonattendance, return them to the treasurer. Make the payments to the directors after the meeting, preferably enclosed in an envelope. Individual corporate policy will indicate how and when payment is to be made.

17.15. Material to Take to Meetings

Take the following material to directors' and stockholders' meetings:

1. Pamphlet copy of the corporation laws of the state in which the corporation is organized.
2. Copy of the certificate of incorporation, with marginal notations of amendments and copies of them
3. Copy of the bylaws, with marginal notations of amendments and copies of them
4. Separate sheet for order of business
5. Rules and regulations of the corporation, if any, governing the conduct of meetings

6. Proof of the mailing of notices of the meeting and, when necessary, of publication

7. The original call for the meeting and, if there has been a demand for a call, the original of the demand

8. The minute book

9. The corporate seal

10. Current papers pertaining to the meeting (see section 17.4)

11. Blank affidavits, oaths, and the like

17.16. Drafting Resolutions Before Meetings

The lawyer will compose all resolutions involving legal technicalities, but there are many simple resolutions that you should maintain in the computer. The forms in section 17.37 include examples of resolutions that almost all corporations adopt. Complete and print out all simple resolutions that are indicated by the agenda and submit them to the lawyer before finalizing them. Frequently, the lawyer submits drafts of resolutions to the office or department of the corporation that originated the proposition, to insure that the resolution expresses the correct view.

Resolutions to Satisfy Outside Person or Organization

Certain actions may require the passage of a resolution in a form satisfactory to some outside person or organization. For example, the opening of a bank account by a corporation generally calls for passage of a resolution in the form required by the bank. If such a resolution is to come before the meeting, get the required form before the meeting. After the board passes the resolution, fill in the blanks. To avoid copying the resolution into the minutes, you can get two blank forms of the resolution, fill in both forms, and affix one copy to the minutes, making it a part of the minutes by reference. The original of the resolution, signed by the appropriate officers of the corporation, is filed with the bank. If you make extra copies of the minutes, however, you will need to make extra copies of the resolution.

17.17. Preparation for Taking Notes at Meetings

In advance of the meeting, prepare either a skeleton of the minutes or a memorandum form for entering notes. The *skeleton*, or outline, is a rough draft of the minutes with the spaces to be filled in with details as they develop at the meeting. A skeleton is particularly useful when the program of a meeting is prearranged. Use the models of minutes in section 17.37 (see nos. 1 and 10) as a guide in preparing the skeleton and store a copy of the outline in the computer for future use.

A memorandum form for entering notes is shown in Figures 17.1 and 17.2. The memorandum includes the nature of the meeting (regular or special) and how notice was given (regular or personal) or whether a waiver was secured, and all that is necessary to show the facts is a check mark. The resolutions submitted to the meeting are numbered to correspond with the numbers of the resolutions on the memorandum. The notes on this memorandum supply the secretary with all the information necessary for writing

	SECRETARY'S MEMORANDUM		
	MEETING OF BOARD OF DIRECTORS		
		Stated	Reg. Notice
		Annual	Personal
ORGANIZATION		Special	Waiver
DATE	19—	Hour	Standard
PRESENT	No. present	Necessary for quorum	
CHAIR			
SECRETARY			
MINUTES			
STATEMENTS			
RESOLUTIONS			
#1	Proposed by	Seconded by	
		For	
	Votes	Against	
#2	Proposed by	Seconded by	
		For	
	Votes	Against	
#3	Proposed by	Seconded by	
		For	
	Votes	Against	

Figure 17.1.   Secretary's Memorandum for Entering
Notes of Minutes at Meeting (Page 1).

```
RESOLUTIONS
CONTINUED
        #4    Proposed by          Seconded by
                                   For
              Votes                Against


        #5    Proposed by          Seconded by
                                   For
              Votes                Against


        #6    Proposed by          Seconded by
                                   For
              Votes                Against


        #7    Proposed by          Seconded by
                                   For
              Votes                Against
NOTES

ADJOURNMENT
              Fees      Per member present
DISBURSEMENT  Expenses   "     "  present  Sundries Total

                        (Signed).....................
                                        Secretary
```

Figure 17.2.   Secretary's Memorandum for Entering
Notes of Minutes at Meeting (Page 2).

minutes of the meeting. In some cases the proceedings also may be recorded
on tape to assist in preparation of the minutes.

17.18. Taking Notes at Meetings

Verbatim notes of a meeting are not generally necessary except at
stockholders' meetings of large corporations and at board meetings when
there is dissension among the directors. Expert stenographers are sometimes
brought to stockholders' meetings to take the notes.

In taking notes at a meeting, make no attempt to put everything down
in full, but do take important statements verbatim. Also make a verbatim
record of resolutions that are framed at the meeting. A tape recorder is

helpful in this respect. When someone at the meeting asks that his or her views be made a part of the record, the secretary should record those remarks in full. Do not hesitate to record in the minutes the full details of what transpires at the meeting.

Do not permit the meeting to proceed to the next subject unless you have a clear understanding of what has been done. By prearranged signal let the person chairing the meeting know that you do not have a clear understanding of an action that was taken or a statement that was made. It is helpful to have reports and other data handy from which you can quickly extract facts and figures, check spelling of names, and so on. At small meetings, a seating chart helps identify the people who are speaking during the meeting.

Make a separate notation of any action that is to be taken immediately after the meeting.

MINUTES

17.19. The Minutes

Minutes of stockholders' meetings, directors' meetings, and committee meetings may be stored in the computer, with a hard copy kept in separate looseleaf minute books. The pages of a minute book may be numbered for convenience. Any good quality paper may be used. Special paper designed especially for minute books is smooth, heavy, and durable and usually has an outside ruled margin. Manufacturers and suppliers that specialize in corporate forms can provide this paper. Special minute book paper is generally thicker than regular paper, and a laser printer may be necessary to accommodate the increased density.

17.20. Arrangement of Contents of Minute Book

The contents should be arranged in a looseleaf binder as follows:

1. Insert a certified copy of the articles of incorporation in the first pages of the book, or merely copy the articles for inclusion.

2. Next insert a copy of the bylaws.

3. Then insert the minutes of the meeting of incorporators or of other organization meetings.

4. Continue with the minutes of the stockholders' meetings, beginning each set of minutes on a new page.

5. Finally, begin the section on minutes of directors' meetings.

17.21. Content of Minutes

The content and form of minutes are fairly well standardized (see model no. 1 in section 17.37). The order of the contents follows:

1. Begin with the time and place of the meeting.

2. Establish that the meeting was properly called and that notice was given or waived. When the bylaws do not require notice of regular directors' meetings, omit this item from the minutes.

3. Give the names of the chair and the secretary of the meeting.

4. List those present. Also list absentees at directors' meetings. In minutes of stockholders' meetings, list those represented by proxy as well as those present in person and, also, the amount of stock represented. Note that a quorum was present or represented by proxy.

5. State that the minutes of the previous meeting were read and that they were unanimously approved, or that they were corrected as transcribed into the minutes, or that reading was dispensed with.

6. Follow with a clear, accurate, and complete report of all business transacted, arranged in accordance with the order of business established in the bylaws.

17.22. Preparation of Draft of Minutes

Write the minutes immediately after the meeting while events are still fresh in your mind.

If you do not attend the meeting, write the minutes by expanding the lawyer's notes. For example, the notes may show that a certain resolution was adopted unanimously. The minutes would be expanded to read:

On motion duly made and seconded, the following resolution was
    unanimously adopted:
RESOLVED, That . . .

To write minutes from notes made by another, you must have before you all papers, documents, and reports that were discussed at the meeting. If the lawyer takes notes on the memorandum form described in Figures 17.1 and 17.2, the task of expanding the notes is simple.

Submit a draft of the minutes to the lawyer for review and correction. Put the minutes in the minute book only after a draft has been approved by the lawyer or appropriate corporate officer.

17.23. How to Prepare Minutes in Final Form

Some of the large corporations have strict rules about the uniformity of arrangement of minutes. Independently of rules, a secretary should take particular pains with formatting details and the arrangement, spacing, and general appearance of the minutes. The following is a suggested list of rules relating to the format:

1. Capitalize and center the heading designating the meeting.

2. Indent paragraphs about 1 inch.

3. Indent names of those present or absent about 1 1/2 inches.

4. Double-space the text, including preambles to resolutions.

5. Single-space and indent, but do not quote inserts such as letters, waivers of notice of meetings, oaths of inspectors of election, and the like. Leave at least four line spaces before and after the insert. When the insert is a printed paper, the text following the printed insert should start on a new page.

6. Double-space between each paragraph, and triple-space between each item in the order of business.

7. Indent resolutions about 1 1/2 inches and single-space them.

8. Capitalize the words *Board of Directors* and the word *Corporation* when reference is made to the corporation whose minutes are being written. References to specific officers of the corporation may be capitalized or in lower case, but the capitalization should be consistent.

9. Leave about 1 1/2 inches for the outside margin.

10. Put captions in the margin in capitals.

11. Capitalize all letters in the words *WHEREAS* and *RESOLVED,* followed by a comma, and begin the word *That* with a capital.

12. When sums of money are mentioned in a resolution, write them first in words and then in figures in parentheses.

17.24. Correction of Errors in Minutes

The minutes of a meeting are usually approved at the next meeting. The chair informally directs the correction of simple errors. If the error can be corrected immediately, make the correction at the meeting and offer the minutes, as changed, for approval. If the error involves a revision of the minutes, report the corrections of the minutes of the previous meeting in the minutes of the current meeting. A form of resolution correcting the minutes of a previous meeting is shown in section 17.37 (see model no. 17).

Inserting Corrections in the Minute Book

On the hard copy of the minutes filed in the minute book, strike out the erroneous material by drawing a red line through each line of the incorrect material. Write the correct minutes in between the red lines. Make a reference in the margin of the corrected minutes to the minutes of the following meeting, to show where the correction was ordered.

When it is impractical to make the corrections this way, strike out the erroneous material in red and make a note in the margin showing where the revised minutes appear. Then insert the corrected minutes on a separate page at the end of the original minutes. Do not throw away the pages that were incorrectly written. Retain the original pages and indicate that they are obsolete by reference to the minutes of the meeting at which the errors were corrected.

17.25. Certified Extract of Minutes

Directors authorize by resolution the transaction of various items of business on behalf of the corporation, and the resolutions passed by the directors are embodied in the minutes of the meetings. It is frequently necessary to produce evidence of the authority granted in the form of a certified extract of the minutes or a copy of the resolution. The certification is usually by the secretary of the corporation. Figures 17.3 and 17.4 on pages 410 and 411 illustrate a certified extract of minutes. It may be prepared on plain letter-size paper or on the corporation's letterhead.

CERTIFIED EXTRACT OF MINUTES

I, the undersigned, Secretary of GLASSER & SONS, INC.,

a corporation duly organized and existing under the laws of

the State of New York, and having its principal place of

business in the City of New York, hereby CERTIFY that the

following is a true copy of a certain resolution duly adopted

by the Board of Directors of the said corporation in accord-

ance with the Bylaws at, and recorded in the minutes of,

a meeting of the said Board duly held on   , 19   ,

and not subsequently rescinded or modified:

RESOLVED:

That an account be opened in the name of
the Glasser & Sons, Inc., with the EAST RIVER
SAVINGS BANK at 41 Rockefeller Plaza, in the
Borough of Manhattan, City of New York, and
that the funds of the said Glasser & Sons, Inc.,
may be deposited therein and that all drafts
and other instruments for the payment of money
shall be signed by the following officers:-

Jules MacDonald   President
Janet Lewis   Secretary & Treasurer
John Bennett   Asst. Secretary &
                   Asst. Treasurer
Ellen Farnsworth   Vice-President
Joseph Hart   Asst. Treasurer of
                   Committee of Managers

And the Bank is hereby authorized to pay such
drafts and instruments when so signed (including those drawn to cash or bearer or to the
individual order of the officer or officers
signing the same) and also to receive the same

Figure 17.3.   Certified Extract of Minutes (Page 1).

17.26. Indexing of Minutes

If minutes of meetings are voluminous, keep a computerized index so
that any business that has been passed upon may be referred to easily and

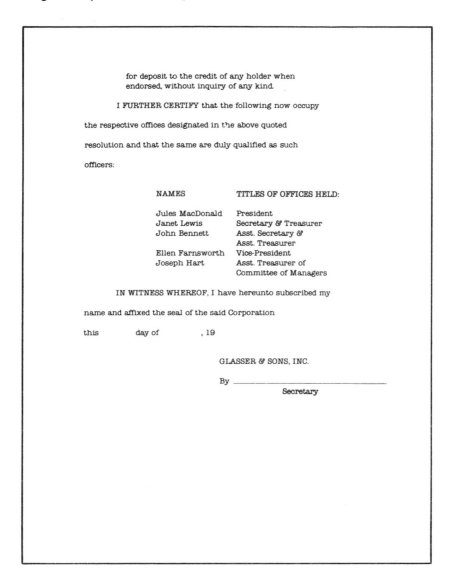

for deposit to the credit of any holder when
endorsed, without inquiry of any kind.

I FURTHER CERTIFY that the following now occupy

the respective offices designated in the above quoted

resolution and that the same are duly qualified as such

officers:

NAMES	TITLES OF OFFICES HELD:
Jules MacDonald	President
Janet Lewis	Secretary & Treasurer
John Bennett	Asst. Secretary &
	Asst. Treasurer
Ellen Farnsworth	Vice-President
Joseph Hart	Asst. Treasurer of
	Committee of Managers

IN WITNESS WHEREOF, I have hereunto subscribed my

name and affixed the seal of the said Corporation

this   day of   , 19

GLASSER & SONS, INC.

By _____
                Secretary

Figure 17.4.   Certified Extract of Minutes (Page 2).

quickly. The making of the index is facilitated by marginal captions in the
minutes. The index contains the subject matter taken from the captions and
a reference to the page on which the caption appears. When the minutes are

stored in the computer, they can usually be searched for a particular subject specified in the index.

ISSUANCE AND TRANSFER OF STOCK OF A SMALL CORPORATION

17.27. Authority to Issue Certificate

A large corporation has a transfer agent, usually a bank, that issues and transfers shares of stock. The lawyer frequently has this responsibility for a small corporation. He or she issues an original certificate of stock for a definite number of shares to a certain person when authorized to do so by resolution of the directors or of the stockholders.

17.28. Stock Certificate Book

A looseleaf book of blank stock certificates is kept for each class of stock. The certificates and corresponding stubs are numbered consecutively. The number of shares is usually left blank so that certificates may be issued for various amounts. Figure 17.5 is a reproduction of a stock certificate. In a small corporation with only a few stockholders, the stock certificate book usually serves as a transfer record and as a stock ledger.

17.29. Original Issue and Transfer of Stock

An original issue of stock refers to a share of stock that has never before been issued. The certificate of incorporation authorizes the corporation to issue a stated number of shares. All of these shares need not be issued immediately, but as each is issued, it is considered an original issue. When the person to whom it is issued sells or gives it to someone else, it becomes a transferred share.

State Transfer Tax

Some states have a transfer tax on stock. Whether or not the state tax is payable depends on the state in which the transfer is made. Thus a transfer in New York of a Delaware corporation's stock is subject to the New York transfer tax, although Delaware does not have a tax. It is impractical to give the rate of taxation for each state here, but you can get the information from the state statutes.

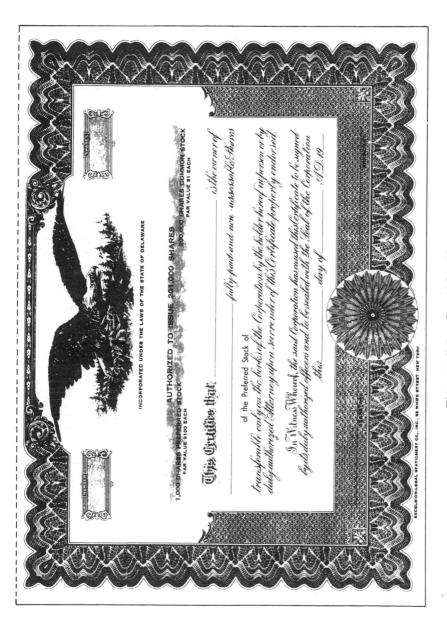

Figure 17.5. Stock Certificate.

413

Almost every law imposing these taxes gives some official the right to call for books and documents on a moment's notice. For example, state inspectors may call on New York transfer agents and ask to see the stock transfer books to ascertain whether the proper stamps have been affixed to meet stock transfer requirements. If you are the custodian of a corporation's books, it is your duty (1) to see that the proper documentary stamps are affixed and (2) to present the books for inspection upon presentation of the proper credentials.

Dissolution of Corporation

When a corporation decides to end its existence, it must be formally dissolved. The state corporation law will specify how this is done. Articles of dissolution may be filed by the incorporators, or a statement of intent to dissolve may be filed by written consent of the shareholders or by act of the corporation. Similarly, a corporation may merge with another corporation. Forms for all of these procedures may be found in booklets designed to implement the law in your state, and they should be entered in your computer library.

17.30. Issuance of Certificate of Stock

Here are the steps necessary to issue a stock certificate.

1. Enter the name and address of the person to whom the certificate is issued and the number of shares for which it is issued on the stub.

2. Remove the certificate from the stock book.

3. Type on the face of the certificate the name of the person to whom it is issued, the number of shares it represents, and the date.

4. Have the certificate signed by the officers whose signatures are required.

5. Impress the corporate seal in the space provided.

6. If possible, have the receipt on the stub of the certificate signed. If the person in whose name the certificate is issued is not present to sign the stub, photocopy the receipt section. Enclose the original receipt with the certificate and request the person in whose name the certificate is issued to sign and return it. Replace the photocopy when the original is signed and returned.

7. Affix to the stub and cancel the documentary stamps. (See Chapter 18.)

8. Send certificates by registered mail.

17.31. Transfer of Certificate

The back of the certificate has a form for assignment or transfer of stock from one holder to another (Figure 17.6). When shares of stock are transferred, the corporation issues a new certificate. The holder of a 100-share certificate might want to transfer, say, 50 shares and keep the other 50. In that case, two new certificates of 50 shares each are issued—one to the transferee and one to the original owner.

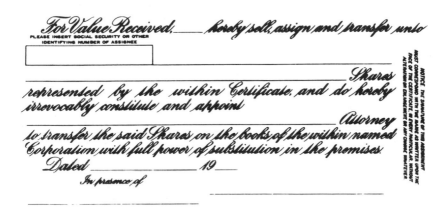

The designations and the powers, preferences and rights, and the qualifications thereof are as follows: The non-voting mana shares, as a class, shall be entitled to such dividends as from time to time may be declared by the board of directors of the Corporat: irrespective of whether or not dividends are declared and paid on any and all classes of voting stock of Preferred Shares. The of the Management Shares can only be officers or employees of the Corporation and said shares are subject to call by the Board of Di at any time at the same price at which they were issued. The deposit at any bank in Puerto Rico to the credit of the registered he any then outstanding Management Shares of an amount equivalent to the price at which said shares were issued, shall have the e making valueless and void any certificate or certificates representing any shares outstanding against which such deposit shall ha' made. The holders of such Management Shares are not entitled to vote at any meeting of stockholders, have no interest whatsoever corporate surplus nor in the assets of the Corporation other than to the extent of the amount paid for said shares. The Management of this Corporation shall be issued from time to time as authorized by the Board of Directors of the Corporation, and the persons t said shares are issued, receive them subject to the conditions hereinabove mentioned and subject to the further condition that said must be surrendered at such time as when said officer or employee ceases to be an officer or employee of the Corporation, it being stood that if said Certificate or Certificate of Management Shares of the Corporation are not surrendered by a person who ceases t officer or an employee of the Corporation, said certificate shall be of no value in his possession and shall not be entitled to such di as therafter may be declared by the Corporation on the holders of Management Shares.

The amount of the authorized stock of the Company may be increased or decreased by the affirmative vote of the holder: then outstanding Class A Voting Stock, Class B Non-Voting Stock. It shall not be required, for any amendment to these articles corporation, the vote of the then holders of Management Shares, irrespective of whether or not such amendment may affect the rig privileges of the holders of said Management Shares.

Figure 17.6. Back of Certificate Showing Transfer Form.

When a certificate is transferred, follow the procedure outlined on the preceding pages for the original issuance of a certificate. Notice that the stub to a transferred certificate calls for more information than the stub to an original issue. In addition, take the following steps:

1. Write or stamp "Canceled" in ink across the face of the old certificate.

2. Date and initial the canceled certificate.

3. Tape the canceled certificate to its stub in the stock certificate book, as nearly in the certificate's original position in the book as possible.

4. Affix the state documentary stamp to the canceled certificate and cancel the stamp. The stamp tax will apply only to the shares that are transferred, not to the certificate for the new shares that the original owner might keep. (See Chapter 18 for cancellation of stamps.)

17.32. Separate Form of Assignment

When you handle the lawyer's personal securities, you will probably deal with a broker. Securities transferred through a broker are transferred in blank because the transferor does not know to whom they will be delivered. A transfer in blank might be made on a form of assignment separate from the stock certificate, instead of on the assignment that is printed on the back of the certificate. The broker will supply you with printed forms for this purpose. If the certificates are sent to the broker by mail, registered or otherwise, send the assignment in blank separately. The reason for this is that only nonnegotiable securities should be sent through the mail. A security endorsed on the back in blank or a security accompanied by a separate assignment in blank is negotiable. The wording of a separate assignment is similar to that of the assignment on the back of a certificate. Figure 17.7 illustrates an assignment separate from a stock certificate.

THE CORPORATION CALENDAR

17.33. Need for a Corporation Calendar

The need for a corporation calendar is evident to anyone whose office has the responsibility of seeing that certain acts of a corporation are done at

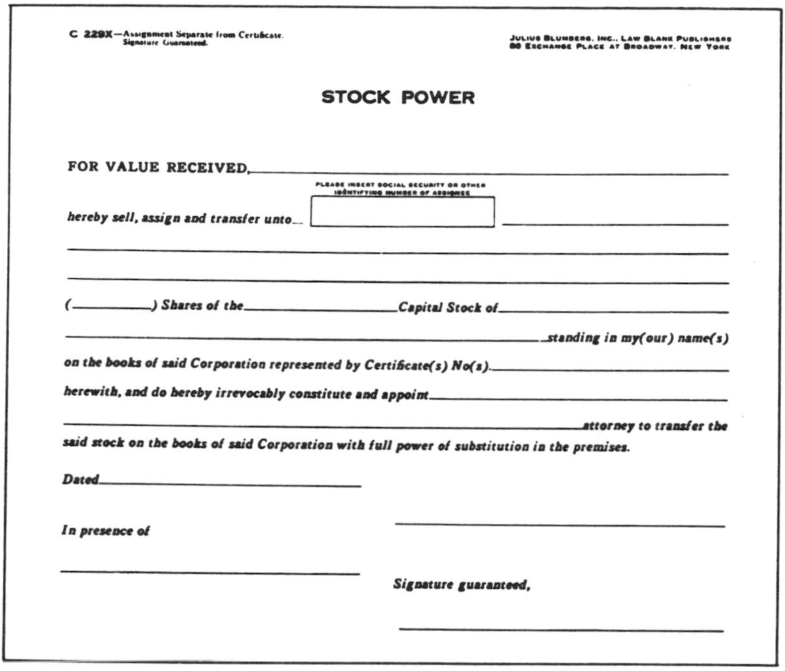

C 229X—Assignment Separate from Certificate. Signature Guaranteed.

JULIUS BLUMBERG, INC., LAW BLANK PUBLISHERS
80 EXCHANGE PLACE AT BROADWAY, NEW YORK

STOCK POWER

FOR VALUE RECEIVED,__________

PLEASE INSERT SOCIAL SECURITY OR OTHER IDENTIFYING NUMBER OF ASSIGNEE

*hereby sell, assign and transfer unto*__________

(_____) *Shares of the*__________*Capital Stock of*__________

__________*standing in my(our) name(s)*

*on the books of said Corporation represented by Certificate(s) No(s).*__________

*herewith, and do hereby irrevocably constitute and appoint*__________

__________*attorney to transfer the said stock on the books of said Corporation with full power of substitution in the premises.*

*Dated*__________

In presence of

____

Signature guaranteed,

____

Figure 17.7. Assignment Separate from Certificate.

certain times. The acts for which the lawyer is responsible generally relate to the following subjects:

1. Directors' and stockholders' meetings
2. Expiration and renewal of contracts, leases, and the like
3. Tax matters
4. Reports

In some cases the lawyer attends to these matters personally; in others, he or she merely advises the principals of the corporation that the matter should be attended to by a certain date.

It is advisable to keep the follow-ups for the corporation on a computerized or other form of calendar separate from the appointment and court diary (Chapter 3). If the lawyer has these follow-up responsibilities for more than one corporation, however, one calendar will serve for the several corporations.

I7.34. How to Keep the Corporation Calendar

If your calendar is computerized, follow the requirements of your software. If you use a hard-copy system, arrange it so that you are reminded of things to do on the correct date without having to search the files each day. With an index-card-file system, for example, you would arrange the index cards chronologically behind monthly tab cards. A card should contain sufficient information, in addition to the date, to give the lawyer a correct idea of what he or she is to do or what the secretary and paralegal are to do. The cards are made up as a transaction occurs or as the need for the card arises. Thus if the lawyer is custodian of the corporate documents and you are given a lease to put in the safe, you will note the expiration date of the lease and make up a card for that particular day.

Acts that are to be done at certain times but for which no definite day is specified may be entered on a monthly reminder card. Suppose that in a certain state the corporation is required to file a statement with the secretary of state each time a change in officers occurs. You will make a note of the requirement on a card without a date and at the beginning of each month move it along to the next month. If you prefer, you might make a note on 12 separate cards and file one for each month.

At the beginning of each month, examine all of the items in the calendar for the succeeding two months to allow ample time for taking action on the reminders furnished by the cards. Time-consuming tasks that must be done by a certain date should be entered sufficiently in advance to permit the work to be finished on time.

17.35. Where to Get Dates for the Corporation Calendar

You will have to ask the lawyer to give you the date for many of the calendar entries, but you can get some of them from the material in the information folder (see section 17.1) and from the sources indicated below. In any event, the lawyer should verify the dates, because severe penalties result from failure to perform some of these acts at the required time.

Annual stockholders' meeting. See the bylaws.

Regular directors' meeting. See the minutes of first meeting of directors or stockholders.

Expiration and renewal dates. See the documents or abstracts of them in the information folder.

Annual report to stockholders. The annual report is published as soon after the end of the fiscal year as possible. Work on it begins considerably before the close of the fiscal year, the length of time depending on the elaborateness of the report.

Annual report to state authority. Check the general corporation law for the state of incorporation, a pamphlet copy of which should be in the information folder.

Tax matters and reports to federal and state governments. For accurate, up-to-date information, a looseleaf tax service would probably serve your purpose best. These services cover all taxes imposed by federal, state, and local governments and contain tax calendars. If your office maintains a corporation, its library will probably contain a service of this kind. If not, and if the service is not available in a nearby law library, write to the particular tax authority for the information desired.

CHANGE OF CORPORATE NAME

17.36. When the Corporate Name Is Changed

The states provide by statute the manner in which a corporation may change its name and indicate the procedure to be followed. The attorney will give you detailed instructions about the legal procedure because the directions outlined by the statute must be strictly followed. Numerous other changes are made necessary by the adoption of a new name. The corporation personnel looks after many of them, such as changes in bank accounts, stationery, and the like, but some of the changes are handled in the law office. Matters to which you should attend might include the following:

1. Changes in corporate seal
2. Change in contracts
3. Change in leases
4. Change in deeds to real property
5. Need to order new stock certificate book
6. Need to write to stockholders

CORPORATION FORMS

17.37. Model Corporation Forms

The following are forms commonly used for directors' and stockholders' meetings. All of these forms should be stored in your computer and in any other forms file or looseleaf notebook that you maintain. Note that any headings in brackets shown in the following examples may appear as marginal notes in the minute book.

No. 1. Minutes of First Meeting of Incorporators of a Corporation

[Time and Place of Meeting]

The first meeting of incorporators of the .... was held at ...., in the City of ...., State of ...., at ..... o'clock in the ..... noon of the .... day of ...., 19...., pursuant to a written waiver of notice, signed by all of the incorporators, fixing the place and time.

The following incorporators were present in person or by proxy:

Name of Incorporator	Name of Proxy*
....	....
....	....
....	....

being all of the incorporators named in the Certificate of Incorporation.

[Temporary Officers]

On motion unanimously carried, Mr./Ms./Mrs. .... was elected Chair, and Mr./Ms./Mrs. ...., Secretary of the meeting.

[Waiver of Notice]

The Secretary presented the waiver of notice of the meeting signed by all of the incorporators, and it was filed as part of the minutes. The Secretary was ordered to file as a part of the minutes any proxies that had been accepted.

---

*If the incorporator was present in person, write "In person" in the column. If not, write the name of the person who represented him as proxy.

[Certificate of Incorporation Reported Filed]

The Chair reported that the Certificate of Incorporation of the Corporation was filed in the office of the Secretary of State of the State of .... on the ..... day of ...., 19..; that a certified copy thereof was filed for record in the office of the recorder of Deeds in the County of ...., on the ..... day of ...., 19..; and that a copy of the Certificate was ordered to be inserted in the minute book as part of the records of the meeting.

[Adoption of Bylaws]

The Secretary presented a proposed form of the Bylaws for the regulation and management of the affairs of the Corporation, which was read, section by section, and unanimously adopted and ordered to be made a part of the permanent records to follow the Certificate of Incorporation in the minute book.

[Election of Directors]

Motions were declared by the Chair to be in order for the nomination of directors of the Corporation to hold office for the ensuing year and until their successors are elected and qualify. The following persons were nominated: [*Insert names of nominees.*]

No further nominations having been made, a ballot was taken. All of the incorporators having voted and the ballots having been duly canvassed, the Chair declared that the above-named persons were elected directors of the Corporation by the unanimous vote of all incorporators.

Upon motion duly made, seconded, and unanimously carried, it was

[Issuance of Capital Stock]

RESOLVED, That the Board of Directors be and it hereby is authorized in its discretion to issue the capital stock of this Corporation to the full amount or number of shares authorized by the Certificate of Incorporation, in such amounts and for such considerations as from time to time shall be determined by the Board of Directors and as may be permitted by law.

[Adjournment]

There being no other business to be transacted and upon motion duly made, seconded, and carried, the meeting was adjourned.

....
Secretary of the Meeting

No. 2. Waiver of Notice of First Meeting of Incorporators

We, the undersigned, being all of the incorporators of the ...., a corporation organized under the laws of the State of ...., do hereby severally waive all of the statutory requirements as to notice of the time, place, and purpose of the first meeting of incorporators of the said Corporation and the publication thereof and consent that the meeting shall be held at ...., the the City of ...., State of ...., on the ..... day of ...., 19.., at ..... o'clock in the ..... noon; and we consent to the transaction of any and all business that may properly come before this meeting. Dated ...., 19..

....
....
....

No. 3. Waiver of Notice of First Meeting of Directors

We, the undersigned, constituting all of the duly elected directors of ...., do hereby severally waive notice of time, place, and purpose of the first meeting of directors of said Corporation and consent that the meeting be held at ...., in the City of ...., State of ...., on the ..... day of ...., 19.., at ..... o'clock in the ..... noon; we do further consent to the transaction of any business requisite to complete the organization of the company and to any and all business that may properly come before the meeting. Dated ...., 19..

....
....
....

No. 4. Notice of Annual Meeting of Stockholders

The annual meeting of the stockholders of .... Corporation, for the election of directors and the transaction of such other business as may properly come before the meeting, will be held at the Corporation's registered office at ...., in the City of ...., State of ...., on the ..... day of ...., 19.., at ..... o'clock in the ..... noon.

If you cannot be present at the meeting, please sign and return the accompanying proxy in the enclosed self-addressed envelope.

....
Secretary

No. 5. Notice of Special Meeting of Stockholders Indicating Purpose of Meeting

NOTICE IS HEREBY GIVEN that a special meeting of the stockholders of the .... Company, a corporation of the State of .... has been called and will be held on ...., 19.., at ..... o'clock .....M, at the registered office of the Company at ...., City of ...., State of ...., for the following purposes:

[*Insert purpose of meeting.*]

To transact any other business that may come before the said meeting.

If you are unable to be present in person, please sign the enclosed form of proxy and return it in the enclosed self-addressed envelope.

By order of the Board of Directors.

....
Secretary

Dated.........., 19..

No. 6. Affidavit of Secretary That Notice of Annual Meeting of Stockholders Was Mailed

STATE OF ....
COUNTY OF ....

.........., being duly sworn, states that he/she is the Secretary of the .... Corporation, a corporation organized and existing under the laws of the State of ...., having its principal office in the State of ....; that on the ..... day of ...., 19.., he/she caused notice of the annual meeting of the stockholders of the said Corporation, a copy of which is hereto attached and is hereby made a part of this affidavit, to be deposited in the United States Post Office at .... [*City*], in a sealed envelope, postage prepaid, duly addressed to each stockholder of record of the said Corporation at his or her last-known post office address as the same appeared on the books of the Corporation.

....

Subscribed and sworn to before me
this ..... day of ...., 19..

....
Notary Public
My commission expires ...., 19...

No. 7. Affidavit of Secretary of Publication of Notice of Stockholders' Meeting.

STATE OF ....
COUNTY OF ....
............, being duly sworn, states that he/she is the Secretary of ....
Corporation, a corporation organized and existing under the laws of the
State of ....; that pursuant to the order of the Board of Directors of said
Corporation, he/she caused the notice of the .... [*insert annual or
special*] meeting of stockholders, a copy of which is hereto annexed and
made a part of this affidavit, to be published in the ...., a newspaper
published in the City of ...., and circulating in the County of ....,
being the county in which said Corporation is located, for a period of ....,
beginning the ..... day of ...., 19.., as required by .... [*insert words
"the laws of the State of ....." or "the Bylaws of the Corporation*].
Sworn to me before this
..... day of ...., 19..   ....
        ....   Secretary
        Notary Public
        My commission expires ...., 19...

No. 8. Proxy for Special Meeting of Stockholders

KNOW ALL MEN BY THESE PRESENTS, That ...., the undersigned,
stockholder in the .... Corporation, does hereby appoint .... and
.........., or either of them, true and lawful attorneys, with power of
substitution for .... and in .... name to vote, as .... proxy, at the
Special Meeting of the Stockholders in said Corporation, to be held at the
City of ...., State of ...., on the ..... day of ...., 19.., or at any
adjournment thereof, with all the powers that .... should possess if
personally present.
Dated this ..... day of ...., 19..

                                                        ....

No. 9. Notice of Special Meeting of Directors, Specifying Purposes

                                        .... [*City*] .... [*State*]
To ...., ..., and ....
Directors of ....Corporation:
        NOTICE IS HEREBY GIVEN That, in accordance with the
provisions of Article ....., Section ....., of the Bylaws of the ....
Corporation, and in accordance with the requirements of the laws of the
State of ...., a special meeting of the Board of Directors of the said
Corporation will be held at its office and principal place of business, ...

[*Street*], ... [*City*], ... [*State*], on the ..... day of ...., 19.., at .....
o'clock in the ..... noon, for the purpose of:

1. [*Insert particular purpose of meeting.*]

2. To transact such other business as may lawfully come before said
meeting.

....
Secretary

No. 10. Minutes of Annual Meeting of Directors

[Time and Place of Meeting]

The .... annual meeting of the Board of Directors of the ....
Corporation was held at the office of the Corporation, ..., in the City of
.........., State of ...., on the ..... day of ...., 19.., at ..... o'clock in the
..... noon, immediately following the adjournment of the annual meeting of
the stockholders.

[Quorum]

The following directors, being all of the directors of the said
Corporation, were present:

....
....
....
....
....

[Chair; Secretary]

Mr./Ms./Mrs. ...., President of the Corporation, presided, and
Mr./Ms./Mrs. .... acted as Secretary of the meeting.

[Notice of Meeting]

The Secretary presented the notice of the meeting pursuant to which
the meeting was held. The same was ordered to be entered in the minutes
and is as follows:

[*Insert notice here.*]

The Chair laid before the meeting the minutes of the annual meeting
of the stockholders of the Corporation, held on the ..... day of ...., 19..,
showing the election of the following persons as directors of the

Corporation, to hold office for the term of .... year(s), and until their successors shall be elected and shall qualify.

....

....

....

....

....

[Election of Officers]

Upon motion duly made, seconded, and unanimously carried, the Board of Directors proceeded to elect the following officers of the Corporation: President, Vice President, Secretary, and Treasurer.

Mr./Ms./Mrs. .... was nominated for the office of President of the Corporation. No other nominations being made, and upon motion duly made, seconded, and unanimously carried, Mr./Ms./Mrs. .... was elected President of the Corporation and was declared duly elected to the office.

[Repeat the minutes given above for each officer.]

Each of the officers so elected was present and thereupon accepted the office to which he or she was elected.

Upon motion duly made, seconded, and unanimously carried, the Board of Directors proceeded to fix the salaries to be paid to the President, Vice President, Secretary, and Treasurer, for the year 19...

[Compensation of Officers]

The Chair announced that the salary of each officer would be voted on separately and that the officer whose salary was under consideration would not participate in the vote. Mr./Ms./Mrs. ...., President, thereupon left the room.

Upon motion duly made, seconded, and affirmatively voted on by all of the directors then present, it was

[Salary of President]

RESOLVED, That the salary of Mr./Ms./Mrs. ...., President of the Corporation, be fixed at $..... for the year beginning ...., 19.., and ending ...., 19.., payable in semimonthly installments on the fifteenth day and the last day of each calendar month.

The vote having been taken, Mr./Ms./Mrs. .... was recalled to the meeting.

The Vice President then left the room.

[Repeat the minutes given above for each officer.]

[Adjournment]

There being no further business, the meeting was, upon motion, adjourned.

....
President
....
Secretary

No. 11. Resolution of Directors Authorizing Sale and Issue of Stock to Persons Determined by Executive Committee

RESOLVED, That this Corporation sell and issue .... (..........) shares of the Preferred Stock of this corporation at par and .... (..........) shares of Common Stock having no par value at .... dollars ($..........) per share, payable in cash at the time of purchase, to such persons, firms, or corporations as the Executive Committee shall determine, and the President and the Secretary of this Corporation are hereby authorized to execute and deliver certificates of stock to purchasers upon receipt of full payment for shares purchased.

No. 12. Resolution of Directors Amending a Particular Bylaw upon Authorization of Stockholders

WHEREAS, The holders of more than two-thirds of the subscribed capital stock of the Corporation have, by a resolution adopted at a meeting duly called upon notice, authorized and directed the Board of Directors of this Corporation to amend Section ..... of Article ..... of the Bylaws, it is

RESOLVED, That the aforesaid Section ..... of Article ..... of the Bylaws be amended in accordance with the said resolution of the stockholders, to read as follows:

[Insert new bylaw.]

IT IS FURTHER RESOLVED, That the Secretary of the Corporation be and he hereby is authorized and directed to copy the said Section ..... of Article ..... of the Bylaws, as amended, in the book of Bylaws of the Corporation, and properly to certify the same.

No. 13. Directors' Resolution Accepting Resignation of a Member of Board

RESOLVED, That the resignation of .... as a member of the Board of Directors of the .... Corporation, as evidenced by his/her letter to the Corporation, dated the ..... day of ...., 19.., be and it hereby is accepted, and the Secretary of this Corporation is hereby instructed to notify .... of the acceptance of his/her aforesaid resignation.

No. 14. Directors' Resolution Accepting Resignation of Officer

RESOLVED, That the resignation of Mr./Ms./Mrs. .... as ....
[*insert office*] be and it hereby is accepted to take effect on the ..... day of
.........., 19...

No. 15. Directors' Resolution Expressing Gratitude for Services of Resigning Officer

WHEREAS, ... has, for the past .... (..........) years, been
President of the Company, and whereas the said .... declines to be a
candidate for reelection, this Board of Directors wishes to enter the
following resolution in the minutes.

RESOLVED, That we recognize the excellent, energetic, and
intelligent service that .... has rendered the Company during his/her
incumbency. We believe the high position the Company has attained has
been in large measure due to his/her earnest efforts and untiring devotion.

RESOLVED FURTHER, That in recognition of his/her services to
the Company, the aforesaid .... be elected Chair to preside at the
meetings of the Board for the ensuing year.

No. 16. Blanket Resolution of Directors Authorizing Issuance of Duplicate Certificate in Event of Loss

RESOLVED, That, in the event of the loss, mutilation, or destruction
of any certificate of stock of .... Corporation, a duplicate thereof may be
issued, provided the owner makes a sufficient affidavit setting forth the loss,
mutilation, or destruction of the original certificate and gives a surety bond
to the Corporation to such amount as may be determined by the ....
[*indicate officer*].

No. 17. Excerpt of Minutes Showing Adoption of Minutes of Previous Meeting as Corrected

RESOLVED, That the minutes of the meeting of ...., held on the
..... day of ...., 19.., be and they are hereby adopted and approved in their
entirety, except that the words "..........” be eliminated from the resolution
.... [*specify subject matter of resolution for identification*] contained
therein.

No. 18. Resolution of Directors (or Stockholders) Extending Sympathy upon Death of Associate

WHEREAS, The directors of the .... Corporation wish to record
their deep sorrow at the death on ...., 19.., of their esteemed associate
.........., who since ...., 19.., served as director of this Corporation, be it

RESOLVED, That the Board of Directors of this Corporation hereby gives formal expression of its grievous loss in the death of .... and does hereby note in its records the passing from this life of someone who was esteemed by his/her associates, loved by his/her friends, and respected by all.

RESOLVED, FURTHER, That a copy of this resolution be tendered to his/her family as a humble expression of the Board's heartfelt sympathy in its bereavement.

18 Assisting in Real Estate Practice and Foreclosures

The legal secretary and paralegal are very valuable to a lawyer engaged in real estate practice. By becoming familiar with the various legal documents involved in real estate transactions and the procedure necessary to consummate the transaction, they can relieve the lawyer of practically all routine work, with very little guidance.

In Chapter 9, we gave basic information about legal instruments generally. In this chapter, we describe specific real estate instruments, with information and suggestions that will help you assume part of the responsibility for their preparation. Regardless of how capable you are, observe this rule: Always get the lawyer's approval of an instrument both before it is signed and after it is executed, before recording it.

The following sections discuss deeds, mortgages, leases, purchase and sale agreements, closings, and foreclosure actions. Although realtors and bank mortgage departments handle many of these matters, the lawyer's secretary and the paralegal must be familiar with the various legal documents and procedures involved in real estate practice.

REAL ESTATE INSTRUMENTS

18.1. Pattern Followed for Each Instrument

The following information is given for the instruments that are discussed in this chapter: The instrument is defined, and the parties to it are described. The forms and kinds of a particular instrument are noted, with a list of the information needed to fill out a printed form. Any important statements or clauses common to the instrument are described.

REAL PROPERTY DESCRIPTIONS

18.2. How Land Is Described

A description of real property appears in many legal instruments that you prepare and constitutes an important part of the instrument. The descriptions are often complicated and difficult to follow. Usually, they are copies from some other document or from an abstract of title. An understanding of how these descriptions are evolved will make it easier for you to copy them and will lessen the possibility of an error. Accuracy is essential.

Land is identified according to section and township or by metes and bounds. In towns and subdivisions, lot and block identification is also used. Property is never identified solely by street and number because the names and numbers of streets might change.

18.3. Section and Township Description

In the eighteenth century, when the United States began to sell public lands, it was necessary to adopt some conventional method of describing the tracts that were sold. A *rectangular system of surveys* was devised for the public land states, which include Alabama, Alaska, Arizona, Arkansas, California, Colorado, Florida, Idaho, Illinois, Indiana, Iowa, Kansas, Louisiana, Michigan, Minnesota, Mississippi, Missouri, Montana, Nebraska, Nevada, New Mexico, North Dakota, Ohio, Oklahoma, Oregon, South Dakota, Utah, Washington, Wisconsin, and Wyoming.

The survey divided the public lands into rectangular tracts, located with reference to base lines running east and west and *prime* or *principal meridians* running north and south. The prime meridians are numbered, as Third Prime Meridian, or named, as San Bernardino Meridian. The rectangular tracts are divided into six-mile squares, known as *townships*. A row of townships running north and south is called a *range,* and the ranges are numbered east and west from the prime meridians. The townships are divided into 36 sections, each one mile square, or 640 acres. The sections are numbered from 1 to 36, beginning with the section in the northeast corner of the township, proceeding west to the boundary of the township; the next row is numbered from west to east and so on. (See Figure 18.1.) The sections in turn are divided into half and quarter sections, and the quarters into quarter-quarter sections, designated by their direction from the center as northwest, southwest, northeast, and southeast.

The description of a given five acres of land identified by the section and township (government survey) description might read:

The East Half of the Northeast Quarter of the Northeast Quarter of the Northeast Quarter of Section One, Township 39 North, Range 12 East of the Third Prime Meridian.

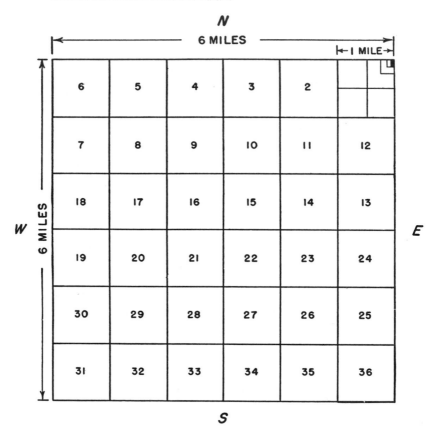

Figure 18.1.   Diagram of Township Divided into Sections.

The shaded portion of the diagram in Figure 18.1 represents the parcel described above, assuming that the diagram is Township 39 North, Range 12 East.

Land identification in the 29 public land states in which the government survey description is used is thus precise and orderly; it is possible to designate any plot of land as small as five acres with perfect accuracy; no two parcels are described in exactly the same terms because they are identified with reference to a specific prime meridian.

18.4. Metes and Bounds Description

Before the government survey, the land in the area comprising the 13 colonies (18 states) was held under original grants from the Crown to the colonists. In these states—Connecticut, Delaware, Georgia, Kentucky, Maine, Maryland, Massachusetts, New Hampshire, New Jersey, New York, North Carolina, Pennsylvania, Rhode Island, South Carolina, Tennessee, Vermont, Virginia, and West Virginia—and in Texas[1] each parcel of land is different in size and shape and is described by *metes and bounds*. A metes and bounds description is not correlated to any system of meridians and base lines, but each tract of land is described by the lines that constitute its boundaries. Metes are lineal measures and bounds are artificial and natural boundaries. A natural landmark, such as a tree or river, or an artificial landmark, such as a fence, stake, railroad, or street, often marks the corners and angles. These marks are known as *monuments*. A description by courses and distances constitutes part of a metes and bounds description. The direction from the starting point in which the boundary line runs is a *course;* the length of the line is a *distance.* Figure 18.2 illustrates a metes and bounds description.

18.5. The Plat System

Tracts of land described by metes and bounds or the rectangular survey system may be further divided into streets, blocks, and lots. Maps or plans of these divisions are called *plats*. A *plat book* is a record maintained showing the location, size, and name of the owners of each plat of real

---

[1]The United States never had original title to the land in Texas because it was annexed as an independent republic.

ALL that lot or parcel of land, situate, lying and being in the Town of Oyster Bay, County of Nassau, State of New York, bounded and described as follows:

BEGINNING at a point in the center line of Buena Vista Avenue distant two hundred sixty-one and thirty hundredths (261.30) feet southerly from the point of intersection of said line with the center line of Jones Road; running thence along the center line of Buena Vista Avenue South twenty-five (25) degrees thirty-three (33) minutes East four hundred fifty-two and seventy-eight hundredths (452.78) feet to a point; running thence North sixty-eight (68) degrees thirty-two (32) minutes East three hundred ten and eleven hundredths (310.11) feet to a point in the center line of a driveway; running thence generally along the center line of said driveway the following courses and distances:

A. North forty-five (45) degrees forty-two (42) minutes West, 50 feet;

B. North thirty-nine (39) degrees two (02) minutes West, 50 feet;

C. North thirty-four (34) degrees sixteen (16) minutes West, 50 feet;

D. North twenty-eight (28) degrees fifty-eight (58) minutes West, 40 feet;

E. North twenty-six (26) degrees seventeen (17) minutes West, 100 feet;

F. North Thirty-two (32) degrees six (06) minutes West, 50 feet;

G. North fifty-five (55) degrees thirty-four (34) minutes West, 50 feet;

H. North Sixty-one (61) degrees thirty-two (32) minutes West, 50 feet;

I. North eighty (80) degrees thirty-three (33) minutes West, 50 feet;

J. South seventy-nine (79) degrees eleven (11) minutes West, 50 feet;

K. South sixty-five (65) degrees thirty-two (32) minutes West, 50 feet; and

L. South sixty-four (64) degrees forty-seven (47) minutes West, 77 feet, to a point in the center line of Buena Vista Avenue, the point or place of beginning;

Containing, in area, approximately two and seven hundred seventy-four thousandths (2.774) acres;

Being and intended to be all of Plot No. 5, as shown on a map entitled "Plot Plan," Property of John Doe Estate, Town of Oyster Bay, Nassau County, New York, made by James Brown, Surveyor, November 1, 1940, as revised January 13, 1942, and December 31, 1945.

Figure 18.2.   Metes and Bounds Description.

property in a given area. A *plat description* might read: Lot Ten (10), Block Eight (8), Bay Shore Subdivision, as recorded in Volume 5 of Plats, Page 39, records of Blank County, State of . . .

18.6. How to Prepare Real Property Descriptions

Unless instructed otherwise, observe the following style in preparing descriptions of real property for use in deeds and other instruments:

1. Single-space, with a double-space between paragraphs.

2. Do not abbreviate *Street, Avenue, Road, Boulevard,* in the text.

3. Write the words *North, Northeast, South, West, Southwest,* and the like, with initial capitals, but do not capitalize the words *northerly, northeasterly,* and the like.

4. Capitalize *Quarter, Township, Section, Range,* and the name or number of a prime meridian.

5. Write courses as follows: "South twenty (20) degrees, thirty-three (33) minutes, forty-five (45) seconds West." In offices that use only the abbreviated form, or both, use a single quotation mark for minutes and a double quotation mark for seconds (S 20° 33' 45" W).

6. Write distances as follows: "One hundred thirty-three and twenty-nine one hundredths (133.29) feet."

7. When several courses and distances are given in succession, introduced by a phrase such as ". . . the following several courses and distances . . . ," each of the courses and distances is written separately, indented and single-spaced, separated one from the other by a double space, and each course and distance is ended with a semicolon. The sentence after the last course and distance is flush with the left margin of the text preceding the itemized courses and distances. (See Figure 18.2.)

8. Many law offices use figures, symbols, and abbreviations, rather than spelling out everything as described above, because of the limited space on a printed form, especially when reference is made to a recorded survey plan. A description might then read: "South 20° 33' 45" West, 50 ft," with reference to the plan where the description is written out in full. A better and more common practice is to reference the plan and also write out the description. But follow the practice of your office.

18.7. How to Check Land Descriptions

A typographical error in the description of land can cause trouble and even result in a lawsuit. The importance of checking the description cannot be overemphasized. It is easy to make an error in copying that is not always discernible from merely reading the description. For example, the government survey description in section 18.3 contains the phrase "of the Northeast Quarter" three times. It would be easy to omit the phrase once but difficult to realize the omission in reading over the description; yet the omission would double the amount of land conveyed by the deed. Nor is it advisable for one person to compare the description line by line. The safest method of checking the accuracy of a land description is to have someone read aloud to you the original copy, slowly enough to permit you to follow your copy carefully.

If you have a plat or diagram showing the location of the parcel described, you can check the accuracy of the description from that, especially if the identification is by government survey. To compare a government survey description with the map designation, read the parts of the description in reverse order—that is, begin with the township and range and work backward to the designated plot.

DEEDS

18.8. What Is a Deed?

A *deed* is a formal written instrument by which title to real property is conveyed from one person to another. A *purchase and sale agreement* is an agreement to convey title, whereas a deed is the conveyance itself. In almost every state a deed is the only method by which real estate may be voluntarily transferred, although courts of equity have the authority to order the transfer or conveyance.

18.9. Parties to a Deed

The parties to a deed are the *grantor,* who conveys his or her interest in the property, and the *grantee,* to whom the conveyance is made. The grantor is the seller, and the grantee is, usually but not necessarily, the purchaser. The purchaser may buy the land for the grantee. Only the grantor signs the deed, unless the grantee makes special covenants (see section 18.15).

The *grantor* may be a natural person, a partnership, or a corporation. The individual must be of legal age and of sound mind. Sometimes the grantor makes the deed in a representative capacity, for example, as the guardian of a minor. In such case, the first paragraph of the deed recites the capacity in which the grantor makes the deed. Whether or not the grantor's spouse must join in the deed depends on the law of the state where the land is situated. Generally, it is necessary for the spouse to join, and for that reason the marital status of the grantor is stated in the deed as *single, widow, widower*, or *divorced and not remarried*.

The *grantee* may be a natural person, a partnership, or a corporation. A minor or insane person may be a grantee, although he or she cannot be a grantor. In some states a deed cannot be made to a partnership in the firm name but must be made to the individual partners. A conveyance would not be made to "Hillside Estates," for example, but would be made to "Marcus Wylie and Joan Boyle, doing business as Hillside Estates." In some states foreign corporations are not permitted to acquire title to land unless they have received authority to do business in that state.

18.10. Forms of Deeds

Follow the form of deed used in your state and office. In addition to having a long form of deed, many states provide by statute for a short form of deed, known as a *statutory form,* to save space required for recording deeds. By statute, certain covenants and warranties are made part of the deed and, although not set forth in detail in the deed, are binding on the grantor and his or her heirs. Since the statute is actually part of the deed and a state statute is not effective outside of the state enacting it, a statutory form of deed can be used only in the specific state that makes statutory provision for it.

18.11. Kinds of Deeds

There are various kinds of deeds; those commonly used are the *warranty deed* and the *quitclaim deed. Fiduciary deeds* executed by third parties, such as the executor of an estate, or a trustee, are also relatively common.

A *warranty deed* is the most desirable from the standpoint of the purchaser. It not only transfers title in fee simple but also covenants and warrants that the grantor has the right to transfer the title to the property and that the grantee will enjoy the premises quietly, forever. Should anyone later make a claim against the property, the grantee can sue the grantor for breach of his or her warranty.

A *quitclaim deed* conveys whatever interest, if any, the grantor has in the property. It does not warrant the title against adverse claims. A quitclaim deed may be used to obtain a release from a person who is believed to have some interest in or claim to the property, whether real or not. By this form of deed, the grantor "quits" or releases any claim he or she might have to a given piece of real property. These deeds do not obligate the grantor in any way, but if he or she should have full title, the quitclaim deed will operate as a full and complete conveyance of title.

A *fiduciary deed* transfers title of real estate belonging to a deceased or incapacitated person. A *trust deed* conveys property held by a trust.

18.12. Printed Form of Deed

Printed forms of deeds are sometimes used. (See Figure 18.3.) With the information called for by the following checklist, you should have no difficulty in filling in the printed forms. The lawyer will provide any special clauses with reference to encumbrances, covenants, and the like. When printed forms are used, the description is often prepared on a computer and appended to the deed. A reference to the appendix is then made on the form itself, for example: "For more particular description, see Appendix A, attached hereto and made a part hereof."

Some printed forms are drawn especially for use by corporations, others for use by individuals.

Printed forms of deeds with special provisions, such as cutting of timber or harvesting of crops or oil rights, are also available in localities in which there is a need for them.

18.13. Information Needed for Form

Follow this checklist in filling in a printed form of deed.

1. Whether grantee is an individual, a partnership, or a corporation

Know all Men by these Presents:

THAT

for consideration paid, grant to

with warranty covenants to the said

(wife
(husband   of said grantor, release to said grantee all right of

(dower
(curtsey   and homestead and other interests therein.

Witness   hand and seal   this   day of   19

WITNESS:

....

....

....

STATE OF NEW HAMPSHIRE   COUNTY OF

On this the   day of   , 19   , before me,

the undersigned officer, personally appeared

known to me (or satisfactorily proven) to be the person   whose name   subscribed to the within instrument and acknowledged that   he   executed the same for the purpose therein contained.

In witness whereof I hereunto set my hand and official seal.

....

....

Justice of the Peace

Figure 18.3.   Printed Form of Deed.

2. Full name and residence of grantor, including street address in large cities

3. Full description of the grantor's office and authority if he or she is conveying in a representative capacity

4. Marital status of grantor

5. Full name of spouse if spouse must join in the conveyance

6. Full name and residence of grantee

7. Date of deed

8. Description of property

9. Whether deed is to be a warranty, quitclaim, or other type of deed, the form for each being different

10. Consideration to be expressed in deed

11. When and where deed is to be acknowledged

12. Names and official positions of officers signing and acknowledging deed, if grantor is a corporation

18.14. Deeds Prepared by Computer

Deeds are commonly prepared on the computer, and the format will be in your computer library, along with stock provisions. When a number of deeds containing similar basic provisions, differing only in property description, are to be prepared, the computer greatly simplifies the process. Once the master deed is prepared, individual descriptions can be inserted along with the names of the individual grantee(s), to create separate deeds for each parcel or unit conveyed. This is common practice in condominium conveyances whereby title is granted to individual units in a building or complex. Condominium deeds will also reference the condominium documents that have been recorded. Covenants and restrictions common to all of the units may also be recorded and referenced in the individual deeds (rather than rerecording the entire document with every conveyance).

18.15. Statements and Clauses in Deeds

You should become familiar with key statements and clauses in deeds.

Consideration

The *consideration* is the payment made by the purchaser for the property. It is usually a sum of money, but it might take some other form, such as the cancellation of debt owed by the seller to the purchaser. A deed frequently states a nominal consideration because the parties do not want the actual consideration to be known.

> WITNESSETH, That the Grantor(s), in consideration of five thousand dollars ($5,000), lawful money of the United States, paid by the Grantee, does hereby grant . . .

> . . . for the sum of one dollar ($1), to me in hand paid, and other good and valuable consideration, do hereby grant . . .

> . . . That the Grantor(s), in consideration of her natural love and affection for the Grantee, does hereby . . .

Encumbrance

Frequently, there is an indebtedness against property that is being sold, or taxes or assessments are owed on it. These are *encumbrances* on the property. Easements and restrictions or covenants are also considered encumbrances. The deed recites the agreement between the parties regarding them. The person who holds the encumbrance is the *encumbrancer*. The statement of encumbrances, if any, either follows the property description or is made a part of the habendum (see below). It is usually written by the lawyer.

> The said premises are conveyed subject to a mortgage thereof in the sum of ten thousand dollars ($10,000), with interest, made by David Jones to Leon Holt, dated the fifteenth day of January, 19.., and recorded in Book 27 of conveyances, page 359, in the office of the Clerk of said county.

> Subject to a purchase money mortgage made by the Grantee to the Grantor delivered and intended to be recorded simultaneously herewith, . . .

Habendum Clause

The habendum clause derives its name from the Latin phrase *habendum et tenendum* and, accordingly, begins with the words "to have and to hold." Its purpose is to define the extent of the interest conveyed. When special circumstances surround the transfer of the property, the lawyer dictates a substitute habendum.

TO HAVE AND TO HOLD the premises herein granted unto the Grantee, his heirs and assigns, forever.

TO HAVE AND TO HOLD the granted premises, with all the rights, easements, and appurtenances thereto belonging, to the said William V. Croft, his heirs and assigns, to his and their own use forever.

SUBJECT, HOWEVER, to all rights of the lessees, tenants and occupants of, or in said granted premises, or in any part, or parts, thereof.

Meaning and Intending Clause

The meaning and intending clause summarizes what the grantor intends to convey, usually by referencing an earlier conveyance.

Meaning and intending to convey all and the same premises conveyed to the grantor by warranty deed of Julia Davis, dated April 6, 19.., and recorded in Book 18, Page 277, in the Hudson registry of deeds.

Covenants

The *covenants* are the promises made by the grantor and grantee. The usual covenants by the grantor, which are printed in the deed, relate to the title to the property and to its quiet and peaceful enjoyment by the grantee. The grantor might make special promises not included in the usual printed form, such as agreeing to construct and maintain roadways. Covenants by the grantee are less common than covenants by the grantor. The most frequent use of covenants by the grantee is in connection with the sale of lots in subdivisions; they usually relate to the type of structure that may be erected on the premises and the uses that may be made of the property. These covenants are not included in the usual printed form of deed, but special deeds that contain them are usually prepared for the sale of lots in a specific subdivision. The following is an example of a covenant by a grantee:

And the said grantee does hereby for himself, his heirs and assigns, covenant with the said grantor, his heirs, executors, and administrators, that he will not, at any time hereafter, erect, or cause, or suffer, or permit, to be erected upon the hereby granted premises, or any part thereof, any building other than a brick or stone private dwelling house, not less than three stories in height.

Restrictions and Conditions

Property is often sold subject to certain restrictions and conditions to be observed by the grantee. They usually relate to types of buildings that may be constructed, purposes for which the property may be used, and the subsequent sale of the property.

Exceptions and Reservations

Property is frequently sold subject to certain exceptions and reservations. They might relate to easements, rights of way, growing crops, timber, minerals, and the like. They are not included in the usual printed form of deed; the lawyer writes them.

Testimonium Clause

The testimonium clause to a deed is similar to the testimonium clause to any written instrument. (See Chapter 9.)

18.16. State Taxes

Many states have imposed a state tax as a source of revenue. If your state requires revenue stamps, they are usually affixed to the deed at the registry of deeds at the time of recording.

18.17. Cancellation of Stamps

State stamps are usually canceled by machine at the registry of deeds. This process takes place at the time of recording, and the stamps are also affixed to the deed at this time.

18.18. Recording of Deed

A purchaser has a deed recorded for his or her own protection and pays the recording fee. If the purchaser is your firm's client, the lawyer will probably ask you to have the deed recorded. Before a deed is recorded, however, the person recording must check the registry to be sure that there is nothing of record since the title search was completed that would cloud the title. If you are asked to record a deed, you should know how to update the title before you put the deed on the record. Usually, deeds should be recorded promptly after they are executed. A delay in recording could give rise to unpleasant surprises for the grantee who might find a lien on the property recorded after conveyance or some other activity that could affect his or her title.

18.19. How to Prepare a Deed

Unless instructed otherwise, follow these directions when preparing a deed. Obviously, some of them apply only to typed or computer-prepared deeds, some to printed forms, and some to both.

1. Use legal- or letter-size paper according to your office or the registry preference.

2. Follow the directions for filling in a printed form in Chapter 10.

3. Do not forget the responsibility and distribution line at the top of the first page. This goes on the office copy only of the printed form. (See Chapter 10.)

4. Double-space.

5. Prepare the land description in accordance with the directions in section 18.6.

6. Number all pages of the deed at the bottom, and if it has several pages, number them "page ___ of ___."

7. If you are using a printed form, be sure to make the "Z" after the land description. (See Chapter 9.)

8. Do not forget to have at least two lines of typing on the signature page. (See Chapter 9.)

9. Prepare a signature line for the grantor. (See Chapter 9.) The grantee does not sign a deed except in special circumstances.

10. Affix the seal in accordance with directions in Chapter 9, when it is required.

11. Remember that a corporation's seal is generally affixed to an instrument.

12. Include witness lines and an attestation clause, when required. (See Chapter 9.)

13. Prepare a certificate of acknowledgement. (See Chapter 9.)

14. Collate.

15. Check and double-check spelling of names.

16. Get someone to compare the land description with you. (See section 18.7.)

17. Endorse the back of a printed form (see Figure 18.4, p. 446).

18. Arrange for the grantor to come in and sign the deed and acknowledge it.

19. Get the lawyer's approval of the instrument before it is signed. Have the grantor sign the original only.

20. Check if the grantor's signature agrees with the name typed in the deed.

21. Have the deed notarized. If you are a notary, take the acknowledgment, following instructions in chapter 9.

22. Prepare a closing statement.

23. After signature and acknowledgment, conform copies to the original. (See section 10.18 in Chapter 10.)

24. Get the lawyer's approval and then have the deed recorded. (See Chapter 9.) Do not forget to put a notation on the back of the deed asking that it be returned to you. (The secretary to the lawyer for the grantee attends to the recording.)

25. Make three copies—the original for the grantee, a copy for the grantor, and a copy for your files.

26. See that revenue stamps are affixed and canceled at the time of recording.

27. When the deed is returned by the recorder, note the book and page of recording and send the original recorded deed to the grantee with a covering letter. (See Chapter 9.)

A closing can be very formal, in which case all last-minute details are worked out among the parties, documents are executed, and distribution of proceeds made. Checks may be required for a mortgageholder, a taxing entity such as a municipality, and a broker (commission).

FINANCIAL STATEMENT AS OF ...... *June 8* ...... 19......

CREDIT				Purchase Price	DEBIT	
Paid on signing Contract	5,000	00		Purchase Price	$100,000	00
Mortgage held by ...*N. C. B.*	20,000	00		......		
Int. from *3/5* ...... @ ...*9*...%	280	00		......		
Mortgage held by ...... @ ......%				......		
Int. from ...... @ ......%				......		
Purchase money mortgage	25,000	00		Taxes as adjusted		
Security on lease				Water charges as adjusted		
				Sewer rents as adjusted		
Rent from ...*June 8*......						
...*to June 30*......	3,833	33		Insurance *Northwestern*		
Taxes as adjusted *$3,000 for 6 mos.*				*$360 paid Bill — for 3 years*		
2 mos., 7 days	566	67		*10 months, 7 days*	102	33
Water charges as adjusted						
Sewer rents as adjusted				Fuel		
Assessments	7,500	00		TOTAL DEBIT	100,102	33
Rent security				TOTAL CREDIT, brought over	62,180	00
Total credit	$62,180	00		BALANCE PAID TO SELLER	$37,922	33
Disbursements by purchaser				Disbursements by seller		
Revenue stamps				Revenue stamps		
Drawing papers				Recording papers		
Recording papers						
Title Company bill						

Closing of title under the within contract is hereby adjourned to ...... 19 ...... at ...... o'clock

at ...... all adjustments to be made as of 19

Dated, ... 19

For value received, the within contract and all the rights, title and interest of the purchaser hereunder are hereby assigned, transferred and set over unto ...... and said assignee hereby assumes all obligations of the purchaser hereunder.

Dated, ... 19

IN PRESENCE OF

.... Purchaser

.... Assignee of Purchaser

Figure 18.4. Memorandum of Closing Figures.

446

MORTGAGES

18.20. What Is a Mortgage?

A *mortgage* is a conditional conveyance. It is given by a borrower or debtor as security to ensure the payment of a debt, with a provision that the conveyance will become void on the payment of the debt by the date named. In early English times, the debtor actually turned over his property to the lender, who would keep the income and profits from it. The land was "dead" to the owner and gave him no return; hence the word *mort-gage,* meaning "dead pledge." A mortgage may be given on real estate or on personal property, but a mortgage on personal property is referred to as a *chattel mortgage,* whereas a mortgage on real estate is referred to simply as a *mortgage.* Some mortgages cover both real and personal property, for example, a mortgage on a furnished apartment building.

The word *mortgage* also refers to the instrument used to make the conveyance. The debt is evidenced by promissory notes; the mortgage is the security instrument that secures payment of the notes. Whenever you prepare a mortgage, therefore, you also prepare a promissory note to be signed by the mortgagor, and there are standard forms for promissory notes, which should be in your computer library, especially for debts to be secured by a real estate or chattel mortgage. In some states the debt is evidenced by a bond instead of a promissory note. The bond takes the place of the note. Frequently, the bond and mortgage are combined in one instrument, which is referred to as a *bond and mortgage.*

18.21. Parties to a Mortgage

The parties to a conventional mortgage are the *mortgagor,* who is the debtor or borrower, and the *mortgagee,* who is the lender. The mortgagor owns the property that is being mortgaged and gives a mortgage to the mortgagee, usually in return for a loan.

The parties to a deed of trust are the mortgagor and the trustee. Some states, Colorado for example, have designated officials, known as *public trustees,* to whom the estate is conveyed under a deed of trust.

18.22. Designation of the Parties

Extreme care should be exercised to see that the name of the mortgagor appears exactly as it appears in the instrument under which he or she claims title to the land; otherwise, the mortgagee's title might be defective if it becomes necessary for him or her to foreclose. The mortgagor's name should be exactly the same in the body of the mortgage, in the signature, and in the acknowledgment. If the mortgage is a purchase money mortgage (section 18.24), the names of both parties should be given precisely as they appear in the deed from the mortgagee to the mortgagor.

The requirements relative to the grantor and grantee in a deed apply generally to the mortgagor and mortgagee. (See section 18.9.)

18.23. Forms of Mortgages

Practice has given rise to the use of forms that differ widely in detail in the various states. Any instrument that is actually intended as security for a debt, however, will generally be construed as a mortgage.

The forms of mortgages most commonly used are the form that might be termed the *conventional mortgage* and the form various called a *trust deed, deed of trust, trust indenture,* or *trust mortgage.*

A *conventional mortgage* is essentially a deed from the borrower to the lender that contains a provision, known as the defeasance clause, that the mortgage will be void on payment of the debt. The additional provisions, which appear in fine print in the printed form, vary with the state.

A *deed of trust* conveys the land to a third party instead of directly to the lender. The third party holds the property in trust for the lender until the debt is paid in accordance with the terms of the trust deed. In some states, the deed of trust is more commonly used than the conventional mortgage deed: Alabama, California, Colorado, District of Columbia, Illinois, Mississippi, Missouri, Montana, New Mexico, Tennessee, Texas, Virginia, West Virginia, and Wisconsin. In the other states a deed of trust is seldom used except in connection with large transactions, such as railroad mortgages, that involve a large number of creditors. It would be impracticable to convey part of the legal title to each lender or bondholder. A trust deed may be used when the lender is a governmental body such as the Federal Housing Administration.

Some states have *short statutory forms* of mortgage, which save space when recorded. Since these forms are amplified by statute, they are not used outside the state of origin. Some real estate practitioners feel the short statutory form does not protect the mortgage sufficiently.

18.24. Purchase Money Mortgage

A *purchase money mortgage* is one that is given in part payment of the purchase price of the property. For example, if the purchase price is $100,000, the purchaser might pay $30,000 cash and give the seller a purchase money mortgage for $70,000. The deed and the purchase money mortgage are executed simultaneously. The grantee in the deed is the mortgagor; the grantor in the deed is the mortgagee. All names and descriptions of property in the purchase money mortgage must agree with those in the deed. A purchase money mortgage has certain priorities that other mortgages may not have. It also has priority over existing judgments and other debts of the mortgagor. On the other hand, as a rule, the mortgagee cannot get a deficiency decree against the mortgagor when he or she forecloses a purchase money mortgage, which the mortgagee can usually get under other mortgages. (See "Foreclosure Actions.") A *deficiency decree* is a decree or judgment against a debtor for amounts owed in excess of what can be realized by liquidation of the mortgaged asset (property). A purchase money mortgage may contain a statement similar to the following example, which distinguishes it from a mortgage given for an existing debt.

This mortgage is a purchase money mortgage, which is given and intended to be recorded simultaneously with a deed this day executed and delivered by the mortgagee to the mortgagor, covering the property above described; this mortgage being given to secure a portion of the purchase price expressed in said deed.

18.25. Printed Mortgages

Printed forms of conventional mortgages and deeds of trust are used extensively. Follow carefully the proper procedure for filling in printed forms.

Upon instructions from the lawyer, you should be able to complete the printed form of an ordinary mortgage or deed of trust without difficulty. The lawyer will write any special clauses that he or she wants to include in the instrument.

Long printed mortgage forms are used by banks and finance companies that sell the mortgages on the secondary market. They must generally be acceptable to quasi-governmental agencies called the Federal National Mortgage Administration (FNMA, or Fannie Mae) and the Federal Home Loan Mortgage Corporation (FHLMC, or Freddie Mac).

Private mortgages do not necessarily need all of the provisions on the printed forms (which are designed to cover all contingencies in any state), especially if the state statutes have a statutory form of mortgage that covers all of the standard provisions without detailed enumeration.

18.26. Information Needed for Mortgage or Deed of Trust

To complete the printed form of mortgage or deed of trust, you will need the information listed here. You can probably obtain it from the lawyer's notes and other information in the file; otherwise, you will have to ask the lawyer or, at his or her direction, the client.

1. Full name of mortgagor and mortgagee; also of trustee in the case of a trust deed

2. County and state of residence of mortgagor and mortgagee; in a large city, their street address; also residence of trustee in the case of a trust deed

3. Full description of the mortgagor's office and authority if he or she is conveying in a representative capacity

4. Marital status of mortgagor

5. Full name of spouse if spouse must join in the conveyance

6. If purchase money mortgage, whether spouse is to join

7. Date of mortgage

8. Amount of mortgage

9. Period mortgage is to run; maturity date

10. Rate of interest and when payable

11. Description of property

12. Date and place mortgage is to be acknowledged

13. If mortgagor is corporation, name and title of officers signing and acknowledging

14. If mortgage contains power of sale, number of days notice to be given in newspaper (this is determined by statute) and where newspaper is published

15. If there is to be an affidavit of title, who is to make it

18.27. Computer-Prepared Mortgages and Deeds of Trust

Printed forms of mortgages and deeds of trust are frequently inadequate for the special conditions of the transaction. The lawyer will then draft the instrument. The information is usually lengthy and requires special care in transcription. Instead of writing or dictating certain parts of the mortgage, the lawyer will probably tell you to copy from a printed form or access the form stored in the computer. The lawyer might say, "Copy the defeasance clause from this form." When preparing the instrument, follow the general style of a printed form.

Deeds of trust that are given to secure a bond issue are long and involved and are printed especially for a specific bond issue. The lawyer writes the first draft and revises it, usually several times. You can assist the lawyer in this laborious task by providing an especially careful and accurate transcription of any notes, thus enabling him or her to devote full attention to the content of the draft without the distraction of typographical errors. Law offices that do a large volume of real estate work have clauses stored in the computer and assemble the document using this library of forms.

18.28. Statements and Clauses in Mortgages

You should become familiar with important statements and clauses in mortgages.

Description of Debt

A mortgage is given to secure a debt, and the mortgage instrument must describe and identify the debt precisely. The description includes the rate and time of payment of interest and clearly states the time of payment of the debt. Some forms call for a copy of the note secured by the mortgage to be copied in the body of the instrument.

. . . An indebtedness in the sum of fifty thousand dollars ($50,000), lawful money of the United States, to be paid on the first day of November 19.., with interest thereon to be computed from November 1, 19.., at the rate of ten percent (10%) per annum, and to be paid semiannually thereafter, according to a certain note bearing even date herewith, . . .

Defeasance Clause

The provision in the mortgage that it will become void upon payment of the debt is known as the *defeasance clause*—the mortgage will be defeated upon payment of the debt. Printed forms usually contain an adequate defeasance clause.

Provided always, that if said mortgagor, ..., shall pay .... a certain promissory note, a copy of which is on the reverse side hereof, and shall perform and comply with each and every stipulation, agreement and covenant of said note and of this mortgage, the estate hereby created shall be void, otherwise the same shall remain in full force and effect.

. . . provided, that if I shall punctually pay said notes according to the tenor thereof, then this mortgage shall be void.

Consideration

A mortgage recites the consideration for which it was given. Statement of the consideration usually names the amount of the indebtedness but occasionally recites a nominal consideration.

. . . for and in consideration of the aforesaid debt of fifty thousand dollars ($50,000), and the better securing the payment of the same with interest . . .

. . . for the better securing the payment of the sum of money mentioned in the said bond, or obligation, with the interest thereon, and, also, in consideration of one dollar ($1) paid by the Second Party, the receipt whereof is hereby acknowledged . . .

Acceleration Clause

Mortgages contain a clause providing that if principal or interest payments are not made when due, or if any obligation on the part of the mortgagor is not fulfilled, the entire amount of the mortgage becomes payable immediately. The maturity date of the mortgage is *accelerated,* if the mortgagor defaults. This clause is the *acceleration clause.* It is usually printed in the instrument.

That the whole of said principal sum shall become due after default in the payment of any installment of principal or of interest for ..... days, or after default in the payment of any tax, water rate, or assessment for ..... days, after notice and demand.

Description of Property

An explanation of land descriptions and how to prepare them is given in sections 18.2 and 18.3. Accuracy in the description of mortgaged property is as important in a mortgage as in a deed. A purchaser takes possession of the premises purchased, thus giving notice to all the world of his or her rights. But a mortgagee must depend on the recording of the instrument to give notice of such rights.

Prepayment Privilege

The mortgagor sometimes likes to pay off the mortgage, or part of it, before maturity but does not have this right unless the terms of the mortgage specifically grant it. Mortgages and mortgage notes frequently provide that the debt is payable *on or before* the maturity date, or they contain a specific clause giving the mortgagor this right. This clause is the prepayment privilege. A comparable provision in trust deeds securing issues of bonds permits *redemption* of the bonds before maturity dates. The privilege enables a mortgagor to refinance his or her debt when money is cheaper or to sell the property free and clear of any mortgage. Printed forms do not usually include the prepayment privilege.

The mortgagor is hereby authorized and permitted to pay the debt hereby secured, or any part of it, not less than ..... dollars at any one time, whenever and at such time and times as he may choose, and the mortgagee hereby agrees to accept such payment or payments, and thereupon the interest shall cease upon such part of the debt as may be so paid; and upon the full payment of said debt, with all interest up to the date of actual payment, he will discharge this mortgage.

Partial Release

The mortgagor frequently wants to sell part of the mortgaged land. For example, the developer of a subdivision sells lots that are part of a subdivision covered by a blanket mortgage. The prepayment privilege (see above) does not release any of the mortgaged land from the mortgage until the entire mortgage is paid. Therefore, to permit the mortgagor to sell part of the land, some mortgages contain a *partial release* clause. The clause permits the release of a specified portion of the premises covered by the mortgage upon payment of a specified sum.

Said mortgagor reserves the right to release all or any part of the said land from the operation of this mortgage, in case said land is subdivided, upon payment to mortgagee of a sum of money to be agreed upon for each lot, the sum to be determined according to the size and location of the lot as soon as the said land is subdivided. Said mortgagee has agreed to sign a plat of said premises prepared by mortgagor.

Other Statements and Clauses

A mortgage might contain, also, some or all of the clauses in a deed, such as the habendum, or the covenants, or the testimonium clause. (See section 18.15.)

18.29. State Tax

In some states a mortgage registration tax is in effect. It is payable by the mortgagee at the time the mortgage is recorded. Some states do not permit the mortgagee to collect the tax from the mortgagor.

18.30. How to Prepare a Mortgage

Follow the instructions for preparing a deed in section 18.19, substituting "mortgagor" for "grantor," "mortgagee" for "grantee," and "mortgage" for "deed." In addition, note the following: (1) If the mortgage is a purchase money mortgage, compare the names of the mortgagor and mortgagee with the names of grantor and grantee. (2) If the mortgage is not a purchase money mortgage, the mortgagor's spouse may also have to sign the document.

LEASES

18.31. What Is a Lease?

A *lease* is a binding contract, written or oral, for the possession of lands and improvements on the one side and the recompense by rent or other compensation on the other side. When the lease is evidenced by a written instrument binding the parties to fulfill certain covenants or agreements, that instrument is known as a *lease*. Leases range from the letting of an apartment for a 1-year to a 99-year lease on vacant property. They may cover real property, personal property, or both, but a lease of real property is most common. Leases of realty give the lessee a *leasehold estate in the premises*.

18.32. Parties to a Lease

The parties to a lease are the *lessor,* who owns the property, and the *lessee,* who rents it. The lessor, or owner, leases the property *to* the lessee, or tenant; the lessee leases the property *from* the lessor.

A party to a lease may be a natural person, a partnership, or a corporation. Leases on behalf of minors or insane persons must be made by a guardian. The officers of a corporation enter into a lease on its behalf pursuant to authorization of the board of directors or stockholders. An administrator cannot make a lease because his or her function is to wind up the estate, not to lease real property. An executor or testamentary trustee must have specific authority given to him or her by the will to make a lease.

18.33. Classification of Lease

Leases can be classified according to duration, type of property, and rental payment.

Duration

Leases may be short term or long term. Although there is no definite duration that takes a lease out of the short-term class, a lease of 10 or more years is generally considered a long-term lease. In a number of states a lease for more than seven years must be recorded. The fundamental distinctions are in the responsibilities assumed by the lessee and in the bond and security requirements. Under a short-term lease the lessor usually requires the lessee to deposit with him one, three, or six months' rental at the time the lease is executed, whereas under a long-term lease the lessee is required to furnish a bond or collateral in an amount equal to about three years' rental. The most common practice is for the lessee to deposit with a bank or other financial institution negotiable securities of the required amount.

A special type of long-term lease is the 99-year lease, which has been used extensively in the development of business districts in large cities. These leases are made on parcels of valuable real estate strategically located for business expansion. They contemplate the erection or improvement of buildings upon the property by the lessee.

Type of Property

Leases May be classified as *commercial* or *residential,* according to the type of property covered by the lease. Short-term leases may be either commercial or residential leases, but long-term leases are almost exclusively commercial leases.

Rental Payment

The majority of leases call for the payment of a definite amount of rental, which continues at a uniform rate throughout the term of the lease. The amount is called a *flat rental.* Other leases, especially long-term leases, provide that the rental will start at a comparatively low figure and gradually increase. A rental provision of this type is called a *graded rental.* Another method of fixing the amount of rental is to require the tenant to pay a specified percentage of the gross income from sales made upon the premises. A lease with this requirement is called a *percentage lease.* These leases generally cover premises occupied by retail businesses, such as chain stores and department stores. Percentage leases generally run for 10 or more years.

For residential leases especially, state law may control certain terms of the lease. In particular, the amount of deposit that may be required and the means for holding the deposit may be set out in the statute.

18.34. Printed Form of Lease

Printed forms of leases covering almost any kind of property are available and are frequently used for short-term leases. Many firms print their own leases in a form prepared by the lawyer. The lawyer's secretary is more likely to be concerned with the drafting and printing out of a form than with filling in a standard lease such as a lease on an apartment.

18.35. Standard Lease Clauses

Usually, the lawyer drafts both the short-term and long-term leases that are prepared in the office. Many of the clauses in a lease are standard (see below) and should be stored in the computer. A variety of other clauses is necessary to express the agreement between the parties, especially in long-term leases. Ninety-nine-year leases and many other long-term leases are extremely technical legal instruments, their preparation requiring a lawyer who is a specialist in the field. You will probably have to prepare several drafts before the lawyer and the client are satisfied.

18.36. Standard Clauses in Commercial Leases

Here is a list of the standard clauses that appear in most commercial leases. Although each clause might not be in a separate paragraph, in all probability the lease will contain words covering each of these subjects.

1. Term or duration
2. Rent
3. Water, electricity, heat
4. Alterations
5. Repairs
6. Damage or liability—that is, the provision fixing the liability for injury to persons or property
7. "To let" sign before expiration of lease
8. Assignment of the lease
9. Surrender of the premises upon expiration of the lease
10. Rules and ordinances
11. Fire—that is, the agreement about the respective rights of the parties if the building should be destroyed by fire or "other action of the elements"
12. Elevators and heat
13. Insurance
14. Default in payment of rent
15. Bankruptcy of lessee
16. Peaceful possession or quiet enjoyment of the premises
17. No waiver—that is, the provision that the consent of the lessor to a variation of the terms in one instance is not a waiver of terms and conditions of the lease

18. Subordination to mortgages

19. Sprinkler system

20. Condemnation or eminent domain proceedings—that is, the rights of the respective parties if the city, county, state, or federal authority should condemn or take possession of the premises

21. Security deposited by lessee

22. Property taxes

18.37. Style of Computer-Prepared Lease

When a lawyer drafts a lease, he or she simplifies the location of specific provisions by grouping them in a particular order. In planning the style in which to produce the lease, your objective should be to simplify further the location of specific provisions. You can do this by indicating the subject of each provision in the margin. Another style involves making side headings of the subjects and underscoring them. Still another style is to center each subject heading. Usually, the clauses are numbered consecutively throughout the lease. The numbering may be any style that you choose: I, II; FIRST, SECOND; ONE, TWO; 1., 2.; (1), (2).

18.38. Execution, Acknowledgment, and Recording of Lease

A lease of land or commercial property is executed with the formalities of a deed. State statutes vary, but generally, the following apply:

1. Both the lessor and lessee sign the lease.

2. A lease is sealed unless the state statute does not require a deed to be sealed.

3. A lease is witnessed unless the state statute does not require a deed to be witnessed.

4. If the duration of the lease is more than one year (longer in some states), the lessor and lessee acknowledge it, and the lessee should have it recorded.

5. A lease may be signed by an agent with written authority.

The execution of the standard short-term lease, such as a lease on an apartment, is not so formal. Both the lessor and lessee sign, and usually the signatures are witnessed. Otherwise, there are no formal requirements. The directions about acknowledgments and recording apply only to leases that must be recorded.

18.39. How to Prepare a Lease

Follow the instructions for preparing a deed in section 18.19, substituting "lease" for "deed," "lessor" and "lessee" for "grantor" and "grantee," and so on. These special additional instructions apply to the preparation of leases: (1) Make four copies—an original for the lessee, a copy for the lessor, a copy for the broker, and a copy for your files. (2) Both the lessor and lessee must sign the lease. Therefore, you will need to prepare signature lines and certificates of acknowledgment for both lessee and lessor. Lessor and lessee should each sign three copies. (3) Revenue stamps, mentioned in section 18.19, are applied to deeds, not leases.

PURCHASE AND SALE AGREEMENTS

18.40. What Is a Purchase and Sale Agreement?

In real estate sales there is almost always an agreement to buy and sell before the actual conveyance is made. This agreement, called a *purchase and sale agreement,* may be an informal memorandum or merely a receipt for a deposit on the purchase price, which is not prepared in the lawyer's office. Often it is prepared on a printed form setting forth the customary terms of such an agreement. It is usually prepared by the real estate broker and signed by the buyer and seller. The seller's lawyer enters the picture when he or she is asked to draw the deed and purchase money mortgage, if any; the buyer's lawyer, when asked to pass upon the seller's title to the property and his or her right to convey it. The lawyer may be asked to review a purchase and sale agreement for a client before it is signed, whether the lawyer's client is a buyer or seller. Many times the lawyer is asked to prepare a formal agreement, or contract of sale. He or she usually draws the contract when the property is very valuable, if the property is income producing, or if it is to be sold on the installment plan. An agreement to enter into an important lease is also necessary, before the lease itself is entered into. Under the statute of frauds these agreements, whether formal or informal, must be in writing or they are not enforceable.

Purchase and sale agreements fix a date—called the *closing date*—at which time title to the property is actually conveyed. The lawyer's secretary and the paralegal will have many preparations to make for the closing. Since your preparations depend to a large extent on the contents of the purchase and sale agreement, you should first become familiar with this document. Read carefully the form of contract used in your locality.

18.41. Need for a Purchase and Sale Agreement

When an owner decides to sell and a buyer decides to purchase real estate, they agree upon the terms of sale—the purchase price, the amount of cash to be paid, how the balance will be paid, what will be done about mortgages on the property—and upon numerous other details. The transfer of the property cannot be effected immediately because the seller must produce evidence of his or her right to sell, and the buyer wants his or her attorney to examine this evidence; the buyer needs time in which to arrange the necessary financing; the seller must collect various data regarding insurance, taxes, rents, and the like; instruments of conveyance must be prepared. Neither party wants the other to back out of the deal in the interim. Therefore, they enter into a contract of sale, commonly called a purchase and sale agreement, that sets forth in detail the terms under which the property will be conveyed. Great care is exercised in the drafting and preparation of a purchase and sale agreement because the conveyance will be made upon the terms set forth in the agreement.

18.42. Types of Contracts of Sale of Land

There are two principal types of contracts for the sale of land. One type, the *purchase and sale agreement,* contemplates the immediate transfer of title to the buyer, with the buyer to pay the entire purchase price in cash, or part in cash and part by a purchase money mortgage. The contract binds the parties while the buyer is having the title examined and arranging for financing through a lending institution.

The other type of contract of sale is an *installment contract.* The purchase price is paid in installments, and the title remains with the seller until the entire purchase price has been paid or until the unpaid purchase price has been reduced to an amount agreed upon in the contract of sale. This type of sale is now heavily regulated and has become less common.

18.43. Parties to a Purchase and Sale Agreement

The necessary parties to a purchase and sale agreement are the seller or vendor and the buyer or purchaser or vendee. Both seller and purchaser sign the contract because each has certain obligations to perform. Since the seller agrees to convey title, the seller must be a natural person or corporation with the power and ability to make a deed of conveyance (section 18.11). When a married person enters into a purchase and sale agreement, it is necessary for the spouse to sign the contract in those states where the spouse must sign the deed of conveyance.

The buyer must be an adult of sound mind or a corporation with power to purchase real estate. Although an infant or an incompetent may be the grantee of real property, he or she cannot enter into a purchase and sale agreement because he or she does not possess contractual powers. Trustees and executors rarely have power to buy land.

The broker who brings about the agreement is naturally interested in its consummation. Although the broker is not a party to the contract, provision is usually made in the contract for payment of his or her commission.

18.44. How to Prepare a Purchase and Sale Agreement

Each locality has a contract form approved by the local real estate board. Printed forms are available from office-supply stores and, also, from abstract and title companies. The forms are easy to complete and require little explanation. The lawyer will give you the information necessary to complete the form.

Make four copies—original and duplicate original for the seller and buyer, a copy for the broker, and a copy for your files. Both the seller and the buyer sign the contract and, usually, the seller's spouse. Generally, an acknowledgment is not necessary, because ordinarily, the contract is not recorded. Unless you receive specific instructions from the lawyer, be guided by the form. If the form adopted in your locality has an acknowledgment printed on it, fill in the acknowledgment. The form will also indicate whether it should be witnessed.

When the lawyer prepares the contract, follow the instructions for preparing deeds (section 18.19).

18.45. Information Needed for Form

You will need the following information to complete the agreement:

1. Date of contract

2. Name and residence of seller

3. Name of seller's spouse if spouse must join in deed that is to be delivered

4. Name and residence of the buyer

5. Description of property to be conveyed and evidence of title

6. Purchase price, the exact amount being named

7. Amount to be paid when contract is signed (earnest money)

8. Amount to be paid at closing, when deed is delivered

9. Whether existing mortgage, if any, is to be assumed or property purchased subject to it

10. How balance is to be paid and when

11. Name of trustee in those states where a deed of trust is the security instrument

12. Unpaid taxes and assessments

13. Fire insurance data

14. Name of broker and commission

15. Closing date

16. Expiration date of offer

17. Date of possession

18.46. Earnest Money

An element of all purchase and sale agreements is a cash deposit by the buyer as an indication that he or she intends to go through with the purchase if the seller furnishes good title to the property. The deposit is designated *earnest money*. It is also referred to as a *binder,* although this term is more frequently applied to a deposit made under informal agreements than to deposits made in connection with formal contracts drawn up by the lawyer. If the buyer fails to consummate the deal, the earnest money is retained by the seller; if the buyer does perform his or her part of the contract, the earnest money is applied as part payment of the purchase price. If the seller cannot convey good title to the property, the deposit is returned to the buyer. The amount of earnest money depends on the agreement between the parties. It is ordinarily sufficient to compensate the seller for the loss he or she might sustain should the buyer fail to go through with the deal.

18.47. Escrow for the Sale of Real Property

One of the most common uses of *escrow* (see Part 5, "Glossary of Legal Terms") is in connection with real estate transactions. Frequently, the buyer's deposit is placed in escrow, so there will be no difficulty about a refund should it prove impossible for the seller to deliver clear title to the property. Sometimes the purchase and sale agreement is put in escrow so it cannot be recorded until the deal is consummated, because the recorded contract might be a cloud on the title. Sometimes, especially in transactions involving very valuable property, both the seller and the buyer deposit bonds in escrow to prevent either party from being damaged by the failure of the other party to consummate the sale. The ramifications of escrows for the sale of real property are manifold, but necessary components are the following:

1. A valid and enforceable contract for the purchase and sale of land.
2. An escrow agreement
3. A disinterested third party, usually a bank, to act as escrow holder, *escrowee*. Neither buyer nor seller can act as escrowee.

When the lawyer in your office acts as escrow holder, you should deposit funds placed with him or her in escrow in the trust account, not in the firm's regular account.

TITLE CLOSINGS AND EVIDENCE OF TITLE

18.48. What Is a Title Closing?

The purchase and sale agreement designates a certain day, and sometimes hour, when the deed will be delivered, the balance of the purchase price paid, and the mortgages, if any, are released or delivered. This transaction between the seller and purchaser, and their representatives, is known as the *title closing* or *closing of title*. All of the formalities necessary to the conveyance of property are attended to at the closing. It usually takes place at the title company, at the office of the lawyer for the seller, or at the bank holding the mortgage or its attorney's office. Papers to be signed must be ready for signature; other papers, such as receipts and insurance policies, must be produced; and a closing statement must be prepared. The date on which the title closing takes place is known as the *closing date*. Before the closing, the purchaser must have proof that the seller has good title to the property.

18.49. Evidence of Title

Every purchaser insists on satisfactory evidence that the seller has good title to the land that he or she is selling. Proof of good title is just as important to a mortgagee. There are four kinds of evidence of title—*abstract and opinion, certificate of title, title insurance,* and *Torrens certificate.* To a great extent, the acceptability of a particular kind of evidence of title depends on the local custom.

The mortgagee, usually a bank, will do its own title search before granting a mortgage. Often a buyer will assume that the bank's search is adequate to protect him or her. But considering the size of the buyer's investment, it is generally considered worthwhile for the buyer to contract for an independent title search.

The mortgagee will probably insist that the buyer pay for title insurance to protect its interest. For a relatively small additional amount, a one-time payment, the buyer can protect his own interest in the title.

18.50. Abstract of Title

The evidence of title most commonly used in the United States is the *abstract of title.* An *abstract* is a condensed history of the title to a particular tract of land. It consists of a summary of the material parts of every recorded instrument affecting the title. It begins with a description of the land covered by the abstract and then shows the original governmental grant and all subsequent deeds, mortgages, releases, wills, judgments, mechanics' liens, foreclosure proceedings, tax sales, and other matters affecting title. Only a summary of these items is shown. A deed, for example, is summarized as follows:

DONALD HALL AND JANE HALL, HIS WIFE to KENNETH CLARKE	WARRANTY DEED Dated Sept. 15, 1860 Ack. Sept. 18, 1860 Rec. Sept. 20, 1860 Bk. 21, page 23

Conveys a large plot of land including the premises under examination.

The abstract concludes with the abstracter's certificate. This discloses what records the abstracter has and has not examined. For example, if the abstracter certifies that he or she has made no search of federal court proceedings affecting the property, it may be necessary to write to the clerk of the district court, who will supply the search for a small charge.

Abstract companies, lawyers, title insurance companies, and public officials prepare abstracts. Abstract companies and title insurance companies do by far the greatest portion of the abstracting, except in a few states where there are no abstract companies.

Always keep the name, address, and telephone number of the abstract company, or other abstracter, used by your firm in your desk directory. If you are employed by the lawyer for the purchaser or the mortgagee in communities where abstracts are acceptable evidence of title, you will frequently have to order abstracts. When you order the abstract, make a follow-up entry in your diary or an extra copy of the letter for your follow-up file. It is important to get the abstract as soon as possible because the deal cannot be closed until the purchaser's attorney has examined the abstract of title. When the abstract is received, charge the cost to the client; the lawyer will pay the abstracter.

You will find that purchase and sale agreements frequently provide that the seller will furnish an abstract of title. This usually means that he or she will give the purchaser an abstract of title to the date that the seller obtained the property. The purchaser will have it brought down to date. You will then be asked to order a continuation or an extension. The original abstract is sent to the abstract company and the company recertifies its accuracy and brings it down to date.

Your letter ordering an abstract of title, or a continuation, might read as follows:

We are enclosing an abstract of title for the west three rods of Lots 30 and 31, Cecil Hedgwick's Addition to Saco, York County, Maine, according to the recorded plat thereof.

Please continue this to date for the land owned by Mary Hartz and return it to us as soon as possible.

18.51. Opinion of Title

When the attorney receives the abstract, he or she examines it and prepares an *opinion* about the validity of the title. If the lawyer finds any difficulty, such as a deed that was improperly acknowledged or a discrepancy in the description of the property, he or she states these defects. They constitute *clouds* on the seller's title and must be removed by affidavits, quitclaim deeds, or court procedure to quiet title. The attorney also sets forth in his or her opinion any liens and mortgages on the property, because the title is subject to them. Usually, the purchase and sale agreement mentions the liens and mortgages and provides for their disposition. The opinion will also refer to easements, covenants or restrictions on the property that may affect the use the buyer may make of it.

The lawyer writes the opinion of title, which is usually in the form of a letter. If there are no defects in the title, you might be asked to draft a routine opinion-of-title letter. A sample letter follows.

Mr. and Mrs. Harold Wallace
Box 600
Freeport, ME 04032

Dear Mr. and Mrs. Wallace:

We have examined the abstract of title continued by the Saco Abstract and Title Company of Saco, Maine, to date of June 15, 19.., at 8:00 A.M., for the following described premises:

The west three (3) rods of Lots Thirty (30) and Thirty-one (31), Cecil Hedgwick's Addition to Saco, York County, Maine, according to the recorded plat thereof.

From such examination, we find the title thereto to be in Mary Hartz, subject to the following:

1. There are ancient and minor errors in this title, but we do not consider any of them sufficiently important to affect the merchantability of the title.

2. There are no liens or encumbrances of record against said premises.

3. The abstract shows no unpaid taxes for 19.. and prior years. The summer taxes for 19.. will be due July 1, 19.. and may be checked with the city treasurer, as may also special assessments.

It is therefore our opinion that a merchantable title exists in said above-named titleholder, subject to the exceptions above noted. This opinion is based on the abstract continued as aforesaid and does not cover rights of persons in possession, line fences, location of buildings, or any other matter or thing not contained in said abstract.

Sincerely yours,

18.52. Mechanics and Materialman's Liens

It is customary to require an affidavit from the seller that all bills from people working on the property or supplying materials for construction have been paid and that nothing is outstanding. The reason is that contractors and suppliers who have not been paid have an automatic lien on the property for a limited time before they must put it on the record to perfect it.

18.53. Hazardous Substances

Under federal law, the owner of property is responsible for removal of hazardous materials found on real estate, even if that particular owner had no involvement in placement of the materials. Especially in conveyances of industrial or commercial property, the buyer will want expert examination of the property to insure that there is no hazardous waste and will require a statement from the seller to that effect.

18.54. Certificate of Title

In some localities an abstract is dispensed with. The attorney examines the public records and issues a *certificate*, which is merely the lawyer's opinion of title based on the public records he or she has examined. The lawyer does not guarantee the title but is liable for damages caused by his or her negligence. If the lawyer's certificate failed to show a mortgage that was recorded, for example, he or she would be liable to a purchaser who relied on that certificate and purchased the property without knowledge of the mortgage. Abstract companies also issue certificates of title. A certificate of title should not be confused with title insurance policies issued by title companies.

18.55. Title Insurance Policies

Title guarantee companies issue title insurance policies, which guarantee against defects in title. They are called *title guarantee policies* or *guaranty title policies*. They are issued to owners and to mortgagees.

A title policy not only guarantees against defects in the title, but the company issuing it usually undertakes to defend at its own expense any lawsuit attacking the title. A title company will not insure a defective title.

The attorney for the buyer, or the mortgagee, orders the policy of insurance from the title company, and the title company then searches its records and makes any surveys necessary to the issuance of the title insurance. Lending institutions generally require title insurance sufficient to protect their interest in the mortgaged property.

18.56. Torrens Certificate

In addition to the system of transferring title under the recording acts, another system is known as the *Torrens system*, originated by Sir Robert Torrens. A landowner who wishes to register under the Torrens system first obtains a complete abstract of title to the land. He or she then files in the proper public office an application for the registration of title. After certain legal procedure, the court orders the registrar of titles to register the title. The registrar makes out a certificate showing the title as found by the court. These certificates are bound in books and are public records. The registrar delivers a duplicate certificate to the owner. When land that has been registered under the Torrens system is sold, the deed itself does not pass title to the land. The deed must be taken to the registrar's office, and he or she issues a new certificate to the grantee. The deed is not returned to the grantee but remains in the registrar's office. Likewise, a mortgage or judgment lien is not effective until a notation has been entered on the certificate of title in the registrar's office. The Torrens system, originally established to simplify property titles, is now rarely used. It is confined to only a few metropolitan areas.

18.57. Preparations for Closing

As soon as you prepare or receive a purchase and sale agreement, the closing of which is of interest to a lawyer in your office, enter the date of the closing in your diary. The following checklists show some of the preparations you will have to make before the closing.

Checklist of Preparation by Staff of Seller's Attorney

In the following checklist the asterisks indicate items that are to be delivered to the buyer at the closing.

*1. Prepare the deed (section 18.19).

  2. Prepare the purchase money mortgage and bond or note, if any (section 18.30).

*3. Prepare, or obtain from the seller, a list of tenants, rents paid and unpaid, and due dates.

*4. Obtain from the mortgagee, holding any mortgage that the purchaser assumes, a certificate that is properly acknowledged, showing payment on account or the amount actually due at the closing date.

  5. Prepare a memorandum of closing figures (sections 18.58-18.65). A copy of the memorandum might be mailed to the attorney for the purchaser, thus saving time in adjusting figures at the closing.

*6. Prepare a letter to tenants advising them to pay future rent to the purchaser.

*7. Prepare an assignment of any service contracts, such as exterminator's contracts, that are to be assigned to the purchaser.

  8. Prepare form 1099-B, required by the U.S. Internal Revenue Service from all sellers of real estate.

  9. Notify the seller of the exact time, date, and place of the closing. Tell him or her to bring to the closing the following papers:

   a. Receipts for last payment on mortgages

  *b. Insurance policies and assignments of them

  *c. Last receipts for taxes, special assessments, gas, electricity, and water

  *d. Leases and assignments

  *e. Securities deposited by tenants as security for rent, which might be in the form of cash

 10. If the seller is an individual, tell the seller that his or her spouse must also be present at the closing to sign the deed.

 11. If the seller is a corporation, indicate the two officers who are to sign the deed and who, therefore, should be present at the closing. Also, advise the officers to bring the corporation's seal.

 12. Notify others who might be present on behalf of the seller of the closing date—broker, accountant, title closer.

Checklist of Preparations by Staff of Purchaser's Attorney

These steps should be followed by the office of the purchaser's attorney:

1. Order the abstract of title (section 18.50).

2. Prepare the opinion of title after the lawyer writes it (section 18.51).

3. Prepare a memorandum of closing figures (sections 18.58-18.65). This might be mailed to the seller's attorney, thus saving time in adjusting figures at the closing.

4. Notify the purchaser of the exact time, date, and place of the closing. Tell him or her to bring to the closing the following:

    a. Certified check for the approximate amount that will be due to the seller. You can get the figure from the memorandum of closing figures.

    b. Blank check (to be filled in at closing for any additional amount owed the seller).

5. If the purchaser is a corporation, indicate the two officers who are to sign the purchase money mortgage and who, therefore, should be present at the closing. Also advise the officers to bring the corporate seal with them.

6. Notify others who might be interested in behalf of the buyer of the closing date—accountant, insurance broker, title closer.

7. Prepare for the attorney a checklist of papers that are to be delivered to the buyer at the closing. This list will include the items marked with an asterisk in the foregoing checklist of preparations by the seller's staff.

PREPARATION OF CLOSING STATEMENT

18.58. What Is a Closing Statement?

A purchase and sale agreement, or a contract for lease, provides that certain charges against the property and the income from it should be adjusted or prorated. For example, if the seller has paid the insurance for a year in advance, he or she is entitled to receive an adjustment from the buyer.

If the seller has collected the rents for a month in advance, the buyer is entitled to an adjustment. This prorating or adjustment results in credits in favor of each party and charges against each party. A statement of the charges and credits is known as a *closing statement,* sometimes called a *settlement sheet.*

Forms of closing statements vary. Printed forms are available and are widely used. Many offices use a form developed by the federal Housing and Urban Development Agency (HUD), whether or not federal subsidy is involved, because it provides for unformity and extensive detail. When the printed forms do not provide for all items that must be entered on the closing statement, the statement is prepared by computer or typewriter. This situation frequently arises in large, complicated transactions. The statement cannot be prepared in final form until the closing is held, because all necessary information is not available. It is prepared on the basis of the figures agreed upon by all parties at the closing. The lawyer for each party usually calculates the adjustments, however, and prepares a memorandum of them before the closing. You will probably have the responsibility of calculating the adjustments. The lawyer will tell you what items are to be adjusted, and he or she will check your figures. Figure 18.4 illustrates a printed form on the back of a contract that may be used for a memorandum of the closing figures. A form of this kind is sometimes used as a closing statement too. See also the HUD settlement statement illustrated in Figure 18.5 on pages 472 and 473.

18.59. How to Calculate Adjustments

The practice of computing adjustments and the date of adjustment varies with the locality. In many localities, adjustments are made as of the day immediately preceding the day on which title is closed. In other words, the buyer receives the income and is charged with the expenses incurred beginning with and including the day on which title passes to him.

It is much easier to compute interest, taxes, water rates, and insurance by the 360-day method, each month representing $\frac{1}{12}$ of the annual charge, and each day one-thirtieth of the monthly charge, than by the 365-day method. This is the practice adopted by many local real estate boards. Rent is usually computed on the basis of the days in the particular month in which title is closed. Although the 360-day method of computing interest, taxes, water rates, and insurance is used, when the period for which computation

INSTRUCTIONS
1. Detach worksheet and complete before typing. 2. At Final Settlement combine respective copies of sets A & B and distribute as indicated.

Form Approved OMB NO. 63-R-1501

A.	U.S. DEPARTMENT OF HOUSING AND URBAN DEVELOPMENT SETTLEMENT STATEMENT	B. TYPE OF LOAN

B. TYPE OF LOAN

1. ☐ FHA   2. ☐ FMHA   3. ☐ CONV. UNINS.

4. ☐ VA   5. ☐ CONV. INS.

6. FILE NUMBER: 7. LOAN NUMBER:

8. MORT. INS. CASE NO.:

C. **NOTE**: This form is furnished to give you a statement of actual settlement costs. Amounts paid to and by the settlement agent are shown. Items marked "(p.o.c.)" were paid outside the closing; they are shown here for informational purposes and are not included in the totals.

D. NAME OF BORROWER: E. NAME OF SELLER: F. NAME OF LENDER:

G. PROPERTY LOCATION: H. SETTLEMENT AGENT: I. SETTLEMENT DATE:

PLACE OF SETTLEMENT:

J. SUMMARY OF BORROWER'S TRANSACTION:	K. SUMMARY OF SELLER'S TRANSACTION:
100. **GROSS AMOUNT DUE FROM BORROWER**	400. **GROSS AMOUNT DUE TO SELLER**
101. Contract sales price	401. Contract sales price
102. Personal property	402. Personal property
103. Settlement charges to borrower (line 1400)	403.
104.	404.
105.	405.
Adjustments for items paid by seller in advance	Adjustments for items paid by seller in advance
106. City/town taxes to	406. City/town taxes to
107. County taxes to	407. County taxes to
108. Assessments to	408. Assessments to
109.	409.
110.	410.
111.	411.
112.	412.
120. **GROSS AMOUNT DUE FROM BORROWER**	420. **GROSS AMOUNT DUE TO SELLER**
200. **AMOUNTS PAID BY OR IN BEHALF OF BORROWER**	500. **REDUCTIONS IN AMOUNT DUE TO SELLER**
201. Deposit or earnest money	501. Excess deposit (see Instructions)
202. Principal amount of new loan(s)	502. Settlement charges to seller (line 1400)
203. Existing loan(s) taken subject to	503. Existing loan(s) taken subject to
204.	504. Payoff of first mortgage loan
205.	505. Payoff of second mortgage loan
206.	506.
207.	507.
208.	508.
209.	509.
Adjustments for items unpaid by seller	Adjustments for items unpaid by seller
210. City/town taxes to	510. City/town taxes to
211. County taxes to	511. County taxes to
212. Assessments to	512. Assessments to
213.	513.
214.	514.
215.	515.
216.	516.
217.	517.
218.	518.
219.	519.
220. **TOTAL PAID BY/FOR BORROWER**	520. **TOTAL REDUCTION AMOUNT DUE SELLER**
300. **CASH AT SETTLEMENT FROM OR TO BORROWER**	600. **CASH AT SETTLEMENT TO OR FROM SELLER**
301. Gross amount due from borrower (line 120)	601. Gross amount due to seller (line 420)
302. Less amounts paid by/for borrower (line 220) (	) 602. Less reduction amount due seller (line 520) (
303. **CASH** (☐ FROM) (☐ TO) **BORROWER**	603. **CASH** (☐ TO) (☐ FROM) **SELLER**

(Continued on following page)

Figure 18.5.   Sample Closing Statement.

U.S. DEPARTMENT OF HOUSING AND URBAN DEVELOPMENT
SETTLEMENT STATEMENT
PAGE 2

L. SETTLEMENT CHARGES

		PAID FROM BORROWER'S FUNDS AT SETTLEMENT	PAID FROM SELLER'S FUNDS AT SETTLEMENT
700.	TOTAL SALES/BROKER'S COMM. based on price $ @ % =		
	Division of commission (line 700) as follows:		
701.	$ to		
702.	$ to		
703.	Commission paid at Settlement		
704.			
800.	**ITEMS PAYABLE IN CONNECTION WITH LOAN**		
801.	Loan Origination Fee %		
802.	Loan Discount %		
803.	Appraisal Fee to		
804.	Credit Report to		
805.	Lender's Inspection Fee		
806.	Mortgage Insurance Application Fee to		
807.	Assumption Fee		
808.			
809.			
810.			
811.			
900.	**ITEMS REQUIRED BY LENDER TO BE PAID IN ADVANCE**		
901.	Interest from to @ $ /day		
902.	Mortgage Insurance Premium for mos. to		
903.	Hazard Insurance Premium for yrs. to		
904.	yrs. to		
905.			
1000.	**RESERVES DEPOSITED WITH LENDER FOR**		
1001.	Hazard Insurance mos. @ $ /mo.		
1002.	Mortgage Insurance mos. @ $ /mo.		
1003.	City property taxes mos. @ $ /mo.		
1004.	County property taxes mos. @ $ /mo.		
1005.	Annual assessments mos. @ $ /mo.		
1006.	mos. @ $ /mo.		
1007.	mos. @ $ /mo.		
1008.	mos. @ $ /mo.		
1100.	**TITLE CHARGES**		
1101.	Settlement or closing fee to		
1102.	Abstract or title search to		
1103.	Title examination to		
1104.	Title insurance binder to		
1105.	Document preparation to		
1106.	Notary fees to		
1107.	Attorney's fees to		
	(includes above Items No.:)		
1108.	Title insurance to		
	(includes above Items No.:)		
1109.	Lender's coverage $		
1110.	Owner's coverage $		
1111.			
1112.			
1113.			
1200.	**GOVERNMENT RECORDING AND TRANSFER CHARGES**		
1201.	Recording fees: Deed $; Mortgage $; Release $		
1202.	City/county tax/stamps: Deed $; Mortgage $		
1203.	State tax/stamps: Deed $; Mortgage $		
1204.			
1205.			
1300.	**ADDITIONAL SETTLEMENT CHARGES**		
1301.	Survey to		
1302.	Pest inspection to		
1303.			
1304.			
1305.			
1400.	**TOTAL SETTLEMENT CHARGES** (enter on line 103, Section J and line 502, Section K)		

The Undersigned Acknowledges Receipt of This Settlement Statement and Agrees to the Correctness Thereof.

Buyer   Seller

Figure 18.5. Sample Closing Statement. *(cont.)*

is made is more than one month, the time is computed by full months and by the actual number of days in each partial month. For example, the period between March 15 and June 3 is two months (April and May) and 20 days (17 days in March and 3 days in June).

Calculations of taxes, interest, insurance, and rents follow. Other adjustments are calculated in the same manner. For the purpose of the examples, we will assume that title closes June 8.

18.60. Example of Calculation of Tax Adjustment

There are two basic methods for computing tax prorations. There is the due date method and the fiscal year method. They may vary from state to state. The due date method prorates the taxes based on the actual date that the taxes are due. The fiscal year method of proration allocates taxes according to the period the taxes represent, regardless of the date that they are due.

Assume that the state uses the due-date method and taxes in the locality are payable semiannually, April 1 and October 1. The seller paid taxes on April 1 for the preceding six-month period. During the current six-month period the seller is responsible for taxes from April 1 to, but not including, June 8, the closing date. He or she will have to allow the buyer the amount of the taxes for that period—two months (April and May) and seven days. Assuming that the taxes for the six-month period amount to $1,500.00, the taxes for one month are $250.00 ($1,500 ÷ 6); for one day, $8.33 ⅓ ($250 ÷ 30). An adjustment of $558.34 is made in favor of the purchasers [(2 x $250) + (7 x $8.33 ⅓)].

But suppose that the seller had paid taxes six months in advance. He or she would be entitled to recover taxes from and including June 8 through September 30, or for a period of three months (July, August, and September) and 23 days (June 8 through June 30). Allowance of $941.67 would be made in favor of the seller [(3 x $250) + (23 x $8.33 ⅓)].

18.61. Example of Calculation of Interest Adjustment

Suppose that there is a mortgage of $20,000 on the property, with interest at 9 percent payable quarterly on the 15th of December, March, June, and September. When title closed on June 8, interest had been paid to but not including March 15. The purchaser is entitled to an allowance for interest from and including March 15 through June 7, or for a period of 2 months (April and May) and 24 days (17 days in March and 7 days in June). The interest on $20,000 at 9 percent per annum is $150 per month, $5 per day ($150 ÷ 30). The interest for 2 months and 24 days is $420 [(2 x $150) + (24 x $5)]. An adjustment of $420 is made in favor of the purchaser.

The bank will supply a figure for payoff of an existing mortgage as of the date of closing. Mortgages are always paid off and released at closing except in the rare instance when the mortgagee allows the buyer to assume the seller's mortgage.

18.62. Example of Calculation of Insurance Adjustment

Suppose that there is a fire policy on the property that had been paid up for three years. The expiration date of the policy is August 1, 1993. The seller is therefore entitled to an adjustment of insurance for 13 months and 23 days (June 8, 1993, the date of the closing, to August 1, 1993). The premium is $10 per month [$360 ÷ (12 x 3)], or 33 ⅓¢ per day ($10 ÷ 30). An adjustment of $137.67 [(13 x $10) + (23 x 33 ⅓¢)] is made in favor of the seller.

18.63. Example of Calculation of Rent Adjustment

The seller had collected the rents in advance for the month of June. They amounted to $5,000.00. The purchaser is entitled to an adjustment for the period from and including June 8 through June 30, or 23 days. Since June has only 30 days, the rent per day is $5,000 ÷ 30, or $166.66 ⅔ per day. The purchaser is entitled to an adjustment of $3,833.33 (23 x 166.66⅔). If there is more than one tenant, you will have to prorate the rent for each separately, unless the rents had all been collected for the same period.

18.64. Miscellaneous Payments

Certain miscellaneous items are paid by the seller and others by the purchaser. These items do not constitute part of the actual closing figures because they are not charges or credits to the property itself, and they are not included in the calculation of the amount due by the buyer to the seller. However, each party must be given a memorandum of the payments for which he or she is responsible.

Checklist for Miscellaneous Payments by Seller

The seller is usually responsible for the following items:

1. Broker's commission
2. Attorney's fees (attending closing, etc.)
3. Fee for drawing deed
4. Recording fee on purchase money mortgage
5. Revenue stamps on purchase money mortgage

Checklist of Miscellaneous Payments by Purchaser

The purchaser is usually responsible for the following items:

1. Abstract
2. Fee for drawing purchase money mortgage (payable to mortgagee's attorney)
3. Attorney's fees (examination of abstract, attending closing, etc.)
4. Recording fee and documentary stamps on deed

FORECLOSURE ACTIONS

18.65. What Is a Foreclosure Action?

The forced sale of property to satisfy the payment of a mortgage (or deed of trust) or other default under the terms of the mortgage (or deed of trust) is a *foreclosure*. In some states the foreclosure is by advertisement and sale, held in accordance with the legal technicalities prescribed by the state statutes. In the majority of states, foreclosure is by litigation.

The first action in a foreclosure situation is a demand letter to the mortgagor. If the mortgagor does not cure the default in a timely manner, a foreclosure action may be instituted by the lender or mortgagee. Foreclosure proceedings must follow the statutory requirements precisely.

The preliminary steps in foreclosure litigation are fairly similar in all jurisdictions, but the procedure between the commencement of the action and the sale vary considerably not only with the jurisdiction but with the circumstances of the case. For that reason, emphasis here is on the preliminary procedure. The steps in the following sections will guide you, but you should be certain that your procedure adheres to the statute in your jurisdiction.

18.66. Papers Necessary for Institution of Foreclosure Action

The lawyer will need the following papers and documents before starting a foreclosure action:

1. Bond or note
2. Mortgage or deed of trust
3. Assignment, if any
4. Abstract of title
5. Receipted bills for taxes, assessments, water rates, interest, insurance, and the like paid by the mortgagee or his or her assignee

These papers constitute the nucleus of your file in the case. As soon as you receive a new matter slip (Chapter 2) about the case, ask the lawyer if you should get them from the client, so that they will be on hand when he or she is ready to start the action.

18.67. Information Needed to Prepare Papers in Foreclosure Action

You will need the following information to prepare the preliminary papers in a foreclosure action:

1. Venue
2. Parties plaintiff
3. Parties defendant
4. Description of property
5. Description of note or bond
6. Description of mortgage, including recording information
7. How the mortgage is in default

18.68. Venue

You can get the *venue* from the description of the property in the mortgage. An action to foreclose a mortgage is always brought in the state and county in which the property is located. A foreclosure is an equity action and in those states that have separate courts for law and equity, the action is brought in the chancery court.

18.69. Parties to a Foreclosure Action

The parties in a foreclosure action are the plaintiff and the defendant.

Parties Plaintiff

The holder of the mortgage—the mortgagee or his or her beneficiary or assignee—is the *plaintiff* in a foreclosure action. The suit must be brought in the name of the actual owner of the mortgage. If a mortgage is held by William Walsh as Trustee for Carl Sloane, the action is brought by William Walsh, Trustee for Carl Sloane, not by William Walsh. If the mortgage is owned jointly, perhaps by husband and wife, the action is brought in the name of both owners.

Parties Defendant

Every person who has an interest in the property covered by a mortgage is made a *party defendant* to the foreclosure action. This might include the mortgagor; the mortgagor's heirs, devisees, or legatees; wife of the mortgagor; *cestui que trustent;* persons in possession as tenants or occupants; the People of the State; and others. You can get the names of known defendants from the certification of defendants (section 18.75); the lawyer will give them to you if there is no certification.

18.70. Fictitious Names

Since someone frequently has an interest that the plaintiff does not know about, or someone whose name is unknown has an interest in the property, several *fictitious names* are added as defendants. The reason for adding the fictitious names is that additional defendants can be brought into the action without the necessity of serving an amended complaint on all defendants. Perhaps an interested party's last name is known but not his or her first; a fictitious first name is given to that defendant:

"Gerald" Thomas, first name "Gerald" being fictitious, defendant's real first name being unknown to the plaintiff.

Sometimes an unknown person is identified by a description:

"Abraham Bryant," name fictitious, defendant's real name being unknown to the plaintiff, person intended conducting a stationery store at No. 35 East 18 Street.

The complaint usually alleges that the names are fictitious. The true name is substituted for the fictitious name as soon as it is learned. In all subsequent papers filed in the case, the caption reflects the substitution.

18.71. Description of Note or Bond

The foreclosure complaint contains a complete description of the note or bond secured by the mortgage. A note is usually copied verbatim. Only the gist of the bond is set forth, including the name of the person signing it, the amount, the date, rate of interest and when payable, date of maturity. You can get the wording from a good form book or your computer forms file, but unless your office does considerable foreclosure work, the lawyer will provide the terms of the bond. Check the names, dates, and amounts against the original bond.

18.72. Description of Mortgage

A description of the mortgage sufficient to identify it is set forth in the complaint and other papers. The description includes the name of the mortgagor, name of the mortgagee, date of execution, maturity date. The description also shows when and where the mortgage was recorded—the date, the clerk's office, book (*Liber*) and page number. In some jurisdictions a copy of the mortgage is attached to the complaint as an exhibit.

If the plaintiff is the assignee of the original mortgage, the foreclosure complaint alleges the fact of the assignment, thus showing the plaintiff's right to sue.

18.73. Description of Property

Get the description of the property from the mortgage. It is advisable to keep the copy in your file and in the computer so that it will be readily available whenever you prepare a paper in the case. Follow the directions given in section 18.6 for copying land descriptions. An accurate description is particularly important in a foreclosure action because the action is defective if the description has an error in it.

18.74. When Is a Mortgage Considered in Default?

Failure of the mortgagor to meet any obligation under a mortgage is a default. The default may be in payment of principal, interest, taxes, insurance, or in the observance or performance of any of the conditions of the mortgage. If the mortgagor fails to pay the taxes when due, he or she is in default. Under the acceleration clause (section 18.28), the entire amount of the mortgage then becomes due, and the owner may foreclose for the entire amount, not merely for the amount that is in default.

PROCEDURE IN FORECLOSURE ACTION

18.75. Title Search for Foreclosures

When the mortgagor delivered the mortgage to the mortgagee, he or she either turned over to the mortgagee an abstract of title to the premises or the mortgagee conducted his or her own title search. Banks taking mortgages have their own title-search requirements. Before the lawyer begins foreclosure proceedings he or she will want that abstract brought up to date. Write a letter to the abstract company similar to the letter ordering a continuation of abstract when a purchase and sale agreement is entered into (section 18.50). In those few states where there are no abstract companies, other arrangements are made for the title search.

Upon request, most title companies will also furnish a certification of defendants, or a foreclosure report, as it is called in some localities. The certification lists the necessary and proper parties defendant to the foreclosure action and the interest of each in the premises. It also discloses the legal capacity of each defendant. (See section 13.6 in Chapter 13.) When you order the continuation of abstract, ask the lawyer if he or she wants a certification of defendants. The lawyer might prefer to prepare the list of parties defendant from the abstract, rather than have the title company make the certification.

18.76. Preparation of Complaint

The complaint in a foreclosure action is largely standardized. The lawyer will provide any unusual parts. The complaint is prepared in the same style and on the same kind of paper as a complaint in any civil action (Chapter 14).

Caption

The caption of the complaint includes the fictitious names as well as the names of the known defendants. The exact wording varies, but the following styles are typical.

HENRY MASON,

Plaintiff,

vs.

JOHN MASON, doing business under the trade name or style of John's Stores, "JOHN DOE," "RICHARD DOE," and "EARL DOE," said three last named defendants being fictitious, said defendants' true names being unknown to plaintiff, they being intended to designate tenants of portions of the premises described in the complaint,

Defendants.

HENRY MASON,

Plaintiff,

against

JOHN MASON and HELEN MASON, husband and wife, DOE ONE, DOE TWO, DOE THREE, and DOE FOUR,

Defendants.

18.77. Number of Copies

To know how many copies of the complaint to prepare, besides your office copy, you will have to know the answer to these practice questions:

1. How many copies are filed in court?
2. May we dispense with service against any group of defendants?

Foreclosure actions frequently have numerous defendants, and the preparation of a copy of a long complaint for each of them works a hardship on the plaintiff. To relieve the plaintiff, some jurisdictions have adopted practice rules that make it unnecessary to serve the complaint on every defendant.

18.78. Preparation of Summons

The *summons* in a foreclosure action is prepared like the summons in any civil action. (See the directions in Chapter 14.)

18.79. Filing and Service of Complaint and Summons

After the complaint and summons are prepared, proceed as in any civil action. (See directions in Chapter 14.) Remember to make diary and suit register entries.

18.80. Follow-up of Process Service

Follow-up of process service is necessary in all civil actions but is particularly important in foreclosure actions because of the number of defendants. Numerous foreclosure actions are delayed because service of process is lax. It is your responsibility to see that the process server makes every effort to effect service expeditiously on all defendants. Request weekly reports on the progress of service. Insist that you be informed immediately when, where, and upon whom service is made and that the process server make affidavit of service as soon as service is made. The process server should inform you of any difficulties that may arise, such as questions with respect to identity. In those jurisdictions where process is served by the sheriff or other county official, you cannot follow the matter as closely as when your office employs the process server. (Remember to make appropriate diary and suit register entries.)

18.81. Party Sheet

Numerous parties defendant in a foreclosure action make it advisable to keep a special record, which might be called a *party sheet,* of service on and appearance by each defendant. (This record is not to be confused with the party sheet that is filed in court in some jurisdictions.) Use a wide sheet of paper for the record. Head the sheet:

PARTY SHEET

Action No. ..... Plaintiff's .... Premises (brief description) ....
Office File No. .....

Rule the sheet into vertical columns, with the following columnar headings:

Defendants (specify legal status, such as infant, corporation, trustee)

Interest in premises (owner, tenant, etc.)

Address where served

When served

How served

By whom served

Affidavit of service made before .... (*notary's name*)

Last day to answer

Appeared by .... (*name of defendant's attorney*)

Address and telephone number of attorney

Date appearance entered

Remarks

A glance at the party sheet will tell the lawyer the status of service and appearance of each defendant.

18.82. Other Steps in Foreclosure Proceedings

After the complaint and summons have been filed and served, the procedure in foreclosure litigation varies. The following steps are among those that will have to be taken, depending on the jurisdiction and the circumstances of the case.

1. Application for receivership. If the property involved is income producing, the plaintiff will ask for the appointment of a receiver to collect the income and make the necessary disbursements.

2. Application for appointment of guardian ad litem. If the parent of an infant defendant will not ask for the appointment of a guardian ad litem, the plaintiff does.

3. *Ex parte* motion to obtain leaver to sue "arm of court," such as a trustee in bankruptcy.

4. Entry of default judgment.

5. Reference to compute or reference to master in chancery.

6. Hearing before referee or master. The lawyer will want the following papers to take to the hearing:

   a. Referee's oath

   b. Referee's report ready for signature

   c. Bond or note

   d. Mortgage or deed of trust

   e. Assignments

   f. True or photocopies of (c), (d), and (e), so that the originals may be withdrawn when the hearing is over

   g. Receipted bills for taxes, assessments, water rates, penalties or interest, if any, paid by mortgagee

   h. Receipt for payment of insurance if paid by mortgagee

   i. Summons with affidavit of service

   j. Check to order of referee

7. Judgment or decree of foreclosure and sale.

8. Publication of notice of sale.

9. Sale.

18.83. What to Do in Foreclosure Action

Here is a checklist of what you will have to do when your office handles a foreclosure action.

1. Make file and process as any other new matter (Chapter 2).

2. Keep diary entries (Chapter 4) and progress record (Chapter 12).

3. Order abstract of title continuation.

4. Prepare all papers, as directed by the attorney.

5. See that complaint and summons are filed and served.

6. In states where foreclosures are advertised, arrange for publication in a local newspaper and keep copies for the files when notice is published.

7. Make sure to keep a record of all process served on defendants; if any are missed, their interest in the property may not be foreclosed.

8. Have copies (computer printout or photocopy) made of mortgage or deed, trust, bond or note, and assignments.

9. Prepare party sheet and keep it up to date.

10. If a receiver is appointed, keep after him for regular reports.

11. Gather together papers for the lawyer to take to the hearing.

12. Make bookkeeping entries of all disbursements and receipts, just as in any case (Chapter 7).

19 Assisting with Probate and Estate Administration

The property left when a person dies is known as a *decedent's estate*. Whether the deceased died *testate* (having a will) or *intestate* (without a valid will), it is usually necessary that a competent person or corporation be charged with the duty of administering the deceased person's estate. (See Chapter 11 for instructions concerning the preparation of wills.) The objects of the administration are, first, to collect the assets of an estate and pay the claims against it; and, second, to determine the persons to whom any residue of the estate belongs and deliver it to them. The administration of an estate is under the jurisdiction of the probate court (known as the surrogate's court in New York), and it is only through proceedings in this court that the executor or administrator can function.

Proceedings in probate courts, although similar, vary in detail not only from state to state but from county to county. The courts have printed forms for almost all of the papers that are filed in the administration of an estate. You can prepare many of them without detailed instruction from the lawyer. The procedure described here is similar to the practice in New York County, but you should follow the procedure and use the forms required in your locality.

ADMINISTRATION OF ESTATE

19.1. Distinction Between Executor and Administrator

The general term used to describe any person appointed to administer an estate, whether testate or intestate, is *personal representative* or *legal representative*. In many states the term *personal representative* has replaced

486

both of the terms *executor* and *administrator*. In other states, if the decedent left a valid will naming the person or corporation whom the testator wanted to administer the estate, the person or corporation named in the will is an *executor*. The testator may name as many executors as desired. Often an individual names both the spouse and a bank as coexecutors. The spouse thus has a voice in the administration of the estate, and the bank can advise the spouse and handle the considerable amount of work involved in the administration. Frequently, an alternate executor is named in case the first is unable to serve.

If a decedent died intestate, the court will appoint a person who is entitled to share in the estate known in some states as *administrator*. If the decedent left a will but did not nominate an executor, or if the person named is incompetent or refuses to act or dies, the court will appoint an administrator *cum testamento annexo, c.t.a* (with the will attaced, *w.w.a*). The abbreviations *c.t.a.* and *w.w.a* refer to the same thing.

In those states where the terms *executor* and *administrator* are used, there is little practical difference between the authority and duties of each, except that a will may confer on an executor powers in addition to those the law gives. The executor, although nominated by the testator, receives authority to act by petitioning the probate court for *letters testamentary*. The administrator receives authority to act by petitioning for *letters of administration*. The will controls the distribution the executor (or administrator, c.t.a.) makes of the property, whereas state inheritance statutes control the distribution the administrator makes.

19.2. The Lawyer's Part in the Administration of an Estate

Almost every lawyer is at some time the personal representative (or executor or administrator) of one or more estates. The lawyer's most common role in the administration of an estate, however, is as counsel to a personal representative. Every personal representative, corporate or individual, requires the services of an attorney in the administration, settlement, and distribution of the estate. The attorney probates the will; files the petition for letters testamentary or letters of administration; institutes the necessary proceedings, such as tax proceedings and accounting proceedings; and advises the personal representative about the legality of his or her acts. The personal representative receives a commission from the estate, except when agreeing to serve without compensation. If acting as personal representative, the attorney may perform the necessary legal services and receive proper compensation in addition to a commission.

19.3. Estate Taxes

Both state and federal governments tax estates. During administration, the estate may be taxed as an entity like any other. It will have an Employer Identification Number (EIN), which is applied for on Form SS-4. Federal estate taxes are assessed on estates over a certain amount, $600,000 in 1991. State taxes vary as to what estates are taxed and at what rates. Lawyers who have an extensive estate planning practice will be very sophisticated in the area of taxation and tax planning for their clients.

PROBATE OF WILL

19.4. The Personal Representative's Right to Act

The personal representative named in a will cannot take over the administration of an estate without first indicating an intention to act and receiving the sanction of the court. Three documents are necessary to establish the personal representative's right to act: (1) the will itself, (2) the decree admitting it to probate, and (3) letters testamentary. The will is generally considered the source and measure of a personal representative's power, but the will must first be proved. It is proved by a legal proceeding in probate court known as *probate of will*. The proceeding culminates in a decree by the court admitting the will to probate and directing that letters testamentary issue to the personal representative. The letters testamentary are the evidence of the personal representative's authority.

19.5. Probate of Will

The attorney for the estate generally prepares and submits to the personal representative the necessary papers in the proceeding to probate the will. The probate proceeding is initiated by the filing of the will itself, together with a copy of it, certified to be a correct and true copy. (Figure 19.1 on page 490 shows entries made in the suit register record [Chapter 12] in a probate proceeding.) A petition for the probate of the will is also filed with the will and the copy. Simultaneously, a transfer tax affidavit is filed. The inheritance tax is not based on the affidavit. A special proceeding is needed for that. Legal notice of the probate proceeding must be served on all interested parties and affidavit of service (or waiver of service) filed with the court. Sworn depositions of one or more witnesses to the will must also be filed, unless the will was a "self-proving will" in a form established by statute in many states. If there are no objections to the admission of the will within the time specified, the will is admitted to probate by a decree of the court to that effect. The person named as personal representative in the will then files a bond (unless waived in the will) and an oath, and letters testamentary as personal representative issue to the person who is named. A corporate fiduciary named as personal representative does not generally have to file a bond.

19.6. Parties to a Probate Proceeding

The proponent of the will, that is, the person or corporation seeking to have the will probated, is the *petitioner*. The petitioner is usually the person or corporation named in the will as personal representative. There are three groups of interested parties who must be informed of the probate proceeding so that they may protect their interests:

1. Heirs-at-law of the deceased including the surviving spouse and those individuals who would have inherited if the decedent had died intestate. This group includes the heirs-at-law who are also named in the will as legatees, because they might take less by the will than they would have inherited if there had been no will.

2. The executors and trustees named in the will who do not sign the petition.

3. Legatees or devisees who are not distributees. They are the legatees or devisees named in the will who would not have inherited if the decedent had died intestate. They are interested in the proceeding because they lose their legacies if the will is not admitted to probate.

19.7. Copy of Will and Affidavit

Some states require a copy of the will to be filed in the probate court with the original will. In most jurisdictions a photocopy may be filed. In the administration of a large, complicated estate, where numerous copies of the

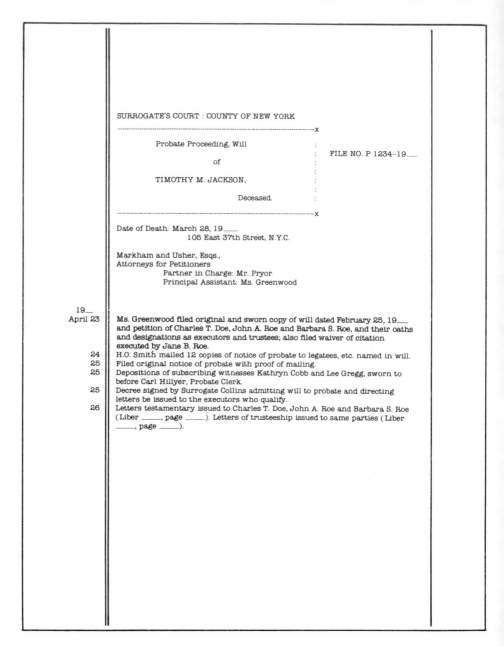

SURROGATE'S COURT : COUNTY OF NEW YORK

---x

      Probate Proceeding, Will   :

             of   :   FILE NO. P 1234--19___

      TIMOTHY M. JACKSON,   :

                     Deceased.   :

---x

Date of Death: March 28, 19___
               105 East 37th Street, N.Y.C.

Markham and Usher, Esqs.,
Attorneys for Petitioners
        Partner in Charge: Mr. Pryor
        Principal Assistant: Ms. Greenwood

19___		
April 23		Ms. Greenwood filed original and sworn copy of will dated February 25, 19___ and petition of Charles T. Doe, John A. Roe and Barbara S. Roe, and their oaths and designations as executors and trustees; also filed waiver of citation executed by Jane B. Roe.
	24	H.O. Smith mailed 12 copies of notice of probate to legatees, etc. named in will.
	25	Filed original notice of probate with proof of mailing.
	25	Depositions of subscribing witnesses Kathryn Cobb and Lee Gregg, sworn to before Carl Hillyer, Probate Clerk.
	25	Decree signed by Surrogate Collins admitting will to probate and directing letters be issued to the executors who qualify.
	26	Letters testamentary issued to Charles T. Doe, John A. Roe and Barbara S. Roe (Liber ___, page ___). Letters of trusteeship issued to same parties (Liber ___, page ___).

Figure 19.1.   Progress Record in Probate of Will.

will are needed, the will is photocopied or, less commonly, printed. Photocopy the will after the signature and data written in ink are complete.

19.8. Petition for Probate of Will

The petition for probate sets forth certain factual data about the testator and the testator's heirs, legatees, and devisees and prays that the will be admitted to probate and that letters testamentary be issued to the executor. If trustees are named in the will, the petition also prays for letters of trusteeship.

1. Be especially careful about names, addresses, and values of legacies and devisees.

2. Note that the lawyer will give you (a) the name and address of the petitioner or petitioners; (b) the name of the testator, the testator's residence at the time of death, and the time and place of his or her death; (c) the names, addresses, ages, and degree of kinship to the decedent of the heirs-at-law and of those interested in the will; (d) the addresses of the other legatees and devisees. This information and the copy of the will give you the facts necessary to fill in the form, unless the will is complicated. The lawyer will write any additional necessary information.

3. Note that the relationship of the distributees shows how to fill in the information on surviving relatives. A surviving spouse always shares in a decedent's estate. The distributees, other than the surviving spouse, take in the following order: (1) children and issue of deceased children; (2) father, mother; (3) brothers, sisters, and issue of deceased brothers and sisters; (4) uncles, aunts, and issue of deceased uncles and aunts.

4. Do not make an allegation concerning relatives of a deceased who are not entitled to inherit, and do not make an allegation about a surviving mother or father, or others, because in this case they cannot inherit. If there were no surviving children or issue of a predeceased child, and no surviving mother or father, the brothers and sisters would be listed as distributees. It would then be necessary to allege that there were no surviving children or issue of a deceased child and no surviving mother or father.

It would not be necessary to allege that there were no surviving aunts or uncles and no issue of a deceased aunt or uncle, because they could not inherit, unless specifically named in the will.

5. Get the names of the legatees and devisees from the copy of the will.

6. Note that the petition indicates the kind of legacy, as well as its value. You can get this information from the will. Thus the testator might leave the residue of the estate in trust for the testator's spouse, the remainder to go to the children upon the death of the spouse. The petition would show that the spouse was the *beneficiary of a residuary trust* and that the children were given a *remainder interest in the residuary trust.* If the testator does not place the residue of the estate in trust but leaves it outright to someone, the petition indicates that the person is the *residuary legatee.* When specific personal property, rather than a sum of money, is bequeathed, the bequest is indicated in the petition as a *specific legacy.*

7. Arrange for the petitioners to come in and sign the petition.

8. Have the petitioners verify the petition.

9. Make an original for the court and a copy for your office file.

10. File the original of the petition, the original and certified copy of the will, and the transfer tax affidavit (see section 19.9) in the probate court.

11. Mark on your office copy the date the petition was filed.

12. Make an entry in the suit register and your computerized schedule.

19.9. Transfer Tax Affidavit

A *transfer tax affidavit,* filed with the petition, is a sworn statement about the totals of realty and personalty affected by the will and of the names, amounts of legacies, residences, and relationship of those who receive gifts under the will. The affidavit supplies the state taxing authorities with data to be used by them for taxing purposes. It is prepared on a printed form supplied by the taxing commission.

19.10. Citation and Waiver in Probate Proceeding

Probate in some states may require that the surviving spouse, distributees, and executors and trustees named in the decedent's will must be given notice of the petition for probate by service of a *citation*. The citation is a legal writ citing those to whom it is addressed to appear in court on a certain date and show cause why the will should not be admitted to probate. It does not command an appearance as a summons does. Those who do not want to contest the will need not appear in court. A citation is issued by the clerk of the court but is prepared by the petitioner's attorney.

Any person above age 18 may serve a citation. Service is made by delivering a copy to the person upon whom it is served. If an infant is a distributee, the citation is addressed to the infant but is served on the parent with whom the infant resides or upon the infant's guardian. If an infant is above age 14, service is made upon the distributee, as well as the distributee's parent or guardian.

Service of Citation by Publication and Mailing

If any of the distributees live outside the state, or if there are any heirs or next of kin whose names and place of residence are unknown, service is by publication and mailing. The procedure is similar to that in a civil action. (See "Service by publication," Part 5, "Glossary of Legal Terms.")

Adults may waive the issuance and source of a citation in the matter of proving the last will and testament of the deceased, but infants may not. Thus before the citations are prepared, waivers are secured.

19.11. How to Handle a Waiver of Citation

Follow these steps in processing a waiver of citation:

1. Make an original for the court and an office copy.
2. Have those who waive citation sign the original in the presence of two witnesses.
3. Take the acknowledgment of those signing the waiver.
4. Conform the office copy, marking on it the date the original is filed. (See section 10.18 in Chapter 18.)
5. File the original in court.
6. Make an entry in the suit register and your computerized schedule.

19.12. How to Handle a Citation

Follow these steps in preparing a citation:

1. Make an original for the court, a copy for each person to be served, and an office copy.
2. Note that the return date may be any date within the time allowed by the court rules.
3. Get the clerk of the court to sign the original.
4. Conform the copies and give the original and copies (except the office copy) to the person who is to serve the citation. (See section 10.18 in Chapter 18.)
5. Prepare an affidavit of service, which is usually printed on the back of the citation, and have the person who served the citation sign and swear to the affidavit in the presence of a notary.
6. Conform the office copy, marking on it the date the original is filed in court. (See section 10.18 in Chapter 18.)
7. File the original in court.
8. Enter in your diary the return date of citation, and make an entry in the suit register and computerized schedule.

19.13. Preparations for Hearing

The hearing, if any, in an uncontested probate proceeding is informal. The lawyer for the petitioners appears before the clerk of the court with the witnesses to the will. The date of the hearing is the return day indicated in the citation. (In some jurisdictions the clerk of the court sets the date for hearing at the time the petition is filed.) Although many states no longer require hearings for uncontested wills, you may be called upon to assist with a hearing. In that case you will have to make certain preparations before the hearing:

1. Prepare the deposition of witnesses.
2. Notify the witnesses to the will.
3. Prepare and mail the notice of probate.
4. Prepare the oath of the executor.
5. Prepare the decree.

6. Prepare the letters testamentary and also letters of trusteeship if the petition prays for them.

19.14. Notice of Probate

The legatees and devisees who are not heirs-at-law must be given notice that the will has been offered for probate. A printed form of notice calls for the names and addresses of the proponents (the petitioners) and for a list of the names and addresses of the legatees, devisees, and beneficiaries who have not been cited or have not waived citation.

1. Send the notices by mail, if desired. The attorney for the petitioners makes an affidavit of service by mail on the back of the notice.

2. Notarize the affidavit made by the attorney.

3. Make an original for the court, a copy for each person listed in the notice, and an office copy; conform the office copy. (See section 10.18 in Chapter 18.)

4. Place the original with the papers that the lawyer will take to the hearing.

5. Make an entry in the suit register and computerized schedule that the notices were mailed.

19.15. Deposition of Witnesses to the Will

As soon as you know the date of the hearing, notify the witnesses to the will of the time and place of the hearing. You can get their names and addresses from the will. If the witnesses are not available, the lawyer will have to take other legal steps to prove the will. Make an entry of the notice in your suit register and computerized schedule.

Printed forms of depositions are available.

1. Do not date the depositions. They are signed and sworn to before an officer of the court, who dates them at that time.

2. Prepare an original and an office copy for each witness. Thus if there are two witnesses, you will prepare two sets of depositions.

3. Place the originals with the papers that the lawyer will take to the hearing.

4. Draw checks to witnesses for the fee allowed by law. The lawyer will probably take the checks to the hearing and pay the witnesses

at that time; otherwise, mail the checks after the depositions are taken.

19.16. Oath of Personal Representative

A personal representative, or an executor, must take an oath to perform his or her duties faithfully. Printed forms are usually available.

1. Prepare an original and an office copy for each executor. Thus if there are two executors, you will prepare two sets of oaths.
2. Have each executor sign the original of the oath in the presence of a notary public. In New York the executor must also certify that his or her domicile address is in New York.
3. Conform the office copies. (See section 10.18 in Chapter 18.)
4. Place the originals with the papers the lawyer will take to the hearing.
5. Make an entry in the suit register and computerized schedule that the oaths have been executed.

19. 17. Decree Admitting Will to Probate

A *decree* in a probate proceeding serves the same purpose as an order or judgment in a civil action. A favorable decree admits the will to probate and directs that letters testamentary issue to the executor nominated in the will. The probate judge (the surrogate in New York) signs the decree, but the petitioner's attorney prepares it. Printed forms are available.

1. Do not date the decree. It will be dated when the judge signs it.
2. Make an original for the court and a copy for your office file.
3. Place the original with the papers the lawyer will take to the hearing.
4. The decree might not be signed for several days after the hearing. Make a follow-up entry in your diary for a few days after the hearing and inquire of the clerk of the court if it has been signed.
5. Mark on your office copy the date the decree was signed.
6. Make an entry in the suit register and computerized schedule.

19.18. Letters Testamentary

After the judge signs the decree, the clerk of the court issues *letters testamentary* to the personal representative. The attorney for the personal representative prepares the letters. They are the evidence of the personal representative's authority to act. Anyone dealing with the personal representative as the representative of the estate will require a certificate to that effect that letters have been issued and are still in force. Certificates are available from the clerk of the court for a small fee.

1. If there are two or more executors, name all of them in the letters.

2. Do not date the letters. The clerk of the court will date them when they are issued.

3. Prepare an original, or duplicate original, for each personal representative, an office copy, and a sufficient number of copies to be certified by the clerk of the court. Thus if there are two personal representatives, prepare three copies in addition to the copies to be certified. There must be a certified copy for each bank account, each security issue, each safe deposit box, and the like.

4. Place the original and duplicate original with the papers that the lawyer will take to the hearing. The clerk will sign a copy for each personal representative named in the letters and return them to your office.

5. Conform your office copy. (See section 10.18 in Chapter 18.)

6. Deliver a signed copy to each personal representative. If the lawyer is a personal representative, he or she will retain one of the signed copies.

7. Make entries in the suit register and computerized schedule.

19.19. Notice to Creditors

As soon as letters testamentary are issued, notice to creditors should be published in a local newspaper. Creditors of the decedent are given a certain time in which to file any claims they may have against the decedent. Enter in your diary the last day the creditors have to present claims.

Newspapers usually have a printed form of notice to creditors that you can fill in without any difficulty. Within a specified time after the last publication, affidavit of publication is filed with the clerk of the court. The publisher makes the affidavit of publication and delivers it to either the clerk of the court or the attorney. Enter in your diary the date by which the affidavit must be filed; also make entries in the suit register and computerized schedule.

APPOINTMENT OF ADMINISTRATOR

19.20. Application for Letters of Administration

When a person dies without leaving a will or, in many states, dies intestate, a person who is an adult (18 or older in most states) of sound mind, and entitled to share in the estate, may ask to be appointed administrator of the estate. One does this by applying to the probate court for *letters of administration.* The procedure is governed by statute and may differ in some of the states. In many states *letters of authority* are used for both testate and intestate estates.

19.21. Parties

The person who files an application for letters of administration, or authority, is known as the *petitioner*. There are no plaintiffs and defendants—the petitioner does not bring a suit against someone else—but there are other necessary and interested parties. Those nearer of kin to the deceased than the petitioner have a prior right to be appointed; those of an equal decree of kinship have an equal right to be appointed. The kin of the decedent in these two categories are, therefore, necessary parties to the proceeding and are made parties to it by the service of a citation unless they waive citation (section 19.10).

All of those who are entitled by law to share in the intestate's estate—the *distributees*—are interested parties to the proceeding, although they may not be entitled to letters of administration. For example, a minor child of the deceased, or a minor child of his prior deceased child, are distributees of the estate and are interested parties. They are not served with citations because they cannot serve as administrators, but they are given notice of the application for letters of administration.

19.22. Who Has Prior Right to Letters of Administration?

The statutes provide the order of priority by which distributees of the decedent's estate are entitled to letters of administration. The usual order is as follows:

1. Surviving spouse
2. Children
3. Grandchildren
4. Parents
5. Brothers and sisters
6. Nephews and nieces

19.23. Necessary Papers in Application for Letters of Administration

Printed forms of papers that must be prepared by the attorney and filed in an application for letters of administration are usually available, and the courts prefer that they be used. The forms are not uniform, varying even from county to county within a state, but they are similar. In every state, there is a petition for letters of administration, an oath of administrator, and a notice in some form to interested parties.

19.24. How to Handle a Petition; Oath; Designation of Clerk

The lawyer will give you the information necessary to fill in the form.

1. Fill in the blanks not only in the petition but also in the form of verification, oath, and designation of clerk, even if they are on separate forms.
2. Have the petition verified.
3. Prepare an original and one copy of the petition.
4. Arrange for the client to come in and sign the petition when it is ready.
5. Have the petitioner sign on the line designated in the presence of a notary public; also immediately beneath the verification, immediately beneath the oath, and immediately beneath the designation of the clerk for service of process.

6. If you are a notary, ask the petitioner to swear to the petition and to the oath and to acknowledge the designation of the clerk.

7. Notarize the instrument.

8. Conform the office copy. (See section 10.18 in Chapter 18.)

9. File the original in court.

10. Get the court file number from the clerk and enter it on the back of the office copy.

11. Make an entry in the suit register and computerized schedule.

12. Note that in some states the clerk of the court sets a hearing date when the petition is filed. If this is the practice in your state, enter the hearing date in your diary.

19.25. Renunciation

Many states provide that a person who is entitled to letters of administration, or authority, may renounce this right. An individual does this by signing a simple printed form. The renunciation makes it unnecessary to serve a citation on those who renounced.

19.26. Citations

All interested parties must be notified of the application for letters. the method of notifying them varies, however, from state to state. When printed forms of citations are used, they are similar to the form used in a proceeding to prove a will.

1. Do not put a caption on the citation.

2. Address the citation to those distributees who have a right prior or equal to that of the petitioner to letters of administration. You can get the names and addresses of those to whom the citation is to be addressed from the petition.

3. Note that the return date of the citation may be any date within the time allowed by the court rules. In some jurisdictions the date is set by the clerk of the court when the petition is filed.

4. Make an original for the court, a copy for each person to whom the citation is addressed, and an office copy.

5. Get the court clerk to sign the original.

6. Conform the copies and serve them. (See section 10.18 in Chapter 18.)

7. Make an affidavit of service.

8. Enter the return date in your dairy.

9. Make an entry in the suit register and computerized schedule and follow the court calendar just as in a contested action.

19.27. Notice of Application for Letters of Administration

If distributees who do not have a right to letters of administration equal to that of the petitioner are not served with a citation, they are *notified* of the application. Printed forms are available.

1. Date the notice of application at any time subsequent to the filing of the petition, before the issuance of the letters.

2. Make an original for the court, a copy for each distributee entitled to the notice, and an office copy.

3. Have the petitioner sign the notice.

4. Mail copies of the notice to each distributee entitled to it at the address given in the petition.

5. Make an affidavit that the notice was mailed.

6. Conform the office copy and file the original in court. (See section 10.18 in Chapter 18.)

7. Make an entry in the suit register and computerized schedule.

19.28. Letters of Administration

If there is no opposition to the appointment of the petitioner as administrator, the court enters a decree directing that *letters of administration* issue to the petitioner. The letters of administration serve the same purpose for an administrator that letters testamentary do for the executor. The attorney for the petitioner prepares the decree and the letters in the same manner as when a will is admitted to probate and letters testamentary are granted.

As soon as letters of administration are granted, notice to creditors must be published. (See notice to creditors after letters testamentary are granted in section 19.19.) Make the appropriate diary entries and entries in the suit register and computerized schedule.

20 Handling Commercial Collections

Commercial items, that is, past due accounts, that the lawyer undertakes to collect for others are referred to as *collections*. Collections may be turned over to the lawyer by local clients, or they may be forwarded from another town by a collection agency or by another lawyer. Commercial collections have become a specialty in the legal profession. Some law offices handle collections almost exclusively. Because retail and consumer claims are governed by requirements outlined in the Fair Debt Collection Practices Act, as amended in 1985, it is important to recognize that these types of claims differ from commercial claims.

Unless suit is filed, collections may be handled on a contingent fee basis. Although some commercial items involve large amounts, the majority of them are for small sums, with a correspondingly small fee. It is, therefore, desirable in the case of small items to curtail the usual office procedure as much as is consistent with efficiency. If the office handles a significant load of collections, they may be segregated from the other cases and handled in a special manner. The procedure is routine and, after it has been established, the secretary and paralegal can assume responsibility for the entire operation of the collection department.

COLLECTION PROCEDURES

20.1. Commercial Law Lists

Lawyers who want to handle the collection of commercial items obtain representation on one or more bonded commercial law lists. It is from these

502

lists that out-of-town lawyers select an attorney in the debtor's locality to handle the claim. It is also from these lists that the lawyers in your office will select attorneys to whom to forward accounts against debtors in other jurisdictions.

Usually, the forwarder of an item will mention the law list from which the lawyer's name was obtained. Some lists produce better results than others. You, therefore, should keep a record of the items the lawyer receives through each list and the fees earned by reason of representation on that list. The lawyer can then determine whether continued representation on a special list is warranted. A simple record is sufficient and may be kept up to date on the computer. Keep a separate page or file for each law list and note on it the forwarder, the item (creditor, debtor, and amount), and, when the matter is closed, the amount of the fee. You might also keep a hard copy of the lists in a folder in the front of the file drawer in which the collection cases are filed.

20.2. Office Procedures Affecting Collections

The office procedures affecting collections involve the following:

1. Files
2. Follow-up system
3. Acknowledgment of claim
4. Letters to debtor
5. Reports to forwarder
6. Records of collections
7. Remittances to forwarder
8. Forwarding collection items
9. Suit

20.3. How to File Collection Matters

As soon as a collection item is received, set up your computer or other file for it. Offices with a lot of collections, especially for local clients, would organize the files by client name and cross-file as needed. File folders, too, would be filed alphabetically by name. When a numerical system of filing is used for collections, a cross-reference index of alphabetical names is essential. If suit is brought on a collection, the case is handled like any other litigated matter. (See Chapter 4 for a description of a follow-up filing system.)

20.4. Acknowledgment of Claim

Promptness in acknowledging a collection is very important because the forwarder wants to know that the matter is receiving immediate attention. The acknowledgment might read:

Dear Mr. Hill:

Re: Jones Brothers, Inc. v. F. M. Wilson
Amount $1,500

We acknowledge receipt of the above claim and accept the claim for collection on the basis of the Operative Guides of the Commercial Law League of America.

Since you are recognized as the client's agency, we will report developments and make remittances directly to you.

Sincerely yours,

Elwood & Adams

Firms that handle a large volume of collection accounts often use a snap-out form, with the firm's name and address printed at the top, for acknowledgments, initial collection letters, and file identification.

20.5. Collection Letters

In a comparatively small community the attorney frequently knows the debtor against whom there is a collection claim. Handling the collection is often tempered by the personal relationship, but in normal cases the lawyer proceeds promptly and vigorously. Your computer library should include models of a standard series of collection letters that can be adapted to each particular case. If you are called upon to draft any letters, keep these premises in mind:

1. Since the purpose of the letter is to collect money, do not hesitate to ask for a check.

2. Do not take the attitude that the account "probably has been overlooked," because numerous demands for payment are made before the account is given to an attorney.

3. Use *dated action*. Tell the debtor that a certain action is expected by a given date or within a given number of days, not in the "near future."

4. Avoid the *divided urge* in a collection letter. Suggest only one course of action—do not mention an alternative. Do not, for example, tell the debtor that you expect a check by a certain date and then suggest that he or she should telephone if payment is impossible.

5. Keep the period between letters short—from five to ten days.

A first letter to the debtor from the attorney on May 3 might read:

Dear Mr. Wilson:

Jones Brothers, Inc., has retained us to collect your past due account in the amount of $1,500.

Since this account has been delinquent for six months, it is imperative that you give it your immediate attention. Please let us have your check in full by May 8.

Sincerely yours,

After this letter is written, mark your file for follow-up for May 10. If the debtor does not reply by that date, you might send another letter that reads:

Dear Mr. Wilson:

We have received no reply to our letter of May 3 concerning your past due account with Jones Brothers, Inc., in the amount of $1,500. If we do not receive a response, we will be forced to take appropriate action.

Sincerely yours,

20.6. Reports to the Forwarder

The forwarder is interested in developments. Therefore, as soon as contact is made with the debtor, write to the forwarder telling what the prospects for collection are. The forwarder in turn may send copies of any reports you make to the client.

20.7. Installment Payments

Suit to collect a small sum is a last resort. It is expensive, and the judgment may be as difficult to collect as the debt. For this reason, attorneys will play along with a debtor and accept partial payments. Usually, the arrangement is that the debtor will pay a certain amount at regular intervals. In fact, an arrangement of this type is often made even after judgment is obtained against the debtor. It is your responsibility to bring up the file for attention on the dates that payments are due. If a payment is not made as promised, you should communicate with the debtor, either by telephone or mail, and keep a record of such communications on file (see Figures 20.1, 20.2, and 20.3).

20.8. Record of Collections

A payment on an account, whether in full or part, is noted in the computer file and on any file card, folder, or envelope (Figures 20.1, 20.2, and 20.3) as soon as it is received. If you use a plain folder, simply enter the date and the amount received. All such entries should be made in ink. The payments are also entered in the journal and posted to the client's ledger account in the same manner as payments in any other kind of case. The amount of bookkeeping involved by accepting partial payments is simplified when bookkeeping is computerized.

When a collection is made, put it in the trust account. It is the client's money and should not be commingled with the firm's funds. The fee may be deposited to the firm account.

20.9. Remitting

As soon as any money is collected, remit promptly to the forwarder, after deducting the fee. This is essential in handling collections. If it is necessary to collect an account in installments, report the details to the

PLAINTIFF	DEFENDANT
me _____	Name _____
dress _____	Address _____
ne No. _____ Claim No. _____	Phone No. _____ Occupation _____

CLAIM	FORWARDER OR RECEIVER
ceived _____ Amount $_____	Name _____
ture _____	Address _____
	Over _____ List _____

No.

FORM LETTERS USED
knowledged Receipt _____
st Letter to Debtor _____
cond Letter to Debtor _____
commended Suit _____ Cost $_____
knowledged Suit Papers _____ Reported Suit filed _____
t Cost _____ Affidavit _____ Invoices _____ Statement to _____
ported Judgment _____
ported Execution Issued _____
ported Remittance Direct _____ of $_____
ported Bankruptcy _____ Requested P.C.P.A. _____
knowledged P.C.P.A. _____ Divided of ___ %

COURT PROCEEDINGS
t Filed _____
urt _____
mmons Returnable _____
ue Changed to _____
ntinued to _____
gment _____ for $_____ and Cost $_____
pealed by _____ to _____ Court _____
position on Appeal _____
cution Issued _____ to _____
as Execution Issued _____ to _____
rlus Execution Issued _____ to _____
nscript Filed _____ in _____ County
cution on Transcript Issued _____ to _____

BANKRUPTCY — ASSIGNMENT — PROBATE
of Claim Power Attorney Filed _____
th _____
ount $_____ Acknowledgment Received _____
bable Dividend of _____ % Due _____

CREDITS DIRECT

Date	Nature	Amount

PAID IN FULL DIRECT

Date _____

Amount _____ $_____

Fee Due _____ $_____

Expense _____ $_____

TOTAL _____ $_____

Posted _____

Fee Paid _____

PAID _____

REMITTED _____

CLOSED _____

HANDLED BY:

FOLLOW DATES

A B C D E F G H I J K L M N O P Q R S T U V W X Y Z

Figure 20.1. Front Page of Standard Vertical Collection Folder No. 1.

Courtesy of Commercial Law League of America

DEBTOR'S NAME	ADDRESS		A
CREDITOR	ADDRESS		B
FORWARDER	ADDRESS		C
SENT TO	ADDRESS		D

AMOUNT OF CLAIM	INTEREST	DATE OF CLAIM	DATE DUE	DATE RECEIVED	LIST	
NATURE OF CLAIM (Check Proper space)	ACCOUNT	AFFIDAVIT	NOTE	ACCEPTANCE	DRAFT	JUDGMENT
COLLECTION DATE	COSTS ADVANCED	REGISTERED		PROOF FILED		

Right margin vertical text: Debtor's Name and Address

CORRESPONDENCE WITH — Forwarder / Debtor / General

CALLS MADE

SUIT MEMORANDA

COURT		
SUIT FILED	RETURNABLE	
CONTINUANCES		
TRIAL	JUDG. COSTS	$ $
EXECUTION ISSUED	..	$
SUPPLEMENTARY		
CITATION	COSTS	$
GARNISHMENT	COSTS	$
FINAL DISPOSITION		
TOTAL	JUDG. & COSTS	$

Index letters G through Z down right side; numbers 1–31.

CASH ACCOUNT — DATE / MEMO / REC'D. / DISB.

FOLLOW UP DATES

REMARKS:

Vertical text: STICK GUMMED TAPE ON BACK LEAF OF FOLDER OPPOSITE INDEX LETTER IN POSITION

Forwarder's Number / Office Number

COMMERCIAL LAW LEAGUE OF AMERICA—STANDARD VERTICAL COLLECTION FOLDER NO. 2 LETTER SIZE

Figure 20.2. Inside Page of Standard Vertical Collection Folder No. 2.

Courtesy of Commercial Law League of America

Debtor's Name and Address

| 1 | 2 | 3 | 4 | 5 | 6 | 7 | 8 | 9 | 10 | 11 | 12 | 13 | 14 | 15 | 16 | 17 | 18 | 19 | 20 | 21 | 22 | 23 | 24 | 25 | 26 | 27 | 28 | 29 | 30 | 31 |

Office Number

Forwarder's Number

Creditor's Name

Address

Amount of Claim $_____

Nature

Forwarder's Name

Address

| Name of List | Date Received |

General Information, Suit, Calls Made, Promises, Etc.

Date

Letters Written and Received

Date

CASH ACCOUNT

DATE	From	Folio	Amount Received	Amount Disbursed	Folio	DATE	To and for What

SUIT MEMORANDUM

Court _____

Summons Issued _____

Returnable _____

Adjournments _____

Trial _____

Jugmt. $_____ Costs $_____

Transcript Recorded _____

Execution Issued _____

Returnable _____

Supplementary _____

Final Disposition _____

COMMERCIAL LAW LEAGUE OF AMERICA—STANDARD VERTICAL COLLECTION FOLDER, NO. 3 LETTER SIZE

Figure 20.3. Front Page of Standard Vertical Collection Folder No. 3.

Courtesy of Commercial Law League of America

forwarder and have an understanding about when and how often an accumulation of small payments will be remitted.

20.10. Fees

Collection fees are all negotiable. You will have to calculate the lawyer's fee before remitting to the forwarder, because only the net is remitted. Assume that your firm's fees are based on the following schedule:

33 ⅓% up to $75

$25 on claims of $75 to $125

20% on the first $300 (if claim is for more than $125)

18% on $300 to $2,000

13% over $2,000

If you collect $800 on a claim, for example, you will deduct, according to the above schedule, $150 for a fee and remit $650. The $150 fee is run through the books like any other fee (Chapter 7). The fee is calculated on the basis of the collections in each case, not on the total of collections for a certain client. If a claim goes to litigation, the collections lawyer will expect a noncontingent suit fee of 5 to 10 percent of the claim, in addition to filing fees and other costs, before suit is filed.

20.11. Forwarding an Item for Collection

Sometimes a claim is received for collection against a debtor in another locality. The lawyer then consults the law lists and selects the name of an attorney in the debtor's locality, to whom the claim is sent. You will set up a file for a claim that is forwarded, just as you do for claims that were forwarded to your office, and follow them in the same manner. Your letter forwarding the claim should give the name and address of the creditor, name and address of the debtor, amount of the claim, law list from which the attorney's name was selected, and the terms upon which the claim is forwarded. Your letter might read:

Dear Ms. Rawlings:

Client: Henderson Jewelers, Inc.
West Palm Beach, Florida 33602

Debtor: David Goldstein
324 Fourth Street, N.W., Birmingham, Alabama 35215

Amount: $1,400.89

We are forwarding to you for collection the above account. This claim is sent to you on the basis of two-thirds of our fee.

Please acknowledge and keep us informed of developments. If you are unable to handle this account, we will appreciate it if you return it promptly. Please do not institute suit before informing us.

We obtained your name from the . . . . . Law List.

Sincerely yours,

The documentary evidence necessary to collect the account should be forwarded with your letter. The evidence depends on whether the suit is on open account or on an instrument. In the case of suit on open account, you should forward (1) copies of the original written order for the merchandise, if any; (2) copies of the invoice; and (3) copies of the bills of lading. If the suit is on an instrument—for example, on a dishonored trade acceptance or promissory note—the necessary documents are (1) the trade acceptance or note, (2) the bank's memorandum of nonpayment, and (3) copies of any notices of dishonor sent to the buyer and to accommodation endorsers, if any.

When your office forwards a collection to an attorney whose name is taken from the law list, check the name on the law list. If the attorney handles the account satisfactorily, you will know to whom to forward the next claim that your office has against a debtor in that locality.

UNCONTESTED SUIT

20.12. When the Lawyer Recommends Suit

Lawyers seldom write more than two collection letters. If the debtor does not make some arrangement for payment, the lawyer recommends suit or returns the claim to the forwarder. This decision is made by the lawyer. Tell the forwarder the prospects of collection by suit. Also indicate what advance court costs will be required and what papers will be needed. The defendant in a suit on a collection item rarely has a defense against the claim and thus lets the suit go by default. It will save time if you get all papers that are needed in the ordinary course of a default judgment before suit is actually filed. They vary with the jurisdiction. The lawyer will tell you what papers are needed, or you can get the information from other collection files. The legal procedure is not complicated, and you should be able to draw the necessary court papers without detailed instructions from the lawyer.

Many collection suits are small enough to be filed as small claims. The procedure in small claims court is simpler and less costly than the procedure used in suing for larger amounts. The small claims limit may be as high as $2,500, depending on state law. Courts have special forms to be used in filing small claims actions. They can usually be obtained from the local clerk of court.

20.13. Complaint and Summons

A short-form complaint is usually permissible. A brief statement of the indebtedness is alleged instead of a statement of the specific facts required by code pleading (Chapter 14). The statement may be given on the back of the printed form of summons. The causes of action, or counts, generally alleged in suits on collection items are for:

1. Goods sold and delivered
2. Account stated
3. Open book account
4. Account for services

20.14. Preparation and Service of a Summons and Short-Form Complaint

Use a printed form of summons and type the complaint in the space provided on the back for that purpose. The service, affidavit of service, and filing of a short-form complaint in a collection suit is the same as in any other action (see Chapter 14). If it is the practice in your office to make a litigation file of all collection suits in which a summons is served, enter the return date of the summons in your diary and open a suit register sheet or computerized record for the case. If your practice is not to transfer uncontested cases, mark the file for follow-up on the return date of the summons.

Remember that the period of time to answer begins the date the summons is served, not the date it is prepared.

Keep in close touch with your process server and immediately recall the summons from him or her if the account is paid before service of the summons. If by chance the summons is served on the defendant after the account is paid, the summons and affidavit of service should not be filed in court. The lawyer will depend on you to keep track of these matters, and your records must be accurate and up to date to know the status of an account or an action at any time.

20.15. Information Needed to Draw a Complaint and Summons

The following information is necessary to draw a complaint and summons in a suit on a collection item:

1. *The court in which to bring the action.* This will depend on the amount of the claim and the jurisdiction of the local courts. Usually, suit on a collection item may be brought in a municipal court or a justice of the peace court.

2. *The court district.* This is needed if the city is divided into districts with a municipal court in each.

3. *The amount of the debt.* A collection item is for a *liquidated amount*—the amount is certain as distinguished from an indefinite amount to be determined by the court or jury, as in the case of an action for damages in an accident case. The file shows the amount of the debt.

4. *The rate of interest and the date from which it is to be charged.* The rate is the legal rate of interest in the state in which the debt was contracted, unless a lower rate had been contracted for. Interest runs from the date the debt became due.

5. *The wording of the complaint.* The wording varies with the jurisdiction and with the cause of action, but the counts are short and you will become familiar with the wording in your state very quickly. Stock phrases should be in your computer, and you can check the computer for the wording in similar cases. You will notice that in an action on an account for merchandise, which is the most common action, the legal phraseology is "goods, wares, and merchandise," whether the merchandise is hardware, grocer-

ies, drugs, or wearing apparel. When you prepare a count for a new cause of action, add it to your computer library.

20.16. Judgment by Default

If the defendant decides to contest the suit, a copy of the answer will be delivered to your office. In municipal court, however, the defendant may go to the court and make his or her answer orally, at any time before court closes on the return day of the summons. Therefore, you will not know until the day after the return day whether the defendant has answered or has defaulted. If appropriate in your jurisdiction, on the day after the return day ask a law clerk to go to the court and find out if the defendant appeared. Or you can get the information yourself by going to the court and looking at the papers in the court file under the index number of the case. If the defendant has not answered, prepare a judgment by default.

20.17. How to Prepare a Judgment by Default

In some jurisdictions there are two types of judgments by default. One can be signed by the court clerk, and one must be signed by the court. A printed form is generally available, and you can get the necessary information from your file.

1. Calculate the interest at the legal rate, from the date indicated in the summons.
2. Itemize the cost disbursed by your office and include the total in the amount of the judgment.
3. Make an original and two copies.
4. Get the clerk of the court to sign the original and file it in court.
5. Conform the two copies. (See section 10.18 in Chapter 18.)
6. Fill in the notice of entry of judgment in the space provided on the back of the judgment.
7. Mail one copy to the defendant. The other copy is for your office file.

After the judgment by default is entered, the plaintiff is known as a *judgment creditor* and the defendant as a *judgment debtor*. If the judgment debtor does not pay the judgment, the attorney for the judgment creditor may ask the clerk of the court to issue a writ of execution. Should the execution be returned unsatisfied, the attorney will commence supplementary proceedings, if it appears that the judgment debtor has any assets out of which the judgment may be collected. If the debtor has no such assets, he is considered *judgment proof*.

Some states permit a court, on petition of the creditor, to inquire into the financial condition of the debtor. If the court finds the debtor is able to make payments at regular intervals, usually weekly, the court may order him or her to do so. Failure to obey such an order may result in a finding of contempt of court and the imposition of appropriate penalties.

Part 5

LEGAL FACTS
AND SECRETARIAL AIDS

Forms of Address: Honorary and Official
Positions

Latin Words and Phrases

Glossary of Legal Terms

Courts of Record and Judicial Circuits

Forms of Address: Honorary and Official Positions

The following list gives the correct forms of written address, salutation, and complimentary close for letters to court officials:[1]

Chief Justice, U.S. Supreme Court

The Chief Justice of the United States
The Supreme Court of the United States
[Address]
Sir/Madam:
Yours very truly,
Dear Mr./Madam Chief Justice:
Sincerely yours,

Associate Justice, U.S. Supreme Court

Madam Justice Short
The Supreme Court of the United States
[Address]
Madam:
Yours very truly,
Dear Madam Justice/Dear Justice Short:
Sincerely yours,

---

[1] From the *Prentice Hall Style Manual*, by Mary A. De Vries © 1992. Reprinted by permission of the publisher, Prentice Hall, a division of Simon & Schuster, Englewood Cliffs, NJ.

Retired Justice, U.S. Supreme Court

The Honorable Adam Long
[Local Address]
Sir:
Yours very truly,
Dear Justice Long:
Sincerely yours,

Chief Justice, Chief Judge, State Supreme Court

The Honorable Adam Long
Chief Justice of the Supreme Court of Arizona
[Address]
Sir:
Yours very truly,
Dear Mr. Chief Justice:
Sincerely yours,

Associate Justice, Highest Court of a State

The Honorable Eve Short
Associate Justice of the Supreme Court of Ohio
[Address]
Madam:
Yours very truly,
Dear Justice/Dear Justice Short:
Sincerely yours,

Presiding Justice

The Honorable Adam Long
Presiding Justice, Appellate Division
Supreme Court of California
[Address]
Sir:
Yours very truly,
Dear Justice/Dear Justice Long:
Sincerely yours,

Judge of a Court

This does not apply to the U.S. Supreme Court.

The Honorable Eve Short
Judge of the United States District Court
    for the Northern District of South Carolina
[Address]
Madam:
Yours very truly,
Dear Judge Short:
Sincerely yours,

Clerk of a Court

Adam Long, Esq.
Clerk of the Superior Court of Iowa
[Address]
Dear Sir:
Yours very truly,
Dear Mr. Long:
Sincerely yours,

Latin Words and Phrases

Latin words and phrases that you are most likely to use or hear in the legal profession are listed below. Foreign words and phrases are frequently italicized in printed material (underlined if your computer does not have this capability). Those that have become anglicized, however, are written in roman type the same as other text. Some words are not italicized unless they are used in an expression; "animus," for example, is not italicized when written alone but is italicized in the phrase *animus furandi*.

a fortiori. With stronger reason; much more.
a mensa et thoro. From bed and board.
a priori. From what goes before; from the cause to the effect.
a vinculo matrimonii. From the bonds of marriage.
ab initio. From the beginning.
actiones in personam. Personal actions.
ad faciendum. To do.
ad hoc. For this (for this special purpose).
ad infinitum. Indefinitely; forever.
ad litem. For the suit; for the litigation (A guardian *ad litem* is a person appointed to prosecute or defend a suit for a person incapacitated by infancy or incompetency.)
ad quod damnum. To what damage; what injury. (A phrase used to describe the plaintiff's money loss or the damages he claims.)
ad respondendum. To answer.
ad satisfaciendum. To satisfy.
ad valorem. According to value.
aggregatio menium. Meeting of minds.
alias dictus. Otherwise called.
alibi. In another place; elsewhere.
alii. Others.

aliunde. From another place; from without (as evidence outside the document).

alius. Another

alter ego. The other self.

alumnus. A foster child.

amicus curiae. Friend of the court.

animo. With intention, disposition, design, will.

animus. Mind; intention.

animus furandi. The intention to steal.

animus revertendi. An intention of returning.

animus revocandi. An intention to revoke.

animus testandi. An intention to make a testament or will.

anno Domini (A.D.). In the year of the Lord.

ante. Before

ante litem motam. Before suit brought.

arguendo. In the course of the arguement.

assumpsit. He undertook; he promised.

bona fide. In good faith.

bona vacantia. Vacant goods. (Personal property that no one claims, which escheats to the state.)

capias. Take; arrest. (A form of writ directing an arrest.)

capias ad satisfaciendum (ca. sa.). Arrest to satisfy. (A form of writ.)

causa mortis. By reason of death.

caveat. Let him beware; a warning.

caveat emptor. Let the buyer beware.

cepit et asportavit. He took and carried away.

certiorari. To be informed of; to be made certain in regard to. (See glossary of legal terms.)

cestui (pl. *cesuis*). beneficiaries. (Pronounced "setty.")

cestui que trust. He who benefits by the trust.

cestui que use. He who benefits by the use.

cestui que vie. He whose life measures the duration of the estate.

civiliter mortuus. Civilly dead.

Consensus, non concubitus, facit nuptias vel matrimonium. Consent, not cohabitation, constitutes nuptials or marriage.

consortium (*pl.* consortia). A union of lots or chances (a lawful marriage).

contra. Against.

contra bonos mores. Against good morals.

contra pacem. Against the peace.

coram non judice. In presence of a person, not a judge. (A suit brought and determined in a court having no jurisdiction over the matter is said to be *coram non judice,* and the judgment is void.)

corpus. Body

corpus delicti. The body of the offense; the essence of the crime.

corpus juris. A body of law.

corpus juris civilis. The body of the civil law.

Cujus est solum, ejus est usque ad coelum. Whose the soil is, his it is up to the sky.

cum testamento annexo (c.t.a.). With the will annexed. (Describes an administrator who operates under a will rather than in intestacy.)

damnum absque injuria. Damage without injury. (Damage without legal wrong.)

datum (*pl.* data). A thing given; a date.

de bonis non administratis. Of the goods not administered. Frequently abbreviated to *de bonis non.*

de bono et malo. For good and ill.

de facto. In fact; in deed; actually.

de jure. Of right; lawful.

De minimis non curat lex. The law does not concern itself with trifles.

de novo. Anew; afresh.

de son tort. Of his own wrong.

dies non. Not a day (on which the business of the courts can be carried on).

donatio mortis causa. A gift by reason of death. (A gift made by a person in sickness, under apprehension of death.)

duces tecum. You bring with you. (A term applied to a writ commanding the person upon whom it is served to bring certain evidence with him to court. Thus we speak of a *subpoena duces tecum.*)

dum bene se gesserit. While he shall conduct himself well; during good behavior.

durante minore aetate. During minority.

durante viduitate. During widowhood.

e converso. Conversely; on the other hand.

eo instanti. Upon the instant.

erratum (*pl.* errata). Error.

et alii (et al.). And another.

et cetera (etc.). And other things.

ex cathedra. From the chair.

ex contractu. (Arising) from the contract.

ex delicto. (Arising) from a tort.

ex gratia. As a matter of favor.

ex necessitate legis. From legal necessity.

ex officio. From office; by virtue of his office.

ex parte. On one side only; by or for one party.

ex post facto. After the act.

ex rel (short for *ex relatione*). On information of; on behalf of a party or parties.

et uxor (et ux.). And wife.

et vir. And husband.

felonice. Feloniously.

feme covert. A married woman.

feme sole. A single woman (including one who has been married but whose marriage has been dissolved by death or divorce).

ferae naturae. Of a wild nature.

fiat. Let it be done. (A short order or warrant of a judge, commanding that something shall be done.)

fieri. To be made up; to become.

fieri facias. Cause to be made. (A writ directed to the sheriff to reduce the judgment debtor's property to money in the amount of the judgment.)

filius nullius. The son of nobody; a bastard.

filius populi. A son of the people.

flagrante delicto. In the very act of committing the crime.

habeas corpus. You have the body. (See glossary of legal terms.)

habendum clause. Clause in deed that defines extent of ownership by grantee.

habere facias possessionem. That you cause to have possession. (A writ of ejectment.)

habere facias seisinam. That you cause to have seisin. (A writ to give possession.)

honorarium (*pl.* honoraria). An honorary fee or gift; compensation from gratitude.

idem sonans. Having the same sound (as names sounding alike but spelled differently).

Ignorantia legis neminen excusat. Ignorance of the law excuses no one.

illicitum collegium. An unlawful association.

Impotentia excusat legem. Impossibility is an excuse in law.

in bonis. In goods; among possessions.

in esse. In being; existence.

in extremis. In extremity (in the last illness).

in fraudem legis. In circumvention of law.

in futuro. In the future.

in loco parentis. In the place of a parent.

in pari delicto. In equal fault.

in personam. A remedy where the proceedings are against the person, as contradistinguished from those against a specific thing.

in praesenti. At present; at once; now.

in re. In the matter.

in rem. A remedy where the proceedings are against the thing, as distinguished from those against the person.

in rerum natura. In nature; in life; in existence.

in specie. In the same, or like, form. (To decree performance *in specie* is to decree specific performance.)

in statu quo. In the condition in which it was. (See *status quo.*)

in terrorem. In terror.

in toto. In the whole; completely.

in transitu. In transit; in course of transfer.

indebitatus assumpsit. Being indebted, be promised, or undertook. (An action in which plaintiff alleges defendant is indebted to him.)

indicia. Marks; signs.

infra. Below.

innuendo. Meaning.

inter. Among; between.

inter vivos. Between the living.

interim. In the meantime.

intra. Within; inside.

ipse dixit. He himself said (it). (An assertion made but not proved.)

ipso facto. By the fact itself.

ita est. So it is.

jura personarum. Rights of persons.

jura rerum. Rights of things.

jurat. Portion of affidavit in which officer administering the oath certifies that it was sworn to before him

jure divino. By divine right.

jure uxoris. In his wife's right.

jus (pl. *jura*). Law; laws collectively.

jus accrescendi. The right of survivorship.

jus ad rem. A right to a thing.

jus civile. Civil law.

jus commune. The common law; the common right.

jus gentium. The law of nations; international law.

jus habendi. The right to have a thing.

jus proprietatis. Right of property.

levari facias. Cause to be levied; a writ of execution.

lex loci. Law of the place (where the cause of action arose).

lex loci rei sitae. The law of the place where a thing is situated.

lex mercatoria. The law merchant.

lis pendens. Litigation pending; a pending suit.

locus delicti. The place of the crime or tort.

locus in quo. The place in which.

locus sigilii (L.S.). The place for the seal.

mala fides. Bad faith.

mala in se. Wrongs in themselves (acts morally wrong).

mala praxis. Malpractice.

mala prohibita. Prohibited wrongs or offenses.

malo animo. With evil intent.

malum in se. Evil in itself.

mandamus. We command. (See glossary of legal terms.)

manu forti. With a strong hand (forcible entry).

mens rea. Guilty mind.

nihil dicit. He says nothing. (Judgment against defendant who does not put in a defense to the complaint.)

nil debet. He owes nothing.

nisi prius. Unless before. (The phrase is used to denote the forum where the trial was held as distinguished from the appellate court.)

nolle prosequi. To be unwilling to follow up, or to prosecute. (A formal entry on the record by the plaintiff or the prosecutor that he will not further prosecute the case.)

nolo contendere. I will not contest it.

non compos mentis. Not of sound mind.

non est factum. It is not his deed.

non obstante. Notwithstanding.

non prosequitur (*non pros.*). He does not follow up, or pursue, or prosecute. (If the plaintiff fails to take some step that he should, the defendant may enter a judgment of *non pros.* against him.)

nudum pactum. A nude pact. (A contract without consideration.)

nul tiel record. No such record.

nul tort. No wrong done.

nulla bona. No goods. (Wording of return to a write of *fieri facias.*)

nunc pro tunc. Now for then.

obiter dictum. Remark by the way. (See *dictum* in glossary of legal terms.)

onus probandi. The burden of proof.

opus (pl. opera). Work; labor.

ore tenus. By word of mouth; orally.

pari delicto. In equal guilt.

particeps criminis. An accomplice in the crime.

pater familias. The father (head) of a family.

peculium. Private property.

pendente lite. Pending the suit; during the litigation.

per annum. By the year.

per autre vie. For another's lifetime. (See also *pur autre vie.*)

per capita. By the head; as individuals. (In a distribution of an estate, if the descendants take per capita, they take share and share alike regardless of family lines of descent.)

per centum (percent). By the hundred.

per contra. In opposition.

per curiam. By the court.

per diem. By the day.

per se. By itself; taken alone.

per stirpes. By stems or root; by representation. (In a distribution of an estate, if distribution is *per stirpes,* descendants take by virtue of their representation of an ancestor, not as individuals.)

postmortem. After death.

postobit. To take effect after death.

praecipe or *precipe.* Command. (A written order to the clerk of the court to issue a writ.)

prima facie. At first sight; on the face of it.

pro. For.

pro confesso. As confessed.

pro forma. As a matter of form.

pro hac vice. For this occasion.

pro rata. According to the rate or proportion.

pro tanto. For so much; to that extent.

pro tempore (pro tem.). For the time being; temporarily.

prochein ami. Next friend.

publici juris. Of public right.

pur autre vie. For, or during, the life of another. (See also *per autre vie.*)

quaere. Query; question; doubt. (This word indicates that a particular rule, decision, or statement that follows it is open to question.)

quantum meruit. As much as he deserved.

quantum valebant. As much as they were (reasonably) worth (in absence of agreement as to value).

quare. Wherefore.

quare clausum fregit. Wherefore he broke the close. (A form of trespass on another's land.)

quasi. As if; as it were. (Indicates that one subject resembles another, but that there are also intrinsic differences between them. Thus we speak of quasi contracts, quasi torts, and so on.)

quid pro quo. What for what; something for something. (A term denoting the consideration for a contract.)

quo warranto. By what right or authority. (See glossary of legal terms.)

quoad hoc. As to this.

quod computet. That he account.

reductio ad absurdum. Reduced to the absurd.

res. A thing; an object; the subject matter.

res gestae. Things done; transactions.

res ipsa loquitur. The thing speaks for itself.

res judicata. A matter adjudicated.

scienter. Knowingly.

scilicet (SS. or ss.). To wit. (The abbreviation *sc.* is not used in legal papers.)

scintilla. A spark; the least particle.

scire facias. Cause to know; give notice. (A writ used to revive a judgment that has expired.)

se defendendo. In self-defense; in defending oneself.

semper. Always.

semper paratus. Always ready. (A plea by which the defendant alleges that he has always been ready to perform what is demanded of him.)

seriatim. Severally; separately.

sigillum. A seal.

simplex obligato. A simple obligation.

sine die. Without day. (Without a specified day being assigned for a future meeting or hearing.)

situs. Situation; location.

stare decisis. To abide by decided cases.

status quo. State in which (the existing state of things at any given date). (See *in statu quo.*)

sub judice. Under consideration.

sub modo. Under a qualification; in a qualified way.

sub nom. Under the name.

sui juris. Of his own right (having legal capacity to act for himself).

supersedeas. That you supersede. (A writ commanding a stay of the proceedings.)

supra. Above.

terminus a quo. The starting point.

ultra vires. Without power; beyond the powers of. (See glossary of legal terms.)

venire facias. That you cause to come (a kind of summons).

Verba fortius accipiuntur contra proferentem. Words are to be taken most strongly against the one using them.

versus (vs., v.). Against.

vi et armis. By force and arms.

via. A road; a right of way; by way of.

vice versa. On the contrary; on opposite sides.

videlicet (*viz.;* contraction of *videre* and *licet*). It is easy to see (that is, namely).

virtute officii. By virtue of his office.

viva voce. by the living voice; by word of mouth.

voir dire. To speak the truth. (Denotes a preliminary examination to determine the competency of a witness.)

Glossary of Legal Terms

The following pages give clear and concise definitions and explanations of words and terms that you will hear in your daily work in a law office. Many of the words are not, strictly speaking, legal terms but are used in the preceding text with special legal significance. The words in the texts of the definitions that are in small caps are defined in their respective alphabetical positions in this glossary.

Abrogation. The annulment or repeal of a law or obligation. The COMMON LAW, for example, is abrogated by statute.

Acceleration clause. A clause in contracts evidencing a debt such as mortgages and installment contracts, that results in the entire debt becoming immediately due and payable when a condition of the contract is breached. Without an acceleration clause, the mortgagee or seller would have to sue for the amount of each payment as it became due or would have to wait until the entire debt matured.

Account stated. An account balance, as determined by the creditor, that has been accepted as correct by the debtor. In law, the *account stated* operates as an admission of liability by the debtor. He is barred from disputing the accuracy of the computation, the bar being raised either by the debtor's explicit approval of the account or by his failure within a reasonable time to indicate any exception to it.

Acknowledgment. The act by which a person who has signed an instrument goes before an authorized officer, such as a notary public, and declares that he executed the instrument as his free act and deed. *See also* Index.

Adjective law. *See* SUBSTANTIVE LAW.

Administrative law. The rules and regulations framed by an administrative body created by a state legislature or by Congress to carry out a specific statute. For example, the federal income tax law is administered by the Internal Revenue Service. The bureau issues regulations and rules that have the weight of law as long

533

as they keep within the scope of the income tax statute. Frequently, such regulations interpret in a specific way the legislature's general intent when it enacted the statute. Thus administrative bodies that are primarily executive may also have powers that resemble legislative or judicial authority. Local boards are also administrative, and work before them is administrative law.

Administrator. A person appointed by the court to settle the estate of a deceased person who has left no valid will or whose named executor fails to serve. *See also* Index.

Affidavit. A written statement signed and sworn to before some person authorized to take an oath; frequently required as proof when no other evidence of a fact is available. *See also* Index.

Affirmance. *See* RATIFICATION.

Agency. The relationship that exists when one person authorizes another to act for him. The one granting the authority is the *principal;* the one authorized to act is the *agent.* For an agent to act, a third party, with whom he contracts, is necessary. An agency relationship is created when a person gives a POWER OF ATTORNEY or a PROXY and in other situations. An agency may be *general*—the agent has broad powers to represent the principal; or the agency may be *special*—the agent represents the principal for a specific purpose or for a series or routine tasks. The principal is liable for the acts of the agent within the scope of the agency. An agency is also an establishment engaged in doing business for another, such as a collection agency, or an administrative division of government, such as the Environmental Protection Agency.

Alien corporation. A business organization incorporated outside the United States and its territories. The state statutes make no distinction between an alien and a FOREIGN CORPORATION, except in a few states that do not recognize alien corporations.

Allegation. A statement made by a party who claims it can be proved as fact. *See also* Index.

Allonge. (French) A piece of paper attached to a bill of exchange or a promissory note on which to write endorsements when there is no room on the instrument itself.

Ancillary. Auxiliary; subordinate. The term *ancillary letters* is used to apply to letters testamentary or letters of administration (*see* Index) that are taken out in a state other than that of the decedent's domicile but in which he had assets or debts. Those letters are subordinate or supplementary to the letters issued in the decedent's domicile. The term *ancillary* also applies to court proceedings that are auxiliary to the main action—for example, a bill of discovery is ancillary to the principal action.

Antitrust laws. Laws designed to prevent restraint of trade, monopoly, and unfair practices in interstate commerce. The antitrust statutes are the Sherman Act (Antitrust Act of 1890); the Clayton Act; the Federal Trade Commission Act; the Robinson-Patman Act; the Miller-Tydings Act; the Wheeler-Lea Act.

Assault and battery. An assault is a threat made with the apparent intention of doing bodily harm to another. An essential element of assault is real or apparent ability on the part of the person making the threat to do bodily harm to another. Mere words do not constitute an assault. A *battery* is the wrongful touching of another's person or clothing as a result of assault. A battery always includes an assault, but an assault may be made without a battery. A person guilty of assault and battery is liable for damage to the injured party. Assault and battery may also be a crime punishable by the state.

Assignment. The transfer of property or some right or interest in property to another. Assignments are made (a) by the act of the parties, as in the case of a tenant assigning his lease to another; or (b) by operation of law, as in the case of death or bankruptcy. The party transferring his right is the *assignor;* the party to whom the rights are transferred is the *assignee.* To be valid, an assignment must be executed by a party having legal capacity, and it must be supported by consideration.

Attachment. The process of seizing or taking into custody. An attachment is a legal proceeding that a creditor uses to have the property of a debtor seized under court order, pending a determination of the creditor's claim. The attachment is recorded in the public records as notice that a claim has been made that, if found valid, will affect the value of the property attached. An attachment creates or perfects a LIEN on property. Attachment of property or money held by a third party, such as a bank, is called *trustee process.*

Attestation. The act of signing a written instrument as witness to the signature of a party, at his request; for example, witnessing signatures to a contract or a will. *See also* Index.

Attorney-in-fact. One who is appointed by another, with the authority to act for him in matters specified in the terms of the appointment. (*See* AGENCY; *see also* Index.)

Bailment. A delivery of personal property for some particular purpose, upon a contract, express or implied, that the property will be returned to the person delivering it after the accomplishment of the purpose for which it was delivered. An essential of a bailment is that return of the property or an accounting in accordance with the terms of agreement is contemplated. The person delivering the property is a *bailor;* the person receiving it is a *bailee.* If under the terms of the contract the bailee is obligated to pay a sum of money instead of returning the goods, the obligation is a debt and not a bailment. Thus a conditional sale is distinguished from a bailment in that the purchaser must pay the purchase price at which time he acquires title to the property. The parties to a consignment of goods expect that the goods will be sold for the account of the consignor or returned to him; a consignment is therefore considered a bailment. A bailee is liable for breach of his contract to keep the property in a particular manner in a particular place for a particular purpose. The following transactions are bailments: lease of a car for hire; deposit of goods for storage or safekeeping; pledge of stocks as collateral. Title to the property remains in the bailor.

Bankruptcy. *Bankruptcy* is a state of insolvency in which the property of a debtor is taken over by a receiver or trustee in bankruptcy for the benefit of the creditors. This action is taken under the jurisdiction of the courts as prescribed by the National Bankruptcy Act.

Voluntary bankruptcy. Voluntary bankruptcy is brought about by the filing of a petition in bankruptcy by the debtor. The form of the petition is prescribed by the act. By filing a voluntary petition, the debtor seeks, first, to have his assets equally distributed among all his creditors but on the basis of established priorities and, second, to free himself of his debts. He is thus able to begin his business life anew, free of those debts discharged in bankruptcy.

Voluntary bankruptcy is open to all individuals, firms, partnerships, and corporations, except banks of all kinds, credit unions, and insurance, railroad, and municipal corporations. No special amount of indebtedness is required; a person owning one dollar or several million dollars may file a petition in voluntary bankruptcy.

Involuntary bankruptcy. Involuntary bankruptcy is brought about by the filing of a petition by the creditors against an insolvent debtor. Farmers, charitable corporations, banks of all kinds, railroads, and domestic insurance companies may not be subjected to involuntary bankruptcy. If there are fewer than 12 creditors, 1 creditor may file the petition; if there are more than 12, 3 creditors must join in the filing. Before creditors can throw a debtor into bankruptcy, these conditions must exist: (1) There must be general inability to pay its debts as they become due or the appointment of a custodian to take charge of the debtor's property. (2) The creditor or creditors filing the petition must have provable unsecured claims aggregating $5,000.

Bill of sale. A formal document issued by a seller to a buyer as evidence of transfer to the latter of title to the goods described in the instrument. A bill of sale may be used in the case of any sale of PERSONAL PROPERTY.

Blue-sky laws. Laws that have been enacted by most of the states to protect the public from fraud in the offering of securities. Such laws are an exercise of the POLICE POWER of the states; they supplement interstate regulation of securities offerings, securities exchanges, and speculative practices, through the Securities and Exchange Commission. Protection is achieved through (1) specific legislation—blue-sky laws; and (2) through enforcement of the statute of frauds.

Breach of contract. The failure or refusal by one of the parties to a contract to perform some act the contract calls for without legal excuse. A contract may also be breached by preventing or obstructing performance by the other party; or by "anticipatory" breach, as the unqualified announcement by a seller, before delivery date, that he will not deliver the goods.

Breach of a contract by one party may discharge the other from performance. Or the injured party may sue for damages representing the loss directly incurred from the breach. Damages cannot be obtained for speculative or possible losses that cannot be shown to have resulted directly from the breach.

Breach of warranty. When a WARRANTY made by a vendor proves to be false, the warranty is said to be breached. For the breach, the buyer has a choice of four remedies: (1) accept or keep the goods and set up the breach to reduce the purchase price; (2) keep the goods and recover damages for the breach of warranty; (3) refuse to accept the goods if title has not passed and bring an action for damages for breach of warranty; (4) rescind the contract, or if the goods have been delivered, return them and recover any part of the purchase price that had been paid. The buyer can claim only one of these remedies.

Business trust. *See* MASSACHUSETTS TRUST.

Bylaws (corporate). Rules adopted by a corporation to regulate its conduct as a corporate entity and to define and determine the rights and duties of its stockholders and the rights, powers, and duties of the directors and officers. They are permanent, except insofar as they may be amended. They are never public laws or regulations—hence the term *bylaws. See also* Index.

Caveat emptor. (Latin for "let the buyer beware.") This COMMON LAW doctrine or maxim imposes on the buyer the duty of examining what he buys. It is applied where the seller makes no express warranty and is not guilty of fraud. Exceptions to the *caveat emptor* doctrine are made under the following circumstances: (1) A fiduciary relationship exists between the parties, as between principal and agent, attorney and client, trustee and beneficiary. (2) The defects are not obvious and the buyer has not had an opportunity for thorough inspection. (3) The sale was made by sample or by description. (4) The sale was for a specific purpose.

Cease and desist order. An order by an administrative agency or court prohibiting a person or business from continuing to pursue a particular course of action or activity.

Certificate of stock. *See* CORPORATION; *see also* Index.

Certiorari. A writ issued by a superior court to an inferior court directing it to send to the former court the record of a particular case. A *writ of certiorari* is an extraordinary remedy resorted to in cases obviously entitled to redress where no direct appellate proceedings are provided by law. A writ of certiorari cannot be used as a substitute for an appeal or a writ of error. A litigant is entitled to a writ of error as a matter of right, but a writ of certiorari lies within the court's discretion.

The dissatisfied party in the lower court petitions the appellate court for a writ of certiorari. If, on the face of the record, the appellate court determines that the lower court has nor proceeded in accordance with the law, it will consent to issue the writ and hear the case. If the record itself does not indicate that the petitioner has been wronged by the proceeding, the court will deny the petition for writ of certiorari. The denial is, in effect, an affirmance of the lower court's decision on the point of law before the appellate court, but the issuance of the writ does not mean that the appellate court will decide in favor of the petitioner. The court may then order the certiorari dismissed, or return it to the lower court with instructions, or render a final judgment, which must finally govern the case.

Chattel. An article of tangible PERSONAL PROPERTY, as distinguished from real property (land and improvements) and intangibles (stocks, bonds, and the like).

Chose in action. PERSONAL PROPERTY that is not susceptible to physical possession and that requires some form of action to acquire or recover possession. Some of the most important choses in action are contracts, promissory notes, checks, trade acceptances, stocks, bonds, bank accounts, and the right of legal action to recover money or property.

Civil law. The law of the Romans under Emperor Justinian was condensed and digested into a code known as Corpus Juris Civilis. The laws of Justinian were lost in the Western Empire during the early Dark Ages, but a complete copy was found about 1137. The laws were then revised and became the basis of jurisprudence for most of continental Europe. The present law on the Continent is therefore referred to as the Roman or civil law. *See* COMMON LAW for development of law in England. Louisiana is the only state in the United States that bases its law on the civil law.

Civil wrongs. Those that concern the relationship between individuals as such, as distinguished from wrongs against the public (*see* CRIMINAL LAW). Civil wrongs infringe on private rights and duties; remedy against them is sought by private action. TORT and BREACH OF CONTRACT are among the more common civil wrongs.

Close corporation. A corporation whose capital stock is held by a limited group, in contrast to one whose stock is generally sold to the public. Frequently, the owners are also the managers. Usually, a close corporation is small, although some are large. Ford Motor Company, for instance, was a close corporation until 1956.

Collateral. Property pledged as security for payment of a debt. Mortgaged real estate is collateral for money loaned to the owner.

Common law. A system of law, or body of legal rules, derived from decisions of judges based on accepted customs and traditions. It was developed in England. It is known as the *common law* because it is believed that these rules were generally recognized and were in full force throughout England. Common law is now the basis of the laws in every state of the United States, except Louisiana, which bases its laws on the early laws of France. Statutes have been enacted to supplement and supersede the common law in many fields; the common law, however, still governs where there is no statute dealing with a specific subject. Although the common law is written, it is called the *unwritten law* in contradistinction to STATUTORY LAW enacted by the legislatures.

Common law trust. *See* MASSACHUSETTS TRUST.

Community property. In some states a system exists whereby all earnings of either husband or wife constitute a common fund of the husband and wife. The property is known as *community property.* The central idea of the system is the same in all states where community property exists, but statutes and judicial decisions have directed the development of the system along different lines in the various states. For example, in some states only property that is acquired by the exertion or labor of either party is *common,* whereas in other states income from separate property is also considered community property. Generally, either husband or wife may have "separate" property, such as that belonging to either of them at the time of marriage, real estate acquired in a state that does not recognize community property, or property given to or inherited by either at any time. Property acquired in exchange for separate property is separate property; that acquired in exchange for community property is community property. In some states the husband may dispose of or encumber the community property, but the wife may not; nor may community property be attached for the wife's debts, except for those contracted for necessities for herself and her children.

Competent parties. *See* CONTRACT.

Conditional sale. An installment sale. The buyer usually gives the seller a promissory note secured by a conditional sale contract or a chattel mortgage. A *conditional sale contract* is a contract for the sale of goods under which the goods are delivered to the buyer but the title remains in the seller until the goods are paid for in full or until the conditions of the contract are fulfilled. When a chattel mortgage is used, the seller transfers the goods to the buyer who, in turn, executes a chattel mortgage in favor of the seller. This instrument gives the seller a lien on the goods.

The seller's choice of a security depends on the laws in his state. He studies the laws and selects the type of instrument that provides the most protection with the least inconvenience. The instrument usually includes a provision that if an installment is not paid when due, the entire debt becomes payable at once. This clause, called the ACCELERATION CLAUSE, is essential in any installment contract. Otherwise the seller would have to sue for the amount of each installment as it became due or would have to wait until the entire debt matured.

Constructive. The term *constructive* generally applies to that which amounts in the eyes of the law to an act, although the act itself is not necessarily performed. The law presumes an act to have been performed and applies the term to many situations to prevent a miscarriage of justice.

Some of the circumstances under which the law will presume an act are indicated by the following: constructive abandonment, constructive delivery, constructive desertion, constructive eviction, constructive fraud, constructive gift, constructive notice, constructive possession, constructive process, constructive receipt of income, constructive service, and constructive trusts. To illustrate, a few of these terms are explained.

Constructive delivery. Arises when actual, or manual, delivery is impossible or undesirable. Constructive delivery includes those acts that are equivalent to actual delivery, although they do not confer real possession. Acts that bar a lien or a right to stoppage in transit, such as marking and setting apart goods as belonging to the buyer, constitute constructive delivery.

Constructive notice. Notice that arises from a strictly legal presumption that cannot be controverted. The presumption is one of law and not of fact, as distinguished from implied notice that arises from an inference of facts. The presumption of constructive notice is conclusive against the actual facts. Thus a mortgage recorded with the proper public authorities is constructive notice of the mortgagee's interest in the property.

Constructive receipt. Constructive receipt of income usually constitutes taxable income under the various tax laws. For example, at any time during the year commissions may be credited on a firm's books to a salesperson who may draw upon the firm to the amount of the credit. The commission is said to be constructively received. Whatever amount is credited to the salesperson would have to be reported by him as income in the year the amount was credited on the books, even if the money was not drawn until the following year.

Contract. An agreement, enforceable at law, by which two parties mutually promise to give some particular thing or to do or abstain from doing a particular act. A contract may be formal or informal; it may be oral or written, sealed or unsealed, except that state statutes, usually designated as the STATUTE OF FRAUDS, require certain agreements to be in writing. A contract may be *executed*—one that has been fully carried out by both parties; or *executory*—one that is yet to be performed. It may be executed on the part of one party and executory on the part of the other. For example, the purchase of merchandise on credit, followed by delivery, is executed on the part of the seller and executory on the part of the buyer. A contract may be *express*—all the terms definitely expressed in the oral or written agreement—or *implied*—the terms not expressed but implied by the law from the actions of the parties. For example, when a person gets on a bus, his action implies a contract with the transit company.

To be enforceable at law, a contract must have the following elements:

Offer and acceptance. Before a contract can be formed, there must be an offer by one party, called the *offeror,* to do or to refrain from doing a certain thing and an acceptance of the proposal by another party, called the *offeree.*

An offer is considered open until it is revoked, rejected, or accepted or until after the lapse of a reasonable time. The only case in which an offeror cannot withdraw an offer before acceptance is the case in which he has entered into an option contract, which is an agreement supported by the payment of a sum of money, or for some other consideration, to hold an offer open for a definite period. As a general rule, an offer, once accepted, cannot be withdrawn or revoked.

An acceptance is an indication by the offeree of his willingness to be bound by the terms of the offer. The acceptance may take the form of an act, of the signing and delivery of a written instrument, or of a promise communicated to the offeror. Silence on the part of the offeree is not an acceptance unless the previous dealings between the parties create a duty upon the part of the offeree to accept or reject the offer. The acceptance must be unequivocal and must show an intention to accept all the terms of the offer. In the language frequently used by the courts, there must be a "meeting of the minds" of the offeror and the offeree.

Competent parties. All persons are presumed to have unlimited power to contract—except infants, insane persons or persons with impaired mental faculties, intoxicated persons, married women (see below), and corporations.

Under common law, a person is in his infancy until he reaches the age of 21, although some states provide that women become of age at 18, and other states provide that marriage removes the infancy status. Contracts by infants are not void, but generally, they may be disaffirmed by the infant. An infant is not bound by an executory contract unless he affirms the contract after coming of age; failure to affirm implies disaffirmance. An infant may disaffirm an executed contract during infancy or within a reasonable time after he attains his majority; failure to disaffirm within a reasonable time implies affirmance. Contracts for necessities, such as food, clothing, shelter, medical care, or education, may be binding upon an infant.

Like infants, insane persons are not absolutely incapable of making contracts; their contracts are voidable, not void, and they may be held liable for necessities. A person who is so drunk that he is deprived of his reason and does not understand the nature of his acts is in the same position as a mental incompetent; he may disaffirm his contracts if the disaffirmance does not injure third persons and provided he disaffirms immediately upon restoration of his faculties.

Under the COMMON LAW a married woman was deemed incapable of binding herself by contract, her contracts being regarded as void rather than voidable. But the statutes in most states have modified the common law. In general, a married woman may now contract as freely as a single woman, but in some states she cannot contract with her husband, enter into partnership with him, or act as surety for him.

A corporation's ability to contract is limited by its articles of incorporation and by various statutes.

Legality of subject matter. A contract is illegal if it calls for the performance of an act forbidden by law or against public policy. Gambling and wagering contracts and usurious contracts (*see* USURY), for example, are generally held to be illegal. In some states any contract entered into on Sunday is illegal. Federal and state laws make those contracts illegal that restrain trade, fix prices, or result in unfair practices.

Consideration. Something of benefit to the person making a promise must be given, or some detriment must be suffered by the person to whom a promise is made to make a contract binding. *Consideration* is the price, motive, or matter inducing the contract; it may consist of (a) doing some act that one is not obligated to perform, (b) refraining from doing something that one would otherwise be free to do, (c) giving some money or property, (d) giving a promise. The value of the consideration is generally immaterial.

Contracts under seal. The placing of a SEAL on a contract has lost the significance formerly attached to it, but it is still customary, especially in certain corporation transactions, and required in some states on contracts of major importance. Deeds, mortgages, and other conveyances of real estate are among the contracts that may require a seal.

Conversion. The unlawful taking or possession of another's CHATTEL. When a seller has passed title but refuses to make delivery, the buyer may sue him for conversion. Conversion may also take the form of unauthorized destruction or alteration of another's property.

Corporation. *Business corporations* are organizations formed under a state statute for the purpose of carrying on an enterprise in such a way as to make the enterprise distinct and separate from the persons who are interested in it and who control it; ". . . an artificial being, invisible, intangible, and existing only in contemplation of law." *The Trustees of Dartmouth College* v. *Woodward* (1918) 17 U.S. 518, 636.

The ownership of the corporation is represented by its capital stock, which is divided into identical units or groups of identical units called *shares*. These shares are represented by written instruments called *certificates of stock*. The owners of the shares are called the *stockholders*. Every stockholder has the right to transfer his shares—a right based on the inherent power of a person to dispose of his property. Since the shares of stock of a corporation can be transferred by sale or otherwise from one owner to another without affecting the corporate existence, the corporation enjoys continuous succession. The existence of the corporation is not disturbed by death, insanity, or bankruptcy of individual stockholders or by change of ownership. *See also* Index.

Public corporations include all of the subdivisions of the state, such as cities and towns, tax districts, and irrigation districts. They also include government-owned corporations, such as the Federal Deposit Insurance Corporation and the Federal Savings and Loan Insurance Company.

Corporations not for profit are those organized for purposes other than the pecuniary gain of their members. Those who are interested in and control the corporation are referred to as its members, rather than as its stockholders or shareholders as in a corporation for profit. These corporations include religious, civil, social, educational, fraternal, charitable, and cemetery associations.

Counterclaim. A defendant may take advantage of a suit against him to ask the court for relief against the plaintiff, when otherwise he would be compelled to institute an action of his own. For example, the maker of a note might claim that the payee is indebted to him for certain sums in connection with a matter not related to the note. The cause of action set up by the defendant, to be tried at the same time as the cause of action alleged by the plaintiff, is a counterclaim.

Court bond. Litigants at law are often required to file a bond or other security guaranteeing that, if unsuccessful in litigation, they will pay to the other party the monetary damages awarded by the court. These bonds are known as *court* or *judiciary bonds*. Another class of court bonds are known as *probate bonds*. They are issued to executors, administrators, and other fiduciaries to guarantee the faithful performance of their legal duties.

Criminal law. The statutes and general dicta that forbid certain actions or conduct as detrimental to the welfare of the state and that provide punishment therefor. Criminal acts are prosecuted by the state, as opposed to CIVIL WRONGS, which are prosecuted by an individual. A wrong may be both a criminal wrong and a civil wrong as in ASSAULT AND BATTERY. A crime may be a *treason*, a *felony*, or a *misdemeanor*. The Constitution states that treason "shall consist only in levying war against them or in adhering to their enemies, giving them aid and comfort." *Felonies* are crimes punishable by death or by imprisonment in a federal or a state prison. They include murder, grand larceny, arson, and rape. *Misdemeanors* are crimes of lesser importance than felonies and are punishable by fine or imprisonment in the local jail. They include petty larceny, drunkenness, disorderly conduct, and vagrancy. Violation of traffic ordinances, building codes, and similar city ordinances are not crimes but are termed *violations, petty offenses, public torts,* or *mala prohibitia.*

Cumulative voting. A system of voting for directors of a corporation under which each stockholder is entitled to a number of votes equal to the number of shares he owns multiplied by the number of directors to be elected. He may cast all the votes for one candidate—cumulate them—or he may distribute his votes among the candidates in any way he sees fit. This system enables the minority stockholders to elect one or more of the directors. The right to cumulative voting cannot be claimed unless provided for (1) by statute, (2) by the corporation's charter or bylaws, or (3) by contract among all the stockholders, provided the agreement is not otherwise illegal.

Curtesy. The right that a husband has in lands of his deceased wife when they have had children capable of inheriting the converse of dower.

Cy pres doctrine. (French for "as near as.") An ancient doctrine applicable to the construction of instruments in equity, whereby the intention of the party making the instrument is carried out as nearly as possible when it is impossible to carry out his precise intention. The doctrine, though ancient, is especially useful in modern times as a device to render charitable trusts useful. For example, if funds left to a charitable trust are insufficient to carry out the provisions of the testamentary trust, the fund does not necessarily revert to the estate but may be used for a charitable purpose similar to that provided for in the trust. The doctrine is not accepted in all states.

Damages. The sum allowed by law as compensation for an injury or loss caused by the unlawful act or negligence of another. The amount of damages to be recovered is usually a matter for the jury to determine.

Decree. The court's decision in EQUITY. A decree usually directs the defendant to do or not to do some specific thing, as opposed to a judgment for damages in a court of law. A decree is final when it disposes of the case, leaving no question to be decided in the future; for example, a decree ordering SPECIFIC PERFORMANCE of a contract. A decree is *interlocutory* when it leaves unsettled some question to be determined in the future, such as a temporary INJUNCTION. *See also* Index.

Deed. A formal written instrument by which title to real property is conveyed from one person to another. The parties to a deed are the *grantor*, who conveys his or her interest in the property, and the *grantee*, to whom the conveyance is made. *See also* Index.

Defamation. *See* LIBEL AND SLANDER.

del credere. (Italian) A term applied to an agent who, for a higher commission, guarantees his principal that he will pay for goods sold on credit if the buyer does not. Del credere agencies are common in businesses that employ commission merchants or agents whose relatively independent financial status enables them to guarantee their customers' accounts.

Deposition. Testimony taken under oath, usually outside of a courtroom. *See* DISCOVERY.

Dictum. An opinion expressed by a court that is not necessary in deciding the question before the court. When, in addition, such opinion does not relate to the questions before the court, it is called *obiter dictum* (Latin for "remark by the way"). Dicta carry legal weight in courts deciding subsequent questions but not to the extent that court decisions do. Court decisions are binding precedents; the dicta expressed in the opinion are not.

Disaffirmance. The act by which a person who has entered into a voidable contract indicates that he will not abide by the contract. (*See* VOID; VOIDABLE.) For example, an infant may refuse to honor a contract by disaffirmance when he reaches majority.

Discharge of contract. The release of the parties to a contract from their obligations under it. Contracts may be discharged by the following methods: (1) *Performance.* The carrying out of the terms of the contract. (2) *Agreement.* The parties may agree to discharge one another from further liability under the contract. There must be sufficient consideration for the agreement. (3) *Impossibility of performance.* When a contract is based on an implied condition that certain factors shall continue to exist during the life of the contract, and those factors cease to exist, performance is impossible and the contract is discharged. (4) *Operation of law.* A change in the law in effect at the time the contract was made may bring about a discharge of the contract, or a law itself may operate as a discharge. Thus a contract to build a garage on a certain site would be discharged by a zoning ordinance forbidding the erection of a garage within that zone. (5) *Breach.* If one party breaches a contract the other may be discharged. (*See* BREACH OF CONTRACT.)

Discovery. A procedure designed to obtain facts known by the defendant or referred to in papers in his possession. The information may be obtained by written interrogatories, requests for production of documents, or depositions. Any or all methods may be used in a given case.

Dishonor. Refusal to pay a NEGOTIABLE INSTRUMENT when due. Notice of dishonor is usually given to endorsers and drawers, who, in addition to the maker, are liable on the instrument. Notice of dishonor may be given orally or in writing. If it is not given, endorsers and drawers are discharged from liability. (*See also* PROTEST.)

Doing business. *See* INTERSTATE COMMERCE; INTRASTATE COMMERCE.

Domestic corporation. A corporation organized under the laws of a particular state is a *domestic corporation* in that state. When this corporation does business in another state, it is a *foreign corporation* there. (*See* FOREIGN CORPORATION.)

Duress. Coercion causing action or inaction against a person's will through fear. Duress may take the form of physical force, imprisonment, bodily harm, improper moral persuasion, or the threat of any of them. Threat of criminal prosecution constitutes duress, but threat of civil prosecution does not. A contract made under duress is voidable at the option of the party subjected to duress.

Earnest (earnest money). The payment that one contracting party gives to another at the time of entering into the contract to bind the sale and that will be forfeited by the donor if he fails to carry out the contract. The money is applied to the purchase price if the donor lives up to his bargain. *See also* Index.

Eminent domain. The power of federal, state, and local governments to appropriate property for public use or the public welfare. When such property is taken, the owner is reimbursed according to a fair appraisal and has the right to sue for a greater amount. PUBLIC UTILITY (public service) corporations are also given the power of eminent domain.

Endorsement. *On negotiable instrument.* Writing one's name, either with or without additional words, on a NEGOTIABLE INSTRUMENT or on a paper (called an ALLONGE) attached to it. By an endorsement, the endorser becomes liable to all subsequent holders in due course for payment of the instrument if it is not paid by the maker when properly presented and if he is given notice of DISHONOR.

Blank endorsement. The writing of one's name on an instrument, or an allonge, without any additional words. Its effect is to make the paper payable to the bearer. Thus as finder or thief might transfer the note to a third party for a consideration, and the third party might then enforce payment against the maker or the endorser.

Special endorsement. The designation of a certain person to whom the instrument is payable. Thus if an instrument is endorsed "Pay to John Jones" or "Pay to the order of John Jones," followed by the endorser's signature, no one but John Jones can receive payment for the instrument or transfer it.

Restrictive endorsement. An endorsement that transfers possession of the instrument for a particular purpose. Examples: "Pay to John Jones only. Sam Brown." "Pay to National City Bank for collection. Sam Brown." "For deposit only. Sam Brown." A restrictive endorsement terminates the negotiability of the instrument.

Qualified endorsement. An endorsement that qualifies or limits the liability of the endorser. If an endorser endorses an instrument "without recourse," he does not assume liability in the event the maker fails to pay the instrument when due.

Conditional endorsement. A special endorsement with words added that create a condition that must happen before the special endorsee is entitled to payment. The endorser is liable only if the condition is fulfilled. Example: "Pay to Greenwood Cotton Growers Association upon delivery of warehouse receipt for twenty-five standard bales cotton, strict to middling. John Jones."

Irregular or accommodation endorsement. An endorsement made for the purpose of lending the endorser's credit to a party to the instrument. It is also called an *anomalous endorsement.* A regular endorsement transfers title to the instrument, whereas an accommodation endorsement is for additional security only. An accommodation endorser is never the maker, drawer, acceptor, payee, or holder of the instrument he endorses.

Equity. 1. *Legal. See* Index.

2. *Accounting and finance.* The value of the owner's interest in property in excess of all claims and liens against it. Examples: (2) An owner's equity in his home is its present value less the amount of the mortgage. (b) The equity of the stockholders of a business is its net worth; hence the interest of the stockholders as measured by capital and surplus or the value of the assets of the business in excess of its liabilities. Sometimes, however, equity refers to the unlimited interest of common stockholders. (c) The equity of a person who has bought securities on margin is the present market value of the securities less the sum borrowed from the broker to make the purchase.

Error, writ of. A writ commanding an appellate court to examine the record to correct an alleged error of law.

Escheat. The return of land to the state if the owner dies without legal heirs. Unclaimed personal property may also go to the state. Escheated personal property is called *bona vacantia.*

Escrow. A conditional delivery of something to a third person to be held until the happening of some event or the performance of some act. To place an instrument or a fund in escrow is to deliver the instrument or fund to a person charged with its custody and disposition under the terms of a specific agreement, known as the *escrow agreement.* For example, a grantor may deliver a deed in escrow to a trust company until the grantee makes certain payments on the purchase price, at which time the trust company delivers the deed to the grantee. *See also* Index.

Estate by the entirety. *See* TENANCY BY THE ENTIRETY.

Estoppel. A bar raised by law preventing a person from taking a position, denying a fact, or asserting a fact in court inconsistent with the truth as established by judicial or legislative officers or by his own deed or acts, either express or implied. Example: *A* sells *B* a house that he (*A*) does not own, giving *B* a covenant and warranty deed in which he warrants that he has title to the house. Later, *A* obtains title from the actual owner and attempts to eject *B* on the ground that *A* is now the true owner and *B* is not. *A* would be estopped from disputing what he formerly warranted, namely, that he was the true owner when he sold the house.

Ex parte. (Latin for "of the one part.") Done for or on behalf of one party only. The term is applied to a proceeding, order, or injunction that is taken for the benefit of one party only. An injunction is granted *ex parte* when only one side has had a hearing. When *ex parte* appears in the title of a case, the name following is that of the party upon whose application the case was heard.

Execution, writ of. When a judgment is obtained by one party against another, the successful party is known as a *judgment creditor* and the other party as a *judgment debtor.* If the judgment debtor does not pay the judgment, the attorney for the judgment creditor may get the clerk of court to issue execution to a designated officer of the law, usually the sheriff, constable, or marshal. The execution is a printed form, easily filled out upon the basis of the information in the file. If the officer to whom the execution is issued can find no property of the judgment debtor against which to levy, he returns the execution "unsatisfied." The lawyer may then commence a SUPPLEMENTARY PROCEEDING.

Fee simple. The absolute ownership of real property. It gives the owner and his heirs the unconditional power of disposition and other rights. (*See* REAL PROPERTY.)

Felony. *See* CRIMINAL LAW.

Force majeure. (French) Superior or irresistible force. Corresponds in a general way to "Act of God"; for example, an earthquake, or the sudden death of a person. If a party to a contract is prevented from executing it by a *force majeure*, he may not be held liable for damages.

Foreign corporation. A corporation doing business in a state of the United States other than the state in which it was created or incorporated. It must comply with certain terms and conditions imposed by the sate. The state statutes make no distinction between a foreign and an alien corporation (a corporation organized outside the United States and its territories); both are regarded as foreign, except in those few states that do not recognize alien corporations.

Garnishment. The right of a creditor to compel a third party owing money to, or holding money for, a debtor to pay the money to the creditor instead of to the debtor. (*See* EXECUTION.) The third party against whom the proceedings are brought is called the *garnishee*. Not only wages and salaries but trust fund, insurance disability payments, and the like may be garnished. The laws that govern the right of garnishment differ considerably in the various states, and in some states it is referred to as a *factoring process* or a *trustee process*.

Guaranty. The term is used interchangeably with suretyship by courts and lawyers as well as laypersons, although there may be a distinction about the degree of liability wherein the surety is primarily liable upon the engagement and the guarantor is secondarily liable and not chargeable with nonperformance until notice is given. A contract of guaranty or of suretyship is a contract whereby one person agrees to be responsible to another for the payment of a debt or the performance of a duty by a third person. It must be in writing and is not enforceable if made orally.

The term *guaranty* (or *guarantee*) is often loosely used in the sense of WARRANTY. In a strict legal and commercial sense, it is of the essence of a contract of guaranty that there should be a principal, liable directly to perform some act or duty. An agreement by a third party guaranteeing the honest and faithful performance of a contract of sale is a contract of guaranty; an agreement in a sales contract "guaranteeing" the efficient performance of a product for a certain number of years is a contract of warranty.

Habeas corpus. (Latin for "You have the body.") A writ commanding the person having custody of another to produce the person detained at a certain place and time so the court may determine if the detention is lawful.

Holder in due course. The transferee of a NEGOTIABLE INSTRUMENT who acquires the instrument under the following conditions: (1) The paper must be complete and regular on its face. (2) It must be purchased before maturity. (3) The purchase must be in good faith for a valuable consideration. (4) The purchase must be made without notice of defects in the title or of defenses against payment to the transferor. A holder in due course may enforce collection of the instrument against prior parties regardless of their claims, defenses, and offsets against one another. A transferee may acquire the rights of a holder in due course without being one himself. Example: *A*, the holder in due course of a note procured by the payee through fraud, endorses the note to *B*, who knew of the fraud and hence was not a holder in due course. *B*, however, acquires *A's* right as a holder in due course to collect the note regardless of the fraud, provided *B* had no part in the fraud.

Exception: Some states have amended their consumer protection laws to allow a buyer of goods to assert any defenses he would have against the seller, as against seller's assignee, even though the latter has met the above criteria as a holder in due course.

Inchoate. Begun but not completed, as a contract not executed by all the parties. An instrument that the law requires to be recorded is an *inchoate instrument* until it is recorded, in that it is good only between the parties and privies (*see* PRIVITY). A wife's interest in her husband's lands that becomes a right of dower upon his death is an *inchoate right of dower* during his lifetime. An interest in real estate that may become a vested interest unless barred is an *inchoate interest*. Other phrases are *inchoate equity, inchoate lien, inchoate title.*

Indemnity. An undertaking, either express or implied, to compensate another for loss or damage or for expenses or trouble incurred either in the past or in the future. Under a contract of indemnity, the indemnity is the obligation or duty resting upon a particular person or company to make good any loss or damage another has suffered or may suffer upon the happening of a specific event. The person giving the indemnity (agreeing to indemnify) is the *indemnitor*, corresponding to an insurer; the person who receives the indemnity or protection is the *indemnitee*, corresponding to the insured. The term *indemnity* also applies to the sum paid as compensation or remuneration in the event of loss or damage to the indemnitee. The indemnity may be payable to the indemnitee or to someone else in behalf of the indemnitee. For example, the payments that are made to an injured working person under worker's compensation insurance are indemnities. They are payable to the worker in behalf of his employer, who is the indemnitee.

Indenture. A formal written instrument between two or more parties that involves reciprocal rights and duties, such as a lease. In ancient times the practice was to write two or more copies of the instrument on the same piece of parchment. The copies were then separated by tearing the parchment in irregular fashion, so the indentions of each torn part would fit the other. Hence the name *indenture*. (*See also* Index.)

Infant's contract. *See* CONTRACTS.

Injunction. A writ issued by a court of equity restraining a person or corporation from doing or continuing to do something that threatens or causes injury or requiring the defendant to do a particular act. Injunctions may be classified as *prohibitory* and *mandatory*. A *prohibitory injunction* restrains the commission or continuance of an act. Thus a prohibitory injunction may restrain a board of elections from placing a certain candidate's name on the ballot. A *mandatory injunction* commands acts to be done or undone. For example, a mandatory injunction may compel a property owner to open a road that he had closed by constructing a fence across it, thus depriving another property owner of the use of the road.

Injunctions may also be classified as (1) temporary restraining orders, (2) preliminary injunctions, and (3) permanent injunctions. A *temporary restraining order* (TRO) may be granted without notice to the opposite party for the purpose of restraining the defendant until the court has heard an application for a temporary injunction. A *preliminary injunction* is granted on the basis of the application before the court has heard the case on its merits. It restrains the defendant during the litigation of a case and may be either dissolved or made permanent when the rights of the parties are determined. Temporary injunctions are also called preliminary, interlocutory, or injunction *pendente lite*. *Permanent injunctions* are granted on the merits of the case. They are often called *final injunctions*.

Insurable interest. A person has an insurable interest if he might be financially injured by the occurrence of the event insured against. Under American law if an insurable interest is not present, the contract is a mere wager and is not enforceable.

In property. Insurable interest must exist at the time the loss occurs. Title to the property insured is not necessary; an owner, lessee, mortgagee, or purchaser has an insurable interest. Thus the interest (1) may be contingent, as the interest of a purchaser under a contract of sale; (2) may be conditional, as the interest of a seller under a contract of CONDITIONAL SALE until the conditions of the sale have been met; (3) may arise from possession, as in the case of a bailee (*see* BAILMENT).

In life. Insurable interest must exist at the time the policy is written but need not exist at the time death occurs. Every person has insurable interest in his own life and may name anyone he chooses as beneficiary. Other examples of relations giving rise to an insurable interest are those of (1) employer and valued employee, (2) several partners of a partnership, (3) creditor and debtor, (4) corporation and its officers, (5) wife and husband, (6) dependent children.

Interlocking directorates. Boards of directors of two or more corporations have one or more directors in common. Through this method of control, the will of the common dominant stockholders is executed.

Interlocutory decree. *See* DECREE.

Interstate commerce; intrastate commerce. The Constitution gives the federal government power to regulate "commerce among the several states" (Art. I, sec. 8). But it does not define either commerce or interstate commerce. The courts decided originally that commerce meant buying and selling. Hence if the buying and selling is part of an interchange of commodities or intangibles between states, it is *interstate commerce*. Today, interstate commerce includes transportation of persons and property, transmission of power, and communication—radio, television, telephone, and telegraph.

Interstate commerce also comprises general movements of commodities. For example, on different occasions the courts have upheld the regulation of both buying and selling of livestock at the stockyards and the buying and selling of grain futures. Both operations, even though local, are part of the general flow of commerce that supplies produce to the consumer markets.

A company is engaged in *intrastate commerce,* as distinguished from interstate commerce, if most of its business (isolated cases of interstate commerce do not count) takes place entirely within a state and is not part of an interchange or movement of tangible or intangible commodities.

As a general rule a state cannot prohibit foreign corporations (corporations chartered in other states) from doing interstate business within its borders; however, it can prohibit them from doing intrastate business unless they meet certain qualifying conditions. Usually, the conditions include (1) registration and filing of certain documents with state officials, (2) designation of an agent to accept service of summons, (3) payment of certain fees and taxes. If a corporation "does business" in a state without qualifying, that is, meeting the state's requirements, it may become subject to certain fines or it may lose the right to sue in state courts on contracts made within the state.

The regulatory laws and court decisions are not consistent in their definition of what interstate commerce is, although the tendency is toward uniformity.

Joint adventure (venture). An association of two or more persons for a given, limited purpose, without the usual powers, duties, and responsibilities that go with a PARTNERSHIP. Thus if two people buy a specific piece of real estate for resale at a profit, they become parties to a joint adventure. But if they enter into an agreement whereby each contributes money and services in establishing and carrying on a real estate business, they become members of a partnership.

Joint and several. An obligation or liability incurred, either under contract or otherwise, by two or more parties together and separately is said to be *joint and several*. The parties may be held jointly responsible or severally responsible. Thus partners are jointly and severally liable on partnership transactions, whereas a subscriber to a charity is severally liable—the subscriber is not jointly liable with the other subscribers for their subscriptions. Or a bond may be joint and several, in which case the obligors are liable either individually or together, at the option of the obligee.

Joint estate. *See* JOINT TENANCY.

Joint stock company. A form of business organization created by an agreement of the parties. This agreement is commonly called articles of association. This type of company is similar to the CORPORATION in the following respects: (1) The ownership is represented by transferable certificates. (2) Management is in the hands of a board of governors or directors elected by the members (shareholders). (3) The business continues for its fixed term notwithstanding the death or disability of one or more of the members. It is unlike the corporation and like the PARTNER-SHIP in that each shareholder is personally liable for the company's debts.

In many states the laws affecting taxation and regulation of corporations make the definition of a corporation broad enough to include joint stock companies. These states regard a joint stock company organized in another state as a FOREIGN CORPORATION. In other states a joint stock company may conduct business in the state without being subject to restrictions imposed upon corporations.

Joint tenancy. If two or more persons acquire the same estate at the same time, by the same title or source of ownership, each having the same degree of interest (including right of survivorship) as the others, and each having the same right of possession as the others, the estate is called a *joint estate* or *tenancy*. The distinguishing characteristic of a joint tenancy is that upon the death of one of the joint tenants, his or her interest automatically passes to the others by survivorship. The courts do not favor joint tenancies and in many jurisdictions permit joint tenants to defeat the right of survivorship by mortgage or conveyance. Some of the states have passed retroactive statutes making existing undivided interests TEN-ANCY IN COMMON unless a contrary intent plainly appears in the instrument sufficient to negate the presumption of a tenancy in common. (*See also* TENANCY BY THE ENTIRETY.)

Judgment. An adjudication by a court after a trial or hearing of the rights of the parties. Broadly speaking, an adjudication by a court of law or of EQUITY is considered a judgment, but technically, an adjudication by a court of equity is a DECREE. The sentence in a criminal case is the judgment. If, following judgment, the debtor fails or refuses to pay the award of the court, the judgment or debtor may direct that a writ of execution be issued by the clerk of court. Pursuant to the terms of the writ, the sheriff may seize and sell any property of the debtor not exempt by law in satisfaction of the judgment. If the party against whom a judgment is rendered appeals to a higher court, execution of the judgment is stayed pending the higher court's decision. *See also* Index.

Judgment by default. After a SUMMONS has been served by the sheriff and returned to the court, the court has JURISDICTION over the defendant. If the defendant fails to defend a civil case by filing proper pleadings, or fails to appear within a definite time, a judgment is given against him in his absence. This judgment is called *judgment by default. See also* Index.

Jurisdiction. The authority of a court as established by federal or state constitution and statute; or the political entity within which the particular court is authorized to act, such as a state or a district. *See also* Index.

Laches. Unreasonable delay in bringing suit or seeking remedy in an equity court. For a defendant to plead laches as a defense to a suit, he must show that he suffered from the plaintiff's delay in bringing suit.

Letters patent. *See* PATENTS.

Libel and slander. That which tends to injure the reputation of a living person or the memory of a deceased person and to expose him to public hatred, disgrace, ridicule, or contempt or to exclude him from society is known as *defamation. Slander* is oral defamation of one person by another in the presence of a third person or persons; *libel* is written or printed defamation of one person by another, published before a third person or persons. A corporation is a person in this sense. For a slanderous statement to be actionable, it must be false and must cause injury to the person to whom the statement refers. In libel actions, no injury need be proved, although proved injury will affect the amount of any damages awarded. (*See also* LIBELOUS LETTERS.)

Libelous letters. For a letter to be libelous (*see* LIBEL AND SLANDER), it must have been read by someone other than the person defamed. The reader may be a stenographer who takes the libelous writing by dictation and transcribes the notes, although some courts have taken the view that publication to a stenographer does not subject the writer to liability unless the letter was prompted by actual malice.

License, business. Federal, state, or city approval and permission are necessary to engage in certain businesses that are of sufficient concern to the public to justify regulation. Permission and approval are issued in the form of a license, for which a fee is charged.

Lien. A charge imposed on property by which the property is made security for the discharge of an obligation. Some liens, particularly those on personal property, must be accompanied by actual possession of the property: a *lienor* (the holder of a lien) who parts with possession loses his lien. Other liens, particularly those on real estate, need not be accompanied by possession: the lienor gives notice of the lien he claims by a public record of it. Some of the common liens are vendor's lien, MECHANIC'S LIEN, mortgage lien (*see* Index: Mortgage), and TAX LIEN.

Life estate. An interest in property, real or personal, that lasts only for the duration of the owner's life. A life estate may also be for the duration of another's life or may terminate with the happening of a certain contingency. For example, a life estate may terminate upon the marriage of the owner. This estate may be created by an act of the parties, as by deed, will, or gift, or by operation of law, as by dower or curtesy. The owner of a life estate (called the LIFE TENANT) has the current use of the property and is responsible for its maintenance, including taxes and carrying charges. He also gets the income from the property but cannot ordinarily sell the property or do anything to impair its permanent value. However, the life tenant may be allowed to sell or consume property to support himself if the deed or will so provides. He cannot dispose of the property at his death. The person or persons to whom the estate passes upon termination of the life estate is determined when the life estate is created. The estate that is left at the termination of the life estate is called a *remainder;* the person to whom it passes is a *remainderman* (plural: *remaindermen*)

Life tenant. The owner of a LIFE ESTATE. Beneficiaries with life interests under trusts are sometimes called *equitable life tenants.*

Limited partnership. A partnership in which the liability of one or more special partners for debts of the firm is limited to the amount of his investment in the business. Special partners have no voice in the management of the partnership. They merely invest money and receive a certain share of the profits. There must be one or more general partners who manage the business and remain liable for all its debts.

A limited partnership is organized under state statutes, usually by filing a certificate in a public office and publishing a notice in a newspaper. The statutes, codified in many states as the Uniform Limited Partnership Law, must be strictly observed. A limited partnership is regarded as a general partnership in states other than the state in which it is organized; therefore, it must register and form a limited partnership with the same firm members under the laws of each state in which it wishes to do business.

As in a general partnership, the death, insanity, or bankruptcy of any one of the general partners dissolves the limited partnership. (*See* PARTNERSHIP.)

Liquidated damages. An amount the parties to a contract have agreed upon that shall be paid in satisfaction of a loss resulting from a BREACH OF CONTRACT. The amount must be in proportion to the actual loss; otherwise the agreement is unenforceable.

Mandamus. (Latin for "We command.") A writ issued by a court of superior jurisdiction to a public or private corporation, or an official thereof, or an inferior court, commanding the performance of an official act that the person or body named in the writ had failed or refused to perform. It is an extraordinary WRIT, which is issued in cases in which the usual and ordinary procedures do not afford remedies to the party aggrieved. The writ of mandamus is known as a remedy for official inaction. It was introduced to prevent disorder from a failure of public officials to perform their duties and is still an important legal remedy for the protection of the public and the individual against exploitation and abuse by official inaction. Mandamus is an "extraordinary" writ; it may not be used to force a discretionary act.

A mandamus may also enforce a private right. It compels the performance by a corporation of a variety of specific acts within the scope of the corporation's duties. For example, a stockholder may institute a mandamus proceeding to compel a corporation to submit to an inspection of its books and records.

The writ is either peremptory or alternate. The *peremptory mandamus* compels the defendant to perform the required act; the *alternate mandamus* compels him to perform the act or show cause on a certain day why he should not perform it. The alternate writ is usually issued first.

Massachusetts trust. A business association formed under a deed of trust, which is really a contract between the trustees and beneficiaries. It is also known as a business trust or a common law trust. Its structure closely resembles that of a CORPORATION. The interests of the beneficiaries are represented by certificates frequently called certificates of stock, which may be divided into several classes of common and preferred stock and may be listed on stock exchanges. The trustees correspond to the directors and the certificate holders to the stockholders. The trustees manage the property and pay dividends out of the profits. They usually appoint and remove the officers. Unlike a corporation, the management is permanent. The trustees are personally liable in dealing with outsiders unless they clearly indicate that they are acting as trustees and that the creditors shall look only to the trust property for all payments.

Massachusetts trusts are regarded as corporations under many taxing statutes and federal acts.

The duration is limited by statute in most states, but the parties interested at the time the trust expires can agree to another trust.

Mechanic's lien. The statutory lien of a contractor, subcontractor, laborer, or materialman, who performs labor or furnishes material for the permanent improvement of real property for hire or with the consent or at the request of the authorized agent. The lien attaches to the land and improvements. A mechanic's lien is for the amount of the contract plus interest. Notice of the lien must be filed in the public filing place prescribed by statute. If a mechanic's lien is not discharged, it may be foreclosed subject to all prior liens. Like a mortgage, a mechanic's lien may be released or waived.

Merger. The absorption of one or more corporations by another existing corporation, which retains its identity and takes over all the rights, privileges, franchises, properties, and liabilities of the absorbed companies. The absorbing corporation continues its existence, whereas the other companies terminate their existence. For example, companies *A*, *B*, and *C* agree to combine so companies *A* and *B* are absorbed by *C*. When the plan becomes effective, companies *A* and *B* go out of existence and company *C* remains. The remaining company takes care of the creditors of the constituent companies.

The procedure designated by statute to bring about the merger must be followed. The percentage of the stockholders fixed in the law must approve the agreement. Where the statute so provides, stockholders who dissent to the plan may obtain cash for the appraised value of their shares, instead of shares in the remaining company.

Minutes of corporate meetings. *Minutes* are the official record of the proceedings at a meeting of an organized body, such as the stockholders or directors of a corporation. It is not essential to the validity or binding effect of acts done by an organized body that minutes be kept, but accurate minutes avoid future misunderstandings. They are particularly useful if the corporation institutes suit or is sued upon a matter recorded in the minutes. Ordinarily, minutes are PRIMA FACIE EVIDENCE of what transpired at the meeting; frequently, they are the best evidence. *See also* Index.

Misdemeanor. *See* CRIMINAL LAW.

Muniments of title. Written evidence by which title to real property may be defended. The word *muniments* is derived from the Latin verb *munio,* meaning "to fortify." Hence muniments of the title fortify or strengthen rights in property. The expression as generally defined refers to deeds of conveyance, wills, legislative grants, and other documents relating to the title to land.

Negotiable instrument. A written instrument, signed by a maker or drawer, containing an unconditional promise or order to pay a certain sum of money, which can be passed freely from one person to another. Each transferee becomes the holder until he or she transfers the instrument to a new holder. If payable to the bearer, the instrument may be negotiated simply by delivery; if payable to order, it is negotiated by endorsement of the holder, completed by delivery.

The Uniform Commercial Code governs negotiable instruments in all states and territories except those few states that still retain the older Uniform Negotiable Instruments Law. The code states the manner in which a negotiable instrument shall be transferred, and it fixes the rights and duties of the maker, the payee, the holder, and the endorser. For example, under the law an endorser of a negotiable instrument vouches for its genuineness. If it is a forgery, the endorser is liable to a HOLDER IN DUE COURSE of the instrument after delivery.

Strictly speaking, documents of title (such as order bills of lading and warehouse receipts) are not negotiable instruments because they do not contain an order to pay a sum of money. However, various statutes have given certain documents of title the quality of negotiability. They are known as quasi-negotiable instruments.

Negotiation. The transfer of a written instrument in a manner that makes the transferee the holder or the instrument. If payable to order, an instrument is negotiated by endorsement and delivery; if payable to the bearer, by delivery alone. An instrument is not negotiated until it is transferred by the person to whom it is issued. Thus *A* makes a note payable to *B* and delivers it to him. Subsequently, by negotiation, *B* transfers the note to *C*, and *C* to *D*, and so on. As opposed to transfer by ASSIGNMENT, the innocent transferee by negotiation takes the paper free of defenses that are good against the transferor.

Novation. The substitution of a new contract, or debtor or obligor, for an existing one. The substitution must be agreed to by all the parties. Example: *A* sells a car to *B*, who makes a small down payment and agrees to pay the balance in installments. Finding himself unable to make the payments, *B* sells the car to *C*, who agrees to make the payments to *A*. If *A* agrees to release *B* from the contract and to look to *C* for payment, a novation is created.

Obiter dictum. *See* DICTUM.

Offer and acceptance. *See* CONTRACT.

Omnibus. A term applied to that which contains two or more independent matters. The term is applied, for example, to a legislative bill that relates to two or more subjects.

Option. An agreement, usually in consideration for the payment of a certain sum of money by the offeree, to hold an offer open for a definite period. The offer ceases to be an offer and becomes a contract of option; it cannot be withdrawn until the option period expires. Although an option is generally based on a consideration, a few states require no consideration if the contract is in writing. Others recognize an option under seal as binding because a seal, at COMMON LAW, indicates consideration. The consideration for an option is not returnable to the optionee if he fails to take up the option; it is, however, usually applied to the purchase price if the offer is accepted.

Ordinance. A law or statute. The word is commonly used to apply to enactments of a municipality.

Partnership. "An association of two or more persons to carry on as co-owners a business for profit" (Uniform Partnership Law). A partnership is organized by oral or written agreement among the parties. Agreement may also be implied from the acts and representations of the parties. Partnerships are governed by fairly uniform laws, which are codified in many states by the Uniform Partnership Law. A partnership may carry on business in any state without paying greater taxes than residents of the state pay.

Each partner of a general partnership is fully liable personally for all partnership debts regardless of the amount of his investment. (*See* LIMITED PARTNERSHIP.) All types of capital produced or acquired by the partnership becomes partnership property. Real estate is generally acquired in the individual names of the partners or in the name of one partner who holds the property in trust for the partnership.

In the absence of a specific contract, partners share profits and losses equally. It is customary, however, to provide in the partnership agreement that profits and losses shall be distributed pro rata according to the amount of capital contributed by each or in any other ratio to which they agree. Partners have no right to salaries unless they are agreed upon, even though one partner may devote all of his time to the business and the other may devote little or none. The agreement may provide for the division of profits after allowing each of the partners an agreed-upon salary.

Partnerships are dissolved without violation of the partnership agreement by (1) withdrawal of one of the members under some circumstances, (2) operation of law through death or bankruptcy of one of the partners or a change in the law that makes the partnership's business illegal, (3) court decree granted because of incapacity or insanity of one of the partners, gross misconduct, or neglect or breach of duty.

Patents. A *patent* is an exclusive right granted by the federal government for a fixed period to make, use, and sell an invention. A person who perfects a new machine, process, or material, or any new and useful improvements of them, or who invents or discovers and reproduces a distinct and new variety of plant, may make application to the government for a patent for it. The person to whom a patent is granted is called the *patentee*. Patent rights are issued in the form of letters and run to the patentee, his heirs, and assigns generally for a period of seventeen years.

Perjury. The act of willfully giving, under oath, false testimony. A statement that one does not remember certain facts when one really does is *perjury*; conversely, swearing one remembers something when in fact one has no recollection of it is also perjury. Honest but erroneous expression of opinion is not perjury. A statement substantially true but literally false is not necessarily perjury. Federal and some state statutes provide for punishment for perjury by fine or imprisonment.

Personal property. A right or interest, protected by law, in something that is not land or anything permanently attached to land and is capable of ownership (*see* REAL PROPERTY). Personal property is generally movable. It may be tangibles (also called *chattels*), such as money, gold, merchandise, or any movable object susceptible to physical possession, or intangibles, such as contracts or stocks (*see* CHOSE IN ACTION). Personal property may be an interest in land: a 99-year lease may be personal property. Products of the soil become personal property when severed from the land; trees and crops that are sold while attached to the land constitute real property, but when severed from the land, they constitute personal property.

Title to personal property may be acquired by the following methods: (1) *appropriate or original possession:* although almost all property today belongs to someone, there are still some kinds of property, such as wild game and fish, that may be appropriated; (2) *discovery:* the finder of lost property acquires a title that is good against everyone except the rightful owner; (3) *creation:* a person is entitled to that which he produces by his physical or mental labor, unless the product is produced during the course of his employment or under some other contract; then it belongs to his employer or the party for whom he contracted to create the property; (4) *gift;* (5) *sale or exchange;* (6) *will;* (7) *operation of law:* when a person dies without making a will, his property passes by operation of law to certain relatives. Or if a person becomes bankrupt, his property, with certain exceptions, passes to a trustee for the benefit of creditors. A person's property may also be taken from him by legal process (*see* EXECUTION, 1).

Pleadings. *See* Index.

Pledge. The placement of personal property by the owner with a lender as security for a debt. Pawned articles and stocks and bonds put up as collateral for a loan are the most common pledges. Essentials of a pledge are (1) a debt or obligation to be secured; (2) the thing pledged; (3) the pledgor (the one who gives the pledge) and the pledgee (the one who receives the pledge); (4) transfer of possession of the property (if actual physical possession is practically impossible, the pledge may acquire CONSTRUCTIVE possession); (5) retention of title in the pledgor; (6) the pledgor's right to redeem the pledge; (7) a contract, express or implied, covering the transaction.

When stock is pledged as collateral, the pledgee has the right and is bound to collect the dividends and apply them to the loan, in the absence of an agreement to the contrary between the pledgor and pledgee. This is the legal theory. As a matter of practice, the stockholder makes an assignment of the stock in blank and the stock is not transferred on the books of the corporation unless the pledgor defaults; the stockholder pledgor therefore continues to collect the dividends.

Police power. That power which any governmental body has to protect the property, life, health, and well-being of its citizen by legislation. State minimum wage laws have been held by the United States Supreme Court to be a proper exercise of the states' police powers. Under police powers states license doctors and lawyers, barbers and beauticians, and the like, and only those who obtain a license are authorized to practice their profession or trade. City ordinances that require certain standards of cleanliness in restaurants or that impose building restrictions are regulations issued under police power. The extent of a governing body's police power is limited by the state constitutions and by the Fourteenth Amendment to the Constitution of the United States, which protects personal liberties and freedoms. The power of Congress to regulate and control business activities is not a police power but is a power granted by the several states and by the Constitution.

Power of attorney. A written instrument in which the principal (the person giving the power of attorney) authorizes another to act for him. The instrument may be a blanket authorization, but more commonly it authorizes the agent to represent the principal in one specific transaction, as in the closing of a real estate deal, or to do a certain act continuously, as in the signing of checks. The person appointed is commonly called an ATTORNEY-IN-FACT. A power of attorney may be revoked at the will of the principal, unless it was given to the agent for a consideration. The death of the principal constitutes an instantaneous revocation, but there is no revocation when consideration was given for power.

Preemptive right. The right of each stockholder, upon the issuance of additional shares by the corporation, to purchase his proportion of the new stock to maintain his relative interest in the corporation. Example: If A owns $10,000 of the $100,000 worth of stock issued and outstanding, and the corporation increases its authorized capital stock of $200,000, A will have a right to purchase one-tenth of the new issue, or an additional $10,000 worth of stock, before the stock may be offered to outsiders. The stockholder has a right to purchase the stock at the price fixed by the corporation, and if he fails to take it, it cannot be offered to anyone else upon more favorable terms. He must be given reasonable notice of his right to subscribe and a reasonable opportunity to exercise the right. Stockholders who are not in a position to take and pay for the stock to which they are entitled may sell the rights to anyone who can. A stockholder may also waive his preemptive right by agreement with the corporation.

The preemptive right is governed by statute in many states. Frequently, the certificate of incorporation regulates the preemptive right in accordance with the governing statute. In the absence of regulating statute and charter provisions, the court decisions determine under what circumstances the preemptive right exists; these decisions in many instances are conflicting.

Pretrial. A system to expedite the progress of a case. Before the trial of a case, the judge calls counsel for both sides into conference for the purpose of settling issues that are either unnecessary or not disputed. Counsel agree on undisputed and indisputable facts common to both parties; on exhibits, about the authenticity of originals and accuracy of copies; and on various other matters that ordinarily consume considerable time in the trial of a case. For example, in an automobile accident case, the ownership of the car is admitted, without necessity of putting a witness on the stand to testify about the ownership.

Pretrial has not yet been accepted officially in all states, but some judges use it in jurisdictions where court rules neither require nor specifically sanction it. Rule 16 of Federal Rules provides for pretrial, making the use of it optional with each judge. There is no set form for pretrial, the procedure varying from state to state and from judge to judge.

At the end of the pretrial conference, the judge prepares an order embodying the results of the conference. There is no uniformity in the method of preparing it. The order is official and controls the case to the same extent as any other order.

Prima facie evidence. Evidence deemed by law to be sufficient to establish a fact if the evidence is not disputed. For example, the placement of a corporate seal on an instrument is prima facie evidence that the instrument was executed by authority of the corporation.

Private law. *See* PUBLIC AND PRIVATE LAW.

Privity. Mutual or successive relationship to the same right of property, or the power to take advantage of and enforce a promise or warranty. Identity of interest is essential. There must be a connection or bond of union between parties about some particular transaction. Thus privity of contract exists between a lessor and lessee, because the parties are mutually interested in the lease. Privity of contract also exists between a lessor and an assignee of the lease, because the assignee succeeded to the rights of the lessee. Heirs, executors, and assigns succeed to the rights and liabilities of a contract whether or not it so states. They are thus *privies* to the contract.

Privity affects legal rights and duties and, in many cases, determines whether a party may sue or be sued. Thus a privy has the same right to relief against mistake of fact as the original party to a contract. A stranger to a contract has no right to sue for fraud, but a privy does. An injunction extends to all persons in privity with the parties enjoined. Evidence may be admissible or inadmissible because of privity. Privity may be an element in an action for negligence or in the substitution of parties in a legal action.

Probate bond. *See* COURT BOND.

Process server. A person authorized by law to serve papers in court proceedings. In most states process servers are county officials such as a sheriff. In some states service of process has been delegated to private process servers.

Proprietorship, sole. One of the three most common forms of business organization. Ownership of the business is vested in one proprietor. The other two common forms of business organization are PARTNERSHIP and CORPORATION.

Protest. A formal certificate attesting the DISHONOR of a NEGOTIABLE INSTRUMENT after NEGOTIATION. A protest is usually made by a notary public but may be made by a responsible citizen, in the presence of two witnesses. The certificate states the time and place of presentment, the fact that presentment was made and the manner thereof, the cause or reason for protesting the bill, and the demand made and the answer given or the fact that the drawee or acceptor could not be found. The protest is attached to the dishonored instrument or a copy of it. Notice of protest is then sent to the parties who are secondarily liable (drawer and endorser). Protest is required only when a bill of exchange or check drawn in one state (or country) and payable in another is dishonored, but as a matter of business practice domestic instruments are often "protested." The word *protest* is loosely applied to the process of presenting an instrument for payment, demanding payment, and giving notice to the drawer or endorser. Example: Buyer accepts a trade acceptance drawn by Seller. Seller endorses and discounts the acceptance at Doe Bank, which sends it to Roe Bank for collection. Roe Bank's notary public (usually an employee) presents the instrument to Buyer for payment, which is refused. The notary then *protests* (using the term loosely); he makes out the certificate, attaches it to the instrument, and sends notice of protest to Seller, who is secondarily liable, through Doe Bank. In this case, Seller is the drawer and the endorser.

Public and private law. *Public law* is the law that relates to the public as a whole, rather than to a specific individual. It involves the authority of the federal and state governments to make laws and of federal and state executives to issue orders, as well as ADMINISTRATIVE LAW and CRIMINAL LAW. *Private law* is that body of the law that pertains to the relationship between individuals as such. It includes laws relating to contracts, sales, agency, negotiable instruments, and business organizations.

Public utility (public service corporation). A private corporation that renders service to an indefinite public, which has a legal right to demand and receive the service or commodities of the corporation. Public utilities are subject to special laws that do not apply to other corporations, and they are closely supervised by governmental agencies. They owe a duty to the public that they may be compelled to perform. For example, a railroad company cannot abandon part of its route without authority from the Interstate Commerce Commission. On the other hand, public utilities are given certain powers of a public nature, for example, the power of EMMINENT DOMAIN. Public utilities include railroads; bus lines; airlines; gas and electric companies; hydroelectric, water, and irrigation corporations.

Quasi. (Latin) Almost; like; resembling. Thus we speak of certain federal agencies, such as the Federal Trade Commission, as being "quasi-judicial" bodies because they have powers, resembling those of a judicial body, to enforce certain rules and regulations. Or we speak of certain documents of title as being "quasi-negotiable instruments"—they are invested by statute with certain characteristics of negotiability but are not NEGOTIABLE INSTRUMENTS as that term is defined by the Uniform Commercial Code.

Quiet title, action to. An equity proceeding to establish the plaintiff's title to land by bringing into court an adverse claimant and compelling him either to establish his claim or to be estopped from asserting it. Whenever a deed or other instrument exists that may throw a cloud over the complainant's title or interest, a court of equity will clear the title by directing that the instrument be cancelled or by making other decree required by the rights of the parties. For example, when a real estate mortgage is valid on its face but has ceased to be a lien, it may be cancelled as a cloud on the title by an action to quiet title.

Quitclaim deed. *See* Index.

Quo warranto. (Latin for "by what authority.") A WRIT of inquiry as to the warrant or authority for doing the act complained of. The writ tests the right of a person to hold an office or franchise or to exercise some right or privilege derived from the state. Quo warranto affirms an existing right to an office, or it sets aside wrongful claims of a pretender. An information in the nature of a quo warranto has replaced the old writ, but the terms *information in the nature of a quo warranto* and *quo warranto* are used interchangeably and synonymously and have substantially the same purpose. The power to file a quo warranto is incident to the office of the attorney general, but the privilege of instituting the proceeding upon the refusal of the attorney general to act has been granted to private individuals in their capacity as taxpayers and citizens.

Quorum. The number of persons who must legally be present at a meeting to transact corporate business or the business of any assembly of persons. When the membership of the assembling group or body consists of a definite number of persons as required by law—for example, a board of directors or the United State Senate—a majority (more than half) of the members are required to make a quorum, unless the controlling law expressly states that another number constitutes a quorum. At COMMON LAW, when the membership of the assembling body consists of an indefinite number of persons (that is, the law requires no definite number)—as the stockholders of a corporation—any number constitutes a quorum; however, the BYLAWS, and frequently the statutes or charter, customarily make an express provision concerning a quorum. In the case of a stockholders' meeting, the designated quorum usually relates to the amount of stock represented at the meeting and not to the number of stockholders.

Ratification. The approval of an act that had not been binding previously; ratification, or affirmance, reverts and becomes effective as of the date the act was performed. An infant may ratify, or affirm, his contracts after he reaches his majority; a principal may ratify, or affirm, the unauthorized acts of an agent; a corporation may ratify, or affirm, the unauthorized acts of its officers. A corporation could not ratify or affirm the acts of its incorporators before the corporation was formed because it was not in existence and could not possibly have entered into a contract at that date. It may, however, *adopt* the acts of the incorporators.

Regulations. *See* ADMINISTRATIVE LAW.

Real property. The land, APPURTENANCES, and constructed improvements attached to it. All other property is PERSONAL PROPERTY. Hence in addition to the land, real property includes the buildings, natural growth, minerals, and timber that have not been separated from the land and the air space above the land. Apples on the tree constitute real property, whereas harvested apples become personal property. (*See also* Index: Real estate.)

An interest in real property is an *estate* and runs the entire gamut of varying rights from an estate in FEE SIMPLE (absolute ownership) to a LEASEHOLD (the right to use property during a fixed term for a specific consideration). An *estate* is only a designation of a particular type of interest in property; it is not a legal entity. Other forms of estates are modifications and limitations of a fee simple estate. (*See* LIFE ESTATE; TENANCY BY THE ENTIRETY; JOINT TENANCY; TENANCY IN COMMON.)

Remainderman. *See* LIFE ESTATE.

Replevin. A court action to recover possession of property unlawfully taken or detained. Title to the property must be in the person bringing the action. Thus if title passes to the buyer and the seller refuses to deliver the goods, the buyer may bring an action in replevin to get possession of the goods. Or the seller, under a conditional sale contract by which he retains title to the goods until payment is made, may recover the goods by an action in replevin if the buyer does not make the payments called for by the contract.

Rescission. An action in equity whereby a court is asked to annul a contract entered into through fraud, misrepresentation, or excusable error. For example, if a person enters into a contract of partnership and then discovers that material facts were misrepresented, he brings an action in rescission. Rescission may be absolute or qualified. Thus in *rescission of a contract of sale,* the seller resumes title and possession of the goods as though he had never parted with them, but he has no claim for damages. In *qualified rescission,* he resumes title and possession but does not rescind the entire contract because he reserves the right to sue for damages. A contract may also be rescinded by mutual consent.

Residuary estate. That part of a testator's estate remaining after payment of the legacies and debts. The testator usually makes certain bequests and then names the person or institution that shall receive the remainder, or residue, of his estate. That person or institution is the *residuary legatee.*

Restrictive covenant. A provision in an agreement limiting or restricting the action of one of the parties to the agreement. Thus a seller of a business may agree not to engage in the same business within a certain number of years. Or a deed may contain a covenant restricting the type of building that may be placed on the property. A restrictive covenant of this type is said to "run with the land"—subsequent purchasers are bound by the covenant whether or not it is expressly set forth in the deed to them.

Royalties. Payments or rentals made to the owner of a patent for the privilege of manufacturing or renting the patented article. The term is also applied to payments made to authors and composers for the sale of copyrighted material and to payments under gas, oil, mining, or mineral leases.

Service of process. The law compels the giving of notice of a suit to a defendant, which makes him a party to the suit and compels him to appear in court or suffer judgment by default. The means of compelling in court is called *process.* (*See* SUMMONS; SERVICE BY PUBLICATION; *see also* Index.)

Service by publication. Generally, service of process or other notice is personal or upon the agent of the party to be served, but where personal service is impossible, service may be had in many cases by publication. The paper to be served is published in a designated newspaper a required number of times. Certain other legal formalities are also observed, such as mailing the paper to the party's last known address. Usually, service by publication is permitted if the party to be served is a nonresident or is absent from the jurisdiction or if his address is unknown. Proof of publication is made in the form of an affidavit by the publisher.

Silent partner. A partner who has no voice in the management of the partnership business. Unless he is also a limited partner (*see* LIMITED PARTNERSHIP), a silent partner is equally responsible with the other partners for the debts of the partnership.

Slander. *See* LIBEL AND SLANDER.

Specific performance. The performance of a contract according to its exact terms. A court of equity will enforce specific performance, whereas a court of law awards damages to the injured party to a contract. Specific performance is never enforced in contracts for personal services. It is usually confined to sales of real property and unique personal property such as an antique.

Star page. The line and word at which the pages of a first edition of a law book begin are frequently indicated by a star in differently paginated later editions. The original page number is indicated in the margin. In citing a few well-known works, the edition is left out and the star page is referred to: 1 Bl. Comm. *150.

Statute of frauds. A statute, enacted with variations in all the states, providing that certain contracts cannot be enforced unless they are in writing signed by the party against whom the contract is sought to be enforced. The writing need not be a formal document signed by both parties—a written note or memorandum of the transaction signed by the party to be bound by the agreement is sufficient. The laws in the various states are fairly uniform in requiring the following contracts to be in writing.

1. A special promise to be responsible for the debt or default of a third person.

2. An agreement by an executor or administrator to become liable out of his own property for the debts of the estate.

3. A contract, the consideration for which is marriage. Engagement contracts are not included.

4. Contracts for the sale of real estate or any interest therein.

5. Contracts that cannot be performed within one year.

6. Contracts involving the sale of personal property in excess of a certain amount (which varies in the different states), when no part of the property has been delivered and no part of the purchase price has been paid.

In addition, many states require the following contracts to be in writing:

1. An agreement to bequeath property or to make any provision for someone by will.

2. An agreement to pay upon attaining legal majority a debt contracted during infancy.

3. The creation of a trust of real estate. (*Note:* Few states require a writing for trust of personal property.)

4. The promise to pay a debt that has been outlawed by the statute of limitations or barred by bankruptcy.

5. An assignment of wages to be earned in the future.

6. A mortgage of personal property.

7. The employment of real estate brokers to negotiate the sale or purchase of real estate.

Statute of limitations. A state statute that limits the time within which legal action may be brought, either upon a contract or tort. State and federal statutes also limit the time within which certain crimes can be prosecuted. The purpose of the time limitation is to make it impossible to bring suit many years after a cause of action originates, during which time witnesses may have died or important evidence may have been lost. When a debt is involved, it is possible to interrupt (or "toll") the running of the statute—that is, to lengthen the period in which action may be brought—by obtaining a payment on the debt or a promise to pay. A promise to pay a debt that has been barred by the statute of limitations does not require new consideration (*see* CONTRACT), but many states require such a promise to be in writing. The statutes often differentiate between oral and written contracts.

Statutory law. Rules formulated into law by legislative action. The Constitution of the United States and the constitutions of the various states are the fundamental written law. All other law must be in harmony with the constitutions, which define and limit the powers of government. State constitutions must be in harmony with the Constitution of the United States. Congress, cities and towns, and other governmental units find in the constitutions their authority, either express or implied, to enact certain laws. These legislative enactments are called *statutes* and constitute the greater part of the written or statutory law. Statutory law supplements and supersedes COMMON LAW. (*See also* ADMINISTRATIVE LAW.)

Subornation. The crime of procuring another to commit perjury. Thus one speaks of *suborning* witnesses.

Subpoena. A writ or order commanding the person named in it to appear and testify in a legal proceeding.

Subrogation. The substitution of one person in another's place. Example: *A*'s car is insured by an insurance company against collision. *A*'s car is negligently damaged by *B*. The insurance company pays $850 for repairs to *A*'s car. The insurance company is subrogated to *A*'s position and may prosecute the claim for damages against *B*.

Substantive law. The part of the law that creates, defines, and regulates rights and duties. Substantive law is opposed to *procedural,* or *adjective, law,* which provides the method of administering and protecting the rights, duties, and obligations created by substantive law. All statutes of a general nature are substantive law; those regulating administrative and court proceedings are adjective law. All case law, except the decisions interpreting administrative regulations, codes of procedure, and court rules, are substantive law. For example, the right of administration of an estate is substantive; the procedures by which the estate can be administered are procedural law. The distinction between the two is narrow and often hard to define.

Summary proceeding. A form of legal proceeding in which the established procedure is disregarded, especially in the matter of trial by jury. The term is applied to the process by which a landlord may dispossess a tenant instead of having to resort to eviction, which is a long drawn-out proceeding.

Summons. A legal notice requiring a person to answer a complaint within a specified time. A copy of the summons must be left personally with (served upon) the person against whom it is directed. A corporation is served with process when a copy of the summons is left with an agent of the corporation found in the county. In a few jurisdictions the summons may be left with an adult member of the defendant's household or with some person at the defendant's place of business. An attorney-at-law is often authorized to accept service of a summons for a client. When the summons is served, the process server endorses the summons when, where, and upon whom served, with an affidavit to that effect. This procedure is called the "return of the summons." After return of the summons, the court has jurisdiction over the defendant. *See also* Index.

Supplementary proceeding. When an execution of judgment is returned unsatisfied, the judgment creditor has the right to force the judgment debtor to submit to an examination for the purpose of discovering any assets that may be applied to the payment of the debt. The legal procedure by which the judgment creditor exercises this right is known as a *supplementary proceeding*—it is supplementary to the execution of judgment. (*See* ISSUE OF EXECUTION.)

Suretyship. *See* GUARANTY.

Syndicate. An association of individuals formed to conduct and carry on some particular business transaction, usually of a financial character. A syndicate more nearly resembles a JOINT ADVENTURE than any other business organization. Syndicates in general are temporary associations or firms. They usually terminate automatically when the purpose for which they were formed has been accomplished.

Tax lien. A claim against REAL PROPERTY that accrues to the taxing agency (municipality, township, city) from taxes that are assessed against the property. If the lien is not paid when due, the taxing agency may sell the property at a TAX SALE.

Tax sale. A sale of property by a taxing authority, usually at auction, for nonpayment of taxes.

Tenancy in common. An estate held by two or more persons by separate and distinct title, with unity of possession only. If a deed is made to two or more persons who are not husband and wife, and nothing is said in the deed concerning the character of the estate created by the deed, the estate created is a *tenancy in common*. The co-owners are tenants in common. They need not have acquired their titles at the same time or by the same instrument. Their shares need not be equal. For example, one co-owner may have an undivided one-tenth interest and the other the remaining undivided nine-tenths interest. Tenants in common are entitled to share the possession of the property according to their shares in the property. Except for their sharing of possession and income, however, the situation is almost as if each tenant in common owned a separate piece of real estate. Each tenant in common may convey or mortgage his share, and the share of each is subject to the lien of judgments against him. Upon the death of one of the tenants in common, his interest passes to his heirs and legatees and not to the other tenant in common.

Tenancy by the entirety. An estate held by husband and wife by virtue of title acquired by them jointly after marriage. Upon the death of either spouse, his or her interest automatically passes to the other by survivorship. A tenancy by the entirety cannot be terminated without the consent of both parties. Thus neither spouse can defeat the right of survivorship by mortgage or conveyance without the consent of the other. The courts do not look with disfavor upon a tenancy by the entirety as they do upon a JOINT TENANCY. Not all states recognize tenancy by the entirety or "tenancy by the entireties," as it is sometimes called.

Testamentary trust. *See* TRUST.

Tort. A civil wrong inflicted otherwise than by a breach of contract. Elements of tort are (1) a wrongful act or a wrongful failure to act and (2) an injury to some person. Tort gives the injured party the right to sue for any damages resulting from the defendant's breach of some duty. Persons (including minors) and corporations are liable for torts. Example: A visitor to a department store (even one having no expressed intention to make a purchase but intending merely to examine the merchandise) can recover damages from the proprietor for injuries caused by the negligent maintenance of the store premises. Action arises not from breach of contract but from breach of duty.

Treason. *See* CRIMINAL LAW.

Trespass. The common meaning of trespass is the unauthorized entry upon the land of another. It also means an unlawful and violent interference with the person or property of another. In the practice of law an *action in trespass* is brought to recover damages for injuries sustained by the plaintiff as the immediate result of trespass.

Trust. A holding of property subject to the duty of applying the property, the income from it, or the proceeds for the benefit of another, as directed by the person creating the trust. A trust is created when *A* transfers property to *X*, the trustee, and *X* undertakes to apply the property and income from it for the purposes and in the manner directed by *A*. The elements of an ordinary trust are (1) the trustor (also called settlor, donor, or grantor), who furnishes the property to be put in trust; (2) the subject matter or property that is put in trust (called the *trust principal, corpus, or res*); (3) the trustee, who holds the property and administers the trust; and (4) the beneficiaries, for whose benefit the trust exists. A trust may be created by oral declaration, by writing, or by operation of law. It may be established by will (testamentary trust) or by deed (*inter vivos* or living trust). Some men put property in trust to pay the income to their wives for life and then to pay the principal to their children. In these situations the wives would be *income beneficiaries* (or "equitable life tenants") and the children would be *remaindermen*. (*See* LIFE ESTATE.)

Ultra vires. Without power, beyond the powers of. A term used to apply to a contract or act beyond the powers of a corporation as expressed or implied in its certificate of incorporation or by statute. For example, if a corporation contracts a debt in excess of the maximum allowed by statute, the contract is *ultra vivres*—beyond the power of the corporation. If neither party to the contract has performed, either the corporation or the other party may declare the contract void. After both parties have performed, the courts will not rescind the contract; the weight of authority is to the effect that after one party has performed the other party cannot repudiate the contract by claiming that it was *ultra vires*. Directors may be held personally liable for loss to the corporation occasioned by an *ultra vires* act.

An *ultra vires* contract made by a municipal corporation is not binding upon the municipality, although the other party has performed.

Uniform laws. Conflicting state statutes have led to the adoption, in many fields of business and commercial interest, of similar laws by the various states. The laws are known as *uniform laws*. Some of the more important uniform laws are the Uniform Commercial Code, the Uniform Partnership Act, the Uniform Stock Transfer Act, and the Uniform Warehouse Receipt Act.

Usury. Contracting for or receiving something in excess of the amount of interest allowed by law for the loan or forbearance of money, as in the sale of goods on credit or under the installment plan. In the majority of states, a lender who charges a usurious rate of interest loses his right to collect any interest, although a few states permit him to collect the legal rate. In some states, both principal and interest are forfeited. Service charges, investigation fees, and commissions charged by an agent are not usually considered interest and may be added to the legal rate without usury. In some states the parties to a contract may agree upon a rate of interest higher than the legal rate but within a statutory limit; in a few states they may agree on any rate. In some states loans to corporations, but not to individuals, may be made at more than the legal rate. Certain types of loans, such as small personal loans, are not covered by the usury law but are subject to special laws.

Void; voidable. That which is void is of no legal force or effect; that which is voidable may be rendered void. For example, a gambling or wagering contract is void (*see* CONTRACT); whereas an infant's contracts are merely voidable at his election (*see* CONTRACT).

Voting trust. A method devised for concentrating the control of a company in the hands of a few people. A voting trust is usually organized and operated under a *voting trust agreement.* This is a contract between the stockholders and those who manage the corporation, called the voting trustees. The stockholders transfer their stock to the trustees, giving them the right to vote the stock during the life of the agreement. The trustees, in turn, issue certificates of beneficial interest, called *voting trust certificates,* to the stockholders, who are entitled to the dividends. All stockholders may become parties to the agreement, which is generally subject to statutory regulation. The trust is usually for a definite period. When it is terminated, the certificate holders are notified to exchange their trust certificates for certificates of stock.

Waiver. The surrender, either expressed or implied, of a right to which one is entitled by law. Thus a stockholder might sign a waiver of notice of meeting, or he might impliedly waive that notice by participation in the meeting. The essence of waiver is conduct that indicates an intention not to enforce certain rights or certain provisions of an agreement. A widow may waive her right to share in the estate of her husband; a buyer may waive delivery on a certain date by accepting the goods at a subsequent date. *See also* Index.

Warranty. Affirmation of a material fact or promise by the seller, which acts as an inducement for the buyer to make a purchase. A warranty may be *express* (a direct statement made by the seller) or *implied* (one that is indicated by the nature of the contract). The Uniform Commercial Code has added a class of warranties, neither express nor implied, consisting of warranties of title and against infringement. Warranties relate to many things: fitness of the goods sold for a special purpose; merchantability of the goods; title to real or personal property (*see* specific titles in Index); and quiet enjoyment of premises. All representations made by an applicant for insurance, whether material or not, are deemed warranties. The term *guaranty* is loosely used in the sense of warranty. The common guaranty of a product is, strictly, a warranty and not a guaranty. (*See* GUARANTY.) Any warranty made by a seller that proves to be false gives the buyer a right of legal action.

Without recourse. A phrase used in an ENDORSEMENT that relieves the endorser from assuming liability in the event the maker fails to pay the instrument when due.

Writ. An order issued by a court, or judge, in the name of the state, for the purpose of compelling the defendant to do something mentioned in the order.

"Yellow-dog" contract. An oral or written contract under which either party, as a condition of the employment relationship, agrees to join or remain a member of some specific labor organization or some specific employer organization or agrees not to join any labor organization or any employer organization. It is illegal under the Norris-LaGuardia Act and under many state anti-injunction laws.

Courts of Record and Judicial Circuits (Tables I, II, III and IV)

I. FEDERAL COURTS OF RECORD IN THE UNITED STATES AND THEIR MEMBERS

Court	*Members*
Supreme Court of the United States	Chief Justice
	Associate Justices
United States Court of Appeals for the District of Columbia	Circuit Justice
	Chief Judge
	Circuit Judges
United States Court of Appeals for the (First) Circuit	Circuit Justice
	Chief Judge
	Circuit Judges
United States District Court for the (Southern) District of New York)	Chief Judge
	District Judges
United States District Court for the District of (Maryland)	Chief Judge
Or where the state is all in one district	Judges
United States Court of Claims	Chief Judge
	Associate Judges
United States Court of Customs and Patent Appeals	Chief Judge
	Associate Judges
United States Customs Court	Chief Judge
	Judges
United States Court of Military Appeals	Chief Judge
	Associate Judges
The Tax Court of the United States	Chief Judge
	Judges
Temporary Emergency Court of Appeals of the United States	Chief Judge
	Associate Judges

II. STATE COURTS OF RECORD IN THE UNITED STATES AND THEIR MEMBERS

(Asterisks indicate intermediate appellate courts.
Municipal courts are not included.)

State	Court	Members of Court
Alabama	Supreme Court	Chief Justice
		Associate Justices
	*Court of Appeals	Presiding Judge
		Associate Judges
	Circuit Courts	Judges
	Probate Courts	Judge
Alaska	Supreme Court	Chief Justice
		Associate Justices
	Superior Court	Judges
Arizona	Supreme Court	Chief Justice, Justices
	Court of Appeals	Judges
	Superior Courts	Judges
Arkansas	Supreme Court	Chief Justice
		Associate Justices
	Circuit Courts	Judges
	Chancery Courts	Chancellors
	Probate Courts	Judges
California	Supreme Court	Chief Justice
		Associate Justices
	*Courts of Appeal	Presiding Justice
		Justices
	Superior Courts	Judges
Colorado	Supreme Court	Chief Justice, Justices
	Court of Appeals	Judges
	District Court	Judges
	Superior Courts	Judges
	County Courts	Judges
	Probate Courts	Judges
	(Denver only)	
Connecticut	Supreme Court	Chief Justice
		Associate Justices
	Superior Court	Judges
	Courts of Common	
	Pleas	Judges
	Probate Courts	Judges

State	Court	Members of Court
Delaware	Supreme Court	Chief Justice
		Associate Justices
	Court of Chancery	Chancellor
		Vice Chancellor
	Superior Court	President Judge
		Associate Judges
	Registers' Courts	Register of Wills
District of Columbia	U.S. District Court	Chief Judge
		Judges
	District of Columbia Superior Court	Chief Judge
		Associate Judges
Florida	Supreme Court	Chief Justice, Justices
	*District Courts of Appeal	Chief Judge, Judges
	Circuit Courts	Judges
	County Courts	Judges
	Probate Courts	Judges
Georgia	Supreme Court	Chief Justice
		Presiding Justice
		Associate Justices
	*Court of Appeals	Chief Judge
		Presiding Judge
		Judges
	Superior Courts	Judges
	Probate Courts	Probate Judges
Hawaii	Supreme Court	Chief Justice
		Justices
	*Circuit Courts	Judges
	District Courts	District Judges
Idaho	Supreme Court	Chief Justice
		Justices
	District Courts	Judges
Illinois	Supreme Court	Chief Justice
		Justices
	*Appellate Courts	Judges
	Circuit Courts	Judges
	Court of claims	Chief Judge
		Judges
Indiana	Supreme Court	Chief Justice
		Associate Judges
	*Court of Appeals	Chief Judge
		Presiding Judge
		Associate Judges

State	Court	Members of Court
Indiana (cont.)	Superior Courts	Judges
	Circuit Court	Judges
	Probate Courts	Judges
Iowa	Supreme Court	Chief Justice
		Justices
	*Court of Appeals	Judges
	District Courts	Judges
Kansas	Supreme Court	Chief Justice
		Justices
	*Court of Appeals	Judges
	District Court	Judges
Kentucky	Supreme Court	Chief Justice
		Associate Justices
	*Court of Appeals	Commissioners of Appeals
		Special Commissioners
	Circuit Courts	Judges
	District Courts	Judges
Louisiana	Supreme Court	Chief Justice
		Associate Justices
	*Court of Appeal	Judges
	(New Orleans only)	
	District Courts	Judges
Maine	Supreme Judicial Court	Chief Justice
		Associate Justices
	Supreme Court	Justices
	State District Courts	Chief Judge, Judges
	Probate Courts	Judges
Maryland	Court of Appeals	Chief Judge
		Associate Judges
	Court of Special Appeals	Judges
	Circuit Courts	Chief Judges, Judges
	Orphans' Courts	Judges
Massachusetts	Supreme Judicial Court	Chief Justice
		Associate Justices
	*Appeals Court	Justices
	Superior Court	Chief Justice
		Associate Justices
	Probate Courts	Judges
	Land Court	Judge, Associate Judges
Michigan	Supreme Court	Chief Justice
		Associate Justices
	Court of Appeals	Justices

State	Court	Members of Court
Michigan (cont.)	Circuit Courts	Circuit Judges
		Judges
	Court of Claims	Judge
	Probate Courts	Judges
Minnesota	Supreme Court	Chief Justice
		Associate Justices
	District Court	Judges
	County Courts	Judges
	Probate Courts	Judges
Mississippi	Supreme Court	Chief Justice
		Associate Justices
	Circuit Courts	Judges
	Chancery Courts	Chancellors
	County Courts	Judges
Missouri	Supreme Court	Chief Justice
		Presiding Judge
		Associate Judges
	*Court of Appeals	Presiding Judge
		Associate Judges
	Court of Common Pleas	Judges
	Circuit Courts	Judges
	Probate Courts	Judges
Montana	Supreme Court	Chief Justice
		Associate Justices
	District Court	Judges
Nebraska	Supreme Court	Chief Justice
		Associate Justices
	District Court	Judges
	County Courts	Judges
Nevada	Supreme Court	Chief Justice
		Associate Justices
	District Court	Judges
New Hampshire	Supreme Court	Chief Justice
		Associate Justices
	Superior Court	Chief Justice
		Justices
	District Court	Justices
	Probate Courts	Presiding Judges
New Jersey	Supreme Court	Chief Justice
		Justices
	*Superior Court,	Senior Judge
	Appellate Division	Judges

State	Court	Members of Court
New Jersey (cont.)	Superior Court, Chancery Division	Judges
	Superior Court, Law Division	Judges
	County Courts	Judges
	Surrogate's Courts	Surrogates
New Mexico	Supreme Court	Chief Justice
		Justices
	*Court of Appeals	Chief Judge
		Judges
	District Court	Presiding Judge
		Judges
	Probate Courts	Judges
New York	Court of Appeals	Chief Judge
		Associate Judges
	*Supreme Court, Appellate Division	Presiding Justice
		Justices
	Supreme Court	Justices
	County Courts	Judges
	Surrogates' Court	Surrogates
	Court of Claims	Judges
	City and District Courts (in larger cities and counties)	Judges
North Carolina	Supreme Court	Chief Justice
		Associate Justices
	*Court of Appeals	Judges
	Superior Courts	Judges
North Dakota	Supreme Court	Chief Justice
		Judges
	District Court	Judges
	County Courts	Judges
Ohio	Supreme Court	Chief Justice
		Justices
	*Court of Appeals	Judges
	Court of Claims	Judges
	Courts of Common Pleas	Judges
Oklahoma	Supreme Court	Chief Justice
		Vice Chief Justice
		Justices
	*Criminal Court of Appeals	Presiding Judge
		Judges
	*Court of Appeals	Judges
	District Courts	Judges

State	Court	Members of Court
Oregon	Supreme Court	Chief Justice
		Associate Justices
	*Court of Appeals	Judges
	Tax Court	Judges
	Circuit Courts	Judges
	County Courts	County Judges
Pennsylvania	Supreme Court	Chief Justice
		Justices
	Superior Court	Presiding Judge
		Judges
	Commonwealth Court	Judges
	Courts of Common Pleas	Judges
Rhode Island	Supreme Court	Chief Justice
		Associate Justices
	Superior Court	Presiding Justice
		Justices
	Family Court	Judges
	District Court	Judges
	Probate Courts	Judges
South Carolina	Supreme Court	Chief Justice
		Associate Justice
	Circuit Courts	Judges
	County Courts	Judges
	Probate Courts	Judges
South Dakota	Supreme Court	Presiding Judge
		Judges
	Circuit Courts	Judges
Tennessee	Supreme Court	Chief Justice
		Associate Justices
	*Court of Appeals	Presiding Judge
		Associate Judges
	*Court of Criminal Appeals	Judges
Tennessee	Chancery Courts	Chancellors
	Circuit Courts	Judges
	County Courts	Judges
	Probate Courts, Shelby and Davidson Counties	Judges
Texas	Supreme Court	Chief Justice
		Associate Justices

State	Court	Members of Court
Texas (cont.)	*Court of Civil Appeals	Chief Justice Associate Justices
	Court of Criminal Appeal	Presiding Judge, Judges Commissioners
	District Courts	Judges
	County Courts	Judges
Utah	Supreme Court	Chief Justice Justices
	District Court	Judges
	Circuit Courts	Judges
Vermont	Supreme Court	Chief Justice Associate Justices
	Superior Courts	Judges
	Probate Courts	Judges
Virginia	Supreme Court	Chief Justice Justices
	Circuit Courts	Judges
Virgin Islands	District Court	Judge
	Territorial Courts	Judges
Washington	Supreme Court	Chief Justice Associate Judges
	Court of Appeals	Judges
	Superior Courts	Judges
West Virginia	Supreme Court of Appeals	President Judges
	Circuit Courts	Judges
	County Commissions	Commissioners
Wisconsin	Supreme Court	Chief Justice Associate Justices
	*Court of Appeals	Judges
	Circuit Courts	Judges
	County Courts	Judges
Wyoming	Supreme Court	Chief Justice Associate Justice
	District Courts	Judges

III. JUDICIAL CIRCUITS AND THE STATES AND TERRITORIES IN EACH CIRCUIT

District of Columbia Circuit	District of Columbia
First Circuit	Maine, Massachusetts, New Hampshire, Puerto Rico, Rhode Island
Second Circuit	Connecticut, New York, Vermont
Third Circuit	Delaware, New Jersey, Pennsylvania, Virgin Islands
Fourth Circuit	Maryland, North Carolina, South Carolina, Virginia, West Virginia
Fifth Circuit	Louisiana, Mississippi, Texas
Sixth Circuit	Kentucky, Michigan, Ohio, Tennessee
Seventh Circuit	Illinois, Indiana, Wisconsin
Eighth Circuit	Arkansas, Iowa, Minnesota, Missouri, Nebraska, North Dakota, South Dakota
Ninth Circuit	Alaska, Arizona, California, Hawaii, Idaho, Montana, Nevada, Oregon, Washington, Guam, Northern Mariana Islands
Tenth Circuit	Colorado, Kansas, New Mexico, Oklahoma, Utah, Wyoming
Eleventh Circuit	Alabama, Florida, Georgia

IV. STATES AND TERRITORIES AND JUDICIAL CIRCUIT IN WHICH EACH IS LOCATED

State	Circuit	State	Circuit
Alabama	Eleventh Circuit	Nevada	Ninth Circuit
Alaska*	Ninth Circuit	New Hampshire*	First Circuit
Arizona	Ninth Circuit	New Jersey	Third Circuit
Arkansas	Eighth Circuit	New Mexico	Tenth Circuit
California	Ninth Circuit	New York	Second Circuit
Colorado*	Tenth Circuit	North Carolina	Fourth Circuit
Connecticut	Second Circuit	North Dakota	Eighth Circuit
Delaware	Third Circuit	Northern Mariana	Ninth Circuit
Florida	Eleventh Circuit	Islands*	
Georgia	Eleventh Circuit	Ohio	Sixth Circuit
Guam*	Ninth Circuit	Oklahoma	Tenth Circuit
Hawaii	Ninth Circuit	Oregon*	Ninth Circuit
Idaho*	Ninth Circuit	Pennsylvania	Third Circuit
Illinois	Seventh Circuit	Puerto Rico*	First Circuit
Indiana	Seventh Circuit	Rhode Island*	First Circuit
Iowa	Eighth Circuit	South Carolina	Fourth Circuit
Kansas	Tenth Circuit	South Dakota	Eighth Circuit
Kentucky	Sixth Circuit	Tennessee	Sixth Circuit
Louisiana	Fifth Circuit	Texas	Fifth Circuit
Maine*	First Circuit	Utah*	Tenth Circuit
Maryland*	Fourth Circuit	Vermont	Second Circuit
Massachusetts*	First Circuit	Virginia	Fourth Circuit
Michigan	Sixth Circuit	Virgin Islands	Third Circuit
Minnesota	Eighth Circuit	Washington	Ninth Circuit
Mississippi	Fifth Circuit	West Virginia	Fourth Circuit
Missouri	Eighth Circuit	Wisconsin	Seventh Circuit
Montana	Ninth Circuit	Wyoming*	Tenth Circuit
Nebraska	Eighth Circuit		

*Only one district court.

Index

A

ABA/net, 29
Abbreviations
  spacing in citations, 367
  in titles, 108
Ab initio, meaning of, 523
Absence of employer, letters written during, 128-133
Abstract of title, 464-465
Acceleration clause, mortgages, 452-453
Acceptance, letters of, 146-147
Account errors, letters about, 133-135
Accounting equipment, 19
Accounts payable, in cash journal, 152
Accounts receivable
  in cash journal, 152
  rules related to, 151
  taking trial balance, 157-158
Acknowledgments, 198-205
  authentication, 205
  compared to affidavits, 206
  date of, 200-201
  date of expiration or commission, 203
  designation of person making, 201-203
  laws related to, 198
  notary's seal, 203, 205
  person making acknowledgment, 204
  person taking acknowledgment, 204-205
  placement of, 203-204
  purpose of, 198
  signature of officer, 203
  venue, 199-200
Actiones in personam, meaning of, 523
Action number, 263
Ad faciendum, meaning of, 523
Ad hoc, meaning of, 523
Ad infinitum, meaning of, 523
Ad litem, meaning of, 523
Administrative law, 6-7

Administrator of estate, 498-501
  citations, 500-501
  compared to executor, 486-487
  letters of administration, 498
    application for, 499
    granting of, 501
    notice of application for, 501
    prior right to, 499
    renunciation of, 500
  parties, 498
  as party in lawsuit, 277
  petition/oath/designation of clerk, 499-500
  prior right to letters of administration, 499
Ad quod damnum, meaning of, 523
Ad respondendum, meaning of, 523
Ad satisfaciendum, meaning of, 523
Ad valorem, meaning of, 523
Affiant, 279
Affidavits, 205-209
  authentication, 207
  averment of oath, 206
  compared to acknowledgments, 206
  example of, 208
  jurat, 207
  name of affiant, 206
  nature of, 205
  notary signature, 207
  preparation of, 207-209
  procedure for, 324-325
  signature of affiant, 206
  statement of facts, 206
  for use in court, 325-326
    parts of, 325
    preparation of, 325-326
  venue, 206
A fortiori, meaning of, 523
Agenda, corporate meeting, 401
Agent, in power of attorney, 227
Aggregatio menium, meaning of, 523
Alias dictus, meaning of, 523

585

Alias summons, 300
Alibi, meaning of, 523
Alien corporation, 377
Alii, meaning of, 523
Aliunde, meaning of, 524
Alius, meaning of, 524
Allegations, defined, 294
Alphabetical system of filing, 86-87
   advantages of, 86
   alphabetical system, 87
   method for, 86-87
Alter ego, meaning of, 524
Alumnus, meaning of, 524
A mensa et thoro, meaning of, 523
American Bar Association
   Code of Professional Ethics, 4
   Code of Professional Responsibility, 7
   database of, 29
American Digest, 176-177
   Decennial Digest, 176
   General Digest, 176-177
   index of, 176
   organization of, 176-177
   scope of, 176
   use of system, 177
American Federal Tax Report, 175
American Jurisprudence, 182
American Labor Cases, 175
American Law Reports, 174-175, 182, 364
Amicus curiae, 276
   meaning of, 524
   role of, 276
Animo, meaning of, 524
Animus, meaning of, 524
Animus furandi, meaning of, 524
Animus revertendi, meaning of, 524
Animus revocandi, meaning of, 524
Animus testandi, meaning of, 524
Anno Domini, meaning of, 524
Announcements, in building law practice, 7-9
Answer, 302-312
   certificate of service, 309, 310, 311
   defendant's first pleading, 302, 305
   example of, 306-308
   methods of serving, 309, 311
   parts of, 305
   preparation of, 305, 309
   procedure with, 311-312
Ante, meaning of, 524
Ante litem motam, meaning of, 524
Appeal
   brief, 353-360
   citations, 360-369
   parties for, 275
   record on appeal, 350-352

assignments of errors and directions to clerk, 352
   nature of, 350-351
   preparation of record, 352
   review procedure, 345-350
      change in caption of case, 347-348, 349
      designation of parties in, 348
      diary entries, 347
      methods for review, 346-347
      notice of appeal, 348-350
      rules of court, 345-346
      service on opposing counsel, 350
   use of term, 346
Appellant, defined, 274
Appellate court, 256
   intermediary appellate courts, 346-347
   supreme appellate courts, 259
   See also Appeal
Appellee, defined, 348
Applications software, 25
Appointments
   client arrives without appointment, 46-48
   client early for appointment, 50
   diary entry, 71
   lawyer late for, 53-54
   reminders to lawyer, 77
Appreciation, letters of, 137-139
A priori, meaning of, 523
Arguendo, meaning of, 524
Articles of association, 380
Articles of incorporation, 380-386
Assignments of error, in appeal, 352
Associate justice, forms of address, 519-520
Associate lawyers, 12
Assumpsit, meaning of, 524
Attention line, letters, 112
Attestation clause
   legal instruments, 196-197
   wills, 237
Attorneys. *See* Lawyers
Authentication
   acknowledgments, 205
   affidavits, 207
Averment of oath, affidavits, 206
A vinculo matrimonii, meaning of, 523

B

Bailiffs, role of, 251
Ballentine's Law Dictionary, with Pronunciations, 184
Bank account, for corporation, 392
Banker's Directory, 185
Bar, admission requirements, 4-5
Bar Register, 184

Barrister, 262
Bauds, modems, 24
Beneficiaries, of will, 231
Bibliographies, formatting, 42
Billing client. *See* Fees, billing client
Bill of particulars
  demand for, 317, 319-320, 330
  See also Discovery
Binder, purchase and sale agreements, 462-463
Black's Law Dictionary, 184
Blind copy, abbreviation for, 118
Block format, letters, 101, 103
Board of directors
  meetings
    fees for, 402
    first meeting, 392
    notice of, 400
    quorum, 400
Bona fide, meaning of, 524
Bona vacantia, meaning of, 524
Bookkeepers, 13
Bookkeeping
  basic rules for, 151
  billing client
    copies of bills, 164
    invoice, 165-166
    itemized charges made to client, 167
    preparation of bill, 162
    retainer, 162, 164
  bookkeeping equipment, 19
  capital account, 161
  cash journal, 151-153
  and computers, 30-31
  cost of services
    daily time sheet, 162
    to find out cost of lawyer's time, 161-162
    to find time and cost of services, 161
    posting time charges, 162
  double-entry bookkeeping, debits and credits, 150-151
  drawing account, 158
  general ledger, 153-154
    posting to, 155, 157
  payroll record, 158-161
  petty cash fund, 167-168
  profit and loss statement, 158
  subsidiary ledger, 154-155
  trial balance, 157-158
    of accounts receivable, 157-158
Books of index
  American Digest, 176-177
  Corpus Juris Secundum System, 180-182
  Shephard's Citations, 177-180
Brief, 353-360
  definition of, 353

  oral argument, application for, 356, 360
  parts of, 353
  preliminaries to, 353
  preparation of
    citations, 356, 358
    copies, 354
    cover and binding, 356, 359
    draft, 354
    example of page, 353
    filing and service, 356
    formatting, 354
    table of contents, 356, 357
  purpose of, 345, 353
  time factor in, 354
Bulletins, filing of, 88
Business corporations, 375
Business position, inside address of letter, 109
Bylaws, corporation, 390-391

C

Calculators, printing, 19
Calendar
  calendar number, 265
  computerized, 67
  corporate. *See* Corporation calendar
  of court, 265-266
Calendar call, 265-266
  answering of, 266
  daily and weekly calls, 265
  pretrial conference, 266
Capias, meaning of, 524
Capias ad satisfaciendum, meaning of, 524
Capital account, 161
Capitalization
  ills, 241
  in legal papers, 224-225
  minutes of meeting, 408
Caption, 284-289
  change in, for appeal, 347-348
  of complaint, 294
  examples of styles, 286-289
  in foreclosure action, 481
  index number, 285
  minutes of meeting, 408
  of orders, 339
  for papers filed in federal district court, 287, 289
  preparation guidelines, 285-287
  of summons, 297
  title of case, 285
  title of pleading, 285
  venue, 284-285
Carbon copy, abbreviation for, 118
Cash
  in cash journal, 152

Cash, *(cont.)*
 payments, rules related to, 151
 received, rules related to, 151
Cash journal, 151-153
 items in, 152-153
Causa mortis, meaning of, 524
Caveat, meaning of, 524
Caveat emptor, meaning of, 524
CBX systems, 16
Central processing unit, 23-24
Cepit et asportavit, meaning of, 524
Certificate of incorporation, 380
Certificate of service, 309, 310, 311
Certificate of title, 467
Certification, extract of minutes of
 meeting, 409-410
Certorari, meaning of, 524
Cestui, meaning of, 524
Cestui que trust, meaning of, 524
Cestui que trustent, in foreclosure action, 478
Cestui que use, meaning of, 524
Cestui que vie, meaning of, 524
Chancery courts, 258
Charters, 380
Chief justice, forms of address, 519, 520
Circuit courts, 253
Citations, 360-369
 administrator of estate, 500-501
 for brief, 356, 358
 for cases in official reports, 363-365
  date, 364
  federal courts, 364
  jurisdiction and court, 364
  name of parties, 363
  parallel citations, 364
  selective case series, 364-365
  spot page reference, 363-364
  volume and page, 363-364
 for codes, 362-363
 for constitution, 362
 databases, use of, 361
 definition of, 360
 formatting
  examples of, 368-369
  italicizing and underscoring, 366-367
  placement of citations, 367
  spacing of abbreviations, 367
 importance of accuracy of, 360-361
 for law reviews, 366
 for legal newspapers, 366
 main sources for, 360
 for named reporters, 365
 National Reporter System, 361-362
 Practice Manual of Standard Legal Citations,
  364
 in probate of will, 493-494
 reports, 361
 for slip decisions, 366
 for statutes, 362-363
 string citations, 365
 for treatises, 366
 Uniform System of Citations, 360, 364
 for unpublished cases, 365
Civic affairs, and lawyers, 10
Civiliter mortuus, meaning of, 524
Claims court, 254
Clerk of court, 263-265
 and appeal
  directions to clerk, 352
  filing brief, 356
  preparation of record, 352
 forms of address, 520
 index system of, 263-264
 minute books, 265
 register of, 264-265
 role of, 251, 263
Clerks, 13
Client files
 new case, 32-35
  form for, 34
  information needed for, 33
  intake information, 32-33
  routing procedure, 33, 35
Closely held corporation, 375
Closing case, progress records, 273
Closing date, and purchase and sale agreements,
  460
Closing file, 95
Closing statement, 470-476
 calculation of adjustments, 471, 474
 calculation of insurance adjustment, 475
 calculation of interest adjustment, 474-475
 calculation of rent adjustment, 475
 calculation of tax adjustment, 474
 example of, 472-473
 miscellaneous payments, 475-476
 nature of, 470-471
 printed forms, 471
Code of Administrative Rules, 7
Code of Federal Regulations, 6-7, 182-183
Code of Professional Ethics, American Bar Association, 4
Code of Professional Responsibility, American
  Bar Association, 7
Codes
 citations for, 362-363
 compilation of, 170
Codicil, wills, 242
Collating, legal papers, 225
Collections

acknowledgment of claim, 504
collection charges, lawyers, 11, 510
collection folder, pages of, 507-509
collection letters, 504-505
commercial law lists, use of, 502-503
filing collections material, 503-504
forwarding item for, 510-511
installment payments, 506
judgment proof, 515
laws related to, 502
office procedures related to, 503
record of, 506
remittance to forwarder, 506, 510
reports to forwarder, 506
suit for, 511-515
    complaint and summons, 512
    information for complaint and summons,
        513-514
    judgment by default, 514-515
    service of summons, 512-513
    time for, 511-512
Commercial law lists, use of, 502-503
Commercial leases, 456
Compilations of laws, 170
    finding laws, 171
Complainant, defined, 274
Complaint
    defined, 292
    parts of, 294-295
    preparation of, 295-297
    procedure with, 300-301
Complimentary close, 114
    familiar closes, 114
    formal closes, 114
Computers
    and bookkeeping, 30-31
    database management, 28-29
    deed preparation, 440
    and desktop publishing, 27
    diary/calendar programs, 67
    and document assembly, 26-27
    for document storage and retrieval, 17
    and file management, 27-28, 82
    hardware
        central processing unit, 23-24
        disk drive, 22-23
        keyboard, 23
        modem, 24
        monitor, 23
        printer, 24
    lease preparation, 458
    mailing activities, 29-30
    mail service, 18
    mortgage preparation, 451
    and optical scanners, 22

PC fax, 19
    security, 25
    software, 24-25
    spreadsheets, 30-31
    virus, 25
    and word processing, 25-26
Confidential, notation on envelope, 107
Conforming copies, court papers, 290
Congratulations, letters of, 141-143
Congressional Directory, 184
Consensus, meaning of, 524
Conservator, wills, 236
Consideration
    deeds, 441
    mortgages, 452
Consortium, meaning of, 524
Constitution, citations for, 362
Contacts with client
    client access to files, 51-52
    client arrives without appointment, 46-48
    client early for appointment, 50
    general guidelines for, 45-46
    hysterical client, 50
    impatient client, 53-54
    introduction to client, 44-45
    payment for special work, 51
    presents to secretary, 51
    social invitation from client, 50
    stranger requesting legal advice, 48-50
    unreasonable important client, 54
Contingent fee, lawyers, 11
Continuation sheet, 21
    page heading for letters, 119
Contra, meaning of, 524
Contra bonos mores, meaning of, 524
Contra pacem, meaning of, 524
Conventional mortgage, 448
Copies
    of bills, 164
    brief, 354
    court papers, 290
    in foreclosure action, 481-482
    legal papers, 223-224, 225
    of wills, 240
Copy-distribution notation, letters, 118
Copying material
    general rules, 43
    take-ins/inserts, 39-40, 41
Coram non judice, meaning of, 525
Corporate meetings, 396-406
    agenda, preparation of, 401
    directors' fees, 402
    director's meetings
        notice of, 400
        quorum at, 400

Corporate meetings, *(cont.)*
  folder for, 397-398
  materials needed for, 402-403
  meeting room
    preparation of, 402
    reservation of, 401-402
  notes
    memorandum form for, 404-405
    preparation for note-taking, 403-404
    procedure for taking notes, 405-406
  notices, preservation of, 401
  preparation for, 397
  resolutions before meetings, drafting of, 403
  stockholder's meeting
    notice of, 398
    proxies/proxy statement, 399
    quorum at, 398-399
    waiver of notice of, 398
  types of, 396-397
Corporate secretary, duties of, 395-396
  corporate meetings, 396-406
  corporation calendar, 416-419
  information folder, contents of, 396
  minutes of meetings, 406-412
Corporation
  articles of incorporation, 380-386
    application for Employer Identification Number, 385
    execution of, 383-384
    filing papers, 384-386
    preparation of, 380, 383
  bank account, resolution for opening, 392
  bylaws, 390-391
  checklist for incorporation, 377-378
  corporate outfit, 387-388
  dissolution of, 414
  first meeting
    of board of directors, 392
    minutes of, 391-392
  forms of
    business corporations, 375
    closely held corporation, 375
    not-for-profit corporations, 374
    professional corporation, 375
    public corporation, 374
    publicly owned corporation, 375
    subchapter S corporation, 375
  incorporators, 376
  laws related to, 376, 377
  name of corporation, 378-380
    changing name, 419
    clearance for name, procedure for, 379-380
    laws related to, 379
    words required and prohibited in, 378
  nature of, 374

  organization meeting, 386-389
    participants in, 387
    preparation of, 387
    purpose of, 386-387
    waiver of notice of, 388-389
  as party in lawsuit, 277-278
  separate form of assignment, 416
  state of incorporation, 376-377
    alien corporation, 377
    domestic corporation, 377
    foreign corporation, 377
  steps in organization of, 375-376
  stock certificates
    authority to issue, 412
    issuance of, 414-415
    original issue, 412
    preparation of, 392-393
    stock certificate book, 412
    transfer of, 415-416
    transfer tax, 412, 414
  words required and prohibited in, 378-379
    clearance for name, 379-380
Corporation calendar, 416-419
  purpose of, 416-417
  sources of dates for, 418-419
  upkeep of, 418
Corporation forms
  affidavit of secretary of publication of notice of stockholders' meeting, 424
  affidavit of secretary that notice of annual meeting was mailed, 423
  blanket resolution of directors authorizing issuance of duplicate certificate in event of loss, 428
  directors' resolution accepting resignation of member of board, 427
  directors' resolution accepting resignation of officer, 428
  directors' resolution expressing gratitude for services of resigning officer, 428
  excerpt of minutes showing adoption of minutes of previous meeting as corrected, 428
  minutes of annual directors' meeting, 425-427
  minutes of first meeting of incorporators, 420-421
  notice of annual meeting of stockholders, 422
  notice of special meeting of directors, 424-425
  notice of special meeting of stockholders indicating purpose of meeting, 423
  proxy for special meeting, 424
  resolution of directors amending bylaw upon authorization of stock, 427
  resolution of directors authorizing sale and issue of stock to persons determined by executive committee, 427

resolution of directors extending sympathy on death of associate, 428-429
waiver of notice of first meeting of directors, 422
waiver of notice of first meeting of incorporators, 422
Corpus, meaning of, 525
Corpus delecti, meaning of, 525
Corpus juris, meaning of, 525
Corpus juris civilis, meaning of, 525
Corpus Juris Secundum System, 180-182
    index of, 181
    organization of, 180-181
    scope of, 180-181
    use of system, 181-182
Counterclaims
    and answer, 305, 308
    parties to, 275
Counts, defined, 294
County courts, 258
Course, in land survey, 433
Court
    American court system, 252-255
        courts of intermediate review, 259
        courts of special jurisdiction, 258-259
        district courts, 254-255
        federal courts, 254
        inferior courts, 257
        state courts, 253-254
        superior courts, 257-258
        supreme appellate courts, 259
    court calendar, 265-266
    definitions of, 247-248
    equity, concept of, 260-261
    inferior court, 257
    jurisdiction
        limitations on, 256-257
        original jurisdiction, 256
        in personam jurisdiction, 255
        in rem jurisdiction, 256
        sphere of authority, 256
        subject matter jurisdiction, 256
    personnel
        attorneys, 251, 262
        bailiffs, 251
        clerk of court, 251, 263-265
        court reporter, 251
        defendant, 252
        judge, 250, 261-262
        jury, 250-251
        plaintiff, 251, 252
    proceedings, nature of, 248-250
    progress records, 267-273
    superior court, 257-258
    term of, 266

Courtesy, and telephone, 55
Court of appeals, 254, 255
Court of intermediate review, 259
Court of special jurisdiction, 258-259
Court order, 338
Court papers, 189
    and civil practices and procedures, 291
    masters of pleadings, storage of, 291
    parties
        to a cross action, 275
        amicus curiae, 276
        bringing or defending lawsuit, 274
        corporations, 278
        executors/administrators/trustees/personal representatives, 277
        husband and wife, 277-278
        intervening party, 275
        minors and incompetents, 276-277
        parties on appeal, 275
        partnerships, 278
    preparation of
        caption, 284-289
        conforming copies, 290
        copies, 290
        folding, 290
        legal backs, 290
        line spacing, 289
        margins, 289
        numbering of pages, 290
        paper for, 284
        printed litigation blanks, 291
    verifications, 279-284
Court reporter, role of, 251
Court work
    diary entry, 72
    reminders to lawyer, 79
Covenants, deeds, 442-443
Covers, brief, 356, 359
Creditors, and probate of will, 497-498
Criminal courts, 258
Cujus est solum, ejus est usque ad coelum, meaning of, 525
Cum testamento annexo, 487
    meaning of, 525
Curator, 277
Current Legal Forms, 183
Cursor, 23
Customs court, 254

D

Daily time sheet, 162
Daisywheel printer, 24
Damnum absque injuria, meaning of, 525

Database, 28-29
  commercial databases, 29
  for forms files, 29
  for legal research, 170, 361
  relational database, 29
  software for, 28
Dated action, in collection letter, 505
Dateline, letters, 106
Datum, meaning of, 525
DBase IV, 28
De bono et malo, meaning of, 525
De bonus non administratis, meaning of, 525
Debts, and will, 235
Declaration, 293-294
Declination, letters of, 147-148
Decrees
  admitting will to probate, 496
  compared to judgments, 342
Deed of trust, 448
Deeds, 436-446
  computer prepared, 440
  forms of, 437
  nature of, 436
  parties to, 436-437
  preparation of, 444-445
  printed forms of, 438-440
    information needed for form, 438, 440
  recording of, 443-444
  statements and clauses
    consideration, 441
    covenants, 442-443
    encumbrance, 441
    exceptions and reservations, 443
    habendum clause, 441-442
    meaning and intending clause, 442
    restrictions and conditions, 443
    testimonium clause, 443
  state taxes, 443
  types of
    fiduciary deed, 437, 438
    quitclaim deed, 437, 438
    trust deed, 438
    warranty deed, 437, 438
De facto, meaning of, 525
Defeasance clause, mortgages, 452
Defendant
  defined, 274
  in foreclosure action, 478
  role of, 252
  third-party, 275
Deficiency decree, mortgages, 449
De jure, meaning of, 525
De miniums non curat lex, meaning of, 525
Demurrer, 312
  defined, 292

De novo, meaning of, 525
Deponent, 279
Depositions, 332
  notice of deposition, 332, 333-334
Desktop publishing, 27
De son tort, meaning of, 525
Devisee, of will, 231
Dialog, 29
Diary
  computerized diary, 67
  example page, 68
  format for entries, 69-70
  information for entries, 70-71
  information in, 67, 69
    appointments, 71
    court work, 72
    family dates, 72
    holidays, 72
    meetings, 72-73
    payment dates, 73
    renewal dates, 73
    tax dates, 73
  nature of, 66-67
  and recurring events, 69
  tickler card files used with, 74-75
  work accomplished, 73-74
Diary entries, for appeal, 347
Dictation, 35-37
  confusing words in, 37-39
  dictation equipment, 19-20, 35
  errors in, 36-37
  length of dictation session, 36
  and recurring phrases/clauses/paragraphs, 39
Dies non, meaning of, 525
Direct Inward Dialing, 16
Directory of Directors, 184
Discovery, 317, 330-332
  depositions, 332
  forms of, 330-331
  interrogatories, 331
  purpose of, 330
  request for admissions, 331-332
  request for production of documents, 331
Disk drives, types of, 23
Dismissed for want of prosecution, (DWP), 265
Dispositive clauses, wills, 235
Distance, in land survey, 433
Distributees, defined, 498
District courts, system of, 254-255
District of Columbia, courts of, 252, 254
Ditto marks, use and misuse of, 225
Divided urge, in collection letter, 505
Docket, 267
Docket clerks, 12
Docket envelope, 96-98

Docketing, computerized, 27-28
Docket number, 42, 263-264
Document assembly, and computers, 26-27
Documentation, software, 24
Document creation
    checking document, 43
    copying document, 43
    dictation, 35-37
    formatting documents, 40-43
        bibliographies, 42
        front matter, 42
        rules for, 40, 42
        tables, 42-43
    looseleaf formbook for, 35
    take-ins/inserts, 39-40, 41
Domestic corporation, 377
Donatio mortis causa, meaning of, 525
Dot matrix printer, 24
Drafts
    brief, 354
    error correction, 223
    line spacing, 223
Drawing account, 158
Duces tecum, meaning of, 525
Dum bene se gesserit, meaning of, 525
Durable power of attorney, 228
Durante minore aetate, meaning of, 525
Durante viduitate, meaning of, 525

E

Earnest money, purchase and sale agreements,
    462-463
E converso, meaning of, 525
Electronic mail, nature of, 30
Ellipsis points, and omissions, 221-222
Employer Identification Number
    application for, 385
    opening bank account, 392
Enclosure notation, in letters, 116
Enclosures
    in letters, 119-120
    size factors, 119-120
Encumbrance, deeds, 441
Endorsements, and legal backs, 225
Envelope
    format for optical character reading, 111
    personals and confidential notation, 107
    street address, 111-112
Environmental Law Reporter, 175
Eo instanti, meaning of, 525
Equipment of office
    bookkeeping/accounting equipment, 19
    dictation equipment, 19-20
    facsimile machines, 18-19

filing and retrieval equipment, 17
mailing equipment, 17-18
photocopy machines, 18
telephone equipment, 16
word processing equipment, 20-21
Equity, 260-261
    compared to law, 261
    principles of, 260-261
Erratum, meaning of, 525
Error correction
    drafts, 223
    minutes of meeting, 409
Escrow, purchase and sale agreements, 463
Escrowee, defined, 463
Esquire, use of, 107-108
Estate administration
    administrator of estate, 498-501
    estate taxes, 488
    lawyer's part in, 487-488
    probate of will, 488-498
Estate taxes, 488
Et alii, meaning of, 525
Et cetera, meaning of, 525
Ethics, and law office, 3-4
Ex cathedra, meaning of, 525
Exceptions and reservations, deeds, 443
Ex contractu, meaning of, 525
Ex delicto, meaning of, 525
Executor
    compared to administrator, 486-487
    defined, 487
    as party in lawsuit, 277
    wills, 236
Ex gratia, meaning of, 525
Ex necessitate legis, meaning of, 526
Ex officio, meaning of, 526
Ex parte, meaning of, 526
Ex parte motion, 321, 484
Expert witnesses, role of, 252
Ex post facto, meaning of, 526
Ex rel, meaning of, 526
Ex uxor, meaning of, 526
Ex vir, meaning of, 526

F

Facsimile
    facsimile machines, 18-19
        PC fax, 19
        types of, 19
    transmission form, 117
Fair Debt Collection Practices Act, 502
Family courts, 258
Family dates, diary entry, 72
Family Law Reporter, 175

Fax copy, abbreviation for, 118
Federal cases, reporters for, 173-174
Federal courts
  citations from, 364
  system of, 254
Federal Energy Guidelines, 175
Federal Practice Digest, 176
Federal Reporter, 174
Federal Rules of Civil Procedure, 260, 292, 330
Federal Supplement, 174
Federal Tax Course, 175
Fees
  billing client
    copies of bills, 164
    invoice, 165-166
    itemized charges made to client, 167
    preparation of bill, 162
    retainer, 162, 164
  finding cost of services
    daily time sheet, 162
    to find out cost of lawyer's time, 161-162
    to find time and cost of services, 161
    posting time charges, 162
  lawyers, 10-11
  telephone questions about, 62
Fees earned, in cash journal, 153
Felonice, meaning of, 526
Feme covert, meaning of, 526
Feme sole, meaning of, 526
Ferae naturae, meaning of, 526
Fictitious names, foreclosure action, 478-479
Fiduciary deed, 437, 438
Fieri, meaning of, 526
Fieri facias, meaning of, 526
File-drawer, labels for, 90
File guide, labels for, 90
File management, and computers, 27-28, 82
Filing
  alphabetical system, 86-87
    advantages of, 86
    method for, 86-87
    transferring files, 87
  classification of files, 80-81
  collection items, 503-504
  control removal of material from, 95, 99
  docket envelope, 96-98
  filing and retrieval equipment, 17
  general correspondence files, 88
  litigation filing envelope, 93-94
  new cases. *See* Client files, new case
  numerical system, 82-86
    advantages of, 82
    key number assignment, 82-83
    method for, 82-84
    numbers assigned to cases, 84-85

    transferring files, 85-86
  out guides, 95, 99
  personal files, 87-88
  of printed materials, 88
  setup for
    arrangement of papers in folders, 92, 95
    closing file, 95
    index tabs and labels, 89-93
    preparation of materials for filing, 88-89
Filius nullius, meaning of, 526
Filius populi, meaning of, 526
Findings of fact and conclusions, 336-337
  preparation of, 336-337
  procedure with, 337
  purpose of, 336
First pleading by plaintiff, 293-294
Flagrante delicto, meaning of, 526
Flat rental lease, 456
Floppy disks, 22, 23, 28
FluShot, 25
Folders
  in filing, 92, 95
  labels for, 90
Folding, court papers, 290
Follow-up files
  material placed in, 75-76
  operation of system, 76-77
  setup for, 75
Follow-up letters, 136-137
Footnotes, creating, 40, 42
Foreclosure action, 476-485
  default of mortgage, time of, 480
  documents needed for, 477
  fictitious names, 478-479
  information needed for, 477
  mortgage, description of, 479
  nature of, 476-477
  note, description of, 479
  parties to, 478
  procedure
    activities in, 484-485
    filing of complaint and summons, 482
    follow-up of process service, 482
    number of copies, 481-482
    party sheet, 482-483
    preparation of complaint, 480-481
    preparation of summons, 482
    steps in, 483-484
    title search, 480
  property, description of, 479-480
  venue, 477-478
Foreign corporation, 377
Foreign words
  Anglicized, 220
  italicized, 220

Form 2553, 375
    S corporation, 386
Form books, 183
    Current Legal Forms, 183
    practice manuals, 183
Forms
    forms files, database for, 29
    looseleaf formbook for, 35
    See also Corporate forms
Forms of address
    associate justice, 519-520
    chief justice, 519, 520
    clerk of court, 520
    judge, 520
    presiding justice, 520
Form SS-4, 385
Forwarding fee, lawyers, 11
Front matter
    components of, 42
    formatting, 42
Full-block format, letters, 101, 102
Funeral expenses, and will, 235
Furniture, law offices, 15

G

Gender unknown, and inside address, 110-111
General correspondence files, 88
General ledger, 153-154
    client's ledger sheet, 156
    items for, 153-154
    posting to, 155, 157
General partnership, 374, 393
General power of attorney, 228
General term, 267
Graded rental lease, 456
Grantee, defined, 436, 437
Grantor, defined, 436, 437
Guardian, wills, 236
Guardian ad litem, in lawsuit, 276-277

H

Habeas corpus, meaning of, 526
Habendum clause
    deeds, 441-442
    meaning of, 526
Habere facias possessionem, meaning of, 526
Habere facias seisinam, meaning of, 526
Handwritten wills, 231
Hard disks, 22, 23, 28
Hazardous substances, title closings, 467
Headnotes, 171
Holidays, diary entry, 72

Holographic will, 231
Honorarium, meaning of, 526
How to Find the Law, 184
Hysterical client, dealing with, 50

I

Idem sonans, meaning of, 526
Identification line, letters, 115-116
Ignorantia legis neminen excusat, meaning of, 526
Illicitum collegium, meaning of, 526
Impotentia excusat legem, meaning of, 526
In bonis, meaning of, 526
Incompetents, as party in lawsuit, 276-277
Incorporators, 376, 387
Indebitatus assumpsit, meaning of, 527
Indents
    bibliographies, 42
    paragraphs, 40
Indexes, to compilations of laws, 171
Indexing, minutes of meeting, 410-412
Index number, caption in court papers, 285
Index system, of clerk of court, 263-264
Index tabs, for files, 89-93
In esse, meaning of, 526
In extremis, meaning of, 526
Inferior court, 257
Information folder, about corporation, 396
Infra, meaning of, 527
In fraudem legis, meaning of, 526
In futuro, meaning of, 526
Inheritance tax, and probate of will, 489
Initials, in titles, 108
Inkjet printer, 24
In loco parentis, meaning of, 526
Innuendo, meaning of, 527
In pari delicto, meaning of, 527
In personam, meaning of, 527
In personam jurisdiction, 255
In praesenti, meaning of, 527
In re, subject line of letter, 114
In rem, meaning of, 527
In rem jurisdiction, 256
In rerum natura, meaning of, 527
Inside address of letter, 107-112
    business position, 109
    street address, 111-112
    titles, 107-109
    women, forms of address, 109-111
In specie, meaning of, 527
Installment contract, sale of land, 460
Installment payments, collections, 506
In statu quo, meaning of, 527

Insurance adjustment, calculation for closing
    statement, 475
Intake information, for new client, 32-33
Integrated Services Digital Network, 16
Inter, meaning of, 527
Interest adjustment, calculation for closing state-
    ment, 474-475
Interim, meaning of, 527
Interlocutory, judgments, 342-344
Internal Revenue Service, requirements for com-
    puterized records, 31
Interrogatories, 331
    preparation of, 331
    purpose of, 331
In terrorem, meaning of, 527
Intervening party, 275
Intervenor, defined, 275
Inter vivos, meaning of, 527
Intestate, defined, 486
In toto, meaning of, 527
Intra, meaning of, 527
In transitu, meaning of, 527
Introduction, 42
    letters of, 143-144
Inventory management, 21
Invitation, letters of, 144-146
Invoice
    and computers, 30-31
    example of, 165-166
Ipse dixit, meaning of, 527
Ipso facto, meaning of, 527
Ita est, meaning of, 527
Italics
    for citations, 366-367
    foreign words, 220
    quotations in legal papers, 221

J

Job hunters, handling of, 53
Judge, 261-262
    compared to justice, 261-262
    forms of address, 520
    role of, 250
Judge's order, 338
Judgment creditor, defined, 514
Judgment debtor, defined, 514
Judgments, 342-344
    compared to decrees, 342
    interlocutory, 342-344
Jura personarum, meaning of, 527
Jura rerum, meaning of, 527
Jurat
    affidavits, 207
    meaning of, 527

Jure divino, meaning of, 527
Jure uxoris, meaning of, 527
Jurisdiction of court
    original jurisdiction, 256
    in personam jurisdiction, 255
    in rem jurisdiction, 256
    sphere of authority, 256
    subject matter jurisdiction, 256
Jury, role of, 250-251
Jury instructions, 337-338
    preparation of, 338
Jus, meaning of, 527
Jus accrescendi, meaning of, 527
Jus ad rem, meaning of, 527
Jus civile, meaning of, 527
Jus commune, meaning of, 527
Jus gentium, meaning of, 527
Jus proprietatis, meaning of, 527
Justice
    compared to judge, 261-262
    forms of address, 519-520
Juvenile courts, 258

K

Keyboard, computer, 23

L

Labels
    file-drawer labels, 90
    folder labels, 90
    format for writing on, 90
    guide labels, 90
Labor Law Reports, 175
Labor Relations Reports, 175
Land courts, 258
Laser printer, 24
Law, compared to equity, 261
Law blanks, printed, 226
Law books, sales people, 52
Law clerks, 12
Law Dictionary for Non-Lawyers, 184
Law firm
    business organization of, 11-12
    deportment for, 14
    paralegals, 13
    personnel of, 12-13
    secretary, duties of, 13-14
Law List, The, 184
Law offices
    equipment
        bookkeeping/accounting equipment, 19
        computer, 21-31

dictation equipment, 19-20
facsimile machines, 18-19
filing and retrieval equipment, 17
mailing equipment, 17-18
photocopy machines, 18
telephone equipment, 16
word processing equipment, 20-21
furniture, 15
physical layout, 14-15
supplies
inventory management, 21
types of paper, 21
Law Reports Annotated, 364
Law reviews, citations for, 366
Lawsuit, documents
affidavits, 325-326
answer, 302-312
discovery, 330-332
judgments and decrees, 342-344
jury instructions, 337-338
motions, 312-325
notice of appearance, 301-302
notice of trial, 332-336
orders, 338-342
requests for findings and rulings, 336-337
stipulations, 326-330
summons and complaint, 293-301
Lawyers
administrative law, 6-7
admission to bar, requirements of, 4-5
building practice, 7-9
and civic affairs, 10
fees, 10-11
law degrees, 5
legal training of, 4
relationships with clients, 10
role in court, 251
specialization, 6-7
trial lawyer, 262
Lawyer's List, The, 185
Leases, 454-459
classification
according to duration, 455-456
according to rental payment, 456
according to type of property, 456
computer prepared, 458
execution of, 458-459
parties to, 455
preparation of, 459
printed form, 456
purpose of, 454-455
standard clauses, 456-458
state statutes related to, 458
types of
commercial leases, 456

flat rental lease, 456
graded rental lease, 456
percentage lease, 456
residential leases, 456
Legal advice
requested by stranger, 48-50
telephone requests for, 61-62
Legal backs
court papers, 290
and endorsements, 225
Legal instruments
acknowledgments, 198-205
affidavits, 205-209
execution of, 191-197
attestation clause, 196-197
formatting document for signatures,
194-195
sealing, 195-196
signatures, 194
testimonium clause, 190, 191, 193-194
nature of, 189
and notary public, 209-212
parties to, 190
preparation of, 190-191
recording of, 212-214
mailing to recording office, 213
model letter for, 213-214
purposes of, 212
recording vs. filing, 212
secretary's role in, 212-214
Legal newspapers, citations for, 366
Legal papers
preparation of
collating, 225
conforming, 225
copying, 223-224
ditto marks, 225
drafts, 223
error correction, 223
law blanks, printed, 226
legal backs, 225
line spacing, 218
marginal/tabular stops, 217
margins, 216
numbering pages, 216-217
number of copies, 215
paper, 215-216
paragraphs, 216
punctuation/capitalization, 224-225
quotations, 220-222
responsibility/distribution line, 217-218
space for fill-ins, 219
spacing rules, 218-219
tabulated material, 217
underscoring, 219-220

Legal research
  American Digest, 176-177
  American Jurisprudence, 182
  books of index, 176
  citation, method for, 182
  Code of Federal Regulations, 182-183
  compilation of laws, 170
  Corpus Juris Secundum System, 180-182
  databases, 170
  form books, 183
  locating laws, 171
  looseleaf services, 175-176
  reference books, 184-185
  reports of decided cases, 171-175
  selected cases series, annotated, 174-175
  Shepard's Citations, 177-180
  subject reports, 175
  treatises, 183-184
Legal Research in a Nutshell, 184
Legal secretary, duties of, 13-14
Legatee, of will, 231
Letterhead, copying, 225
Letters
  formats
    block format, 101, 103
    full-block format, 101, 102
    modified-block format, 101, 104
    official-personal format, 101, 105
  opinion letters, 101, 106
  parts of
    attention line, 112
    complimentary close, 114
    continuation page heading, 119
    copy-distribution notation, 118
    dateline, 106
    enclosure notation, 116
    enclosures, 119-120
    identification line, 115-116
    inside address, 107-112
    mailing notation, 116, 118
    personal notation, 107
    postscript, 118
    reference line, 106-107
    salutation, 112-114
    signature, 114-115
    subject line, 114
  punctuation, 106
Letters of administration, 487
Letters testamentary, probate of will, 487, 497
Letter writing
  letters written by secretary about account errors,
    133-135
  acknowledgement of correspondence, 128-
    130
  follow up letters, 136-137
  letters about omission of enclosures, 136
  letters concerning appointments, 130-133
  letters of acceptance, 146-147
  letters of appreciation, 137-140
  letters of congratulation, 141-143
  letters of declination, 147-148
  letters of introduction, 143-144
  letters of invitation, 144-145
  letters of sympathy, 140
  reply to notice of meeting, 135-136
  overuse of same word/expression, 126
  sentence length in, 127
  specialized terminology, 127
  straightforward language of, 120
  terms to avoid in, 120-125
  unnecessary words and phrases in, 125-126
  using two words of same meaning, 126
Levari facias, meaning of, 527
LEXIS, 29, 170, 361
Lex loci, meaning of, 528
Lex loci rei sitae, meaning of, 528
Lex mercatoria, meaning of, 528
Limited partnership, 374, 393
Limited power of attorney, 228
Line spacing
  court papers, 289
  drafts, 223
  minutes of meeting, 408
  and preparation of legal papers, 218
  quotations in legal papers, 220
Lis pendens, meaning of, 528
Litigants, defined, 255
Litigation blanks, printed, 291
Litigation filing envelope, 93-94
Litigation papers. *See* Court papers
Living will, 232
Locus delecti, meaning of, 528
Locus in quo, meaning of, 528
Locus siglii, meaning of, 528
Long distance calls
  billing practices, 58
  record of, 56, 57
Looseleaf services, types of, 175-176
Lotus, 28

M

Magistrate court, 256, 257
Mailing activities, computers, 29-30
Mailing equipment, 17-18
Mailing lists, computerized, 29-30
Mailing notation, letters, 116, 118
Mala fides, meaning of, 528
Mala in se, meaning of, 528
Mala praxis, meaning of, 528

Mala prohibita, meaning of, 528
Malo animo, meaning of, 528
Malum in se, meaning of, 528
Managing clerk, 12
Mandamus, meaning of, 528
Manu forti, meaning of, 528
Margins
  court papers, 289
  of documents, 40
  minutes of meeting, 408
  and preparation of legal papers, 216
  quotations in legal papers, 220
Marking material, take-ins/inserts, 39-40, 41
Married couple, as party in lawsuit, 277-278
Martindale-Hubbell Law Directory, 9, 185
Materialman's liens, 467
Meaning and intending clause, deeds, 442
Mechanics liens, 467
Meetings
  diary entry, 72-73
  letters
    about omission of enclosures, 136
    reply to notice about, 135-136
  See also Corporate meetings; Minutes of meetings
Megabyte, 23
Megahertz, 24
Memory, computer, 23-24
Mens rea, meaning of, 528
Merge feature, word processing software, 30
Mesdames, use of, 108
Message memo, 58, 59
Messengers, 13
Messrs., use of, 108
Metes and bounds description, survey for land, 433
Microfiche, 17
Microfilm, 17
Miniaturization equipment, 17
Minors, as party in lawsuit, 276-277
Minute books
  arrangement of contents, 406-407
  clerk of court, 265
  corporation, 387
Minutes of meeting, 406-412
  certified extract of, 409
  draft of minutes, preparation of, 407-408
  error correction, 409
  formatting, 408-409
  indexing, 410-412
  minute book, arrangement of, 406-407
  order of contents, 407
  storage of, 406
Miss, use of, 110
Mixed punctuation, 106
Model Business Corporation Act of 1969, 376
Modified-block format, letters, 101, 104

Money, form for writing sums of, 409
Monitor, computer, 23
Monuments, in land survey, 433
Moody's Manuals, 185
Mortgagee, defined, 447
Mortgages, 447-454
  computer prepared, 451
  default of mortgage, time of, 480
  deficiency decree, 449
  definitions of, 447
  forms of
    conventional mortgage, 448
    deed of trust, 448
    short statutory forms, 448
  nature of, 447
  parties to, 447-448
  preparation of, 454
  printed forms, 449-450
    information needed for, 450
  purchase money mortgage, 449
  statements and clauses of
    acceleration clause, 452-453
    consideration, 452
    defeasance clause, 452
    description of debt, 451
    description of property, 453
    partial release, 453-454
    prepayment privilege, 453
  state tax, 454
Mortgagor, defined, 447
Motions, 312-325
  assented to motions. *See* Stipulations
  ex parte motions, 321
  information for preparation of, 322, 324
  motion for more definite statement, 317-321
    parts of, 317-318
    preparation of, 318
    procedure for, 318, 320
    purpose of, 317
  motion to dismiss, 312-317
    defined, 292
    example of, 314-316
    grounds for, 312
    parts of, 312
    preparation of, 313
    procedure with, 313, 317
  and objections, 321-322, 323
  procedure for, 324-325
  purpose of, 321
  return day of, 322
  types of, 321
Mrs., use of, 110
Ms., use of, 110
Municipal courts, 258

N

National Reporter Blue Book, 174
National Reporter System, 171, 173, 361
Nihil dicit, meaning of, 528
Nil debet, meaning of, 528
Nisi prius, meaning of, 528
Nolle prosequi, meaning of, 528
Nolo contendere, meaning of, 528
Non compos mentis, meaning of, 528
Non est factum, meaning of, 528
Non obstante, meaning of, 528
Non prosequitur, meaning of, 528
Notary public, 209-212
  and acknowledgments, 203, 205
  and affidavits, 207
  guidelines for notarizing, 211
  lawyers as, 209
  letter of law in notarizing, 210-211
  role of, 209-210
Note of issue, 265, 332, 335, 336
  example of, 335
  procedure with, 332, 336
  purpose of, 332
Note-taking
  corporate meeting
    memorandum form, 404-405
    preparation for, 403-404
    procedure for, 405-406
    skeleton, 403-404
Not-for-profit corporations, 374
Notice of appeal, 348-350
Notice of appearance, 301-302
  federal, 304
  preparation of, 302
  purpose of, 301-302
  state, 303
Notice of deposition, 332, 333-334
Notice of entry, 341
Notice of probate, 495
Notice of settlement, 339, 340
Notice of trial, 265, 332-336
  and clerk of court, 332
  note of issue, 332, 335, 336
  pretrial conference, 332
Notice to creditors, probate of will, 497-498
Nudum pactum, meaning of, 528
Nulla bona, meaning of, 528
Nul tiel record, meaning of, 528
Nul tort, meaning of, 528
Numbering of pages
  court papers, 290
  and preparation of legal papers, 216-217
Numerical system of filing, 82-86
  advantages of, 82

  key number assignment, 82-83
  method for, 82-84
  numbers assigned to cases, 84-85
  transferring files, 85-86
Nunc pro tunc, meaning of, 528
Nuncupative will, 231

O

Oath
  alternate terms used in, 284
  and verifications, 284
Obiter dictum, meaning of, 528
Objections, and motions, 321-322, 323
Office manager, 12
Official-personal format, letters, 101, 105
Omissions
  of paragraphs, 222
  in quotations, 221-222
Onus probandi, meaning of, 528
Open punctuation, 106
Operating-system, 25
Opinion letters, 101, 106
Opinion of title, 465-467
Optical character reading, format of
    address for, 111
Optical scanners, 22
Opus, meaning of, 528
Oral argument, in appeal, 356, 360
Oral wills, 231
Orders, 338-342
  compared to judgment of decree, 338
  court order, 338
  judge's order, 338
  preparation of, 339
  procedure with, 339, 341-342
  proposed order, 339, 340
Ore tenus, meaning of, 528
Original jurisdiction, 256
Out guides, 95, 99
Overhead expense, in cash journal, 153
Oyer and terminer, 258

P

Paper
  continuation sheet, 21
  for court papers, 284
  and preparation of legal papers, 215-216
  types used, 21
Paragraphs
  omissions in, 222
  and preparation of legal papers, 216

Paralegals, 12
  education of, 13
  office of, 14
  role of, 13
Pari delicto, meaning of, 528
Partial release, mortgages, 453-454
Particeps criminis, meaning of, 529
Parties
  administration of estate, 498
  to an instrument, 190
  in appeal, 348
  in citations of reports, 363
  in complaint, 294
  to deeds, 436-437
  to foreclosure action, 478
  in lawsuits, 274-278
  to lease, 455
  to mortgage, 447-448
  in power of attorney, 227, 230-231
  to probate of will, 489
  to purchase and sale agreement, 461
  in verifications, 279
Partnership
  general partnership, 374, 393
  limited partnership, 374, 393
  partnership agreement
    contents of, 393-394
    preparation of, 394
  as party in lawsuit, 277-278
Party sheet, in foreclosure action, 482-483
Pater familias, meaning of, 529
Payment dates, diary entry, 73
Payroll record, 158-161
PBX systems, 16
Peculium, meaning of, 529
Pendente lite, meaning of, 529
Per annum, meaning of, 529
Per autre vie, meaning of, 529
Per capita, meaning of, 529
Percentage lease, 456
Per centum, meaning of, 529
Per contra, meaning of, 529
Per curiam, meaning of, 529
Per diem, meaning of, 529
Periodicals, filing of, 88
Per se, meaning of, 529
Personal files, 87-88
Personal notation, letters, 107
Personal representatives
  oath of, 496
  as party in lawsuit, 277
Per stirpes, meaning of, 529
Petition, 293-294
Petitioner
  administration of estate, 498

  defined, 274, 348
  in probate of will, 489
Petty cash fund, bookkeeping, 167-168
PHINET, 170, 361
Photocopy machines, 18
Physical layout, law offices, 14-15
Pica type, 217
Plaintiff
  defined, 274
  in foreclosure action, 478
  role of, 251, 252
  third-party, 275
Plat system
  plat book, 433
  plat description, 434
  survey for land, 433-434
Pleading, 189
Plotters, 24
Pluries summons, 300
Postmortem, meaning of, 529
Postobit, meaning of, 529
Post-office box number, in address, 112
Postscript, letters, 118
Powers of attorney, 227-229
  durable power of attorney, 228
  general power of attorney, 228
  limited power of attorney, 228
  meaning of, 227
  parties to, 227
  preparation of, 228-229
  statements and clauses, 228
Practice Manual of Standard Legal Citations, 364
Practice manuals, 183
Practice of law, building practice, 7-9
Praecipe, meaning of, 529
Prayer for relief, 295
Precatory provisions, wills, 236-237
Preface, 42
Prepayment privilege, mortgages, 453
Presents to secretary, from clients, 51
Presiding justice, forms of address, 520
Pretrial conference, 266, 332
Prima facie, meaning of, 529
Principal, in power of attorney, 227
Printers, computer, types of, 24
Pro, meaning of, 529
Probate court, 258
Probate of will, 488-498
  citation
    citation and waiver in proceeding, 493
    preparation of, 494
    service of citation, 493
    waiver of citation, handling of, 493
  copy of will and affidavit, 489, 491
  decree admitting will to probate, 496

Probate of will, *(cont.)*
  deposition of witnesses to will, 495-496
  letters testamentary, 497
  notice of probate, 495
  notice to creditors, 497-498
  oath of personal representative, 496
  parties to, 489
  personal representative's right to act, 488
  petition for, 491-492
  preparation for hearing, 494-495
  probate proceeding, 488-489
  transfer tax affidavit, 492
Prochein ami, meaning of, 529
Pro confesso, meaning of, 529
Professional association, 375
Professional corporation, 375
Profit and loss statement, 158
Pro forma, meaning of, 529
Progress records, 267-273
  closing case, 273
  entries for, 269
  example of, 270-271
  guidelines for making entries, 269, 272-273
  opening case in, 268-269
  physical features of, 267
  sheet for, 268
  terms used for, 267
Pro hac vice, meaning of, 529
Proofreaders, 12
Proposed order, 339, 340
Pro rata, meaning of, 529
Pro tanto, meaning of, 529
Pro tempore, meaning of, 529
Proxy
  proxy statements, 399
  stockholder's meeting, 399
Public corporation, 374
Publici juris, meaning of, 529
Publicly owned corporation, 375
Public trustees, defined, 447
Puerto Rico, courts of, 252, 254, 255
Punctuation
  of legal papers, 224
  letters, 106
  mixed punctuation, 106
  open punctuation, 106
  wills, 241
Pur autre vie, meaning of, 529
Purchase and sale agreements, 436, 459-463
  and closing date, 460
  compared to installment contract, 460
  earnest money, 462-463
  escrow, 463
  information needed for, 461-462
  nature of, 459-460

  parties to, 461
  preparation of, 461
  purpose of, 460
Purchase money mortgage, 449
Purpose clause, in incorporation, 377

Q

Quaere, meaning of, 529
Quantum meruit, meaning of, 529
Quantum valebant, meaning of, 529
Quare, meaning of, 529
Quare clausum fregit, meaning of, 529
Quasi, meaning of, 530
Questions presented, 352
Quid pro quo, meaning of, 530
Quitclaim deed, 437, 438
Quoad hoc, meaning of, 530
Quod computet, meaning of, 530
Quorum
  at director's meeting, 400
  at stockholder's meeting, 398-399
Quotation marks, quoted material, 221
Quotations in legal papers, 220-222
  formatting, 40
  indication of errors, 221
  italics, 221
  line spacing, 220
  margins, 220
  omissions, indication of, 221-222
  quotation marks, 221
Quo warranto, meaning of, 530

R

Random access memory, 23-24
Re, subject line of letter, 114
Reader, 17
Reader-printer, 17
Read only memory, 23-24
Real estate
  closing statement, 470-476
  deeds, 436-446
  foreclosure actions, 476-485
  leases, 454-459
  mortgages, 447-454
  purchase and sale agreements, 459-463
  real property descriptions, 431-436
  title closings, 463-470
Real property descriptions, 431-436
  checking land descriptions, 436
  identification of land, 431
  metes and bounds description, 433
  plat system, 433-434

preparation of, 435
section/township description, 431-433
Receptionist, 13
Reciprocal wills, 231-232
Recording legal instrument. *See* Legal
    instruments, recording of
Recording of deed, 443-444
Recordkeeping, computerized, 30-31
Record on appeal, 350-351
Rectangular system, land surveys, 431-433
Red-inking, wills, 243-244
Reductio ad absurdum, meaning of, 530
Reference books, 184-185
    basic information, 184
    names/addresses references, 184-185
Reference line, letters, 106-107
Register, of clerk of court, 264-265
Register of actions. *See* Progress records
Relational database, 29
Reminders
    for appointments, 77
    for court work, 79
    importance of, 77
    for tasks, 77, 79
Renewal dates, diary entry, 73
Rent adjustment, calculation for closing
    statement, 475
Rental payment, types of leases, 456
Reports
    American Federal Tax Report, 175
    American Jurisprudence, 182
    American Labor Cases, 175
    American Law Reports, 174-175, 182
    citations for, 363-365
    Federal Reporter, 174
    Federal Supplement, 174
    Lawyer's Edition, 173, 182
    locating alternative citations, 174
    National Reporter Blue Book, 174
    National Reporter System, 171, 173
    organization of, 171, 173
    scope of, 171
    Shephard's Citations, 174
    subject reports, 175
    Supreme Court Reporter, 173
    United States Reports, 173
    use of reports and reporters, 173-174
Reprographic copy, abbreviation for, 118
Request for admissions, 331-332
Request for production of documents, 331
Res, meaning of, 530
Research. *See* Legal research
Res gestae, meaning of, 530
Residential leases, 456
Residuary clause, wills, 235-236

Residuary legatee, 492
Residuary trust, 492
Res ipsa loquitur, meaning of, 530
Res judicata, meaning of, 530
Respondent, defined, 348
Responsibility and distribution line, and prepara-
    tion of legal papers, 217-218
Restrictions and conditions, deeds, 443
Retainer, 162, 164
    lawyers, 11
    trust accounts, 162, 164
Return day of motion, 322
Revenue stamps, deeds, 443
Revised Model Business Corporation Act of 1984,
    376
Revocation clause, wills, 233
Rolodex, directory of important numbers, 63-65
Rule days, 299

S

Sales people
    handling of, 52-53
    telephone calls from, 62-63
Salutation, 112-114
    forms of, 113
    to women, 113-114
Scienter, meaning of, 530
Scilicet
    abbreviation for, 199
    meaning of, 530
Scintilla, meaning of, 530
Scire facias, meaning of, 530
S corporation, Form 2553, 386
Screening calls, 58-60
Seal, corporate, 387
Sealing the instrument, 195-196
    corporation seal, 196
    individual seal, 196
Securities Exchange Commission, and incorpora-
    tion, 383
Security, computers, 25
Se defendendo, meaning of, 530
Semper, meaning of, 530
Semper paratus, meaning of, 530
Sentences, length, in letters, 127
Sequestering of witnesses, 252
Seriatim, meaning of, 530
Service mail, affidavit for, 351
Services charged, in cash journal, 153
Sessions, 266-267
Shareholders, 387
Shepard's Citations, 174, 177-180
    database, 170
    page from, 179

Shepard's Citations, (cont.)
   purpose of, 177-178
   use of system, 178, 180
Short statutory forms, mortgages, 448
Sigillum, meaning of, 530
Signature
   of acknowledgment, 203
   firm name in, 115
   legal instruments, 194
   letters, 114-115
   on affidavits, 206
   and titles, 115
   typing in name, 115
   will, 237
Simplex obligato, meaning of, 530
Sine die, meaning of, 530
Situs, meaning of, 530
Slip decisions, citations for, 366
Social invitation from client, 50
Software, 24-25
   applications software, 25
   documentation, 24
   operating-system, 25
Solicitor, 262
Spaces for fill-ins, and preparation of legal papers, 219
Spacing, and preparation of legal papers, 218-219
Specialization, lawyers, 6-7
Spell checker, work processing software, 26
Sphere of authority, 256
Spot page reference, in citation, 363-364
Spreadsheets, 30-31
   creation of, 31
Standard clauses, leases, 456-458
Standard Federal Tax Reporter, 175
Stare decisis, meaning of, 530
State codes, compilation of, 182-183
State courts, system of, 253-254
State legislative manuals, 185
State of incorporation, 376-377
State taxes
   and deeds, 443
   mortgages, 454
Stationery, paper, types of, 21
Status quo, meaning of, 530
Statutes
   citations for, 362-363
   compilation of, 170
Statutory form, deeds, 437
Stay writs, 346
Stipulations, 326-330
   parts of, 329
   preparation of, 329
   procedure with, 330
   purpose of, 326

Stock clause, in incorporation, 378
Stockholders, 387
Stockholder's meeting. *See* Corporate meetings, stockholder's meeting
Stock of corporation
   authority to issue, 412
   certificates, 392-393
   issuance of, 414-415
   original issue, 412
   preparation of, 392-393
   stock certificate book, 387
   stock ledger, 387
   transfer of, 415-416
   transfer tax, 412, 414
Street address, 111-112
Subchapter S corporation, 375
Subject line, 114
Subject matter jurisdiction, 256
Sub judice, meaning of, 530
Sub modo, meaning of, 530
Sub nom, meaning of, 530
Subscribers, 387
Subsidiary ledger, 154-155
   items for, 154-155
Sui juris, meaning of, 530
Suit register. *See* Progress records
Summons, 293-301
   alias summons, 300
   first pleading by plaintiff, 293-294
   in foreclosure action, 482
   parts of summons, 297
   pluries summons, 300
   preparation of, 297, 299
   procedure with, 300-301
   return day of, 299-300
Superior court, 257-258
Supersedeas, meaning of, 530
Supra, meaning of, 530
Supreme appellate courts, 259
Supreme Court, 254, 259
Supreme Court Digest, 176
Supreme Court Reporter, 173, 361
Survey for land
   metes and bounds description, 433
   plat system, 433-434
   rectangular system of, 431-433
   section/township description, 431-433
Switching systems, for telephone equipment, 16
Syllabus, 171
Sympathy, letters of, 140

T

Table of contents, 42
   brief, 356, 357

Tables
    creating, 42-43
    formatting, 42-43
Tabs, and preparation of legal papers, 217
Tabulated text, and preparation of legal papers, 217
Tax adjustment, calculation for closing statement, 474
Tax court, 254
Tax dates, diary entry, 73
Tax expense, in cash journal, 153
Teamwork in law office, 3
Telephone contacts
    answering calls for lawyer, 58
    asking purpose of call, 60-61
    callers asking legal advice, 61-62
    directory of important numbers, 63-65
    and dishonest vendors, 62-63
    importance of, 54
    irate clients, 62
    long distance calls, record of, 56, 57
    making calls for lawyer, 63
    message memo, 58, 59
    notes of all incoming calls, 58
    placing calls for lawyer, 55-56
    questions about fees, 62
    rules of courtesy, 55
    screening calls, 58-60
    toll calls placed by clients, 56
Telephone equipment
    law offices, 16
    technological advances, 16
    types of systems, 16
Telephone numbers on file
    law business numbers, 63-64
    lawyer's personal telephone numbers, 65
    office administration numbers, 64-65
Terminus a quo, meaning of, 530
Term of court, 266-267
Testamentary trust, 235
Testate, defined, 486
Testator, of will, 230-231
Testimonium clause
    deeds, 443
    legal instruments, 190, 191, 193-194
    in power of attorney, 228
    wills, 237
That, in dictated material, 37
Third-party actions, 275
Tickler card files
    setup for, 74
    use with diary, 74-75
Time computation, in summons, 299-300
Time sheet, daily, 162
Title closings, 463-470
    abstract of title, 464-465
    certificate of title, 467
    evidence of title, 464
    hazardous substances, 467
    mechanics and materialman's liens, 467
    opinion of title, 465-467
    preparation for, 468-470
    purpose of, 463-464
    title insurance policies, 467-468
    Torrens certificate, 468
Title of case, caption in court papers, 285
Title of pleading, caption in court papers, 285
Title page, 42
Titles
    business titles, 109
    inside address of letter, 107-109
    and signature of letter, 115
    wills, 233
Title search, for foreclosures, 480
Torrens certificate, 468
Trade Regulation Reporter, 175
Transfer tax
    on stock, 412, 414
    and probate of will, 488, 492
Treatises, 183-184
    citations for, 366
    purposes of, 183-184
Trial lawyer, 262
Trial term, 267
Trust, testamentary, 235
Trust accounts, 162, 164
Trust deed, 438
Trustees, as party in lawsuit, 277
Trust fund account, in cash journal, 152
Trust provisions, wills, 235
Tutor, 277
Typewriters, electronic type, 20-21

U

Ultra vires, meaning of, 531
Underscoring
    for citations, 366-367
    and preparation of legal papers, 219-220
Uniform Acknowledgment Act, 198
Uniform Partnership Act, 373, 393
Uniform System of Citations, A, 184, 360, 362, 364, 368
United States Code, 170
United States Code Annotated, 170
United States Code Service, 170
United States Government Printing Office Style Manual, 220
United States Law Week, 176
United States Reports, 173

United States Small District Court, 254
Unpublished cases, citations for, 365

V

Venire facias, meaning of, 531
Venue
   acknowledgment, 199-200
   affidavits, 206
   caption in court papers, 284-285
   foreclosure action, 477-478
VERALEX, 170, 361
Verba fortius accipiuntur contra proferentem,
      meaning of, 531
Verifications, 279-284
   in complaint, 295
   formatting, 280-283
   forms of, 279-280
   and oath, 284
   parties in, 279
   purpose of, 279
Versus, 224
   meaning of, 531
Via, meaning of, 531
Vice versa, meaning of, 531
Videlicet, meaning of, 531
Vi et armis, meaning of, 531
Virex, 25
Virtute officii, meaning of, 531
Virus, computer, 25
Viva voce, meaning of, 531
Voice-data systems, 18
Voice-mail systems, 18
Voir dire, meaning of, 531

W

Warranty deed, 437, 438
Webster's New Collegiate Dictionary, 184
WESTLAW, 29, 170, 361
Wills, 229-244
   attestation clause, 237
   body of, 233-235
   codicil, 242
   dispositive clauses, 235
   executor, 236
   guardian, 236
   handwritten wills, 231
   introductory paragraph, 233

living will, 232
oral wills, 231
parties in, 230-231
payment of debts/funeral expenses, 235
precatory provisions, 236-237
preparation of, 237-242
   copies, 240
   guidelines for, 241-242
   signature page, 238-240
   witnessing will, 240
purpose of, 229-230
reciprocal wills, 231-232
red-inking, 243-244
residuary clause, 235-236
revocation clause, 233
self-proving will, 489
signatures, 237
testimonium clause, 237
titles, 233
trust provisions, 235
See also Probate of will
Witnesses
   expert witnesses, 252
   role in court, 252
   sequestering of, 252
   to will, 240
      deposition of, 495-496
Women
   forms of address, 109-111
   proper salutation, 113-114
Word processing
   and computers, 25-26
   equipment for, 20-21
Word processing software
   merge feature, 30
   tables, 42-43
Words, confusing pairs of, 37-39
Writ, 293-294
Writ of certiorari, 346
Writ of habeas corpus, 346
Writ of mandamus, 346
Writ of prohibition, 346
Writ of quo warranto, 346

Z

Zip code, in address, 112
Z ruling, 226